THE BOOK OF GENESIS,

AND

PART OF THE BOOK OF EXODUS:

A Revised Version, with Marginal References,

AND AN

EXPLANATORY COMMENTARY.

BY

HENRY ALFORD, D.D.,

LATE DEAN OF CANTERBURY.

WIPF & STOCK · Eugene, Oregon

Wipf and Stock Publishers
199 W 8th Ave, Suite 3
Eugene, OR 97401

The Book of Genesis and Part of the Book of Exodus
A Revised Version with Marginal References and an Explanatory Commentary
By Henry Alford, 1872
Public Domain
ISBN 13: 978-1-60608-033-7
Publication date 7/21/2008

FOREWORD

Dean Henry Alford is best remembered as one of the world's great New Testament Greek scholars. Few knew that he was working on a commentary on the whole Old Testament when he died. This volume is all that he was able to complete before he heard the voice which John of Patmos heard as of a trumpet, as of many waters -- saying, 'Come up hither. . . .' Henry Alford died in 1871.

Alford's commentary on Genesis shows the same depth of study that characterizes his work on the New Testament. He delves into the Hebrew, the original language of the book, into the Samaritan Hebrew texts, into the Greek of the Septuagint version and into the Vulgate and Syriac versions for the benefit of the reader. No reader can expect fully to agree with all of Alford's conclusions, yet every reader can profit measurably and meaningfully from his research. Often Alford's quotations from the older scholars will give interesting access to scholarly materials not available to most Bible students. His qoutation of Kalitsch on the term 'Great Whales' in Genesis 1:21 is a good example. Alford says: "No scientific classification must be thought of; 'The Hebrew term denotes both mammifer and non-mamifer' Kalitsch."

The thoughtful student will recognize that Alford knew that he did not have all of the answers to the problem of the harmonization of science and the Scriptures. Regretfully, he will see Alford stand at an impasse on the subject. Again he quotes Kalitsch: " 'We have willingly renounced the attempt to discover that harmony [between Scripture and Science]; and both science and Biblical exposition will gain by this candid understanding.' " Time has proven clearly that only unbelieving science has gained by this unwise approach. Almost three generations of research on the problem have been lost, as well as the generations of students who have been deluded by the current scientific hypothesis of origins. Indeed, the remarkable development of unbelief and the rejection of the authority of the text of the Old Testament through the documentary hypothesis have been given unwarranted freedom for development and exposition in this environment of "candid understanding."

The careful student will also find cause for regret in Alford's wavering position on the text itself for he hesitantly accepts a very limited amount of the documentary theory's pronouncements just as Delitzsch did. Both were troubled and influenced by the rise of unbelief in their day. Undoubtedly this great scholar would have taken a different position on these problem areas if he had been endowed with the 100 years "hindsight" available to us today.

In spite of these problems which mar the work in a few places, Dean Alford's commentaries on Genesis and part of Exodus will prove to be of significant value to the serious student. A brief examination of his discussion of the Table of the Nations will demonstrate the depth of research available through this work. Klock and Klock are to be commended for making available to late twentieth century Bible students another excellent work on Genesis by a great nineteenth century scholar.

Bernard E. Northrup, Th.D.
Director of Graduate Studies
Central Baptist Seminary
Minneapolis, Minnesota

PREFACE.

In February, 1870, Dean Alford undertook to write an explanatory Commentary on the Old Testament. The first volume was intended to include the Pentateuch. In the course of the year he completed the Book of Genesis, revised it for the press, and placed the first sheet in the printers' hands: he also wrote the Commentary as far as the twenty-fifth chapter of the Book of Exodus; when his work on earth ended, on Jan. 12th, 1871.

It is due both to his memory and to those for whose instruction he laboured, that the unfinished volume should be published exactly as he left it.

Pains have been taken to make the publication as accurate as possible. But if errors are observed, it will be borne in mind that the difficulty of printing from the manuscript was not slight, and the difficulty of correcting the press was increased by an unforeseen occurrence to the manuscript.

It was the Dean's intention to prefix to the Book of Genesis, a general Introduction: but no part of it was actually written. Many important questions, at which he only glances in the Commentary, were to be discussed in the Introduction. Among them were "all general matters respecting the Creation of the World and Man"—"science and revelation"—"the use of the name Elohim in the first chapter"—"the distinctness of the accounts of the Creation in the first two chapters"—"Paradise and the Fall"—"the trees of Life and Knowledge"—"the Sons of God"—"the Flood and its extent"—"the Confusion of Tongues and Dispersion"—also "the Anthropomorphism of the early part of Genesis," and "the hypothesis of the composition of the book by two writers, distinguished as the Elohist and the Jehovist, or even by more than two."

A book which he valued highly—Theophylact's Commentaries on St. Paul—was first published in England under circumstances so similar to those in which this Commentary is submitted to the Reader, that I venture to introduce it with the words of the preface of that book:—

"Virum omni literarum genere excultum, inter media optimæ frugis molimina abreptum, etiam ignoti flebunt. At vero mei muneris esse duxi (qui in istiusmodi studiis illi inservierim) non tam defunctum ignavo questu prosequi, quàm quæ voluerit, meminisse; quæ mandaverit exequi. Hinc animus mihi accendebatur hosce Commentarios quos ille bono publico destinaverat pro mediocritate meâ potiùs excolere quàm unà cum ipso sepelire. Priores ipsius curas, atque etiam secundas experti erant; manus tantum deerat suprema. Unde licèt fortassis haud usque adeò absolutos, non tamen omnino neglectos, prodire comperies."

W. T. B.

Kensington, June, 1872.

THE FIRST BOOK OF MOSES,

CALLED

GENESIS.

I. 1 [a] In the beginning God [b] created the [c] heavens and the
[c] earth. 2 And the earth was [d] waste, and [d] empty; and

a Prov. viii. 23. John i. 1, 2. Heb. i. 10. b ver. 21, 27; ch. v. 1, 2. Isa. xl. 26; xlv. 18. See note. c ch. xiv. 19, 22. 2 Kings xix. 15. Jer. xxiii. 24. d Jer. iv. 23. Isa. xxxiv. 11.

Title] The book is called in the Hebrew Bereshith, **In the beginning**, from its first word. It was also known by the Rabbis as "**The Book of Creation.**" The present name is derived from the Septuagint version, which inscribes it Genesis Kosmou, **the genesis of the world.**

I. 1—II. 2.] *First, or Introductory portion.* The creation of the world and of man.

I. 1, 2.] *History previous to the six days' works.* The assignment of this portion of the narrative has been curious. Many have regarded ver. 1 as an announcement of the original creation of matter, and ver. 2 as opening with the first day. Others have included ver. 1 in the first day's works, and have regarded the opening words as meaning *First of all.* But, inasmuch as every one of the six days' works opens with **And God said**, it is required by the symmetry of the narrative that the first day's work should begin at ver. 3, and that vv. 1, 2, should be regarded as introductory matter. It is no objection to this that in Exod. xx. 11, xxxi. 17, God is said in six days to have "made" heaven and earth. See on the former of these places. This being so, we have in it three propositions. First, (*a*) originally God created the heaven and the earth. Secondly, (*b*) at a certain time formlessness and darkness prevailed. Thirdly, (*c*) the Divine Spirit wrought upon this chaotic state. And thus the way is prepared for the six-days' work. (*a*) **1. In the beginning**] i. e. as in reff., absolute, at the first beginning of things. **God**] **Elohim**, the Divine Name used throughout the whole of this first portion, I. 1—II. 3. **created**] The Hebrew verb does not of necessity signify creation out of nothing. It is the same word which is used, Ps. li. 12, "Create in me a clean heart, O God;" Jer. xxxi. 22, "Jehovah hath created (brought about) a new thing in the earth;" Isa. lxv. 18, "I create (make) Jerusalem a rejoicing." But in the sense of *creating* at all, it is used of God only: and Gesenius thinks that in passages like this, the sense of creation out of nothing must be taken as intended by it. If not so here, what distinction would there be between this proposition and the narrative which follows, specifying as it does the arrangement and furnishing of that matter which is here said to have been created? **the heavens and the earth**] =, see reff., the whole world, the universe. The Hebraists tell us that there is in Hebrew no one word expressing this meaning. And therefore the expressions "heaven" and "earth," occurring here in an idiomatic formula, are not to be taken singly out and argued on as when they afterwards occur singly in the following narrative. **Heavens** is properly plural, and is so rendered in the A. V. in ch. ii. 1, and frequently elsewhere. It is not possible to preserve absolute uniformity in such renderings; but in solemn formulæ like the present, it is well to be precise. (*b*) **2.**] At a certain time, or, as first created, **the earth**—that which we now

e ch. viii. 2. Job xxviii. 14. Jonah ii. 5.
f ch. xli. 38. Num. xxiv. 2. Exod. xxxi. 3. Judg. iii. 10. Isa. lxi. 1 (Luke iv. 18). Ps. civ. 30.
g Deut. xxxii. 11.
h Ps. xxxiii. 9; cxxvii. 15; cxlviii. 8. John i. 1. Heb. xi. 3. 2 Pet. iii. 5.
i 2 Cor. iv. 6.

darkness *was* upon the face of the [e] deep. And the
[f] Spirit of God [g] moved upon the face of the waters.
3 ¶ And God [h] said, Let there be light: and [i] there was

know and inhabit, but then in embryo, in chaos—**was waste and empty** (literally, **wasteness and emptiness**). This is the true rendering. The expression *without form* seems to have been borrowed from the apocryphal Book of Wisdom (xi. 17). The Septuagint version has *invisible and unarranged.* In the Hebrew, the words have not only much the same meaning, but also a kindred sound; *tohu va bohu.* Besides this, **darkness was upon the face of,** rested upon and covered, **the deep**—(see ref.), the abyss of waters which enveloped the waste earth. The word thus rendered is derived from a root signifying *perturbation, commotion*—a raging deep of wild waters and storm. (*c*) **2.**] *The first action of God to bring order and light out of chaotic darkness.* **And the Spirit of God**—so, beyond question, the words are here to be rendered. The English reader need hardly be told that *spirit* is originally and literally *breath,* or *wind;* but that it has in usage and in Scripture acquired the meaning which we now commonly assign to it, of an immaterial, sentient, and active being; and when joined with *of God,* as here, the term becomes a theological one, variously indeed revealed and understood in the various ages of revelation, but always importing a personal agency of God. (See the reff., in which this meaning has its examples.) **moved upon** (lit. *fluttered over,* as a bird over her young, see ref. Deut., which is the only recurrence of the same form of this verb. The meaning evidently is, that the Spirit of God exerted an incubating or vivifying influence, preparatory to the great calling forth of organism and life which was to follow). This primeval chaotic form of matter, and evocation of life by a Divine influence, are common to the ancient Gentile cosmogonies. The Divine influence is personified as Eros (love), and is called the eldest of the gods. **3—31.**] THE SIX DAYS' WORK. And, herein, **3—5.**] *The first day's work:* the creation of LIGHT. **and God said**] It is well to mark the significance of these words, which form the introduction to each creative act. They are altogether anthropomorphic: translating a Divine method of proceeding, which is naturally removed out of our realm of cognizance into language expressing an analogy with human acts. Human commands are given to intelligent agents by the material organ of the voice: here God, who is a Spirit, is represented as exerting His power over non-intelligent matter by the utterance of words. This example, obvious as it is, of the anthropomorphism of the whole narrative, has, from our familiarity with the phrase, been overlooked. [Kalisch remarks, in his able commentary, "In the history of creation, God is said to hover (ver. 2); to speak (ver. 3, 6, &c.); to see and examine (ver. 4, 18, &c.); to give names (ver. 5, 8, &c.); to approve of His works (ver. 4, 12, &c.); to deliberate with Himself (ver. 26); to rest, and to repose Himself (ii. 2, 3); and even to make garments for the first pair (iii. 21). By these anthropomorphistic phrases, the biblical text loses nothing of its grandeur, and gains immeasurably in distinctness and perspicuity; it describes Divine manifestation for human beings and in a human medium."] Observe, that there is a material difference between this absolute proposition "**God said,**" and that other, "*God said unto Moses,*" or the like. God may have communicated His will to His intelligent creatures by the vehicle of sound, if it so pleased Him. But here we are on totally different ground. Observe, also, that this form of conveying to us the Divine procedure entirely precludes the idea of the creatures being emanation from God Himself. It implies a freely-acting Personality on the part of the Creator. In this employment of the Divine word as the agent in creation we see the first germs of the mysterious doctrine of the Personal Word as now known to us in the N. T. revelation. Compare the reff. **Let there be light**] The simplicity and sublimity of this record of the first act of the six-days' work has been observed even by those outside the faith of the Bible. With regard to the act itself, we may remark that the sacred writer first relates the creation of a world of matter, and then out of it, in a waste and dark condition, the separat-

light. 4 And God saw the light, that *it was* good: and
God divided between the light and the darkness. 5 And
God called the light Day, and the darkness he called
Night. And it was evening, and it was morning; one

ing of light and darkness, of waters above and waters below, of earth and seas, of day and night. Then we have the general before the elementary creation, the elementary before the special. It is in vain to inquire scientifically, as some have done, of what kind this first-created light was. We are not here in the realm of science, nor is the anthropomorphic arrangement of this Divine revelation of the facts of creation to be set parallel with our upward feelings after the ways and works of the God of Nature. **4.**] The oversight and approval by God of each of the works of creation, as made, is recorded again and again, in the spirit of the whole narrative, according to the analogy of human workmanship. But not only so. The sacred writer has it, from the first, in his purpose to affirm the absolute goodness of the Divine works: and this formula is only another and a more detailed method of saying that all creation followed the behest and the character of its maker, Himself all good.

and God divided] As above noticed, this *division*, this specific arrangement out of confusion, is the general character of these former days of creation. The scientific inquiry how this division were possible without the heavenly bodies, whose creation follows on the fourth day, is both a misuse of science and a misunderstanding of the narrative. No such matter-of-fact priority is here in question; light and darkness, as here spoken of, are not merely dependent on the presence or absence of the sun, but are phenomena of human sense and objects of human thought, distinct from each other. That they are so, is the effect of the creative act of God. By what arrangements He made provision for their alternation, does not enter here.

Between the light and the darkness is literally, **between the light and between the darkness.** **5.**] Here, again, we see the spirit of the narrative. We are still on the ground of purely elementary and general distinction, and the words will not bear pressing into literal accuracy. It is not always day where there is light, nor always night where there is darkness. But God made light to be the distinguishing mark of day, and darkness of night. The objection that the efficient causes of the succession of day and night have not yet been mentioned as created—as it does not stand in the way of the sacred writer, so neither should it in ours. This, again, is not enough remembered. The sacred writer could speak of this division: he could imply this succession through three days and a half; and yet he had no scruple to record *after all this* (ver. 14), that God said, Let there be lights . . . *to divide the day from the night.* Surely we are not called upon to be wiser than he was, nor to reconcile that as a difference which was none to him. He had reason for writing as he did; and the question for us is, What was that reason? By God **calling** the light Day, &c., is implied that God made the light (as above) to be the distinguishing mark of that which we call Day, &c. **and it was evening . . .**] This, which is, as it were, the *burden* or *refrain* of the six strophes in the narrative, is especially instructive, as it here occurs for the first time. For how shall we seek, if we are to seek, to press it in this case to a literal interpretation? There can be none, unless indeed the primeval darkness is to be taken as the evening, and the creation of light as the morning. And if that be so, then surely all attempt at literal interpretation is at an end. For neither was that darkness an evening, nor that light a morning, except in a sense altogether figurative and non-literal; and hardly even then, for evening darkens onward into night; which could in no sense be said of that primeval darkness; for it brightened into morning. From this consideration alone it would follow that the idea of a common day of 24 hours being intended, is quite foreign to the purpose. But this consideration does not stand alone. Such an hypothesis would be involved in the absurdity of limiting God's rest on the seventh day to a day of the same length, whereas we know that that rest is enduring. Again, let it be observed that the whole notion of equality of endurance, or of close succession, of these "days" of creation, is

day. 6 ¶ And God said, Let there be an expanse in the
midst of the waters, and let it be a division between the
waters and the waters. 7 And God made the expanse,
and divided between the waters under the expanse and
the waters above the expanse: and it was so. 8 And God
called the expanse Heaven. And it was evening, and

imaginary, and imported into the narrative. The story of creation is arranged in these periods, familiar to us; the great personal cause of every step in it is God, and God's will. But it is as irrelevant and as foolish to inquire minutely into the lower details following on a literal acceptance of the terms used in conveying this great truth to our minds, as it would be to take the same course with the words "God said,"—to inquire in what language He spoke, and to whom. It never can be too much impressed on the reader that we are, while perusing this account, in a realm separated by a gulf, impassable for human thought, from the matter-of-fact revelations which our senses make to us. We are listening to Him who made the world, as He explains to us in words, the imperfect instruments of our limited thoughts, His, to us, inscrutable procedure. **it was evening, and it was morning**] Many commentators have illustrated this order of making up the day by a similar way of speaking among many nations. But, as Kalisch well observes, such illustrations are not to be trusted: for if many used this arrangement, quite as many used the converse order. The choice would be ruled by considerations which may or may not be traceable. It may seem natural to end the day with the disappearance of the sun: it may seem natural also to begin the day at the moment when the darkness begins to wane into light. Some have reckoned their days from sunrise to sunrise, some from noon to noon. It is enough for the illustration of our text, that the Hebrews reckon them from sunset to sunset; and for Hebrews our text was written. **one day**] I have preferred giving throughout the literal rendering of these Hebrew formulæ. That adopted by the A. V., though passable in a *version*, does not tell us exactly what the text tells us. The definite article, "**the**," does not appear at all in it till ver. 31; and the use of that article throughout tends to give more idea of a definite pre-arranged week than is furnished by the text. **6—8.**] *The second day's work*: the creation of HEAVEN. **6. An expanse**] The Hebrew word is derived from a verb which signifies to *beat*, or to *spread out by beating*. And this, which our version, after the Septuagint and the Vulgate, calls a *firmament*, implies a solid vault. "The Hebrew idea of heaven was as of a substance (Exod. xxiv. 10), a firm vault fixed on the water-flood which surrounds the earth (Prov. viii. 27), firm as a molten looking-glass (Job xxxvii. 18), borne by the highest mountains, which are therefore called pillars and foundations of heaven (2 Sam. xxii. 8; Job xxvi. 11); doors and windows are attributed to it (ch. vii. 11, xxviii. 17; Ps. lxxviii. 23)." Knobel. Some have thought that by the word which the LXX. used they intended merely a solid of three dimensions, as distinguished from a mere surface; and so the Jew Philo interprets the word. But this hardly agrees with the passages quoted above, nor would there be in this case any contrast between the firmament and the waters, seeing that they are, in *this sense*, solid also. As the word *firmament* now stands in our A. V. it conveys no idea, having become in our usage synonymous with *heaven*. **and let it be a division**] The Hebrew expresses that the expanse is to be a *permanent* separation. **between the waters and the waters, &c.**] The region above the expanse was regarded as the storehouse of rain, which from thence descends to swell the waters below. The expanse of heaven separates these two, and thus the clear blue sky becomes visible. Beware of applying to such a record speculation about the watery material of the planets, or the like. The description is given by God according to the thoughts of them to whom it was given; and is altogether out of the realm of physical science. The LXX. insert here, *And God saw that it was good.* But these words are not found in the Hebrew; proba-

it was morning; a second day. [9] ¶ And God said, Let
the waters under the heaven be gathered together unto
one place, and let the dry *land* appear: and it was so.
[10] And God called the dry *land* Earth; and the gathering
together of the waters called he Seas: and God saw that
it was good. [11] And God said, Let the earth bring forth
grass, the herb yielding seed, the fruit tree yielding fruit
after his kind, whose seed *is* in itself, above the earth:
and it was so. [12] And the earth brought forth grass,
herb yielding seed after his kind, and the tree yielding
fruit, whose seed *is* in itself, after his kind: and God saw
that *it was* good. [13] And it was evening, and it was
morning; a third day. [14] ¶ And God said, Let there be

bly, because we are not at a point of completion; the upper and lower waters are separated, but on earth it was not yet good, for the dry land had not appeared.

9—13.] *The third day's work:* THE DRY LAND and THE SEAS: and VEGETATION. Observe the symmetry of the whole. This third day, on which plants were made, answers to the sixth, on which animals and man were created. **9.**] The earth was as yet a mere watery desert. It was necessary that the land and water should be separated, before the products of the earth could appear. Kalisch well remarks, "We have no right to ask how vegetation could exist and thrive before the creation of the sun; according to the biblical statement, the world and its contents were miraculously formed by the will of God; they are not the result of mere natural laws: and that order of the days seems just designed and intended to teach that the vegetation was called forth by the Omnipotence of God, and not by the influence of the solar rays."

10.] In the poetical expansion of this brief account, Ps. civ. 5—9, the method of this division between water and dry land is described to be the ascending of the mountains and subsidence of the valleys, and the consequent "parting" of the waters to the latter. See also Prov. viii. 24—29. But, as Kalisch again observes, we are not by either of these descriptions set at unity with the conclusions of science. The continents and seas have not always been relatively fixed; and the rock formations, even beneath the ocean, are not only full of animal and vegetable fossil remains, but are themselves evidences of long ages of deposit when they formed part of continents. "We have willingly renounced," he continues, "the attempt to discover that harmony [between Scripture and Science]; and both science and biblical exposition will gain by this candid understanding."

11.] **Let the earth bring forth** represents the endowing of the earth with power so to do. It is disputed, whether here *two* or *three* kinds of vegetable productions are specified. Some believe the first, here rendered **grass**, to represent *vegetation* in general, and to include the two subordinate kinds, the herb and the fruit-tree. Others, and it seems to me with more probability, regard the first as pointing to the universal covering of the earth, which, as was anciently believed, was of spontaneous growth without seed, while the second and third specify the herbs or "vegetables" which are propagated by seed, and the race of trees which bear both seed and fruit. **above (upon, A. V.) the earth.**] It is doubtful, again, whether these words represent the stature of the tree rising above the earth, as distinguished from that of the herb and the grass,—or belong to all the varieties of vegetation mentioned. The former view is supported by the use of the same Hebrew expression in ver. 20, "that may fly *above the earth;*" I have therefore kept the same rendering here as there.

14—19.] *The fourth day's work:* THE HEAVENLY BODIES. From this point, the second half of Creation's week begins: the

lights in the expanse of the heaven to divide between the
day and the night; and let them be for [j] signs, and for
[k] seasons, and for days, and years: 15 and let them be for
lights in the expanse of the heaven to give light upon the
earth: and it was so. 16 And God made the two great
lights; the greater light to [l] rule the day, and the lesser
light to [l] rule the night: *he made* the stars also. 17 And
God set them in the expanse of the heaven to give light
upon the earth, 18 and to rule over the day and over the
night, and to divide between the light and the darkness:
and God saw that *it was* good. 19 And it was evening, and
it was morning; a fourth day. 20 And God said, Let the
waters [m] swarm with [n] moving creatures that [o] have life,
and let fowl fly above the earth towards the expanse of

j Job iii. 3. Jer. x. 2. Matt. xxiv. 29.
k So Lev. xxiii. 2, 4, 37, 44. Num. x. 10; xv. 3; xxix. 39. Ps. civ. 19. Jer. viii. 7.
l Job xxxviii. 33.
m So ch. ix. 7. Exod. i. 7.
n So Lev. v. 2; xi. 29, &c.
o ch. ii. 7; ix. 3.

divisions of it answering to those of the first half. On the first day light was made: on the fourth, it is divided into its various vessels for the use of the world. On the second, the expanse of heaven was arranged, dividing the waters: on the fifth, the waters and the air are peopled with the winged tribes. On the third, the land and its vegetation is called into being: on the sixth, animals to people that land, and feed on its products; and, lastly, man, for whom all is made.

Observe, again, that in this section all is *geocentric*, related from the position also of man, with reference to this earth only, and as judged of by man's eye and measurement. Of astronomy or its facts there is here not a word. **14. lights**] *luminaries*, repositories of light. **for signs, &c.**] These terms have been variously interpreted. Kalisch thinks the most likely understanding of them, "for signs of the seasons, days, and years;" but Knobel and Keil, as it seems, more probably take "**signs**" as importing the tokens given by the heavenly bodies, which are so often mentioned in Scripture (see reff.). **seasons**] not merely times naturally marked, or days and years would not be also specified, but festal times; the word is derived from a verb signifying to *constitute*, to *appoint*: see reff., in all which places the same Hebrew noun occurs, and is thus rendered in A. V., except in Ps. civ. 19, where it is "He appointed the moon for *seasons*." Other appointed times, having reference to man or beast, may also be included, as the times of the migration of birds (Jer. viii. 7, where A. V. thus renders the word), the rutting-time of beasts, the periods of women, &c. **days and years** need no explanation. **15.**] Observe, all these services of the heavenly bodies are for the earth and for man. Of aught else there is no account taken. **16—18.**] The final words of this verse in the Hebrew are simply,—"**and the stars.**" Notice, again, how the myriads of fixed stars, and firmaments, are spoken of merely with reference to *giving light upon the earth*, and to serve man's purposes. "Biblical astronomy is derived from mere optical appearance; the eye alone is the judge; the moon is represented as the second of the great heavenly orbs, and as a luminous body; the stars are nothing else but her companions; and their only end is to shed their chaste lustre on our small planet." Kalisch.

20—23] *The fifth day's work:* FISHES AND BIRDS. **20. Let the waters**] As on the second day of the first triad, the waters below were separated from the waters above, and the expanse of air was constituted between the two; so on this, the second day of the second triad, those waters and air were peopled with living creatures. Observe, this is the first introduction of animal life: creation rising in a climax from the lowest to the highest. **teem with**] It is impossible to represent exactly the force of the Hebrew. The verb and the following substantive have the same sound, which feature cannot be preserved in English. The verb

heaven. 21 And God [p] created the great [q] whales, and
every living creature that moveth, with which the waters
teem abundantly, after their kind, and every winged
fowl after his kind: and God saw that *it was* good.
22 And God blessed them, saying, Be fruitful, and mul-
tiply, and fill the waters in the seas, and let fowl multiply
in the earth. 23 And it was evening, and it was morning;
a fifth day. 24 ¶ And God said, Let the earth bring forth
living creatures after their kind, cattle, and creeping
things, and beasts of the earth after their kind: and it
was so. 25 And God made the beasts of the earth after
their kind, and cattle after their kind, and all the creeping
things that creep upon the [r] ground after their kind: and
God saw that *it was* good. 26 ¶ And God said, Let us

p ver. 1, reff.
q Exod. vii. 9. Isa. xxvii. 1. See Ezek. xxxii. 2. Jer li. 34.
r So ch. ii. 19. Exod. xx. 21. 1 Sam. iv. 12. Neh. ix. 1.

is probably not to bring forth abundantly, but to *creep*, or *creep* [*with*], i. e. to *swarm* [with]: it is used of the frogs in Ex. viii. 3, *the river shall swarm* [with] *frogs;* and of men in reff. The substantive derived from the verb usually denotes *creeping things* (reff.). "Plainly," says Quarry, "it is the similarity in the manner of moving, with a wavy or serpentine action of the body, that gives rise to the double use of the word, while the signification which the verb has, to swarm, or produce abundantly, is plainly derived from the abundant offspring of such creatures, the numerous fry of fishes or young of worms being perhaps the chief ground for this use of the word. It is employed here for the sake of the alliteration, which cannot be preserved in a translation without departing from the sense of either the verb or the noun." **that have life**] literally, **a living soul**, where *soul* represents the animal principle, the vital element: see in ch. ii. 7. There is no trace in the original of the fowl being created out of the water, as the A. V., by inserting *that*, "*fowl that may fly*," gives. **towards the expanse**] Literally, to the face of the expanse, i. e. to the under face, which is turned towards us. There may be, as some have thought in classing both fishes and birds under one, as *moving creatures*, reference to the similarity of their motion; birds swimming in the air with their wings as fishes with their fins in the water. **21. Great whales**] The word thus rendered is derived from a verb signifying *extension*, and is used to denote any great monsters; as, e. g. *serpents*, ref. Exod.: *crocodiles*, ref. Isa.: *dragons*, ref. Jer. No scientific classification must be thought of; "the Hebrew term denotes both mammifer and non-mammifer." Kalisch. **22.**] Here we first hear of a blessing, and a command to multiply; for here we first have the power of spontaneous propagation. The words **in the earth** are a testimony against the connection of the creation of the fowls with the *waters*.

24—34.] *The sixth day's work:* THE ANIMALS OF THE EARTH, AND MAN. On this third day's work of the second triad of the week, see above, on ver. 14. **living creatures**] The same expression as before, **living soul**: expressing the complex idea of all creatures thus brought into being, that they had *animal life*. They are subdivided into three classes: **cattle**—the non-predaceous, graminivorous animals: **beasts of the earth**,—the beasts of prey, and **creeping things**, worms and reptiles.

25.] The word rendered **ground** is not that which has been rendered **earth** throughout the history, but is *Adamah*, soil, the term cognate to *Adam* (see on both, ch. ii. 19).

26—28.] This is the first instance of more than one 'saying' of God during the creative day. **Let us make**] This plural form of deliberation has been variously interpreted:—(1) The idea of a *Trinitarian* explanation lay too close to the inclination and the practice of the Christian Fathers, and those who in modern times have followed them, not to draw them aside. But any such

s ch. v. 3; ix. 6. 1 Sam. vi. 5, 11. Ezek. xvi. 17.
t 2 Chron. iv. 3. Isa. xl. 18.

make man in our [s]image, after our [t]likeness: and let them have dominion over the fish of the sea, and over the fowl of the heaven, and over the cattle, and over all the earth, and over the creeping things that creep upon the

intimation here would be in the highest degree unnatural and incongruous. The doctrine of the Holy Trinity, which lies at the very root of the New Covenant, was gradually and insensibly opened even in the Old Testament. But to discover, in such expressions as this, inlets into the secrets of the Godhead, is to violate the proportion and analogy of faith. (2) Some have thought it the plural of *majesty:* against which it is urged as an objection, that the repetition of the plural again "*in* **our** *image, in* **our** *likeness,*" seems to require a deeper reason than one of mere form; or (3) of agreement with the plural form of **Elohim,**—which cannot stand, seeing that in ch. xi. 7, we have the same deliberative plural connected, not with the plural form **Elohim,** but with the singular **Jehovah;** or (4) of *communication,* understanding that God took counsel with the heavenly powers. But this, though adopted by the Jewish Targums and Philo, and by the Christian Delitzsch, would both be unbefitting, and is contradicted by what follows: for man was not created in the image of the angels as well as in that of God, but in that of God only; or (5) of mere superfluity, having no meaning at all,—which hardly needs refuting; or (6) as an address to that personified Wisdom of God which is said (Prov. viii. 22, ff.) to have been present with God at the creation: but this in its bare form would be liable to the same objections as lie against the Trinitarian explanation; or (7) of pure *deliberation,* one who deliberates being both speaker and spoken to, and thus having a kind of double personality. This last view is that of Kalisch, who refers to ch. xi. 7, above noticed, and to Ezra iv. 18, vii. 24 (which two seem rather the regal plural of majesty).

I am inclined to think that the habit, testified by the name **Elohim,** and corrected by its usage with singular verbs and adjectives, of connecting plurality, perhaps for the sake of majesty, with the idea of God, would in some measure account for this plural. And it would be no objection, that the same plural occurs with the singular JEHOVAH in ch. xi. 7: because the idea would there rule the deliberative expression, as here. Then, again, do the phrases "*in* **our** *image, in* **our** *likeness,*" necessarily require any more profound account than this; they must necessarily follow the form of the preceding. This shadowed ideal plurality might, as Lange well reminds us, not be altogether unconnected with the fact that besides God, **the spirit of God** has been already mentioned. The fact of Divine deliberation here, and here only, interrupting the continuous flow of God's creative acts, sufficiently indicates the solemnity of that which is to follow. Earth and earth's tribes were prepared; but now there is a king to be set over them,—one like them, but also unlike them: a complex being, made up of the dust of the earth and of the image of God. We may observe, once for all, that the word here rendered **man** is *Adam,* as throughout the whole history of the fall. I have followed Kalisch's example, and have not changed it into a proper name, till we are beyond this portion of Genesis, and he is distinguished in the genealogies from other men. **in our image, after our likeness]** The former substantive means primarily, *a shadow*; hence a sketch, or effigy, or image (see reff.): the latter is literally rendered (reff.).

The distinction between these two phrases, much maintained of old, viz. that the former applies to the physical, the latter to the ethical side of man's likeness to God, appears to be groundless. They are far more probably synonymous. Luther has rendered them "an image which may be like us." That the two words do not differ in meaning, is shown by their indiscriminate use, the former in ver. 27 and in ch. ix. 6, and the latter in ch. v. 1, where the same thing is evidently meant. This likeness consists not in his nobler external form,—for God has none; not in his imperial rule over earth and her inhabitants,—for this would be only a consequence of his likeness to God;—but in his superior spiritual nature, which he has by direct communication from God, as the parallel account, ch. ii. 7, gives it. This spiritual nature, when free from sin, reflect-

earth. 27 So God [u] created man in his image, in the image
of God [u] created he him; male and female [u] created he u ver. 1, reff.
them. 28 And God blessed them, and God said unto them,
Be fruitful, and multiply, and replenish the earth,
and subdue it: and have dominion over the fish of the
sea, and over the fowl of the heaven, and over every living
thing that creepeth upon the earth. 29 ¶ And God said,
Behold, I have given you every herb bearing seed, which
is upon the face of all the earth, and every tree, in the
which *is* the fruit of a tree yielding seed; to you it shall
be for food. 30 And to every beast of the earth, and to
every fowl of the heaven, and to every thing that creep-
eth upon the earth, wherein *there is* life, *I have given* every
[v] green herb for meat: and it was so. 31 And God saw v ch. ii. 5. Prov. xxvii. 25.
every thing that he had made, and, behold, *it was* very
good. And it was evening, and it was morning; the sixth
day. II. 1 AND the heavens and the earth were finished,
and all the [w] host of them. 2 And on the seventh day God w Neh. ix. 6. Isa. xxxiv. 2.

ed in small the spiritual nature of God himself. When sin intervened, it lost its purity and dignity, its holiness and blessedness, but not its basis and form. Christ is the restorer again to it of the Divine image, Col. iii. 10; Eph. iv. 24. The words **all the earth** are rendered by the Syriac version, and are by some commentators understood to imply, the beasts of the earth or of the forests. Otherwise, they are not specified in this catalogue. **27.**] The repetition gives solemnity and importance—the fact was as God in His deliberation had proposed it. **male and female created he them**] There is no absolute assertion here that one pair alone were first created: but it follows in the Jehovistic narrative, ch. ii. 7, 22; and is implied in the Elohistic of ch. v. 3. There is no reason to infer from these words that both sexes were at first united in the man, as some have supposed. This account is independent of the details which follow in ch. ii., and speaks generally. But evidently in the form of *this* narrative, both sexes were created on the sixth day, so that the Jehovistic account, ch. ii. 4, must be regarded not as consecutive on this, but as complete in itself, and beginning from the first.—It has been observed that the parallelism of style begins at this verse, and gives to it a kind of jubilant character. **28.**] The blessing of man and the declaration of his prerogative of dominion next follow. The blessing is double: that of fruitfulness they share with the fishes, fowls; that of dominion is peculiarly their own.

29, 30.] *The assignment of food to man, and the animals.* It appears from this, that vegetable diet alone was originally assigned to man, the vegetable world being shared between him and the inferior animals; man taking the seed-bearing trees and plants, and the animals the "green herbs," literally, **the green of the herb.** Traditions of the same fact are found in various Gentile writers of Greece and Rome, and the ancient practice of Egypt, India, and Syria agrees thereto. **life** is literally "**a living soul.**" **31.**] The approval, given separately to each day's work before, is now not repeated for that of the sixth day, but is spread over the whole, and the approval is intensified by the addition of **very.** The latter clause stands literally **a day, the sixth.**

II. 1.] *General summary.* The word rendered **host** is generally used of the heavens alone. In ref. Neh., we have the expression more conformed to ordinary usage. In ref. Isa., the word rendered *armies* in A. V. is the same: see note there

ended his work which he made; and he [x] rested on the
seventh day from all his work which he made. 3 And
God [y] blessed the seventh day, and [z] sanctified it: because
that on it he rested from all his work which he [a] created
and made.

4 ¶ [b] These *are* the generations of the heavens and of

x Isa. xiv. 4; xxxiii. 8. Lam. v. 14. ch. viii. 22.
y Exod. xxiii. 25. Job i. 10. Ps. lxv. 10; cxxxii. 15. Prov. iii. 33.
z Lev. xxi. 8. Joel i. 14.
a ch. i. 1, reff.
b ch. x. 1; xi. 10, 27; xxv. 12, 19; xxxvi. 1, 9. Num. iii. 1. Ruth iv. 18. 1 Chron. i. 29. See ch. v. 1.

2, 3.] God's rest on, and blessing of, the seventh day. There is no difficulty in the assertion that God **ended** His work on the seventh day. As Keil well remarks, this **ending** had two aspects,—negative, in leaving off creating, and positive, in blessing the seventh day. The Samaritan Pentateuch, as also the LXX., reads *sixth* for seventh, doubtless on account of the apparent difficulty. Others, as Kalisch, understand **ended** as a pluperfect, *had ended:* but this hardly seems necessary. **rested**] Ceased to work, see Lam. v. 14, 15, where the A. V. renders the verb by cease. In none of those places is there any implication of rest owing to weariness, but merely of abstaining from doing what was done before. Still, although we know that the Creator of the ends of the earth is not weary, Isa. xl. 28, it would be vain to deny that by the very terms here the human idea of rest after work is suggested, and was meant to be suggested. The record of creation, which throughout suits the Divine acts to man's ways of thought, here gives the most notable example of this procedure, in the Almighty worker resting from His work. It was to guard against the literal acceptation of this, that our Lord asserted against the Jews, "My Father worketh hitherto, and I work," John v. 17. **3.] blessed** is the same word as before in ch. i. 22, 28. Here it is left to be explained by what follows. Its usage with regard to inanimate things will be found in reff. **sanctified**] Set apart as holy, "separated it from the other days, and gave it a higher significance," as Knobel. This higher significance was not fully brought out till the giving of the Mosaic law: though there are traces of the recurrence of the day being observed in pre-Mosaic times: see on ch. iv. 3; viii. 10, 12. It is useless to deny that the intent of this ordinance, solemnly completing as it did the work of creation, was to be coëval with mankind, the appointed lords of the world thus finished. But it is, by this very consideration, and the reason on which it rests, equally futile to suppose that any subsequent circumstances could change the day thus to be observed. We cannot first say that this sanctification of the seventh day is binding on all men in all time, because its ground concerns God's rest after creation, and then transfer that obligation to another day, to which no such reason applies. With the stricter Mosaic sanctions of the day, we Christians have no concern: but its significance as commemorative of God's rest has no more passed away for us than the significance of the rainbow or any other fact naturally recurring which has been by God clothed with sacred meaning. That the Christian Church has seen fit to observe as a sacred day the *first* which witnessed the resurrection of our Lord, is a matter resting on wholly different grounds, and not to be referred to this ordinance for its sanction: a practice which in the purer times of the Church, and by her best authors, was consistently repudiated. To confound the two is to destroy the landmarks of the symbolism of creation and of the kingdom of grace. "The Church," says Delitzsch well, "keeps the Sunday; but the Sabbath remains the blessed and hallowed Day of Days." **created and made**] Literally, **created to produce,** or **created producing:** a frequent Hebrew mode of speech, used constantly in such phrases as "spoke saying" (lit. spoke to speak), Exod. vi. 10, al.,—"laboured to do," Eccl. ii. 11, &c.

II. **4**—III. **24.**] *Second account of the creation of the world and of man:* PARADISE AND THE FALL. **4. These are the generations**] This is an opening formula, and has reference to what follows: see reff. It is not to be taken as closing the former account and referring back. It is plain that the meaning of the generations must be extended beyond mere *origin;* as it is indeed in many places, e. g. ch. vi. 9; xxv. 19;

the earth when they were created. In the [c] day that God
Jehovah made the earth and the heavens, 5 no plant
of the field was yet on the earth, and no herb of the field
did yet sprout forth : because God Jehovah had not caused
it to rain upon the earth, and *there was* not a man to till
the ground. 6 And there went up a [d] mist from the earth,
and watered the whole face of the ground. 7 And God
Jehovah [e] formed the man of the [f] dust of the ground, and
breathed into his nostrils the breath of life ; and the man
became a living creature. 8 ¶ And God Jehovah planted
a garden in [g] Eden, [h] eastward ; and there he put the man

c Num. iii. 1. Exod. vi. 28. Isa. xi. 16.
d Job xxxvi. 27.
e Isa. xliv. 9, 12 ; liv. 17 ; lxiv. 8. ch. i. 20, 21.
f ch. xxvi. 15. Josh. vii. 6.
g ch. iv. 16. Isa. li. 3. Ezek. xxviii. 13 ; xxxi. 9, 16, 18. Joel ii. 3.
h ch. iii. 24 ; iv. 16 ; xi. 2, reff.

xxxvii. 2. **when they were created**] Lit., **in their creation**. Here the first member of the sentence appears to end : not as in A. V. So Kalisch. But see Num. iii. 1, which seems to favour the other construction. **In the day that**] It is not necessary, as some have done, to suppose that we must take the word **day** literally (see reff.), so as to create a discrepancy between this and the former account. **5**.] Literally, **and every plant of the field was not yet in the earth, and every herb of the field sprouted not yet** : i. e. the earth was as yet void of vegetable life. This might be taken as denoting a point in ch. i., corresponding to the middle of the third day, were it not for the reason which follows : viz. that the earth was as yet dry. In ch. i. the waters at first covered the whole, then (ver. 9) were gathered into one place and the dry land appeared. In that case the "dry land," having but newly emerged from the water, would not be in want of rain. It is lamentable to see commentators attempting, by quibbling on mere words, to deny a substantial difference like this. Thus it is said that because the land is called "dry" there, the account is in accord with this which affirms dryness of it. But who does not see that the term "dry (land)" there is merely one of distinction from "water," and has absolutely nothing to do with the intrinsic quality of the earth composing such land ? On the difference between the earth "dry" and "dried," see note on ch. viii. 14.

6. a mist] The word is rendered by the LXX. and the ancient Syriac version, a *fountain* : but this appears to be incorrect. The moisture rose in vapour, and fell in rain, for so it is implied. **7.** *The creation of the man*] Thus one of the hindrances to vegetation was removed ; and now the other is to be taken away. One is to be supplied to till the ground. **formed**] fashioned, shaped : the word is used in reff. Isa., of workmen forming an image, of weapons formed, of the work of a potter. **a living creature**] see reff., where the Hebrew words are precisely the same. The description is not one bringing out any distinctive attribute of man, but simply one describing the animation of the form shaped out of the dust of the earth, whereby he became, what in ch. i. the various tribes of created things are described as becoming, a living being. The difference, whatever it may be, between him and other living creatures, is not declared in this term, but would be deduced from the agency whereby he was endued with life. Into no other creature do we read that God breathed the breath of life. This verse seems plainly referred to in Job xxxiii. 4. See also Isa. xlii. 5. **8—15.** *The garden of Eden.* **a garden**] This word is rendered in the LXX. and Vulgate *a paradise*,—that name being one common to the Semitic languages (occurring in Neh. ii. 8 ; Eccl. ii. 5 ; Cant. iv. 13) to signify the gardens which surrounded the palaces of kings and the wealthy : see 2 Kings xxv. 4 ; Jer. xxxix. 4. **in Eden**] The word signifies pleasure or delight ; and is thus used in Ps. xxxvi. 8 ; 2 Sam. i. 24. Hence the Vulgate here renders "*a garden of pleasure*," and so the LXX. in ver. 15. But by comparing ch. iv. 16, there can be little doubt that it is here used as a proper name, and denotes a particular spot. Where situated, has been a vexed question, which never can be determined. The various opinions would require pages even to enumerate ; they may

whom he had formed. 9 And out of the ground made
God Jehovah to grow every tree that is pleasant to the
sight, and good for food; the tree of life also in the midst
of the garden, and the tree of knowledge of good and evil.
10 And a river went out of Eden to water the garden; and
from thence it was parted, and became into four heads.
11 The name of the first, Pison: that *is* it which compass-
eth the whole land of [i] Havilah, where *there is* the gold;
12 and the gold of that land *is* good: there *is* [j] bdellium
and the [k] onyx stone. 13 And the name of the second

i ch. xxv. 18. 1 Sam. xv. 7.
j Num. xi. 7 only.
k Exod. xxix. 13. Job xxviii. 16.

be found tabulated in Kalisch. Observe, the name in Hebrew is distinct from that of Eden in Assyria, mentioned 2 Kings xix. 12; Isa. xxxvii. 12; Ezek. xxvii. 23; Amos i. 5. **eastward**] This word is rendered in the Vulgate, *from the beginning*, but scholars seem agreed that this is a mistake: see reff., especially the two first: and that it signifies **in**, or **at**, or **towards the east.** **9.**] Consistency of interpretation requires that we understand the tree of life here and in Rev. xxii. 2 (ii. 7) by the same rule. In this history, it is a tree, the fruit whereof conferred immortality; see ch. iii. 22; as that of the other tree conferred knowledge of the difference between right and wrong. **10—14.**] Compare, throughout, the description of the heavenly paradise in Rev. xxii. 1, 2. It seems futile to seek geographically for four rivers which *rise near* one another, thus rationalizing the description. There was *one river* (not mere contiguous origin): and it, *after it had watered the garden*, was parted into four streams, whose names indicate the most important rivers of the world. **heads** does not signify *sources*, but principal streams, i. e. as we should say, *arms*. **11, 12.**] It is quite uncertain what river is here indicated,—opinions are very various. The most notable are those which identify Pison with 1. the Ganges. This was held by Josephus, Eusebius, Ambrose, Epiphanius, Jerome, Augustine, and others. Kalisch prefers the Indus. Some have thought of the *Phasis*, but only, it would appear, from similarity of sound. **Havilah**] What this is, is equally uncertain. Opinions have been mostly ruled by previous conjecture about the river Pison. The land of Havilah in ref. Gen. forms one boundary of the people of Ishmael, the other being "Shur, which is before Egypt, as thou goest toward Assyria:" in ref. 1 Sam. it is also connected with "Shur, that is over against Egypt." There is a Havilah, a son of Cush the son of Ham, in ch. x. 7; and another, the son of Joktan the son of Eber, ib. 29. On the peoples supposed to be descended from these, see *Havilah*, in Smith's Biblical Dictionary. **12.**] From the description of the gold as good, it is plain that the countries and rivers here spoken of are to be regarded as subsisting when the account was written, not as belonging to a state of things gone by. **bdellium**] In the Hebrew, *Bdolach*. Here, again, we have a dispute as to what is intended. Bdellium is explained by Pliny to be a *gum*, found in Bactriana, Arabia, India, Media, and Babylon. But Gesenius thinks this could not be precious enough to be ranked with the onyx which follows: and therefore inclines to the opinion of the Jewish writers, who believed *pearls* to be intended. In ref. Num., the manna is said to have been *of the colour of bdellium*, which would suit the pearl, but not so well the gum. But Pliny describes it as translucid, like wax; so that there seems no force in this argument. **the onyx stone**] Heb. *Shoham*, generally thus interpreted: this interpretation at least suits the colour,—the name meaning *pale*, and the *onyx* being so named as signifying in Greek *a fingernail*. See reff. **13.**] About Gihon there is less dispute, almost all agreeing that it is the Nile. In Jer. ii. 18, the LXX. render Sihon, which is the Nile, by *Geon*. The land of Cush (eldest son of Ham, ch. x. 6), which it is said to encompass, is the country of the South, comprising Ethiopia and all that was known to the Hebrews in their direction. See reff. Kalisch mentions and illustrates the ancient

river, Gihon: the same *is* it that compasseth the whole
land of [l]Cush. 14 And the name of the third river,
Hiddekel: that *is* it which floweth in front of Assyria.
And the fourth river, that *is* Euphrates. 15 And God
Jehovah took the man, and put him into the garden of
Eden to till it and to guard it. 16 And God Jehovah
commanded the man, saying, Of every tree of the garden
thou mayest freely eat: 17 but of the tree of the know-
ledge of good and evil, thou shalt not eat of it: for in the
day that thou eatest thereof thou shalt surely die.
18 ¶ And God Jehovah said, *It is* not good that the man
should be alone; I will make him an [m] help [n] like unto him.
19 And out of the ground God Jehovah formed every
beast of the field, and every fowl of the air, and brought
it unto the man to see what he would call it: and what-

l Isa. xviii. 1; xliii. 3; xlv. 16. Esth. i. 1, al.

m Ps. xxxiii. 20; lxx. 5; cxv. 9—11.

n Isa. xl. 17; Neh. xii. 9.

popular belief that the Ganges and Nile, or Indus and Nile, were part of the same great river. **14.**] HIDDEKEL is generally believed to be the TIGRIS. The name is formed by prefixing the epithet "*swift*" (Chad) to the name of the river, Digla, or Dekel, the universally-received name of the Tigris, which already signified "*swiftness*." There is a difficulty in the rendering of the A. V., *toward the east of Assyria*, seeing that the Tigris bounded Assyria on the *west*. The marginal rendering, *eastward to Assyria*, devised to escape the difficulty, seems hardly allowable. The word rendered *toward the east* also means "in front." It is used in Ps. cxxxix. 5, in this sense, and Isa. ix. 12; and Kalisch maintains that it has this meaning here. So also Knobel, and others. The fourth river has no local notice attached to it, as being thoroughly known to the Hebrews. **15.**] The second object is now accomplished, a man to till the ground. The other part of the duty of the man is stated with reference to present circumstances, under which a garden requires watching and protecting. Knobel understands it to have been the guarding his charge against the tribes of beasts which were about to be created. **16, 17.**] *The primal command to the man.* The only difficulty in these verses is presented by the concluding words. Man did not die in the day when he ate thereof. The simplest solution of the difficulty is found in remembering that death is not only the actual separation of soul and body, but includes all that culminates in that separation. A man may, as we say, "die by inches:" and may be said, especially if passing from a state where death was not the necessary end of his days, to die, when the seeds of death begin to work in him. It is not sufficiently borne in mind, that man's exclusion from the tree of life which could have conferred immortality on him, was the carrying out of this sentence. **18—24.**] *The creation of woman.* **18.**] **like unto him,** literally, **as in front of,** or, over against him; i. e. corresponding to himself. The likeness is both physical and mental. The same word is used in ref. Isa., of one thing set *over against another* by way of comparison: in ref. Neh., of one set of men *corresponding to another*. The Vulgate renders as our text. **19.**] In pursuance of the purpose just announced, Jehovah forms out of the ground the beasts and birds. But for the difficulty of uniting this second narrative with the former one, no one would have dreamt of other than the *prima facie* understanding of this, that at this time, and subsequently to man, the beasts and birds were created. As to the reconciliation of the two, it need not trouble those who, like the sacred writer who originally set together these two accounts, are not slaves of the letter but freemen of the spirit. Those who insist on strict historical consecutiveness in the days

soever the man called every living creature, that *was* the
name thereof. 20 And the man gave names to all cattle,
and to the fowl of the air, and to every beast of the field;
but for the man he found not an help like unto him.
21 And God Jehovah caused a [o] deep sleep to fall upon the
man, and he slept: and he took one of his ribs, and
closed up the flesh in the place thereof; 22 and the rib,
which God Jehovah had taken from the man, [p] formed he
into a woman, and brought her unto the man. 23 And the
man said, This time it is bone of my bones, and flesh of my
flesh: this shall be called Woman, because this was taken
out of Man. 24 [q] Therefore shall a man leave his father
and his mother, and shall cleave unto his wife: and they
shall be one flesh.

o ch. xv. 12. 1 Sam. xxvi. 12.

p Literally, built. See 1 Kings xviii. 32.

q ch. x. 9; xxvi. 33; xxxii. 32.

of creation are obliged here to have recourse to various devices which for us are unneeded. The man was endowed by his Creator with the gift of speech—and that endowment presupposed the perception of the congruity of sounds with the things which to the thoughts of men they represent. Exercising this faculty and perception, the man gives names to the various animals. **20.**] **he**, that is, the man, **found no help like unto him** (self). The process of giving names was, in fact, that of declaring attributes and qualities: and among all these, none occurred bearing with it that correspondence to himself which was sought for. See below on ver. 23. **21, 22.**] Notice again, as characteristic of this second narrative, the formative and tentative processes used. Compare the short and majestic words of the former narrative, "male and female created He them." Jehovah *built* up the rib into a woman. the **rib**, as taken from the side, where is the heart: typifying the close and inseparable connection. Woman is made, not out of the dust of the earth, but out of *man*. Woman did not receive the command to obedience, but through and as part of man. Woman did not take any part in those first utterances which fixed the names of creation, but inherited them from man. There is no part of the sacred narrative warning us more forcibly against bondage to the letter. The whole is parabolic and symbolic. **23.**] **this time it is**,—in contrast with the previous exhibition to him of those who were not helps corresponding to him. **woman**] In the Hebrew, *Ishah*, as being taken out of *Ish*. **24.**] These words may be intended as spoken by the man: or they may be the words of the writer of Genesis. The latter is maintained by Delitzsch, both as suiting best the citation by our Lord, Matt. xix. 5, and because this particle "Wherefore" or "Therefore" commonly introduces parenthetical remarks by the writer: see reff. But Delitzsch seems subsequently to have changed his view; and the coherence of the narrative as well as the solemnity of the saying appears to require that it should be represented as a prophetic saying for all mankind, spoken by their first father. That our Lord quotes it as a word of "Him that made them from the beginning," is in no way against this view; not because, as some, Adam may have spoken by Divine inspiration (of which there is no hint, and which would not, after all, fulfil the saying of our Lord), but because the whole account is one given by God's inspiration as a Divine narrative of the origin of mankind. The mention of *father and mother* in the mouth of Adam is, of course, not to be judged servilely according to the letter, but to be regarded as of a piece with the whole spiritual character of the narrative. Their state was one of innocence void of shame—as that even now of children,—of whom these same words may still be said. **25—III. 24.**] *The Fall.* Ver. 25 is not, as commonly taken, the conclusion of what has gone before, but, as Quarry has

25 And they were both naked, the man and his wife,
and were not ashamed. III. 1 And the serpent was more
[r]subtil than any beast of the field which God Jehovah had
made. And he said unto the woman, Yea, hath God said,
Ye shall not eat of any tree of the garden? 2 And the
woman said unto the serpent, Of the fruit of the trees
of the garden we may eat: 3 but of the fruit of the tree
which *is* in the midst of the garden, God hath said, Ye
shall not eat of it, neither shall ye touch it, lest ye die.
4 And the serpent said unto the woman, Ye shall not DIE:

r Job v. 12; xv 5. Prov. xii. 16, 23, al.

well pointed out, the opening of the following narrative. However solemn the purport of that narrative, the coherence of it is found in, (1) the fact of their nakedness (ii. 25); (2) the discovery of that nakedness (iii. 7); (3) the remedy of that nakedness (iii. 21). **25.**] Of the whole of the account, it is hardly to be doubted that the solemn fact of man's temptation is conveyed to us in terms of parable and allegory. Reverence requires this conclusion, no less than reason. To suppose the narrative realistic and matter of fact is to degrade it from the higher spiritual reality. This view has been held without blame, both in ancient and modern times. Eusebius says, "There is present to each of us a wicked demon, lying in wait for us, a seducer, and a hater of good, and the same that from the beginning plotted against the salvation of man. He (Moses) calls this demon a dragon and a serpent, because he is black and allied to darkness, full of poison and malice. . . . . by his fraud our first parents also fell from their Divine estate;" hereby plainly showing that in his view the spiritual and not the literal interpretation was to be taken. And Cardinal Cajetan says, "It is plain, both by the method of speech of all Scripture, and by that of this narrative, that under the name of the serpent we must not understand the reptile thus called, but the devil." With this interpretation we are content: not inquiring further whether the tempter of man is to be supposed to have assumed the form of a serpent, and in that form to have spoken with Eve, any more than whether the serpent is to be conceived as changing its physical character after the curse. Regarding the whole as a Divine parable setting forth to us the spiritual facts of the fall of man, we are not careful about such matters. See below on ver. 14. It is remarkable, in connection with our Lord's saying in John viii. 44, that the Samaritan Pentateuch has here *liar* instead of serpent: the two words in Hebrew differing only by one letter. Observe, that the name Jehovah is not used by the serpent, nor by the woman, but only by the sacred writer in the course of his narrative. Some commentators have found deep meaning in the non-use of "Jehovah" by the serpent: but they have omitted to observe that it is wanting in the woman's speech likewise. Those who have observed on this, have thought that it was to preserve the Holy name from the desecration of being uttered *to* the serpent. Observe that doubt is the beginning of temptation. Stress has also been laid on the fact that the woman's answer goes further than the Divine prohibition. Kalisch regards this as an exaggeration, showing "the fanaticism of passion and its self-deception;" but he thinks, as *she* did not receive the command, this may have arisen from its being misreported to her. Lange sees in this overdone obedience the first wavering of allegiance. But surely we may turn round such subjectivities as easily the other way, and suppose this additional particular to have been inserted in the ardent desire to obey. Not that I really take it so—but such a consideration serves to show the insecurity of such fine tracking of words to their supposed sources. The same may be said of almost all the minute inferences which have been drawn from this reply. The best exposure of their unsafeness is that some hold Eve's reply to be a sign of her unswerving loyalty, others of her incipient disloyalty to God. **4.**] It is not easy to give in this verse the force of the original, which brings out into promi-

5 for God doth know that in the day ye eat thereof, then
your eyes shall be opened, and ye shall be as God, know-
ing good and evil. 6 And when the woman saw that the
tree *was* good for food, and that it *was* pleasant to the
eyes, and a tree to be desired to [s]make *one* wise, she took
of the fruit thereof, and did eat, and gave also unto her
husband with her; and he did eat. 7 And the eyes of them
both were opened, and they knew that they *were* naked; and
they [t]sewed fig leaves together, and made themselves
girdles. 8 And they heard the voice of God Jehovah
walking in the garden in the cool of the day: and the
man and his wife hid themselves from the presence of God
Jehovah amongst the trees of the garden. 9 And God
Jehovah called unto the man, and said unto him, Where
art thou? 10 And he said, I heard thy voice in the
garden, and I was afraid, because I *was* naked; and I hid
myself. 11 And he said, Who told thee that thou *art*
naked? Hast thou eaten of the tree, whereof I com-
manded thee that thou shouldest not eat? 12 And the
man said, The woman whom thou gavest *to be* with me,
she gave me of the tree, and I did eat. 13 And God

s Neh. viii. 13, marg.; ix. 20. Prov. xxi. 11. Dan. ix. 22, marg.

t Job xvi. 15. Eccl. iii. 7. Ezek. xiii. 8.

nence the threatened punishment as something utterly incongruous to the known effect of the fruit. It may best be done perhaps by laying strong emphasis on the word DIE. Our insertion in the A. V. of "*surely*" does not answer the purpose, because that adverb is apt to be taken with the whole, as if it were, "Surely ye shall not die:" which, though Kalisch thus renders, can hardly represent the meaning. **6.] to make one wise**] There is considerable doubt about the meaning of this word. The LXX., Vulgate, the Targum of Onkelos, and some of the ancient versions, render it **to look upon.** But seeing that the word will certainly bear the other meaning (see reff.), and that the proposed one introduces almost a repetition of the preceding clause, I have kept the A. V.

7.] It seems better, with Kalisch and Gesenius, to take this as the ordinary fig, whose leaves would require uniting for this purpose, than, with Knobel, and others, as the banana or musa, one of whose leaves would be too large for the purpose. The ordinary fig is indigenous over the whole East.

8.] The anthropomorphism of the narrative may be said here to reach its highest example. Eden is the garden of God, and He is represented as gone forth to walk in the cool, literally, the wind, of the day, i. e. in the breeze which springs up in the evening, and invites into the open air. Who can doubt that we are as much in the region of parable here, as when we read of the Householder who planted a vineyard and let it out, or the certain man who came seeking fruit on his fig-tree? **11.**] Literally, **Of the tree, whereof I commanded thee that thou shouldest not eat, of that hast thou eaten?**

12, 13.] Kalisch's remarks here are well worth extracting: "God was in familiar intercourse with man in the happy days of his innocence. He was loved as a father; fear was unknown: the severe rule, 'nobody beholds God and lives,' did not yet exist. As man was scarcely aware of his superiority over the animal creation, so he was hardly impressed with that awe of God which the consciousness of His grandeur inspires. His eyes were not yet opened. He knew neither pride nor humility. He walked in simplicity, careless, but sure of the right path.

Jehovah said unto the woman, What *is* this *that* thou
hast done? And the woman said, The serpent beguiled
me, and I did eat. 14 And God Jehovah said unto the
serpent, Because thou hast done this, thou *art* cursed above
all cattle, and above every beast of the field; upon thy
belly shalt thou go, and [u] dust shalt thou eat all the days of
thy life: 15 and I will put [v] enmity between thee and the

u Isa. lxv. 25. Micah vii. 17. See Ps. lxxii. 9. Isa. xlix. 23; also Ps. cii. 9.

v Num. xxxv. 21, 22. Ezek. xxv. 15; xxxv. 5, only.

But now he was awakened to a sense of duty. He cannot bear the presence of God: it overwhelms his spirit. He hears His step; he hides himself; he answers timidly to the question of God; he fears His anger; he tries to avert it, by laying the fault partly upon his wife and partly *upon God himself;* 'the woman whom thou gavest *to be with* me, she gave me of the tree, and I did eat'; and Eve, not less terrified, accuses the serpent as the cause of the transgression. The voice of conscience troubled for the first time the internal peace. The harmony of the mind was disturbed. We abstain from developing the many and important practical truths contained in this narrative; we cannot wonder that many have here abandoned themselves to the strains of the preacher; it is indeed tempting to pursue the inimitable and unparalleled description of the consequences of sin, the uneasiness and timidity, the cowardice, the internal wretchedness which, as a last resource, impeaches even God as the primary cause of the offence. It is sufficient for us to have indicated the general course of ideas which our section suggests, and to have pointed out the successive stages of innocence, temptation and conflict, sin, remorse, and banishment, which are represented by the Paradise, the serpent, the forbidden fruit, the concealment, and the curse." I may add to these admirable remarks, that if, in the majestic simplicity of the former cosmogony in ch. i., one felt that we were listening to Him who in the beginning made the heavens and the earth, we here feel that every word of the mysterious parable is inspired by Him who "needed not that any should testify of man; for He knew what was in man." **14, 15.**] As, long after, the rainbow, a phenomenon which must have always subsisted since the creation of light and water, was consecrated to a symbol of the covenant between God and man, so here the serpent, which must always since its creation have maintained its present form and habits, was in that form and those habits appointed a symbol of the deceiver's punishment; and so was that enmity between it and mankind, which issues in the wounds of man's lowest part, followed by the crushing out of the serpent's life, consecrated as a pledge of the ultimate triumph of man in the person of the great seed of the woman, over the tempter of souls. Cleave to the letter as historical fact, and all this is lost. Admit the divine parable, and the reference is indisputable. The LXX. have here "upon thy breast and upon thy belly shalt thou go," combining the reading "upon thy breast," which the Vulgate also follows, with the received one. **dust shalt thou eat**] As crawling in the dust, deeper and more abundant in the dry East than with us (see reff.); and thus necessarily mingling all it eats with dust. **15.**] The Messianic import of this curse is recognized in the Targums. The Targum of Jonathan says: "it will be, when the children of the woman observe the commandments of the Law, that they will tread thee on thy head, and when they forsake the commandments of the Law, thou wilt be able to bite them on their heels; but they will be healed, and thou wilt not be healed: and they will, in the days of the Messiah, be able to make a bruise with the heel." Kalisch. Observe, it is **it**, or **he**, viz. the woman's seed, that shall bruise the serpent's head, not *she*, as the Vulgate and the Church of Rome have it here. Even were it *she*, no such application of the words could be made as that Church makes to the Virgin Mary, for it would mean she, the woman then present, by means of her seed which is to come. The deeper or parabolic sense of the words is veiled under that which is ordinary and physical as regards the common relation of the serpent to man.

w Job ix. 17. Ps. cxxxix. 11 (cover) only. woman, and between thy seed and her seed; it shall [w]bruise
thy head, and thou shalt [w]bruise its heel. 16 Unto the
x ch. v. 29. woman he said, I will greatly multiply thy [x]pain and thy
conception; in [x]pain thou shalt bring forth children; and
y ch. iv. 7. Cant. vii. 10, only. thy [y]desire *shall be* to thy husband, and he shall rule over
thee. 17 And unto the man he said, Because thou hast
hearkened unto the voice of thy wife, and hast eaten
of the tree, of which I commanded thee, saying, Thou
shalt not eat of it: cursed *is* the ground for thy sake; in
[x]pain shalt thou eat *of* it all the days of thy life; 18 thorns
also and thistles shall it bring forth to thee; and thou
shalt eat the herb of the field; 19 in the sweat of thy
face shalt thou eat bread, till thou return unto the ground;
for out of it wast thou taken: for dust thou *art*, and unto
dust shalt thou return. 20 And the man called his wife's

16.] **thy pain and thy conception,** i. e. the pain which accompanies thy pregnancy. Some, as Knobel, take the "**and**" as meaning *especially:* thy pain (throughout life, in the physical troubles incident to the sex), and especially thy pregnancy. And yet, though this shall be so, the woman, as a second curse, shall desire again the occasion of this pain; and, thirdly, though thus the subject of all the suffering which accompanies the propagation of the race, she shall be the subordinate, and ruled over by the man. 17—19.] To the man is appointed penal labour, and death for his sin. Before, he was put into the garden, to till it and keep it; but now the soil is to be stubborn, and to defy his labour, and cause him pain and disappointment. Before, he had access to the tree of life, which was to make him immortal (and this was not forbidden him, see on ver. 22): now he is to be driven out from access to it, and to return to the earth again. The word which we render **for thy sake** is, by the differing apprehension of a single turn in a Hebrew letter, translated "*in thy works*" by the LXX., and "*in thy work*" by the Vulgate. 18.] And this labour will be hindered by the curse of the soil, overpowering his tillage with noxious growths. He will eat, not the rich spontaneous fruits of Eden, but the herb of the field—the lesser growths sown by his own toil. 19.] **the sweat of thy face,** because it is on the face that that effect of labour is first and prominently shewn. On the latter part of the verse, see on ver. 22. It is commented on by St. Paul in 1 Cor. xv. 47, "the first man was of the earth, earthy." 20—24.] *The man and his wife are clothed by Jehovah, and are driven out of the garden of Eden.* 20.] The connexion of this verse here has been thought somewhat difficult to assign. Its place has to some appeared to be after ch. iv. 1. Perhaps it is inserted here, because here the man and his wife are first reunited in the narrative after the separate account of their parts in the act of disobedience and its consequences, and in connection with the words of God to the woman, relative to her conception of children. Murphy remarks, "The man here refers to two expressions in the sentences he had heard pronounced on the serpent and the woman. . . It is the woman who is to bear the seed, and this seed is . . to undo what had been done for the death of man, and so re-invest him with *life.* This life was to come by the woman. Again, in the address of the Judge to the woman, he had heard the words, 'thou shalt bear children.' These children are the seed, among whom is to be the bruiser of the serpent's head, and the author of life. . . He gives permanent expression to his hope in the name which he gives to his wife." Similarly Delitzsch: rendering "for she is become the mother of all living," viz. by the

name Eve; because she was the mother of all living. 21
Unto the man also and to his wife did God Jehovah make
garments of [z]skin, and clothed them. 22 ¶ And God Jehovah
said, Behold, the man is become as one of us, to know
good and evil: and now, lest he put forth his hand, and
take also of the tree of life, and eat, and live for ever:
23 therefore God Jehovah sent him forth from the garden
of Eden, to till the ground from whence he was taken.
24 So he drove out the man; and he placed at the east of
the garden of Eden the [a]Cherubim, and a flaming sword
which [b]turned every way, to keep the way of the tree of
life.

z ch. xxvii. 16. Job xli. 7, al.

a Exod. xxv. 18, &c. Num. vii. 89. 1 Sam. iv. 4. 2 Sam. xx. 11 (Ps. xviii. 10). 1 Kings vi. 23, &c. (2 Chron. iii. 7, &c.) 1 Chron. xxviii. 18. Ezek. ix. 3; x. 1, &c.; xi. 22; xxviii. 14, 16.

b Job xxxvii. 12; xxxviii. 14.

words concerning child-bearing just pronounced by God: and regarding the name as given in faith and hope. Knobel thinks the connection is by way of contrast to the preceding verse, which seemed to imply the extinction of the species; but still thinks that after iv. 1 would be its more appropriate place. **Eve**] **Chauah**, i. e. living; rendered by the LXX. *Zoë*, i. e. life; but in chap. iv. 1 by *Eua*. **21.**] The first act of Divine mercy, in answer to man's first word of faith—healing the first wound which the consciousness of good and evil had inflicted. It is hardly allowable to assume, as some have done, that these "coats of skins" were the skins of animals slain in sacrifice. But it is to be observed, that the Targum of Onkelos paraphrases the words as "garments of honour upon the skin of their flesh" (see 1 Cor. xii. 23), thus understanding **the skin** as *their skin*, which the garment covered. **22.**] God is again (see i. 26) introduced as taking counsel, speaking to Himself: here, perhaps, more evidently than there in a communicative sense, seeing that **one of us** widens those addressed by Him, at least to the higher order of spirits, who minister round His throne. To see here, with some of the Fathers, an argument for the Trinity of Persons in the Godhead, is surely far-fetched, and but ill calculated to serve the cause of Christian orthodoxy. This even Delitzsch confesses, and Wordsworth merely states the fact timidly. **lest he put forth his hand. . .**] Then our narrative implies, as St. Paul asserts, 1 Cor. xv. 47, that man was created subject to death, but would by the use of the tree of life have gained immortality. This use was not forbidden him, nor would it have been precluded even after the fall, had he remained in the garden. Some commentators (e. g. Keil and Delitzsch) suggest that in that case, the "living for ever" would have been to him not eternal life, but eternal persistence in the present sinful state: but surely we cannot gather so much from the mysterious narrative. **23, 24.**] Heaven and earth are now disjoined by the sin of man. Paradise was the symbolic setting forth of God's unity with, and dwelling among, man. And now this presence of God on earth is not altogether withdrawn, but is set up to the exclusion of men from its most holy place. As in the temple afterwards, so here, the Holy Place is westward: it is at the east of Paradise that the barrier to God's presence is set up. For the Cherubim, here mentioned, are in Scripture evermore the attendants, and bearers up, of the throne of God (see reff.). The cherubic forms (Ezek. x. 14) are the same as those borne by the four living beings, who surrounded the throne in Rev. iv. 6–8. I have dealt with this matter in my Hulsean Lectures for 1841, and am still of the same opinion, that the placing of these Cherubim at the east of Eden was indicative of ordinances of worship, and a form of access to the Divine presence still open to man, though he was debarred from entrance into paradise. See further on chap. iv. 3, and *Smith's Biblical Dict.*, under "Cherub." **the flaming sword**] lit. **the flame of the sword**, not borne in the hands of the Cherubim, but separate from them, which turned every way—i. e. continually flashing, or coruscant, in all directions. Evidently, from the

IV. 1 And the man knew Eve his wife; and she con-
ceived, and bare Cain, andsaid, I have gotten a man by
the help of Jehovah. 2 And she again bare his brother
Abel. And Abel was a keeper of sheep, but Cain was
a tiller of the ground. 3 And in process of time it came
to pass, that Cain brought of the fruit of the ground an
offering unto Jehovah. 4 And Abel, he also brought of
the [c] firstlings of his flock and of the fat thereof. And

c Deut. xii. 6; xiv. 23.

context, the purpose of the guard was to bar the way to the tree of life against man's entering and partaking of it. But it had at the same time a symbolical and teaching significance as regarded man. It was a provision of access as well as an ordinance of exclusion.

IV. **1—26.**] *The posterity of Adam.* In the whole of this section, with the single exception of Eve's speech, ver. 25 (where Elohim only is used), the name JEHOVAH is used simply, without the addition of Elohim. It is to be regarded as another separate document, distinct alike in its prosaic narrative style (see on vv. 23, 24) from the majesty of the first portion (ch. i.—ii. 3) and the poetic symbolism of the second (ch. ii. 4—iii. 24). **1.**] The *knowledge* of Eve his wife involves the recognition and use of her for that purpose to which God had ordained and especially devoted her. **Cain**] i. e. possession, or acquisition, "gain," to answer to her saying. **by the help of Jehovah**] In the Hebrew the phrase might mean *even Jehovah*, the particle *eth* which precedes the sacred name being the usual sign of apposition in the accusative case. And this possibility has been used to introduce the idea that Eve believed she had borne the Incarnate God, the seed of the woman. But such an idea is by almost all confessed to be alien from the context. No such promise is even latent in ch. iii. 15. So that we have no way but to take the less usual sense of the particle, and to render it **with**, i. e. by the help of. Kalisch has **with**; Wright, **by the help of.** **2.**] **again bare**, literally, "*added to bear.*" Some have thought, because there is no mention of a second conception, that Cain and Abel were twins. But this does not seem necessary. After what went before, the fact only needs stating. Observe, it is not said that *she called* his name Abel (Hevel, *nothingness, vanity*). That name was in all probability given afterwards, owing to his premature end. Notice the difference in ver. 25. **3.**] The words **in process of time** seem best to render the Hebrew **at the end of days.** Kalisch says, "at the end of a certain indefinite time, when both the ease and the affluence of a pastoral life were seen in sufficient contrast to the toils and cares of the husbandman." See his views below, on ver. 4. Cain brought simply some of the fruits of his labour: we are not told that they were the first or the best. This seems, from the beginning of the narrative, to make a difference between the brothers. For **4.**] Abel brought some from among the firstlings of his flock, and from their fat. Kalisch regards the **and** as meaning **especially**. Abel's offering consisted of these first-born themselves, and of their fat. That they were first slain would hence appear; but it lies in the background: a valuable truth, but not belonging to the present comparison between the sacrifices. Abel's was the "better sacrifice" (Heb. xi. 4), as being the best of what he had, which does not appear of Cain's. We must not travel beyond the sacred narrative when we have these indications within it. Cain being an agriculturist, could but do as he did in the *matter* of his offering. The fact of the brothers each bringing of his own as an offering would be disturbed by one having recourse to the other for the material of his offering, as must have been on the hypothesis of Cain's fault having consisted in not bringing a slain sacrifice.

How the acceptance of the one offering and the rejection of the other were shewn we are not told. Some have imagined in the consumption of the one by fire from above, and not of the other; and Theodotion in his version actually has given "*consumed by fire*" as the rendering of the verb, whereas

Jehovah had respect unto Abel and to his offering: [5] but
unto Cain and to his offering he had not respect. And
Cain was very wroth, and his [d] countenance fell. [6] And [d] Job xxix. 24. See Ps. iv. 6.
Jehovah said unto Cain, Why art thou wroth? and why is
thy countenance fallen? [7] If thou doest well, shalt thou
not be accepted? and if thou doest not well, sin lieth at
the door. And unto thee is his desire, and thou shalt rule
over him. [8] And Cain talked with Abel his brother: and

its meaning is simply **regarded,** "looked with favour on." There is no mention of an altar, as in ch. viii. 20, in the case of Noah, so that it seems we must rather think of some appearance or word of Jehovah by which the preference was shewn. As to the preference itself, it is, I think, unavoidable to suppose that there was ground for it in the previous character and the present state of mind of Cain, and that we have a hint of this in ver. 3. Whether, as Kalisch insists at some length, we are to suppose previous hatred and envy of his brother, I am not so sure. There is enough in the narrative to beget that in an unthankful and selfish mind. **Cain was very wroth**] Literally, **it burned** in (or with) **Cain exceedingly**, i. e. his anger was much inflamed. **his countenance fell**] He scowled and hung his head, as men do in displeasure. **6.**] It seems to be implied here and in the following verses that Jehovah was in some way manifested as present. **7.**] There are few verses in the Bible about which there is more uncertainty. It seems difficult to extract sense from any of the various renderings. I can only lay before the reader those of the principal commentators and versions. (*a*) The LXX. give it,—"*If thou hast offered rightly, but hast not divided rightly, hast thou not sinned? Rest quiet: toward thee is his* (or *its*) *resort, and thou shalt rule over him* (or *it*)." (*b*) The Vulgate: "*If thou hast done well, shalt thou not receive? but if badly, will not sin be forthwith present at the doors? but in thy power will be his* (or *its*) *desire, and thou shalt rule over him* (or *it*)." (*c*) Kalisch: "*If thou doest well,* wilt thou not find *acceptance? and if thou doest not well, sin lieth at the door, and to thee is its desire; but thou shalt rule over it,*" interpreting that sin, as a wild beast in ambush, lies at the door, desiring to have thee. (*d*) Knobel: "*Is there not, if thou doest well, lifting up* (*of countenance*)*? but if thou doest not well* (*falling of countenance*)*?* This latter an ellipsis, filled up out of vv. 5, 6. *Sin is lying in wait before the door, and to thee is its desire, but thou shalt rule over it.*" And so very nearly Keil, except that he does not fill in the ellipsis, but makes the last clause depend upon "*If thou doest not well*" .... and similarly also Delitzsch. (*e*) The idea pressed by Abp. Magee on the atonement, that "*sin lieth at the door,*" ought to be rendered "*at the door a sin-offering is crouching,*" and that the words point to the opportunity of atonement by sacrifice seems to be universally repudiated by Hebraists. (*f*) In the uncertainty I have left the A. V. of the former part unaltered. It expresses very nearly the sense as given by the Targum of Onkelos, and seems in no respect to violate the requirements of the original. In the latter portion I have abstained from changing **his** and **him** with *its* and *it*, although the consensus of nearly all commentators is that way, feeling that the words *may* apply to Abel, who, as the younger brother, is described by God as still ready to submit himself to his elder brother. This certainly suits better ch. iii. 16, where nearly the same words occur. I have only supplied *is*, instead of *shall be.* **8.**] Here, again, is a difficulty. The Hebrew word rendered *talked*, or *spoke*, has not properly this meaning. The literal rendering is: **And Cain said unto Abel his brother** ...., in which case there is an ellipsis, nothing which was said being mentioned. And in consequence we have in the Samaritan Pentateuch, in the LXX., the Vulgate, the Syrian Version, and the Targum of Pseudo-Jonathan, these words inserted, "*Let us go into the field,*" and some are in favour of inserting them in the text. But they are not found in a single Hebrew MS., nor in the Targum of Onkelos, nor were they in the Hebrew text used by Origen.

it came to pass, when they were in the field, that Cain
rose up against Abel his brother, and slew him. 9 And
Jehovah said unto Cain, Where *is* Abel thy brother?
And he said, I know not: *Am* I my brother's keeper?
10 And he said, What hast thou done? [e] the voice of thy
brother's blood crieth unto me from the ground. 11 And
now *art* thou cursed from the ground, which hath opened
her mouth to receive thy brother's blood from thy hand;
12 when thou tillest the ground, she shall no more yield
unto thee her strength; a fugitive and a vagabond shalt
thou be in the earth. 13 And Cain said unto Jehovah, [f] My
† punishment *is* greater than can be || borne. 14 Behold, thou

e ch. xviii. 20, 21; xix. 13. Exod. iii. 9. James v. 4. Hab. ii. 11. See Job xvi. 18; Isa. xxvi. 21, also Heb. xii. 24.

f ch. xix. 15. 1 Sam. xxviii. 10. Isa. v. 18.

† or, *Mine iniquity.*

|| or, *forgiven.*

Some have supposed that "*it*" should be supplied after "*said*," viz. that which God had said to Cain,—"Cain told it to Abel;" but this would not seem likely to have been, nor if it had happened, would it come naturally into the narrative. Others have supposed that another verb, composed of nearly the same letters, should be read, signifying that Cain *watched* Abel his brother (so Knobel); but thus we should be entering the realm of conjecture, which must in the criticism of the sacred text be strictly forbidden. Gesenius, in his Lexicon, taking the meaning that Cain told to Abel the words of God, thinks it implied that a temporary reconciliation took place, but that afterwards in the field Cain's suppressed indignation broke out again, and led to the murder. I have again, in the uncertainty, left the A. V., which, whether it exactly render the Hebrew verb or not, expresses what happened. **slew him**] In what manner and with what weapon is not intimated, and it is vain to speculate.

9.] Knobel remarks that the evil in man has made a step onward: Adam and Eve, when challenged, confessed their fault; Cain denies his. **10.**] This way of speech, representing murder, or other crime, crying for vengeance, is common in the sacred text (see reff.). It is in allusion to this voice of Abel's blood that in ref. Heb. the writer describes Christ's blood as speaking better things: reconciliation, and not vengence. **11.**] **cursed from**, i.e. driven out, as an accursed exile from. But more than this. Not only does the ground eject thee from a particular favoured spot (compare "from thy face" below, ver. 14), but she has a quarrel against thee everywhere; that blood (in the Hebrew plural, those streams, drops of blood) which thou hast poured upon her shall curse her for thee, so that she shall no longer yield her strength under thy tillage,—a double curse of the ground for man's sake. Kalisch disputes this, the usually received interpretation, and insists that it was only that particular portion of ground which had received his brother's blood that should be cursed with barrenness for Cain: viz. the land of Eden. But what follows is against this: his vagabond life is connected with the ground not yielding her strength to him. And what additional particular would it be in his punishment, that the district from which he was to be expelled should not yield her strength to him? This detail would act *per contra:* he would be driven from earth which would be barren to him, to that which would be fertile.

The LXX. render the latter clause of the verse, "*groaning and trembling shalt thou be on the earth:*" probably they mistook one of the Hebrew verbs. **13.**] The word rendered **punishment** is the common term for sin, and so may indeed be rendered here, provided we understand *sin*, or *iniquity*, to imply the apprehended magnitude of his sin, now first revealed to him by its punishment. And the words rendered **than I can bear** may also have the meaning given in the margin. Gesenius prefers both these; and they are adopted by the LXX., Vulgate, Syriac Version, the Targum of Onkelos, and many ancient expositors. But the A. V. seems to fit the context better, seeing that he goes on to complain of the heaviness of the sentence against him. **14.**] **from thy face I shall be hid** seems certainly to point to some

hast driven me out this day from the face of the ground;
and from thy face shall I be hid; and I shall be a fugitive
and a vagabond in the earth; and it shall come to pass,
that every one that findeth me shall slay me. 15 And
Jehovah said unto him, Therefore whosoever slayeth Cain,
vengeance shall be taken on him sevenfold. And Jehovah
appointed a [g] sign unto Cain, that no one finding him should [g] (token) Exod. iii. 12. Deut. xiii. 2. 1 Sam. ii. 34; x. 9, al.
kill him. 16 ¶ And Cain went out from the presence of
Jehovah, and dwelt in the land of Nod, on the east of
Eden. 17 And Cain knew his wife; and she conceived,
and bare Enoch: and he builded a city, and called the

especial location of God's manifested presence in Eden (see on ch. iii. 24). Kalisch is very indignant at this interpretation, designating it as "an almost heathen idea, that the presence of God is bound to a certain spot, which He has chosen for His residence, or the sphere of His activity." But surely he forgets the "place where I have put my name," and the prevalence of this idea throughout the Mosaic dispensation (see Jonah i. 3, 10). Cain's fear that every one that should find him should slay him, seems to belong to a later period when the earth should be peopled, for as yet he was the only man on earth besides Adam and Eve. Perhaps the *history itself* belongs to this later period. If so, we have repeated goings back to the earlier time again, e. g. vv. 17, 25. **15.**] We may ask, with some degree of surprise, why God granted this uncommon indulgence to a murderer, who had insidiously killed his own brother? Did not God Himself give the distinct precept, "He who sheddeth man's blood by man shall his blood be shed"? Why was it necessary to take such anxious precautions to save a life forfeited according to human and Divine right? There is a peculiar point in the words: "He who *killeth* the *murderer* (Cain), vengeance shall be taken on him seven-fold." "We hesitate to speak with decision where the text is silent." Kalisch. Equally mysterious is the sign which God gave to Cain. It appears to have been some pledge on God's part which reassured him. The A. V. appears not to be justified in "*set a mark upon.*" **16—24.**] *Cain's dwelling and posterity.* He is described as going eastward further still, as our first parents were driven eastward, and the presence of God was set up on the east of Eden. The name **Nod** signifies *flight* or *exile.* The Vulgate does not give any proper name, but renders, "*dwelt as a fugitive in the earth on the east side of Eden.*" But from the express naming of a city in the next verse, it is probable that some thus named territory is intended. Knobel connects the whole with China, "the oldest and best known Cainitish people." But all is in uncertainty. We have evidently here only fragments, too brief to be intelligible, of ancient prehistoric documents.

17.] Of the wife of Cain we know nothing: no daughters of Adam and Eve have been as yet mentioned; but we read of such at ch. v. 4. The narrative proceeds, as with regard to Cain's fear expressed in ver. 14, as if the world were already peopled.

Enoch] i. e. dedication, or initiation. "The resemblance of names in the two families of Cain and Seth are remarkable. In the family of Cain we have Enoch and Lamech, Irad, Mehujael, Methusael; and in the family of Seth we have Enos, Cainan, Mahalaleel, Jared, Enoch, Methuselah, Lamech. Two names are here identical, Enoch and Lamech; in a third there is a likeness of two syllables." Bp. Wordsworth. There is not the least ground for the idea started by Ewald, and supported by others, that the two families were really one and that we have here two accounts in error. The names do not occur in like places in the genealogies; and examples of similar names in different lives are common enough in Scripture. "There is a Judith among the daughters of Heth (ch. xxvi. 34); a Korah among the sons of Levi (Exod. vi. 31) and among those of Esau (ch. xxxvi. 5); a Kenaz in the family of Esau (ch. xxxvi. 11) and in that of Judah (Num. xxxii. 12)." Keil. And on

name of the city, after the name of his son, Enoch.
18 And unto Enoch was born Irad: and Irad begat Mehu-
jael: and Mehujael begat Methusael: and Methusael be-
gat Lamech. 19 ¶ And Lamech took unto him two wives:
the name of the one *was* Adah, and the name of the
other Zillah. 20 And Adah bare Jabal: he was the father
of such as dwell in tents, and *of such as have* [h]cattle.
21 And his brother's name *was* Jubal: he was the father of
all such as handle the [i]harp and [j]pipe. 22 And Zillah, she
also bare Tubal-cain, a [k]forger of every kind of [l]instru-
ment in brass and iron: and the sister of Tubal-cain *was*
Naamah. 23 And Lamech said unto his wives,

h ch. xxvi. 14; xlvii. 17. Exod. xxxiv. 19.
i ch. xxxi. 27. 1 Sam. x. 5. Ps. cxxxvii. 2. Isa. xxiii. 16, al fr.
j Job xxi. 12; xxx. 31. Ps. cl. 4, only.
k a sharpener. 1 Sam xiii. 20. Job xvi. 9. Ps. vii. 12; lii. 2, only.
l here only. See note.

any hypothesis concerning our Lord's brethren there must have been repetitions of the names Judah, Joses, Simon in the Holy family. "The similarity of names shows nothing more than that the two branches of the human race maintained intercourse with one another." Keil. **Builded** is literally "was building," and does not seem to imply that he finished the building. Here, again, it would seem as if the world were more populous than by the place of the narrative we should suppose. **19.**] Polygamy originates in the race of Cain, and in the same line various occupations and arts take their beginning. Keil notices that the names of Lamech's wives indicate already a state of luxury and enjoyment. **Adah** signifies *adornment* or *beauty* (it was also the name of the Hethite wife of Esau, ch. xxxvi. 2, 4), and **Zillah**, *tinkling sound* (but according to Gesenius, *shadow*). **20.**] **Jabal**, probably meaning *profit*: the word used for "the *increase* of the earth" (Deut. xxxii. 22). He introduced the nomad pastoral life of the eastern tribes. Keil suggests that the eating of flesh may be well implied as introduced, which seems not to have been from the first. The word rendered **cattle** simply signifies in the primitive meaning *possessions*, but as the sole possessions of nomads are flocks and herds, became the usual word for cattle (see reff.). **21.**] **Jubal**, signifying *musical sound*: the word is represented in our *jubilant, jubilee.* **the harp**] This Hebrew word (*Kinnohr*) occurs 41 times in the Bible, and is always rendered *harp* by our translators. It follows from the context of several of the places (see in reff.) that it was a smaller instrument than the harp at present, being carried during dancing or processional motion,—more what we understand by the *lyre.* **pipe**] Perhaps a combination of pipes, like our "Pan's pipe." In all the reff. the A. V. has "*organ.*" But that instrument in the modern acceptation is an invention of later ages. The word *(ngoogahv)* is connected by Kalisch and others with a root meaning *to blow*, and must be taken as representing *wind* instruments, as the other does *stringed* instruments. **22.**] The derivation of **Tubal-cain** is acknowledged on all hands to be entirely obscure, and it would exceed the limit of the present work to give the discussion on it. The syllable *cain* is omitted by the LXX. The sense may be as in A.V., but the revised text is preferred by the Hebraists, the sharpener being taken not figuratively, as *instructor*, but literally, as a *forger* or *polisher*; and the latter noun, which is literally only "cutting," that which cutteth, being understood of the tool, not of its maker. **brass**] This word, which occurs very commonly, is always rendered *brass* in the A.V. In strict accuracy it ought to be *copper*, as the mixture of copper and zinc, now known as brass, was not known to the ancients. But the word brass is so familiarized to us, that I have not thought it well to make the change. **the sister**] Why this sister is named does not appear, nor need we be anxious to inquire, among these primæval fragments. The name **Naamah** signifies *pleasant*, or *lovely*. The scope of this notice of the Cainite race seems to be to represent them as advancing in all worldly arts and arms, and becoming exceedingly prosperous on earth: but unconnected with the worship of Jehovah. The race are never

Adah and Zillah, Hear my voice;
Ye wives of Lamech, hearken unto my speech:
For I have slain a man for my wound,
And a young man for my bruise,
24 For Cain shall be avenged sevenfold,
And Lamech seventy and sevenfold.

25 ¶ And Adam knew his wife again; and she bare a son,
and called his name Seth: For God, *said she*, hath ap-
pointed me another seed instead of Abel, whom Cain slew.
26 And to Seth, to him also there was born a son; and he
called his name Enos: then began men to [m] call upon the

[m] ch. xii. 8; xiii. 4; xxi. 33; xxvi. 25. Ps. lxxix. 6. Isa. xii. 4.

named again after this chapter. **23, 24.**] Here, again, we have a mysterious particular introduced, which has never received even a probable interpretation. The conjecture which seems at any rate not to *contradict* any probability is that Lamech had slain some man in self-defence; and here in a poetical form he represents to his wives his innocence, and his conviction that if Cain's slaughter by an avenger of blood were forbidden, much more must his own be. The renderings "*to my wounding*," "*to my hurt*," in the A. V., are generally regarded as erroneous. "As Drechsler remarks, the history of the Cainite race begins with a deed of murder, and ends with a song of murder," Wright: who with many modern scholars, Ewald included, understands the words as a song of blasphemous triumph on the invention of the sword, and renders the verb in the future, *I will slay*. This alone may serve to show how entirely the interpretation and reference are wrapped in uncertainty, and also to read a lesson to all positive and rash interpreters of other parts of this primæval history, which, perhaps only from our own ignorance, appear to us more clear in meaning and reference. This saying of Lamech's presents strikingly the characteristic parallelism of Hebrew poetry, and has consequently been generally arranged as a lyrical fragment. **25, 26.**] The narrative returns to the first progenitors of mankind, and their further posterity, in the line of which the future history is to be continued. It seems as if the writer of Genesis had retained this portion of the document prior to the new narrative in ch. v., in order to bind the portions together. (See on ch. v. 1 ff.) We may notice that here first is the first man called by the proper name Adam, without the article: Ha-Adam, the man, having in every case where he is directly introduced been heretofore used. **Seth**] *Appointed* or *substituted*. The words are put into the mouth of Eve, without any notice to indicate that they are hers. Observe, that she uses the name Elohim, whereas at the birth of Cain she used Jehovah; can any reason be assigned for this? that given by Knobel, because the Sethites were Elohists, would be a reason for the name appearing in any insertion in ch. v., but not here, where we are still apparently in the portion belonging to the history of Cain and Abel. Keil's reason that Elohim, God, who had made up the loss, is the contrast to Cain, man, who had occasioned it (so also Delitzsch), has perhaps more likelihood, but hardly seems to reach the root of the matter. Least of all will the fair-judging reader agree with Bp. Wordsworth, who tries to convince him that because the one name occurs in a passage otherwise devoted to the other, therefore no distinction is to be traced between the Elohistic and Jehovistic documents. I would rather seek the reason in supposing that this joining link between the history in ch. iv. and that in ch. v. itself belongs to some independent document. **26.**] Another link with the next independent account in ch. v. **Enosh** signifies *man*, but usually on the side of our weakness and nothingness. See Ps. viii. 5, where the word is used. So that, as Delitzsch observes, the meaning is not far removed from that of Abel. The words that follow to the end have seemed to the commentators full of mystery. The expression "to call on the name of Jehovah" is found in the Pentateuch only in the Jehovistic parts (see reff.), n so (register): Neh. vii. 5.

name of Jehovah. V. 1 This *is* the [n] book of the genera-
tions of Adam. In the day that God created Adam, in the
likeness of God made he him; 2 Male and female created
he them; and blessed them, and called their name Adam, in
the day when they were created. 3 ¶ And Adam lived an

and in the sense of making prayer to Him. The notice, here inserted by the Jehovist writer, seems merely to indicate that at this time, coincidently with the apostasy of the Cainite race, there began to be a distinct and formal worship of Jehovah, that God-fearing line being founded, in and down which the true worship of the Lord descended. It is not that then first the name of Jehovah was known; for we have Eve using it at the birth of her first-born; but that it then first became a formal and distinctive name in men's worship. There is nothing corresponding to "*men*" in the Hebrew; it is literally, then began to call, &c., no subject to the verb being specified. So widely differing have been the interpretations, that the Targum of Onkelos paraphrases, "*Then the children of men ceased to call on the name of Jehovah.*"

V. **1—32.**] *The generations from Adam to Noah* (Elohistic). See on ver. 29. From this point the sacred narrative follows only the line of the descendants of Seth, the callers upon the name of Jehovah; this line alone is important for the purpose of the tracing down of God's covenant with man, and the bringing in of the father of the faithful. Of such patriarchs there are ten from Adam to Noah, and again (ch. xi. 10, ff.) ten from Noah to Abraham.

1. The book of the generations] Similarly the Gospel of St. Matthew begins: meaning the register, a genealogy. The recapitulation shows that we have here a complete document, not a continuation merely of that which has gone before. **2.**] This is a recitation of ch. i. 27, 28, as far as "blessed them." The word Adam is the same throughout these two verses, without the article. God called man Adam when he was created, he being so named in the narrative of the act of his creation, ch. i. 27.

3, ff.] The chronology of these ten patriarchs is much disturbed by the varieties which we find in the Samaritan Pentateuch and in the LXX. The accompanying table will show the differences.

	Present Hebrew text.			Samaritan Pentateuch.			LXX.		
Names.	Age at birth of son.	Rest of life.	Whole life.	Age at birth of son.	Rest of life.	Whole life.	Age at birth of son.	Rest of life.	Whole life.
Adam . .	130	800	930	130	800	930	230	700	930
Seth . . .	105	807	912	105	807	912	205	707	912
Enos . . .	90	815	905	90	815	905	190	715	905
Cainan . .	70	840	910	70	840	910	170	740	910
Mahalaleel. .	65	830	895	65	830	895	165	730	895
Jared . .	162	800	962	62	785	847	162	800	962
Enoch . .	65	300	365	65	300	365	165	200	365
Methuselah .	187	782	969	67	653	720	167	802	969
							(or 187	782)	
Lamech . .	182	595	777	53	600	653	188	565	753
Noah . .	500	450	950	500	450	950	500	450	950
Age of, at Flood	100			100			100		
Total from Creation to Flood	1656			1307			2242		

It will be seen, by the notes on ch. xi. 10, that there are differences of equal importance in the genealogy of ten post-diluvian patriarchs. Now, the object of the present edition of the Old Testament is not so much to enter on disquisition on matters of this kind, as to draw inference from the phenomena which may be useful to an English reader for the practical benefit of his faith. And such an inference in the

hundred and thirty years, and begat *a son* in his likeness,
after his image; and called his name Seth: 4 And the
days of Adam after he had begotten Seth were eight hun-
dred years: and he begat sons and daughters: 5 And all
the days that Adam lived were nine hundred and thirty
years: and he died. 6 And Seth lived an hundred and
five years, and begat Enos: 7 And Seth lived after he be-
gat Enos eight hundred and seven years, and begat sons
and daughters: 8 And all the days of Seth were nine
hundred and twelve years: and he died. 9 ¶ And Enos
lived ninety years, and begat Cainan: 10 And Enos lived
after he begat Cainan eight hundred and fifteen years, and
begat sons and daughters: 11 And all the days of Enos
were nine hundred and five years: and he died. 12
¶ And Cainan lived seventy years, and begat Mahalaleel:
13 And Cainan lived after he begat Mahalaleel eight

present case seems to be this: that we have, in the presence of such uncertainty as this, absolutely no right to assert the numerical accuracy of these dates. Quarry has well pointed out that as we do not undervalue the Divine authority of the Gospels of St. Matthew and St. Luke, because of the demonstrable inaccuracy, as to matter of fact, of the genealogies of our Lord given by those two Evangelists; so neither need the Divine authority of the Book of Genesis be undervalued, because of the manifest uncertainty of all these technical chronological enumerations. We happen to *know* that in St. Matthew's genealogy three whole generations are omitted to make the three *fourteens* square with one another. How can we tell what similar process, or what other process, may not have been employed, to square the ten antediluvian and the ten postdiluvian patriarchs? How can we tell what difference in conventional ways of reckoning, at present untraceable by us, may have assigned to Noah and Abraham, who were contemporaries during 58 years, to the former a life of 950 years, to the latter a life of 175 years? On such matters, and where we are involved in such uncertainties, it surely becomes Christians to suspend their judgment,—"not to be unwise, but understanding what the will of the Lord is,"—and above all, to abstain from harsh and unfavourable expressions towards those who differ from them in method or in result of their search after truth. See, on the whole details, Mr. Stuart Poole's able article on "Chronology," in *Smith's Biblical Dictionary*. **3. in his likeness, after his image**] Do these words imply a continuation of the Divine likeness and image, or a discontinuation? The word "*own*" of course implied, but not expressed in the Hebrew, and inserted in the A. V. for perspicuity, tends to throw the bias somewhat too strongly in the latter direction, and to bring out a contrast where it may not necessarily be implied. On the one side we have Kalisch, "The Divine image impressed by God as the first man was inherited by his descendants; for Adam begat Seth in his image and his likeness;" and Knobel, even more decidedly, holding that to insist on the identity was the object of the insertion of these words. On the other side, we have several of the older commentators, and recently Keil, Bp. Wordsworth, and Prof. Murphy. Keil gives a slightly moderated view — that it is meant that Adam transmitted the Divine image through his own condition—which includes the deterioration introduced through sin. But perhaps it is more natural, seeing that the Divine image is expressly predicated of man again, ch. ix. 6, and as a reason for a permanent institution, to understand the words simply of the transmission of the image of God, in which Adam was himself created. **12. Mahalaleel**] *praise of*

hundred and forty years, and begat sons and daughters:
14 And all the days of Cainan were nine hundred and ten
years: and he died. 15 ¶ And Mahalaleel lived sixty and
five years, and begat Jared: 16 And Mahalaleel lived
after he begat Jared eight hundred and thirty years, and
begat sons and daughters: 17 And all the days of Maha-
laleel were eight hundred ninety and five years: and he
died. 18 ¶ And Jared lived an hundred sixty and two
years, and he begat Enoch: 19 And Jared lived after he
begat Enoch eight hundred years, and begat sons and
daughters: 20 And all the days of Jared were nine
hundred sixty and two years: and he died. 21 ¶ And
Enoch lived sixty and five years, and begat Methuselah:
o ch. vi 9, only. See Mic. vi. 8. 22 And Enoch o walked with God after he begat Methuse-
lah three hundred years, and begat sons and daughters:
23 And all the days of Enoch were three hundred sixty
and five years: 24 And Enoch o walked with God: and

El (God). **22—24.**] A special notice is given of Enoch, "seventh from Adam." The dread monotony of "and he died" is now first broken through, as Delitzsch well observes. His further commentary is worth extracting: "Enoch's life had another issue. He **walked with God**; this expression, only found in the antediluvian history (see reff.), is more than to *walk before God* (ch. xvii. 1; xxiv. 40) or to *walk after* . . . (Deut. viii 19). It betokens the most intimate communion of life with God, as it were a walking beside God who still walked among men (ch. iii. 3). [We may notice that the LXX. render **walked with** "*pleased*," and that this is adopted in Heb. xi. 5, 6.] The name HA-ELOHIM evermore recalls the contrast of the created and worldly to God; in the N. T. it would be said that his walk was *in heaven*. To this walk corresponded his end of life: he suddenly disappeared (on this expression, **was not**, compare reff.), God had taken him away. With the other patriarchs long life is a blessing from God; Enoch's early end (his 365th year corresponds about to our 33rd) was no premature death: he was in some manner, surprising and inexplicable to his contemporaries, taken hence, and taken into nearer proximity to God, with whom he had here walked. It is not said that he was taken up to heaven: heaven was at that time not yet in the later sense the place of blessedness, the essential participation of God's revelation of Himself in glory. Heaven and earth were not yet, in respect of their personal self-witness of God, separated as they afterwards were. God snatched away Enoch from this nether world of sin and evil, to which he, as we know from Jude 14, f. (compare Sirach, xliv. 16), had proclaimed the future coming of God to judgment, and set him in His own immediate presence, where is no sin or evil, and that without his becoming a prey to death, Heb. xi. 5. He excepted him, therefore, from the law of death, shewing that though He had subjected man to this law, He bound not Himself to it,—that personal immortality was an attainable gift of grace, that for them who walked with Him in the life of the body, a higher existence was reserved." And Kalisch well observes, "We are convinced, that the 'taking away' of Enoch is one of the strongest proofs of the belief in a future state, prevailing among the Hebrews; without this belief the history of Enoch is a perfect mystery, a hieroglyph without a clue, a commencement without an end." On all matters regarding the very curious apocryphal Book of Enoch, see Dr. Westcott's article in *Smith's Biblical Dictionary*, and the Introduction to the Epistle of Jude in my New Testament for English readers. **25.**] Some have traced

[p] he *was* not; for God took him. 25 And Methuselah [p] ch. xliii. 13, 32. Job vii. 8.
lived an hundred eighty and seven years, and begat
Lamech: 26 And Methuselah lived after he begat La-
mech seven hundred eighty and two years, and begat sons
and daughters: 27 And all the days of Methuselah were
nine hundred sixty and nine years: and he died. 28
¶ And Lamech lived an hundred eighty and two years,
and begat a son: 29 And he called his name Noah, saying,
This *same* shall relieve us from our work and the toil of
our hands, because of the ground which Jehovah hath
cursed. 30 And Lamech lived after he begat Noah five
hundred ninety and five years, and begat sons and
daughters: 31 And all the days of Lamech were seven
hundred seventy and seven years: and he died. 32 And
Noah was five hundred years old: and Noah begat Shem,
Ham, and Japheth. VI. 1 And it came to pass, when
men began to multiply on the face of the ground, and
daughters were born unto them, 2 That the [q] sons of God [q] Job i. 6; ii. 1; xxxviii. 7. See Ps. xxix. 1; lxxxix. 6.
saw the daughters of men that they *were* fair; and they

in the name **Methuselah**—*man of sending forth* [Bp. Wordsworth adds (*of water*), but this seems pure fancy]—a prophetic intimation of the flood, seeing that he died the same year as the flood began. But all this is untrustworthy. Gesenius interprets the name, *the man of the weapon* (missile). Such ground needs the utmost caution in treading. **29.**] **Noah,** i. e. *rest.* The sacred writer connects the name with another root signifying *to comfort* (see below), "caring," as Simonis (quoted in Gesenius) observes, "more for the reality of things than of words." The construction is,—shall comfort us from, i. e. *shall comfort us by relieving us from.* This is nearest expressed in English by "**relieve us from,**" as Kalisch. This last commentator understands the name, as given, to be prophetic of a relief of the human race from the necessity of living on vegetable food, requiring the hard labour of incessant tillage, and the coming permission to eat the flesh of animals. Surely this is most fanciful. Even if we are to understand ch. ix. 3, ff. as the first *Divine sanction* for the practice of eating flesh, who shall say that the practice did not prevail long before? Observe, that the name Jehovah is here found. It was Jehovah Elohim who had cursed the ground, ch. iii. 17. And thus the occurrence of the name is a sign of minute accuracy, which should not be overlooked. It may point to a "Jehovistic" insertion or correction of the "Elohistic" narrative. **32.**] The mention of the *three* sons, unprecedented as yet, serves to preface us for their playing some notable part in the history which is to follow: also for the continuation of the "book of generations," no longer in one main line, but in three branches. See ch. x. 1, ff. Of these sons, Ham was the youngest (see ch. ix. 24); Shem the eldest (see ch. x. 21, in our text).

VI. **1—IX. 29.**] The life-time of Noah. The causes of the Flood, its history and its consequences. On the mixed Jehovistic and Elohistic character, see Introduction. **1—7.**] *The causes of the Flood.* And herein (1–4) the unnatural union of sons of God with daughters of men, by which giants and men of renown came upon earth. With regard to these **sons of God,** I have maintained in the Introduction to the Epistle of Jude, N. T. for English readers, vol. ii. part 2, that they are most probably to be understood as being *angels.* In no other way, in spite of the

took them wives of all which they chose. 3 And Jehovah
said, My spirit shall not always strive with man, for that
he also *is* flesh: yet his days shall be an hundred and

arguments to the contrary by Hengstenberg, Quarry, and others, can we understand the contrast between the sons of GOD and the daughters of MAN: for however the distinction may have been drawn between the godfearing race of the Sethites and the ungodly race of the Cainites, nothing approaching any justification of such names for the two has been adduced. And again, only thus can St. Jude's expression respecting Sodom and Gomorrha, that they *committed fornication in like manner to these angels*, be explained. The great objection to this, which was the opinion of the early fathers, and of Philo and Josephus, seems to be that it opens the way to the idea that the narration is mythical and not historical. But is this really so? And if it were so, is it to overbear the plain sense of words, and the common sense of interpretation? What wonder would it be,—what would it be worthy of narration,—that these took place, mixed marriages between the godly and ungodly? Has not this been already testified by the community of names in the Sethite and Cainite lines? And what issue such as is here stated, could have been the result of those mixed marriages? Again, in order to carry through what I cannot help calling this makeshift interpretation, the word "*men*," in ver. 1, must be limited to the Cainite line, whereas it is plainly and unmistakeably used of the whole human race, and as about to distinguish the human race from some other order of beings to be presently mentioned. We conclude, therefore, moved by these considerations, and by the others adduced by Dr. Kurtz, that these sons of God were beings of a higher order than man. We are here in the region, as Bp. Wordsworth has well argued in his long note on the flood, of the miraculous, and our simple understanding of the same text is not to be overthrown by considerations deduced from our present ordinary conception of things. To what ultimate inference this leads us is no concern of the interpreter. On the phrase **sons of God**, see reff. **3.**] Here is another verse over which much controversy has been spent. The two streams of interpretation may be thus described: 1. (corresponding to the translation, *My spirit shall not always rule in man while he is also flesh*) The Spirit of God, the Lord who giveth life, was not any longer to preside in man in the flesh for so long a period as it had hitherto done, approaching a thousand years; but his life shall henceforth be reduced to a hundred and twenty years. So, in the main, the LXX., the Vulgate, Kalisch, Knobel, and many others; and so Delitzsch, but he understands the former clause to mean that God would withdraw His Spirit of life from the whole race of man, i. e. destroy the race,—and the latter clauses as below. 2. (corresponding to the translation, *My spirit shall not always strive with man, for that* [because] *he also is flesh*) The Spirit of God, the author and suggester of all that is good in man, was not any longer to strive with a race who had by their carnal corruption shewn themselves to be flesh. **also**] i. e. as well as the lower tribes (so Knobel); but in this prospect of the withdrawal of God's striving Spirit in man, his days (of gracious respite) should be 120 years. Thus this latter view regards the words as spoken 120 years before the flood, i. e. in the 480th of Noah's life. So Kimchi, and most modern interpreters. The whole verse is a battle-field of commentators, and it seems impossible to decide. It is, as so often in the interpretation of difficult O. T. texts, Hebraist against Hebraist, one great scholar insisting on a meaning for a word which another great scholar entirely denies that it can ever have. We may say here, by way of laying down some landmarks for the interpretation, 1. That the *spiritual* meaning, of God's (warning) Spirit striving with man, is something quite alien as yet from the primæval narrative. 2. That the interpretation of "his days," as meaning his time of grace intervening before judgment is inflicted, is not after the analogy of ch. v., where "the days of" is used ten times in the sense of "the life of." 3. That this last interpretation cannot be said to square with the following history, in which the lives of the patriarchs far exceed the limit of 120 years. **4.**] The context shews (so Knobel and others. Lange, &c., maintain the contrary, that the giants were on the earth

twenty years. 4 The [r] giants were in the earth in those [r] Num. xiii. 33.
days, and also after that the sons of God came in unto the
daughters of men, and they bare *children* to them, these were
the mighty men which *were* of old, men of renown. 5 ¶ And
Jehovah saw that the wickedness of man *was* great in the
earth, and *that* every [s] imagination of the thoughts of his [s] ch. viii. 21. Deut. xxxi. 21; only in Pentat. 1 Chron. xxviii. 9; xxix. 18. Ps. ciii. 4 (frame). Isa. xxvi. 3; xxxi. 16 (thing framed). Hab. ii. 18 (work).
heart *was* only evil continually. 6 And it repented Jehovah
that he had made man on the earth, and it grieved him at
his heart. 7 And Jehovah said, I will destroy man whom
I have created from the face of the ground; both man,
and beast, and the creeping thing, and the fowls of the
air; for it repenteth me that I have made them. 8 But
Noah found grace in the eyes of Jehovah. 9 ¶ These *are*
the generations of Noah: Noah was a righteous man,
perfect in his generations: Noah walked with God.
10 And Noah begat three sons, Shem, Ham, and Japheth.
11 The earth also was corrupt before God, and the earth

previously to those marriages) that these giants (see ref.: the word appears to be connected with a root signifying *to fall*, and so is variously interpreted,—*violent men*, who fall upon others,—or *apostates*, men who have fallen), men of great stature and power, are spoken of as the offspring of the unhallowed unions indicated above. Knobel takes this verse to mean that these giants who were the first offspring of the unions, propagated their race upon earth, and became parents of the mighty men of old, men of renown. Delitzsch, who participates the above view concerning these unions, understands the description in the latter part of the verse to be that of the giants themselves. We may remark, in the midst of all this whirl of interpretations, that it is impossible not to connect such notices as this with the subsequent frequent intimations of giant races in and among the nations bordering on Palestine. See Num. xiii. 33; Deut. ii. 11; iii. 11, 13; Josh. xii. 4; xiii. 12; xv. 8; xvii. 15; xviii. 16; 2 Sam. xxi. 16 (end); 1 Chron. xx. 4 (end). It may be said that such a connexion is at once precluded by the intervention of the Deluge; but it must not be forgotten that even among the posterity of Noah there was an accursed race.

5.] **imagination** seems exactly the word: it is literally *formation*, product of the thought; see reff. **continually**] literally, **every day**. **6.**] The anthropopathism of this verse is striking. See Exod. xxxii. 14; 1 Sam. xv. 29, and the true account of the matter in Num. xxiii. 19. **7.**] The whole living world is involved in the punishment of man's wickedness: with

8.] One exception—Noah, and, as involved in his rescue, his family. **9—22.**] *The generations of Noah; the beginning of the history of the Flood.* (Elohistic: assigned to the writer of ch. i.—ii. 3; ii. 1, and of ch. v.). On the opening, see on ch. v. 1.

perfect in his generations] The word rendered **generations** is not the same as that thus rendered before in this verse. It is the word commonly found in the sense of a *generation of men*, not of a series of genealogical successions. The clause is here usually interpreted of Noah's blameless character among the generations of men with whom he lived. **walked with God**] See on ch. v. 22. **10.**] The three sons of Noah are here mentioned again because of their position as the forefathers of the new earth, in connexion with Noah, whose righteousness was to rescue himself and family from the coming catastrophe. **11.**] A more detailed account of that which ver. 5 has already by implication revealed. The ten generations which had passed had been a downward progress into universal depravity. Delitzsch

t Ezek. xxii. 26. Zeph. iii. 4. Jer. xxii. 3.
u Exod. xxxii. 7. Deut. xxxii.5, al. fr.
v here (ch. vi.—ix.) and Exod. ii. 3, 5, only.
w = here only. See Exod. xxx. 10, reff.
x (see note) Exod. xxv. 2; xxxvii. 2.
y see ch. xliii. 16. Deut. xviii. 29, &c.

was filled with [t] violence. 12 And God looked upon the
earth, and, behold, it was [u] corrupted; for all flesh had
corrupted its way upon the earth. 13 And God said unto
Noah, The end of all flesh is come before me; for the
earth is filled with violence through them; and, behold,
I will destroy them with the earth. 14 ¶ Make thee an
[v] ark of gopher wood; cells shalt thou make in the ark, and
shalt [w] pitch it [x] within and without with [w] pitch. 15 And
this *is the fashion* which thou shalt make it *of*: The length of
the ark *shall be* three hundred cubits, the breadth of it fifty
cubits, and the height of it thirty cubits. 16 [y] Light shalt
thou make for the ark, and in a cubit shalt thou finish it
above; and the door of the ark shalt thou set in the side
thereof; *with* lower, second, and third *stories* shalt thou

points out the fearful contrast in ver. 12 to ch. i. 31. The reluctance which our translators shewed to writing "*its*" has here given rise to an ambiguity; "*his* way" is often understood as *God's* way. **13. through them**] is literally **in their presence**, i. e. by their conscious agency. **with**] i.e. together with. **the earth**] Meaning here, by the earth, not the very substance of the earthitself, but the superficial contents of it—fields, building, trees, &c. **14—22.**] *Command to Noah to build the ark, and specification of the same.* The word for **ark**, *tehvah*, is found only in the history of Noah and in that of Moses. See reff. It appears to have been originally not a Hebrew but an Egyptian word. **gopher wood**] "The word **gopher** occurs in this passage only; its root seems to signify to *cover*: it is evidently a tree which yields a resinous, pitch-like substance, as the lime, fir, and cedar. . . . it signifies here most likely the *cypress*, which was in some parts of Asia exclusively used as the material of ships; in Athens for coffins; and in Egypt for the mummy-cases, for which purpose it was peculiarly adapted, on account of its great durability and hardness." Kalisch. **cells**] literally, **nests**, i. e. compartments. **within and without**] is expressed by a Hebrew idiomatic expression signifying **from the house and from the street**, as also in reff. The word rendered **pitch**, as both verb and substantive, is nearly relative to *gopher* above. It gets its meaning from *covering*: a substance smeared over the surface. **15.**] Assuming the cubit at 21 inches, which seems the most approved account of it, the ark would be 525 ft. long, 87 ft. 6 in. broad, and 52 ft. 6 in. high, not far from the size of Canterbury Cathedral, except that it would be many feet less in height. It would be considerably larger than the largest British man of war. "The Great Eastern, however, is both larger and deeper than the ark, being 680 feet in length (691 on deck), 83 in breadth, and 58 in depth. Solomon's temple, the proportions of which are given in 1 Kings vi. 2, was the same height as the ark, but only one-fifth of the length, and less than half the width."—Prof. Perowne, in *Smith's Biblical Dictionary*, art. "Noah," which see for much interesting matter on this part of the history. **16. light**] Not a window, which gives the absurd idea of there being but one window in the ark. The word used in ch. viii. 6 is a different one. See there. This term, here in the singular, is used in the dual number 23 times in the O. T., and every time in the sense of *noon day*, i. e. the doubling of light. See reff. Noah was to make, i. e. to provide for giving, light to the ark. This might be done either by a series of windows (see on ch. viii. 6) or by leaving a vertical space on each side, on the ridge of the roof, and covering this on the top. When the commentators say that some translucent material must have been employed, or the rain would have come in, they forget that such a raised lantern along the ridge, especially if protected by eaves

make it. [17] And, behold, I will bring the flood of waters
upon the earth, to destroy all flesh, wherein *is* the breath
of life, from under the heaven; every thing that *is* in the
earth shall die. [18] But with thee will I establish my
covenant; and thou shalt come into the ark, thou, and
thy sons, and thy wife, and thy sons' wives with thee.
[19] And of every living thing of all flesh, two of every *sort*
shalt thou bring into the ark, to keep *them* alive with
thee; they shall be male and female. [20] Of fowls after
their kind, and of cattle after their kind, of every creeping
thing of the earth after his kind, two of every *sort* shall come
unto thee, to keep *them* alive. [21] And take thou unto thee
of all food that is eaten, and thou shalt gather *it* to thee;
and it shall be for food for thee, and for them. [22] Thus
did Noah; according to all that God commanded him, so
did he. VII. [1] And Jehovah said unto Noah, Come thou
and all thy house into the ark; for thee have I seen

slightly overhanging, would admit very little water. This idea would also explain the following words, "in a cubit shalt thou finish it above;" viz. that the height of the lantern, the vertical dimension of the "light," was to be a cubit, running the whole length of the ark. **shalt thou make it**] That is, the ark, not the door.
18.] This is the first *mention* of a **covenant** between God and man, although one was implied in the narrative of the events immediately following the fall. To Christians, who see in the rescue from the flood a type of baptism, this word is of interest. **19.**] This command is differently given in the Jehovist account, ch. vii. 2, 3, but referred to again in *these same* terms, not in those, in the resumption of the Elohistic narrative, ch. vii. 8, 9. Let the reader beware of the well-meant desires by which it has been attempted to show that there is no such variety in the accounts. When we once consent to break down the barriers of simple-minded truth and to commit pious frauds to save the literal accuracy of Scripture, we let go all evidence, and all fair judgment thereupon. If two may mean seven, and seven two, what need is there for us to mark, learn, and inwardly digest Scripture at all? The discrepancy is recognized by the best of the orthodox commentators, e. g. Delitzsch says, on ch. vii. 1—9, "I hold it undeniable that ch. vii. 1—9 belongs to the Supplementa, and that it, in respect of the contradiction between vii. 1—9 and vi. 9, ff., vii. 10—16, as to the number of the beasts to be included, is similarly situated to ch. ii. 5, ff, and i. 1, ff. in respect of the contradiction as to the Creation. These contradictions point to different sources, but admit of harmonizing in the spirit of the narrative. The original document spoke of only two of each kind taken in by Noah, the Supplementa specifies this more clearly from sources which gave more particulars, &c."—Genesis, p. 190. That *some* solution of the discrepancy was *possible* and was accepted, is evident by the fact of the insertion of the two accounts in immediate contiguity by the sacred writer. **20.**] Here we have again the phraseology of ch. i.
21.] All food that is eaten would at this time probably comprehend only vegetable food,—herbs and fruits. **22.**] Refers mainly to the building of the ark; but also includes prospectively what the same writer by-and-by relates in detail, ch. vii. 7—9.

VII. **1—10.**] *Entry of Noah into the Ark; command of God to bring in the clean beasts by sevens, and the unclean by two; and fowls by sevens.* The foundation of the passage is Elohistic (compare ver. 9), but the subsequent hand of the Jehovist is evident in the passage 1—6.

righteous before me in this generation. 2 Of every clean
beast thou shalt take to thee by sevens, the male and his
female: and of beasts that *are* not clean, two, the male
and his female. 3 Of fowls also of the air by sevens, the
male and the female; to keep seed alive upon the face of
all the earth. 4 [z] For yet seven days, and I will cause it
to rain upon the earth forty days and forty nights; and
every living substance that I have made will I destroy
from off the face of the ground. 5 And Noah did accord-
ing unto all that Jehovah commanded him. 6 And Noah
was six hundred years old when the flood of waters was
upon the earth. 7 ¶ And Noah went in, and his sons,
and his wife, and his sons' wives with him, into the ark,
because of the waters of the flood. 8 Of clean beasts, and
of beasts that *are* not clean, and of fowls, and of every
thing that creepeth upon the earth, 9 there went in two
and two unto Noah into the ark, the male and the female,
as God had commanded Noah. 10 And it came to pass
after seven days, that the waters of the flood were upon
the earth. 11 ¶ In the six hundredth year of Noah's life,
in the second month, the seventeenth day of the month,
the same day were all the [a] fountains of the great deep
broken up, and the [b] windows of heaven were opened.

z ch. ii. 5. Amos iv. 7.

a ch. viii. 2. Lev. xi. 36. Josh. xv. 9. Ps. lxxxvii. 7.
b ch. viii. 2. 2 Kings vii. 2, 19. Eccl. xii. 3. Isa. xxiv. 18; lx. 8. Hos. xiii. 3 (chimney). Mal. iii. 10, only.

2.] The distinction between clean and unclean cannot for one moment be treated as an anachronism, introduced here out of the Mosaic law. Those who are prepared to think so humbly of the writer of the Pentateuch surely forget that he and those who came after him must have been aware of such an absurdity. Rather is the distinction a testimony to the subsistence at that time of sacrificial arrangements, which would necessitate such a distinction. That sacrifice *was* in view is clear from ch. viii. 20. We must imagine of these *sevens* as seven *pair*, otherwise they could not have come "male and his female." And the Hebrew expression is "seven and seven," whereas in the subsequent clause it is not "*two and two*," but simply "**two.**" (It is to be noted that the LXX., Vulgate, and Syriac versions read "*two and two.*") **6.**] literally, **son of six hundred years.** **7—10.**] We have here again the resumption of the original Elohistic account. See ch. vi. 20. This **two and two**, though it looks like the fulfilment of the command in vi. 19, 20, need not be inconsistent with the taking in of *seven pair* of clean animals in ver. 2. **11—24.**] Principally Elohistic. "The flood began on the 17th day of the 2nd month, which was later called *Jar*: it corresponds with April or May; it is not the Marheshvan, or October, which is never designated as the second, but the eighth month; for the year is, throughout the Bible, counted from Nisan, not from Tishri." Kalisch. See on Exod. xii. 2. **11. fountain**] The great deep, i. e. the ocean, was conceived as having its springs in the earth; see Job xxxviii. 16; Prov. viii. 28; and the meaning is, that these fountains were (lit.) rent open, and caused the sea to flood the earth from beneath, as the rain from above. **windows**] Not the same word as so rendered ch. viii. 6. This word, *arubboth*, is derived from a root signifying weaving or plaiting, and comes to mean a window from the lat-

12 And the rain was upon the earth forty days and forty
nights. 13 In the selfsame day entered Noah, and Shem,
and Ham, and Japheth, the sons of Noah, and Noah's
wife, and the three wives of his sons with them, into the
ark; 14 they, and every beast after his kind, and all the
cattle after their kind, and every creeping thing that
creepeth upon the earth after his kind, and every fowl
after his kind, every bird of every sort. 15 And they
went in unto Noah into the ark, two and two of all flesh,
wherein *is* the breath of life. 16 And they that went in,
went in male and female of all flesh, as God had com-
manded him: and Jehovah shut him in. 17 And the
flood was forty days upon the earth; and the waters in-
creased, and bare up the ark, and it rose above the earth.
18 And the waters prevailed, and increased greatly upon
the earth; and the ark went upon the face of the waters.
19 And the waters prevailed [c] exceedingly upon the earth;
and all the high mountains, that *were* under the whole
heaven, were covered. 20 Fifteen cubits upward did the
waters prevail; and the mountains were covered. 21 And
all flesh died that moved upon the earth, both of fowl, and
of cattle, and of beast, and of every creeping thing that
creepeth upon the earth, and every man: 22 all in whose
nostrils *was* the breath of the spirit of life, of all that *was*
in the dry *land*, died. 23 And he destroyed every living
substance which was upon the face of the ground, both

c lit. *much much*. See ch. xvii. 2, 6, 20; xxx. 43. Exod. i. 7. Num. xiv. 7.

ticed or reticulated material with which windows were formerly closed. The waters being divided (ch. i. 6) into those above and below the expanse of heaven, both contributed to the flood of the deluge. **12. was**] i. e. fell. It endured, on the earth, more than three times as long, ver. 24. **13.**] i. e. in the seventeenth day of the second month, as above in ver. 11. By **the three wives** we see that monogamy was preserved in the God-fearing family. Ver. 14 is a complete enumeration of the animals which went in. The last words may be also rendered, as by Kalisch, *every bird, every winged creature*. The close of ver. 16 is remarkable, as introducing into this Elohistic portion the name JEHOVAH. Knobel remarks that the clause also betrays the strong anthropomorphism of the Jehovist writer. One would rather say perhaps that he has in mind the *covenant* which God had established with Noah, and of which this shutting him in was a pledge: Jehovah being especially the covenant name of God. The phrase is literally, **Jehovah shut behind him.** It should be remarked that in the progress of the narrative Noah possesses the power of opening and closing the ark. See ch. viii. 6, 13. So that this act can only be regarded as an assurance of security to Noah and his family. **17. was**] See above, ver. 12. Went on increasing. No expressions could well be stronger than those here used to assert the universality of the flood. **20.**] Fifteen cubits, i.e. upwards of 26 feet, above the tops of the highest mountains.

man, and cattle, and the creeping things, and the fowl of
the heaven; and they were destroyed from the earth: and
Noah only remained *alive*, and they that *were* with him in
the ark. 24 And the waters prevailed upon the earth an
hundred and fifty days. VIII. 1 And God [d] remembered
Noah, and every living thing, and all the cattle that *was*
with him in the ark: and God made a wind to pass over
the earth, and the waters asswaged; 2 the fountains also
of the deep and the windows of heaven were closed, and
the rain from heaven was stopped; 3 and the waters re-
tired from off the earth continually: and after the end of
the hundred and fifty days the waters were abated. 4 And
the ark rested in the seventh month, on the seventeenth
day of the month, upon the mountains of Ararat. 5 And
the waters decreased continually until the tenth month:
in the tenth *month*, on the first *day* of the month, were the
tops of the mountains seen. 6 ¶ And it came to pass at
the end of forty days, that Noah opened the window of the

d = ch. xix. 29; xxx. 22. Exod. ii. 4. 1 Sam. i. 19.

VIII. **1—19.**] *Subsidence of the Flood, and of the Ark: the going forth of Noah.* (The whole section is Elohistic.) **1. a wind**] The ordinary means of clearing away the rain-cloud and producing dry weather. **2.**] See on ch. vii. 11. **3. continually**] Literally, *in going and returning.* The hundred and fifty days included the forty days of the rain's falling. For, seeing that Noah entered the ark and the flood began on the 17th day of the 2nd month, we have (counting the month at 30 days) 13 days of the 2nd month + 120 for the 3rd, 4th, 5th, and 6th months, + 17 for the 7th + 150 days. **4, 5.**] It seems to be implied that at the time indicated, the ark first took the ground—obviously on the highest peak of Ararat; then the waters continuing to decrease, on the first day of the 10th month the tops of the mountains (generally) were seen. Ararat] "The name in its Biblical sense may be most correctly considered as descriptive generally of the Armenian highlands, the lofty plateau which overlooks the plain of the Araxes on the N., and of Mesopotamia on the S." Mr. Bevan's article, in *Smith's Biblical Dictionary,* which see. The Ararat consists of two unequal peaks, the higher 16,254 French feet high, and covered with perpetual snow, —the lesser 12,284 feet high. Delitzsch observes: "There is no point in the old world which lies in the interior and yet so truly island-like, surrounded by great waters, which seem to have fallen on all sides from its height. And there is no point in the old world which has a central position in reference to so many great features of land and sea. It is the highest mountain-top, with the exception of the Himalayas, in the old world." See also Kalisch's long and graphic note. **5.**] In seventy-two days after the grounding of the ark, on the highest peak the tops of the surrounding lower mountains became generally visible. Then **6.**] forty days after that Noah makes the first trial of the state of the earth. As before observed on ch. vi. 16, the word here rendered **window** is different from that which we have there translated **light**. This may have been one division or portion of that larger aperture perhaps extending the length of the ark. There is no reason whatever to infer that there was but one such aperture of the limited size which one man might open. We may be allowed to remind the reader that our own common usage is to speak of opening "the window," though there may be many windows in the room. This "window" might even be a mere open-

ark which he had made: 7 and he sent forth the raven,
which went forth to and fro, until the waters were dried
up from off the earth. 8 Also he sent forth the dove from
him, to see if the waters were abated from off the face of
the ground; 9 but the dove found no rest for the sole of
her foot, and she returned unto him into the ark, for the
waters *were* on the face of the whole earth: then he put
forth his hand, and took her, and pulled her in unto him
into the ark. 10 And he stayed yet other seven days; and
again he sent forth the dove out of the ark; 11 and the
dove came in to him in the evening; and, lo, in her mouth
was a fresh olive leaf: so Noah knew that the waters were
abated from off the earth. 12 And he stayed yet other
seven days; and sent forth the dove; which returned not
again unto him any more. 13 ¶ And it came to pass in
the six hundredth and first year, in the first *month*, the
first *day* of the month, the waters were dried up from off

ing closed by a shutter, a kind of door; the LXX. seems to have regarded it as such. 7. **the raven**, a bird of prey, perhaps "*went going and returning*," or **went to and fro** on the earth feeding on the carcases. Kalisch understands the words to mean that she came back from time to time, to the ark, for her food. But this is hardly probable, or we should have read of her returning, as in the case of the dove. The carcases would naturally be found on the tops of the mountains, which we know were by this time visible above the waters. 8, ff.] Though it is not here mentioned, it must be inferred from ver. 10 that the sending forth of the dove was 7 days after that of the raven. The dove forms in its habits a strong contrast to the raven, being domestic, and a frequenter of woods and plains, whereas the other is wild and solitary. He sent her to see whether the plains were yet dry. The olive is reputed by Theophrastus and Pliny to grow under water. "It does not appear," says Kalisch, "that the ancient Hebrews regarded olive branches as a symbol of peace and joy, though it is generally known that the classical nations connected with them those ideas, and though it appears that the later Jews adopted from the Greeks this notion, among many others (2 Macc. xiv. 4)." He quotes from *Wilkinson*, *Ancient Egyptians*, that the olive probably became an emblem of peace because of the great amount of time and care which the restoration of olive plantations require after a frontier invasion, or agricultural neglect. "What messenger of returning happiness could be more appropriate than a dove, the lovely type of purity and atonement, through the Spirit of God, offering an olive-leaf, the symbol of the renewed fruitfulness of the earth?" Kalisch. The olive-tree grows in Armenia: not on the heights of Ararat, nor so high as the walnut, mulberry, and apricot, but on the lowest hills and in the plains. So that the dove had a long day's flight to find her olive leaf. The leaf was **fresh**, so that there had been time for a tender shoot to be put forth. This, and the mere fact of the top of an olive tree being above the water, showed him that the waters were indeed decreased. 12. **yet other seven days**] So that since the end of the forty days in ver. 6 three weeks had passed. These intervals unquestionably give support to the idea that the sabbatical rest was observed by Noah. 13.] Bp. Wordsworth remarks, "Probably there was so much evaporation from the action of the sun on the water, that he could not see to any great distance from his lofty position, and on account of the mist could not discover whether the plains beneath him were dry: it was not till the waters were asswaged

the earth: and Noah removed the [e] covering of the ark,
and looked, and, behold, the face of the ground was dry.
14 And in the second month, on the seven and twentieth
day of the month, was the earth [f] dried up. 15 And God
spake unto Noah saying, 16 Go forth of the ark, thou, and
thy wife, and thy sons, and thy sons' wives with thee.
17 Bring forth with thee every living thing that *is* with
thee, of all flesh, *both* of fowl, and of cattle, and of every
creeping thing that creepeth upon the earth; that they
may increase abundantly in the earth, and be fruitful, and
multiply upon the earth. 18 And Noah went forth, and
his sons, and his wife, and his sons' wives with him: 19
every beast, every creeping thing, and every fowl, *and*
whatsoever creepeth upon the earth, after their kinds,
went forth out of the ark. 20 ¶ And Noah builded an
altar unto Jehovah; and took of every clean beast, and of
every clean fowl, and offered burnt offerings on the altar.
21 And Jehovah [g] smelled a sweet savour; and Jehovah
[h] said in his heart, I will not again curse the ground any

e Exod. xxvi. 14; xxxv. 11; xxxvi. 19; xxxix. 34; xl. 19. Num. iii. 25; iv. 5, 10, 11, 12, 25, only.
f Isa. xix. 5. Jer. xxiii. 10; l. 38. Joel i. 20, al.
g See Lev. i. 9, reff.
h ch. xxiv. 45; xxvii. 41. 1 Sam. xxvii. 1 Hos. vii. 2, al.

from the earth that he could see that the face of the ground was dry." **the covering**] This word (see reff.) is elsewhere used only of coverings of leather and skin, as in the case of the tabernacle. And perhaps we are to think of the covering of the ark as of like material. **14.**] The difference between the state of the earth in ver. 13 and here was that when Noah first looked the "dry land" appeared: but at this latter date it had become quite dry, i. e. had acquired its usual state of dryness. This difference may serve to illustrate the interpretation of ch. ii. 5, as compared with ch. i. 9. See there. By this date we have the whole duration of the flood from the 17th day of the 2nd month of the 600th year of Noah's life, to the 27th day of the 2nd month of the 601st, i. e. one year and ten days.

15—19.] *The going forth from the ark.* **20—22.**] *Noah's sacrifice to Jehovah, who is appeased thereby, and covenants no more to destroy the earth.* This portion is Jehovistic, introducing the first mention of altar and sacrifice. It appears to be inserted between two consecutive verses (viii. 19 and ix. 1) of the Elohistic record, for it is not true, as Delitzsch maintains, that the blessing and covenant of ch. ix. necessarily presuppose the thank-offering of Noah, and its favourable reception. All in the Elohistic narrative proceeds consecutively without the supplement. But this does not take at all from the authority of that supplement. The sacrificial notices inserted afterwards are of equal weight and authenticity with the original and simpler account. **20.**] The notice of **every clean beast and every clean fowl** is in strict accordance with that in ch. vii. 2, 3.

21.] The expression is anthropomorphic in its first usage, but became figurative afterwards (see reff.). Nor did the New Testament reject that phrase, even in reference to its most sacred idea, for it says: "Christ has given Himself for us as an offering and a sacrifice to God for a **sweet-smelling savour** (Eph. v. 2)." Kalisch. It of course indicates the gracious acceptance of the thank-offering of the patriarch. "God saw with delight the piety of the only family which had escaped the universal calamity: and He determined never again to expose the earth to so fearful a destruction, but to be mindful of the weakness of the human heart. . . . He received the sin-offering of Noah as an atonement for the wickedness of the former generations: the sin of man was no more to be measured after the test of

more for man's sake; for the imagination of man's heart
is evil from his youth; neither will I again smite any
more every thing living, as I have done. 22 While the
earth remaineth, seedtime and harvest, and cold and heat,
and summer and winter, and day and night shall not
cease. IX. 1 And God blessed Noah and his sons, and
said unto them, Be fruitful, and multiply, and replenish
the earth. 2 And the fear of you and the dread of you
shall be upon every beast of the earth, and upon every
fowl of the air, upon all that moveth *upon* the earth, and
upon all the fishes of the sea; into your hand are they
delivered. 3 Every moving thing that liveth shall be to
you for food; even as the [i] green herb I give you all
things. 4 Only flesh with the life thereof, the blood
thereof, shall ye not eat. 5 And surely your blood of

[i] ch. i. 30. Exod. x. 15. Num. xxii. 4. Ps. xxxvii. 2. Isa. xv. 6, only.

justice, but after that of mercy. God had, during several centuries, judged him after his innate Divine attributes; He now intended to view him with regard to his human imperfections: He was aware that though the spirit is willing, the flesh is weak. God proclaimed, that man cannot gain salvation by his own righteousness, but by the Divine mercy." Kalisch. To this striking Jewish commentary the Christian can supply the only foundation, the Great Sacrifice, which was being already gradually figured out before the eyes of men, and would in due time be revealed on the cross.

On **said in his heart**, see reff. It is equivalent to *thought*, *determined*. **22.**] The LXX. version, literally following the Hebrew, translates "*All the days of the earth*," to which exactly correspond the last words of our Lord to His disciples, "Behold, I am with you *all the days*," Matt. xxviii. 20. The Hebrews distinguished two seasons only (see Zech. xiv. 8; Amos iii. 15; Isa. xviii. 6), summer and winter, with the heat and cold, the seed-time and harvest, respectively belonging to them. These had been thrown out of their regular succession by the flood. Not so day and night, which, however, are added to complete the series of regularly ordained changes.

IX. **1—17.**] *The blessing of Noah and his family—ordinances concerning eating flesh and abstaining from the blood*; and (8—17) *the covenant of the rainbow*. The whole of this is Elohistic, and continues naturally from ch. viii. 19. **2. all that moveth upon the earth**] literally, all with which the earth moveth. See on ch. i. 21. **3.**] This subsequent enlargement of the original provision of man's food (ch. i. 29) assumes, not that flesh had not been eaten by man before the Flood, but that such eating now first received Divine sanction. See Bp. Wordsworth's note here. **4.**] Among the principal places where this command is iterated, and its reason assigned, see Levit. xvii. 10, 11, 14; Deut. xii. 23—25. The prohibition was afterwards extended to fat also (see Levit. iii. 17; vii. 22—27); but this extension seems never to have been regarded. See on these places. The law against eating blood was among those reserved as binding on the primitive Christian Church (see Acts xv. 20, 29; xxi. 15), and is rigorously observed by all Jews at the present day. Besides that the forbidding of the blood bears testimony, as Kalisch well says, to the original inviolability of every animal life, the sacred reference of blood as the means of Atonement doubtless underlay this commandment. This is not the place to enlarge upon the matter, but every Christian will be able to fill in the outline.

5.] The principle just laid down that the blood is the life, is enlarged to the declaration of vengeance being exacted for the shedding of man's blood. "The blood of a human being cries for revenge to heaven (iv. 10; Heb. xii. 24), the soul of the slain raises its voice (Job xxiv. 12; Rev. vi. 9),

your lives will I require; at the hand of every beast will
I require it, and at the hand of man, at the hand of his
brother man, will I require the life of man. 6 Whoso shed-
deth man's blood, by man shall his blood be shed: for in the
image of God made he man. 7 And you, be ye fruitful, and
multiply; bring forth abundantly in the earth, and multi-
ply therein. 8 ¶ And God spake unto Noah, and to his sons
with him, saying, 9 And I, behold, I establish my covenant
with you, and with your seed after you; 10 and with every
living creature that *is* with you, of the fowl, of the cattle,
and of every beast of the earth with you; from all that go
out of the ark, to every beast of the earth. 11 And I will
establish my covenant with you; neither shall all flesh be
cut off any more by the waters of a flood; neither shall
there any more be a flood to destroy the earth. 12 And
God said, This *is* the token of the covenant which I give
between me and you and every living creature that *is* with
you, for perpetual generations: 13 I have given my bow
in the cloud, and it shall be for a token of a covenant be-
tween me and the earth. 14 And it shall come to pass,
when I bring a cloud over the earth, and the bow is seen

the blood of the innocent victim hangs at the skirt of the murderer's garments (Jer. ii. 24), the blood is identical with the life of the individual itself (Ps. xciv. 21; Matt. xxiii. 35)." Kalisch. **at the hand of every beast**] This agrees with the enactment of the Mosaic law. See Exod. xxi. 28—32. The last clause of this verse has been very variously rendered; the A. V. is approved by Kalisch; but the text is the better rendering of the Hebrew; and so Knobel. **6.**] In the words **by man shall his blood be shed,** we can hardly, as Bp. Wordsworth suggests, trace the institution of magistrates who would take cognizance of murder, though such an institution must ere long spring out of the obligation; but rather is this the institution of the duty of the avenger of blood, who was the next of kin to the murdered. See Num. xxiv. 19; Deut. xix. 6, 11—13; Josh. xx. 1—9.

The reason assigned in the latter half of the verse has been already adduced in the note on ch. v. 3, as shewing that man is still in the image of God. If that image were lost, this reason would not apply to the matter in hand. **7.**] In contrast to the last and foregoing verses: men were placed on the earth not to fight and destroy one another, but to fill the earth. **10.**] The meaning of the latter clause is that the covenant, beginning by being made with all that go out of the ark, is to extend to all the animal world that should hereafter be upon earth. **12—17.**] *The rainbow set as the sign of the covenant.* **13.**] Kalisch remarks that the past tense, I have given (or set) my bow in the cloud, seems to imply that it is recognized as having been there before the Flood, though now first made into a sign. But Keil takes another view. "The setting of the rainbow for a token of the covenant of promise that there should no more be an universal flood, assumes that it then for the first time appeared on the vault and the clouds of heaven. From this follows, not that it never rained before the Deluge, which would be scarcely reconcileable with ch. ii. 5, but that the atmosphere before the flood was differently constructed from that after it; with which idea the

in the cloud: 15 I will remember my covenant, which *is*
between me and you and every living creature of all
flesh; and the waters shall no more become a flood to de-
stroy all flesh. 16 And the bow shall be in the cloud;
and I will look upon it, that I may remember the ever-
lasting covenant between God and every living creature
of all flesh that *is* upon the earth. 17 And God said unto
Noah, This *is* the token of the covenant, which I have
established between me and all flesh that *is* upon the
earth. 18 ¶ And the sons of Noah, that went forth of the
ark, were Shem, and Ham, and Japheth: and Ham *is* the
father of Canaan. 19 These *are* the three sons of Noah:
and of them was the whole earth overspread. 20 And

parts of natural history harmonize which point to a difference in the earth's superficial climate before and after the Flood." And so likewise Delitzsch. But this would certainly imply that there had been no *rain*, as one understand rain, before the Flood. If we are to maintain that the rainbow now first appeared, the earth must have been watered by mere mists for nearly 17 centuries. **18—27.**] *Noah's sons. His drunkenness: the sin of Ham: he is cursed by his father.* This portion is plainly due to the Jehovist. This is testified both by the sacred name, ver. 26 (see there), and by the especial notices in vv. 18, 22, which have been supposed to be due to the relation of the children of Israel to the Canaanites in after time. The allusion to the meaning of the name Japhet in ver. 27 is also characteristic. "This portion of the chapter proceeds evidently from the pen of the Jehovist: it is inserted by him to prepare the reader here already for the future glory of Israel; he approaches nearer to one of the chief ends of the Pentateuch; and he proves that the origin of Israel's ascendancy and of Canaan's degradation dates so far back as the family of the second founder of the human race." Kalisch. **18.**] On the sons of Noah, see on ch. v. 32. The prominence given to Canaan, the younger son of Ham (ch. x. 6), is remarkable. These notices inserted by the sacred writer, "Ham is the father of Canaan," "Ham, the father of Canaan," would perhaps be accountable as above; but the terms of Noah's prophecy would necessarily belong to the original account, and can hardly be due to any subsequent circumstances. It seems to me that we are bound to suppose some participation on the part of Canaan himself, in the act of dishonouring Noah. Delitzsch inclines to the view that the curse of Ham, Noah's *youngest* son (ver. 24), is retributively pronounced on *his youngest* son, Canaan (20 ff.). The same commentator has well remarked that this season after the Flood, like that immediately following the Creation, is the time of decisive events pregnant with weighty consequences; in the one the fate of mankind, in the other that of nations, is decided upon apparently trivial and every-day antecedents. It is peculiar to the primæval times, that the weightiest and widest-spread consequences depend on common and accidental incidents, which yet involve, on their small scale, the same conflicts between spiritual powers, as in our more extended, more numerically important combinations.

It is not apparent, from our narrative, whether Noah is to be regarded as the *first* planter of the vine, and discoverer of the power of wine. The supposition has been widely made, but in great part as an excuse for what happened. We may observe thus much; that if the filling of the earth with violence and wickedness before the Flood is to be regarded as having taken place without the influence of wine, the share of the alcoholic element in human depravity is very considerably lightened; indeed it may be said that mankind has been worse without wine than with it. I should rather regard our narrative as indicating that Noah, in the prosperity which followed the Flood, had allowed himself to fall into some of the sinful habits

j See Zech. xiii. 5. Noah began *to be* an [j] husbandman, and he planted a vine-
yard: 21 and he drank of the wine, and was drunken;
and he was uncovered within his tent. 22 And Ham, the
father of Canaan, saw the nakedness of his father, and told
his two brethren without. 23 And Shem and Japheth
took the garment, and laid *it* upon both their shoulders,
and went backward, and covered the nakedness of their
father; and their faces *were* backward, and they saw not
their father's nakedness. 24 And Noah awoke from his
k = 1 Sam. i. 14; xxv. 37. [k] wine, and knew what his [l] younger son had done unto
l ch. xxvii. 15, 42; xlii. 13, 32; xliv. 2. 1 Sam. xvii. 14. him. 25 And he said,

Cursed *be* Canaan;

Servant of servants shall he be unto his brethren.

26 And he said,

of those against whom he had formerly testified. **an husbandman** is literally "*a man of the ground*," or "*the field*," see reff. Armenia always was, and still is, productive of wine, even in parts as much as 4000 feet above the sea. **21.**] It has very generally been alleged as an excuse for Noah, that he was unacquainted with the intoxicating power of wine. But see above. **22.**] Luther says here, "The son would never have derided his father in his shame, had he not first banished from his mind that reverence and deference which by God's command should be in children towards their parents." What he did was only an index to his character; open acts give *occasion* for punishment, but the punishment is earned by, and is administered for, the depravity out of which open acts spring. **told his two brethren**] clearly not that they might do what they did, nor in any such spirit; but jestingly and undutifully. **23.**] **the garment,** viz. which Noah had thrown off. **24.**] **his wine,** the effects of his wine, see reff. **his younger son**] literally, *his little son*, or *his son the little* [one]. The same expression with the same meaning is found in reff. He knew this perhaps (for so seems the spirit of the narrative) prophetically, and not by ordinary information; and he pronounces the curse on Ham (see above) not so as to affect all his posterity, but his *youngest son*, Canaan. And the form of the curse is that he shall be the lowest of servants to both his brethren. The prophetic speech of Noah is poetical, or rather rhythmical, as that of Lamech was, ch. iv. 23, ff. **25.**] "The Canaanites alone, of all the Hamites, were considered impious and wicked; their destruction was decreed as soon as the cup of their iniquity was full (ch. xv. 16; compare Lev. xviii. 24—30); they suffered both for their own sin and that of the founder of their race. The long-suffering of God did not hasten their perdition. He allowed them to grow and prosper during the ten generations from Noah to Abraham, and the five following centuries from Abraham to Joshua; their fields and vineyards yielded abundant harvests, and their land was full of strong and populous cities; but their evil deeds accumulated, and they forfeited the land which their vices had contaminated." Kalisch. The curse, as matter of world-history, has more or less followed all the Hamite races. "The Canaanites were under Joshua, and under the Shemite race of Israel, partly destroyed, partly reduced to the most abject state of slavery (Josh. ix. 21 ff.; compare Judges i. 28, 30, 33, 35); and their remnants were subjected to the same lot by Solomon (1 Kings xi. 20 f.). The Phœnicians, who belonged to Canaan, with the Carthaginians and Egyptians, were subdued by the Japhetic Persians, Macedonians, and Romans, and the rest of the Hamite races shared the same lot, and do so even now, as e. g. the negroes and other African races under the yoke of the hardest slavery." Keil. **26.**] The blessings, in their turn, are introduced by the formal, "**And he said.**"

Blessed be Jehovah God of Shem;
And let Canaan be servant unto him.
27 Let God enlarge Japheth,
And let him dwell in the tents of Shem;
And let Canaan be servant unto him.
28 ¶ And Noah lived after the flood three hundred and
fifty years. 29 And all the days of Noah were nine
hundred and fifty years: and he died. X. 1 Now these

In the first blessing of Shem, through whom should come the line of the covenant, he blesses, not Shem, but Jehovah, the covenant God, in whom, so to speak, Shem and his race are included; "instead of making prominent the blessedness of Shem, he makes prominent the source of that blessedness." Knobel. The words, **And Canaan shall be servant unto him,** follow both blessings as a sort of refrain or burden; keeping up the tone of malediction which the occasion had set. **27.**] There is here an allusion to the meaning of the name Japhet, which signifies *enlargement* or *expansion.* This is characteristic of the Jehovistic narrative. See ch. iv. 1, 25; v. 29. Observe it is here Elohim, not Jehovah; for Jehovah Elohim is the covenant God of the Shemite race of Israel, Elohim became to them Jehovah; not so with the race of Japhet, till the time when the Covenant should be with all flesh. On the next clause there has been some doubt as to the interpretation. Who is the subject of the proposition, "*he* **shall dwell**"? Is it *God* (Elohim)? or is it *Japheth?* Many have taken the former; God shall pitch His tabernacle in the tents of Shem; which was so in early times, patriarchal and mosaic, and then notably when "the Word was made flesh and dwelt (tabernacled) among us." But to this there are serious objections. The greatest is, that the name Elohim has been deliberately substituted for Jehovah since the last verse; and if any such meaning as that in question had been intended, Jehovah would certainly have been used. Again, such a meaning would really make this, Japhet's portion of the paternal blessing, only an addition to that of Shem. So that we must suppose Japhet to be the subject of the verb "*shall dwell.*" And then the prophecy may portend either a multiplying of the race of Japhet by the promised enlargement, so as to overflow into the settlement of Shem (which however would look like an abridgment of the blessing of Shem), or a fusion and fraternization of the two races by simultaneity of dwelling or religion. That this latter, the intercourse of Europe and Asia, has been the great text of ages of history, and is to this day taking the form indicated in the prophecy, is no mean argument for the secular part of the interpretation, while the grafting in of the Japhetic races into the blessing of Jehovah, God of Shem, by Him in whom all are blessed, seems fully to satisfy the spiritual meaning.

Ver. 28, 29 are assigned, on account of their similarity, to ch. v., and the mention of "the Flood" to the original or Elohistic narrative.

X. *The table of the nations, as descended from the son of Noah:* extending over West Asia, North Africa, and Europe. Elohistic, with the exception of an insertion ver. 8—12. See also on ver. 25. This is shewn by the superscription, and closing formulæ, ver. 5, 20, 31, 32; by the expression, "*the Flood,*" ver. 1, 32. Also we may notice that the genealogy lies insulated here; for evidently the incident involving Canaan, in ch. ix. 19—27, is an anticipation of our ver. 6; while on the other hand the divisions of the world here narrated are anticipations of the narrated cause of the dispersion in ch. xi. 1—9.

The order of the generations of the sons of Noah here followed is Japhet, Ham, Shem. The reason of this arrangement beginning with Japhet, is that he was the eldest of the three. Ham follows next, in order that the main subject, the line of Shem, may be free for treatment, the object of secondary interest having been first disposed of, according to the practice of the sacred writer, —see an example in the treatment of the Cainites before Seth, ch. iv. v.

are the generations of the sons of Noah, Shem, Ham, and
Japheth: and unto them were sons born after the flood.
2 The sons of Japheth; Gomer, and Magog, and Madai,
and Javan, and [m] Tubal, and [m] Meshech, and Tiras. 3 And

m 1 Chron. i. 5. Isa. lxvi. 19. Ezek. xxvii. 13; xxxii. 26; xxxviii. 2, 3; xxxix. 1.

It is, of course, and ever must be, doubtful whether many of the names here given are to be regarded as those of persons or of nations. As Delitzsch remarks, the line between ideal and historical points of unity of nations is never in antiquity strongly drawn. The two are curiously intermingled in the Canaanitish portion of the list, vv. 15—18. And in vv. 13, 14, the apparently personal names at last blend into Philistim and Caphtorim. In the following commentary I shall simply mention the principal similarities between the recorded names and those of the ancient nations as they have been given us by the best authorities.

2—5.] *The sons of Japheth.* The similarity of the name Japheth and the *Iapetus* of the Greeks and Romans (the progenitor of the human race), is too strong to be overlooked. The name GOMER has been traced in the *Kimmerians* of Homer and the classics, also in the *Cymry* or *Cymrian*, even now used by the Welsh, as their national name. MAGOG is supposed to indicate the *Scythians*, and the second syllable to have affinity with *Cau*casus, which is even now called *Gogh*, in the vernacular of the Caucasian tribes. MADAI is traced in the *Medes*, who in old Persian were called *Mada*. JAVAN is one of the most easily identified as the *Ionian* race, called by the old poets *Iaones:* this name in the Eastern tongues, e. g. the Hebrew and other Semitic dialects, as in Sanskrit, old Persian, and Egyptian, designated the whole of the Grecian people. TUBAL and MESECH, which names frequently come together in the O. T. (see reff.), have not been satisfactorily traced, but as the list seems to run from North to South, would naturally belong to the South of Europe. But the names nearest allied to these are the *Moschi* and *Tibareni*, two Colchian tribes mentioned by Herodotus as constituting a satrapy in the Persian empire, and as serving in the army of Xerxes. Sir H. Rawlinson, in his edition of Herodotus, says that they are constantly associated, under the names of *Muskai* and *Tuplai*, in the Assyrian inscriptions (see art. "Tubal" in *Smith's Biblical Dictionary*). But Knobel is disposed to look for them as above among the S. European nations, and to find them in the Iberians and Ligurians. So that we are in uncertainty. **Tiras**] Various guesses have been made as to what nation is represented by this name of a son of Japhet. Josephus gives the *Thracians*, Knobel thinks the *Agathyrsi*. The range of the *Taurus*, the river *Tyras* (Dniester), the *Tyrite*, and even the *Tyrseni* or *Tyrrheni*, have been thought of. See in *Smith's Biblical Dictionary*. **3.**] Now we come to the descendants of Japhet in the second generation, but in two branches only; beyond which the genealogy is not carried. **Ashkenaz**] There seems strong reason to believe that the *Germanic* races are designated by this term. The original place of Ashkenaz was in Armenia, see ref., where it is classed with Ararat. Some think it to be a compound word, and *as* to be the first portion carrying the distinctive name, and *Kenaz*, (*genos* in Greek, kin or kind in English), signifying *race* or *people;* and connect the As with Asia. In North Asia Minor there was a lake *Ascanius*, which name again occurs in the story of Troy as that of the son of Æneas. The central part of Asia Minor, where dwelt the Mysians and Phrygians, was called Ascania according to Frankish traditions, says Knobel; after the fall of Troy, a portion of the Franks came thence to Pannonia, and subsequently to the Rhine. The ancient Saxon legends make, it is true, the Saxons indigenous, but name the first king Aschan or Aschanes, and the name is traceable also in old northern traditions, of a people the Asians, who came from the other side of the Don, and were the first German inhabitants of *Scan*dinavia. It is somewhat remarkable that the Jews to this day call Germany *Askenaz.* **Riphath**] By this name, according to Knobel, the Celtic race seem to be designated. They dwelt originally on the *Riphæan*, *Ripæan*, or *Carpathian* mountains, and, according to an account given by Plutarch, spread thence westward, one branch over North and N.-West Europe, and

the sons of Gomer; [n] Ashkenaz, and [o] Riphath, and [p] Tog-
armah. 4 And the sons of Javan; [q] Elishah, and [r] Tar-
shish, [s] Kittim, and [t] Dodanim. 5 By these were the isles
of the Gentiles divided in their lands; every one after his
tongue, after their families, in their nations. 6 ¶ And the
sons of Ham; [u] Cush, and Mizraim, and [v] Phut, and

n Jer. li. 27. o See 1 Chron. i. 6. p Ezek. xxvii. 14; xxxviii. 6. q Ezek. xxvii. 7, only. r 1 Kings x. 22; xxii. 48. 1 Chron. i. 7. Ps. xlviii. 8; lxxii. 10. Isa. ii. 16; xxiii. 1, 6, 10, 14; lx. 9; lxvi. 19. Jer. x. 9. Ezek. xxvii. 12, 15; xxxviii. 13. Jonah i. 3; iv. 2, only. s Num. xxiv. 24. 1 Chron. i. 7. Isa. xxiii. 1, 12. Jer. ii. 10. Ezek. xxvii. 6. Dan. xi. 30. 1 Macc. i. 1; viii. 5. t 1 Chron. i. 7. Ezek. xxii. 15. (Dedan.) u ch. ii. 13. 1 Chron. i. 8, 9. 2 Chron. xii. 3; xiv. 9, 12, 13; xvi. 8. Esth. i. 1; viii. 9. Job xxviii. 19. Ps. lxviii. 31; lxxxvii. 4. Isa. xi. 11; xviii. 1; xx. 3—5; xxxiii. 9; xliii. 3; xlv. 14. Jer. xiii. 23; xlvi. 9. Ezek. xxix. 10; xxx. 4, 5, 9; xxxviii. 5. Nah. iii. 9. Zeph. iii. 10. v 1 Chron. i. 8. Jer. xlvi. 9. Ezek. xxvii. 10; xxx. 5; xxxviii. 5. Nah. iii. 9, only (Isa. lxvi. 19; see there).

another into France. Much doubt is cast on this view by some of the other commentators, who however have nothing so probable to substitute for it. **Togarmah**] Almost beyond doubt the Armenians, who themselves make their founder the son of *Thorgom.* To this view the mention of Togarmah in reff. Ezek. corresponds; for in the former they are represented as trading in the fairs at Tyre with horses and horsemen and mules, which have always been the staple of Armenia, and in the latter they are spoken of as "of the north quarters," and ranked with Gomer. **4.**] The first mentioned name of a son of Javan, **Elishah,** has been variously connected with the Greek race; Josephus supposed it to represent the *Æolians:* and to this Knobel also agrees. Others have traced the name in *Elis,* or even in *Hellas.* In ref. Tyre is said to have been covered with "blue and purple from the isles (or sea-coasts) of Elishah." The Æolians in ancient times were much more widely spread than afterwards over Greece and Asia Minor, the N.W. corner of which was from them called *Æolis.* **Tarshish**] We may notice that this name is coupled by **and** to Elishah, but is not so coupled to what follows. Knobel hence infers some affinity with the preceding. He interprets this with Tarshish of the *Tyrrhenians* or *Tyrsenians* (see above on *Tiras*), who as well as the Æolians were a Pelasgic race. Elsewhere in the O. T. he seems to regard Tarshish as others do, as being Tartessus in Spain. See note on Jonah i. 3. I have given in the reff. all the places where the word occurs in the O. T. **Kittim**] is taken as representing primarily the Phœnician settlers in the isles of the Levant, traceable (so Josephus) in *Citium* the capital of Cyprus, but mainly the Carians, the people who succeeded them in the occupation of these islands. The LXX. and Vulgate render the word variously in various places; e. g. in ref. Num. the Vulgate has, "they shall come in ships out of Italy;" and in ref. Dan. the LXX. has, "and Romans shall come," and the Vulgate, "ships and Romans." In 1st ref. 1 Macc. Alexander the Great is said to have come out of the land of Chittim; and in 2nd, Perseus is called king of the Chittians. Josephus says that in his time the islands of the Archipelago were called by the Jews *Chettim.* The name has been supposed originally connected with that of the Hittites (Heb. *Chi*ttites), a branch of the Canaanitish race. **Dodanim**] as coupled to Kittim, seems to represent some people in Greece. The name is also written Rodanim, and is here rendered in the LXX. *Rhodians,* by which name they have also rendered Dedan in ref. Ezek. Dodanim is now generally assumed to answer to the *Dardani,* the *ar* and *o* being interchangeable, as in Barmilcar and Bomilcar, Hamilcar and Hamilco. The Dardani were anciently found in Illyrium and Troy. The *Dodona* in Epirus reminds one of this name, and Kalisch thinks the *Daunians* in Italy may be represented by it. On all these names see the articles in *Smith's Biblical Dictionary.*

5. the isles of the Gentiles] would appear to include the coast of the Mediterranean. The word signifies not only island but also any maritime tracts. The notice in this verse must evidently be regarded as anticipatory of ch. xi. 1. **6—20**] *The sons of Ham.* *Cush*] The well-known designation of the Ethiopians, the farthest South of the children of Ham. "They dwelt," says Knobel, "partly in Asia, e. g. in India, Gedrosia, Carmania, and Southern Arabia, and farther north in Susiana and Babylonia. In these lands the ancients speak of dark-skinned tribes known by them as Ethiopians, who partly vanished in old time, partly remain in fragments even now. But the

Canaan. 7 And the sons of Cush; [w] Seba, and [x] Havilah,
and [y] Sabtah, and [z] Raamah, and [a] Sabtechah: and the
sons of Raamah; [b] Sheba, and [c] Dedan. 8 And Cush

w 1 Chron. i. 9. Ps. lxxii. 10. Isa. xliii. 3. x ver. 29; ch. ii. 11; xxv. 18. 1 Sam. xv. 7. 1 Chron. i. 9, 23. y 1 Chron. i. 9, only. z 1 Chron. i. 9. Ezek. xxvii. 22, only. a 1 Chron. i. 9. b 1 Chron. i. 9. See ver. 28 reff. Ezek. xxvii. 22, 23 (ch. xxv. 3). c ch. xxv. 3. 1 Chron. i. 9, 32. Jer. xxv. 23; xlix. 8. Ezek. xxvii. 15, 20; xxxviii. 13, only.

main body of this race dwelt in Africa, in the present Nubia and Abyssinia. To these African Ethiopians the name Cush in the O. T. usually applies; but in these national tables, the name indicates the Ethiopian race generally, and has a wider meaning. In the division of lands here the sons of Cush are also mentioned, whom the writer enumerates from West to East. "In all the reff. except in the genealogical table in Chron., **Cush** is rendered *Ethiopia* in the A. V. **Mizraim**] This is the name throughout the O. T. for *Egypt* or the Egyptians. Mr Stuart Poole, in his art. in *Smith's Biblical Dictionary*, maintains that the form Mizraim can in no case be a man's name, as neither can any of those (ending in *im*) in vv. 13, 14, but must indicate nations, and that the order here may furnish a clue to the positions. Cush would stand first as the most widely spread of these peoples, extending from Babylon to the Upper Nile; the territory of Mizraim would be the next to the north, embracing Egypt and its colonies on the N. W. and N. E. Phut as dependent on Egypt might follow Mizraim, and Canaan as the northernmost would end the list. The occurrence of the name **Mizraim** in the O. T. is far too frequent to admit of a list of reff. It is everywhere rendered *Egypt* in the A. V. except in Genesis l. 11, where the name is given as it stands in a compound word. **Phut**] has been ordinarily understood to indicate the Libyans. See Mr. Stuart Poole's art. in *Smith's Biblical Dict.*, who inclines to interpret it rather of Nubians. However this may be, "the few mentions of Phut clearly indicate a country or people of Africa, and probably not far from Egypt. They occur only in the list of Noah's descendants and in the prophetic Scriptures;" see the reff., which seem quite to bear out this assertion, and on Isa. lxvi. 19. **Canaan**] The well-known progenitor, or natural name of the Phœnician tribes, occupying the territory from the Mediterranean to the Persian Gulf. See on his descendants below. **7. Saba**] To this name is allotted the north of Ethiopia, including Meroe, which is sometimes called Saba by Josephus. See Mr. Stuart Poole's art. in *Smith's Biblical Dict.* **Havilah**] See on ch. ii. 11. There is another Havilah mentioned in this chapter, ver. 29, as a son of Joktan, see there. This one is taken as representing the district *Khawlan* (which is similar in name) in Yemen; it is "a fertile territory embracing a large part of myrrhiferous Arabia." Mr. Stanley Poole in *Smith's Biblical Dict.* **Sabtah**] This name has been traced in *Sabbatu* or *Sabota*, an important inland city in South Arabia. See Mr Stanley Poole's art. as above. **Raamah**] This name has been identified, by means of the LXX. and Vulgate renderings, *Regma*, as a city so called, and mentioned by the ancient geographers, on the shore of the Persian Gulf. See Mr. Stanley Poole's art. as above. **Sabtechah**] Mr. Poole thinks this name has not been satisfactorily or even proximately traced. From its position here, we should expect a people on the Persian Gulf; and Knobel connects with the name a maritime town and river *Samydaké* mentioned by Ptolemy. But this seems far-fetched. **Sheba**] This Cushite Sheba is not to be confounded with the better known Sheba of ver. 28, on which see; it seems to represent a people on the Persian Gulf, where we are told are the ruins of an ancient city called Seba. In ref. Ezek. Sheba is mentioned as here, in connexion with Raamah, as bringing to Tyre spices, precious stones, and gold. On the reappearance of some of these names in ch. xxv. 3, as children of Keturah, see there. **Dedan**] Much obscurity rests over this name. Mr. Stanley Poole (art. as above) thinks that the view best supported by the facts of the case is, "that Dedan son of Raamah settled on the shores of the Persian Gulf, and his descendants (see ref. Ezek.) became caravan-merchants between that coast and Palestine." Mr. Poole thinks the name is to be traced in the island of *Dadan* on the border of the Gulf. In Jer. xxv. 23, Ezek. xxiii. 15, the name is connected with *islands*.

8—12.] *Parenthetical notice concerning Nimrod.* Its diversity of material from, and disconnexion with, what went before and

begat [d]Nimrod: he began to be a mighty one in the
earth. 9 He was a mighty hunter [e]before the LORD:
wherefore it is said, Even as Nimrod the mighty hunter
before the LORD. 10 And the beginning of his kingdom
was [f]Babel, and [g]Erech, and [h]Accad, and Calneh, in the
land of Shinar. 11 Out of that land he went forth to As-
shur, and builded Nineveh, and the city [i]Rehoboth, and

d 1 Chron. i.10. Micah v. 6, only.
e See ch. vii. 1. 1 Sam. xxvi. 12. Ps. civ. 16. Jonah iii. 3. (Acts vii. 20.)
f See ch. xi. 9.
g Ezra iv. 9, only.
h here only.
i here only (see ch. xxxvi.37).

what follows, and the occurrence of the name *Jehovah*, mark the insertion as due to the Jehovist supplementer. **Nimrod**] See Mr. Bevan's article in *Smith's Biblical Dict.* The expression **he began to be a mighty one in the earth,** is explained that he was the first who established an empire, becoming a conqueror, and joining more cities than one under his rule. **9.**] This notice is generally taken in its simple primary sense, that this great conqueror was also a great follower of the chase, a pursuit which, as Delitzsch remarks, "has remained to this day, true to its origin, the favourite pleasure of tyrants." The expression **before the Lord** is more than a mere intensitive; it signifies that in the sight of Him who overlooks all the world, such greatness was eminent—that the reputation was world-wide. The citation of popular proverbs is found also in ch. xxii. 11; Num. xxi. 27; 1 Sam. x. 12; xix. 24. His first establishment of his kingdom began with these four—**Babel** (universally known as Babylon. The ancient tradition made the Ethiopians founders of Babylon—an Ethiopian King Cepheus: and recognized a migration of the people of Cepheus northwards, Knobel). Belus also, the mythical founder of Babylon, was said to be of Egyptian origin, being the son of Poseidon and Libya. "The name Cush itself was preserved in Babylon and the adjacent countries under the form of Cossæi, Cissia, Cuthah, and Susiana, or Chuzistan." Bevan.
Erech] The earliest seat of empire was in the south part of the Babylonian plain. The large mounds, which for a vast number of centuries have covered the ruins of ancient cities, have already yielded some evidence of the dates and names of their founders, and we can assign the highest antiquity to the towns represented by the mounds of *Niffer* (perhaps the early Babel, though also identified with **Calneh**), *Warka* (the biblical **Erech**), *Mugheir* (Ur), and *Senkereh* (Ellasar), while the name of **Accad** is preserved in the title *Kinzi-akkad*, by which the founder or embellisher of their towns was distinguished (Rawlinson, i. 435). Bevan. See Mr. Grove's art. in *Biblical Dict.* Knobel finds the name **Calneh** in *Chalonitis:* the name of a district north of Babylon, on the east bank of the Tigris. On **the land of Shinar,** see note, ch. xi. 2. **11.**] This verse, as it seems now generally agreed, narrates a further progress towards greatness on the part of Nimrod, in going further northward into and conquering Asshur. The rendering in the A. V. seems to be possible, but mistaken. Four more cities are mentioned as built by Nimrod in Assyria. First, **Nineveh.** It would be beyond the limits of a note to give any full account of the early history of and conjectures respecting Nineveh. Mr. Layard, who has most right to do so, has related both these in his article in *Smith's Biblical Dict.* Nimrod is connected with Nineveh more by the modern name Nimroud, given by the Arabs to the principal mound of ruins, than by any ancient tradition. **Rehoboth**] This word properly signifies *streets*, and is taken by Jerome to mean, in connexion with the following word in the Hebrew, *the streets of the city*, viz. of Nineveh: and it is so rendered by the Vulgate. But it is generally supposed to represent a distinct place; and its locality is very variously assigned. Kalisch says the name was very common, and we have in ref. another instance of its occurrence. This Rehoboth is now generally supposed to represent a portion of the existing ruins of Nineveh. The Samaritan version reads here, for Rehoboth, *Sutcan:* which name is found united with *Calab* on the breast of a statue of the god Nebo, disinterred at Nimroud by Sir H. Rawlinson. Sutcan is supposed to represent Sittacene, a district in southern Assyria. **Calah**] Kalisch identifies this with the large mound, *Kalah Sherghat*, about 55 miles south of

here only (see 2 Kings vii. 6, note).
k 1 Chron. i. 11, 17 (Isa. lxvi. 19). Jer. xlvi. 9 (Ezek. xxvii. 10; xxx. 5). See on ver. 22.
l 1 Chron. i. 11, only.

Calah, 12 and Resen between Nineveh and [j] Calah: the
same *is* the great city. 13 And Mizraim begat [k] Ludim,
and [l] Anamim, and [m] Lehabim, and [l] Naphtuhim, 14 and
[n] Pathrusim, and [o] Casluhim, (out of whom came Philis-

m 1 Chron. i. 11, only. Lubims, 2 Chron. xii. 3; xvi. 8. Nah. iii. 9. Dan. xi. 43. n 1 Chron. i. 12, only. Pathros, Isa xi. 11. Jer. xliv. 1, 15. Ezek. xxix. 14; xxx. 14, only. o 1 Chron. i. 12, only.

Mosul, on the right bank of the Tigris. Calah, he says, possessed one of the most extensive palaces, and is several times mentioned on the black obelisk of the central palace of Nimroud as the residence of the king. But Layard (*Biblical Dict.*, as above) regards Calah as the same with Nimroud.

Resen] This has been identified by some with the ruins of Nimroud, regarding Nineveh itself as being Kouyunjik. But these sites seem at the best very uncertain.

the same is the great city] Knobel refers this to the whole four just mentioned, Nineveh, Rehoboth, Calah, and Resen: *these four places are the site which is named the great city*, viz. Nineveh in the wider sense. See Jonah iv. 11; iii. 3.

13—20.] *Continuation of the sons of Ham.* Resumption of the Elohistic genealogy. In what follows respecting the sons of Ham individual and national names are mixed. All these in vv. 13, 14 are plural in form; and in vv. 16, 17, the names are unmistakably national. **13, 14.**] Sons of Mizraim, on whom see note, ver. 6. **Lubim**] There is some difficulty in assigning the Scripture mention of *Lud* and *Ludim* between this Mizraite people and the Shemite of ver. 22. Mr. Stuart Poole discusses the matter in *Smith's Biblical Dict.*, and thinks it probable that this apparently Egyptian tribe are intended in Jer. xlvi. 9, "Cush and Phut that handle the buckler," and "*the Ludim that bend the bow*," in Pharaoh-Necho's army. In Ezek. xxvii. 10, again, Lud is associated with Phut as in Jer., and, probably again, the African Ludim. In Ezek. xxx. 5 we have a similar association. But (see the article) there are reasons why this must remain uncertain. **Anamim**] Probably a people of North Egypt; but nothing probable has been discovered about their site. **Lehabim**] Now generally identified with the *Lubim* of reff., and supposed to be the Libyans, the inhabitants of N.W. Africa. See art. in *Biblical Dict.* **Naphtuhim**] Kalisch connects this name with the Libyan city *Nassata*, in the north of the province of Meroe, which was the capital of an Ethiopian kingdom. **Pathrusim**] The conclusion of Mr. Stuart Poole in the *Biblical Dict.* (Pathros) is, "On the evidence here brought forward, it is reasonable to consider Pathros to be part of Upper Egypt, and to trace its name in that of the Pathyrite Nome (district in which Thebes was situate). But this is only a very conjectural identification, which future discoveries may overthrow." He thinks that the etymology which connects the name with "that which is southern" must be abandoned.

Casluhim] There is nothing to lead to the identification of this race. They were long supposed to be the Colchians, who are related to have been an Egyptian colony; but this is very doubtful, especially as the Philistines are said to have sprung from these Casluhims, and they certainly never came from Colchis. "The only clue to their position is their place in the list between the Pathrusim and the Caphtorim, whence it is probable that they were seated in Upper Egypt." Stuart Poole. Knobel connects the name with Mount Casius and the town *Cassium*, the territory of which was afterwards called *Cassiotis*. **out of whom (or whence) came Philistim**] The name of the Philistines is derived from a verb signifying to migrate, and so this notice is, as Mr. Bevan remarks (*Biblical Dict.*) "an etymological as well as an historical memorandum." An attempt has been made to set up a transposition here, and to make out that the notice refers to the Caphtorim who follow, because it is said (see ref. on that word) that the Philistines came from them. But we evidently must take this place as we find it. There is no reason why, the settlements being near, the Philistines may not have come from both. **Caphtorim**] have been in former times identified with the Cappadocians, Cyprians, and Cretans: others have supposed the name to be traceable in Coptos. But all appears uncertain. On the derivation of the Philistines from them, see

tim,) and [p] Caphtorim. 15 ¶ And Canaan begat Sidon his
firstborn, and Heth, 16 and the Jebusite, and the Amor-
ite, and Girgasite, 17 and the Hivite, and the [q] Arkite, and
the Sinite, 18 and the [r] Arvadite, and the [s] Zemarite, and
[t] the Hamathite: and afterward were the families of the
Canaanites spread abroad. 19 And the border of the

p Deut. ii. 23. 1 Chron. i. 12. Jer. xlvii. 11. Amos ix. 7.
q 1 Chron. i. 15, only.
r 1 Chron. i. 16, only. See Ezek. xxvii. 8, 11.
s 1 Chr. i. 16, only
t 1 Chron. i. 16, only. Hamath Num. xiii. 21, and frequently.

above. **15, f.**] *The sons of Canaan and the races derived from him.* **Sidon**] The Canaanitish peoples of Phœnician race, though they spoke a Semitic language, were both historically and mythologically originally from the south. Sidon and Tyre were their most ancient cities. Sidon was the only Phœnician city known to Homer. From **Heth** came the Hittites, who dwelt about the mountains of Judah, and especially near Hebron. But from Josh. i. 4 their settlements must have been originally much wider; and from 1 Kings x. 29, 2 Kings vii. 6, there were kings of the Hittites in the days of Solomon and of Joram. The four next-mentioned sons of Canaan dwelt in Palestine: the **Jebusites**, in and around Jerusalem; though defeated by Joshua, they maintained their ground in their city Jebus, were unsuccessfully attacked by the tribes of Judah (Judg. i. 8) and Benjamin (Judg. i. 21; xix. 11), driven out by David, but never entirely extirpated. They are mentioned after the return from Babylon, Ezra ix. 1. The **Amorites**, Knobel thinks, are not the great people of that name E. and W. of the Jordan, but a portion of them only who were mingled with the Canaanites on the mountains of Judah. The name implies, *dwellers on the summits.* See Mr. Grove's interesting article (*Biblical Dictionary*), who, however, does not maintain the above distinction. The **Girgasites** may possibly be connected with the Gergesenes mentioned Mark v. 1, on the E. of the Sea of Galilee. The **Hivites** inhabited Shechem and Gibeon, and had a settlement in the N. near the foot of Hermon and Lebanon. They were not a large people, and are frequently included under the Amorites. The **Arkites** are supposed to be the inhabitants of a town *Arka* or *Arké*, at the N. Western foot of Lebanon, whose ruins are still called Tel Arka. The **Sinites** were in the same neighbourhood, at a town which still preserved the name of *Sini* in Jerome's time, and which existed as a village called Sin near the river Arka, as late as the 15th century. The **Arvadites** dwelt in the island of **Aradus**, off the Phœnician coast. It is a mere rock, only 7 furlongs in circumference, but grew to be a settlement almost rivalling Sidon, by exiles from which it was founded,—and even sent out colonies, of which Tarsus was one. It was ruled by its own kings for many centuries, but yielded, first to the Persians, then to Alexander and to Ptolemy Soter. But, instead of declining, it rose to greater prosperity; it was declared a city of refuge, and probably regained its independence, for it offered alliance and support to Antiochus Epiphanes; but after his time it declined, becoming subject to Syria, Armenia, and Rome, and was finally destroyed under Constans. A village (*Ruad*) still recalls the name, and there are remains of massive Phœnician walls. The **Zemarites** are certainly not *Samaritans*, as the LXX. and Vulgate here render; for it does not correspond with the Hebrew word. They are supposed by Kalisch to have been the inhabitants of *Simyra*, near Antaradus (a town opposite the island of Aradus) or Tortosa. The ruins now bear the name of Sumrah. It was once thought that the Zemarites were the tribes round Edessa, near the river Zamyrus. The **Hamathites** were inhabitants of *Hamath*, the principal city of Upper Syria. It was on the Orontes, and commanded the whole of the valley. For an account of its history see *Smith's Biblical Dictionary* and Kalisch. It was called by the Greeks Epiphania. It still exists; and when Burckhardt visited it in 1812, had 30,000 inhabitants. The concluding notice imports that the Canaanites, who at first dwelt in the neighbourhood of Zidon, spread further over Palestine, viz. as specified in the next verse. **19.**] *The borders southward of the Canaanite extensions.* Gerar was a large city to the south of Palestine, the capital of Abimelech, and probably birthplace of Isaac. Its situation is very uncertain. See Dr. Hayman's art. in *Smith's Biblical*

Canaanites was from Sidon, as thou comest to [u] Gerar,
unto Gaza; as thou goest, unto Sodom, and Gomorrah,
and Admah, and Zeboim, even unto Lasha. 20 These *are*
the sons of Ham, after their families, after their tongues,
in their countries, *and* in their nations. 21 ¶ Unto Shem
also, the father of all the children of [v] Eber, the brother
of Japheth the elder, even to him were *children* born. 22
The children of Shem; [w] Elam, and Asshur, and [x] Arphaxad

u ch. xx. 1, 2; xxvi. 1, 6, 17, 20, 26. 2 Chron. xiv. 13, 14.
v ver. 25; ch. xi. 15, 16. 1 Chron. i. 19.
w ch. xiv. 1, 9. 1 Chron. i. 17, al. fr.
x ch. xi. 10, &c. 1 Chron. i. 18, &c.

Dictionary. But see also note on ch. xx. 1. The four names **Sodom, Gomorrah, Admah,** and **Zeboim,** will be found discussed under ch. xix.; the fifth, **Lasha**, is involved in uncertainty. From the expression **even unto**, it would appear to be beyond the "cities of the plain" first mentioned, and from the meaning of the name, a *fissure* or *break*, we might expect to find it in a ravine. Such conditions would be fulfilled in *Callirhoe*, which was Jerome's conjecture for it. But there are no traces of a town in this neighbourhood. See Mr. Bevan, *Biblical Dictionary*. This verse in the Samaritan Pentateuch stands thus: *The boundary of Canaan was from the river of Egypt to the great river, the river Euphrates.* Kalisch sets this down to a corruption originating in the mistaken idea that the boundaries of the kingdoms of *Israel* were intended. Ver. 20 is a formal conclusion, as ver. 5.

21—31.] *The children of Shem:* placed last, as has been before noticed, to clear away the collateral matter and leave the main subject to be treated. The notice, **the father of all the children of Eber**, manifests the object of the sacred writer, to give the people of the Hebrews, who are included (compare ver. 25 and ch. xi. 16, ff.) among Eber's descendants. But this is doubted by some (see Mr. Brown's art. "Hebrew" in *Biblical Dictionary*), who think that this notice only means that Shem was father of all that dwelt east of the Euphrates (see on ch. xiv. 13). But on this supposition it would be difficult to account for the insertion of the words in this prominent place. The words, **the brother of Japheth the elder**, are taken in three ways: 1. That Shem was *Japhet's elder brother*, i. e. older than Japhet. So Knobel and others. 2. That Shem was *brother of Japhet the elder*, i. e. younger than Japhet. So the LXX. and many commentators. 3. That Shem was brother of Japhet the elder, i. e. younger than Japhet, but older than Ham,—the elder of the two brothers of Japhet. It must, we think, remain uncertain whether Shem or Japhet was the eldest brother. No real difficulty, as Quarry has well shewn (Genesis, &c., p. 192, f.), is occasioned on either hypothesis. Dr. Colenso's assertion that in Abraham's ancestry every person mentioned is the eldest son of his father, is a pure assumption of his own. **22.**] **Elam** "appears to be the province lying S. of Assyria and E. of Persia, which is termed Susis or Susiana by the geographers. It includes a portion of the mountainous country separating the Mesopotamian plain from the high tableland of Iran, together with a fertile and valuable low tract at the foot of the range, between it and the Tigris. The passage of Daniel (viii. 2) which places Shushan (Susa)" in the province of Elam, "may be regarded as decisive of this identification, which is further confirmed by the frequent mention of Elymæans in this district, as well as by the combinations in which Elam is found in Scripture, Gen. xiv. 1; Isa. xxi. 2; Ezek. xxxii. 24." Mr. Rawlinson, *Biblical Dict.* **Asshur**] As we learn from ver. 11, the Assyrians were afterwards conquered by the Hamites. They inhabited the plain E. of the Tigris and N. W. of Susiana. The name imports a plain or level. They afterwards spread N. and N. W. into Syria (see on Amos ix. 7), Cappadocia, and Pontus. Knobel says, "From many names of places, persons, and deities, the Assyrians were Semitic, at all events originally; but some of their elements of language are Aryan, and from Isa. xxviii. 11, xxxiii. 19 (see also xxxvi. 10), their tongue was not understood by the Hebrews." **Arphaxad**] This name is supposed to point to the northern district of Assyria, called *Arrhaphachitis*, adjoining Media, and lying chiefly S. of the Gordiæan Mountains. Some suppose the name to mean *the highland of the Chal-*

and [y] Lud, and Aram. 23 And the children of Aram;
[z] Uz, and Hul, and Gether, and Mash. 24 And Arphaxad
begat Salah; and Salah begat Eber. 25 And unto Eber
were born two sons: the name of one *was* Peleg; for in
his days was the earth divided; and his brother's name
was [a] Joktan. 26 And Joktan begat Almodad, and Sheleph,
and Hazarmaveth, and Jerah, 27 and Hadoram, and Uzal,

y 1 Chron. i. 17. Isa. lxvi. 19. Ezek. xxvii. 10; xxx. 5.
z ch. xxii. 21; xxxvi. 28. Job i. 1, which see. 1 Chron. i. 17.
a 1 Chron. i. 19, 23, only.

dæans. **Lud**] See on ver. 13. Josephus supposed Lud to be the ancestor of the *Lydians*, and there are certain indications which favour the idea; but the existence of a powerful people named *Luden* near Mesopotamia, casts doubt on it, unless by chance the two may be the same, and may have migrated westward. See Mr. Stuart Poole in *Biblical Dict.*

Aram represents the Aramæans, the inhabitants of the country about Lebanon. There were Aramæans also E. of the Euphrates in Mesopotamia. See Mr. Grove's art. in *Biblical Dict.* **23.**] **Uz** was probably between the Idumæans and the Euphrates. On all points respecting it, see on Job i. 1. **Hul**] The strongest evidence as to the site is in favour of the district about the roots of Mt. Lebanon, where the names *Ard-el-Huleh*, a district to the N. of Lake Merom; *Ulatha*, a town noticed by Josephus, between Galilee and Trachonitis; *Golan*, and its modern form *Djaulân*; bear some affinity to the original name *Hul*, or, as it should rather be written, **Chul.** Mr. Bevan, in the *Biblical Dict.* **Gether**] Nothing is known. Absalom was the son of Maacah, daughter of Talmai, king of *Geshur*, which was on the Orontes. But all is conjecture. **Mash**] Josephus connected the name with *Mesene* in Lower Babylonia, far away from the rest of the Aramæan race. But others more probably have traced it in Mt. *Masius* of classical writers, a range forming the N. boundary of Mesopotamia. The name is given as *Meshech* in 1 Chron. i. 17. **24.**] This mention of Arphaxad's sons comes in apparently in order to introduce the geographical notice of Joktan and his posterity, vv. 26—30. The words, **for in his days was the earth** (or **land**) **divided** (*niphlegah*), have given rise to much speculation. It is utterly improbable that they have any reference to the division of the earth between the sons of Noah, seeing that Peleg is in the fifth generation from Noah, and, according to the genealogy in the next chapter, at least 130 or 140 years after the Flood. The most probable interpretation is that the name was owing to a partition of the earth (or, land) between Peleg and his brother Joktan, whose numerous family split off, leaving Peleg in Mesopotamia. See below. **Joktan**] The name signifies the *small*, or younger. He is the reputed ancestor of Arabian tribes occupying the southern part of the peninsula. A province and town of *Kachtan* (which is his Arabic name) still exist. On the Joktanite settlements, see below. Of the thirteen sons of Joktan, **Almodad** is thought to be traceable in *El-mudad*, a famous personage in Arabic history, the reputed father of Ishmael's Arab wife and chief of the Joktanite tribe Jurhum. The name was common among its chiefs, but not among other tribes. **Sheleph**] "The tribe which sprung from him has been satisfactorily identified, both in modern and classical times, as well as the district of the Yemen named after him." Mr. Stanley Poole in *Biblical Dictionary*. The latter appears to have been the district of *Sulaf*, and the former the tribe of *Shelif* or *Shulaf*. **Hazarmaveth**] This name also is satisfactorily identified with the Arabic province *Hadramâut* in Southern Arabia; it is situated East of the modern Yemen; its chief ports are Mirbat, Zafari, and Kisheem. The Greeks and Romans called the people Chatramotitæ or Chatrammitæ. See Mr. Stanley Poole, as above. **Jerah**] The identification is doubtful. A fortress named *Yerakh* has been mentioned; but others have fancied, because **Jerah** signifies *the moon*, that the Jerahites were the Alilaei, a people dwelling near the Red Sea, for Herodotus says of the Arabs that they call the moon *Alilat*. **Hadoram** has not been satisfactorily traced. Kalisch finds them in the *Adramitæ*, but others think this name belongs rather to Hadramâut above.

b 1 Chron. i. 22. Isa. lx. 6. Jer. vi. 20. Ps. lxxii. 10.

and Diklah, 28 and Obal, and Abimael, and [b] Sheba,
29 and Ophir, and Havilah, and Jobab: all these *were*
the sons of Joktan. 30 And their dwelling was from
Mesha, as thou goest unto Sephar a mount of the east.
31 These *are* the sons of Shem, after their families, after
their tongues, in their lands, after their nations. 32 These
are the families of the sons of Noah, after their generations, in their nations: and by these were the nations
divided in the earth after the flood. XI. 1 And the whole

Uzal] The name of Saná, the capital city of Yemen, was anciently *Awzal*. It was called *Auzara* by the classics. **Diklah** signifies a *palm-tree*, and is perhaps traced in a place named *Dakalah* in Arabia, or in several named Nakhleh, another name for a palm-tree. All, however, seems uncertain. **Obal** has not been identified. Bochart thought he had traced him in the Avalitæ, a tribe on the E. African coast opposite to Arabia. **Abimael** is totally uncertain; not even a probable guess has been made. **Sheba**] The kingdom of this name embraced the greater part of Yemen, or Arabia Felix. The people were the Sabæans. It was from this and not from the Cushite Sheba (see on ver. 1) that the Queen of Sheba came to visit Solomon. See Mr. Stanley Poole's art. in the *Biblical Dictionary*. **Ophir**] Very great disputes have arisen about the site of this place; but here, from the accurate specification of the land of the Joktanites which follows, it seems evident that Ophir must be sought in Arabia, not in India, as many have supposed. On the whole matter see Mr. Twisleton's art. in the *Biblical Dictionary*. **Havilah**] See on ver. 11. There is no reason to suppose a different Havilah meant from that one; probably, as in several other cases, the Cushites and Shemites were mixed there. **Jobab** has as yet escaped research. But Mr. Stanley Poole reminds us that Ptolemy has mentioned a tribe the *Jobarite* (or Jobabitæ?) in Southern Arabia. **30.**] **Mesha** seems yet to want satisfactory identification. Mr. Stanley Poole (*Biblical Dictionary*) thinks the nearest approach to it has been the seaport *Musa* or *Muza* mentioned by old geographers, and lying near a mountain now called *Jebel Moosa*, in lat. 13° 40′ N., long. 43° 20′ E. Kalisch thinks it is the Island *Mesene* at the N. W. point of the Persian Gulf. **Sephar** has been better made out. "There appears to be little doubt that the ancient sea-port town called *Dhafári* or *Zafári*, and *Dhafár* or *Zafár*, represents the Biblical site or district." Mr. Stanley Poole, as above, whose article see for collateral matter. "It is situated on the coast, in the province of Hadramaut (see above on ver. 26), and near to the district which adjoins that province on the East, called Esh-Shihr, under a lofty mountain (as here described). There are still ruins attesting its ancient importance (Ibid.). **31.**] The formal close, as at ver. 5, 20: followed, 32, by a general conclusion of a similar kind: completing the Elohistic account of the peopling of the earth by the three sons of Noah: and naturally followed by the taking up again of the generations of Shem, the line of the sacred history, at ch. xi. 10.

XI. **1—9.**] *The confusion of tongues, and dispersion of mankind.* Respecting the general understanding of this narrative, it may be sufficient here to observe that almost all the difficulties supposed inherent in it have been imported into it by making it say more than is contained in it. And we may further observe, that whatever be its meaning it is manifestly to be taken—1. As explanatory of much which has already taken place in ch. x., where, after the account of the dispersion of the descendants of each of the sons of Noah, we have it specified that it was *after their tongues;* and 2. As not asserting anything inconsistent with the substantial unity of tongue among the tribes descended from each son of Noah. In the object that they might not undertake one another's speech, these at least were not included. The insertion, as remarked upon ch. x. 32, is Jehovistic.

1.] The words here are important as furnishing some clue to what has gone before.

earth was of one [c] language, and of one speech. 2 And it
came to pass, as they journeyed eastward, that they found
a plain in the land of Shinar; and they dwelt there.
3 And they said one to another, [d] Go to, let us make brick,
and burn them throughly. And they had brick for stone,
and [e] slime had they for morter. 4 And they said, [d] Go to,
let us build us a city and a tower, whose [f] top *may reach*
unto heaven; and let us make us a name, lest we be scat-
tered abroad upon the face of the whole earth. 5 And the
[g] LORD came down to see the city and the tower, which

c =Job xii. 20. Ps. lxxxi. 5. Prov. xvii. 7. Isa. xix. 18.

d vv. 4, 7. ch. xxxviii. 16. Exod. i. 10 (come on).
e ch. xiv. 10. Exod. ii. 3, only.
f Deut. i. 28. Dan. iv. 22.
g Exod. xix. 20; xxxiv. 5. Num. xi. 25; xii. 5.

There was a time when **the whole earth** was of one language; when "they"—all mankind that then were—journeyed, and came to a certain place, and combined in a certain purpose. No words are needed to shew that this must have been before the dispersion of the descendants of the sons of Noah. What, then, was **the whole earth**? Have we any right to give it one meaning here and another in the history of the Flood? The Hebrew has literally **of one life and one** (plural, as also in the Jehovist portions, ch. xxvii. 44; xxix. 20) **words**. **2.**] The word rendered by the A. V. *from the east* is interpreted by Kalisch *in the east*. The very same expression is translated "*East*," i.e. **eastward**, in ch. xiii. 11, and "**eastward**" in ch. ii. 8. **the land of Shinar**] This word probably means *two rivers*. It seems to have been the Jewish name for Babylonia, as no trace of it is found in the ancient inscriptions. See Prof. Rawlinson's art. in the *Biblical Dict.* The neighbourhood of Babylon is described by Herodotus as a *great plain*. **3. burn them throughly**] The more usual way of hardening the bricks seems to have been sun-drying: but these are to be thoroughly *burnt*, for endurance. Both kinds are found in the ruins of Babylon. **slime**] Herodotus speaks of a tower and a river, both named *Is*, the latter flowing into the Euphrates, and bringing down bitumen in abundance. And other writers testify to the quantity of asphalt found in Mesopotamia. Modern travellers describe the tower and river, and the use of and traffic in the bitumen. Layard observes, that the cement in the ruins is so tenacious that it is almost impossible to detach an entire brick from the mass. See Kalisch.

4.] *Their* purpose seems to have been to gain a centre of permanent habitation, and also a distinguishing memorial or mark by which their repute might be handed down. There doubtless is something of rebellion against *God's* purposes implied in their determination. He would have them spread over the whole earth, while they resolved to be gathered in one spot. The idea of a tower whose top might reach heaven is related here as entertained by them bonâ fide: in other places the expression is used hyperbolically: see reff.

There is no trace in Scripture of the popular idea that their design was to provide an effectual escape from a future deluge. With this description the accounts of Babylon given by classical writers entirely agree. The gigantic walls were of burnt brick, cemented with asphalt, as were also the magnificent temple of Belus, and the hanging gardens. The circumference of the city was according to some 480 furlongs, or 60,000 paces; according to others, 385 or 360 furlongs. The most important edifice was the quadrangular temple of Belus, of which each side was two furlongs in length; out of it rose an enormous massive tower of eight stories, according to Herodotus, of one furlong in diameter, and according to Strabo a furlong (600 feet) high. The ruins of this vast tower are generally supposed to be the enormous mound called the Birs Nimroud. The building of Babylon is generally ascribed by the ancients to Semiramis; but this must mean only its fortifying and strengthening, for the city was confessedly older. It is described ch. x. 10 as built by Nimrod; but in that narrative it has no such importance as here, and is classed with other cities as having been built at the same time. **5.**] The anthropo-

the children of men builded. 6 And the LORD said, Be-
hold, the people *is* one, and they have all one language;
and this they begin to do: and now nothing will be re-
strained from them, which they have imagined to do.
h ch. ii. 4; v. 1; x. 1. 7 h Go to, let us go down, and there confound their lan-
guage, that they may not understand one another's speech.
8 So the LORD scattered them abroad from thence upon the
face of all the earth: and they left off to build the city.
9 Therefore is the name of it called Babel; because the
LORD did there confound the language of all the earth:
and from thence did the LORD scatter them abroad upon
the face of all the earth. 10 ¶ These *are* the generations
of Shem: Shem *was* an hundred years old, and begat Ar-
phaxad two years after the flood: 11 And Shem lived after

morphism of the narrative is here apparent to all. Even Bp. Wordsworth says, "We are not to suppose locomotion in Him who is Omnipresent: but by such sentences as these, in which the Holy Spirit condescends to man's weakness, He teaches us that God does not punish without examination." No doubt: but where are we to draw the line for such a method of interpretation to stop? How about the next verse, where there is put into the mouth of Omnipotence language of caution, requiring a human device to curb men's becoming too strong for God? May we, must we, not say here also, we are not to suppose precaution in Him who is Omnipotent: but by such sentences as these, in which the Holy Spirit condescends to man's weakness, He teaches us that God must be understood by men as having done that which men under the circumstances would do? And when we have taken this further step, can we avoid taking more? On these words we may observe, that as concerns the narrative itself we have no right at all to spiritualize *them alone*. If the rest of the narrative is to be taken in simplicity and *au pied de la lettre*, so also must they. See further on ch. iii. 8. The **children of men** is, as usual, the *sons of Adam*. **6—8.**] See above, and on God's *taking counsel*.

9.] This statement, of the reason of calling the city Babel, has given rise to some discussion, seeing that the derivation of Babel from the name of Bel or Belus is hardly to be doubted. But perhaps those are on mistaken ground who find difficulties in such matters. It is not unfrequently the custom of Scripture to trace allusion in names which certainly had no part in their original bestowal. In the phrase, therefore, "is the name of it called Babel," may be meant no more than that to Hebrew ears this signification is carried by the name.

10—26.] *The descendants of Shem.* Here again we have a divergence of the same kind as in ch. v., between the Hebrew text, the Samaritan Pentateuch, and the LXX. I subjoin, as I have done there, a table of the differences in the 10 generations (see next page).

This genealogy, it is agreed by Hebraists, belongs to the original or Elohistic document. This is shewn by the title: see reff. Also by other traces, e. g. "*the flood*," &c.

10.] The first four of the descendants of Shem are mentioned ch. x. 22 ff. There is some little consideration necessary in order to fit in the chronological notices of ch. v. 32 and vii. 11. In the former it is said that Noah was 500 years old, and begat Shem, Ham, and Japheth. But clearly this is merely a notice in round numbers, as he could not beget them all three in one year. In vii. 11, the flood begun in the 600th year of Noah's life, the second month. If Shem were the second son, he might be 99 years old or thereabouts. The flood lasted one year and ten days, so that probably by the words **after the flood** here we must understand after the beginning of the

he begat Arphaxad five hundred years, and begat sons and
daughters. 12 And Arphaxad lived five and thirty years,
and begat Salah: 13 And Arphaxad lived after he begat
Salah four hundred and three years, and begat sons and
daughters. 14 And Salah lived thirty years, and begat
Eber: 15 And Salah lived after he begat Eber four hun-
dred and three years, and begat sons and daughters.
16 And Eber lived four and thirty years, and begat Peleg:
17 And Eber lived after he begat Peleg four hundred and
thirty years, and begat sons and daughters. 18 And Peleg
lived thirty years, and begat Reu: 19 And Peleg lived

	Present Hebrew text.			Samaritan Pentateuch.			LXX.		
Names.	Age at birth of son.	Rest of life.	Whole life.	Age at birth of son.	Rest of life.	Whole life.	Age at birth of son.	Rest of life.	Whole life.
Shem . .	100	500	600	100	500	600	100	500	600
Arphaxad . .	35	403	438	135	303	438	135	400	535
								(or 430	565)
								(or 330	465)
Cainan . .	not mentioned			not mentioned			130	330	460
								(or 430	560)
Salah . .	30	403	433	130	303	433	130	330	460
								(or 450	580)
Eber . . .	34	403	434	134	270	404	134	270	404
								(or 370	504)
Peleg . .	30	209	239	130	109	239	130	209	339
Reu . . .	32	207	239	132	107	239	132	207	339
Serug . .	30	200	230	130	100	230	130	200	330
Nahor . .	29	119	148	79	69	148	179	125	304
							(or 79	129	208)
Terah . .	70		205	70	75	145	70	135	205
Call of Abram .	75			75			75		
Total from birth of Shem to Call of Abram .	465			1115			1345, or, according to the Alexandrine reading, 1245		

On these discrepancies, see note on ch. v. 1.

flood. **12. Arphaxad**] See on ch. x. 22. This name, which as there has received a territorial identification, is clearly here that of an individual. Some of the *sons* are mentioned ch. x. 22. It will be observed by the Table that between Arphaxad and Salah the LXX. introduce another name, *Cainan*, and are herein followed by St. Luke in the genealogy of our Lord, iii. 35. Respecting the account to be given of this, see note there in my New Testament for English Readers. **12. Salah**] Signifies *extension*. Knobel adduces a place of this name in N.E. Mesopotamia. **14. Eber**] See on ch. x. 31. This name is distinct (see Mr. Brown, *Biblical Dict.* "Heber") from *Heber*, ch. xlvi. 17 reff., except in Luke iii. 35, where Heber represents this name. **16. Peleg**] See on ch. x. 25. **18. Reu**] This patriarchal name is supposed to be traceable in Roha, the Arabic appellation of Edessa in N. W. Mesopotamia.

after he begat Reu two hundred and nine years, and begat
sons and daughters. 20 And Reu lived two and thirty
years, and begat Serug: 21 And Reu lived after he begat
Serug two hundred and seven years, and begat sons and
daughters. 22 And Serug lived thirty years, and begat
Nahor: 23 And Serug lived after he begat Nahor two
hundred years, and begat sons and daughters. 24 And
Nahor lived nine and twenty years, and begat Terah:
25 And Nahor lived after he begat Terah an hundred and
nineteen years, and begat sons and daughters. 26 And
Terah lived seventy years, and begat Abram, Nahor, and
Haran. 27 ¶ Now these *are* the generations of Terah:
Terah begat Abram, Nahor, and Haran; and Haran begat
i Num. iii. 4. Deut. xxi. 16. Lot. 28 And Haran died [i] before his father Terah in the
land of his nativity, in Ur of the Chaldees. 29 And Abram
and Nahor took them wives: the name of Abram's wife
was Sarai; and the name of Nahor's wife, Milcah, the
daughter of Haran, the father of Milcah, and the father of
Iscah. 30 But Sarai was barren; she *had* no child. 31 And

The LXX. (see also Luke iii. 35) give this name by *Ragau*, which is not far from *Rages*, said also to have been a name of Edessa. But see on ver. 28. **20. Serug**] There is a district and town mentioned by the Arabian geographers *Sarug*, a day's journey north of Haran. On the legendary statements connected with his having taught men hero-worship, see Bishop Lord A. Hervey's art. in the *Biblical Dict.*

22. Nahor] Not to be confounded with his grandson of the same name, Abram's brother, ver. 27. **27.**] The narrative now passes to the descendants of Terah, Abram's father. They are particularly specified, because they are to be further dealt with in the subsequent history: Rebekah, Leah, and Rachel being of Nahor's family, and Lot and Milcah of that of Harans. **28. before**] Is literally "in the presence of," and therefore of course before in time. The same expression is used in reff. **Ur of the Chaldees**] Prof. Rawlinson in *Biblical Dict.* discusses the various opinions about this place, and thinks the evidence in favour of *Mugheir*, which bore the ancient name of *Ur* or *Hur*, to preponderate. It is in the low country near the Persian Gulf; is now more than 100 miles inland, but was once on the sea: there is a mound with ruins, some of the most ancient yet discovered. The bricks bear the name of a certain *Urukh*, the earliest of the Chaldæan monumental kings, —and Ur was his capital. "Ur retained its metropolitan character for 200 years, and even after it became second to Babylon, was a great and sacred city. It remained a place of burial for many ages, and the ruins are mainly now those of tombs." See the art. above mentioned. Some hold that the name refers to the Roæi or Arrhoæi; if so, what has already been said on Ragau will require modifying. **29.**] Sarai was, according to ch. xx. 12, the daughter of Terah by another wife than Abraham's mother, and was ten years younger than her husband (ch. xvii. 17). **Iscah** is nowhere else mentioned. Josephus and the Targums hold her to have been identical with Sarai, but that cannot have been by what has been noticed above. Marriage with near relatives was the practice of Terah's family. See ch. xxiv. 3, 4; xxviii. 1, 2. **30.**] This remark is inserted as important to the following history.

31.] Terah was an idolater (Josh. xxiv. 2), so that this his journey can hardly be supposed to have been an obedience on *his*

Terah took Abram his son, and Lot the son of Haran his
son's son, and Sarai his daughter in law, his son Abram's
wife; and they went forth with them from Ur of the
Chaldees, to go into the land of Canaan; and they came
unto Haran, and dwelt there. 32 And the days of Terah
were two hundred and five years: and Terah died in Ha-
ran. XII. 1 And JEHOVAH said unto Abram, Get thee
out of thy country, and from the [j] place of thy birth, and

[j] = ch. xi. 28; xxiv. 4, 7; xxxi. 3, 13; xxxii. 10. Num. x. 30. Ruth ii. 11. Jer. xxii. 10; xlvi. 16. Ezek. xxiii. 15.

part to that Divine intimation which we learn, from the subsequent Jehovist account, was made to his son. It may have been that the two designs coincided, as Kalisch supposes, or it may have been that Abram persuaded his aged father to accompany him. It appears that Nahor also went to Haran. Compare ch. xxiv. 10; xxvii. 43; xxix. 4, 5. That the call of Abram took place in Ur and not in Haran, as Keil and others maintain, is clear from ch. xv. 7 (see also Neh. ix. 7; Acts vii. 2), which expression it is impossible to explain away, as Keil and Delitzsch endeavour to do. **Haran** (in Greek Charran, see Acts vii. 2) was in Mesopotamia (ch. xxiv. 10), or more strictly in Padan-aram (ch. xxv. 20), in the beautiful country between Mount Masius and the Euphrates. The name has never changed, the town being still called Harrân; and the Chaldæan language and worship prevailed there to a late time. It was famous for the defeat of the Roman army under Crassus by the Parthians. See Prof. Rawlinson's art. in *Biblical Dict.*

32.] Why they stopped in Haran does not appear. It is possible that the death of Terah there may suggest the reason. Or the halt may have been made owing to local political circumstances. From ch. xii. 5 it appears that Abram spent a considerable time there before his onward journey.

they went together] These words, rendered *they went forth with them* in the A. V., have occasioned some dispute as to their precise meaning. The text gives that preferred by Knobel and Kalisch—*they went with each other*, i. e. **together.** Some suppose *with them* to mean with the unnamed members of Terah's family, viz. Nahor and his: but it is well replied that had they been intended they would have been specified. Keil preferred to understand "they (Lot and Sarai) went forth with them" (Terah and Abram), and so doubtless the A. V. intended.

XII. **1**—XIII. **18.**] ABRAM'S CALL AND MIGRATION. From this time the name Jehovah prevails, and it becomes evident that the tracing down of the covenant of God with the chosen people is that which forms the thread of the narrative. There are apparent from time to time fragments of another narrative, worked in by the sacred writer; but much caprice and doubtful assertion has been indulged in by able writers, such as Ewald and Knobel, in assigning the various portions of the narrative to different writers. And on the other hand, orthodox commentators, such as Keil, strangely deny, in the face of all evidence, the incorporation by the Jehovist of elder documents. Delitzsch, equally orthodox, acknowledges, and carefully traces out, the different elements of the narrative. This we shall also endeavour to do as we proceed.

XII. **1.**] This command was given to Abram not in Haran, but in Ur: see above, and add to what was there said, that the terms of the command itself involve this. For we read (ch. xi. 31) that the whole family reached Haran *on their way to Canaan.* But this command must apply by the words, "a land that I will shew thee," to a time when the direction of the journey was unknown. The force of it was still abiding and working upon Abram, and when the cause of his detention in Haran was over, he went forth thence, leaving his father there. On the statement of Stephen, Acts vii. 4, that this was so, and the subterfuges of commentators to justify it, see my note there in New Testament for English Readers. The figures are as follows: Terah lived 70 years, and begat Abram, Nahor, and Haran (ch. xi. 26); lived 205 years, and died in Haran (xi. 32): Abram was 75 when he left Haran (ver. 4). So that Abram having

from thy father's house, unto a land that I will shew thee:
2 and I will make of thee a great nation, and I will bless
thee, and make thy name great; and thou shalt be a bless-
ing: 3 and I will bless them that bless thee, and curse him
that curseth thee: and in thee shall all families of the
earth be blessed. 4 So Abram departed, as JEHOVAH had
spoken unto him; and Lot went with him: and Abram
was seventy and five years old when he departed out of
Haran. 5 And Abram took Sarai his wife, and Lot his
brother's son, and all their substance that they had ga-
k Ezek. xxvii. 13 (Rev. xviii. 13; Macc. x. 33). thered, and the [k] souls that they had gotten in Haran;
and they went forth to go into the land of Canaan; and
into the land of Canaan they came. 6 ¶ And Abram
l ch. xviii. 24; xix. 12; xxix. 22. passed through the land unto the [l] place of Shechem, unto

been born about Terah's 70th year, about 70 + 75 = about 145, Terah's age when Abram left Haran. Bp. Wordsworth and others attempt to get over the difficulty by supposing Abram to have been the youngest of the three sons of Terah, and to have been begotten when his father was 130. And yet this very son regards it as impossible that he himself should beget a son at 99. (See ch. xvii. 1, 17.) Not to say further, that by this argument all the deductions drawn in Scripture from the miraculous birth of Isaac would entirely disappear (see Rom. iv. 17—21; Heb. xi. 11, 12). For us plain people, who believe our Bibles, it is enough to follow their data, and to assume that Terah lived 60 years after Abram's departure from Haran. **the place of thy birth**] Such is the general meaning of this word: see reff. In some places it seems to signify *kindred* as Gen. xliii. 7; Esther viii. 6.

2, 3.] The promise to Abram ranges itself in six particulars, forming three pairs of parallels. I. (1) Making into a great nation, (2) personal blessing; II. (3) greatness of name, (4) being a source of blessing; III. (5) blessing of his well-wishers and discomfiture of his enemies, (6) being a general blessing to all men. The unfolding of the fulfilment of this promise, afterwards made special in its last member to the seed of Abraham (ch. xxii. 18, xxvi. 4), is the great subject of all Scripture. On the prophetic meaning of the concluding words, see below and on ch. xxii. 18. The words **in thee shall all families of the earth be blessed** have given occasion, as was to be expected, for much contention on the part of the rationalist interpreters. Knobel, who is the best example of them, would understand them, that all families of the earth should *bless with* (or, *in*) *thee*, i.e. wish themselves blessed in, by the example of, Abraham; wish for themselves blessedness like his. This rendering he defends by ch. xlviii. 20, "*In thee shall Israel bless*, saying, God make thee as Ephraim and as Manasseh." The objection to this is that the verb is in the passive voice, not *bless*, but *be blessed*. And although in the repetition of the promise, ch. xxii. 18, xxvi. 4, the passive voice is not used, but the reflexive, that does not by any means exclude from those places the sense which this requires, much less does it require force to be put on the plain words here by doing away with the passive sense. On those places, see notes there. On such a matter we may further remark, that we may well leave the New Testament writers, to whom Hebrew was familiar, to decide for us which of the senses should prevail. And this has been plainly and emphatically done. See Acts iii. 25; Gal. iii. 8, 14. Notice that literally the expression is, "all the families of the **ground**," so that the blessing is an echo of the primal curse, ch. iii. 17.

5. the souls that they had gotten] Were slaves: see reff. Abram's stay in Haran must, from this verse, have been considerable. **6. the place of Sichem**] Gesenius interprets this expression, which appears to be found only here, as the *neighbourhood of*

the [m] oak of Moreh. And the Canaanite *was* then in the
land. 7 And JEHOVAH appeared unto Abram, and said,
Unto thy seed will I give this land: and there builded he
an altar unto JEHOVAH, who appeared unto him. 8 And

m ch. xiii. 18; xiv. 13; xviii. 1. Deut. xi. 30. Judg. iv. 11; ix. 6, 37. 1 Sam. x. 3.

Sichem; Keil, as the *site* where afterwards stood Sichem; most others, as if "the place of" were redundant, *the place, Sichem*, and this seems favoured by the occurrence of the word in this sense in reff. See also ch. xxxiii. 18. SHECHEM was one of the oldest towns in Palestine, in a narrow valley between the mounts Gerizim and Ebal, about seven miles south of Samaria. It was in early times inhabited by the Hivites (ch. xxxiv. 2): there Jacob bought a parcel of a field and built an altar (xxxiii. 19). In the division of the land, Shechem was in the lot of Ephraim, but was assigned to the Levites, and became a city of refuge (Josh. xxi. 20, 21). The mountains of Ebal and Gerizim were of great interest as being the appointed spots for the declarations of blessings and curses on the observers and breakers of the law (Deut. xxvii. 11; Josh. viii. 33—35). Here Joshua assembled the people before his death and pledged them to serve the Lord (Josh. xxiv. 1, ff.). Here Jotham delivered his parable against the rule of Abimelech (Judg. ix. 7, ff. 22, ff.: see Stanley, Sinai and Palestine, p. 236). The city was destroyed by Abimelech (cf. ver. 45). But we find all Israel meeting at Shechem (1 Kings xii. 1, ff.) to make Rehoboam king. After the captivity the place was occupied by Samaritans. The "men from Shechem," Jer. xli. 5, who were coming up to the house of the Lord and were slain all but ten by Ishmael, were probably Samaritans of the mixed race, the result of the Babylonians sent by Shalmaneser (2 Kings xvii. 24) dwelling among the people of the land. On the New Testament interest attached to the place see notes on John iv. 2, and on its modern history as Nablous, the art. by Prof. Hackett in *Smith's Biblical Dict.* **the oak]** Thus the best Hebrew authorities seem agreed in rendering the word, and not *plain*. The same is the case in all the places mentioned in reff. The only question is whether the tree should not rather be named the *terebinth* than the *oak*. The matter seems very doubtful, and cannot be discussed in a note. See Mr. Houghton's art. "Oak" in the *Biblical Dict.*, and Kalisch's long and interesting note on sacred trees.

There is also a difference respecting **Moreh.** Knobel thinks it is not a proper name, and renders, "*the oak of the teacher*," comparing "*the oak of the witches*," Judg. ix. 37, which he regards as identical with this. But the view that Moreh is a proper name has generally prevailed. Mr. Grove, in the *Biblical Dict.*, thinks that the name may not be unconnected with "the land of Moriah," in ch. xxii. 2. He also remarks, that perhaps a trace of this ancient name is discernible in the word *Morthia*, which appears on some ancient coins as a title of Neapolis. There seems to be no connexion with the hill of Moreh in Judg. vii. 1: see there. **the Canaanite was then in the land]** See ch. xiii. 7; xxxiv. 30. This notice was most probably added to shew that the land was not empty at that time, but that the subsequent promise implied a displacement of inhabitants then in possession. This, of course, enhanced Abram's faith, and made his obedience more admirable. Nothing can be more natural than such a notice: and there is not the slightest reason for supposing it to be an interpolation of later date than the narrative itself. The promise of ver. 7 was an expansion of that in ver. 1 into concrete particulars. It was repeated to Abraham, ch. xiii. 15, 17; xv. 18; xvii. 8; to Isaac, xxvi. 3; to Jacob, xxviii. 13; xxxv. 12.

7. Abraham **builded an altar to Jehovah** in Shechem, as did Jacob afterwards, ch. xxxiii. 20. There was afterwards a sanctuary of Jehovah in Shechem (see Josh. xxiv. 1, 26), the beginning of which was doubtless this first act of the Patriarch's worship. Bethel [Jerusalem], Hebron, and Beersheba were similarly places known as hallowed to the worship of Jehovah. See ver. 8; ch. xiii. 18; xiv. 18 [ch. xxii. 1, ff., but see on Moreh above]; xxi. 33; xxvi. 25. **who appeared unto him]** See ch. xxxv. 1. **8, 9.]** *His journey southwards.* No motive is assigned for the journey further south. Possibly the famine had already begun which drove him (ver. 10)

he removed from thence unto a mountain on the east of
Beth-el, and pitched his tent, *having* Beth-el on the west,
and Hai on the east: and there he builded an altar unto
JEHOVAH, and called upon the name of JEHOVAH. 9 And
Abram journeyed, going on still toward the south.
10 ¶ And there was a famine in the land: and Abram
went down into Egypt to sojourn there; for the famine
was grievous in the land. 11 And it came to pass, when
he was come near to enter into Egypt, that he said unto
Sarai his wife, Behold now, I know that thou *art* a fair
woman to look upon: 12 therefore it shall come to pass,
when the Egyptians shall see thee, that they shall say,
This *is* his wife: and they will kill me, but they will save
thee alive. 13 Say, I pray thee, thou *art* my sister: that
it may be well with me for thy sake; and my soul shall

into Egypt. **Beth-el,** so named here by anticipation, for it was at this time called Luz, and did not become Beth-el till after Jacob's vision (see ch. xxviii. 19), was in the direct thoroughfare of Palestine (see Judges xxi. 19). On the situation of Abram's tent, see notes, ch. xiii. 10. **on the west**] literally, *from the sea*, which is the universal westward boundary of Palestine. Would Moses, who was born and bred in Egypt, have used this expression? The exact site of **Hai** (or Ai) is unknown. The various conjectures will be given on Joshua vii. 2. The same notice that it is on the *east side of Beth-el* is there given. **9. the south**] literally, the dry country, the desert.

10—20.] *Abram's sojourn in Egypt. The deliverance of Sarai.* The account of the pressure of famine on the nomad patriarch and the seeking of plenty in the more permanently settled Egypt is in singular accord with two subsequent parts of the history—(1.) When Isaac (ch. xxvi. 1), on the occurrence of another famine, is forbidden to go down to Egypt; (2.) When Joseph's brethren during time of famine go to buy corn in Egypt. Keil remarks that the custom of flying to Egypt for food is even now exemplified by the Bedouin tribes when dearth arises. The history respecting Sarai reappears in another form in ch. xx. 1, ff., at the court of Abimelech, king of Gerar: and, in substance, again in ch. xxvi. 1, ff., also at the court of an Abimelech, king of Gerar, but happening to Isaac and Rebekah. Abraham himself explains in ch. xx. 13 that the giving out of Sarah as his sister had been a matter settled between them at the beginning of his wanderings. It is vain, as some of the orthodox commentators (e. g. Keil) have done, to try to soften down Abram's untruthfulness. Bp. Wordsworth well remarks, Abram came forth from a land of idolaters. He was surrounded by idolaters in Canaan, and by idolaters in Egypt, and, we may add, was himself born of idolatrous parents. And wherever idolatry abounds falsehood abounds. Sarai was at this time upwards of 65 years old, for (ch. xvii. 17) she was ten years younger than Abram, who was 75 when he left Haran (ver. 4). It seems the worthiest and most reverent way of regarding considerations of this kind, to remember, with Kalisch, that we are in a region of primæval history not to be measured out by our present rules of verisimilitude, without using that recollection, as he does, to impugn the credibility of the narrative as one of facts. If, as Knobel has observed, the writer "perhaps conceived a certain divine grace to have dwelt about the progenitress of the people of God," why might not his conception have just as well represented the fact as not? What right have we to assume that all heroic ideas about primæval men and ages are ideas only? That such ideas are found in works of mere human fiction is surely no proof that they never corresponded to fact at all. We may hesitate to believe that the

live because of thee. 14 ¶ And it came to pass, that,
when Abram was come into Egypt, the Egyptians beheld
the woman that she *was* very fair. 15 The princes also of
Pharaoh saw her, and commended her before Pharaoh:
and the woman was taken into Pharaoh's house. 16 And
he entreated Abram well for her sake: and he had sheep,
and oxen, and he asses, and menservants, and maidserv-
ants, and she asses, and camels. 17 And JEHOVAH plagued
Pharaoh and his house with great plagues because of Sarai
Abram's wife. 18 And Pharaoh called Abram, and said,
What *is* this *that* thou hast done unto me? why didst thou
not tell me she *was* thy wife? 19 Why saidst thou, She *is* my
sister? so I might have taken her to me to wife: now there-
fore behold thy wife, take *her*, and go thy way. 20 And Pha-
raoh commanded *his* men concerning him: and they sent
him away, and his wife, and all that he had. XIII. 1 And
Abram went up out of Egypt, he, and his wife, and all

old men of Troy declared Helen's beauty, at 100, worth the world's battle, but this scepticism need not affect our reception of the Scripture primæval history. We may observe, and ought not to conceal, the entirely selfish nature of the arrangement. It is not made to save Sarai but to save Abram by the more easily sacrificing her. If she were known as his wife, she could be had only by destroying him; if as his sister, the end might be accomplished without affecting his safety, nay, with probable good results for his worldly prosperity. The slight semblance of truth by which the falsehood was upheld (see ch. xx. 12) only testified that it was known to be a falsehood in the conscience. "Pharaoh is the common title of the native kings of Egypt in the Bible, corresponding to P-RA or PH-RA of the hieroglyphics." Mr. Stuart Poole, *Biblical Dict.*, who further remarks on this Pharaoh, that while there are no clear indications in the Scripture narrative for the identification of this Pharaoh, there are strong chronological presumptions that he was one of the Shepherd kings, probably Salatis, the head of their first and most powerful line. These are confirmed by the notice which follows, ver. 16, that he gave Abraham *camels*, for that animal was hateful to the subsequent Egyptians on account of its great value to their enemies, the Shepherds, and nowhere appears on any of their monuments. The most probable date of Abram's visit is about 2080, which would accord with the time of Salatis. **16.**] The presents are much the same as the items of the patriarchal wealth given elsewhere, e. g. ch. xxiv. 35; xxxii. 15; Job i. 3; xlii. 12. It is to be observed that in these enumerations we nowhere find horses mentioned, though they were the pride of Egypt. This result fully bears out what we said above of the selfish nature of Abram's compact. **17.**] We may perhaps venture to guess at the nature of these plagues by the fuller account in ch. xx. 18. According to Josephus, the cause of them was revealed to Pharaoh by the priests. The words **so might I**, &c., might also be rendered, *and I took her to me to wife.* This Pharaoh did, although, as we may fairly supply from the subsequent account (compare ver. 17 with ch. xx. 6), that he was providentially withheld from consummating his marriage with her.

20.] The concluding words seem to imply in the Hebrew that Pharaoh's men escorted him and his out of the land.

XIII. **1—13.**] *The return of Abram to Canaan: his severance from Lot.* He returned to the "dry country," the desert

that he had, and Lot with him, to the south. 2 And Abram
was very rich in cattle, in silver, and in gold. 3 And he
went on his journeys from the south even to Beth-el, unto
the place where his tent had been at the beginning, be-
tween Beth-el and Hai; 4 unto the place of the altar, which
he had made there at the first: and there Abram called on
the name of JEHOVAH. 5 ¶ And Lot also, which went with
Abram, had flocks, and herds, and tents. 6 And the land
was not able to bear them, that they might dwell together:
for their substance was great, so that they could not dwell
together. 7 And there was a strife between the herdmen
of Abram's cattle and the herdmen of Lot's cattle: and
the Canaanite and the [n] Perizzite dwelled then in the land.
8 And Abram said unto Lot, Let there be no strife, I pray
thee, between me and thee, and between my herdmen and
thy herdmen; for we *be* brethren. 9 Is not [o] the whole land
before thee? separate thyself, I pray thee, from me: if
thou wilt take [p] the left hand, then I will go to the [p] right;
or if *thou depart* to the right hand, then I will go to the left.
10 And Lot lifted up his eyes, and beheld all the region

n ch. xxxiv. 30. Josh. xvii. 15—18. Judg. i. 4, 5. 1 Kings ix. 20. 2 Chron. viii. 7, al.

o ch. xx. 15; xxxiv. 10; xlvii. 6.

p ch. xxiv. 49. Num. xx. 17; xxii. 26.

south of Palestine (see ch. xii. 9). **2.**] The word rendered **rich** is the same as that rendered "*grievous*" in ch. xii. 10: heavy in material, to move and to feed.

3. his journeys] After the manner of a nomad, not in one journey, but in many marches—*by stations*. On the place spoken of, see ch. xii. 8, and note below on ver. 10. Kalisch remarks, "It is evident from the tenor of the text that Abram's premeditated aim was the service which he intended to solemnize; and the words '*he invoked the name of the Lord*' imply a more profound devotion than an ordinary prayer: they are hence used only on certain predominant occasions, and tend here to prove that Abram returned from the land of multifarious idolatry, in which his progeny lost and forgot the true faith, as a pure and believing servant of the Creator."

5.] Lot had become prosperous in the prosperity of Abram. **7.**] The land (i. e. about those parts) was not empty: the Canaanite (ch. xii. 6) dwelt there, and also the Perizzite. This latter is here first mentioned—not in the catalogue in ch. x.; so that the origin of the people indicated is left in obscurity. On the various places in reff. the scattered notices of them will be commented on. From this and other places they seem to have been inhabitants of the southern part of Palestine.

9.] On the modes of expression, see reff. **10.**] "Immediately east of the low grey hills on which the Canaanitish Luz and the Jewish Beth-el afterwards stood, rises,—as the highest of a succession of eminences, each now marked by some vestige of ancient edifices,—a conspicuous hill; its topmost summit resting, as it were, on the rocky slopes below, and distinguished from them by the olive-grove which clusters over its broad surface above. From this height, thus offering a natural base for the patriarchal altar, and a fitting shade for the patriarchal tent, Abraham and Lot must be considered as taking the wide survey of the country 'on the right hand and on the left,' such as can be enjoyed from no other point in the neighbourhood. To the east there rises in the foreground the jagged range of the hills above Jericho; in the distance the dark wall of Moab; between them lies the wide valley of the Jordan, its

round about Jordan, that it *was* well watered every where,
before JEHOVAH destroyed Sodom and Gomorrah, *even* as
the [q] garden of JEHOVAH, like the land of Egypt, as thou
comest unto Zoar. 11 Then Lot chose him all the region
round about Jordan; and Lot journeyed east: and they
separated themselves the one from the other. 12 Abram
dwelled in the land of Canaan, and Lot dwelled in the
cities of the plain, and pitched *his* tents as far as Sodom.
13 But the men of Sodom *were* wicked and sinners before JE-
HOVAH exceedingly. 14 ¶ And JEHOVAH said unto Abram,
after that Lot was separated from him, Lift up now thine
eyes, and look from the place where thou art northward,
and southward, and eastward, and westward: 15 for all the
land which thou seest, to thee will I give it, and to thy
seed for ever. 16 And I will make thy seed as the dust of
the earth: so that if a man can number the dust of the
earth, *then* shall thy seed also be numbered. 17 Arise,
walk through the land in the length of it and in the breadth
of it; for I will give it unto thee. 18 And Abram pitched
his tents, and came and dwelt in the oak-grove of [r] Mamre,

q Isa. li. 3, only. See Ezek. xxviii. 13; xxxi. 8, 9.

r ch. xiv. 13, 24; xviii. 1; xxiii. 17, 19; xxv. 9; xlix. 30; l. 13, only.

course marked by the tract of forest in which its rushing stream is enveloped: and down to this valley a long and deep ravine, now, as always, the main line of communication by which it is approached from the central hills of Palestine—a ravine rich with vine, olive, and fig, winding its way through ancient reservoirs and sepulchres, remains of a civilization now extinct, but in the times of the patriarchs not yet begun. In the south and west the view commanded the bleak hills of Judæa, varied by the heights crowned with what were afterwards the cities of Benjamin, and overhanging what in a later day was to be Jerusalem, and in the far distance the southern range, on whose slope is Hebron. Northward are the hills which divide Judæa from the rich plains of Samaria." Stanley, Sinai and Palestine, p. 218. **the region round about Jordan**] Literally, the circle of Jordan — the environs of Jordan. The LXX. expression (perichorōs) is that occurring in Matt. iii. 5, and rendered there as in our text. Kalisch compares the French *arrondissement*, and the German *Kreis* or *Bezirk*. "He saw not indeed the tropical fertility and copious streams along its course. But he knew of its fame, as of the garden of Eden, as of the valley of the Nile; no crust of salt, no volcanic convulsions had as yet blasted its verdure, or touched the secure civilization of the early Phœnician settlements which had struck root within its deep abyss." Stanley, as before. **well-watered**] A number of streams descend from the mountains of Moab and fertilize it. The garden of Jehovah (reff.) is of course Eden. On Zoar, see note, ch. xix. 22. **12.**] Lot **pitched his tent as far as Sodom**, advanced in his nomadic journeys to Sodom: there we find him, ch. xiv. 12 and xix. 1. The word **plain** here is the same as before, *the region round about,—the district*, as Kalisch. It came to be used without the adjunct "*of the Jordan.*" **14, ff.**] *Renewal of the promise to Abram.* "That dreary view, unfolded then in its primæval desolation before the eyes of the now solitary patriarch, would be indeed peopled with a mighty nation through many generations, with mighty recollections, like the dust of the earth in number, for ever." Stanley, as above. **18. the oak grove**] See on ch. x. 6. **Mamre**, as we learn from ch. xiv. 13, 24, was a person, brother of Eshcol

which *is* in Hebron, and built there an altar unto JEHOVAH.
XIV. 1 And it came to pass in the days of Amraphel king
s Dan. ii. 14. of Shinar, s Arioch king of Ellasar, Chedorlaomer king of

and Aner, and all three brothers were confederates of Abraham (see also ch. xviii. 1). But in the other reff. the name appears simply as that of a place. See on ch. xxiii. 20. **Hebron]** This is the first mention of this famous city. It is situated among the mountains, 20 Roman miles S. of Jerusalem, and the same distance N. of Beersheba. It is one of the most ancient cities in the world. See Num. xiii. 22, where it is said to have been built seven years before Zoan, in Egypt (see there). Its former name was Kirjath-Arba, the city of Arba, the father of Anak, and progenitor of the Anakim (see Josh. xv. 13, 14; xxi. 11). At Hebron Sarah died, on which occasion Abraham bought of Ephron the Hittite the field and cave of Machpelah, for a burial-place. The cave is still there, enclosed within the walls of a mosque. On the entry of the Israelites Hebron was taken by Joshua (Josh. x. 36), and given by him to Caleb (Josh. xiv. 13, f.; xv. 13, 14). It was assigned to the Levites, and made a city of refuge (Josh. xxi. 11—13). Here David established his seat of government, and reigned seven and a half years over Judah (2 Sam. v. 5). For other and later particulars, see Mr. Porter's article, *Biblical Dict.* He says, "About a mile from the town, up the valley, is one of the largest oak trees in Palestine. It stands quite alone in the midst of the vineyards. It is 23 ft. in girth, and its branches cover a space 90 ft. in diameter. This, say some, is the very tree beneath which Abraham pitched his tent; but however this may be, it still bears the name of the patriarch."

XIV. *Invasion of Palestine by four Eastern kings* (1—7). *Their triumph, and capture of Lot* (8—12). *Rescue of Lot by Abram* (13—16). *His meeting with the king of Sodom and with Melchizedek* (17—24). This chapter shews us Abram not only as a sojourner in the land which afterwards his seed was to possess, but as a political power and conqueror: and this, doubtless, not so much for the interest in this world's history, which such an exhibition of him may have, but for the interest thereto attaching in reference to the future kingdom of God. It shews us Abram in conflict with this world's powers and victorious, foreshadowing in the long perspective of prophecy that which the kingdom of Abram's son, Solomon, more nearly represented, the prevalence of Abram's seed and its redemptive work in the world. This portion of the history belongs to the Jehovist in its present form: but evidently he has wrought up a much older document. This will be illustrated in detail as we pass on. Ewald is disposed to think this venerable fragment of history one of the oldest portions of Genesis. In it first we are introduced to this world's matters in the form of action such as our histories deal with.

1.] Of **Amraphel** nothing is known. He was king or chief of Babylonia (see on ch. xi. 2). The name **Arioch** (see ref.) probably means *lion-like:* he was chief of **Ellasar**, probably Larsa, called Larissa by the Greeks, an old Chaldean town, about half-way between *Ur* and *Erek*. "The inscriptions (says Prof. Rawlinson, *Biblical Dict.*) shew it to have been one of the primitive capitals, of earlier date, probably, than Babylon itself." It must not be confounded with *Thelassar*, 2 Kings xix. 2. Our knowledge of **Chedorlaomer** is only conjectural. Traces have been found on the inscribed bricks in Chaldea of a king *Kudur mapula*, who bears also the title of "*ravager of the West*." Even nearer to the name is that of *Kedar-el-Ahmar*, or *the red*, a great hero in Arabian tradition. He was king of Elam (see on ch. x. 22, and art. "Chedorlaomer" in the *Biblical Dict.*) He appears as a settled king of great power, able to make war 2000 miles from his country, and holding other kings, among whom is the king of Babylon, under his supremacy. This pre-eminence was of short duration: Elam fell under Babylon and Assyria, and afterwards (?) under Persia, when Susa (Shushan) the Elamite capital became the seat of empire. **Tidal** is otherwise unknown. His title, **king of nations** (Gozim), seems to imply that he was chief of a number of nomadic tribes. Some have called to mind "Galilee of the nations" (Matt. iv. 15); but this must be only for

Elam, and Tidal king of nations; 2 *that these* made war
with Bera king of Sodom, and with Birsha king of Gomorrah,
Shinab king of Admah, and Shemeber king of
Zeboiim, and the king of Bela, which is Zoar. 3 All these
were joined together in the vale of Siddim, which is the
salt sea. 4 Twelve years they served Chedorlaomer, and
in the thirteenth year they rebelled. 5 And in the four-
teenth year came Chedorlaomer, and the kings that *were*
with him, and smote the [t] Rephaim in Ashteroth Karnaim,
and the Zuzim in Ham, and the Emim in Shaveh Kiriathaim,

t ch. xv. 20. Deut. ii. 10, 20; iii. 11. Josh. xii. 4; xiii. 12; xvii. 15. 2 Sam. xxi. 18. 1 Chron. xx. 4.

illustration, not for identification, as we have obviously in this history nothing to do with Galilee. **2.**] On all these towns, see notes, ch. xix. Of these kings, whose names are not elsewhere found, nothing is known. The last city, Bela or Zoar (see on ch. xix. 22), has no king named, probably on account of its insignificance.

3.] The **vale of Siddim** is named only here. The meaning of the name is doubtful. The Hebraists, Gesenius and Kalisch, suppose it to mean "a plain cut up by stony channels, which render it difficult of transit." The word translated **vale** (*Emek*) is also applied to the plain of Jezreel, and hence is explained to be "a broad, flattish tract, sometimes of considerable width, enclosed on each side by a definite range of hill." This vale of Siddim, at all events, by the very terms of our text, formed a portion of the low land afterwards submerged by the Salt Sea. See on the whole, Mr. Grove's art. in the *Biblical Dict.* The notice, **which is the salt sea,** is one of those added by the writer of Genesis to the ancient document. See vv. 2, 6, 7, and notes. **5.**] The **Rephaims** (see reff.), or *giants*, appear first here in the E. of Palestine, but are afterwards found in connexion with the Philistines in the W. as enemies of Israel. There is no mention of them in ch. x., so that they were not Canaanites. Their last remaining king was Og, whose sway was very extensive (Josh. xii. 4, 5). The **Zuzim** and **Emim** were giant tribes of the Rephaim, dwelling, the former in the country afterwards held by the Moabites (Deut. ii. 10), the latter, called Zamzummims by the Ammonites (Deut. ii. 20), between the Arnon and the Jabbok. **Ashteroth Karnaim,** or Ashteroth of the two horns, is quite unknown as to situation. Knobel says it has been recognized in *Tell Ashteroth*, in the neighbourhood of Damascus. But Mr. Grove, writing at the same date (*Biblical Dict.*, 1860), makes no mention of this recognition. It is elsewhere called Astaroth in Edrei (Deut. i. 4), or simply Ashtaroth (Josh. ix. 10): in Josh. xii. 4, xiii. 12, 31, we have "Ashtaroth and Edrei," as separate cities, pertaining to Og in Bashan. Ashtaroth was his residence (Deut. as above). In later times it was known as *Carnaim*, 1 Macc. v. 43, 44, or *Carnion*, 2 Macc. xii. 26. The adjunct Karnaim probably alludes to the worship of the horned goddess Ashtoreth, or the moon (Astarte): but some refer it to a mountain with two peaks or horns, in the neighbourhood. It is somewhat doubtful whether **Ham** is a proper name at all. The LXX. and Vulgate render the word (Be-ham) "*together with them.*" But the general opinion is, that a place is represented, possibly the Ammonitish capital *Rabbath Ammon*, the ruins of which are now called *Amman.* The Samaritan Pentateuch has here the totally different name *Lishah*, meaning thereby perhaps the *Lasha* of ch. x. 19. **Shaveh Kiriathaim,** or *the plain* Kiriathaim: a city so called is mentioned Num. xxxii. 37 as having been built by the Reubenites, and as pertaining to them, Josh. xiii. 19,—as a Moabitish city, Jer. xlviii. 23; Ezek. xxv. 9; by Eusebius and Jerome as *Kariatha*, 10 miles west of Medeba (which, however, does not appear to lie in a plain). The identification thus seems to be quite uncertain, as it may well be, considering that Kiriathaim simply means *two cities.*

6.] The **Horites** mean *dwellers in caves*, as the inhabitants of Mount Seir (the

6 and the Horites in their mount Seir, unto El-paran, which
is by the wilderness. 7 And they returned, and came to En-
mishpat, which *is* Kadesh, and smote all the country of the
[u] Amalekites, and also the Amorites, that dwelt in [v] Ha-
zezon-tamar. 8 And there went out the king of Sodom
and the king of Gomorrah, and the king of Admah, and the
king of Zeboiim, and the king of Bela (the same *is* Zoar;)
and they joined battle with them in the vale of Siddim;
9 with Chedorlaomer the king of Elam, and with Tidal
king of nations, and Amraphel king of Shinar, and
Arioch king of Ellasar; four kings with five. 10 And the

u Exod. xvii. 8, 14. Num. xxiv. 20. 1 Sam. xv. 3, 8.
v 2 Chron. xx. 2, only.

rugged, full of clefts and caverns) or Petra might well be called. Their expulsion and destruction by the Edomites are recorded in Deut. ii. 12. **El-paran,** the oak (or terebinth) of Paran, the E. limit of the wilderness of Paran. On this latter see note, Deut. i. 1. Here we have another of the explanatory notices which abound in this history. **7.**] If they marched northward, they arrived in the desert of Zin, which formed a part of the great wilderness of Paran. Here lay, on the frontier of the Idumæan land, the old province and town of **Kadesh** or Kadesh-barnea (Num. xiii. 26; xx. 16). It was not distant from the town Gerar (ch. xx. 1), extended from here to the S. districts of Canaan, and formed its southern boundary (Num. xxxiv. 4; Josh. xv. 3). Therefore Moses could from here send the scouts for the exploration of the promised land, and treat with the King of Edom regarding the transit of the Hebrew army (Num. xiii. 20; xx. 14). "The town contained a celebrated well which, from an unknown but no doubt important cause, was called **En-mishpat,** *Well of Judgment,* which more ancient name later gave way to that of Kadesh (*holy*), likewise pointing to the holy character of the place." Kalisch. In connexion with both names, it may be remembered that it was here Moses, in striking the rock, spake unadvisedly with his lips (Num. xx. 10, 11), and was *judged* for his offence: and here also "the children of Israel strove with the Lord, and He was *sanctified* in them" (Num. v. 13). The objection to connecting these incidents with the name seems to be that because of that strife the water did receive a name, viz. that of *Meribah* (ib.). The explanatory words, **which is Kadesh,** have apparently been inserted by the Supplementer. There is some difficulty in the mention of the Amalekites here, seeing that "duke Amalek," who is ordinarily taken as the progenitor of that people, was the grandson of Esau (ch. xxxiv. 12, 16). If that were so, then this mention of the country *of the Amalekites* must be understood as meaning, *which was afterwards that of the Amalekites.* But some (see Mr. Bevan, *Biblical Dict.*) suppose that the assumption with regard to Esau's grandson is unfounded, and that the Amalekites were the ancient inhabitants of the peninsula of Sinai and the wilderness intervening between the southern hill-ranges of Palestine and the border of Egypt. For their subsequent history see reff., and notes thereon. **the Amorites**] See on ch. x. 16, and note on the report of the spies, Num. xiii. 29. Mr. Grove in *Biblical Dict.* regards the name not as indicating a distinct tribe, but as being a local term only, supporting the opinion by the curious blending of the designation Amorite with the various Canaanitish Gentile appellations—Hittite, Canaanite, Hivite, Jebusite. **Hazezon-tamar**] In the only other place where this name occurs (ref.) it is explained to be Engedi. The word is said to mean "*the felling of palm-trees,*" and the place may be the "city of palm-trees" of Judg. i. 16. See Stanley, *Sinai and Palestine,* p. 297, note. **8.**] Here we have another parenthetical notice of the identity of Bela with Zoar. **10.**] There is, perhaps, an implication that the bitumen pits were connected with the overthrow of the kings: they fell *there,* i. e. in the pits, probably by

vale of Siddim *was full of* slimepits; and the kings of
Sodom and Gomorrah fled, and fell there; and they that
remained fled to the mountain. 11 And they took all the
goods of Sodom and Gomorrah, and all their victuals, and
went their way. 12 And they took Lot, Abram's brother's
son, who dwelt in Sodom, and his goods, and departed.
13 ¶ And there came one that had escaped, and told Abram
the Hebrew; for he dwelt in the oak-grove of Mamre the
Amorite, brother of Eshcol, and brother of Aner: and
these *were* confederate with Abram. 14 And when Abram
heard that his brother was taken captive, he armed his
tried *servants*, born in his own house, three hundred and
eighteen, and pursued *them* unto Dan. 15 And he divided

being entangled in them, and unable to escape. From the bitumen found on its surface and shores the sea received the name of Lacus Asphaltites. The sentence is literally, "The vale of Siddim was pits pits of bitumen," i. e. was all pits. The remainder, the three kings of Admah, Zeboiim, and Bela, fled, as Lot afterwards, to the heights of Moab. **13.**] There has been much discussion over the words **Abram the Hebrew**. The simplest explanation of all is that of Knobel, that the term is to be understood in its obvious later sense, as distinguishing Abram from the Gentile races and people who occur in the narrative. Thus we have, "Let the Hebrews hear," 1 Sam. xiii. 3. See also ib. ver. 7, and xiv. 21. The chief objection to this view is that there does not appear here any sufficient reason for such contrast being made. Another explanation is, that Abram is thus called here owing to his descent from Eber, ch. x. 21. It is true that Eber's descendants there seem to be specially mentioned as constituting a race by themselves; but again there would be against this the former objection that no reason exists here for thus distinguishing the patriarch. There remains the solution afforded by the Septuagint rendering, which the Hebrew word will bear, Abram the *crosser-over*, or the *immigrant*, viz. from the other side of the Euphrates. If this were a name by which Abram was known among his Canaanitish contemporaries, and if this remarkable document were, as has been by some supposed, a fragment of Canaanitish history incorporated by the Jehovist, then a reason would be furnished for this title being given. But the question why Abram is here thus called, cannot be considered as satisfactorily solved. On the **oak-grove of Mamre**, see note, ch. xiii. 18. **Eshcol**, the *cluster of grapes*, was in after times the name given by the children of Israel to a valley near Hebron, because of the bunch which the spies brought from thence. But there can hardly be any connexion between the two names. Of **Aner** nothing is known. **confederates with Abram**] Literally, *lords of the oath of Abram*, possessors of a treaty with A. **14. his brother**] i. e. his near relative. See ch. xiii. 8. **armed**] Literally, *poured out* or emptied out. **tried**] Or proved—faithful and skilled. The root of the word signifies *to narrow*, hence to initiate or imbue with. **unto Dan**] If this is the same place as that afterwards named Dan by the Danites, the word must have been substituted here for its older appellation Laish (see Josh. xix. 47). But this (though held by Ewald) seems very improbable, as other ancient names have not been thus changed, but have been parenthetically explained. See vv. 2, 7, 8. And yet we can hardly fix on any other place, as Dan lies almost in the line of the way from Sichem to the neighbourhood of Damascus, along which Abram pursued the kings. Another place, if it be another, Dan-jaan, is by Keil supposed to be this Dan. It is mentioned 2 Sam. xxiv. 6, but corresponds there again very well with the Danite city, formerly Laish. **15.**] He divided himself against them, i. e. split his forces into two portions. **Hobah** has not

himself against them, he and his servants, by night, and
smote them, and pursued them unto Hobah, which *is* on
the left hand of Damascus. 16 And he brought back all
the goods, and also brought again his brother Lot, and his
goods, and the women also, and the people. 17 ¶ And the
king of Sodom went out to meet him after his return from
the slaughter of Chedorlaomer, and of the kings that *were*
with him, at the valley of Shaveh, which *is* the valley of
the king. 18 And Melchizedek king of Salem brought
forth bread and wine: and he *was* the priest of the high
God. 19 And he blessed him, and said, Blessed *be* Abram
of the most high God, possessor of heaven and earth:

been satisfactorily made out. It was to the left hand, i. e. the north, of Damascus. The Hebrews regarded themselves as facing the East, and named the quarters of the compass accordingly. The Jews regard the village of *Jobar*, a few miles N. E. of Damascus, as answering to Hobah. At Burzeh, very near, is a spot held in veneration by the people as having been the "praying-place" of Abraham, where he returned thanks to God after the discomfiture of the kings. See Mr. Porter's art. *Biblical Dict.* **17.**] Nothing is known of the name or the site of the **valley of Shaveh**. It is probable that the word itself (see on ver. 5) means a valley, in which case the valley of Shaveh is a reduplication. In 2 Sam. xviii. 18 we read that Abraham erected for himself a monument in the "valley of the king," but we are not told where it was: see there.

18—24.] *Abram's meeting with Melchizedek. His renunciation of the spoil.* It would exceed the limits of a note to give the many different opinions about this mysterious personage, Melchizedek. "Bearing a title which Jews in after-ages would recognize as designating their own sovereign, bearing gifts which recall to Christians the Lord's Supper, this Canaanite crosses for a moment the path of Abram, and is unhesitatingly recognized as a person of higher spiritual rank than the *friend of God*. Disappearing as suddenly as he came in, he is lost to the sacred writings for a thousand years; and then a few emphatic words for another moment bring him into sight as a type of the coming Lord of David. Once more, after another thousand years, the Hebrew Christians are taught to see in him a proof that it was the consistent purpose of God to abolish the Levitical priesthood. His person, his office, his relation to Christ, and the seat of his sovereignty, have given rise to innumerable discussions, which even now can scarcely be considered as settled." Mr. Bullock, *Biblical Dict.*

It may be stated briefly, that he has been variously supposed to have been Shem, authorized by the dignity of age and by paramount lordship of Canaan, to bless Abram and convey to him his right over the land, (so the Jewish opinion in Jerome's time,—the Samaritan, as reported by Epiphanius,—the later Targums, or Jewish commentaries,—and in modern times, Luther and Melanchthon, Lightfoot, and others),—*an angel* (ascribed to Origen by Jerome), a *Power or Virtue of God*, or even the *Holy Ghost* (various heretics blamed by the Christian Fathers), *the Son of God*, in human form (some of the ancients, to whose opinion Ambrose inclines, as well as some modern critics), the *Messiah* (a Jewish opinion), *Ham*, or *Enoch*, or *Job*. But we may safely treat all these as fanciful and unneeded. The typology connected with Melchizedek does not require that he himself should be regarded as any superhuman person, but merely exalts the human circumstances under which he appears into symbols of superhuman things. Everything combines to shew that Melchizedek was a Canaanitish king who had retained the worship of the true God, and combined in his own person the offices of king and priest. It is to be observed that there is not used regarding him, nor does he use, the title of Jehovah, but that of the HIGH GOD, a title found also in the question ad-

20 And blessed be the high God, which hath delivered
thine enemies into thy hand. And he gave him tithes
of all. 21 And the king of Sodom said unto Abram, Give
me the persons, and take the goods to thyself. 22 And
Abram said to the king of Sodom, I [w] lift up mine hand
unto JEHOVAH the high God, the possessor of heaven and
earth, 23 [x] That I will not *take* from a thread even to a
shoelatchet, and that I will not take any thing that *is* thine,

w Exod. vi. 8. Num. xiv. 30. Deut. xxxii. 40. Dan. xii. 7.

x So ch. xxi. 23; xxvi. 29; xlii. 15. Ps. xcv. 11 (Heb. iv. 5).

dressed (Micah vi. 6) by the Moabitish king Balak, to his prophet Balaam: but that Abram in answering the King of Sodom probably in his presence, affirms the identity of his covenant-God, Jehovah, with the *High God, possessor of heaven and earth,* of whom Melchizedek had spoken.

Respecting Salem, the city of Melchizedek, there is much discussion. Mr. Grove (*Biblical Dict.*) thinks that no satisfactory identification is possible. He quotes Dr. Wolff, who maintains that Salem is not a place, but part of the title, "King of *peace*." This is also held by Bleek and others. The general idea has been in ancient and modern times that Salem is Jerusalem, because it is so called in Ps. lxxvi. 2. Certainly it is: but this is no argument whatever for this Salem being also Jerusalem. Jerome identifies it with the Salem (Saleim in the Greek) near where John the Baptist was baptizing, John iii. 23. He reports that in his time the ruins of Melchizedek's palace were shewn there. But this Salem would be at a great distance from any point where Abram might be met: and if we are to take the account strictly, this incident happened (ver. 17) *after* Abram's return, and consequently in Hebron, which makes it likely that after all Salem may be Jerusalem. On all other points connected with this history, see notes on Heb. vii. 1—4. There the sacred writer adduces this incident as manifesting the superiority of the priesthood of Christ, who (Ps. cx. 4) was to be a priest after the order of Melchizedek, to the Levitical priesthood here represented by Levi's ancestor, Abraham. Melchizedek is greater than Abraham, because Abraham receives blessing at his hand, and pays tithes to him of all his spoil. It is interesting to see the view taken of this incident by Kalisch, a Jew: "Everything is here significant, everything typical: it is obvious that the dim background is designed to veil a grand religious and political future. . . . . Melchizedek brought forth to Abraham bread and wine, not to refresh him or his men, for Abraham had, among the booty of the enemies, seized their large stores of provisions also (vv. 11, 24), but to perform a symbolical ceremony, in which bread and wine had a typical meaning. For bread represents the ordinary daily food, the necessities of physical subsistence, whilst the wine points to the cheering delights of life and to the spiritual cravings of religion, in the rites of which it formed an important object." He also notices that whereas the Canaanitish king served only the most High God, but Abram the same God by the sublimer name of Jehovah, the religious enlightenment of the king of Salem was but a ray of the sun of Abraham's faith. "This is another instance of the extreme carefulness of the Scriptures in the application of the names of the Deity: the serpent was not allowed to profane the holy name (iii. 1—5); Japheth, though blessed, stood not under the direct protection of Jehovah (ix. 27); and Melchizedek, though a believer in God, had not entirely understood the God of the Hebrews.

On the blessing, and the paying of tithes, in their deeper significance, see on Hebrews, as above. **21.**] Certainly the impression is that the offer of the spoils by the king of Sodom takes place at the same time and in the presence of Melchizedek. And this is confirmed by the repetition in Abram's mouth of the name and designation of God used already by Melchizedek. On the prefacing this by the special Divine name, see above. The king of Sodom appears moved by the liberality of Abram to a like generous return. But there is no league between Abram and Sodom, nor will he give his riches to the idolaters about him. This is at least a different spirit from that in which he acquired his riches in Egypt, ch. xii. 16. **I lift up my hand,** i. e. I swear: see reff. The

lest thou shouldest say, I have made Abram rich: 24 Save
only that which the young men have eaten, and the por-
tion of the men which went with me, Aner, Eshcol, and
Mamre; let them take their portion. XV. 1 After these
things the word of JEHOVAH came unto Abram in a vision,
saying, Fear not, Abram: I *am* thy shield, *and* thy ex-
ceeding great reward. 2 And Abram said, Lord JEHOVAH,
y 2 Chron. xxi. 20. Ps. xxxix. 13. z Lev. xx. 20. Jer. xxii. 30. what wilt thou give me, seeing I [y] go [z] childless, and the
steward of my house *is* this Eliezer of Damascus? 3 And
Abram said, Behold, to me thou hast given no seed: and,
lo, one belonging to my house is mine heir. 4 And, be-
hold, the word of JEHOVAH *came* unto him, saying, This
a 2 Sam. vii. 12; xvi. 11. shall not be thine heir; but he that shall [a] come forth out
of thine own bowels shall be thine heir. 5 And he brought
him forth abroad, and said, Look now toward heaven, and
number the stars, if thou be able to number them: and he
said unto him, So shall thy seed be. 6 And he believed in

words do not appear to record a past action, but to describe a present one. Abram then and there makes oath to God. **That I will not take** is literally **If I take**: the act of lifting up the hand in abjuration implying the calling down God's anger on himself if he did that which he abjured. See reff., and compare 1 Kings xix. 2, and like passages. **from a thread to a shoelatchet** (or **lace**)] Meaning, any of even the most vile and trivial things, over which, and which only, the expression extends.

24.] Save only is literally **Not for me: only. . . .** Abram claims, for *himself*, nothing; for his own servants, only that which they had eaten; for his allies, their fair portion of the spoil.

XV. *Promise of an heir to Abram, and solemn covenant of Jehovah with him.*

1.] Literally, **there was a word of JEHOVAH to Abram.** The **vision** was not one in sleep, as is evident from what follows. Apparently the first portion, to verse 9, happens during the night (ver. 5). Then the obedience to the command (ver. 9) takes place during the day, and the night again supervenes in vv. 12—17. God had shewn Himself to be Abram's shield in Egypt and in his late encounter: the reward of which He speaks is to come, and to it Abram's question applies. It is not quite certain whether we should keep the idea that *God* was his reward: Kalisch renders, "*I am thy shield: thy reward will be very great.*" But Keil and Knobel retain the text. **2.]** This is the first time that **Lord JEHOVAH** occurs. **I die** (literally, **go, depart**: see reff.) **childless** (literally, **naked**). **the heir** is lit. **the son of possession.** There is in the original a play upon words: the heir is *ben-meshek*, and the appellation of Eliezer is *Dam-mesek:* such alliteration, as frequently, expressing a certain degree of despondent feeling. In Isa. xvii. 1, Damascus is again introduced in an alliteration; *Masah Dam-masek*, "the burden of Damascus." There is some dispute over the name and designation of this steward. As they stand in the Hebrew the words would be *Damascus Eliezer*. Kalisch is inclined to think that the two words together makes his name, as Hadad-ezer (2 Sam. viii. 3), Chushan-rishathaim (Judg. iii. 10), &c.; and so the LXX. and Vulgate render. But almost all the commentators, however they get at the meaning as a question of Hebrew, believe that **Eliezer of Damascus** expresses the sense. Probably he was a servant acquired at that city during Abram's journeying.

3.] one belonging to my house is literally **a son of my house**, that expression being evidently equivalent not to *one born in my house* (that his own son would be), but to *one attached to, a dependant of, my house.*

JEHOVAH; and he counted it to him for righteousness.
7 And he said unto him, I *am* JEHOVAH that brought thee
out of Ur of the Chaldees, to give thee this land to inherit
it. 8 And he said, Lord JEHOVAH, whereby shall I know
that I shall inherit it? 9 And he said unto him, Take for
me an heifer of three years old, and a she-goat of three
years old, and a ram of three years old, and a turtle-
dove, and a young pigeon. 10 And he took for HIM
all these, and divided them in the midst, and laid each
piece one against another: but the birds divided he not.
11 And the birds of prey came down upon the carcases, but

6.] Keil remarks, "In the strictly maintained objective character of the narratives of Genesis, in accordance with which simple facts without insertion of any subjective judgment are told, this remark seems so surprising that the question presses itself on us, whence Moses has derived it. How did Abram manifest his belief in Jehovah? And how did Jehovah reckon it to him as righteousness? The answer to both questions must not be sought from the N. T., but must be given or implied in the context. What return, then, did Abram make to the promise, or what did he do on its reception? When God for the confirmation of the same in ver. 7 pledged Himself to him as JEHOVAH, who brought him out of Ur of the Chaldees, to give him this land in possession, Abram replied, 'Lord, how shall I know that I shall inherit it?' And then God commanded him, 'Take one,' &c. And Abram took the animals as prescribed and did as God commanded him. By this prompt fulfilment of that which God ordered him to do, Abram shewed, as matter of fact, that he believed Jehovah: and that which God did with the animals which Abram sacrificed was the practical declaration on Jehovah's side that He reckoned Abram's faith as righteousness. The signification of the divine act is finally given in ver. 18: 'In the same day Jehovah made a covenant with Abram.' Accordingly, He shewed that he reckoned Abram's faith for righteousness, in that He made a covenant with him, and took Abram as a party into covenant with Himself." On the N.T. significance of this verse, see notes, Rom. iv 3.

7.] We have before referred to this verse to shew that the command of God to Abram first came when he was at Ur, not afterwards at Haran. **8.**] The same request may be made with two different minds. Zacharias (Luke i. 18) asked this in unbelief; the Blessed Virgin (Luke i. 34), as Abram here, in faith, humbly yearning for further assurance. God, who sees the heart, answers accordingly. **9.**] The animals prescribed are of the three kinds afterwards by the law allowed for sacrifice; and the birds are those repeatedly mentioned in the law as to be brought for offerings. The animals were to be each three years old, denoting, says Kalisch, the perfection of their species. But we Christians cannot shut our eyes to a deeper symbolism in this sacred number, especially when we remember that this part of the covenant symbolism was to be "for ME," i. e. to signify GOD's part of it (see also ver. 10). The universal Eastern custom was to divide the sacrifices, as Abram did, and *both* the contracting parties passed between the halves. Here one alone of the parties, JEHOVAH, thus passed. Abram's part of the covenant was the obedience of faith: and God on account of this entered, He, the righteous God, into bond with Abram, thus made a contracting party with God, and therefore accounted righteous. See above. **10.**] Abram appears to have done this not by special command, but as being aware what purpose the killing of these animals was to serve, viz. that of ratifying a covenant. Abram took these, as commanded, for GOD. So Kalisch. On the practice of cutting the sacrificed animals in two and passing between the parts, see Jer. xxxiv. 18, 19; Ps. l. 5. **11.**] Abram drove them away in the expectation that the sacrifice was about to serve God's purpose; another act of faith. **12.**] The great

Abram drove them away. 12 And when the sun was going
down, sleep fell upon Abram; and, lo, an horror of great
darkness fell upon him. 13 And he said unto Abram,
Know of a surety that thy seed shall be a stranger in a
land not their's; and shall serve them, and they shall
afflict them, four hundred years; 14 and also that nation,
whom they shall serve, will I judge: and afterward shall
they come out with great substance. 15 And thou shalt go
to thy fathers in peace; thou shalt be buried in a good old
age. 16 But in the fourth generation they shall come
hither again: for the iniquity of the Amorites *is* not yet
full. 17 And it came to pass, that, when the sun went
down, and it was thick darkness, behold a smoking furnace,
and a burning lamp that passed between those pieces.
18 In that day JEHOVAH made a covenant with Abram,
saying, Unto thy seed have I given this land, from the
river of Egypt unto the great river, the river Euphrates:

darkness was, as Knobel well explains, to hide the working of the Godhead from mortal eyes—and the horror accompanied it, because of the presence of the terrible God. During the sleep Abram receives the promise. **13.**] Literally, **Knowing know**: see ch. ii. 17. 400 years is the manner of speech of prophecy, taking the greater and round numbers. It really was 430: see Exod. xii. 40. The devices resorted to in order to produce exact agreement are beneath notice. **15.**] See the fulfilment of this in ch. xxv. 8. "The death of Abraham is predicted in one of those remarkable phrases which seem to prove that the Hebrews were not unacquainted with the doctrine of immortality. Here the return of the soul to the eternal abode of the fathers is, with some distinctness, separated from the interment of the body: that both cannot be identical is evident; for whilst Abraham was entombed in Canaan, all his forefathers died and were buried in Mesopotamia; and the reunion of the spirits is in some passages expressed still more clearly by the term being 'gathered to the fathers' after the fact of the death itself had been stated, and with a separate allusion to the act of sepulture (ch. xxv. 8, 9; xlix. 29, 33; Num. xx. 24, 26; xxxi. 2; Luke xx. 3)." Kalisch. **16. the fourth generation**] Was really the end of the fifth century (about 480 years). So that the length of a generation as here reckoned must be understood as being 120 years, the age (according to one interpretation of ch. vi. 3) allotted to man after the Flood. On the **Amorites** as a general name for the Canaanitish tribes, see above, ch. xiv. 13. The whole of their tribes are frequently described as being sunk in grossest immoralities. See Levit. xviii. 24; xx. 23; Deut. ix. 4; xviii. 12, al. **17.**] This fire was a symbol of the presence of Jehovah. See Exod. iii. 2; xiii. 21. **18. the river of Egypt**] Is variously supposed to mean the *Nile* (Keil, Delitzsch, Kalisch, Mr. Stuart Poole in *Biblical Dict.*, and many others, the objection being that the borders of the Land of Promise was never even supposed to extend thus far), or the present *Wady al Arish*, south of Philistia (the objection being that the name given to this small river, if indeed even that can be assumed as certain, is the Nah*al* Mizraim, the *brook* of Egypt, not as here the Nah*ar* Mizraim, the river of Egypt). If the Nile be meant, then Abraham's seed have never permanently reached either of the divinely-appointed boundaries of their inheritance: even if at one time in Solomon's day, 2 Chron. ix. 26, it could be said.

19—21. The Kenites] Were a people curiously connected with Israel in after

19 The [b] Kenites, and the Kenizzites, and the Kadmonites,
20 and the Hittites, and the Perizzites, and the Rephaims,
21 and the Amorites, and the Canaanites, and the Girgas-
hites, and the Jebusites. XVI. 1 Now Sarai Abram's
wife bare him no children: and she had an handmaid, an
Egyptian, whose name *was* Hagar. 2 And Sarai said unto
Abram, Behold now, JEHOVAH hath restrained me from
bearing: I pray thee, go in unto my maid; it may be that
I may obtain children by her. And Abram hearkened to
the voice of Sarai. 3 And Sarai Abram's wife took Hagar
her maid the Egyptian, after Abram had dwelt ten years
in the land of Canaan, and gave her to her husband Abram
to be his wife. 4 ¶ And he went in unto Hagar, and she
conceived: and when she saw that she had conceived, her

b Num. xxiv. 21, 22. Judg. i. 16; iv. 11. 1 Sam. xv. 6; xxvii. 10; xxx. 29. 1 Chron. ii. 55.

times: see reff. and notes there. Their origin is entirely obscure. The **Kenizzites, or Kenezites,** are mentioned again Num. xxxii. 12; Josh. xiv. 6, 14, where we read that Jephunneh, the father of Caleb, was a Kenezite. There is this difficulty respecting them. If these Kenizzites are the descendants of Kenaz (ch. xxxvi. 11), the mention of them here must be an after insertion; if they are distinct from that tribe, then we must regard them as a people who are otherwise utterly unknown to us, and who had became extinct in the time of Moses and Joshua. The **Kadmonites** are otherwise unknown, and mentioned here only. The name indicates an Eastern location. The enumeration here is remarkable both for what it inserts and for what it omits. We have no mention of the *Hivites*, who are in no other place absent from the complete enumeration of the Canaanitish nations. The number of 10 may be here used to signify the completeness of the gift. The number specified is generally 5, 6, or 7. See Exod. iii. 8, 17; xiii. 5; xxiii. 23, 28; xxxiii. 2; xxxiv. 11; Deut. vii. 1; xx. 17; Josh. iii. 10; ix. 1; xxiv. 11, &c. On the **Hittites,** see on ch. x. 15; **Perizzites,** xiii. 7; **Rephaims,** xiv. 5; **Amorites,** x. 16, and on ver. 16; **Girgashites,** x. 16; **Jebusites,** ib.

XVI. 1—16.] *The birth of Ishmael.* It is natural that Sarai should have had a female slave from Egypt. By ch. xii. 16 we learn that Abram was enriched with "maid servants." The name Hagar (flight) belongs to a tribe mentioned 1 Chron. v. 10, 19, 20; xxvii. 31; Ps. lxxxiii. 68; but (see there) their connexion with Hagar is doubtful.

2.] This practice is stated to be not uncommon in the East. It is the less to be wondered at in this case, seeing that Sarai had nowhere as yet been mentioned as the future mother of the seed of promise, and she might imagine that she was the obstacle in the way of its fulfilment. That the proposal comes from her and not from Abram, must be regarded as a token of the simplicity of his faith. He was willing to leave to God the method of fulfilling His promise; whereas Sarai, not seeing a way to it, becomes impatient, and has recourse to a doubtful expedient. **obtain children** is literally, **be built**; the pillars of the house being the offspring. See this figure used ch. xxx. 3; Exod. i. 21; Deut. xxv. 9; 2 Sam. vii. 11, 27; 1 Kings xi. 38. Sarai regards Hagar's possible offspring as *hers*, not foreseeing how the matter would turn out. **3.**] **his wife** must of course be understood in the inferior sense of that relation. There is in the very terms of this verse, **Sarai Abram's wife,** and **gave her to her husband Abram to be his wife,** an implied disapprobation of the course taken. Knobel regards this whole narrative as containing portions of the original record worked in by the Jehovist, and sees in the careful specification of date here, and in the expression **the land of Canaan,** the original hand of the Elohist. **4.**] The many touches of genuine nature in this narrative have compelled even modern unbelief to admit that it is no myth, but a ecord of

mistress was despised in her eyes. 5 And Sarai said unto
Abram, My wrong *be* upon thee: I have given my maid
into thy bosom; and when she saw that she had conceived,
I was despised in her eyes: JEHOVAH judge between me
and thee. 6 But Abram said unto Sarai, Behold, thy maid
is in thy hand; do to her that which is good in thine eyes.
And when Sarai dealt hardly with her, she fled from her
face. 7 ¶ And an angel of JEHOVAH found her by a foun-
tain of water in the wilderness, by the fountain in the way
to Shur. 8 And he said, Hagar, Sarai's maid, whence
camest thou? and whither wilt thou go? And she said, I
flee from the face of my mistress Sarai. 9 And the angel
of JEHOVAH said unto her, Return to thy mistress, and
submit thyself under her hands. 10 And the angel of JE-
HOVAH said unto her, I will multiply thy seed exceedingly,
that it shall not be numbered for multitude. 11 And the
angel of JEHOVAH said unto her, Behold, thou *art* with
child, and shalt bear a son, and shalt call his name Ish-

real life. See a parallel in Hannah's case, 1 Sam. i. 6. **5.**] In saying, **My wrong be** (or, **is**) **upon thee**, Sarai, now perceiving the consequence that she is despised, reminds her husband that he too is involved in this contumely, and in fact in the latter part of the verse passionately attempts to cast the chief blame on him: "I made the offer to thee, but the deed was thine; let God apportion the blame between us." **6.**] Abram assures her that Hagar has entered into no new and rival relation, but is still in her own power, still **thy maid.** On this Sarai maltreated her (it is the same word as "*afflict*," ch. xv. 13, xxxi. 50; and perhaps implies hard bondage, as in those places), and she fled. **7.**] This is the first mention of **an angel of Jehovah.** The Hebrew word (*Maleach*) signifies one sent, an ambassador or emissary. In several places it appears that this emissary of Jehovah is none other than an appearance, carrying the power of the Divine presence. As none can see Jehovah Himself, every such appearance to the eye, or manifestation to the ear, is in fact a mission from Himself. As Christians, we have a further inference from such a circumstance. We know Who it is that is the shining out of the Father's glory, and the expressed stamp of His Deity (Heb. i. 3), even the Divine Word, who is the Declaration of the Father to man (John i. 18; xiv. 9). But the more we feel this in our hearts, the more lightly and reverently should such thoughts be touched. It has not pleased God positively to declare to us that it was the Divine Son who was present in these Divine appearances, and therefore we should not on our parts positively declare, nor build systems upon it. **Shur** is a place, not now known, on the eastern boundaries of Egypt (ch. xxv. 18; Exod. xv. 22; 1 Sam. xv. 7; xxvii. 8). See further on ver. 14 and ch. xx. 1. **8.**] The address **Sarai's maid** both serves to remind her of her position and duty, and is in consonance with the formal character of the narrative in which such relations are again and again expressed (ver. 3). **9.**] There is no difference between the Hebrew expression for the angel here and **an** angel above: in both places the noun is without the definite article. I have inserted it at this second mention in conformity with our English usage. **10.**] lit. **multiplying I will multiply.** On the angel using the first person, as Jehovah, see above, and compare Exod. iii. 2, and notes.

11.] **Ishmael**, or *God heareth*, or *shall hear*, in the sense of taking note of, so as to act thereupon. Compare the similar use of

mael; because Jehovah hath heard thy affliction. 12 And
he will be a wild ass of a man; his hand *will be* against
every man, and every man's hand against him; and he
shall dwell in the presence of all his brethren. 13 And
she called the name of Jehovah that spake unto her, Thou
art the God of my seeing: for she said, Do I here also see,
after my seeing? 14 Wherefore the well was called Beer-
lahai-roi; behold, *it is* between Kadesh and Bered.
15 ¶ And Hagar bare Abram a son: and Abram called his
son's name, which Hagar bare, Ishmael. 16 And Abram *was*
fourscore and six years old, when Hagar bare Ishmael to
Abram. XVII. 1 And when Abram was ninety years old
and nine, Jehovah appeared to Abram, and said unto

hear in Isa. xxxvii. 4, 17. **12.**] The roving fierceness of the wild ass of the desert is described Job vi. 5; xxiv. 5; xxxix. 5, 8. See also Ps. civ. 11; Isa. xxxii. 14. The rendering in the text is that of Kalisch. The A. V., by omitting the central word in the sentence, loses altogether the point of the prophecy. "The character of the Ishmaelites, or the Bedouins, could not be described more aptly or more powerfully. They have preserved it almost unaltered during three or four thousand years. . . . They have defied the softening influence of civilization, and mocked the attacks of the invader. Ungovernable and roaming, obeying no law but their spirit of adventure, regarding all mankind as their enemies, whom they must either attack with their spears or elude with their faithful steeds, . . . the Bedouins are the outlaws among the nations. . . . 'In the desert, everybody is everybody's enemy,' is their proverbial saying." Kalisch.

in the presence of] Is interpreted by Delitzsch as rather meaning *to the east of*, but Kalisch, and the majority of commentators, render as in text, and understand it as describing "the wide and almost indefinite extent of territories through which the Bedouins roam, so that they seem to be everywhere before the eyes of their brethren." Certainly, as Kalisch observes, their limit being said, in ch. xxv. 18, "unto Shur, that is before Egypt," they did not dwell only to the *east* of their brethren. **13.**] "She exclaimed, with mingled feelings of exultation and submission, 'Thou art the God of seeing;' for she said, 'Do I even still see after seeing?' that is, Thou art to me a God whom I saw unpunished: for although I saw Thee I still live and see the light of day." Kalisch. Compare ch. xxxii. 30; Exod. xxxiii. 20; Deut. v. 24; Judg. vi. 22, 23; xiii. 22; Isa. vi. 5. **Do I still see,** i. e. live, as explained in the next verse.

14. Beer-lahai-roi] Literally, "*the fountain for the life of beholding.*" Kalisch. He renders it, *the well of seeing* God *and living.* It is stated to be between Kadesh, i. e. Kadeshbarnea (see ch. xiv. 7; also xxiv. 62; xxv. 11), and Bered. This latter has not been satisfactorily made out. Mr. Grove (*Biblical Dict.*) thinks it to be *El-Chalasah* the ancient *Elusa*, 12 m. S. of Beersheba. Mr. Rowlands claims to have discovered this well about 12 m. from Kadesh, on the road to Jebel-es-Serr (Shur ?)—at a place still called by the Arabs Moilahi Hadjar, Moi (water) being equivalent to Beer (well). See Rev. G. Williams, *Holy City*, i. p. 465.

15, 16.] *The fulfilment of the promise to Hagar.* **15.**] We can surely find no ground here for asserting a discrepancy from ver. 11. Abram obeys the order there given to Hagar.

XVII. **1—25.**] *The covenant sealed by a new name given to Abram, and by circumcision.* The narrative is considered by Knobel to belong throughout, with the exception of the opening words, to the original Elohistic document, and to be unchanged. Abram had waited fourteen years at least for the performance of the promise, and no sign of it had appeared. This appearance of God denoted the fulness of the time for the

c El Shaddai; see ch. xxxv. 11. him, I *am* c God Almighty; walk before me, and be thou
perfect. 2 And I will make my covenant between me and
thee, and will multiply thee exceedingly. 3 And Abram
fell on his face: and God talked with him, saying, 4 As
for me, behold, my covenant *is* with thee, and thou shalt
be a father of many nations. 5 Neither shall thy name
any more be called Abram, but thy name shall be Abra-
ham; for a father of many nations have I made thee.
6 And I will make thee exceeding fruitful, and I will
make nations of thee, and kings shall come out of thee.
7 And I will establish my covenant between me and thee
and thy seed after thee in their generations for an ever-
lasting covenant, to be a God unto thee, and to thy seed
after thee. 8 And I will give unto thee, and to thy seed
after thee, the land wherein thou art a stranger, all
the land of Canaan, for an everlasting possession; and
I will be their God. 9 ¶ And God said unto Abraham,

covenant promise to be put in fulfilment. God here calls Himself **El Shaddai, God All-mighty**, able to perform that which He had promised. I reserve the full explanation of this name for the remarkable place, Exod. vi. 2, 3. There is an appropriateness in its special revelation here, seeing that in order for God's promise to be performed the course of nature itself would have to be changed. "Is anything too hard for Jehovah?" was an appeal made by God Himself during the course of the narrative (ch. xviii. 14). Abram's part of the covenant was to walk before, in the presence of, God in the obedience of faith. See ch. vi. 9; Micah vi. 8; Matt. v. 48; James iii. 2.

2.] Knobel thinks that this was the only narrative of the making the covenant contained in the primeval document, the others having been afterwards added by the Jehovist. That would account for the apparently first introduction here of the promise of multiplying Abram exceedingly, which had been already given both generally, ch. xii. 2, and specially, ch. xv. 5, in the Jehovist supplement. Abram, overcome with the Divine majesty and grace, prostrated himself. See Levit. ix. 24; Ruth ii. 10.

5.] **Abraham** means *father of a multitude*, the latter part of the name signifying "the noise and tumult characteristic of agitated crowds." Kalisch. Henceforth both narrators use no other name for him than Abraham. **8.**] **The land wherein thou art a stranger** is literally, *the land of thy sojournings* or *wanderings*. **9—14.**] *The ordinance of circumcision.* In applying what we know from history to this narrative, we must bear in mind what was before said (ch. ix.) on the covenant character there given to the rainbow. It is as futile to attempt in the face of historical and ethnical facts to deny that circumcision existed before Abraham received it as the sign of God's covenant, as it is to deny in the face of physical facts that the rainbow existed before Noah received it as the sign of God's covenant. Neither our Lord's saying that it was of the Fathers as distinguished from Moses (John vii. 22), nor Stephen's, that God gave Abraham the covenant of circumcision, is the least to the purpose. Whenever and among whomsoever the practice first originated, *Jewish* circumcision was "of the Fathers," and the *covenant of* circumcision was given by God to Abraham. The practice appears to have been at first begun from sanitary motives among the African tribes. The Egyptians and Æthiopians, according to Herodotus, maintained it: "it is in use among the Kafir nations of South Africa, forming a considerable portion of the native

As for thee, thou shalt keep my covenant, thou, and
thy seed after thee in their generations. 10 This *is* my
covenant, which ye shall keep, between me and you
and thy seed after thee; Every man child among you
shall be circumcised. 11 And ye shall circumcise the
flesh of your foreskin; and it shall be a token of the cove-
nant betwixt me and you. 12 And he that is eight days
old shall be circumcised among you, every man child in
your generations, he that is born in the house, or bought
with money of any stranger, which *is* not of thy seed.
13 He that is born in thy house, and he that is bought
with thy money, must needs be circumcised: and my
covenant shall be in your flesh for an everlasting covenant.
14 And the uncircumcised man child whose flesh of his
foreskin is not circumcised, that soul shall be cut off from

population of Africa: and it has been discovered in many southern islands of the Indian seas and the Pacific Ocean." Kalisch, who also adds, "There is scarcely a doubt that in these southern countries the rite of circumcision was introduced from a physical cause. It was not only a matter of expediency, but in some cases of necessity. . . . It prevents painful and often miserable disease . . . . the Christian missionaries who exerted themselves for its abolition in Abyssinia were, by the dangerous physical consequences, obliged to desist from their plans." Abundant testimony of the same kind may be found in Winer, *Realwörterbuch*, art. "Beschneidung." See also Mr. T. T. Perowne, *Biblical Dict.* I may remark that the very manner of introduction of the ordinance here confirms the idea that it is not now heard of for the first time. It is spoken of as a practice recognizable on a slight mention; to be adopted, rather than instituted. The idea, upheld by Bp. Wordsworth, that the Egyptians learnt it from Joseph, in the face of such a testimony as ch. xliii. 32 to the entire distinctness of the national practices, surely needs no refutation. By the words **my covenant** must, of course, be understood *the sign of* my covenant (ver. 11). Circumcision was not the covenant itself, but the seal of the covenant. See the similar expression, Acts vii. 8. On the nature of the sign, see some admirable remarks of Delitzsch in loc. **12.**] The Arab descendants of Abraham observed another rule: see on ver. 25. Compare Levit. xii. 3; Gen. xxi. 4; Luke i. 5, 9; ii. 21; Phil. iii. 5. **14.**] This has been sometimes mistaken to mean that by some special intervention God would punish such a person. But most commentators hold, as Kalisch—"We believe the true sense of the phrase to be that the individual who transgresses the condition or sign of the covenant thereby resigns his connexion with the Hebrew community and ceases to belong to it." So, of modern commentators, Knobel, Murphy, &c. On the other side are Keil, Bp. Wordsworth, &c. If we examine usage, we shall find it slightly in favour of the former view. In Exod. xxxi. 14, 15, *death* is prescribed as the manner of *cutting off* from among the people the Sabbath-breaker: see also xxxv. 2. In Levit. xvii. 4, *cutting off* from among the people is the penalty of killing a clean beast and not bringing it as an offering; but in xxiv. 17, "He that killeth any *man* shall surely be *put to death.*" (See also Exod. xxi. 12; Num. xxxv. 31.) In Levit. xviii. 29 *cutting off* is the punishment for unnatural crime; in Exod. xxii. 19, *death*. So that it would appear as if cutting off generally, but not always, implied death at man's hand. But no inference is justified that judgment at God's hand should follow in cases where it is threatened. The case in Exod. iv. 24 (see there) seems to be exceptional, and anyhow cannot apply here,

his people; he hath broken my covenant. 15 ¶ And
Elohim said unto Abraham, As for Sarai thy wife, thou
shalt not call her name Sarai, but Sarah *shall* her name *be*.
16 And I will bless her, and give thee a son also of her:
yea, I will bless her, and she shall be *a mother* of nations;
kings of people shall be of her. 17 Then Abraham fell upon
his face, and laughed, and said in his heart, Shall *a child*
be born unto him that is an hundred years old? and shall
Sarah, that is ninety years old, bear? 18 And Abraham
said unto Elohim, O that Ishmael might live before
thee! 19 And Elohim said, Sarah thy wife shall bear thee
a son indeed; and thou shalt call his name Isaac: and I
will establish my covenant with him for an everlasting
covenant, *and* with his seed after him. 20 And as for
Ishmael, I have heard thee: Behold, I have blessed him,

where it is the circumcised person and not the parent who is to be "cut off." **15.**] Sarai's name also is changed, to testify to her part in the covenant. It is acknowledged on all hands that SARAH means *a princess:* but as to SARAI, Hebraists are far from being agreed. Gesenius and Ewald interpret it "*contentious*," which seems unlikely in itself; Kalisch, *combating* or *contending*, which is not far off the other, though differently understood, viz. as "contending with difficulties:" and Delitzsch remarks well on this, that the *name of conflict*, Sarai, is changed into the *name of triumph*, Sarah. Others again (as Keil) suppose Sarai to signify princelike (Fürstliche), and Sarah, princess (Fürstinn); others, that Sarai means *my princess*, Sarah, *princess*, absolutely. **17.**] Abraham's feeling is one mingled of reverence and incredulousness. On *this occasion* he hardly justified the high praise of Rom. iv. 19; on that other occasion, "the deadness of Sarah's womb" was hardly in his view. So that the praise must be taken as applied to his whole conduct, and especially his obedience in this case, when assured by God, to the order imposed on him of adopting the sign of the covenant. The laugh was not one of "joyful astonishment," as the words of the question, and the subsequent wish regarding Ishmael, plainly shew. Nor can such an interpretation derive support from our Lord's words in John viii. 56: see note there. I may repeat the observation that the words of this verse are a decisive censure to that lame chronological compromise (see on ch. xi.) which makes Abraham himself born when his father Terah was 130.

18.] This wish has been explained away by some commentators, as if Abraham had meant, O that Ishmael, in addition to the promised seed, might live and prosper before Thee! It really is astonishing how such a departure from the obvious spirit of the words both of Abraham and of God can approve itself to any mind. But the desire to find no flaw in Abraham's faith, has fairly blinded our expositors. It is hardly necessary to state that Abraham's wish is uttered in the half-incredulous spirit of his inward questioning. He yearns for the acceptance of his existing son as the heir of the promise: and to this (see below) is the Divine answer directed. **19.**] God responds first to his inward questioning. That which thou hast doubted shall indeed come to pass: and the son which shall be born shall be named after this thy laughter, which was the expression of thy doubt. For the name Isaac signifies "laughter." Human weakness should, by God's abounding grace, be turned into exultation at His mercy. This, and no other, should be the son of the covenant. **20.**] Thy wish for Ishmael has been heard. Not indeed in the full sense, but in the sense of his being blessed

and will make him fruitful, and will multiply him exceed-
ingly; twelve princes shall he beget, and I will make
him a great nation. 21 But my covenant will I establish
with Isaac, which Sarah shall bear unto thee at this set
time in the next year. 22 And he left off talking with
him, and Elohim went up from Abraham. 23 ¶ And Abra-
ham took Ishmael his son, and all that were born in his
house, and all that were bought with his money, every male
among the men of Abraham's house; and circumcised the
flesh of their foreskin in the selfsame day, as Elohim had
said unto him. 24 And Abraham *was* ninety years old
and nine, when he was circumcised in the flesh of his fore-
skin. 25 And Ishmael his son *was* thirteen years old,
when he was circumcised in the flesh of his foreskin.
26 In the selfsame day was Abraham circumcised, and Ish-
mael his son. 27 And all the men of his house, born in
the house, and bought with money of the stranger, were
circumcised with him. XVIII. 1 And JEHOVAH appeared
unto him in the oak-grove of Mamre: and he sat in the
tent door in the heat of the day; 2 and he lift up his eyes
and looked, and, lo, three men stood by him: and when

abundantly, and becoming a great nation. On his 12 sons, see ch. xxv. 12—16.

21.] But he shall not be the promised seed. That shall be the privilege of Isaac, whose birth is now announced at the set time of one year from the date of the establishment of the covenant. **22.**] **God went up,** viz. to heaven. See ch. xxxv. 13.

23—27.] *Abraham fulfils the Divine command in the obedience of faith.* Here was the sign of his unwavering faith in God's promise and covenant. However momentary doubt may have dimmed his spiritual sight, the direct assurance from God clears it again. He hesitates not to perform the painful operation on himself and all in his house. Nor is there the slightest delay. It is done "the selfsame day." **25.**] The mention of this circumstance may have been made merely to give completion to the formal details of so important a transaction, or as (Kalisch supposes) the sacred historian may have inserted it "to explain the usage of the Arabians, who circumcise their males in the thirteenth year, by the circumstance that Ishmael had then attained that age." But surely the former alternative is far the more probable. The two following verses bear it out, re-stating as they do with careful and formal accuracy what has been already narrated.

XVIII., XIX. SODOM AND GOMORRHA. The section begins by the visit of Jehovah, accompanied by two angels, to Abraham at Mamre. The object of this visit is twofold: first, to announce to Sarah her part in the covenant; secondly, to impart to Abraham the Divine purpose of destroying Sodom and Gomorrha. The whole section is Jehovistic, with the remarkable exception of ch. xix. 29, which is apparently an insertion from the original Elohistic narrative (see there).

1.] On the **oak-grove of Mamre,** see on ch. xiii. 18. The commentators quote from Volney, that it is the custom of the Arabs, when the time for their midday meal approaches, to sit in the entry of their tent in order to see the passers-by, and invite them to share the meal. **2.**] The process of recognition on the part of Abraham is minutely described. The three men on being seen are perceived to be the appear-

he saw *them*, he ran to meet them from the tent door, and
bowed himself toward the ground, 3 and said, Lord, if now
I have found favour in thy sight, pass not away, I pray
thee from thy servant: 4 let a little water, I pray you,
be fetched, and [d] wash your feet, and rest yourselves under
the tree: 5 and I will fetch a morsel of bread, and refresh
ye your hearts; after that ye shall pass on: for therefore
are ye come to your servant. And they said, So do, as thou
hast said. 6 And Abraham hastened into the tent unto
Sarah, and said, Make ready quickly three [e] measures of
fine meal, knead *it*, and make [f] cakes. 7 And Abraham
ran unto the herd, and fetcht a calf tender and good, and
gave *it* unto the young man; and he hasted to dress it.
8 And he took butter, and milk, and the calf which he had
dressed, and set *it* before them; and he [g] stood by them
under the tree, and they did eat. 9 ¶ And they said unto
him, Where *is* Sarah thy wife? And he said, Behold, in
the tent. 10 And he said, I will certainly return unto
thee [h] next year; and behold a son to Sarah thy wife.

d ch. xix. 2; xxiv. 32; xliii. 24. Judg. xix. 21. 2 Sam. xi. 8.
e 1 Sam. xxv. 18. 2 Kings vii. 1, 16. See Isa. xl. 12. Ps. lxxx. 5. Matt. xiii. 33. Luke xiii. 21.
f Exod. xii. 39. Num. xi. 8. 1 Kings xvii. 13; xix. 6. Ezek. iv. 12. Hos. vii. 8, only.
g 1 Kings x. 8. Jer. lii. 12. Heb. xiii. 2.
h 2 Kings iv. 16.

ance of the Divine Presence, and hence Abraham does not merely invite them to his meal, but performs the act of reverence mentioned. The three men, as declared in ver. 22, were the human appearance of Jehovah accompanied by two angels. But it is not in vain that the Church reads this chapter as the Lesson on Trinity Sunday; for though it would be presumption to say that we have related here the appearance of the Blessed Trinity, yet she finds ample justification in the employment of the sacred and mysterious number as connected with the Divine Presence. **3.**] The word by which Abraham addresses the principal personage among the Three is uniformly used in the Hebrew Scriptures as the appellation of Deity, Adonai. **4.**] The address which begun in the singular now passes to the plural. As the Easterns walk in sandals merely, or with the feet bare, the washing of the feet from the dust of travel is always the first care, and especially before meals: see reff. **rest yourselves**] Literally, *lean* [upon your elbows], recline, as the manner mostly was in the East, at meat.

6. three measures] Literally, *three seahs*,—sata—the measure being that in most ordinary household use, and = the third part of an ephah, or slightly over a peck. See reff. **fine meal**] Literally, *meal, fine meal*, i.e. meal, the best we have. The cakes here spoken of are explained to be round and flat, baked upon the hot stones of the hearth. **7. the young man**] viz. who was in attendance. **8.**] The word rendered **butter** is *indurated milk*, it may be in the way of butter or of curd: here probably the former. Kalisch understands sour milk in which the calf was boiled, but in the text the dressing seems to have taken place first, and this was a garnish.

Abraham **stood by them**, waiting upon them, as is the custom of the sheikhs in Arabia even now, when they have distinguished guests. **9.**] The visit had especial reference to Sarah, therefore she is asked for.

10.] The expression rendered by the A. V. "*according to the time of life*" is literally **at the living time** (or **season**), and is explained by the Hebraists to mean when the year now passing away again revives, i. e. during the next year. Kalisch renders, "*and she was behind it*," viz. the tent door. But as that *door* was only an opening made by drawing back the material of the tent, this serves to give a wrong idea. The notice is apparently inserted to signify that the

And Sarah heard *it* in the tent door, which *was* behind
him. 11 Now Abraham and Sarah *were* old *and* advanced
in age; *and* it ceased to be with Sarah after the manner
of women. 12 Therefore Sarah laughed within herself,
saying, After I am [i] worn out shall I have pleasure, my i Job xiii. 28. Ps. xxxii. 3.
lord being old also? 13 And JEHOVAH said unto Abra-
ham, Wherefore did Sarah laugh, saying, Shall I of a
surety bear a child which am old? 14 Is any thing [j] too j Deut. xvii. 8; xxx. 11.
hard for JEHOVAH? At the time appointed I will return
unto thee next year, and Sarah shall have a son. 15 Then
Sarah denied, saying, I laughed not; for she was afraid.
And he said, Nay; but thou didst laugh. 16 ¶ And the
men rose up from thence, and looked toward Sodom: and
Abraham went with them to bring them on the way.
17 And JEHOVAH said, Shall I hide from Abraham that
thing which I do; 18 seeing that Abraham shall surely
become a great and mighty nation, and all the nations

opening of the tent was behind the speaker, and consequently unseen by him. So far from this involving (as Kalisch urges) "a notion incompatible with the omnipresence of God," it is mentioned for the very purpose of introducing a proof of that omnipresence. *Though* she was behind Him, He was fully conscious of her presence there, and of that which she was doing.

11.] That natural recurrence, which indicates, and at its cessation terminates, the power of conceiving children, had ceased to be with Sarah. **12.**] She laughed, not from a different reason from that which caused Abraham's laughter in ch. xvii. 17, but from the same reason. The very same enquiry accompanies the laughter in both cases; and it is utterly futile to attempt, in order to save the consistency of Abraham's faith, to represent the one laughter as owing to "amazement and joy," and the other to unbelief. It is not thus that the intelligent understanding of Scripture is promoted. **my lord**] St. Peter (1 Pet. iii. 6) adduces this expression of Sarah's as an example of reverence for her husband.

13.] Here first is one of the three designated as being Jehovah. **which am old**] Literally, **and I have grown old.**

14.] Bp. Wordsworth well remarks on the adoption of the very words used in the LXX. here, by St. Luke, ch. i. 37, in the speech of the angel Gabriel to the Blessed Virgin. **15.**] Her laughter had been inward only (ver. 12), but it had taken place. She must be conceived as having been by the solemn question of ver. 13 brought out from her hiding-place. Her untrue self-excusing is gently dealt with by Him who knows what is in man, and "upbraideth not."

16—33.] *The doom of Sodom; Abraham's intercession.* **16.**] It would appear at first sight as if no departure had taken place at this moment. The Three rose up from meat, and as intending to leave the spot, and turned their faces towards Sodom, Abraham being prepared to go with them to accompany them on their way. Then Jehovah imparted His counsel to the two, which resulted in the announcement of vv. 20, 21; and at ver. 22 the two depart toward Sodom. Kalisch supposes that the two angels went on, and Abraham with them, and that Jehovah remained, and is represented as deliberating with Himself: Knobel, that the Three went on, and the deliberation took place by the way. And this last is certainly right, from ch. xix. 27, from which the place where Abraham stood before the Lord appears to have been at some distance from his tent. **17. which**

of the earth shall be blessed in him? 19 For I have
chosen him, that he may command his children and his
household after him, that they keep the way of Je-
hovah, to do justice and judgment; that Jehovah
may bring upon Abraham that which he hath spoken
of him. 20 And Jehovah said, Verily the cry of
Sodom and Gomorrah is great, yea, their sin is very
grievous. 21 I will go down now, and see whether they
have done altogether according to the cry of it, which
is come unto me; and if not, I will know. 22 And the
men turned their faces from thence, and went toward So-
dom: but Abraham stood yet before Jehovah. 23 ¶ And
Abraham drew near, and said, Wilt thou also destroy the
righteous with the wicked? 24 Perhaps there shall be
fifty righteous within the city: wilt thou also destroy,
and not spare the place for the fifty righteous that *are*
therein? 25 That be far from thee to do after this manner,
to slay the righteous with the wicked: and that the right-
eous should be as the wicked, that be far from thee: Shall
not the Judge of all the earth do justice? 26 And Je-
hovah said, If I find in Sodom fifty righteous within the
city, then I will spare all the place for their sakes. 27 And
Abraham answered and said, Behold now, I have taken
upon me to speak unto the Lord, which *am but* dust and

I do] i. e. have determined to do, am about doing. **19.**] The Hebraists seem mostly agreed that the rendering of this verse should be as in the text. It is God's *purpose* with regard to Abraham, not His knowledge of the character of Abraham, that is spoken of. This purpose being such as is here affirmed, the being taken into God's counsel with regard to the reason of that which was about to happen to Sodom would tend to further it, by testifying to the Divine hatred of sin.

21.] The word rendered **altogether** is given by the Arabic version *the whole multitude of them.* It is a noun, signifying perfection or consummation. From the tone of Abraham's intercession it would appear as if there were something to be said for this rendering. In Exod. xi. 1, where the word is also rendered "*altogether,*" the same ambiguity exists. **22. the men**] i. e. the angels, at a certain point in the way, left Abraham standing before Jehovah. At this point there was a view over the cities of Sodom and Gomorrah and all the land of the circle of Jordan. Knobel, following Robinson, thinks it might have been the present *Beni Naim,* about three miles East of Hebron. **23—33.**] *Abraham's intercession.* He is moved to this, not by his special interest in Lot, not by the memory of his own exertions in saving this land from the invading kings, but by a noble sense of right, and love of men. There is nothing derogatory to the majesty of God in the Divine answers to him here; no difficulty in them, which does not meet us, every time we attempt to describe an answer to prayer. If the mere outward propriety of the narrative need vindication, we may bear in mind that God is represented as being as yet of uncertain counsel, and awaiting the issue of facts.

25.] There is no grander testimony on record to the majesty of the moral sense in man. **27. the Lord** here and in

ashes: 28 perhaps there shall lack five of the fifty right-
eous: wilt thou destroy all the city for five? And he
said, If I find there forty and five, I will not destroy *it*.
29 And he spake unto him yet again, and said, Perhaps
forty shall be found there. And he said, I will not do *it*
for the sake of the forty. 30 And he said, Let not the
Lord be angry, and I will speak: Perhaps thirty shall be
found there. And he said, I will not do *it*, if I find thirty
there. 31 And he said, Behold now, I have taken upon me
to speak unto the Lord: Perhaps twenty shall be found
there. And he said, I will not destroy *it* for the sake of
the twenty. 32 And he said, Let not the Lord be angry,
and I will speak yet but this once: Perhaps ten shall be
found there. And he said, I will not destroy *it* for the sake
of the ten. 33 And JEHOVAH departed when he had finished
communing with Abraham: and Abraham returned unto
his place. XIX. 1 And the two angels came to Sodom at
even; and Lot sat in the gate of Sodom: and Lot seeing
them rose up to meet them; and he bowed himself with
his face toward the ground; 2 and he said, Behold now,
my lords, turn in, I pray you, into your servant's house,
and tarry all night, and wash your feet, and ye shall
rise up early, and go on your ways. And they said,

vv. 31, 32 is the rendering, not of JEHOVAH, but of ADONAI, as in ver. 3. **dust and ashes** is in the Hebrew, which loves alliteration, *gaphar va-aipher*: dust in my origin, and ashes in my end. **33.**] **JEHOVAH departed,** as ch. xix. 24 shews, to heaven. The expression of the A. V., "*went his way*," is calculated to mislead, besides having, at least in our days, a somewhat colloquial aspect. Kalisch well remarks that God proceeded with far greater leniency than even Abraham's anxiety had the courage to advocate: for He delivered the house of Lot, the only virtuous family which was found in Sodom. He further remarks that the patriarch, so far from, as some have said, shewing the "impudence" of importunity, had asked simply for justice, and not for mercy: "he might at once have insisted on the principle, that the sinners only should die, whatever their number might be: though he had confidence in the Divine attribute of justice, he had not fathomed its whole depth. Comp. Num. xvi. 22; Ezek. xviii. 20."

XIX. *The destruction of Sodom. The incest of Lot.* **1.**] Kalisch renders, "*And two of the angels came*," &c. In his character for hospitality, Lot is the counterpart of Abraham. He sits at the gate, where he might best see approaching strangers. He has no idea who they are: see vv. 2 and 8. But they probably had something beautiful and majestic in their appearance: see on ver. 5. **2.**] He addresses them as **my lords.** The word is the same as that by which Abraham addressed God, ch. xviii. 3, in the singular, but it is differently pointed in the Hebrew, and evidently must be differently understood, as the sentence is in the second person plural, not singular, as there. And accordingly, while the Masoretic editors have a note against Adonai there, "*sacred*," meaning that it is the name of God, here they note the "*profane*," meaning that it is the name of man only. **wash your feet**] See on ch. xviii. 4. They decline his offer of hospitality, as not wishing to become guests of any among

Nay; but we will abide in the street all night. 3 And
he pressed upon them greatly; and they turned in
unto him, and entered into his house; and he made
k ch. xxi. 8; xxvi. 30; xxix. 22. Judg. xiv. 12. them a [k] feast, and did bake unleavened cakes, and
they did eat. 4 ¶ But before they lay down, the men
of the city, the men of Sodom, compassed the house
l Isa. lvi. 11. Jer. li. 31. round, both old and young, all the people [l] from every
quarter: 5 and they called unto Lot, and said unto him,
Where *are* the men which came in to thee this night?
bring them out unto us, that we may know them. 6 And
Lot went out at the door unto them, and shut the door
after him, 7 and said, I pray you, brethren, do not wickedly.
8 Behold now, I have two daughters which have not known
man; let me, I pray you, bring them out unto you, and
do ye to them as *is* good in your eyes: only unto these men
do nothing, because they came under the shadow of my
roof. 9 And they said, Stand back. And they said, This
one came in to sojourn, and he continually judgeth *us*:
now will we deal worse with thee, than with them.
And they pressed sore upon the man, *even* Lot, and came
near to break the door. 10 But the men put forth their
hand, and pulled Lot into the house to them, and shut to
the door. 11 And they smote the men that *were* at the

the Sodomites: but 3] at length yield, and are entertained. This apparently was to try the sincerity of his invitation, and to bring about that sifting of his character which the following shameful incident afforded. **a feast**] Literally, **a drink**, but used in this wider sense in reff. Probably the cause of the absence of leaven was the suddenness of the occasion: see also Exod. xii. 33, 34. **4—7.**] From Levit. 22—25 we learn that the practice of the sin here contemplated was among the principal causes why God exterminated the Canaanitish nations. **from every quarter**] Literally, **from the end**, viz. of the city. See reff. **8.**] It is difficult to give an account of this offer consistently with any estimate of Lot as a "righteous" man. But in our estimating we must remember that the same offer was made, and the thing actually done, in the parallel case at Gibeah of Benjamin, Judges xix. 24, ff. Guided by that other case, we cannot, as some have done, suppose that Lot had any end in view beyond that which the proposal declares, or that it was due to his perturbation of mind, as Augustine suggests. It seems simply to have had in view the averting of a fearful crime (enhanced in this case by its violating the sacred rights of hospitality) by the permission of another crime, the very thought of which we happily in these Christian days cannot find place for in a father's heart.

9. Stand back] i. e. make way for us to enter the house. So Knobel and Gesenius. Others, as Kalisch, interpret the expression, "*Come hither* (to us)." **he continually judgeth** *us*] i. e. is constantly protesting against our customs and practices. The threat which follows is interpreted by Knobel, that they would smite and kill him, whereas they would only mishandle his guests. But Lange remarks that the following words point to quite another (and a darker) meaning. **10, 11.**] The blindness does not appear to have

door of the house with blindness, both small and great:
so that they wearied themselves to find the door. 12 ¶ And
the men said unto Lot, Hast thou here any one besides?
son in law, and thy sons, and thy daughters, and whatsoever
thou hast in the city, bring *them* out of this
place: 13 for we will destroy this place, because the cry of
them is waxen great before the face of JEHOVAH; and
JEHOVAH hath sent us to destroy it. 14 And Lot went
out, and spake unto his sons in law, which married his
daughters, and said, Up, get you out of this place; for
JEHOVAH will destroy this city. And he was as one that
mocked in the eyes of his sons in law. 15 ¶ And when
the [m] morning [m] arose, then the angels hastened Lot, say- m ch. xxxii. 24, 26. Josh.
ing, Arise, take thy wife, and thy two daughters, which vi. 15. Judg. xix. 25, al.
are here; lest thou be consumed in the iniquity of the
city. 16 And while he lingered, the men laid hold upon
his hand, and upon the hand of his wife, and upon
the hand of his two daughters; JEHOVAH being merciful
unto him: and they brought him forth, and set
him without the city. 17 ¶ And it came to pass, when

been literal and final, but to have consisted in a bewildering of their vision, so that they could not find the door. Augustine well says, Had they been struck blind, they would not have wearied themselves to find the door, but would have ceased to seek for it. **12.**] The mention of the son in law before the sons and daughters is somewhat surprising. Lange has proposed to read thus: "*Hast thou here any besides as son in law?*" (i. e. connected with thee by marriage), and then follows the mention of the members of Lot's own family. And this would certainly be a more probable arrangement. **13.**] Observe that the angels speak of themselves at the same time as free agents, and as being sent by Jehovah with a purpose. This is in strict accord with similar utterances of Divine messengers: see ch. xxxii. 24, ff.; Exod. iii. 1—6.

14.] Lot goes out into the city and addresses the husbands of his (married) daughters, but without effect. There is considerable variety of opinion about these sons in law. Some hold them to have been only betrothed to his two daughters before mentioned: and so the Vulgate renders, "*his sons in law, who were about to receive his daughters.*" So also Josephus, and of the moderns, Kalisch, Keil, Lange, Ewald, &c. On the other hand the LXX. keeps the past tense, and is followed by Rosenmuller, Knobel, and Delitzsch. Certainly, in ver. 15, the "*two daughters which are here*" seem to be distinguished from other daughters who were absent. On the whole the more probable view seems that there were husbands of married daughters living in the cities, whereas his two virgin daughters lived with their father at home.

The appearance of mockery seems to have been not altogether due to the unbelief of the sons in law, but partly to some want of earnestness in Lot's manner. He required *hastening*, vv. 15, 16. **15.**] The **morning** is the *dawn;* the Hebrew root signifies splitting or breaking, the streaks of light breaking up the eastern clouds; and it **arose**, because the dawn advances from the horizon upwards. **which are here** is literally **which are found**, in contradistinction to others of his family who were absent. See above on ver. 14. **thou**] Understand, *and thine:* his family are summed up

they had brought them forth outside, that he said,
Escape for thy life; look not behind thee, neither stay
thou in all the plain; escape to the mountain, lest thou
be consumed. 18 And Lot said unto them, Not so, Lord:
19 Behold now, thy servant hath found grace in thy sight,
and thou hast magnified thy mercy, which thou hast
shewed unto me in saving my life; and I cannot escape to
the mountain, lest the evil overtake me, and I die: 20 be-
hold now, this city *is* near to flee unto, and it *is* a little
one: Oh, let me escape thither, (*is* it not a little one?)
and my soul shall live. 21 And he said unto him, See, I
have accepted thee concerning this thing also, that I will
not overthrow this city, for the which thou hast spoken.
22 Haste thee, escape thither; for I cannot do any thing
till thou be come thither. Therefore the name of the city
was called [n] Zoar. 23 ¶ The sun was risen upon the earth
when Lot entered into Zoar. 24 Then JEHOVAH rained upon

n ch. xiv. 2. Deut. xxxiv. 3. Isa. xv. 5. Jer. xlviii. 34, only.

in him. So ch. xxxiv. 30, "*I being few in number.*" **17.**] The word rendered **plain** is the same as that used in ch. xiii. 10, the country round Jordan, the circle or environs of Jordan. "Lot had once seen the plain of Jordan beautiful like the garden of Eden, and had been tempted to go and dwell there. Now he may not remain in it lest he be destroyed: he must leave his paradise, for it is polluted by sin, and will be overwhelmed by fire." Bp. Wordsworth.

the mountain] Of Moab, eastward of the "circuit." **18, 19.**] Lot has by this time recognized his guests as divine, and has also (possibly by reason of some physical appearance preceding the catastrophe) risen to the apprehension of the fearful destruction which was impending. Hence both the reverence and the urgency of his request. He fears that there will not be time to reach the somewhat distant mountains before the catastrophe. **20, ff.**] The plea that Zoar should be spared rested on the part of its smallness. It would not be a passing by of any great amount of wickedness. Its former name was Bela, ch. xiv. 2, and was after this event changed to Zoar, i. e. *littleness*. About the situation of Zoar there is considerable and, as appears to Mr. Grove (*Biblical Dict.*), irremoveable doubt. It was near enough to Sodom for Lot and his daughters to reach it in less time than that between the dawn and the sunrising: but then, where was Sodom? The plain or circuit of the Jordan seems to have been N. of the Dead Sea (see Mr. Grove's article, as above), but Zoar is usually placed to the S. of it. It is one of the points mentioned as bounding Moses' view from Pisgah, Deut. xxxiv. 3 (see other reff.), and is there connected with "the plain of Jericho." Knobel thinks it is to be sought at the S.E. end of the sea at the mouth of the Wady el Asal. "This spot," he says, "is to this day well watered and full of trees and bushes, but unhealthy: it is inhabited and built over by Arabs who have here a fixed village; in winter it is a gathering-place for more than 10 tribes." See much more in Knobel and *Biblical Dict.*

24.] It has been suggested that the conditions of this terrible description would be fulfilled by lightning from heaven igniting the bituminous material of the soil, and it has been intimated that the buildings themselves of the cities may have been constructed of solid asphalt, and thus have fallen a prey to the fire. But the language of the text seems to imply more than this: at the very least, an eruption of bituminous liquid which fell on the cities. The whole is in such immediate connexion with Divine agency, that it is vain to seek an explanation

Sodom and upon Gomorrah brimstone and fire from JE-
HOVAH out of heaven; 25 and he overthrew those cities,
and all the plain, and all the inhabitants of the cities,
and that which grew upon the ground. 26 ¶ But his wife
looked back from behind him, and she became a pillar of
salt. 27 ¶ And Abraham gat up early in the morning to
the place where he stood before JEHOVAH: 28 and he
looked toward Sodom and Gomorrah, and toward all the
land of the plain, and beheld, and, lo, the smoke of the
country went up as the smoke of a [o] furnace. 29 ¶ And [o] Exod. ix. 8, 10; xix. 18, only.
it came to pass, when Elohim destroyed the cities of the
plain, that Elohim remembered Abraham, and sent Lot

in physical causes only. There is no occasion and no justification for supposing that the double mention of Jehovah in this verse points to a variety of Divine persons. The second, **from Jehovah**, can hardly be otherwise than equivalent to "*from Himself.*" The overthrow of these cities has naturally been matter of long and laborious research, which is by no means as yet rewarded with a definite result. This is not the place even to report the different opinions. Ample information will be found in Mr. Grove's article "Sodom" in *Smith's Biblical Dict.*, and in Kalisch's commentary. Two remarks may be made for the reader's guidance: 1. That there is no reason to suppose the cities to have been sunk beneath or overflowed by the Dead Sea; 2. That all evidence tends to shew them to have been N. of the lake, not S., as commonly supposed. Besides Sodom and Gomorrah, Admah and Zeboim were destroyed. See Deut. xxix. 23.

25.] **the plain** again is the circle or environs of Jordan. **26.**] Lot's wife looked longingly back (the word is said to imply a steady earnest look). The pillar of salt is spoken of in the Apocryphal Book of Wisdom, x. 7, "Of whose (the cities') wickedness even to this day the waste land that smoketh is a testimony, and plants bearing fruit that never come to ripeness: and a standing pillar of salt is a monument of an unbelieving soul." Josephus relates that it was standing in his time. The same is asserted by Fathers of the Church, and even modern travellers have not been wanting who have deposed to the same. We may observe, in the spirit of Mr. Grove's article "Lot" in the *Biblical Dict.*, that no details are given us here at all furnishing a foundation for the legends, and tales of travellers, which have been built upon the history. "There is no attempt in the narrative to invest the circumstance with permanence; no statement, as in the case of the pillar erected over Rachel's grave (xxxv. 20), that it was to be seen at the time of the compilation of the history. And in this we surely have an example of that sobriety which characterizes the statements of Scripture, even where the events narrated are most out of the ordinary course." And these remarks are confirmed by the fact, that the salt rock which splits into upright pillars, and which seems to have furnished material for the tales of travellers, lies at the S. end of the Dead Sea, whereas it has been observed above that the "cities of the plain" must have been at the N. end. **27.**] See on ch. xviii. 22. The simple and graphic account shews the entireness of Abraham's faith. He fully expects that the Divine purpose had been accomplished. That which we saw as a proof of this shews that not submersion by water, but combustion by fire, was the method of destruction used. No words could more aptly describe the effect of the igniting of the bituminous matter in the plain than these. This description was manifestly before the prophet Isaiah when he wrote the terrible threat against Edom, xxxiv. 9. **29.**] *Elohistic summary of this history.* This verse is one of the most remarkable instances of an independent and summary account worked into the midst of another and detailed one. It may almost be described as the crucial experiment of the view which I cannot help adopting, viz. that

out of the midst of the overthrow, when he overthrew the
cities in the which Lot dwelt. 30 ¶ And Lot went up out of
Zoar, and dwelt in the mountain, and his two daughters
with him; for he feared to dwell in Zoar: and he dwelt
in a cave, he and his two daughters. 31 And the firstborn
said unto the younger, Our father *is* old, and *there is* not a
man in the earth to come in unto us after the manner of
all the earth: 32 come, let us make our father drink wine,
and we will lie with him, that we may preserve seed of
our father. 33 And they made their father drink wine
that night: and the firstborn went in, and lay with her
father; and he perceived not when she lay down, nor
when she arose. 34 And it came to pass on the morrow,
that the firstborn said unto the younger, Behold, I lay
yesternight with my father: let us make him drink wine
this night also; and go thou in, *and* lie with him, that we
may preserve seed of our father. 35 And they made their
father drink wine that night also: and the younger
arose, and lay with him; and he perceived not when she
lay down, nor when she arose. 36 Thus were both the
daughters of Lot with child by their father. 37 And the
firstborn bare a son, and called his name Moab: the
same *is* the father of the Moabites unto this day. 38 And

this ancient sacred book is made up of Elohistic and Jehovistic materials inwrought and alternated one with the other. Those who question this have to account for the remarkable phenomenon, that on the occurrence of any such summary recapitulation as this we have simultaneously occurring the change of the Divine name from Jehovah to Elohim. There is, in this summary, nothing inconsistent with the detailed account in the midst of which it appears.

30—38.] *The incestuous origin of Moab and Ammon.* **30.**] Lot seems to have been afraid lest Zoar, itself in the burning plain, might, though temporarily spared for his sake, eventually fall a prey to the destruction. He therefore accomplishes the journey which at first he deprecated, and flees to the mountain. This neighbourhood is to this day full of holes and caves. See the interesting article on Caves by Mr. Phillott, in *Smith's Biblical Dict.*

31.] On the vain attempt which has been made by some out of these words, **our father is old**, to construct an argument justifying Stephen's assertion, Acts vii. 4, see note, ch. xii. 1. **37, 38.**] The mother names the child as in ch. xvi. 11. The names, **Moab**, "*from the father*," or "*seed of the father*" (the LXX. add, "*saying, He is by my father*"), and **Ben-ammi**, "*son of my people*" (the LXX. add, "*saying, He is the son of my family*"), contain in themselves traces of the incestuous origin.

On the subsequent history of the Moabites and Ammonites and their hostile encounters with the Israelites, see Mr. Grove's admirable articles in the *Biblical Dict.* It may suffice here to remind the reader that by the Mosaic law, Deut. xxiii. 3—6, inexorable hatred to these two races was enjoined on the children of Israel, not in any reference to their incestuous origin, but because of their hostile conduct to Israel on the way from Egypt. As Kalisch well remarks, "No

the younger, she also bare a son, and called his name
Ben-ammi: the same *is* the father of the children of Am-
mon [p] unto this day. XX. 1 And Abraham journeyed
from thence toward the south country, and dwelled be-
tween Kadesh and Shur, and sojourned in Gerar. 2 And
Abraham said of Sarah his wife, She *is* my sister: and
Abimelech king of Gerar sent, and took Sarah. 3 But
Elohim came to Abimelech in a dream by night, and said
to him, Behold, thou *art but* a dead man, for the woman
which thou hast taken; for she *is* a man's wife. 4 But

[p] ch. xxvi. 33; xxxii. 32; xlvii. 26, al.

word is employed, no allusion made, in the whole of this tale to express disgust, aversion, or hatred: the laws concerning the allowed and forbidden degrees were not yet fixed: Abraham himself lived in a matrimony cursed as an abomination in the Mosaic code (Lev. xviii. 9): the event is related with all the calmness of historical composition." And it must also not be forgotten that in Deut. ii. 9—19, the possessions of the "children of Lot" in Ar and in the land of Ammon are recognized by God, and the Israelites are forbidden to distress or meddle with them. But at the same time the very necessity which there was for bereaving Lot of his self-command shew us beneath the surface that his "righteous soul," even though it could brook much which nature now abhors (see on ver. 8), could not have been brought to consent to that into which he was unconsciously betrayed. The words "unto this day" are noticed as occurring in the portions of the book due to the later supplementary documents: see reff.

XX., XXI. *Abraham at Gerar.* And herein (xx. 1—18) *his second deceit concerning Sarah.* Elohistic. The former account of his deceit in Egypt was, it is to be noticed, Jehovistic. 1.] On **Kadesh** see note, ch. xiv. 7, and on **Shur**, note, ch. xvi. 7. The site of **Gerar** appears to have been found "in a shallow wady (valley) three hours S.S.E. of Gaza: it is now called Khirbet-el-Gerar, *the ruins of Gerar.* At the spot are traces of an ancient city. This is all the information given by the Rev. J. Rowlands, who, so far as I know, is the only person who has as yet visited it." Porter, Handbook of Palestine. The people were Philistines (ch. xxi. 32, 34; xxvi. 1, 14, 15, 18), pastoral (ch. xxvi. 20) but warlike (ver. 22; ch. xxvi. 26). It is to be noticed, however, that in this earlier portion of the Elohistic narrative the name Philistine does not occur, only first at ch. xxi. 32—34. The removal of Abraham from Hebron is traced by some to the proximity of the accursed territory of the cities of the plain. Kalisch remarks, that he was "reminded by their catastrophe that he ought not to bind up his fate too closely with that of any heathen town, and that he should never cease to regard himself as a stranger in a strange land." The **south country** is the district called the *Negeb* (ch. xii. 9; xiii. 1, al.) or dry country. His general abode was limited between Kadesh and Shur, and, at a particular time, he pitched his tent in Gerar. **2.**] Sarah was at this time upwards of 90 years old, ch. xvii. 17. But it must not be forgotten that she had "received strength to conceive seed," and after this bare and nursed Isaac. As usual, some of the commentators, more anxious to shield the Father of the faithful than to deal as Scripture has dealt with him, see in this his second act of deceit an act of faith in God (!) If this were so, it is strange that his faith did not advance a step further and believe that God could preserve Sarah without his lie. **Abimelech**, *the father king*, appears to have been the standing title of the kings of Gerar. He took Sarah, i. e. into his harem, anxious, say some, to be connected in marriage with so powerful a chief as Abraham. But this is mere fancy. **3. thou art a dead man**] i. e. thy sickness (vv. 6, 17) shall issue in death. **the woman**] Or, the wife. **a man's wife**] lit. ruled over by a lord: but the word is used ordinarily of marriage, e. g. in Deut. xxi. 13; xxiv. 1; Isa. lxii. 5; Mal. ii. 11. **4.**] Abimelech's re-

Abimelech had not come near her: and he said, Lord,
wilt thou slay also a righteous nation? 5 Said he not
unto me, She *is* my sister? and she, even she herself said,
He *is* my brother: in the integrity of my heart and in-
nocency of my hands have I done this. 6 And the Elohim
said unto him in a dream, Yea, I know that thou didst this
in the integrity of thy heart; for I also withheld thee from
sinning against me: therefore suffered I thee not to touch
her. 7 Now therefore restore the man's wife; for he *is* a
prophet, and he shall pray for thee, and thou shalt live:
and if thou restore *her* not, know thou that thou shalt
surely die, thou, and all that *are* thine. 8 Therefore
Abimelech rose early in the morning, and called all his
servants, and told all these things in their ears: and the
men were sore afraid. 9 Then Abimelech called Abra-
ham, and said unto him, What hast thou done unto us?
and what have I offended thee, that thou hast brought on
me and on my kingdom a great sin? thou hast done
deeds unto me that ought not to be done. 10 And Abime-
lech said unto Abraham, What sawest thou, that thou
hast done this thing? 11 And Abraham said, Because I
said, Surely the fear of Elohim *is* not in this place; and
they will slay me for my wife's sake. 12 And yet indeed
she is my sister; she *is* the daughter of my father, but not
the daughter of my mother; and she became my wife.

monstrance shews, beneath the surface of the narrative, that the terrible example of the Sodomites had wrought its effect on the neighbouring tribes. He prides himself on his people being free from the sins which had drawn down vengeance on the cities of the plain, and uses much the same argument as Abraham in ch. xviii. 23. He uses the name ADONAI, Lord: see on ch. xviii. 3.

5.] As morality was then understood, Abimelech had committed no crime in taking Sarah, believing her to be Abraham's sister. Nay, he stood justified in comparison with the other parties; there is doubtless a hint of moral guilt in his reference to their part in the transaction. **6.**] See on vv. 17, 18 below. **7.**] This verse is in every way remarkable. It lets us into the wonderful relation of Abraham, the called, and the depositary of the promise, to God. He is said to be a **prophet**, occupying a place of especial favour, so that his intercession would avail with God. And no less remarkable are those that follow, in which the heathen king reproves the prophet, the Friend of God, by an appeal to those first principles of moral right which bind prophets and heathens alike: "thou hast done deeds with me that ought not to be done." Abimelech shines throughout this narrative. His public announcement of the facts to his servants is the act of an injured man conscious of his own rectitude and desirous thoroughly to clear himself. **10. what sawest thou**] i. e. what object hadst thou in view? **11, ff.**] Abimelech's questions were more detailed and required more account to be given than those of Pharaoh in ch. xii., which amounted to little more than a remonstrance. **12.**] Regarding this re-

13 And it came to pass, when Elohim caused me to wander
from my father's house, that I said unto her, This *is* thy
kindness which thou shalt shew unto me; at every place
whither we shall come, say of me, He *is* my brother.
14 And Abimelech took sheep, and oxen, and menservants,
and womenservants, and gave *them* unto Abraham, and
restored him Sarah his wife. 15 And Abimelech said,
Behold, my land *is* before thee: dwell where it pleaseth
thee. 16 And unto Sarah he said, Behold, I have given
thy brother a thousand *pieces* of silver: behold, it *is* to
thee a covering of the eyes, unto all that *are* with thee,
and with all *other*: thus thou art righted. 17 ¶ So
Abraham prayed unto the Elohim: and Elohim healed
Abimelech, and his wife, and his maidservants; and they
bare *children*. 18 For JEHOVAH had fast closed up all the
wombs of the house of Abimelech, because of Sarah Abra-
ham's wife. XXI. 1 And JEHOVAH [q] visited Sarah as he

q ch. l. 24. Exod. iii. 16; iv.13; xiii. 19.

lationship, see on ch. xi. 29, and on its moral significance in our estimate of Abraham's sin, see on ch. xii. 10—20. **13.**] We have in this verse the rare occurrence of a plural verb with the name of God, Elohim, itself a plural form. Those who distinguish different writers in the Pentateuch profess to find this construction only in the portions due to this writer, e. g. ch. xxxv. 7; Exod. xxii. 8; xxxii. 4, 8; and in Josh. xxiv. 19. **14.**] Abimelech is anxious to make restitution for the wrong done to both Abraham and Sarah.
16.] The meaning of the latter part of the verse is much disputed. Kalisch renders, "*Behold, he is to thee a protection to all who are with thee, and with all, and thou wilt be recognized;*" and explains, "he gave to Abraham for her a thousand shekels of silver (for the property of the wife belonged to the husband), and addressed to her a remark embodying the experience he had just made, and the respect with which it inspired him (ver. 18); he said that though she might profess Abraham was her brother, he was her protection against every man; she might be taken by others as his sister, but she would be soon known and convicted of being his wife by the supernatural interference of God." On the other hand, Knobel renders, "It (the gift of 1000 shekels) is to thee a covering of eyes (i. e. shall shut thine eyes that they see not, i. e. shall blind thee that thou care not for what has happened, i. e. shall reconcile and make amends to thee) in reference to all which is with thee and with all (i. e. which has happened to thee and thy companions); thus thou art righted (thine injury atoned for). Similarly Keil, Delitzsch, and Lange. I have therefore preferred this rendering. The LXX. gives it, "*These shall be to thee for an honour of thy countenance, and to all the women that are with thee; and speak the truth in all things.*" The Vulgate, "*This shall be to thee for a veil of the eyes to all that are with thee, and wheresoever thou shalt go; and remember that thou hast been detected.*" **17, 18.**] These verses are to be taken with reference to both sexes. God had visited all with incapacity, which visitation was now removed. The last verse is treated as an addition by way of explanation, on account of the name Jehovah occurring in it only of the whole narrative. However this may be, let the reader beware of the supposed significance in the use of the names of God, so ingeniously found out by some commentators. Any such fancies can be justified by any moderately ingenious person; and in one of the latest commentaries it has been done here by passing entirely over verses 11 and 13, which stood in its way.

had said, and JEHOVAH did unto Sarah as he had spoken.
2 For Sarah conceived, and bare Abraham a son in his old
age, at the set time of which Elohim had spoken to him.
3 And Abraham called the name of his son that was born
unto him, whom Sarah bare to him, Isaac. 4 And Abra-
ham circumcised his son Isaac being eight days old, as
Elohim had commanded him. 5 And Abraham was an
hundred years old, when his son Isaac was born unto him.
6 ¶ And Sarah said, Laughter hath Elohim prepared for
me: all that hear will laugh with me. 7 And she said,
Who would have said unto Abraham, that Sarah should
have given children suck? for I have born *him* a son in
his old age. 8 And the child grew, and was weaned: and
Abraham made a great feast the *same* day that Isaac was
weaned. 9 ¶ And Sarah saw the son of Hagar the
Egyptian, which she had born unto Abraham, mocking.
10 Wherefore she said unto Abraham, Cast out this bond-

XXI. **1—7.**] *Birth and circumcision of Isaac.* The whole of this chapter, with the exception of ver. 1 and vv. 33, 34, belongs to the Elohistic narrative. Those verses have apparently been inserted to fill in and complete the history from Jehovistic sources.

1.] It is said (Knobel) that this sense of the word **visit**, as used of God, is found in the Jehovistic portions only: see reff. In the Elohistic portions (but not in them exclusively) we have the word "*remember*" used for the same idea: see ch. viii. 1, and reff. **2.**] On this **set time**, see ch. xvii. 21. **3.**] This had been pre-ordained, ch. xvii. 19, and the name given, signifying "*laughter*," on account of Abraham's laughing, as there related. See below. **6.**] The laughter after which Isaac had been named (ch. xvii. 17, and we may add ch. xviii. 12) had been that of incredulity; but God's abounding mercy had turned weakness into strength, and made his name an accompaniment of the laughter of joy. To relating this glad result both the narratives contribute: the Elohistic record in ch. xvii. and here, and the Jehovistic in ch. xviii. There is in this little song of thanksgiving (Sarah's *Magnificat*, as Bp. Wordsworth calls it) a poetical character, both in the form of the Hebrew words used and in its arrangement by parallels. To suppose that it was uttered at the moment of Isaac's birth, and that ver. 7 should be "Who will tell Abraham?" &c., is inappropriate. Women do not give their children suck at the time of birth, nor indeed are certain that they shall do so.

8—21.] *Expulsion of Hagar and Ishmael.*

8.] The weaning was often as much as three years (see 2 Macc. vii. 27), or even more, after birth. From 1 Sam. i. 22, compared with ii. 11, it would appear that Samuel was not weaned till he was old enough to be left with Eli, which hardly could be so early as at three. This would make Ishmael sixteen years old or more at the time. The occasion is still kept in the East as a family *feast*. The word so rendered is the same as in ch. xix. 3, where see note. **9.**] One can hardly believe, with the LXX., Vulgate, Knobel, and Gesenius, that the word rendered mocking merely means *playing*, as is the wont of children. It comes from the same root as the name Isaac itself, and might in another context bear such a meaning (as e.g. in Exod. xxxii. 6; Judg. xvi. 25; ch. xxvi. 8); but here there is certainly that beneath the surface of the narrative which should give it the meaning of laughing offensively, mocking, as in ch. xix. 14; xxxix. 14, 17. Certainly St. Paul so understood it, Gal. iv. 29, where he says that "he that was born after the flesh *persecuted* him that was after the

woman and her son: for the son of this bondwoman shall
not be heir with my son, with Isaac. 11 And the thing
was very grievous in Abraham's sight because of his son.
12 ¶ And Elohim said unto Abraham, Let it not be griev-
ous in thy sight because of the lad, and because of thy
bondwoman; in all that Sarah hath said unto thee,
hearken unto her voice; for in Isaac shall thy seed be
called. 13 And also of the son of the bondwoman will I
make a nation, because he *is* thy seed. 14 And Abraham
rose up early in the morning, and took bread, and a skin
of water, and gave *it* unto Hagar, putting *it* on her
shoulder, and the boy, and sent her away: and she de-
parted, and wandered in the wilderness of Beer-sheba.
15 And the water was spent in the bottle, and she cast
the boy under one of the shrubs. 16 And she went, and
sat her down over against *him* at the distance as it were of
a bowshot: for she said, Let me not see the death of the
boy. And she sat over against *him*, and lifted up her
voice, and wept. 17 And Elohim heard the voice of the

Spirit." The narrative does not say, but it may easily be supplied, that Hagar was abetting her son's insolence. The Christian reader will remember the allegorization of this whole history in the passage of St. Paul just referred to. On this matter, see notes there. **11.**] This notice is in exact and characteristic accordance with Abraham's yearning expressed ch. xvii. 18, "Oh that Ishmael might live before thee!"

12.] **in Isaac** (i. e. in the line of Isaac,—not in the line of Ishmael) **shall thy seed** (those who are truly thy descendants, and above all the seed of promise) **be called** (this shall be the line where all that are so named shall be found). **13.**] The same had been promised even more in detail, ch. xvii. 20. It seemed to be a specialty of Abraham's descendants to multiply into nations; the very fact of descent from him is alleged as a reason why Ishmael should become one. **14.**] The divine injunction had taken place in the night, as in ch. xv. 1; xx. 3, 6; xxii. 1; xxvi. 24; xxxi. 11, 24; xlvi. 2. This immediate and energetic obedience is characteristic of Abraham: see ch. xxii. 3, and compare Matt. ii. 14, 21. Some misunderstanding has arisen in interpreting this verse. The LXX. render, "*and he placed the child on her shoulder:*" so also the Targum of Onkelos, the Samaritan Pentateuch, and the ancient Syriac version: so also many commentators. But such a rendering is not necessary, nor is it adopted by the Vulgate nor by most of the principal Hebraists. The lad was led by the hand: see ver. 18. The leathern bottle, as may be seen to this day in the East, and indeed in the S. of Europe, is made of the whole skin of an animal (in this case of course of a small one, such as a goat or kid), the fore leg serving as the tap, and the neck as the mouth of the bottle. **Beer-sheba** is here named by anticipation: see below, ver. 31. Perhaps she wandered hopelessly forth into the wilderness. But the direction was towards her native Egypt, and thither she may have intended to direct her course. Ver. 21 shews that her connexion with it was afterwards re-established. **15.**] **she cast the boy** need not imply that he was a mere child, but only that he was *as* such at this time, exhausted with thirst and powerless. The whole description is most vivid in life and pathos. She would not see his death, and yet she would not let him be altogether out of her presence. **17.**] The

lad; and an angel of Elohim called to Hagar from
heaven, and said unto her, What aileth thee, Hagar?
fear not; for Elohim hath heard the voice of the lad
where he *is*. 18 Arise, lift up the lad, and hold him by
thine hand; for I will make him a great nation. 19 And
Elohim opened her eyes, and she saw a well of water;
and she went, and filled the skin with water, and gave the
lad drink. 20 And Elohim was with the lad; and he
grew, and dwelt in the wilderness, and became a great
archer. 21 And he dwelt in the wilderness of Paran: and
his mother took him a wife out of the land of Egypt.
22 ¶ And it came to pass at that time, that Abimelech
and Phichol the chief captain of his host spake unto
Abraham, saying, Elohim *is* with thee in all that thou
doest: 23 now therefore swear unto me here by Elohim
that thou wilt not deal falsely with me, nor with my son,
nor with my son's son: according to the kindness that I
have done unto thee, thou shalt do unto me, and to the
land wherein thou hast sojourned. 24 And Abraham said,
I will swear. 25 And Abraham reproved Abimelech be-
cause of a well of water, which Abimelech's servants had
violently taken away. 26 And Abimelech said, I wot not

weeping of the lad has not been mentioned, but is naturally understood. **where he is**] lit. **there, where he is**. This would seem as if the distance was considerable.

18.] She was to help him up, in token that he was not to die, but to be reserved for great ends. **19.**] The impression conveyed is that God created a spring of water near her, but this is not necessarily conveyed in the words. It may be that there was a spring near, which she had not seen before in her weariness and despair. **21.**] On the wilderness of Paran, see on Num. x. 12.

22—34.] *The covenant between Abraham and Abimelech.* Abimelech, see ch. xx. 14, 15, had learned that Abraham was favoured of God, and no doubt knew the promise of future greatness that awaited his seed: he is therefore anxious to make a lasting covenant with him. **23.**] **son, and son's son** are literally **offspring and progeny**: Prof. Murphy renders, *kin and kith*. The two Hebrew words mean the same thing, and are found together in two other places, Job xviii. 19 and Isa. xiv. 22, in both which they are rendered by "*son*" and "*nephew*." **25.**] A covenant has two sides, and Abraham proceeds to enforce the part due to him also. Kalisch observes on the passage: "One may hence infer (from Abraham's oath to Abimelech) that for some time at least the southern part of Philistia was not attacked by the Hebrews. But, though the Philistines were never subjugated by them, it is certain that almost incessant hostilities were carried on between both nations. Thus, immediately after the conclusion of the alliance, a contention arose which threatened to result in serious enmity. Abimelech's servants had violently seized a well dug by Abraham. A more serious injury can scarcely be inflicted on a nomad chief, rich in flocks and herds. The possession of a well in arid regions not unfrequently causes strife and warfare between whole tribes, and the protection of his wells is a prominent object of solicitude to an Arab sheikh. Abimelech, therefore, perceived fully the force of Abraham's complaint: he

who hath done this thing: neither didst thou tell me,
neither yet heard I *of it*, but to day. 27 And Abraham
took sheep and oxen, and gave them unto Abimelech;
and both of them made a covenant. 28 And Abraham set
seven ewe lambs of the flock by themselves. 29 And
Abimelech said unto Abraham, What *mean* these seven
ewe lambs which thou hast set by themselves? 30 And
he said, Because thou shalt take *these* seven ewe lambs of
my hand, that they may be a witness unto me, that I have
digged this well. 31 Wherefore he called that place
Beer-sheba; because there they sware both of them.
32 Thus they made a covenant at Beer-sheba: then
Abimelech rose up, and Phichol the chief captain of his
host, and they returned into the land of the Philistines.
33 ¶ And *Abraham* planted a [r] grove in Beer-sheba, and called there on the name of JEHOVAH, the everlasting God. r 1 Sam. xxii. 6; xxxi. 13.
34 And Abraham sojourned in the Philistines' land many
days. XXII. 1 And it came to pass after these things,

was indignant at the injustice of his slaves, of which he had never before been informed. But the patriarch, desirous of obtaining a guarantee which might in future shield his property against Abimelech's subjects also, conducted him to the well (vv. 31, 32), and here concluded with him a treaty, by dividing animals, and passing between the dissected parts; but in order to impart still greater solemnity to the ceremony, he gave besides *seven* lambs to Abimelech, to serve as a proof and a witness that the well belonged to himself." **31.**] **Beer-sheba** (Heb. in this and the other early notices of the place, **Beer shabah**) may mean either *the well of the oath*, as *here* interpreted, or *the well of seven* (from the seven lambs of vv. 29, 30), which is in fact the same thing (seven being the sacred number of completion): see on ch. xxvi. 33. The spot is one of the most interesting in Palestine. It meets the traveller as he enters from the south, and retains its ancient name "as nearly as an Arabic signification will permit, *Bir-es-sebâ*—'the well of the lion,' or, 'of seven.' There are at present on the spot two principal wells, and five smaller ones." Mr. Grove, *Biblical Dict.*, where is a full description. The history of this spot will be dealt with at the various mentions of it: see especially ch. xxvi. 33; 1 Sam. viii. 2; 2 Sam. xxiv. 7; 1 Kings xix. 3; Amos v. 5; viii. 14; Neh. xi. 30. **32.**] From the presence of the captain of the host, we may infer that the covenant was accompanied with official solemnity. It is inferred by Knobel that the mention of the **land of the Philistines** betrays the commencement of the Jehovistic supplement at this verse, which beyond question includes the two following. **33.**] **a grove** best represents the sense of the word *aishel*, which in its simple sense means a tamarisk tree. It occurs only in reff. besides. The title of God here used, the everlasting God, the God of the age, i. e. eternity, is found only in Isa. xl. 28 besides this place. St. Paul uses the equivalent Greek epithet in Rom. xvi. 26. **34.**] During these **many days** Isaac grew up from a child to such an age that he was able to bear the wood for the offering, ch. xxii. 6.

XXII. **1—19.**] *Abraham's obedience to God.* The general remarks of Kalisch are worth quoting: "The readiness of Abraham to sacrifice his son has always been considered as the greatest deed of faith on record, and as an act of self-control at which the mind stands amazed. It became the basis on which the Israelites founded their claims of election among the nations, and the later Jews their hopes of atonement; it

s Exod. xv. 25; xvi. 4; xx. 20. Ps. xxvi. 2.

that the Elohim did [s] try Abraham, and said unto him, Abraham: and he said, Behold, *here* I *am*. 2 And he said, Take now thy son, thine only one, whom thou lovest, Isaac, and get thee into the land of Moriah; and offer

served the Christians as a type of redemption, and salvation through faith; and it is in the religion of Mohammed glorified as the highest example and model of piety. It has indeed exercised a powerful and ennobling influence upon almost all nations and all times."

This section at first sight seems due to the Elohistic portion of this book, but on examination this impression is changed. As Knobel well remarks, nothing but the sacred name Elohim favours such an idea. Everything is full of the Jehovistic character. The strong anthropomorphism, exemplified in God trying Abraham (ver. 1), satisfying Himself by the trial (ver. 12), swearing (ver. 16), and numerous other details dependent on the use of Hebrew words and expressions, plainly declare which portion of the sacred book is before us. The use of the divine names, as in several other cases, is matter of accurate and careful discrimination, as will be seen in the course of the notes.

1.] **after these things** casts the thought back upon the events recently narrated—the long course of indefinite promise—the shorter period during which the promise had become definite and specified—the birth of the son of promise, and his waxing onward amidst the joy and hope of his parents. When all this was at its climax, and trial seemed over, then . . . . **God tried Abraham,** . . . . with a trial of such magnitude that it seemed as if he had never been tried before. **God**] ÈLOHIM. This name is used throughout the former portion of the narrative, in which the general God-fearing of Abraham is in question, and in which God appears as the instigator of a practice foreign to the Covenant in virtue of which His sacred name was Jehovah,—a practice common to the nations outside the Covenant. See further on ver. 11. **did try Abraham**] See reff. The vision was by night: see ver. 3. The command came,—there is no escape from the plain fact,—not from any thought of Abraham's mind, but from God, the true God, Himself. It was one of those mysterious, but surely not to be doubted, communications from the Father of man's spirit, in which he tries and proves His creatures, and none so much as those nearest to Himself. Everything was against the probability of this command being from God. Abraham knew, quite as well as modern rationalists, the cogent à priori reasons why such a command should not, could not (he might be disposed by his own reason to say) proceed from God. But the fact that it did so proceed overbore all à priori considerations, and herein consisted the nobility of Abraham's faith. And is there not abundant analogy for such a proceeding on the part of God? What seems so cruel and uncalled-for as the removal of many a beloved desire of man's eyes with a stroke, and for the same purpose as the command here was given? **2.**] Each designation mounts upward in climax after the other: **thy son, thine only one,—whom thou lovest, Isaac,** the personal designation coming last, and clenching as it were the identification of the very heir of the promise himself. There was in the command no softening, but rather all aggravation, of the trial. **the land of Moriah**] About the situation of this country there is considerable controversy. The landmarks to guide us through it seem to be these: 1. We must search, not for a hill, but for a district. 2. One condition of its genuineness is that it should contain a mountain ("*the place of which God told him*"), visible afar off (ver. 4). And 3. This at three days' journey (at most) from the Philistines' land (not from Beersheba necessarily, for we have no right to assume that Abraham continued to dwell there; indeed, by one ver., 19, it seems improbable that he did). 4. The place was solitary. Abraham left the servants and advanced to it with Isaac alone, to avoid human eyes witnessing what should then take place. Now when with these guides we come to the controversy, we find two rival spots with claims to be adjudged. (*a*) Mount Moriah, where in after-ages Solomon's temple was built: 2 Chron. iii. 1, "Then Solomon began to build the house of Jehovah at Jerusalem in Mount Moriah, where Jehovah appeared unto David his father, in the

him there for a burnt offering upon one of the mountains
which I will tell thee of. 3 ¶ And Abraham rose up
early in the morning, and saddled his ass, and took two
of his young men with him, and Isaac his son, and clave
the wood for the burnt offering, and rose up, and went
unto the place of which the Elohim had told him. 4 Then
on the third day Abraham lifted up his eyes, and saw the
place afar off. 5 And Abraham said unto his young men,
Abide ye here with the ass; and I and the lad will go

place that David had prepared in the threshing-floor of Ornan the Jebusite. And such has been in the main the Jewish, and also the Christian, tradition. The temptation to adopt and defend it has been great both to Jews and to Christians: to the former because it adds another glory to the city of their solemnities, to the latter because of typical associations connecting this sacrifice with that greater one offered in the fulness of time at Jerusalem. But there are weighty considerations against this view: the first and greatest being that in no one place of Scripture, and not, as is plain from the quotation above, in that place where of all others we should look for it, is there the slightest intimation of this sacred association having been connected with the spot. Commentators of strong fancy, e. g. the excellent Bp. Wordsworth, speak of this opinion as "grounded on" 2 Chron. iii. 1, but, as has been seen, without a shadow of a reason. If we apply to this view the tests above enumerated, the case will stand thus: The district in which the temple elevation is found is certainly mountainous, but the particular spot is so far from being seen afar off, that it is surrounded by higher eminences preventing its being seen till one is very near upon it. The third test, that it should be three days' journey, at most, from the Philistines' land, may be said to be satisfied. The distance of Jerusalem from Beer-sheba and its neighbourhood is about 40 miles, which might be divided into 15, 15, and 10. The fourth test, that of solitude, tries this hypothesis severely. If the temple elevation were the place it would be certainly close to, if not part of, the Jebusite city. It is a remarkable feature of the history of this idea, that Christian tradition, for the purposes of its typology, shifted the place from Moriah in Jerusalem to Calvary, and still shows it, even to the thicket in which the ram was caught, close to the church of the Holy Sepulchre. (*b*) The second candidate for identity with the spot of Abraham's sacrifice is Mount Gerizim, over Shechem, or Nablous. There Abraham had dwelt on his first entrance into Canaan; there *Jehovah* had appeared to him, and he had built an altar to him (ch. xii. 5) under the oak of Moreh (see note there). The spot well satisfies the test of being conspicuous from afar off, and is perhaps within the required distance from some parts of the Philistines' land, though not from Beer-sheba (being nearly 80 miles of). The requirement of solitude would also be abundantly satisfied. The strongest point against it, in my mind, is that it is the spot fixed on by Samaritan tradition, which held that "in this mountain men ought to worship, and not in Jerusalem." But this is by no means decisive. And it is curious that the same expression (Machom) which designated Sichem in ch. xii. 6, "*the place of Sichem*," is twice used here in the narrative, "*the place* of which God had told him," "saw *the place* afar off." On the whole, we may venture to say that the matter must be still regarded as a doubtful one. The discussion may be seen well given in Mr. Grove's art. "Moriah" and Mr. Ffoulkes's "Gerizim" in the *Biblical Dict.* **3.**] See on ch. xxi. 14. **4.**] At what time on the third day is not said, but Mr. Grove's remark on ver. 5, that we are not told how many more days were required to reach the spot, is hardly justified by the context, which seems to imply that the place was at all events so near as to make the presence of the young men from that point undesirable; besides that the details, the laying the wood on Isaac, and the taking the *fire*, are against the idea of a considerable distance intervening. It is doubtless in the interest of the Gerizim

yonder and worship, and come again to you. 6 And
Abraham took the wood of the burnt offering, and laid *it*
upon Isaac his son; and he took the fire in his hand, and
the knife; and they went both of them together. 7 And
Isaac spake unto Abraham his father, and said, My
father: and he said, Here *am* I, my son. And he said,
Behold the fire and the wood: but where *is* the lamb for
a burnt offering? 8 And Abraham said, My son, Elohim
will provide himself a lamb for a burnt offering: and
they went both of them together. 9 And they came to
the place which the Elohim had told him of; and Abra-
ham built an altar there, and laid the wood in order, and
bound Isaac his son, and laid him on the altar upon the

hypothesis to lengthen the time of the journey; but the text will hardly bear it. It would seem that Abraham had some presentiment that the lad's life would be spared. Some fancy that his words were a mere excuse without truth, and refer to his dealing in Egypt and at Gerar. Nor would the inconsistency even at such a time be past example. One part of the moral being may be intensely alive, while another is dead and without sensation. **the fire**, which Abraham took in his hand, was a brand, or torch, kindled at the spot where he left the servants. This is entirely against the idea that the distance from that spot to the place of sacrifice might have been a day's journey or more. **7, 8.**] All commentators have remarked on the pathos and grandeur of these verses. The repetition of **his father, my father, my son**;—the artlessness of Isaac's question, — the high resignation of Abraham's answer, and then the result, repeated from before, and (notwithstanding, — still) **they went both of them together**, the father in his noble resolve, the son in his trusting simplicity, these mark the sacred narrative as standing in the very first place for truth and for power. This whole incident is to the Christian mind full of type and suggestion of the most sacred kind. All the more should our fancy be kept in check in interpreting details. The minute parallelizing of these with the majestic facts of our redemption, as carried out by some commentators, tends only to cast dishonour on the joy of the Christian heart, with which the stranger intermeddleth not. I refrain from giving instances throughout, as they might be culled from modern commentaries. I would simply warn the reader by way of example against such fancies as that when Abraham said, "God will provide Himself a lamb for a burnt offering," he "with the eye of faith, quickened by God's Spirit, saw Christ." This, which is Bp. Wordsworth's view, is a violation of the far more reverent tact of St. Ambrose, whom he quotes to justify it, but who says, "Abraham prophesied in substance, not in consciousness." This we are all ready to allow, while we instinctively shrink from that other. It is a more interesting and safer question for us, whether Abraham in these words contemplated any such deliverance as that which really took place. From his subsequent ready compliance in act, it would seem that we must answer this in the negative, and must take refuge in the assurance of the writer to the Hebrews that Abraham "accounted that God was able to raise Isaac up, even from the dead." It is refreshing, after reading long pages of notes full of forced analogies and unreal parallelisms, to go back to the manly simplicity of the apostolic writer, and to feel that here we are on ground common to all who have the faith of Abraham and of Christ. **9.**] God then had revealed to him not only the locality, but the very spot. And it would hardly be the same as that where he had built an altar before (ch. xii. 6, 7), or we should rather read that he *repaired* the altar which he had built. He built an altar, viz. by gathering

wood. 10 And Abraham stretched forth his hand, and
took the knife to slay his son. 11 And an angel of
JEHOVAH called unto him out of heaven, and said, Abra-
ham, Abraham: and he said, Here *am* I. 12 And he
said, Lay not thine hand upon the lad, neither do thou
any thing unto him: for now I know that thou fearest
Elohim, seeing thou hast not withheld thy son, thine only
one, from me. 13 And Abraham lifted up his eyes, and
looked, and behold behind *him* a ram caught in a thicket
by his horns: and Abraham went and took the ram, and
offered him up for a burnt offering in the stead of his son.
14 And Abraham called the name of that place Jehovah-
jireh (i. e. Jehovah seeth): as it is said *to* this day, In the
mount of JEHOVAH it shall be seen. 15 ¶ And an angel of

and building up the stones lying on the mountain-top, a work of a very short time.

10.] The pictures are perhaps hardly right which represent him with the knife elevated to strike his son. Rather may we imagine that the moment was just as he grasped the knife where it lay.

11.] We now first have the covenant God, Jehovah, by special interference arresting the course of that obedience with which He was fully satisfied. The angel of Jehovah speaks with the power and in the person of Jehovah Himself: see esp. Exod. iii. 2, 6, and notes. We have no right to say, in this or any similar instances, that this angel was Christ Himself. The double appellation, **Abraham, Abraham,** served to arrest immediate attention to the urgency of the call. **12.**] "The original 'I have known' denotes an eventual knowing, a discovering by actual experiment." Murphy. **thou fearest God** (Elohim)] This was the great subject of the trial, Abraham's God-fearing character. The Divine name is therefore the general one, and not that of the especial Covenant God.

13.] There is some dispute among Hebraists about the expression **behind** *him*, seeing it is said merely that Abraham "*lifted up his eyes*," not that he turned himself. Kalisch insists on the sense "*in the background*," behind the things immediately present. But in this he seems to stand alone. Prof. Murphy thinks that the voice was heard behind Abraham, causing him to turn round, and then he "lifted up his eyes." The word rendered "*behind*" nowhere else occurs as an adverb of place (Knobel). But it seems beyond doubt that it must be so taken. **14.**] The name, **Jehovah seeth** or **provideth,** recalled to mind not only God's mercy to him, but the fulfilment of his own saying, whether that saying were conscious or unconscious of such meaning, "God will *provide himself* a lamb," &c., the Hebrew verb in both sentences being the same. In the popular saying there is an allusion to the name Moriah, the mountain of vision. It imports proverbially that difficulties and trials will receive their solution on the mountain of Jehovah, or at the place which God has appointed for action. This seems the most probable meaning. Many others have been given, as, e. g. the saying by Kalisch, that it alluded to the worship hereafter to be paid on that mount, "On the mount of the Lord His people shall be seen, or appear;" by Keil, "On the mount where Jehovah appears," denying, as is the usual way of one Hebraist against another, the possibility of the rendering "it will be seen." Again, others propose, "in the mount of the Lord He will be seen," i. e. will appear for His people's deliverance. The result of these varying opinions, as in so many other cases, must be to cause us to repeat, while of necessity giving a provisional preference to one among them, that as yet no satisfactory solution of the meaning of the phrase has been arrived at. **15—19.**] *The renewal of the covenant promised to Abraham on the ground of his obedience in*

JEHOVAH called unto Abraham out of heaven the second
time, 16 and said, By myself have I sworn, [t] saith JEHOVAH,
for because thou hast done this thing, and hast not with-
held thy son, thine only *one:* 17 that in blessing I will
bless thee, and in multiplying I will multiply thy seed as
the stars of the heaven, and as the [u] sand which *is* upon
the sea shore; and thy seed shall possess the [v] gate of his
enemies; 18 and in thy seed shall all the nations of the
earth be blessed; because thou hast obeyed my voice.
19 So Abraham returned unto his young men, and they
rose up and went together to Beer-sheba; and Abraham
dwelt at Beer-sheba. 20 ¶ And it came to pass after
these things, that it was told Abraham, saying, Behold,
Milcah, she hath also born children unto thy brother Na-
hor; 21 Uz his firstborn, and Buz his brother, and Kemuel
the father of Aram, 22 and Chesed, and Hazo, and Pil-
dash, and Jidlaph, and Bethuel. 23 And Bethuel begat
Rebekah: these eight Milcah did bear to Nahor, Abra-
ham's brother. 24 And his concubine, whose name *was*

t Num. xxiv. 3, 28. 2 Sam. xxiii. 1, &c.

u ch. xxxii. 12; xli. 49. Josh. xi. 4, al.

v Matt. xvi. 18. See Ps. lxxxvii. 2. Isa. xiv. 31; xxiv. 12.

this trial. **16.**] "God swears either by Himself (compare Jer. xxii. 5; xlix. 13), or by His eternal attributes, and His wonderful works (Deut. xxxii 40, &c.), whereas man solemnly pledges his faith either by invoking God or the imperishable soul which He has imparted to him (compare ch. xiv. 22; 2 Kings ii. 2; Jer. xxxviii. 16, &c.). These ideas are so natural, that the oath, 'I swear by myself,' may date from the earliest times of a conscious knowledge of God, and in itself in no manner presupposes a later origin." Kalisch. The Christian reader may, for the rationale of such an oath on the part of God, refer to Heb. vi. 13, 14, which comments on this very passage. See also Exod. xxxii. 13, where Moses adduces this oath in prayer for Israel's rescue from destruction. The expression rendered **saith Jehovah** is not the common phrase in narrative, but one betokening poetic or prophetic utterance: see reff. It is the usual phrase in the prophets, "saith Jehovah." **17.**] On the promise see ch. xv. 5. The additional comparison of the sand is found here (see reff.), carrying the thought of multitude still further. Possessing the gate is being master of the access, and so of the city. The gate was the place of public resort, and of council, and so came, as in the expression, the Ottoman Porte, to signify the power of a nation or city. See reff. **18.**] See above, ch. xii. 3. **19.**] It does not appear whether they had set out from Beer-sheba: see on ver. 2. **20–24.**] *Notice of offspring in the line of Abraham's brother Nahor.* The intent of inserting this appears to be in order to keep up connexion with the branch of the family, from which Isaac's wife was to be taken. Milcah was daughter of Haran, and sister to Lot (ch. xi. 27, 29). The remarkable thing about the genealogy is its strict analogy with the family of Jacob. Like that, the house of Nahor has twelve sons: like that, eight by the wife, and four by the concubine. The same number of sons are also reckoned to Ishmael (ch. xvii. 20; xxv. 13—15). Another thing to be noticed is that the same names (in part) are found here which have already occurred either in the pedigree of the race of Shem in ch. x., or in the course of the history.

Uz (or Huz), e. g. is named in ch. x. 23 as one of the children of Aram, and it was from Ur of the Chassidim (Chaldæans) that Abram was called. Whereas here Chesed is a son of Nahor. But there is no reason against the repetition of names in the

Reumah, she bare also Tebah, and Gaham, and Thahash,
and Maachah. XXIII. 1 And Sarah was an hundred and
seven and twenty years old: *these were* the years of the
life of Sarah. 2 And Sarah died in Kirjath-arba; the
same *is* Hebron in the land of Canaan: and Abraham
came to mourn for Sarah, and to weep for her. 3 ¶ And
Abraham stood up from before his dead, and spake unto
the sons of Heth, saying, 4 I *am* a stranger and a so-
journer with you: give me a possession of a buryingplace
with you, that I may bury my dead out of my sight.
5 And the children of Heth answered Abraham, saying
unto him, 6 Hear us, my lord: thou *art* a prince of

line of Shem: we have already two in Abram's family bearing the name of Nahor, Abraham's grandfather and brother: and Ur of the Chassidim may be thus called by anticipation. See Job xxxii. 2. Elihu is said to be a Buzite, of the kindred of Ram (= Aram). Of Kemuel, Pildash, Jidlaph, nothing more is known. Knobel traces Hazo in a district-name, Chazene, of which there was one in Mesopotamia, and one in Assyria. Bethuel appears afterwards in the narrative of ch. xxiv.: see there. Tebah (Thibath), near the city of the Syrian king Hadadezer, 1 Chron. xviii. 8 (called Betah in 2 Sam. viii. 8). Thahash is traced in a town Atachas, N.W. of Nisibis. We have an Aram-Maachah in 1 Chron. xix. 6 (Syria-Maachah in A. V.); the border of Og, king of Bashan, reached as far as to the Maachathites (Josh. xii. 5); the tribe of Manasseh took the country of Argob to the coasts of Geshuri and Maachathi (Deut. iii. 14): see also Josh. xiii. 11, 13, where it is stated that the Geshurites and Maachathites still dwelt among the Manassites. We have the city Abel of Beth-maachah mentioned 2 Sam. xx. 15; 1 Kings xv. 20; 2 Kings xv. 29. It is worth notice that Absalom's mother was *Maacah, daughter* of Talmai, *king of Geshur* (2 Sam. iii. 3), and that Absalom's daughter bore the same name, 1 Kings xv. 2; 2 Chron. xi. 20.

XXIII. *Death of Sarah. Purchase by Abraham of the cave of Machpelah as a buryingplace for her.* Sarah is the only woman whose age is mentioned in the Scripture. She occupies an important place, as the mother of the chosen people (see 1 Pet. iii. 6; Isa. li. 2). **2.**] On **Hebron,** see note, ch. xiii. 18. The words **in the land of Canaan** are added for fulness of description, but not without reference to the fact that thus the mother of the faithful rested in the land promised to her descendants. **Abraham came**] Probably from some nomad excursion in the neighbourhood, or perhaps (but this is not so likely) from Beer-sheba, where he is last heard of as dwelling, ch. xxii. 19. **3.**] Abraham must be thought of as "weeping over the face" of Sarah (2 Kings xiii. 14), and he rises up **from the face** (so reff.) **of his dead.** In this rising up is implied the act of going to the gate of the city where the sons of Heth (or Hittites) were assembled. These sons of Heth were Canaanites (ch. x. 15); from them afterwards Esau took wives, ch. xxvi. 34, 35. **4.**] Abraham knew that the land of Canaan was to be the inheritance of his seed; and the securing a grave in it for his and for himself was an act of faith on his part. The **possession of** a buryingplace clearly had reference to future burials as well as to that now urgent. **5.**] The reply of the children of Heth is deeply respectful to Abraham, and confers on him an unusual favour—admission for his dead into the family sepulchres of the inhabitants; but it does not meet the point at which his request had aimed. There is some difficulty in the word rendered "unto him;" it is unusual in such a connexion. But there seems no reason for departing from the A. V. The LXX. have rendered it as if it were another word of similar sound, and signified "*No;*" "*Not so, my lord.*" But there can be little doubt that this is an instance of the carelessness of which that celebrated version

w Exod. xv. 4. Deut. xii. 11. Isa. xxii. 7. Ezek. xxiv. 5.

God among us: in the [w] choice of our sepulchres bury
thy dead; none of us shall withhold from thee his
sepulchre, but that thou mayest bury thy dead. 7 And
Abraham stood up, and bowed himself to the people
of the land, *even* to the children of Heth. 8 And
he communed with them, saying, If it be your mind
that I should bury my dead out of my sight; hear
me, and intreat for me to Ephron the son of Zohar,
9 that he may give me the cave of Machpelah, which he
hath, which *is* in the end of his field; for as much money
as it is worth he shall give it me for a possession of a
buryingplace amongst you. 10 And Ephron sat among
the children of Heth: and Ephron the Hittite answered
Abraham in the audience of the children of Heth, of all
that went in at the gate of his city, saying, 11 Nay, my
lord, hear me: the field give I thee, and the cave that *is*
therein, I give it thee; in the presence of the sons of my
people give I it thee: bury thy dead. 12 And Abraham
bowed down himself before the people of the land. 13 And
he spake unto Ephron in the audience of the people of the
land, saying, But if thou *wilt give it,* I pray thee, hear me:
I will give thee money for the field; take *it* of me, and I
will bury my dead there. 14 And Ephron answered Abra-

presents so many examples. **a prince of God** seems to signify more than merely "*a mighty prince,*" as A. V. They viewed him as enjoying in a special manner the Divine favour, and possibly, as Kalisch suggests, regarded his residing amongst them as a protection and a safeguard against Divine inflictions: compare Abimelech's confession, ch. xxi. 22. They therefore repudiate his description of himself as a stranger and a sojourner, and manifest a wish to incorporate him among themselves. He therefore, while courteously acknowledging their favourable proposal, now makes known to them his full mind on the matter. His description of himself as a stranger and a sojourner had not been given at random: it had its deep foundations in truth, and was not to be complimented away, but to be adhered to and acted on. **9.**] There were two reasons why Abraham chose Machpelah: it was "*at the end*" of Ephron's field, and so could be parted with at small inconvenience, and it was "*before Mamre,*" i. e. close to the patriarch's own residence. The LXX. and Vulgate render the word **Machpelah,** "*double:*" but it would appear, in error. **10.**] It would seem that the notice, with which this verse begins, alludes not to Ephron having dwelt among the children of Heth, but to his having been present, sitting at the gate. The Hebrew word is the same as that rendered "*sat,*" ch. xviii. 1; xix. 1. **all that went in at the gate** are the inhabitants who assembled there for the purpose of converse and business. See on ch. xxii. 17. It has been remarked that the procedure here is even now acted continually over by the crafty Oriental bargainer. He offers to give the object sought, for nothing; he depreciates its price as a trifle not worth having; and thus obtains at last more than it is worth. "Ephron, unable longer to withstand the temptation, but reluctant openly to exhibit his avarice, with adroit cunning preserved

ham, saying unto him, 15 My lord, hearken unto me: the
land *is worth* four hundred shekels of silver; what *is* that
betwixt me and thee? bury therefore thy dead. 16 And
Abraham hearkened unto Ephron; and Abraham weighed
to Ephron the silver, which he had named in the audience
of the sons of Heth, four hundred shekels of silver, cur-
rent with the merchant. 17 ¶ And the field of Ephron,
which *was* in Machpelah, which *was* before Mamre, the
field, and the cave which *was* therein, and all the trees
that *were* in the field, that *were* in all the borders round
about, were made sure 18 unto Abraham for a possession
in the presence of the children of Heth, before all that
went in at the gate of his city. 19 And after this, Abra-
ham buried Sarah his wife in the cave of the field of
Machpelah before Mamre: the same *is* Hebron in the land
of Canaan. 20 And the field, and the cave that *is* therein,
were made sure unto Abraham for a possession of a bury-
ingplace by the sons of Heth. XXIV. 1 And Abraham
was old, *and* well stricken in age: and JEHOVAH had

the appearance of disinterestedness, while he was exacting a considerable sum from the rich emir; he seemed even impatiently to solicit the honour of furnishing the desired ground. But Abraham understood well his stratagem and its motives, and he at once paid the amount hinted at in current silver, such as merchants give and receive." Kalisch. See the same remark, and the whole transaction thus commented on, in "The Land and the Book," p. 578. **16.**] There was then no coined money, so that ingots of silver were weighed for the price; the phrase "current with the merchant" implying perhaps that the ingots were certified genuine and of proper weight by some mark. But all respecting the primæval habits of payment in commerce is very doubtful. See Mr. Stuart Poole's art. "Money," in *Smith's Biblical Dict.* **17.**] This minute specification seems like a recital of the very formula of sale, and shews the solemn significance of the whole proceeding. By the expression which was in (the) Machpelah, it would seem as if the name belonged not to the cave only, but also to the district or property. See Dean Stanley, "Localities visited in the East in 1862." **before Mamre,** in the face of Mamre, probably implies, eastward of Mamre. Tradition is certainly at fault concerning the sacred sites at Hebron. For while Machpelah is universally believed to be within the walls of the great mosque or Haram, in the city; a spot 15 furlongs off, on the road to Jerusalem, is pointed out, the Ramet el Chalil, the traditional dwelling-place of Abraham, where Josephus mentions the terebinth tree as standing in his time. It is probable that this part is an error, and the other authentic. Vv. 19, 20 relate the burial in like formal terms, the place, city, and country being again specified, and the fact also of the field and cave being secured to Abraham, and by whom. The best and most recent account of the Mosque at Hebron is found in Dean Stanley's "Localities in the East visited in 1862," published as an appendix to his "Sermons in the East."

XXIV. 1—67.] *Abraham's servant is sent to Haran to find a wife of the house of Nahor for Isaac. He brings Rebekah.* This beautiful narrative belongs to the Jehovistic portion, as is abundantly shewn in its progress. **1.**] Abraham was 140 years old: see ch. xxv. 20. **2.**] This might, or might not, be the steward, Eliezer of Damascus, mentioned ch. xv. 2. That was

blessed Abraham in all things. 2 And Abraham said unto
his eldest servant of his house, that ruled over all that he
had, Put, I pray thee, thy hand under my thigh: 3 and I
will make thee swear by JEHOVAH, the Elohim of heaven,
and the Elohim of the earth, that thou shalt not take
a wife unto my son of the daughters of the Canaanites,
among whom I dwell: 4 but thou shalt go unto my coun-
try, and to my kindred, and take a wife unto my son Isaac.
5 And the servant said unto him, Peradventure the woman
will not be willing to follow me unto this land: must I
needs bring thy son again unto the land from whence
thou camest? 6 And Abraham said unto him, Beware
thou that thou bring not my son thither again. 7 ¶ JE-
HOVAH, the Elohim of heaven, which took me from my
father's house, and from the land of my kindred, and
which spake unto me, and that sware unto me, saying,
[x Exod. xxiii. 20, 23; xxxii. 34; xxxiii. 2. Num. xx. 16.] Unto thy seed will I give this land; he shall [x] send his
angel before thee, and thou shalt take a wife unto my son
from thence. 8 And if the woman will not be willing to
follow thee, then thou shalt be clear from this my oath:
only bring not my son thither again. 9 And the servant
put his hand under the thigh of Abraham his master, and
sware to him concerning that matter. 10 ¶ And the serv-
[y See ch. xii. 16.] ant took ten camels of the [y] camels of his master, and de-
parted; for all the goods of his master *were* in his hand:
and he arose, and went to Mesopotamia, unto the city of

nearly 60 years ago. Whoever this was, he was in the fullest confidence of his master, and amply justified it: comp. ver. 10. The whole narrative gives us an eminent example of domestic faithfulness in a God-fearing family, but such an one as we may be thankful that many families among ourselves can parallel. The effect of the fear of God is the same in all lands and ages. **Put thy hand under my thigh**] In these words is euphemistically described a practice of making an oath binding by touching that part of the body which symbolizes power and continuance. For the Jew, a further sanctity was imparted to this confirmation of an oath by that member being the recipient of God's covenant of circumcision. The practice is found besides in ch. xlvii. 29, only. **4.**] See similar expressions in the Jehovistic, ch. xii. 1.

5, 6.] The servant understands the mission of obtaining a wife for Isaac to be so entirely committed to him, that in case the endeavour to bring one back failed, it was a question whether Isaac should not be taken there to choose for himself. This proposal Abraham, in the firmness of his faith in God's promise, strongly repudiates; and in the case supposed (which however [ver. 7] he is confident in God will not arise), absolves the servant from the obligation (ver. 8).

10.] **Mesopotamia** is in the Heb., Aram Naharaim, Aram of the two rivers, lying between the Euphrates and the Tigris.

the city of Nahor is Haran, whither Nahor must have (though this is not related) followed his father Terah: see ch. xi. 31. **11.**] The servant, having been

Nahor. 11 And he made his camels to kneel down with-
out the city by a well of water at the time of the evening,
even the time that women go out to draw *water*. 12 And
he said, O JEHOVAH, the Elohim of my master Abraham,
I pray thee, send me good speed this day, and shew kind-
ness unto my master Abraham. 13 Behold, I stand by the
well of water; and the daughters of the men of the city
come out to draw water: 14 and let it come to pass, that
the damsel to whom I shall say, Let down thy pitcher, I
pray thee, that I may drink; and she shall say, Drink,
and I will give thy camels drink also: her thou hast ap-
pointed for thy servant Isaac; and thereby shall I know
that thou hast shewed kindness unto my master. 15

bred in a school of piety (as Kalisch), commits his way unto God's providence to prosper it. But at the same time he takes the course pointed out by human providence. He goes to the place where and at the time when he was most likely to see the young women of the town. "The principal well was a place (compare Exod. ii. 15; also ch. xxix. 2, ff.) whither the duties of the daughters of the inhabitants called them at certain times of the day. Even the daughters of the chief seldom fail to appear there with their vessels. The well or cistern is for the females what the gate is for the men: here they indulge in friendly conversation and exchange their news; here they are for a short interval released from much of their oriental restraint: and since shepherds also repair hither to water their flocks and herds, it serves in many cases as a convenient place for meetings and appointments, and may in others be the scene of strife, where old feuds and enmities are brought to an issue (Exod. ii. 16, 17). Cisterns were generally closed by a large heavy stone, which was removed by the united strength of the shepherds (xxix. 8), while excavated wells were made more easily accessible, by steps leading down to them. The place where the following event happened seems to have belonged to the latter description: see ver. 16." Kalisch.

14.] The sign proposed by the servant was not chosen at hazard. A maiden who should shew such spontaneous kindness as that here described would be worthy of being Isaac's wife. Notice too the exquisite trust in the gentleness of the favoured family in the assumption that none but one of its members would act as here pointed out. It is unwelcome, but necessary, to have to remind the reader how entirely the beautiful simplicity of the narrative is marred by commentators who tell us that we are not to believe what we are here told, that the servant of himself suggested this sign, but rather that it was intimated by God; because, forsooth, "God is not to be tempted by the presumptuous dictation of modes in which His Providence is to act:" see Judith viii. 10—16, who says, "Do not bind the counsels of the Lord our God; for God is not as man, that He may be threatened." (Bp. Wordsworth.) It is strange that those who would be wise beyond what is written do not see how their uncalled-for hypotheses mar that which is written. If God had previously given Abraham's servant the sign, how is it that he wondered (ver. 29) when the sign which he had prayed for appeared to be fulfilled? and how could he describe himself, ver. 45, as *speaking in his heart* when he uttered these words? It is not with any view of controverting the opinion of one whom I deeply revere and esteem that I quote his words with disapproval, but because a sacred principle of truth in interpretation is involved. We of this generation have to learn to follow, not to lead, Holy Scripture; fearlessly to ascertain what it does say, and then fearlessly to adopt its simple words; to leave off laying down à priori what must, outside the text, have been, and thus making void God's word with our inventions. **15.**] The

¶ And it came to pass, before he had done speaking, that,
behold, Rebekah came out, who was born to Bethuel, son
of Milcah, the wife of Nahor, Abraham's brother, with
her pitcher upon her shoulder. 16 And the damsel *was*
very fair to look upon, a virgin, neither had any man
known her: and she went down to the well, and filled her
pitcher, and came up. 17 And the servant ran to meet
her, and said, Let me, I pray thee, drink a little water of
thy pitcher. 18 And she said, Drink, my lord: and she
hasted, and let down her pitcher upon her hand, and gave
him drink. 19 And when she had done giving him
drink, she said, I will draw *water* for thy camels also,
until they have done drinking. 20 And she hasted, and
emptied her pitcher into the trough, and ran again unto
the well to draw *water*, and drew for all his camels. 21
And the man beheld her in silence, to know whether JE-
HOVAH had made his journey prosperous or not. 22 And
it came to pass, as the camels had done drinking, that the
man took a golden ring of half a shekel weight, and two
bracelets for her hands of ten *shekels* weight of gold;
23 and said, Whose daughter *art* thou? tell me, I pray
thee: is there room *in* thy father's house for us to lodge
in? 24 And she said unto him, I *am* the daughter of
Bethuel the son of Milcah, which she bare unto Nahor.
25 She said moreover unto him, We have both straw and
provender enough, and room to lodge in. 26 And the
man bowed down, and prostrated himself to JEHOVAH. 27
And he said, Blessed *be* JEHOVAH, the Elohim of my mas-
ter Abraham, who hath not left destitute my master of his
mercy and his truth: I *being* in the way, JEHOVAH led me
to the house of my master's brethren. 28 And the damsel
ran, and told her mother's house according to these words.

bearing on the shoulder seems to have been the practice with the Hebrews: see ch. xxi. 14; Exod. xii. 34; Josh. iv. 5. We have also bearing on the head mentioned, ch. xl. 16. **16.**] On "going down to the well," see above. **19.**] The words **until they have done drinking** are by no means without significance. Kalisch remarks, "If it is remembered that camels, though endowed in an almost marvellous degree with the power of enduring thirst, drink, when an opportunity offers, an enormous quantity of water, it will be acknowledged that the trouble to which the maiden cheerfully submitted required more than ordinary patience." **22.**] The ring was a nose-ring: see on ver. 47. The weight specified is a *bekah*, which = ½ a skekel. The presents were not as yet bridal presents: those first come in ver. 53, and could not be given till the consent of

29 ¶ And Rebekah had a brother, and his name *was* Laban :
and Laban ran out unto the man, unto the well. 30 And
it came to pass, when he saw the ring, and the bracelets
upon his sister's hands, and when he heard the words of
Rebekah his sister, saying, Thus spake the man unto me ;
that he came unto the man ; and, behold, he stood by the
camels at the well. 31 And he said, Come, thou blessed
of JEHOVAH ; wherefore standest thou without ? for I have
prepared the house, and room for the camels. 32 ¶ And
the man came into the house: and *Laban* ungirded his
camels, and gave straw and provender for the camels, and
water to wash his feet, and the men's feet that *were* with
him. 33 And there was set before him to eat : but he
said, I will not eat, until I have told mine errand. And
he said, Speak on. 34 And he said, I *am* Abraham's
servant. 35 And JEHOVAH hath blessed my master
greatly ; and he is become great : and he hath given him
flocks, and herds, and silver, and gold, and menservants,
and maidservants, and camels, and asses. 36 And Sarah
my master's wife bare a son to my master when she was
old : and unto him hath he given all that he hath. 37
And my master made me swear, saying, Thou shalt not
take a wife to my son of the daughters of the Canaanites,
in whose land I dwell : 38 but thou shalt go unto my
father's house, and to my kindred, and take a wife unto
my son. 39 And I said unto my master, Peradventure
the woman will not follow me. 40 And he said unto me,
JEHOVAH, before whom I walk, will send his angel with
thee, and prosper thy way ; and thou shalt take a wife for
my son of my kindred, and of my father's house : 41 then
shalt thou be clear from my oath, when thou comest to my
kindred ; and if they give not thee *one*, thou shalt be clear
from my oath. 42 And I came this day unto the well, and
said, O JEHOVAH, Elohim of my master Abraham, if now
thou do prosper my way which I go : 43 behold, I stand
by the well of water ; and it shall come to pass, that the
virgin which cometh forth to draw *water*, and I say to her,
Give me, I pray thee, a little water of thy pitcher to

Laban and Bethuel had been ascertained. **31.**] i. e. he had given orders to that

drink; 44 and she say to me, Both drink thou, and I will
also draw for thy camels: *let* the same *be* the woman whom
JEHOVAH hath appointed for my master's son. 45 And
before I had done speaking in mine heart, behold, Re-
bekah came forth with her pitcher on her shoulder; and
she went down unto the well, and drew *water*: and I said
unto her, Let me drink, I pray thee. 46 And she made
haste, and let down her pitcher from her *shoulder*, and
said, Drink, and I will give thy camels drink also: so I
drank, and she made the camels drink also. 47 And I
asked her, and said, Whose daughter *art* thou? And she
said, The daughter of Bethuel, Nahor's son, whom Milcah
bare unto him: and I put the ring upon her nose, and the
bracelets upon her hands. 48 And I bowed down, and
prostrated myself to JEHOVAH, and blessed JEHOVAH, the
Elohim of my master Abraham, which had led me in the
right way to take my master's brother's daughter unto his
son. 49 And now if ye will shew mercy and truth to my
master, tell me: and if not, tell me; that I may turn to
the right hand, or to the left. 50 Then Laban and Bethuel
answered and said, The thing proceedeth from JEHOVAH:
we cannot speak unto thee bad or good. 51 Behold, Re-
bekah *is* before thee, take *her*, and go, and let her be thy mas-
ter's son's wife, as JEHOVAH hath spoken. 52 And it came to
pass, that, when Abraham's servant heard their words, he
prostrated himself before JEHOVAH to the earth. 53 And
the servant brought forth vessels of silver, and vessels of
gold, and raiment, and gave *them* to Rebekah: he gave
also to her brother and to her mother precious things.
54 And they did eat and drink, he and the men that *were*
with him, and tarried all night; and they rose up in the
morning, and he said, Send me away unto my master.
55 And her brother and her mother said, Let the damsel

effect, on hearing his sister's story. **50.**] Prof. Blunt, in his interesting little volume on "Coincidences in Scripture," adduces the consistent manner in which throughout this narrative a secondary place is allotted to Bethuel, the master of the house, as characteristic of a truthful history, some untold fact, such as possibly the imbecility of Bethuel, being the ground of it. But Knobel justifies it on the ground of the brother exercising guardianship over his sister, as in ch. xxiv. 5, 11, 25; Judg. xxi. 22; 2 Sam. xiii. 22. **53.**] These were the bridal presents destined to ratify the espousal. **55.**] **about ten days** is literally **days, or ten,**—i. e. some days, say ten.

abide with us about ten days; after that she shall go. 56
And he said unto them, Hinder me not, seeing JEHOVAH
hath prospered my way; send me away that I may go to
my master. 57 And they said, We will call the damsel,
and enquire at her mouth. 58 And they called Rebekah,
and said unto her, Wilt thou go with this man? And she
said, I will go. 59 And they sent away Rebekah their
sister, and her nurse, and Abraham's servant, and his
men. 60 And they blessed Rebekah, and said unto her,
Thou *art* our sister, mayest thou become thousands of
myriads, and let thy seed possess the gate of those which
hate them. 61 ¶ And Rebekah arose, and her damsels,
and they rode upon the camels, and followed the man:
and the servant took Rebekah, and went his way. 62 And
Isaac came from the way of the well Lahai-roi; for he
dwelt in the south country. 63 And Isaac went out to
meditate in the field towards the evening: and he lifted
up his eyes, and saw, and, behold, there were camels
coming. 64 And Rebekah lifted up her eyes, and when
she saw Isaac, she lighted off the camel. 65 And she said
unto the servant, What man *is* this that walketh in the
field to meet us? And the servant said, It *is* my master:

58. Wilt thou go with this man?] There is no need to supply anything such as "*now, or stay here a while?*" The man was on the point of departure; would she go with him? **59.]** The nurse's name was Deborah. We read of her death many years after, ch. xxxv. 8. **60.]** The wish for prolific abundance is characteristic in the family to whom this was the special promise. The latter portion of the wish is singularly coincident with the blessing of God on Abraham in ch. xxii. 17. **61.]** Knobel thinks the two portions of this verse parts of two separate narratives, incorporated together. Certainly they look like independent accounts of the same transaction. **62.]** Isaac had been on an excursion which took him to the well where Hagar had been found by the angel (ch. xvi. 14), between Kadesh and Bered, and he was now returning. He dwelt in the Negeb, or south country (see ch. xii. 9), i. e. not at Hebron, but in the neighbourhood of Beersheba. **63.]** The interpretation of the word rendered to **meditate** is very various, and quite uncertain. It is given as here in the LXX. (by the same word which they use in Ps. lxxxvii. 3, 6, 12), the Vulgate, the Samaritan Pentateuch, and the generality of commentators; but Onkelos and the Arabic version give it "*to pray;*" the Syriac, *to take a walk;* while Knobel contends for the sense "*to mourn*" (for his mother), and Gesenius thinks there has been some error in transcription, and that the word ought to be another, signifying "*to make his rounds,*" *to overlook his flocks and herds.* The word occurs but this once in the Bible. As the rendering of the A. V. seems to be more generally adopted than any of the others, I have left it in the text. **64.]** "It is an Eastern custom, prevalent in many parts to this day, that women, when riding on the road, and meeting strange men, descend from their animals, as a mark of respect offered to the stronger sex." Kalisch. But it seems to be more general and to be uniformly done by travellers of both sexes on meet-

therefore she took her veil, and covered herself. 66 And
the servant told Isaac all things that he had done. 67
And Isaac brought her into his mother Sarah's tent, and
took Rebekah, and she became his wife; and he loved her:
and Isaac was comforted after his mother's *death*. XXV.
1 And Abraham took another wife, and her name *was*
Keturah. 2 And she bare him Zimran, and Jokshan, and
z Job ii. 11; viii. 1. Medan, and Midian, and Ishbak, and [z]Shuah. 3 And

ing any distinguished person. **67.**] The wives of Jacob had separate tents, ch. xxxi. 33. This tent would naturally be at Hebron where Sarah died, and there is nothing in the narrative to forbid this, as Knobel thinks; Isaac brought his wife from where he dwelt at the time of her arrival to Hebron. It was now three years since Sarah's death; and some have supposed that the "Jehovist," in thus writing, must have set Sarah's death later, seeing that 30 or 70 days were the usual period of mourning. But our narrative obviously is not treating of a mere formal period of mourning, but of filial sorrow, which is not bounded by time.

XXV. The descendants of Abraham. Herein (vv. 1—4) *Abraham's marriage with Keturah, and their progeny;* (vv. 5—10) *his death and burial;* (vv. 11—18) *the descendants and death of Ishmael;* (vv. 19—34) *the two sons of Isaac.* The portion 1—18 is Elohistic, belonging, as Knobel gathers from various indications, to the original document. **1.**] **Keturah** is called a concubine in 1 Chron. i. 32. It is usually assumed, but merely on the assumption of the history following in chronological sequences, that Abraham espoused Keturah after Sarah's death. And the words, "*Then again*" of the A. V. leave this impression on the English reader. But there is nothing in the original to bear this out. The literal sense is, "**And Abraham added and took a wife,**" i. e. took another wife besides Sarah: but *when* is not said. Indeed, from ver. 6, which says that he sent away the sons of his concubines during his lifetime, it would be most improbable that they should all have been born after Sarah's death. **2, ff.**] This list is not without its difficulties. Of the names mentioned, Sheba and Dedan have before been mentioned, ch. x. 7, as sons of Raamah, the son of Cush, the son of Ham. Such occurrences can only be accounted for by observing that the names here given are those of tribes quite as frequently as those of individuals, and supposing that the Sabeans and Dedanites were of mixed descent from Cush and from Abraham. And this appears to have been actually the case according to the national traditions of Arabia, given by Kalisch, p. 477. These traditions recognize three elements of Arab descent: 1. A primæval race answering to the Cushites of ch. x. 7. 2. The pure Arabs, answering to the Semitic descendants of Joktan, ch. x. 25, ff. And 3. An influx of 12 tribes, sprung from Ishmael, and called the mixed Arabs. These last Kalisch holds to have comprehended also the descendants of Abraham by Keturah. Several of the names here given are untraceable, while others have been recognized in history. The name **Zimran** is supposed to be discovered in the *Zabram* of Ptolemy, a town between Mecca and Medina. Of **Jokshan** nothing certain is known. Some have regarded the name as identical with Joktan of ch. x. 25, ff., but this is hardly probable, and would rather create than remove difficulties. **Medan** appears not to be immediately related to **Midian**, which next follows. Ptolemy mentions a *Madiana* and *Madiama* on the East coast of the gulf of Akabeh. A branch of the **Midianites** is found also in these parts, and a town *Madian* (or *Madiene*, as Josephus), supposed to be the residence of Moses' father-in-law. The better known portion of the Midianites, dwelling further N., in the neighbourhood of the Moabites and Ammonites, as well as the Sinaitic Midianites, will be treated further on in the history. See on Exod. ii. 15. **Ishbak** is supposed to be traced in the valley called Sabak, or Sibak, and other places of a similar name, Shebek, and Esh-Shobak. See Mr. Stanley Poole's article in the *Biblical Dict.*

Shuah was the tribe to which Job's friend, Bildad, belonged, see reff.; and hence

Jokshan begat Sheba, and [a]Dedan. And the sons of De-
dan were [b]Asshurim, and Letushim, and Leummim. 4
And the sons of Midian; [c]Ephah, and Epher, and Hanoch,
and Abidah, and Eldaah. All these *were* the children of
Keturah. 5 ¶ And Abraham [d]gave all that he had unto
Isaac. 6 But unto the sons of the concubines, which
Abraham had, Abraham gave gifts, and sent them away
from Isaac his son, while he yet lived, eastward, unto the
east country. 7 And these *are* the days of the years of
Abraham's life which he lived, an hundred threescore and
fifteen years. 8 Then Abraham gave up the ghost, and
died in a good old age, an old man, and full *of years;* and
was gathered to his people. 9 And his sons Isaac and
Ishmael buried him in the cave of Machpelah, in the field

a Isa. xxi. 13. Jer. xlix. 7, 8. Ezek. xxv. 13.
b Ezek. xxvii. 33.
c Isa. lx. 6.
d ch. xxi. 10. Judg. xi. 2. Gal. iv. 30.

must be looked for near Uz, see ch. x. 23; xxii. 21; and note on Job i. 1. **Sheba** (see above) is connected with those Sabeans, who in Job vi. 19 are mentioned together with the companies of Tema, and in Job i. 15 plundered the herds of the Edomite Job. The "travelling companies of Dedanim" are mentioned in ref. Isa., and in connexion with the "inhabitants of the land of Tema:" in ref. Jer. both people are included in Edom, as also in ref. Ezek. The sons of Dedan (see also above) bear the names of tribes with the plural termination -im; of these the **Asshurim** are mentioned in reff. Ezek. in connexion with Arabia; the **Letushim** are traced by Knobel as the Heteim Arabs, dwellers in the neighbourhood of Leits, four days' journey S. of Mecca, and spreading into other parts of Arabia: and the **Leummim** as the *beni Lâm*, a far-spreading tribe, centralized in the same parts, but extending even into Babylonia and Mesopotamia.

4.] **Ephah** is mentioned in connexion with Midian and Sheba in reff. Isa. as bringing dromedaries in the day of Israel's prosperity. **Epher**] Knobel finds the sons of *Ghiphar* mentioned by the Arab geographers; but of two tribes bearing this name, Mr. Stanley Poole objects (*Biblical Dict.*) that the first is a branch of Amalek, the second is Ishmaelite, but neither is Midianitish.

Hanoch] Or Henoch, 1 Chron. i. 33. Knobel mentions a town *Hanakye* or *Chanuka*, 3 days' journey N. from Medina.

Abidah] This name, as well as **Eldaah**, have not been traced, though again Knobel thinks he has found two tribes corresponding to them. It will be seen from these notices that the descendants of Keturah are to be sought, and that many of their names have been found among the Southern tribes of Arabia. **5—10.**] *Abraham's death and burial.* **5, 6.**] i. e. He made Isaac his chief heir—transmitted to him all that he was possessed of at his death. See reff.

the concubines may be only Hagar and Keturah, but we cannot say that there may not have been others. Their sons were dowered and sent away before Abraham's death, to be out of the way of Isaac. It does not follow (as Knobel) from the fact of Ishmael's presence at his father's funeral, that he was not sent away before: it would be natural that he, as chief of the sons in the second rank, and besides signalized by an especial covenant of blessing from God, ch. xvi. 10; xxi. 18, should return to Hebron on the solemn occasion. Abraham sent them into the East country, i. e. to Arabia. A similar departure of Esau from Jacob is related ch. xxxvi. 6. **7.**] So that it was just a century since Abram's call out of Haran, ch. xii. 4. **8.**] The two verbs, **gave up the ghost, and died,** are identical in meaning: the repetition belongs to the solemnity of the narrative. The English reader may be reminded that "gave up the ghost" is equivalent to "breathed his last," "expired," and has no reference to the *spirit*. **full of years** is merely **full,** satiated, in the Hebrew. The expression **was gathered to his people** does not relate

of Ephron the son of Zohar the Hittite, which *is* before
Mamre; 10 the field which Abraham purchased of the
sons of Heth: there was Abraham buried, and Sarah his
wife. 11 ¶ And it came to pass after the death of Abra-
ham, that Elohim blessed his son Isaac; and Isaac dwelt
by the well [e]Lahai-roi. 12 ¶ Now these *are* the genera-
tions of Ishmael, Abraham's son, whom Hagar the Egypt-
ian, Sarah's handmaid, bare unto Abraham: 13 and these
are the names of the sons of Ishmael, by their names, ac-
cording to their generations: the firstborn of Ishmael,
[f]Nebajoth; and [g]Kedar, and Adbeel, and Mibsam, 14 and
Mishma, and [h]Dumah, and Massa, 15 Hadar, and [i]Tema,

e ch. xvi. 14.
f ch. xxviii. 9; xxxvi. 3; 1 Chron. i. 29. Isa. lx. 7.
g Ps. cxx. 5. Cant. i. 5. Isa. xxi. 16, 17; xlii. 11; lx. 7. Jer. ii. 10, 49; xxviii. 28. Ezek. xxvii. 21.
h (Josh. xv. 52). Isa. xxi. 11.
i Job vi. 19. Isa. xxi. 14. Jer. xxv. 23.

to burial, for this was not so: Abraham's "people" dwelt at this time in Haran, and he was buried at Hebron. Besides which, the fact of burial is here, and in many other places, specified over and above (see ch. xv. 15; xxxv. 29; 1 Kings ii. 10; xi. 43, &c.). Nor is it a mere synonym for dying: for in many places, as here, it is specified over and above the fact, here repeatedly expressed, of death (see ver. 17; ch. xxxv. 29; xlix. 33; Num. xx. 26; Deut. xxxii. 50). The only assignable sense, therefore, is that of reference to a state of further personal existence beyond death: and the expression thus forms a remarkable testimony to the O. T. belief in a future state. **11.**] The Divine blessing which had accompanied Abraham descended to him who is now the possessor of the promises. Isaac's dwelling at the well Lahai-roi (reff.) was apparently only temporary, for in ch. xxxv. 27 we find that his habitual dwelling-place was at Hebron.

12—18.] *The descendants, and death, of Ishmael.* On the number, 12, of the sons of Ishmael, see on ch. xxii. 20. The eldest, **Nebaioth,** has of late become the subject of controversy. It had been universal since Jerome to identify the descendants of Nebaioth with the Nabatheans of Arabia Petræa. But a doubt has been now cast on this. It would be quite beyond our limits to enter on the discussion, which will be found well summarized in Mr. Stanley Poole's art. "Nebaioth," in the *Biblical Dict.* He inclines, till more decisive evidence shall be found against it, to maintain the generally believed identification. From ref. Isa. the Nabatheans were a pastoral people. They are mentioned as allies of the Jews in the Maccabæan period, 1 Macc. v. 24, 25; ix. 35. **Kedar**] The classical geographers class together the Nabatheans and Kedræans, as is also done in reff. Isa., and both appear to have inhabited Arabia Petræa, and had their capital Petra, the Kedræans being to the N.W. and next Palestine. This being so, the mention of them is naturally frequent. See reff., where their principal characteristics may be found. The name signifies *black*, dark-skinned: see especially ref. Cant. The name passed into the Rabbinical appellation for all the Arabs. Of **Adbeel** (= *a miracle*) and **Mibsam** (= *sweet odour*) nothing at all satisfactory is known. **Mishma** may be connected with the Masamani of Ptolemy, N.E. of Medina; and there is a tribe in Arabic writers named the Beni-Mismah; but nothing more is known of them. **Dumah** in ref. Isa. is coupled with Seir, the forest of Arabia, and Kedar; it is Dumaitha or -metha in Ptolemy, and is uncertainly situated, in Arabia Felix or Deserta. See Mr. Stanley Poole's art in *Biblical Dict.* **Massa** is thought to appear in the Masani, a tribe N.E. of Dumah, mentioned by Ptolemy. **Hadar** (written Hadad in 1 Chron. i. 30) seems to be traced in a mountain Hadad, N. of Medina, on the borders of the Syrian desert. To this last is coupled Tema in a way peculiar to these two, and perhaps indicating that they dwelt together, separate from others to whom they are not so coupled. In ref. Job **Tema** is connected with Sheba, and in ref. Jer. with Dedan and Buz. The name is said (Mr. Stanley Poole, *Biblical Dict.*) to be satisfactorily identified with Teyma, a small town on the

Jetur, Naphish, and Kedemah: 16 these *are* the sons of
Ishmael, and these *are* their names, by their towns, and
by their castles; [j]twelve princes according to their nations. j ch. xvii. 20.
17 And these *are* the years of the life of Ishmael, an hun-
dred and thirty and seven years: and he gave up the
ghost and died; and was gathered unto his people. 18
And they dwelt [k]from Havilah unto Shur, that *is* before k 1 Sam. xv. 7.
Egypt, as thou goest toward Assyria: *and* his [l]lot was cast l Judg. vii. 12. Ps. xvi. 6.
in the presence of all his brethren. 19 ¶ And these *are*
the generations of Isaac, Abraham's son: Abraham begat m ch. xxxi. 18; xxxiii. 18; xxxv. 9;
Isaac: 20 and Isaac was forty years old when he took xlvi. 15. See also
Rebekah to wife, the daughter of Bethuel the Aramæan xxviii. 2, 5, 6, 7, and note; also ch. xlviii. 7.
of [m]Padan-aram, the sister to Laban the Aramæan. 21 n Exod. viii. 30; x. 18. Judg.
And Isaac [n]intreated Jehovah for his wife, because she xiii. 8. Job xxxviii. 26.

confines of Syria, in the neighbourhood of Dumah. There, as at Dumah also, are the ruins of a stronghold or *castle* (ver. 16). There seems to be no doubt that **Jetur** represents the Ituræans, between Bashan and Damascus, spreading however N. of that city into Lebanon, progenitors of the modern Druses (Luke iii. 1). Of **Naphish** nothing seems to be known. **Kedemah** (the East) may be connected with the Beni Kedem or children of the East, mentioned as a special tribe of Arabs in Judg. vi. 3, 33; vii. 12. Compare also "they of the East," Isa. xi. 14; "the men of the East," Ezek. xxv. 4, 10. **18.**] See on ch. xvi. 7; xx. 1; also on ch. ii. 11. The exact boundaries indicated are somewhat uncertain. Shur, as above, seems to be the eastern limit of Egypt. **Havilah** is altogether undecided: see art. in *Biblical Dict.* **as thou goest towards Assyria** seems to mean, if thou wert to leave Egypt for Assyria, Shur would be before it, i. e. east of it, facing thee. There is some difficulty in the last clause of the verse. The verb rendered in the A. V. "*died*" is "**fell**." Gesenius, as well as the greater part of modern Hebraists, believes the word to mean here **dwelt**, and the clause to be a taking up again of the prophecy in ch. xvi. 12, where a different verb is used. The same verb as this occurs in reff. 1 Sam., where it is rendered "lay along," namely, camping in their tents. Perhaps the best rendering is that of Kalisch, **his lot was cast**.

19—34.] *The history of Isaac. The birth and fortunes of Esau and Jacob.* The well-known formula, "These are the generations," introduces a new portion of the history, which now resumes the main line of the patriarchal descent. The repetition of the fact of Isaac's birth is in the manner of these resumptions: see ch. v. 2. Of a like kind is the recapitulation in ver. 20 of Isaac's marriage. It would seem as if these portions were intended to be used separately, and each to carry completeness in itself. Kalisch remarks, "These reiterations, natural in themselves, far from causing difficulty, are in harmony not only with the style of the Bible, but of ancient historiography in general, and are in this instance not without a positive gain, for they add the valuable chronological fact, that Isaac was 40 years old when he married Rebekah, a statement of decided importance for the exact understanding of several circumstances connected with Isaac's history." **Padan-aram,** the plain of Aram, designates the champaign country of Syria, i. e. Mesopotamia, "*Aram Naharaim*," Aram of the two rivers, together with the desert at the W. of the Euphrates, as contrasted with the mountain region of Syria reaching westward to the Mediterranean: see reff. In Hos. xii. 12 the same country is designated by Sedeh-Aram, (= *country of Syria*, A. V.) from which Gesenius infers that Padan is equivalent in meaning to Sedeh, field, or champaign.

21.] This barrenness lasted 20 years, as we gather from ver. 26. It was the lot of Sarah, and of Rachel also: see ch. xi. 30;

was barren: and JEHOVAH was intreated of him, and Re-
bekah his wife conceived. 22 And the children struggled
together within her; and she said, If *it be* so, why *am* I
thus? And she went to enquire of JEHOVAH. 23 And
JEHOVAH said unto her,

Two nations *are* in thy womb,
    And two people shall be separated from thy bowels;
And people shall be stronger than people;
o Rom. ix. 12. And [o] the elder shall serve the younger.

24 ¶ And when her days to be delivered were fulfilled, be-
hold, *there were* twins in her womb. 25 And the first
came out red, all over like an hairy garment; and they
called his name Esau. 26 And after that came his
p Hos. xii. 3. brother out, and his hand [p] took hold on Esau's heel; and
his name was called Jacob: and Isaac *was* threescore years
old when he begat them. 27 And the boys grew: and
Esau was a man skilled in hunting, a man of the field;
q Job i. 1, 8; viii. 20. Ps. lxiv. 4. Prov. xxix. 10. and Jacob *was* a [q] harmless man, abiding in (the) tents.
28 And Isaac loved Esau, because he did eat of *his* venison:
but Rebekah loved Jacob. 29 ¶ And Jacob cooked pot-
tage: and Esau came from the field, and he *was* weary:

xxix. 31. The word rendered **intreated,** and elsewhere (reff.) used for *praying*, is in its primary meaning "*burnt incense.*" But the literal sense need not be pressed. **for his wife**] literally, before his wife: it is the same term as occurs in ch. xxx. 38, where Jacob laid the rods before, i. e. in front of, the flocks. But there can be no doubt that the word here has the force of *for* or *in behalf of:* acquiring this meaning through that of "*having reference to,*" "*in regard of.*" **22.**] This antenatal struggle was prophetical of the future enmity of the twin brothers. And Rebekah is represented doubtless as recognizing this presage of misfortune, and making it matter of enquiry from Jehovah. Kalisch interprets her "going to enquire of the Lord" as having recourse to God's prophet Abraham (Luther thought, to *Shem;* some, to *Melchizedek*), who still survived (compare ch. xxi. 5 with ch. xxv. 7, 26; see ch. xx. 17, and compare 1 Sam. ix. 9). Knobel, on the other hand, and Keil, understand that she went to some place where Jehovah was adored and where priests were ready to give responses in His name. The response is in the form of poetical parallelism. **25, 26.**] The whole narrative is symbolical and has reference to the subsequent fortunes of the two peoples. **Esau** signifies *hairy;* **Jacob** imports *heel,* but has also another meaning, that of a *cheat* or *deceiver.* The boys were born 15 years before Abraham's death: see above. **27.**] Esau's life and habits were wild and lawless; Jacob's were harmless and stay-at-home. The adjective rendered "*plain*" in A. V. is literally **perfect,** blameless: it is ordinarily used (see reff.) of a righteous, God-fearing character, but appears here to designate Jacob's gentleness and innocence, as set against Esau's fierce and lawless disposition. This difference was shewn also by their habits: Esau hunted in the field, while Jacob abode in [the] tents. **28.**] literally, **because venison was in his mouth.** **29.**] We have here a striking picture of the habits of the two. Jacob is performing the menial duties of the tent, and has newly prepared a savoury mess of the red lentile or vetch. Esau comes in tired, and longs for the appetizing food. Dr.

30 and Esau said to Jacob, Let me eat, I pray thee, of that
red, that red *pottage;* for I *am* weary: therefore was his
name called Edom (red). 31 And Jacob said, Sell me this
day thy birthright. 32 And Esau said, Behold, I *am* on
the way to die: and what profit shall this birthright do
to me? 33 And Jacob said, Swear to me this day; and
he sware unto him: and he sold his birthright unto Jacob.
34 Then Jacob gave Esau bread and pottage of lentiles;
and he did eat and drink, and rose up, and went his way:
thus Esau despised *his* birthright. XXVI. 1 And there was
a famine in the land, beside the first famine that was in

Tristram says: "There are several varieties recognized, and the Red Lentil is considered the best. . . It is generally used as a pottage, or cooked as the Spaniards cook haricot beans, stewed with oil, and flavoured with red pepper. It is by no means an unsavoury dish." *Nat. Hist. of the Bible*, p. 462. The words here are literally, cooked a cooked (dish): brewed a broo. **30.**] The words run in the Hebrew, Let me eat now of that *edom* (red), that *edom* (red); for I am weary: therefore his name was called *edom* (red). In the heat of hunger he omits the name, and merely asks for the mess by its outward appearance, as that red (stuff). **31.**] Jacob, the quiet but sly man, on the watch for his advantage, seizes the opportunity. We may supply in the background, from the intimation of his mother's favouritism, that the promises attaching to the birthright, unheeded by the free-rover Esau, were thoroughly understood and valued by Rebekah and her son. That such a consideration has two sides to it, one looking towards good, the other towards evil, is an inconsistency found in history because it is found in man. **32.**] This saying of Esau, "**Behold, I am on the way to die,**" may be understood in three ways: they may have (1) a general meaning,—I care only for the present: I shall die, and the birthright will pass on and be of no use to *me;* (2) a particular one, referring to his way of life,—I am meeting death every day in the field, and am not the man to benefit by the birthright, constantly exposed as I am to the risk of life; or (3) one belonging to the occasion then present,—"I am ready to die of faintness and fatigue, and so hold a present meal of more value than a distant contingency." Of these the A. V., by rendering, "I am at the point to die," chooses the third. Kalisch and Keil prefer the first, Knobel the second.

33, 34.] Jacob is not slow to follow up his advantage, and to shew his value for that which Esau despised. The narrative accumulates terms of contempt to shew the lightness and profanity of Esau. He behaved as if it were an ordinary meal and nothing especial had happened. But he had by his conduct thrown himself out of the line of that world's blessing, to record which the sacred writer held his pen.

XXVI. **1—33.**] *Further history of Isaac.* The whole portion is Jehovistic in character. This is shewn both by the Divine name, vv. 2, 12, 24, 25, 28, 29, and by the reference to previous Jehovistic matters, as God's oath to Abraham, ver. 3, Abraham's sojourn in Gerar, ver. 15, &c. Various other tokens of the same are enumerated by Knobel and others.

1—6.] *Renewal of the promise to Isaac in Gerar.* **1. in the land**] viz. of Canaan, where Isaac appears to have been dwelling since ch. xxv. 11. There is great similarity in this part of Isaac's life to that of Abraham. In fact, the son seems to be a faint copy of the father. Like him, he is the inheritor of the Divine promises, and the father of the chosen seed; but there is not in Isaac, as there was in Abraham, any great personal character, and he falls into the track of his father's life and habits, as we so often find in corresponding cases among ourselves. Even his very standing in the blessing of the promise is dependent on the past righteousness of Abraham, ver. 5. It would appear that the design of Isaac in going to Gerar had been to proceed further into Egypt, as

the days of Abraham. And Isaac went unto Abimelech
king of the Philistines unto Gerar. 2 And JEHOVAH ap-
peared unto him, and said, Go not down into Egypt;
dwell in the land which I shall tell thee of: 3 sojourn in
this land, and I will be with thee, and will bless thee; for
unto thee, and unto thy seed, I will give all these coun-
r ch. xxii. 16. tries, and I will perform the [r] oath which I sware unto
Abraham thy father; 4 and I will make thy seed to mul-
s ch. xv. 5; xxii. 17. tiply [s] as the stars of heaven, and will give unto thy seed
t ch. xii. 3; xxii. 18. all these countries; and [t] in thy seed shall all the nations
u ch. xxii. 18. of the earth be blessed; 5 because that Abraham [u] obeyed
my voice, and kept my charge, my commandments, my
statutes, and my laws. 6 And Isaac dwelt in Gerar.
7 ¶ And the men of the place asked *him* of his wife; and
he said, She *is* my sister: for he feared to say, *She is* my
wife; lest, *said he*, the men of the place should kill me for
Rebekah; because she *was* fair to look upon. 8 And it
came to pass, when he had been there a long time, that
Abimelech king of the Philistines looked out at a window,
and saw, and, behold, Isaac *was* sporting with Rebekah

had been done by Abraham under similar distress. It must be remembered that there was an oath of friendliness between Abraham and Abimelech (ch. xxi. 22—24). This can hardly be the same Abimelech: at the time of Abraham's sojourn in Gerar he was an hundred years old, and Isaac was born; sixty years then elapsed before Esau and Jacob were born, and the boys were now grown up. So that it must have been at least eighty years since that former visit, even considering that it lasted many days. But Abimelech seems to have been the royal title among the Philistines, rather than a personal name. In 1 Sam. xxi. 10—15 the name of the king of Gath with whom David took refuge is *Achish;* but in the title of Ps. xxxiv. the same king is called Abimelech. On Phichol, see below, ver. 26.

2.] The command with which the verse ends is general—choose not thine own habitation, but be guided by My Divine intimations.

3. this land] viz. Philistia, Gerar.

all these countries] viz. Canaan and its surroundings: this is the only place where the promise to the chosen seed is thus expressed. The reff. will shew how entirely these promises are a recapitulation of those made to Abraham. The accumulation of words in ver. 5, by which Abram's obedience is described, is one oftener occurring when the law was fully revealed. This was natural, supposing Moses to have been the writer. He would express the Divine sayings in terms familiar to himself.

7—11.] *He gives out his wife as his sister; it is detected, and she is saved.* See on this incident notes on ch. xii. 10, ff. It is at all events characteristic of Isaac to tread almost servilely in the steps of Abraham his father; and it is to be noted, that the fraud has not the same result here as it had on the latter occasion in Abraham's time; for Rebekah was not taken into Abimelech's harem. We may also note two other things: 1. It is *against* this being the same Abimelech, that no suspicion arises at the repetition of the allegation of sisterhood. 2. It is *for* the identity that Abimelech expresses no chance of his own having taken Rebekah, but only of *one of the people* having outraged her. **8, ff.**] There is here no Divine interference: all is human detection and human foresight. There is no

his wife. 9 And Abimelech called Isaac, and said, Be-
hold, of a surety she *is* thy wife: and how saidst thou,
She *is* my sister? And Isaac said unto him, Because I said,
Lest I die for her. 10 And Abimelech said, What *is* this
thou hast done unto us? one of the people might lightly
have lien with thy wife, and thou shouldest have brought
guiltiness upon us. 11 And Abimelech charged all *his*
people, saying, He that toucheth this man or his wife
shall surely be put to death. 12 Then Isaac sowed in that
land, and received in the same year an hundredfold: and
JEHOVAH blessed him. 13 And the man waxed great, and
went forward, and grew until he became very great:
14 and he had possession of flocks, and possession of herds,
and great store of servants: and the Philistines envied
him. 15 And all the wells which his father's servants had
digged in the days of Abraham his father, the Philistines
stopped them, and filled them with earth. 16 And Abime-
lech said unto Isaac, Go from us; for thou art much
mightier than we. 17 ¶ And Isaac departed thence, and
pitched his tent in the valley of Gerar, and dwelt there.
18 And Isaac digged again the wells of water, which they

further meaning in ver. 8 than appears in the words. What passed was no more than is related, but was enough to justify the king's inference.

12—16.] *Isaac's prosperity in Gerar.* **12.**] Knobel remarks that we do not read of Abraham that he sowed the land: he appears only as a nomad with flocks and herds. But we do read it of Jacob and his sons (ch. xxxvii. 7). "The fact," Kalisch observes, "marks a progress in the history of the patriarchs: it is the transition from uncertain migrations to a more settled mode of life; it implies a more permanent interest in the land itself; during one season at least the Hebrew could call his own, not only the grave of his parents, but the soil which gives life and wealth." The neighbourhood of Gaza is to this day exceedingly fertile, and Knobel quotes from Burckhardt cases of as rich a return. Ver. 15 appears to relate, not what the Philistines *had* done, but what they did, in consequence of their envy of Isaac. On the wells, see ch. xxi. 25, ff.; and on the practice of filling up wells as an act of hostility, 2 Kings iii. 25, and Isa. xv. 6, note. It is said to be practised by the Arabs of modern times along the lines of passage of the pilgrims when their demands of black mail are not paid. **17—33.**] *Isaac moves to the valley of Gerar, and thence to Beer-sheba—disputes about wells; final reconciliation, and treaty with Abimelech.* It is evident from our narrative that **the valley of Gerar** was at some distance from Gerar itself, a circumstance which has not been taken into account in Dr. Hayman's art. in *Biblical Dict.* Stanley mentions the *Wâdy Kibab* as being probably that which was known in ancient times as the valley, i. e. the torrent-bed or Wâdy of Gerar (*Sinai and Pal.* p. 159). **18.**] These wells are not mentioned in ch. xxi., but only one, which Abimelech's servants had taken away. There were other occasions of strife of which the history takes no account. Knobel maintains, with his confident "evidently," that the wells mentioned in this verse and those in vv. 19, 21 are identical, and that we have here a mixture of two accounts. But never was an assumption more groundless. It has no support what-

had digged in the days of Abraham his father; for the
Philistines had stopped them after the death of Abraham:
and he called their names after the names by which his
father had called them. 19 And Isaac's servants digged in
the valley, and found there a well of [v] springing water.
20 And the herdmen of Gerar did strive with Isaac's herd-
men, saying, The water *is* our's: and he called the name
of the well Esek [Contention]; because they strove with
him. 21 And they digged another well, and strove for
that also: and he called the name of it Sitnah [Strife].
22 And he removed from thence, and digged another well;
and for that they strove not: and he called the name of it
Rehoboth [Enlargement]; and he said, For now JEHOVAH
hath made room for us, and we shall be fruitful in the
land. 23 And he went up from thence to Beer-sheba.
24 And JEHOVAH appeared unto him the same night, and
said, I *am* the God of Abraham thy father: fear not, for
I *am* with thee, and will bless thee, and multiply thy seed
for my servant Abraham's sake. 25 And he builded an
altar there, and called upon the name of JEHOVAH, and
pitched his tent there: and there Isaac's servants digged
a well. 26 ¶ Then Abimelech went to him from Gerar,
and Ahuzzath his friend, and Phichol the chief captain of

v Lev. xiv. 5. Cant. iv. 15. Jer. ii. 13. Zech. xiv. 8. John iv.10,11.

ever in the context. The two wells of vv. 19, 20 are manifestly new wells. **19.**] **springing**, literally **living**: see reff. **20, 21.**] The Gerar herdsmen may have laid claim to these wells as being in their valley; but when **22.**] Isaac left the valley, there was no longer any such claim possible. Robinson found at the junction of the roads to Gaza and Hebron ruins of a city, now called in Arabic *Ruhaibeh*, and naturally suggesting Rehoboth; but he says there are no traces of a well, the water supply having been by means of cisterns. **23—25.**] Isaac leaves the neighbourhood of Gerar for the neighbouring district of Beer-sheba, apparently from the desire of peaceful habitation and enjoyment of water for his flocks. Here the promise is renewed to him, but again for Abraham's sake. The very place was full of the memories of the great patriarch, who had dwelt and worshipped there, ch. xxi. 33. The occurrence of the Divine intimation induces, as in ch. xii. 8; xiii. 18; see also ch. xxxv. 6, the building of an altar and setting up a place of worship. Here also Isaac seems to have fixed his home for most of the remainder of his life: see ch. xxviii. 10. He died, however, at Hebron, ch. xxxv. 27. The well dug at Beer-sheba by Isaac's servants would seem to have been one of the two larger at present remaining there: see on ch. xxi. 25. It may have been a characteristic act, by way of repeating what had been done by his father.

26.] The motive of this visit seems to have been, that Isaac had now grown sufficiently important, having established himself near their frontiers, for definite relations to be cultivated with him. And the memory of their somewhat churlish dismissal of him, and the quarrels which had happened since, may have made them the more anxious to remove cause of offence from his mind.

Ahuzzath his friend] Thus we have in 1 Kings iv. 5, Zabud son of Nathan "principal officer, and *the king's*

his army. 27 And Isaac said unto them, Wherefore come
ye to me, seeing ye hate me, and have sent me away from
you? 28 And they said, We saw certainly that JEHOVAH
was with thee: and we said, Let there be now an oath be-
twixt us, *even* betwixt us and thee, and let us make a
covenant with thee; 29 that thou wilt do us no hurt, as
we have not touched thee, and as we have done unto thee
nothing but good, and have sent thee away in peace: thou
art now the blessed of JEHOVAH. 30 And he made them a
feast, and they did eat and drink. 31 And they rose up
betimes in the morning, and sware one to another: and
Isaac sent them away, and they departed from him in
peace. 32 And it came to pass the same day, that Isaac's
servants came, and told him concerning the well which
they had digged, and said unto him, We have found
water. 33 And he called it Shebah: therefore the name
of the city *is* Beer-sheba unto this day. 34 ¶ And Esau
was forty years old when he took to wife Judith the
daughter of Beeri the Hittite, and Bashemath the daugh-
ter of Elon the Hittite: 35 which were a grief of mind
unto Isaac and to Rebekah. XXVII. 1 And it came to

friend;" and 1 Chron. xxvii. 33, Hushai the Archite, "the king's companion." The visit was one of official state. On the name Phichol appearing as that of the commander of Abimelech's army both here and in the history of Abraham also, various conjectures have been made. The safest conclusion is that of Mr. Grove (*Biblical Dict.*), that it is a Philistine name of the meaning of which we are ignorant. We have no means of saying whether it may or may not have been an official name. See note on ver. 1: and on Abimelech's speech to Isaac, see above. There is evidently, from ver. 29, a desire to have a different interpretation put on the former, sending him away from the true one. In this characteristic trait Knobel sees inconsistency between this account and that in ver. 16! **31.**] So in ch. xxxi. 46 a meal was the accompaniment of a solemn contract. **33.**] **He called it,** i. e. the well, Shibḡah, oath: see on the whole ch. xxi. 31, note. The account of this second origin of the name Beer-sheba must be regarded as rather an intimation of a coincidence than as to be pressed in its literal sense. It is useless to attempt to evade the difficulty, as some have done by a suggestion which we forbear to characterize, that the former narrative gives the origin only of the name of the *well*, whereas this speaks of the *city*. Far rather would we seek a solution in the fact, so apparent throughout the life of Isaac, that his whole bent and plan seems to have been to copy Abraham his father, and as it were to retrace the lines which he had previously traced.

34, 35.] *The double marriage of Esau.* Esau, like his father, marries at 40. He takes two wives, which is not, as some have said, attributed to him as a sin: Abraham had done the same, and so did Jacob. The sin, and that which brought grief to his parents, was that he took those wives, being himself ungodly, out of the heathen race of the Canaanites. On the names of these wives see note, ch. xxxvi. 2. They were both Hittites, of the children of Heth: see ch. x. 15. They introduced misery into the family tents. We see its depth and power in ch. xxvii. 46.

XXVII. *Jacob's fraud upon his father*

pass, that when Isaac was old, and his eyes were dim, so that
he could not see, he called Esau his eldest son, and said unto
him, My son: and he said unto him, Behold, *here am* I.
2 And he said, Behold now, I am old, I know not the day
of my death: 3 now therefore take, I pray thee, thy
† or, *sword.* weapons, thy † quiver and thy bow, and go out to the
field, and take me *some* venison; 4 and make me savoury
meat, such as I love, and bring *it* to me, that I may eat;
that my soul may bless thee before I die. 5 And Rebekah
heard when Isaac spake to Esau his son. And Esau went
to the field to hunt *for* venison, that he might bring *it*.
6 ¶ And Rebekah spake unto Jacob her son, saying, Be-
hold, I heard thy father speak unto Esau thy brother,
saying, 7 Bring me venison, and make me savoury meat,
that I may eat, and bless thee before JEHOVAH before my

and brother. 1.] Isaac was at this time 137 years old, as appears thus: Joseph was 30 years old when he stood before Pharaoh (ch. xli. 46); there had passed the seven years of plenty, and two years of famine when Jacob came into Egypt and declared himself 130 years old; so that, Joseph being 39 when his father was 130, he was born when his father was 91. But Joseph was born when his father had been 14 years in Mesopotamia (compare ch. xxx. 25 with xxix. 18, 21, 27), so that Jacob was 77 when he fled to Mesopotamia; and as he was born when his father was 60 (ch. xxv. 26),—Isaac must have been at this time 137. At this age his half-brother Ishmael had died (ch. xxv. 17); but Isaac survived yet 43 years (see ch. xxxv. 28). It is literally, his eyes had grown dim from seeing, i. e. so that he could not see. He had not given up Esau as his first-born, notwithstanding the prophecy and the transaction about the birthright. Isaac's character is usually treated as that of the good and weak old man, led captive by his mere sensual predilections. But those who thus estimate forget that the father, as a lover of justice, had every right on his side in maintaining that of which Esau had been unjustly defrauded. The type of his predilections and desires may have been low, as undoubtedly was that of his favourite son's; but while we accept the sacred narrative in this chapter as a record of God's inscrutable ways of bringing about His purposes, we must not for a moment let our plain sense of HIS justice and truth be warped by any theological considerations; we must not withdraw our sympathies from Esau the victim, nor suffer our indignation against the instigator and the perpetrator of the wrong to be blunted. We shall find in the course of the history that whatever great results followed the crime, it did not remain unvisited on the heads of both those guilty persons. 3.] The word rendered **quiver** is found only here: it specifies that which is *hung* on, and has by some been rendered *sword*. But Knobel remarks that the sword is girded on, while the quiver is suspended. Still, one name for a sword was a *hanger*, and perhaps the bow would of itself imply the quiver, without its being mentioned. **venison** is rather a translation by derivation than by sense, which is "*venare mihi venationem*," "hunt me the produce of hunting," i. e. game. Such is exactly represented in the derivation of the word by *venison*, which is *venatio;* but not in the ordinary sense of the word, which is the flesh of deer. In the concluding words of the verse Isaac shews a consciousness of his patriarchal dignity as the holder and transmitter of the Divine covenant-promise, and as the vehicle of fate and blessing in virtue of this office. 5, 6.] Notice **Esau his son, . . . Jacob her son.** 7.] The words **before Jehovah**, if not actually uttered by Isaac, shew Rebekah's sense of the

death. 8 Now therefore, my son, obey my voice according
to that which I command thee. 9 Go now to the flock,
and fetch me from thence two good kids of the goats; and
I will make them savoury meat for thy father, such as he
loveth: 10 and thou shalt bring *it* to thy father, that he
may eat, and that he may bless thee before his death.
11 And Jacob said to Rebekah his mother, Behold, Esau
my brother *is* a hairy man, and I *am* a smooth man:
12 my father peradventure will feel me, and I shall seem
to him as a deceiver; and I shall bring a curse upon me,
and not a blessing. 13 And his mother said unto him, Upon
me *be* thy curse, my son: only obey my voice, and go
fetch me *them*. 14 And he went, and fetched, and brought
them to his mother: and his mother made savoury meat,
such as his father loved. 15 And Rebekah took goodly
raiment of her eldest son Esau, which were with her in
the house, and put them upon Jacob her younger son:

solemnity of the intended blessing, gathered from the tone of him whom she had overheard speaking. The blessing of a father, as before God, would be ratified by, as it would be inspired by, Him in the full consciousness of whose Presence it would be pronounced. **11.**] Jacob urges no such scruple against the voice of his temptress as his son afterwards uttered (ch. xxxix. 9), but is afraid only of the consequences of detection. (The Syriac version and some MSS. of the Samaritan Pentateuch have, "*Thou wilt bring* a curse upon me.") But his wicked mother had provided for all this by a scheme heartless in proportion as it was monstrous and unnatural. She will take advantage of the failing sight and impaired perception of her aged husband for her perfidious purposes. At the same time we cannot help regarding with a sort of admiration her lofty appreciation of that result which she sought, and her self-forgetful devotion (ver. 7) to her beloved son; but it is as we feel the same sort of admiration for Lady Macbeth—with full consciousness of, and never forgetting, her crime. **15.**] It has been a dream of the more fanciful of ancient and modern commentators, that this goodly raiment of Esau consisted of the sacerdotal robes belonging to him as the firstborn in the patriarchal family, and that "the transfer of the sacerdotal robes from Esau to Jacob seems to be typical of the transfer of the priesthood from the Jewish hierarchy to Christ and the Church." Bp. Wordsworth. But to say nothing of the sort of typology which sees in a transfer *to* Israel a type of a transfer *from* Israel, we may fervently exclaim, *absit omen!* at the same time that we remind the reader of the improbability of such an interpretation of the garments, in the absence of any intimation in the text. Besides, would such vestments, supposing them to have existed at all, have been described as "raiment of the eldest son" during his father's lifetime? And even if they could have been so described, is it likely that the ambitious Rebekah would have allowed them to remain Esau's, when the birthright to which they were attached had been, in her view and his own, transferred to Jacob? They were probably best, or state garments of "my lord" Esau, in which he sought the companies of his brother hunters, and redolent (ver. 27) of the aromatic shrubs of the wilderness which they had brushed through. The objection that if so they would be in the keeping of his wives is of no weight. Esau seems still a member of his father's household, of the treasures of which Rebekah was naturally the keeper. **in the house**]

16 and she put the skins of the kids of the goats upon his
hands, and upon the smooth of his neck: 17 and she gave
the savoury meat and the bread, which she had prepared,
into the hand of her son Jacob. 18 ¶ And he came unto his
father, and said, My father: and he said, Here *am* I; who
art thou, my son? 19 And Jacob said unto his father, I *am*
Esau thy firstborn; I have done according as thou badest
me: arise, I pray thee, sit and eat of my venison, that thy
soul may bless me. 20 And Isaac said unto his son, How
is it that thou hast found *it* so quickly, my son? And he
said, Because JEHOVAH thy Elohim brought *it* to me. 21
And Isaac said unto Jacob, Come near, I pray thee, that
I may feel thee, my son, whether thou *be* my very son
Esau or not. 22 And Jacob went near unto Isaac his
father; and he felt him, and said, The voice *is* Jacob's
voice, but the hands *are* the hands of Esau. 23 And he
discerned him not, because his hands were hairy, as his
brother Esau's hands: so he blessed him. 24 And he said,
Art thou my very son Esau? And he said, I *am*. 25 And
he said, Bring *it* near to me, and I will eat of my son's
venison, that my soul may bless thee. And he brought *it*
near to him, and he did eat: and he brought him wine,
and he drank. 26 And his father Isaac said unto him,

This word **house** has surprised Knobel, as inconsistent with the usual term *tent*. He says ch. xxxviii. 11 is not parallel, as that has reference to Canaanitish connexions. But may not the expression be merely a general one? **16.**] "The skins of goats are well adapted to the purpose for which Jacob (?) employs them. For the hair of the Syrian long-eared goat, though often black, is long and soft, and looks and feels not unlike human hair, whence the Romans employed it for wigs and other artificial coverings of the head" (see Cant. iv. 1). Kalisch. **20.**] The baseness of Jacob is here coped by his blasphemy. It is no mean sign of the sublimity of Scripture that no word of disapproval is inserted in cases like this. The condemnation is left to the "discernment of good and evil" which we have "even of ourselves;" and when passed, it is in the history's sequel, amply justified. Jacob's own infinite anguish as the victim of deceit, ch. xxxvii. 34, 35, is the comment on this wicked fraud. Nor was this alone. His subsequent life presents many times the cheater cheated: compare ch. xxix. 25; xxxiv. 30; xlii. 36—38, and the suspicion of fraud, ch. xlv. 26. Observe how the blasphemy is enhanced by the most solemn name of God being used, and His covenant relation to Isaac introduced: **JEHOVAH thy God.** **21.**] The arousing and the lulling of the old man's suspicions, are alike characteristic. He suspected Jacob from habit; but his distrust was lightly appeased by an expedient which would hardly have taken in an intelligent child. Yet though appeased, it is not set at rest. It arises again ver. 24, and even then is with difficulty overcome. The concluding words of this verse, **so he blessed him**, must apparently not be understood as importing that *the blessing* was now given, for *it* evidently follows in vv. 27—29 (compare the reference to it, ver. 37); nor again as being a mere preliminary or summary blessing, afterwards

Come near now, and kiss me, my son. 27 And he came
near, and kissed him: and he smelled the smell of his
raiment, and blessed him, and said,

See, the [w]smell of my son w Cant. iv. 11.
As the smell of a field
Which JEHOVAH hath blessed:
28 And † God give thee † The Elohim.
Of the [x]dew of heaven, x Deut. xxxiii. 13. Hos. xiv. 5. Zech. viii. 12.
And of the fatness of the earth,
And plenty of corn and wine:
29 Let people serve thee,
And nations bow down to thee:
Be lord over thy brethren,
And let thy mother's sons bow down to thee:
Cursed *are* they that curse thee,
And blessed *are* they that bless thee.

30 ¶ And it came to pass, as soon as Isaac had made an
end of blessing Jacob, and Jacob was yet scarce gone out
from the presence of Isaac his father, that Esau his brother
came in from his hunting. 31 And he also had made
savoury meat, and brought it unto his father, and said
unto his father, Let my father arise, and eat of his son's
venison, that thy soul may bless me. 32 And Isaac his
father said unto him, Who *art* thou? And he said, I *am*
thy son, thy firstborn Esau. 33 And Isaac trembled very
exceedingly, and said, Who? where *is* he that hath taken
venison, and brought *it* me, and I have eaten of all before
thou camest, and have blessed him? yea, *and* he shall be

to be expanded; but as anticipatory, and summarizing vv. 27—29; q. d. the main instrument in deceiving Isaac and extracting the blessing from him, was the fact that his hands were, &c. **27.**] On **the smell of his raiment** see note, ver. 15. The word raiment may perhaps include the skins of the goats. As Knobel remarks, all contributed to confirm the old man and obtain the blessing,—the meal, the wine, the kiss, the wild odour. **28.**] The blessing is conveyed, as usual with such sayings, in a form of poetic parallelism. The **dew** and the **fatness of the earth** are in Palestine closely connected. The dews there are like rain (see *The Land and the Book*, p. 491): compare reff. **29.**] From physical the blessing goes on to political prosperity. The Edomites, descendants of Jacob's brother, were subjugated by David (2 Sam. viii. 14; 1 Kings xi. 15; Ps. lx., title). See below on ver. 40. The concluding words were remarkably reproduced by Balaam, Num. xxiv. 9.

30—40.] *Esau's return; his despair at the treachery and at the irrevocable blessing.* The words of the patriarch, spoken in the fulness of Divine inspiration, are irrevocable, however obtained. This is one of the mysterious parts of the narrative; but it only represents to us the constant issue of similar successes in life itself. The wrong is done, the prize is thereby won; there is no reversal of the

blessed. 34 And when Esau heard the words of his father,
he cried with a great and exceeding bitter cry, and said
unto his father, Bless me, *even* me also, O my father. 35
And he said, Thy brother came with subtilty, and hath
taken away thy blessing. 36 And he said, Is not he
rightly named Jacob [Defrauder]? for he hath defrauded
me these two times: he took away my birthright; and,
behold, now he hath taken away my blessing. And he
said, Hast thou not reserved a blessing for me? 37 And
Isaac answered and said unto Esau, Behold, I have made
him thy lord, and all his brethren have I given to him for
servants; and with corn and wine have I sustained him:
and what shall I do now unto thee, my son? 38 And Esau
said unto his father, Hast thou but one blessing, my
father? bless me, *even* me also, O my father. And Esau
y ch. xxi. 16. [y]lifted up his voice, and wept. 39 And Isaac his father
answered and said unto him,

Behold, apart from the fatness of the earth shall be thy
 dwelling,
 And apart from the dew of heaven from above;
40 And by thy sword shalt thou live,
 And shalt serve thy brother;
And it shall come to pass when thou shalt revolt,
 That thou shalt break his yoke from off thy neck.

issue; the enjoyment of the prize may be poisoned by the wrong, but the prize itself is of no less value. On all this compare the N. T. comment, Heb. xii. 17. **35.**] Isaac has now his eyes opened to the double fact,—Jacob's unprincipled fraud and Jacob's destination to inherit the blessing and birthright. **36.**] "*Supplanter*" is perhaps nearer to the meaning, but is not so well understood. **39.**] This is put a poor remnant of blessing after that bestowed upon Jacob. But it has been well observed by Delitzsch that it contains in it the elements of trouble for Jacob's blessing, and thereby begins to visit on the latter the unjust means whereby he obtained it. The arrangement is poetical: see above, vv. 27—29. The opening words most likely signify the very contrary of that by which the A. V. renders them. Esau was to dwell in the barren land of Idumæa, far off from the fertility of his brother's lot. Travellers say that notwithstanding some fertile valleys in the eastern parts, Edom is probably "the most desolate and barren upland in the world" (Seetzen, cited by Keil). So also Shaw describes it, "a solitary, empty waste," and Burckhardt, "a stony desert." No words could more accurately describe the habits of its inhabitants than those of living by their sword, existing as robbers and freebooters. Witness the perils, to this day, of a visit to Petra. On **thou shalt serve thy brother**, see above, ver. 29. The renderings of the following words have been very diverse. The Targum of Onkelos give them, "And it shall come to pass, when his sons shall transgress the words of the law, thou shalt," &c. The ancient Syriac, "If thou shalt repent, thou shalt," &c. The Hebrew verb signifies to *roam at liberty*, to rush wildly about, as cattle free from the yoke. It is thus used in Jer. ii. 31. See note there. It seems that our nearest English

41 ¶ And Esau hated Jacob because of the blessing where-
with his father blessed him: and Esau said in his heart,
The days of mourning for my father are at hand; then
will I slay my brother Jacob. 42 And these words of
Esau her elder son were told to Rebekah: and she sent
and called Jacob her younger son, and said unto him, Be-
hold, thy brother Esau, as touching thee, doth comfort
himself, *purposing* to kill thee. 43 Now therefore, my son,
obey my voice; and arise, flee thou to Laban my brother
to Haran; 44 and tarry with him a few days, until thy
brother's fury turn away; 45 until thy brother's anger
turn away from thee, and he forget *that* which thou hast
done to him: then I will send, and fetch thee from thence:
why should I be deprived also of you both in one day?
46 And Rebekah said to Isaac, I am weary of my life be-
cause of the daughters of Heth: if Jacob take a wife of
the daughters of Heth, such as these *which are* of the
daughters of the land, what good shall my life do me?
XXVIII. 1 And Isaac called Jacob, and blessed him, and

term in this connexion is "to revolt." The Edomites were to be subjugated by Israel, but would in time assert their liberty and succeed in shaking off the yoke. This they did in the reign of Joram, 2 Kings viii. 20, ff. They were brought under again by Amaziah (2 Kings xiv. 7; 2 Chron. xxv. 11). In the latter days of the kingdom of Judah the Edomites were a cause of annoyance (see 2 Chron. xxviii. 17). **41—45.**] *Esau hates and threatens Jacob; his mother sends him away to Haran.* It is again characteristic, that Esau will not afflict his father by taking revenge on Jacob, but will wait till his death. He makes no account of his mother, who was indifferent to him. Kalisch calls in question this rendering, and prefers, "Days of grief are at hand for my father, for I will slay," &c., without any reference to Isaac's death. But the common interpretation seems universally accepted, and certainly suits better. It does not, as Kalisch objects, "presuppose a deliberate calmness and self-control on the part of Esau totally at variance with his character," but only an interference of his passion for revenge on his brother with that of tenderness for his father, a very common incident with impetuous persons. It surely would be far more inconsistent with his character to suppose a side-look at his father's probable distress to be a bitter accompaniment of his feeling of revenge. The historical comment on this threat is found at ch. xxxv. 29. **44.**] by the words **a few days** Rebekah persuades her son to tear himself from home. The punishment of the fraud is beginning. She never saw him again. **45.**] If Esau killed Jacob, she would lose them both, because the custom of the avenging of blood would have compelled Jacob's nearest of kin to kill Esau. **46.**] It is curious to see such commentators as Knobel, maintaining that this speech of Rebekah's is inconsistent with what has gone before. It is simply another fraud upon the feeble Isaac, who was unconscious of the threat of Esau. Rebekah sets up the pretext of Jacob going in search of a wife, which had enough of reality to commend it, to induce his father to send him away without being informed of the more cogent reason. Isaac falls into the trap, and hence his speech to Jacob, ch. xxviii. 1, ff. On Esau's wives, see ch. xxvi. 34 and xxxvi. 2, ff.

XXVIII.—XXXV. *The history of Jacob; his wanderings; his wives and chil-*

charged him, and said unto him, Thou shalt not take a
wife of the daughters of Canaan. 2 Arise, go to Padan-
aram, to the house of Bethuel thy mother's father; and
take thee a wife from thence of the daughters of Laban
† El Shaddai. thy mother's brother. 3 And † God Almighty bless thee,
and make thee fruitful, and multiply thee, that thou may-
est be a multitude of people; 4 and give thee the blessing
of Abraham, to thee, and to thy seed with thee; that thou
mayest inherit the land wherein thou art a stranger,
which God gave unto Abraham. 5 And Isaac sent away
Jacob: and he went to Padan-aram unto Laban, son of
Bethuel the Aramæan, the brother of Rebekah, Jacob's
and Esau's mother. 6 ¶ When Esau saw that Isaac had
blessed Jacob, and sent him away to Padan-aram, to take
him a wife from thence; and that as he blessed him he
gave him a charge, saying, Thou shalt not take a wife of
the daughters of Canaan; 7 and that Jacob obeyed his
father and his mother, and was gone to Padan-aram;
8 and Esau seeing that the daughters of Canaan pleased
not Isaac his father; 9 then went Esau unto Ishmael,
and took unto the wives which he had Mahalath the
daughter of Ishmael Abraham's son, the sister of Neba-
joth, to be his wife. 10 ¶ And Jacob went out from

dren; his return to Canaan; his sojourn at Shechem, at Bethel, at Mamre, where Isaac dies and is buried. And herein, XXVIII. **1—5**] *Isaac blesses Jacob and sends him to take a wife among Laban's daughters at Haran.* There is no inconsistency whatever in this incident as here related, with what has just passed in ch. xxvii. Rebekah had kept the aged Isaac uninformed of the true reason why she sent Jacob away, and had substituted for it her anxious desire that he should not take a wife of the daughters of the land. Isaac acts on this, and in dismissing Jacob, gives him his special blessing, at the same time reiterating the general terms of the patriarchal promise in the form of a solemn wish for him. In this whole portion the Elohistic and Jehovistic elements are generally intermingled. It is not the purpose of this commentary to follow out such considerations in detail. Those who wish for a complete account may find it (allowing for the rationalistic bias) in Knobel's commentary, or more briefly in Kalisch. **2.**] On **Padan-aram**, see on ch. xxv. 20. **3.**] On **El Shaddai**, see note, ch. xvii. 1. **5.**] **Bethuel the Aramæan**, see ch. xxv. 20, where Laban is called by this name; and note there, as above. **6—9.**] *Esau's third marriage.* This proceeding of Esau shews the same characteristic misapprehension of the position, and of his father's mind, as we have seen in him before. It fulfils that mind to the letter, but violates it in the spirit. There is, again, no inconsistency with what has gone before, as some have thought. Esau need not have known that his mother had heard of his threat against his brother: he sees his brother's dismissal to Haran, and its ostensible reason. He knows that his wives were displeasing to his father; and he endeavours in his clumsy way to repair the mischief. On **Mahalath**, see ch. xxxvi. 3.

10—22.] *Jacob's journey, and dream at Luz.* On **Haran**, see ch. xi. 31; xxiv. 10. **11.**] This was not at the end of

Beer-sheba, and went toward Haran. 11 And he lighted
upon a certain place, and tarried there all night, because
the sun was set; and he took *one* of the stones of that
place, and put *it* under his head, and lay down in that
place to sleep. 12 And he dreamed, and behold a ladder
set up on the earth, and the top of it reached to heaven:
and behold the angels of God ascending and descending
on it. 13 And, behold, JEHOVAH stood above it, and said,
I *am* JEHOVAH God of Abraham thy father, and the God
of Isaac: the land whereon thou liest, to thee will I give
it, and to thy seed; 14 and thy seed shall be as the dust
of the earth, and thou shalt spread abroad to the west,
and to the east, and to the north, and to the south: and
in thee and in thy seed shall all the families of the earth
be blessed. 15 And, behold, I *am* with thee, and will
keep thee in all *places* whither thou goest, and will bring
thee again into this land; for I will not leave thee, until
I have done *that* which I have spoken to thee of. 16
¶ And Jacob awaked out of his sleep, and he said, Surely
JEHOVAH is in this place; and I knew *it* not. 17 And he
was afraid, and said, How dreadful *is* this place! this *is*
none other but the house of God, and this *is* the gate of
heaven. 18 And Jacob rose up early in the morning,

the first day's journey; for, as Knobel observes, Jerusalem was several days' journey from Beer-sheba, and Bethel was further on still. **12.**] This symbolical dream of Jacob's has deep meaning, and serves as a revelation to him of God's promises and purposes. This is necessarily implied in the narrative. On the one side is Jacob, a lone man, not sheltered by the walls of a city or of a house, but lying down to rest under the canopy of heaven; on the other is He who never slumbers nor sleeps, keeping watch over Israel, imparting to man grace and help by His heavenly messengers, and receiving men's wants through the same. The whole represents the future fortunes of Israel and the connexion of the chosen people with God. The symbol is alluded to by the Psalmist in Ps. cxxi., and by the prophet Hosea, ch. ii. 4, 5, and in its deeper and fullest meaning by our blessed Lord, in John i. 51.

14.] This was not only a renewal of the promises to Abraham and to Isaac, but an enlargement of them, both in that the blessing to all races on earth (literally, of the earth's surface, on the ground: so also ch. xii. 3; not ch. xviii. 18; xxii. 18; xxvi. 4) is not only said of the seed, but is made personal, **in thee and in thy seed**; doubtless because this was he whose personal name was to designate, as he personally was to multiply into, the whole race of Israel; and also in that there is here contained a guarantee that God would guard Jacob in all his paths, and would bring him back to the land of his birth, and would not forsake him till all His promises should be accomplished. **16. JEHOVAH is in this place** is the predication of an especial and solemn presence, such as all men associate with a spot which is called the house of God. In saying that it was **the gate of heaven,** he does no more than revive the vision of the night: here heaven had been opened to him. **18.**] The putting the stone pillow for a monument derives further signifi-

and took the stone that he had put under his head, and
z ch. xxxi. 45; xxxv. 14. Jos. iv. 9, 20; xxiv. 26, 27. 1 Sam. vii. 12. [z] set it up *for* a monument, and poured oil upon the top of
it. 19 And he called the name of that place Beth-el: but
the name of that city *was called* Luz at the first. 20 And
Jacob vowed a vow, saying, If God will be with me, and
will keep me in this way that I go, and will give me
bread to eat, and raiment to put on, 21 so that I come
again to my father's house in peace; then shall JEHOVAH
be my God: 22 and this stone, which I have set *for* a
monument, shall be God's house: and of all that thou
shalt give me I will surely give the tenth unto thee.
XXIX. 1 Then Jacob lifted up his feet and came into the

cance and endurance by his anointing it, as Moses did the tabernacle and its furniture afterwards, Exod. xxx. 26. We read elsewhere of the custom of setting up stones as memorials: see reff. There is a curious fact in connexion with this narrative, that of the mention by various ancient writers of anointed stones as objects of veneration, which anointed stones were called *Bœtulia* in Greek, and *Bœtyli* in Latin, apparently from their usually being aerolites, and thus were regarded as having come from God's dwelling. Accounts are given of such stones in Phrygia, Phœnicia, Syria, Arabia, Egypt; and the celebrated Caaba at Mecca is an excellent example. The setting up of such pillars has been stated to have been forbidden by the law in after times, on the strength of Levit. xxvi. 1; Deut. xvi. 22, but see at those places. **19.**] The giving of the name Beth-el, the house of God, is again narrated ch. xxxv. 15, and said to have taken place on Jacob's return. That account is purely Elohistic; but there is no reason for regarding it as inconsistent with this. *This* may be well related in anticipation, as Jacob may have given the name lightly and cursorily now, and more formally and finally then, or both narratives may relate but one incident,—the naming of the place Beth-el,—without saying when it happened. **20.**] This vow of Jacob is the first formally recorded in Scripture, and consists of a promise that if he should return safely, Jehovah should be his God, and he would dedicate the tenth of his property to Him. It is of the essence of the vow, that this dedication should be voluntary, contingent on a certain event; and it follows that no deduction can be hence made as to the obligatory nature of payment of tithes. It would have been mockery to dedicate to God what already belonged to Him. The stone was to be the house of God (Beth-Elohim), i. e. a place where God should be worshipped. The subsequent fortunes of Beth-el, thus named and consecrated, were remarkable. It was further hallowed by the erection of an altar on a Divine command to Jacob himself on his return, ch. xxxv. 1, ff.; afterwards it became the resort of those who wished to enquire of God, Judg. xx. 18, 26 (where "the house of God" in both verses ought rather to be *Bethel*): next we meet with it as the (idolatrous) Holy place of the kingdom of the ten tribes, 1 Kings xiii. 32, 33; Amos v. 13 (where see note). The incidents which happened there in the course of that kingdom, and the fulfilment of the prophecies of Hosea (iv. 15; v. 8; x. 5, 8) and Amos (v. 5; vii. 10—13), are admirably commented on in Stanley, *Sinai and Palestine*, pp. 220—223.

XXIX. 1—XXX. **24.**] *Jacob's arrival at Haran, and sojourning with Laban. His service for his wives, Leah and Rachel. The births of his children.* **1. lifted up his feet**] Such expressions are used at the commencement of long or important undertakings, e. g. in Matt. v. 2 Jesus *opened his mouth* and taught them. The **children** (sons) **of the east** here are the inhabitants of Mesopotamia. The expression is generally used of the Arabs E. of Palestine: see reff. **2.**] This well is apparently not the

land of the [a]children of the east. 2 And he looked, and
behold a well in the field, and, lo, there *were* three flocks
of sheep lying by it; for out of that well they watered the
flocks: and the stone upon the well's mouth was great.
3 And thither were all the flocks gathered *from time to*
time: and they rolled the stone from the well's mouth,
and watered the sheep, and put the stone again upon the
well's mouth in his place. 4 And Jacob said unto them,
My brethren, whence *be* ye? And they said, Of Haran
are we. 5 And he said unto them, Know ye Laban the
son of Nahor? And they said, We know *him*. 6 And he
said unto them, *Is* he well? And they said, *He is* well:
and, behold, Rachel his daughter cometh with the sheep.
7 And he said, Lo, *it is* yet high day, neither *is it* time
that the cattle should be gathered together: water ye the
sheep, and go *and* feed *them*. 8 And they said, We cannot,
until all the flocks be gathered together: then they
roll the stone from the well's mouth: and we water the
sheep. 9 ¶ And while he yet spake with them, Rachel
came with her father's sheep: for she kept them. 10 And

a Judg. vi. 3, 33; vii. 12; viii. 10. 1 Kings iv. 30. [Job i. 3. Jer. xlix. 28. Ezek. xxv. 4, 10: *men of the E.*]

same as that in ch. xxiv. 11, ff. It seems to be further from the city, and different in its management. This well is closed by a large stone which is only removed at the assemblage of the flocks and shepherds in the evening. This usage is illustrated in the *Land and the Book*, p. 589: "Cisterns are very generally covered over with a large slab, having a round hole in it large enough to let down the leather bucket, or earthen jar. Into this hole a heavy stone is thrust, often such as to require the united strength of two or three shepherds to remove. The same is seen occasionally over *wells* of 'living water;' but where they are large and the supply abundant no such precaution is needed. It was either at one of these cisterns, or less abundant and more precious wells, that Jacob met Rachel; and being a stout man, nearly (?) seventy years of age, he was able to remove the stone and water the flock." The whole scene is most graphically described. We have a similar one in Exod. ii. 16, ff. Ver. 3 describes, not as the impression is from the A.V., that which took place on this occasion, which would be inconsistent with what follows, ver. 7, 8, but that which was the custom day by day. I have attempted to make this plain by inserting the words *from time to time* in italics. **4.**] The antecedent of **them** is left to be gathered out of the preceding: viz. the herdmen who were with the three flocks. **5.**] **Laban** was actually the grandson of Nahor. The insignificance of Bethuel, Laban's father, is here also kept up as in ch. xxiv. **7.**] On the intelligence of Rachel's coming, Jacob, wishing his interview with her to be private, exhorts the shepherds to water their flocks and depart with them, as it is not yet evening. This they reply they cannot do, because the stone must be rolled away, which is not done till all the flocks were gathered. This their reply seems much more probably grounded on their unwillingness to break the custom (no small consideration with Orientals) than on their lacking strength to move the stone. Nor is there any improbability in Jacob venturing, on the strength of his relationship to Laban and his love for Rachel, to do that from which the shepherds had shrunk.

9.] **for she kept them** is literally, **for she was a shepherdess.** The un-

it came to pass, when Jacob saw Rachel the daughter of
Laban his mother's brother, and the sheep of Laban his
mother's brother, that Jacob went near, and rolled the
stone from the well's mouth, and watered the flock of
Laban his mother's brother. 11 And Jacob kissed Rachel,
and lifted up his voice, and wept. 12 And Jacob told
b Zech. xiv. 16; xxiv. 48. Rachel that he *was* her father's [b]brother, and that he *was*
Rebekah's son: and she ran and told her father. 13 And
it came to pass, when Laban heard the tidings of Jacob
his sister's son, that he ran to meet him, and embraced
him, and kissed him, and brought him to his house. And
he told Laban all these things. 14 And Laban said to
c Judg. ix. 2. 2 Sam. xix. 13. See ch. ii. 23. him, Surely thou *art* my [c]bone and my flesh. And he
abode with him the space of a month. 15 ¶ And Laban
said unto Jacob, Art thou my brother, and shouldest thou
serve me for nought? tell me, what *shall* thy wages *be?*
16 And Laban had two daughters: the name of the elder
was Leah, and the name of the younger *was* Rachel.
17 Leah's eyes were dull: but Rachel was beautiful and
well favoured. 18 And Jacob loved Rachel; and said, I will
serve thee seven years for Rachel thy younger daughter.
19 And Laban said, *It is* better that I give her to thee, than
that I should give her to another man: abide with me.

married daughters of the nomad Arabs to this day keep the flocks. The meeting is in the highest degree touching and natural. The forlorn man, driven from his father's house by peril of his life, was at once met, not only with his own flesh and blood, but with her who in a moment becomes to him the centre of his new and recovered life. The history is drawn from the very deepest wells of human emotion. His service done, and his impassioned manner, justify his taking the privilege of a near relative, and all doubt on this is removed by his own avowal. Observe the continual and studied repetition, "the daughter of Laban his mother's brother,"—"the flock of Laban his mother's brother,"—"her father's brother,"—Rebekah's son,"—"Jacob his sister's son." The joy of meeting is imparted to her whom he met: she *runs* and tells her father. And he again, in his turn, welcomes the wayfarer with the same affectionate ardour.

12.] Her father's **brother** is of course in the wider sense: see next verse and reff.

14.] **the space of a month** is literally **a month of days.** Kalisch denies this, and renders, "a month as regards days," or "time." The difference is trivial.

15.] The sense seems somewhat disturbed by the A. V. The fact of being a relative would rather enhance than diminish the wages, and on this consideration the question of Laban depends, and the answer of Jacob also.

17.] Leah's eyes were feeble, i. e. **dull,** without brilliancy and freshness. In the East the clear expressive lustrous eye is accounted the chief feature in female beauty. It was compared to the eyes of the gazelle: see 1 Sam. xvi. 12. On the contrary, Rachel's beauty was complete: she was beautiful in form and beautiful in look, both in figure and in face.

18, 19.] All this is represented in Eastern customs even now. It is still the custom to serve for a wife. Burkhardt found a young man in Hauran who had served eight

20 And Jacob served seven years for Rachel; and they
seemed unto him *but* a few days, for the love he had to
her. 21 ¶ And Jacob said unto Laban, Give *me* my wife,
for my days are fulfilled, that I may go in unto her.
22 And Laban gathered together all the men of the place,
and made a feast. 23 And it came to pass in the evening,
that he took Leah his daughter, and brought her to him;
and he went in unto her. 24 And Laban gave unto his
daughter Leah Zilpah his maid *for* an handmaid. 25 And
it came to pass, that in the morning, behold, it *was* Leah:
and he said to Laban, What *is* this thou hast done unto
me? did not I serve with thee for Rachel? wherefore
then hast thou beguiled me? 26 And Laban said, It must
not be so done in our country, to give the younger before
the firstborn. 27 Fulfil her week, and we will give thee
this also for the service which thou shalt serve with me
yet seven other years. 28 And Jacob did so, and fulfilled
her week: and he gave him Rachel his daughter to wife
also. 29 And Laban gave to Rachel his daughter Bilhah
his handmaid to be her maid. 30 And he went in also
unto Rachel, and he loved also Rachel more than
Leah, and served with him yet seven other years.

years for his board, and had then married his master's daughter, but had yet more years to serve for her. And Laban's speech yet indicates the rule of Eastern betrothals. The general rule is that first cousins marry; without the consent of those who have this right women are not betrothed to those who are not their kindred. Even after marriage they call one another cousins. **20.**] This verse beautifully represents Jacob's lightheartedness in the presence of his beloved. It is wonderful to our minds to remember that these seven years were from the 78th to the 85th year of Jacob's age. **23.**] "So," remarks Keil, "is the deceiver of Esau deceived, and sin punished by sin." The fraud was rendered possible by the eastern custom of the bride being veiled, aided by the darkness of the night. **24.**] Rebekah (ch. xxiv. 61) had "her damsels;" Leah and Rachel have but one maid each. **26.**] This custom, even now prevalent among the Egyptians, was not announced to Jacob when the conditions of his servitude were fixed, and consequently formed no excuse for Laban's treachery. **27.**] **Fulfil her week, . . .** i. e. attach thyself to her during the accustomed days of the wedding-feast: see Judg. xiv. 12; Tobit xi. 19. **we**] i. e. I and mine. **28.**] So that Jacob in eight days married two wives. Keil well remarks that although we have no right, as Calvin does, to pass severe judgment on this bigamy of Jacob's after the requirements of the Mosaic law, and to designate it incest (see Levit. xviii. 18), yet we must not justify it by the consideration that God's blessing turned it into a means of multiplying the patriarchal family. It arose owing to treachery on Laban's part, and owing to abandonment to the love of beauty on the part of Jacob (for Rachel seems to have been far less worthy of his love than Leah): and it turned, in its results, into a veritable "school of crosses," as Keil calls it, to Jacob. **30.**] After his second marriage he served seven years more for Rachel, having for that service received her in prepayment. **31—35.**] *The birth of Leah's*

31 ¶ And when JEHOVAH saw that Leah *was* hated, he
opened her womb: but Rachel *was* barren. 32 And
Leah conceived, and bare a son, and she called his
name Reuben [Behold a Son]: for she said, Surely JE-
HOVAH hath looked upon my affliction; now therefore
my husband will love me. 33 And she conceived again,
and bare a son; and said, Because JEHOVAH hath heard
that I *am* hated, he hath therefore given me this
son also: and she called his name Simeon [Hearing].
34 And she conceived again, and bare a son; and said,
Now this time will my husband be joined unto me, be-
cause I have born him three sons: therefore was his name
called Levi [Joining]. 35 And she conceived again, and
bare a son: and she said, Now will I praise JEHOVAH:
therefore she called his name Judah [Praised]; and ceased
bearing. XXX. 1 And when Rachel saw that she bare
Jacob no children, Rachel envied her sister; and said
unto Jacob, Give me children, or else I die. 2 And
Jacob's anger was kindled against Rachel: and he said,
Am I in God's stead, who hath withheld from thee the
fruit of the womb? 3 And she said, Behold my maid
Bilhah, go in unto her; and she shall bear upon my
knees, that I may also have children by her. 4 And she
gave him Bilhah her handmaid to wife: and Jacob went
in unto her. 5 And Bilhah conceived, and bare Jacob a

four sons. The whole narrative is full of God's justice and of man's weakness and unworthiness. The plain and hated wife-sister is blessed with children; the husband's heart is won towards her; the beautiful and beloved one is led, through crosses and failings, and her husband's anger, to a humbler mind (ch. xxx. 23, 24), God in time compensating her for her affliction. **32.**] There is much behind these words of Leah's: doubtless the penalty of her share in the deceit had been severe, in the entire alienation, after the first, of her husband. **33.**] The sight of his first-born son draws Jacob again to the dis-favoured Leah, but does not attach him to her. **34.**] But on the birth of the third son she believes this will take place.

34.] All hitherto had been a struggle for the poor wife, issuing, so it would appear, in success at the third birth; and now, at the fourth, she breaks out into praise. It must be owned that Leah appears by no means to disadvantage in this part of the narrative.

XXX. **1.**] It is remarkable, that as soon as Rachel had *children* (literally, sons) she did die. It is impossible to read this and not to form an unfavourable estimate of Rachel. There is at the same time an impetuosity and an ungodliness in her speech to her husband. **2. in God's stead**] i. e. having the place and power of God.

3—8.] *The sons of Bilhah.* No blame is attached in the sacred text to this procedure, which was but a following of what Sarah had done previously. Nay, from Leah's speech in ver. 18 it would appear to have been regarded rather as a meritorious act. But it would necessarily

son. 6 And Rachel said, God hath judged me, and hath
also heard my voice, and hath given me a son: therefore
called she his name Dan [Judge]. 7 And Bilhah Rachel's
maid conceived again, and bare Jacob a second son. 8 And
Rachel said, With wrestlings of God have I wrestled with
my sister, and I have prevailed: and she called his name
Naphtali [Wrestling]. 9 When Leah saw that she had
left bearing, she took Zilpah her maid, and gave her
Jacob to wife. 10 And Zilpah Leah's maid bare Jacob a
son. 11 And Leah said, In luck! and she called his name
Gad [Luck]. 12 And Zilpah Leah's maid bare Jacob a
second son. 13 And Leah said, For my happiness, for the
daughters will call me happy: and she called his name
Asher [Happy]. 14 ¶ And Reuben went in the days of
wheat harvest, and found mandrakes in the field, and
brought them unto his mother Leah. Then Rachel said
to Leah, Give me, I pray thee, of thy son's mandrakes.

carry with it disastrous results in a family, even under polygamy. And such results seem pointed at in ch. xxxvii. 2: see there. **upon my knees**] Onkelos interprets, "that she may bear, and I will be the nurse;" i. e. I will take her child on my lap as my own. **have children by her** is literally, as in ch. xvi. 2, **be built up by her.**

8.] **wrestlings of God** are more than great wrestlings, as A. V. They signify wrestlings in a matter of God; in this case, as to the maternity of God's people. The LXX. render, "*God hath helped me;*" The Vulgate, "*God hath compared me with my sister;*" but both appear to be wrong. It is to be noticed, says Keil, that Rachel merely speaks of Elohim (God), while her sister regards her four sons as the gift of JEHOVAH. See below on ch. xxxi. 34. **9—13.**] *The sons of Zilpah.* **11.**] The A. V. has followed the Samaritan Pentateuch, which here reads a different word from the Hebrew. The familiar rendering of the latter seems the only expressive way of giving the sense. Where this is the case I have not shrunk from using the words. We need not dilute the meaning of the text because the words happen to be in trivial use among us.

14—21.] *The transaction respecting the mandrakes, introducing the birth of two more sons and a daughter by Leah.* Kalisch has the following remarks: "Reuben, the eldest son of Leah, finding in the fields certain fruits (*Dudaim*, or mandrakes) believed to possess the power of promoting conception, brought them to his mother, who had for some time been afflicted with barrenness. Her first impulse was to employ them for its removal. She therefore replied to Rachel, who begged them of her, with a certain indignation, mingled however with faithful love for her husband. But she was far from attaching a decisive or essential value to the fruit; and when therefore her sister, with her usual tenacity, insisted upon obtaining them, she readily ceded them to her, relying for fruitfulness upon the mercy of God rather than the powers of nature, a sentiment which she distinctly expressed when she gave birth to her fifth son. Rachel, still enslaved by pagan superstitions, as she later stealthily carried away the idols of her father (xxxi. 19), and purchasing the mandrakes with a certain sacrifice, expected from them a deliverance from her sterility; but she had still to learn that offspring are granted by the beneficence of God alone, and that the products of nature are unavailing without His aid." **mandrakes**] "This plant (*mandragora officinalis*) is of the family *Solanaceæ* (to which the potato belongs), and is of very peculiar appearance. It sends up in early spring a broad disk of leaves,

15 And she said unto her, *Is it* a small matter that thou
hast taken my husband? and wouldest thou take away
my son's mandrakes also? And Rachel said, Therefore
he shall lie with thee to night for thy son's mandrakes.
16 And Jacob came out of the field in the evening, and
Leah went out to meet him, and said, Thou must come
in unto me; for surely I have hired thee with my son's
mandrakes. And he lay with her that night. 17 And
God hearkened unto Leah, and she conceived, and bare
Jacob the fifth son. 18 And Leah said, God hath given
me my hire, because I have given my maiden to my
husband: and she called his name Issachar [There is re-
ward]. 19 And Leah conceived again, and bare Jacob the
sixth son. 20 And Leah said, God hath endued me *with*
a good dowry; now will my husband dwell with me, be-
cause I have born him six sons: and she called his name
Zebulun [Dwelling]. 21 And afterwards she bare a
daughter, and called her name Dinah. 22 ¶ And God
remembered Rachel, and God hearkened to her, and
opened her womb. 23 And she conceived, and bare a son;
and said, God hath taken away my reproach: 24 and she
called his name Joseph; and said, JEHOVAH shall add to

lying flat on the ground, somewhat like those of the primrose, but more than double their size. In the centre of these come out the blossoms singly, some with a stalk two or three inches long, some with scarcely any stem. They are cup-shaped, of a rich purple colour. The fruit is of the size of a large plum, quite round, yellow, and full of soft pulp. It has a peculiar but decidedly not an unpleasant smell, and a pleasant sweet taste. . . . The mandrake is universally distributed in all parts of Palestine, and its fruit is much valued by the natives, who still hold to the belief, as old as the time of Rachel, that when eaten it ensures conception. . . . We found it in flower at Christmas in warm situations, and gathered the fruit in April and May. Wheat harvest is therefore the period of its ripening generally." Tristram, *Natural Hist. of the Bible*, p. 467. **15.**] It would seem then as if Jacob habitually lived with Rachel again at this time. **17.**] Either the words **God hearkened unto Leah** presuppose a prayer on her part, or perhaps they are used merely in the more general sense of ch. xvi. 11, "The Lord hath heard thy affliction."

18.] Leah here treats this new gift of a son as a reward for her self-denial in giving Zilpah to her husband; but this hardly seems in accord with her saying to Jacob in ver. 16, where her "*hire*" is that of her husband at the price of the mandrakes.

20.] The fact of Jacob dwelling with Rachel and not with herself, is still on her mind. There is a double allusion in the name **Zebulun**. The words **endued** and **dowry** are from the root Zavad, he gave; and the word **dwell** is from the root Zaval, he dwelt; l and d are often interchanged, as in the names Odysseus and Ulysses for the same man. **21.**] It is not usual to enumerate female descendants. Dinah's name is mentioned for the sake of the history in ch. xxxiv. Jacob had more daughters: compare ch. xxxvii. 35, with xlvi. 7.

22—24.] *Birth of Joseph.* Here again we have a double derivation for the name, one from *Asaph, took away*, the other from *Yasaph, added.* This is treated by Knobel

me another son. 25 ¶ And it came to pass, when Rachel
had born Joseph, that Jacob said unto Laban, Send me away,
that I may go unto mine own place, and to my country.
26 Give *me* my wives and my children, for whom I have
served thee, and let me go: for thou knowest my service
which I have done thee. 27 And Laban said unto him, I
pray thee, if I have found favour in thine eyes, *tarry:* I
have [d] learned by divination that JEHOVAH hath blessed [d] ch. xliv. 15. 1 Kings xx. 33. See Num. xxiii. 33; xxiv. 1.
me for thy sake. 28 And he said, Appoint me thy wages,
and I will give *it*. 29 And he said unto him, Thou knowest
how I have served thee, and how thy cattle was with me.
30 For *it was* little which thou hadst before I *came*, and it
is *now* increased unto a multitude; and JEHOVAH hath
blessed thee since my coming: and now when shall I pro-
vide for mine own house also? 31 And he said, What
shall I give thee? And Jacob said, Thou shalt not give
me any thing: if thou wilt do this thing for me, I will
again feed *and* keep thy flock. 32 I will pass through all

as indicative of compilation from two sources, as he finds also indicated by the use of Elohim in her first sentence, and Jehovah in her second. Keil, who denies this, refers her use of Elohim to her looking principally to the past, and that of Jehovah to her founding her faith for the future on her husband's God. But apart from this being very far-fetched in itself, how does it agree with her stealing her father's idols in the next chapter? **25—XXXI. 55.**] *Jacob's demand of Laban for his dismissal. Their intrigues and disputes, and final agreement. Jacob's departure.* **25.**] The 14 years which bound Jacob to Laban had now expired. **27.**] Laban confesses by this speech that the demand of Jacob was rightly founded. There is no word in the original corresponding to "*tarry*." The proper supply of the abrupt clause may be, "do it not," which would amount to the same. The word rendered by the A. V. "*I have learned by experience*," literally means I have used divination, I have learned by consulting omens: see reff. Laban had received what he considered intimations from his gods, that Jehovah, Jacob's God, was blessing him for Jacob's sake. In this conviction of Jacob's value to him, he (ver. 29) leaves his wages to be fixed by himself. **29, ff.**] In our estimate of Jacob's conduct, we must remember what passed in these verses. It was with the distinct view of "providing for his own house also" that Jacob made this compact. Laban might have known, and doubtless did know, that it would be hard driven; and a man with flocks and herds surely could not be ignorant of the stratagem which Jacob meant to, and did, employ. In fact, his very precaution in ver. 36 shews that he was aware of the influence of the spotted cattle.

30.] **since my coming** is literally **at** (or *in*) **my foot.** This may mean also, as Kalisch, *wherever I went.* **31, 32.**] Jacob's proposal, while it appears at first sight generous and disinterested, yet must not be judged except by its own terms. It has been treated by some (e. g. Keil) as if Jacob's hire were to be merely the then present abnormal cattle, and as if the extension of the agreement into the future were an encroachment. But surely the very nature of the case implies that the "hire" was to last as long as the service lasted. Indeed as much is implied in ver. 33, where future time (see there) is carefully included.

32.] With regard to the characters of the cattle, we are told (Tristram, *Nat. Hist. of Bible*, p. 144) that the colour of the sheep

thy flock to day, removing from thence all the speckled
and spotted cattle, and all the dark cattle among the sheep,
and the spotted and speckled among the goats: and *of*
such shall be my hire. 33 So shall my righteousness an-
swer for me in time to come, when thou comest for my
hire to inspect it: every one that *is* not speckled and
spotted among the goats, and dark among the sheep, that
shall be counted stolen with me. 34 And Laban said, Be-
hold, I would it might be according to thy word. 35 And
he removed that day the he goats that were ringstraked
and spotted, and all the she goats that were speckled and
spotted, *and* every one that had *some* white in it, and all
the brown among the sheep, and gave *them* into the hand
of his sons. 36 And he set three days' journey betwixt
himself and Jacob: and Jacob fed the rest of Laban's
[e] Hos. iv. 13, only. flocks. 37 ¶ And Jacob took him rods of [e] green poplar,
[f] here only. [g] Ezek. xxxi. 8, only. and of the [f] almond and [g] plane tree; and pilled white
strakes in them, and made the white appear which *was* in

in the East is generally white, as that of the goats is black. "But though black sheep are uncommon, tawny (or as they are called in Genesis, brown) are very numerous in every flock." **33.**] **in time to come,** literally, **to-morrow**, but clearly meaning as rendered: for if the division were made that day, the literal morrow could not be in question. **when thou comest for my hire, to inspect it**] So (but *to* my hire) Kalisch. Onkelos, similarly, *when thou comest for my hire, which shall be before thy face.* So also Keil.

35, 36.] The whole proceeding is that of one cunning man against another. Laban does not leave the matter in Jacob's hands, as proposed ver. 32, but takes it into his own, and entrusts that part of the flock which is Jacob's hire to his (Laban's) sons, putting them at a distance from his own flock, which remains with Jacob, and keeping them studiously separate, to prevent the result which nevertheless Jacob's superior cunning brought about in the end.

37—43.] *Jacob's stratagem, and its success.*

37.] Gesenius believes the first-mentioned of these trees to be the styrax or storax. Tristram thinks the poplar better answers the conditions, seeing that in ref. Hosea the tree is described as a large one, under which idolatrous rites are performed, whereas the storax is only a shrub, rarely more than 12 feet high. Besides, one kind of poplar, the *populus euphratica*, has its name from its abundance in that very country where Jacob peeled the rods, in Haran, between the Euphrates and the Tigris. The second tree, rendered *hazel* in A. V., is more probably, as given by the Vulgate, Onkelos, the Samaritan Pentateuch, and the old Syriac version, **almond**. "We did not," says Dr. Tristram, "observe the true hazel wild in Southern or Central Palestine, nor was it likely to occur in Mesopotamia, though it is common in the Galilean and Lebanon districts." The Hebrew word, *luz*, occurring only here, is to this day the Arabic name for the almond tree. Keil renders it *walnut tree*, but this can hardly be, for the peeling of the walnut rods would produce not white, almost beyond doubt, but a dark colour. The third tree (*'armōn*) is the oriental plane, and is thus rendered by almost all the versions. "We never saw the chesnut in Palestine excepting planted in orchards in Lebanon; while the plane tree, though local, is frequent by the side of streams and in plains, both on the coast and in the northern parts of the country. . . . The Hebrew name, *'armōn*, sig-

the rods. 38 And he set the rods which he had pilled be-
fore the flocks in the gutters in the watering troughs
when the flocks came to drink, that they should conceive
when they came to drink. 39 And the flocks conceived
before the rods, and brought forth cattle ringstraked,
speckled, and spotted. 40 And Jacob did separate the
lambs, and set the faces of the flocks toward the ring-
straked and all the brown in the flocks of Laban; and
he put his own flocks by themselves, and put them not
unto Laban's cattle. 41 And it came to pass, whenso-
ever the stronger cattle did conceive, that Jacob laid the
rods before the eyes of the cattle in the gutters, that they
might conceive among the rods. 42 But when the cattle
were feeble, he put *them* not in: so the feebler were
Laban's, and the stronger Jacob's. 43 And the man in-
creased exceedingly, and had much cattle, and maidserv-
ants, and menservants, camels, and asses. XXXI. 1 And
he heard the words of Laban's sons, saying, Jacob hath
taken away all that *was* our father's; and of *that* which
was our father's hath he gotten all this [h] glory. 2 And [h] Isa. x. 3; lxvi. 12.
Jacob beheld the countenance of Laban, and, behold, it *was*
not toward him as [i] before. 3 And JEHOVAH said unto [i] Exod. xxi. 29, 36. Josh. iv. 18, al.
Jacob, Return unto the land of thy fathers, and to thy

nifies *naked*, and it is a characteristic of the plane tree that it annually sheds its bark." Tristram, *Nat. Hist. of Bible*, p. 345.

38.] The effect produced is illustrated by many writers on natural history, and is said to prevail especially among sheep. **40.**] There is some difficulty in this verse. The meaning seems to be, that when these abnormal lambs were produced, Jacob separated them, and took care that the flocks (of Laban) should always look towards them (setting them to leeward of Laban's flocks), and all his dark sheep he took care to present to the sight of Laban's flocks, keeping the two apart, so that ordinarily Laban's flocks saw nothing but streaked and brown cattle. Thus he further helped out his stratagem above detailed. The words **in the flock of Laban** are puzzling, unless they refer to the whole sentence, as if a comma were after **brown**. One can hardly venture to render them "*towards the flock of Laban*," as Kalisch. **41, 42.**] It is probable that the device here mentioned had no reference (as some suppose, and as the Vulg. and Onkelos render in the main) to the two lambing times, the stronger lambs being yeaned in autumn and the feebler in spring: but simply regarded the distinction between the stronger and the weaker individuals on each occasion. If a difficulty be suggested by the probability that these would be promiscuously mingled, it is easy to reply that Jacob as the shepherd had power to classify the flock as he pleased. **43.**] literally, **the man broke forth**, expanded, **largely largely**. It has been observed that in the whole of this narrative of Jacob's stratagems, the sacred names do not once occur.

XXXI. **1—16.**] *Alienation of Laban. Jacob is divinely commanded to return home; he takes counsel with his wives.* **1. this glory**] See reff., literally, **weight.** Bp. Wordsworth appositely refers to St. Paul's "*weight of glory*," 2 Cor. iv. 7. **2.**] **as before** is literally, as in reff., **yesterday**

kindred; and I will be with thee. 4 And Jacob sent and
called Rachel and Leah to the field unto his flock, 5 and
said unto them, I see your father's countenance, that it *is*
not toward me as [i] before; but the God of my father hath
been with me. 6 And ye know that with all my power
I have served your father. 7 And your father hath de-
j Num. xiv. 22. Neh. iv. 12. Job xix. 3. Zech. viii. 23. ceived me, and changed my wages [j] ten times; but God
suffered him not to hurt me. 8 If he said thus, The
speckled shall be thy wages; then all the cattle bare
speckled: and if he said thus, The ringstraked shall be
thy hire; then bare all the cattle ringstraked. 9 Thus
God hath taken away the cattle of your father, and given
them to me. 10 And it came to pass at the time that the
cattle conceived, that I lifted up mine eyes, and saw in a
dream, and, behold, the rams which leaped upon the
cattle *were* ringstraked, speckled, and grisled. 11 And the
angel of God spake unto me in a dream, *saying*, Jacob:
And I said, Here *am* I. 12 And he said, Lift up now thine
eyes, and see, all the rams which leap upon the cattle *are*
ringstraked, speckled, and grisled: for I have seen all
that Laban doeth unto thee. 13 I *am* the God of Beth-el,
where thou anointedst the pillar, *and* where thou vowedst
a vow unto me: now arise, get thee out from this land,

and the third day, i. e. the day before. **4.**] He sent for his wives out of the family tent, which was apparently at this time (ver. 19) joined to that of Laban,—that he may take freer counsel with them. Notice the order of the names, reversing Laban's saying, ch. xxix. 26. **6.**] The whole speech of Jacob is inconsistent with the view maintained, e. g. by Kalisch, that he had cheated and overreached Laban throughout. And vv. 7, 8 reveal to us another contribution to our judgment on this matter. Laban had done all he could to overreach on his side: he had frequently (ten times is used to signify very often, see reff.) and capriciously changed the form of Jacob's hire; but all to no purpose: God defeated his schemes and turned them against himself. This fact, thus brought into witness by Jacob, but not previously recorded here, is regarded by Knobel as having been in the original documents, but omitted by the compiler of Genesis. **10, ff.**] He relates to his wives, not a vision seen years before, as some represent it, but the substance of the vision which he has just seen, and which had been the occasion of his sending for his wives. This is evident from ver. 13, where he relates God's command to him to leave Mesopotamia. Nor is there any real difficulty in this view, as even Keil fancies there is. He insists on the present tense, **doeth**, ver. 12, as shewing that this could not have been at the end of, but must have been during the progress of, the years of service. But we have no reason to think that Laban's behaviour towards him altered at the end of the time, or even that there *was* any "end of the time." Strictly speaking, Laban's endeavour to defraud him extended throughout. **11. the angel of God**] See ch. xxi. 17, and note, ch. xvi. 7. Here, as elsewhere, the angel, or messenger, plainly speaks in the person of God Himself. **13.**] The heart of Jacob is encouraged, and the command of God to him is carried home with

and return unto the land of thy kindred. [14] And Rachel
and Leah answered and said unto him, *Is there* yet any
portion or inheritance for us in our father's house? [15] Are
we not counted of him strangers? for he hath sold us, and
hath quite devoured also our money. [16] For all the riches
which God hath taken from our father, that *is* our's, and
our children's: now then, whatsoever God hath said unto
thee, do. [17] ¶ Then Jacob rose up, and set his sons and
his wives upon camels; [18] and he carried away all his
cattle, and all his goods which he had gotten, the cattle of
his getting, which he had gotten in Padan-aram, for to
go to Isaac his father in the land of Canaan. [19] And
Laban went to shear his sheep: and Rachel had stolen the
[k] images that *were* her father's. [20] And Jacob deceived the
heart of Laban the Aramæan, in that he told him not that
he fled. [21] So he fled with all that he had; and he rose up,
and passed over the river, and set his face *toward* the mount

k Judg. xvii. 5, &c. 1 Sam. xv. 23; xix. 13, 16. 2 Kings xxiii. 24. Ezek. xxi. 21. Hos. iii. 4. Zech. x. 2, only.

power, by the assurance that He who is now speaking to him is the same God who received his worship and his vow when he left the land to which he is now ordered to return. **14, ff.**] The answer of his wives is the only loyal one they could make, and is again entirely against the idea of guilt on Jacob's part. It is simply founded on the facts which have gone before in the history. Their father had sold them to Jacob: they were entirely severed from him, and he spared no pains to shew them this; Jacob's earnings, which were theirs also, their father was endeavouring to defraud them of. So that their consent is freely given to do that which God had commanded their husband.

15.] **quite devoured** is literally, **eating hath eaten**, as so often. **17—21.**] *Jacob's flight from Haran.* **19.**] Laban had left the encampment and gone to his flocks to superintend the shearing. Rachel, who apparently was still at least partly an idolatress, carried away her father's Teraphim, or household idols ("as Æneas carried away the Penates out of Troy." Knobel), that she might be under the protection of her paternal gods.

The history and archæology of the Teraphim are very curious. Both will be found entered into in Smith's *Bibl. Dict.* vol. ii. pp. 195—197, in Mr. Stuart Poole's article on Magic. The results only can be here stated. The derivation of the word Teraphim is wholly uncertain. The images called by that name are nowhere described: but from ref. 1 Sam. it would seem that they were of considerable size, large enough to be taken for the figure of a man. They were probably objects of pre-Abrahamite idolatry, put away by order of Jacob (Gen. xxxv. 2—4), but retained even in Joshua's time (Josh. xxiv. 14), and notwithstanding his exhortation, abandoned only for a space (Judg. xvii., xviii.). They were also known to the Babylonians, being used by them for divination (Ezek. xxi. 21). In ref. Zech. we find them consulted for oracular answers, as also apparently in ref. 2 Kings. Mr. Poole does not think there is any evidence that they were worshipped. As in this first recorded case of Laban, so in subsequent ones, their use seems to have been simultaneous with the acknowledgment of the true God. See *The Land and the Book*, p. 369, where an illustration is given.

21.] **Mount Gilead** is the eastern frontier of Palestine towards the desert. Kalisch objects that Mount Gilead is S. of the Jabbok, whereas Jacob did not cross the Jabbok till after his interview with Laban, who overtook him in Mount Gilead. The only solution seems to be that pointed out by

Gilead. 22 And it was told Laban on the third day that
Jacob was fled. 23 And he took his brethren with him,
and pursued after him seven days' journey; and they
overtook him in the mount Gilead. 24 And God came to
Laban the Aramæan in a dream by night, and said unto
l ch. xxiv. 50. 2 Sam. xiii. 22. him, Take heed that thou speak not to Jacob [l] either good
or bad. 25 ¶ Then Laban overtook Jacob. Now Jacob
had pitched his tent in the mount: and Laban with his
brethren pitched in the mount of Gilead. 26 And Laban
said to Jacob, What hast thou done, that thou hast de-
ceived my heart, and hast carried away my daughters, as
captives *taken* with the sword? 27 Wherefore didst thou
flee away secretly, and steal away from me; and didst not
tell me, that I might have sent thee away with mirth, and
with songs, with tabret, and with harp? 28 and hast not
suffered me to kiss my sons and my daughters? thou hast
m Deut. xxviii. 32. Neh. v. 5. Job xii. 6. Prov. iii. 27. Micah ii. 1. now done foolishly in *so* doing. 29 It is [m] in the power of
my hand to do you hurt: but the God of your father spake
unto me yesternight, saying, Take thou heed that thou
speak not to Jacob either good or bad. 30 And now,
though thou wouldest needs be gone, because thou sore
longedst after thy father's house, *yet* wherefore hast thou
stolen my gods? 31 And Jacob answered and said to

Deut. iii. 12, 13, that Mount Gilead also extended N. of the Jabbok. Eusebius describes it as "joining to Lebanon."

the river is the Euphrates. **22—55.**] *Laban pursues and overtakes Jacob. Their dispute, and final reconciliation.* **23.**] Laban's **brethren** must be understood in the wider sense, i. e. as comprehending his near relatives. It would appear that Jacob had made ten days' journey. **24.**] Compare the similar warning of God to Abimelech, ch. xx. 3. The phrase **to speak neither good nor bad** imports non-interference: see reff. The manifest sense in both these places seems to forbid that which Knobel would give here, see that thou pass not from saying good, viz. in the ordinary words of greeting, to saying bad, in anger and dispute. **26.**] Laban's speech is a compound, as Delitzsch observes, of paternal feeling and hypocrisy. **27.**] On **tabret,** see Exod. xv. 20. "The custom of accompanying friends at their departure with music and song is still observed in the East." Kalisch. These words of Laban's must clearly be ascribed to the latter of the above-mentioned sources. **28.**] By **sons** must be understood grandsons.

29.] As to the phrase which opens this verse, the Hebraists are, as usual in any doubtful point, entirely at issue. Laban says, **my hand is** *le-El;* i. e. either *as God,* or *as strength.* It is as to these two meanings that the difference lies. If we take the former, the sense is, there is no limit to my action except the strength of my hand; it is to me as God. If the latter, the sense is as in the A. V., my hand is sufficient in power to do you hurt. In the uncertainty, I retain the A. V. In the reff., where the same expression occurs, there is the same diversity of interpretation.

the God of your father seems to shew that Laban was not a worshipper of Abraham's God. **30.**] Jacob's flight might have been excusable, but what account could be

Laban, Because I was afraid: for I said, Peradventure
thou wouldest take by force thy daughters from me.
32 With whomsoever thou findest thy gods, let him not
live: before our brethren discern thou what *is* thine with
me, and take *it* to thee. For Jacob knew not that Rachel
had stolen them. 33 And Laban went into Jacob's tent,
and into Leah's tent, and into the two maidservants' tents;
but he found *them* not. Then went he out of Leah's tent,
and entered into Rachel's tent. 34 Now Rachel had taken
the images, and put them in the camel's furniture, and
sat upon them. And Laban searched all the tent, but
found *them* not. 35 And she said to her father, Let it not
displease my lord that I cannot rise up before thee; for
the custom of women *is* upon me. And he searched, but
found not the images. 36 ¶ And Jacob was wroth, and
chode with Laban: and Jacob answered and said to Laban,
What *is* my trespass? what *is* my sin, that thou hast so
[n] hotly pursued after me? 37 Whereas thou hast searched
all my stuff, what hast thou found of all thy household
stuff? set *it* here before my brethren and thy brethren,
that they may judge betwixt us both. 38 These twenty
years *have* I *been* with thee; thy ewes and thy she goats
have not cast their young, and the rams of thy flock have
I not eaten. 39 That which was torn *of beasts* I brought
not unto thee; I bare the loss of it; of my hand didst

n 1 Sam. xvii. 53, only.

given of his theft of Laban's gods?

31, ff.] Jacob first replies to the former part of Laban's question. Having in his innocence the stronger side as to the latter part, he lays the stress on that. **32.**] **our brethren**, i. e. thy brethren and my brethren—those who accompany us both: see ver. 37. **33.**] It is somewhat remarkable that the real culprit should have been the last suspected. It may serve to shew that the same duplicity which rescued Rachel under the search also had successfully gained for her a character for freedom from such an act. **34.**] "For the greater comfort of ladies or children performing long journeys on camels, a kind of couch or large chair is fastened on the saddle of the animal, and often one on each side; and in order to secure protection againt wind, rain, or the rays of the sun, the couch is appropriately overhung with curtains, so that it is not unlike a curtain-bed, while Arabic writers compare it to a house, or a palm tree: the light is let in by openings at the side; and as it is very commodious for reposing, it is not unfrequently used in the tents at times of encampment." Kalisch. **36.**] Those who observe the divine requital of Jacob's fraud on his father will note here the contemptible position into which he is brought, that of one deceiving another because he is deceived himself. All this virtuous indignation against Laban is founded on Rachel's lie. **hotly pursued after me** is literally **flamed out after me**: see reff. The whole of this speech, the Hebraists point out to us, is half-poetical, and its language highly rhetorical; hence such expressions as "the fear of Isaac:" see below. **39.**] In Exod. xxii. 13 it is provided that one en-

thou require it, *whether* stolen by day, or stolen by night.
40 *Thus* I was; in the day the heat consumed me, and the
frost by night; and my sleep departed from mine eyes.
41 Thus have I been twenty years in thy house; I served
thee fourteen years for thy two daughters, and six years
for thy cattle: and thou hast changed my wages ten times.
42 Except the God of my father, the God of Abraham, and
o Isa. viii. 13. the [o] fear of Isaac, had been with me, surely thou hadst
sent me away now empty. God hath seen mine affliction
and the labour of my hands, and rebuked *thee* yesternight.
43 ¶ And Laban answered and said unto Jacob, *These*
daughters *are* my daughters, and *these* children *are* my
children, and *these* cattle *are* my cattle, and all that thou
p = xxii. 12; xxvii. 45. Exod. xiv. 11. seest *is* mine: and what can I [p] do this day [p] unto these
my daughters, or unto their children which they have
born? 44 Now therefore come thou, let us make a cove-
nant, I and thou; and let it be for a witness between me
and thee. 45 And Jacob took a stone, and set it up *for* a
monument. 46 And Jacob said unto his brethren, Gather
stones; and they took stones, and made an heap: and
they did eat there upon the heap. 47 And Laban called
it Jegar-sahadutha [Heap of witness]: but Jacob called

trusted with the care of herds may bring that which was torn in pieces for witness, and should be free from making it good. The practice casts light on such passages as Amos iii. 12. On the latter clauses see also Exod. xxii. 12. **40.**] "It is well known," says Keil, "that in the East, the hotter the day the colder the night." **41.**] On the change of wages, and the ten times, see on ver. 7. **42. the fear of Isaac**] On the character of the expression, see above, and reff.; and a similar use of the word "fear" as an *object of* fear in Ps. xxxi. 11; Prov. i. 26, 27. Onkelos interprets here, "He whom Isaac feared." There may be something characteristic in this appellation of God as applied to Isaac. He was *the God* of Abraham. Abraham believed Him, and obeyed His commands; Isaac was less personally prominent in matters of the covenant, and seems throughout his course to have trodden somewhat timidly in the footsteps of his greater father. **43.**] Laban, returning to a better mind, confesses the folly of injuring Jacob's possessions, which after all are *his own*, sprung from him, and making part of his reputation. So he proposes a reconciliation and a covenant. The phrase **do unto**, in the bad sense of inflicting harm upon, is found in reff. **44.**] **let it**, viz. the covenant. **45.**] **a stone**, which is the token of the covenant, standing in its place. On stones set up for monuments, see on ch. xxviii. 18. **46.**] **his brethren** here seems to include Laban and his company: see ver. 54. **47.**] It is remarkable that in giving these names Laban chooses the Chaldee, Jacob the Hebrew, for the same meaning, "**the heap of witness.**" "These words," says Keil, "are the oldest testimony that in Mesopotamia, the mother country of the Patriarchs, Aramaic or Chaldee was spoken, while in Canaan, the country of Jacob's birth, Hebrew was the vernacular. And hence we may conclude, that Abraham's family had adopted the Hebrew from the Canaanites (i. e. the Phœnicians)." It has been remarked that the name **Galeed** is closely connected with *Gilead*. This would furnish another example

it Galeed [Heap of witness]. 48 And Laban said, This
heap *is* a witness between me and thee this day. There-
fore was the name of it called Galeed; 49 and q Mizpah
[Watchtower]; for he said, JEHOVAH watch between me
and thee, when we are absent one from another. 50 If
thou shalt afflict my daughters, or if thou shalt take *other*
wives beside my daughters, no man *is* with us; see, God
is witness betwixt me and thee. 51 And Laban said to
Jacob, Behold this heap, and behold *this* monument, which
I have cast betwixt me and thee; 52 this heap *be* witness,
and *this* monument *be* witness, that I will not pass over
this heap to thee, and that thou shalt not pass over this
heap and this monument unto me, for harm. 53 The God
of Abraham, and the God of Nahor, the God of their
father, be judges betwixt us. And Jacob sware by the fear
of his father Isaac. 54 Then Jacob offered sacrifice upon
the mount, and called his brethren to eat bread: and they
did eat bread, and tarried all night in the mount. 55 And
early in the morning Laban rose up, and kissed his sons
and his daughters, and blessed them: and Laban departed,
and returned unto his place. XXXII. 1 And Jacob went

q Judg. x. 17; xi. 11, 34; xx. 1, 3. (Josh. xiii. 26 ?) 1 Macc. v. 35.

of the allusive ascription of names which we have before noticed in commenting on the various origins ascribed to the name Beer-sheba. **49, 50.**] These verses have a parenthetical character, and would seem to have been a subsequent insertion, to connect the name Mizpah with the event. They present some difficulty, but not so much as at first sight may appear. We are surprised to find that the Hebrew allusion in the name Mizpah is taken up by the Aramæan (Chaldaic) Laban, who has just named the heap in Chaldee as distinguished from Jacob's Hebrew. But the words may mean this, that the name Mizpah (rather Ham-mizpah, with the definite article, **the Mizpah**) was given to it also, because of Laban's words which follow. The name was by no means an uncommon one. Mr. Grove, in the *Biblical Dict.*, gives no less than six distinct examples in Palestine. We might adduce a parallel in the very common appellation of "*Beacon*," or "*Beacon hill*," in our own country. Mr. Grove thinks that the name belonged to the place before, and that the word is "seized and played upon, in the address of Laban to Jacob, after the manner of these ancient people." At all events the name is found long after as belonging to a place in Gilead: see ref. Judges. It is doubtful whether, as some maintain, Mizpah is identical with Ramoth-Gilead: see this discussed at Deut. iv. 43. **absent**] literally, hidden. **50. afflict**] i. e. ill-treat. **53.**] Laban calls to witness the gods (the verb is in the plural in the original) of Abraham and Nahor and their father Terah; but Jacob swears only by the true God, Him whom Isaac his father feared. **54.**] It hardly seems plain whether this is to be regarded as a sacrifice in the proper sense or only a slaying of victims for the feast. The **brethren** clearly include Laban and his party. **55.**] Here again the sons are the grandsons.

XXXII. *Jacob meets the host of God* (1, 2). *He fears the encounter with Esau* (3—8); *prays for deliverance from him* (9—12); *prepares a present, and sends it and his company over the ford Jabbok* (13—23); *wrestles with an angel, and has his name changed to Israel* (24—32). **1.**] Jacob

on his way, and angels of God met him. 2 And when
Jacob saw them, he said, This *is* God's camp: and he
called the name of that place Mahanaim [Two camps].
3 And Jacob sent messengers before him to Esau his
brother unto the land of Seir, the country of Edom.
4 And he commanded them, saying, Thus shall ye speak
unto my lord Esau; Thy servant Jacob saith thus, I have
sojourned with Laban, and stayed there until now: 5 and
I have oxen, and asses, flocks, and menservants, and wo-
menservants: and I have sent to tell my lord, that I may
find grace in thy sight. 6 ¶ And the messengers returned
to Jacob, saying, We came to thy brother Esau, and also
he cometh to meet thee, and four hundred men with him.

was under the immediate protection of God, and the holy angels were round about his path. There is also significance in the fact that he was now about to enter the land of promise where God was especially pleased to tabernacle among men. This incident may be connected with the promise of ch. xxviii. 15, "I will bring thee again into this land." The LXX. version (alone) contains the singular and interesting clause after "his way,"—"and he lifted up his eyes and saw a camp of God encamped,"—"and the angels," &c. **2.**] The name given by Jacob records his impression, not that the angels were God's host, but that the *place* was God's **camp**: and he names the place *two camps*, i. e. either from the meeting of his own encampment with that of God, or perhaps, as some of the Hebraists seem to think, merely as a plural of dignity or majesty. **Mahanaim** was situated S. W. of Mizpah in Gilead, and to the N. (Mr. Grove, *Bibl. Dict.*, thinks the S., according to his differing view of the place of meeting of Jacob and Laban) of the river Jabbok, in the portion of Gad (Josh. xiii. 26, 30). Its sanctity was kept up by its being appointed one of the Levitical cities, and thus in a sense continuing to be "God's camp" (see Josh. xxi. 38; 1 Chron. vi. 63, 80). It was Ishbosheth's royal city during his short reign of two years (2 Sam. ii. 8, 12), and served as David's refuge when driven out before Absalom (2 Sam. xvii. 24, 27; 1 Kings ii. 8), being then a large walled city (2 Sam. xviii. 4). It was one of Solomon's twelve commissariat stations (1 Kings ii. 7, 14). For further interesting particulars, see Mr. Grove's article as above. He has some very interesting remarks on the curious features of this narrative: the mere passing mention of the camp of God, while the "two camps" into which his own followers were divided are several times dwelt upon (ver. 7, 10, 22); the same word used for the angels (messengers) of God and the messengers of Esau (vv. 1, 3, 6); the remarkable interchange and parallelism between the face of God (ver. 30) and the face of Esau as the face of God (ch. xxxiii. 10); the very name of the torrent, seemingly derived from the *wrestling* of the patriarch with the angel. "It is," says Dean Stanley (cited by Mr. Grove), "as if there were a correspondence throughout between the human and the divine, the inner and outer parts of the event, the host of God and the hosts of Jacob, the messengers of God and the messengers of Jacob, the face of God and the face of Esau." **4.**] Jacob sends the messengers in a spirit doubtless to be ascribed to his consciousness of his guilt, and his fear of its consequences. It is somewhat surprising to find Esau already dwelling in Mount Seir, seeing that we are told, in ch. xxxvi. 6—8, that the reason of his going there was the overcrowding of Gerar from the joint greatness of Jacob and Esau. But the consideration alleged by Keil and Delitzsch, after others, that Esau's alienation and absence from his father's house was probably gradual, may perhaps be taken as in some measure solving the difficulty. It is fair, however, to state that it is not a *sufficient* solution. Esau's home

7 Then Jacob was greatly afraid and distressed: and he
divided the people that *was* with him, and the flocks, and
herds, and the camels, into two camps; 8 and said, If Esau
come to the one camp, and smite it, then the other camp
which is left shall escape. 9 ¶ And Jacob said, O God of
my father Abraham, and God of my father Isaac, *even*
JEHOVAH, which saidst unto me, Return unto thy country,
and to thy kindred, and I will deal well with thee: 10 I
am too little for all the mercies, and for all the truth,
which thou hast shewed unto thy servant; for with my
staff I passed over this Jordan; and now I am become two
camps. 11 Deliver me, I pray thee, from the hand of my
brother, from the hand of Esau: for I fear him, lest he
will come and smite me, mother with children. 12 And
thou saidst, I will surely do thee good, and make thy seed
as the sand of the sea, which cannot be numbered for
multitude. 13 ¶ And he stayed there that same night;
and took of that which [r] came into his hand a present [r] 1 Kings x. 14. Ps. xc. 12 (see note).
for Esau his brother; 14 two hundred she goats, and

and centre of operations is *here* plainly **Mount Seir**: there he is found, and thence **he** sets out with his large following, whereas *there*, in ch. xxxvi., he took all his persons and his substance and went into the country from the face of his brother Jacob: and it is added, "Thus dwelt Esau in Mount Seir." It is hardly creditable that by some of the orthodox commentators this difficulty is not even noticed. **7.**] Some think that the prospect of meeting Esau's lawless hordes of Bedouins distressed Jacob. But doubtless the common view is right, which regards him as shrinking from his offended brother, in memory of his threat (ch. xxvii. 41, 42), and believing that this large host was intended for an attack upon him. Esau's real motive seems to have been to enhance his generous reconciliation by a demonstration of his power to hurt if he would. The word *Mahanah* (see ver. 2) is used throughout these verses as signifying the parts of Jacob's company, and ought to have been carefully preserved in the A. V., as it is by the LXX. It is caprice of this kind, rendering this word "*host*" in ver. 2, "*band*" in ver. 7, and "*company*" in ver. 8, which has so obscured the meaning of Scripture for English readers.

9—12.] *Jacob's prayer.* Observe the exactness of this address to God as contrasted with Laban's appellation of Him in ch. xxxi. 53. **10.**] The Hebrew expression is **little among all the mercies**, &c., i. e. too little to have received, less than all. In saying **two camps** he does not use the form Mahanaim as in ver. 2, but *sh'nay Mahanoth*, taking a different form. This is worth notice, in connexion with the remarks quoted on ver. 2. **11.**] The concluding words, **mother with children**, like "*root and branch*," betoken utter extirpation of a family or a community: compare Hosea x. 14. **13—23.**] *His present, and his preparations for meeting Esau.* **there**] i.e. at Mahanaim, which by the spirit of the narrative could not be far from both Jordan and Jabbok. The expression, **which came into his hand**, imports which he had earned and gotten. I have changed "*to*" for **into**, as expressing this somewhat more clearly. The words of the A. V. seem rather to import, which came uppermost, which were the first to present themselves; whereas the gift was most carefully selected and ordered. The whole purpose is evidently to deprecate wrath.

14, 15.] We are told that the proportionate numbers are those best calculated for breeding. The arrangements and orders in vv. 16—20

twenty he goats, two hundred ewes, and twenty rams,
15 thirty milch camels with their colts, forty kine, and ten
bulls, twenty she asses, and ten foals. 16 And he delivered
them into the hand of his servants, every drove by them-
selves; and said unto his servants, Pass over before me,
and put a space betwixt drove and drove. 17 And he com-
manded the foremost, saying, When Esau my brother
meeteth thee, and asketh thee, saying, Whose *art* thou?
and whither goest thou? and whose *are* these before thee?
18 then thou shalt say, *They be* thy servant Jacob's; it *is*
a present sent unto my lord Esau: and, behold, also he *is*
behind us. 19 And so commanded he the second, and the
third, and all that followed the droves, saying, On this
manner shall ye speak unto Esau, when ye find him.
20 And say ye moreover, Behold, thy servant Jacob *is* be-
hind us. For he said, I will appease him with the pre-
sent that goeth before me, and afterwards I will see his
face; peradventure he will accept of me. 21 So went the
present over before him: and himself stayed that night
in the camp. 22 And he rose up that night, and took his
two wives, and his two womenservants, and his eleven
sons, and passed over the ford Jabbok. 23 And he took
them, and sent them over the brook, and sent over
that he had. 24 ¶ And Jacob was left alone; and there

are just those best calculated to mollify an angry man. Esau is to meet each generous present separately, that the effect may be again and again repeated. Each time with the same deferential words, and the same assurance that Jacob was not about to shrink from meeting him. All this lies in his own reasoning, ver. 20. **21.**] There is no reason, with Bp. Wordsworth, to suppose that he *fortified* himself there, because the word **camp** occurs here: it has occurred throughout, as noticed above; and he would hardly fortify himself in a position he meant to leave before meeting the enemy.

22.] His two women-servants, Bilhah and Zilpah, belonged to his own family, being the mothers of his sons. The sons were all of tender age at this time. The river or torrent Jabbok was "the border of the children of Ammon" (Deut. iii. 16; Josh. xii. 2: see also Num. xxi. 24; Deut. ii. 37). It intersects the mountain-range of Gilead. Its modern name is Wady Zurka. Its banks are fringed with thickets of cane and Oleander, and are clothed above with oak forests. See Porter's Handbook, and his art. in the *Biblical Dict.* **24—32.**] *Jacob wrestles with an angel. Change of his name.* It would appear that Jacob remained on the hither bank of the torrent, when he had sent over all that he had. It was for him a solemn crisis, and he sought retirement and solitude. To give, as Kalisch, an entirely spiritual meaning to the wonderful scene which follows is little better than trifling with it. Whatever be the interpretation of this history, which is perhaps the strongest example of anthropomorphism in the whole of Scripture, there can be no doubt that if the sacred narrative be good for anything, it has its two sides, the spiritual and the outward. Not *only* did

wrestled a man with him until the breaking of the day.
25 And when he saw that he prevailed not against him, he
touched the hollow of his thigh ; and the hollow of Jacob's
thigh was out of joint, as he wrestled with him. 26 And
he said, Let me go, for the day breaketh. And he said,
I will not let thee go, except thou bless me. 27 And he
said unto him, What *is* thy name ? And he said, Jacob.
28 And he said, Thy name shall be called no more Jacob,
but Israel [Contender with God]: for thou hast con-
tended with God and with men, and hast prevailed.
29 And Jacob asked *him,* and said, Tell *me,* I pray thee,
thy name. And he said, Wherefore *is* it *that* thou dost
ask after my name ? And he blessed him there. 30 And
Jacob called the name of the place Peniel [Face of God]:
for I have seen God face to face, and my life is preserved.
31 And as he passed over Penuel the sun rose upon him,
and he halted upon his thigh. 32 Therefore the children

the incident betoken a mighty crisis in Jacob's inner life, but it also was accompanied by supernatural tokens of the kind indicated in the narrative. The **man** here spoken of is an appearance of God, that appearance of which we have before spoken, whose words are uttered in the Person and name of God Himself. **24.**] The word for **wrestled** is only found in this place, and is said to be an ancient form. From it (*Javayk*) is the name of the torrent, Jabbok. **25.**] In this symbolic struggle we may perhaps discern the spiritual meaning. Jacob had too much, and often in his life, wrestled with and resisted God, and God prevailed against him by the power of afflictions—crippling him in his family and his personal happiness—causing him to enter into life maimed, rather than being whole to be lost. And the power and struggles of Jacob's faith prevailed to hold the blessing from God, but not without that faith being saddened by repentance. The triumph was greater than the defeat: for by the former he obtained the name of the Contender with God, which holy theocratic name descended to his posterity, and became their natural appellation. **the hollow of the thigh**] Where passes the *nervus ischiadicus*, the greatest of the sinews, descending through the leg to the ankle. **26.**] The immortal must not be seen by mortals in that day which lights them to ordinary work: their apparitions occur in the night when this world's light is withdrawn. The idea has been universal, and here finds the sanction. Jacob's was the true pertinacity of faithful effectual prayer. Compare Hosea xii. 4, where his prevailing is ascribed to his "weeping" and making supplication unto the angel. **28.**] **Israel**, from *Sara,* the same word which gave meaning to the name Sarai, and El, God. So that the meaning is doubtful between "a Prince of God," and "a Contender with God." **29.**] The name of the divine messenger is not to be told to men: so in Judges xiii. 17, 18. See also Exod. iii. 13, 14 ; Levit. xxiv. 11 ; Isa. ix. 6 ; Rev. xix. 12. **30.**] On the remarkable parallelisms in this passage between the divine and the human, see note, ver. 2. **31.**] No account has been given by the Hebraists of the change in the spelling of the name Peniel to Penuel. It has been suggested that the latter may have been the commonly recognized local name, and that the slight change to Peniel may have been made to suit the etymological derivation. Commentators have drawn attention to the parallel case of St. Paul, who after an abundance of divine revelations, received a thorn in the flesh, 2 Cor. xii. 7. **32.**]

of Israel eat not *of* the sinew of the hip, which *is* upon the
hollow of the thigh, unto this day: because he touched
the hollow of Jacob's thigh in the sinew of the hip.
XXXIII. 1 And Jacob lifted up his eyes, and looked, and,
behold, Esau came, and with him four hundred men. And
he divided the children unto Leah, and unto Rachel, and
unto the two handmaids. 2 And he put the handmaids
and their children foremost, and Leah and her children
behind, and Rachel and Joseph behind. 3 And he passed
over before them, and bowed himself to the ground seven
times, until he came near to his brother. 4 And Esau ran
to meet him, and embraced him, and fell on his neck,
and kissed him: and they wept. 5 And he lifted up his
eyes, and saw the women and the children; and said, Who
are those with thee? And he said, The children which
God hath graciously given thy servant. 6 Then the
handmaidens came near, they and their children, and they
bowed themselves. 7 And Leah also with her children
came near, and bowed themselves: and after came Joseph

This practice has no sanction in the law, but is, "unto this day" in which we live also, rigidly observed by the Jews. A strict Jew cannot, for that reason, eat of a leg of mutton which has come from a Christian butcher.

There is some doubt about the appellation of the sinew in this verse, from an uncertainty as to the meaning of the Hebrew root of the word used. The more probable sense of the term is that given in the text, which is preferred by Gesenius, Knobel, Keil, Kalisch, and other Hebraists. But Gesenius confesses that "*the sinew which shrank*" (A. V.), or *which failed*, is also a legitimate rendering.

XXXIII. *Meeting of Jacob and Esau* (1—16). *Jacob settles at Shechem* (17—20).

1, 2.] The arrangement is one of distrust and timidity. The least cared for are put in the brunt of the possible danger. But there is no cowardice: he advances to the front himself. It is not asserted, but may be fairly taken as implied, that Rachel and Joseph were behind Leah and her children. The Hebrew is as our text, the same word being used for **behind** in both cases. Compare ver. 7. **3.**] He bowed himself, after the Eastern fashion, bending the body so that the face nearly touches the ground. He did this seven times, to denote the completeness of his humiliation, and his deep sense of the guilt by which he had merited his brother's displeasure. The text gives us to understand that these obeisances were made not on the same spot, but one after another as he approached Esau. **4.**] Very different is the behaviour of the reckless and generous Esau. We can hardly read this description without being reminded of another penitent in Luke xv. 20, to whom the same gracious reception was granted. The very words used by our Lord in the Greek there are the same as those of the LXX. here. The Masoretic editors of the Hebrew text have set dots over the word "*kissed-him*," which are generally explained as expressing a doubt of the genuineness of the kiss. Surely it need not be doubted, but is entirely in keeping with Esau's character. A very curious substitution for the word was given by some of the Jewish commentators, "*he bit him*:" and the Targum of Jonathan explains the weeping of Jacob to be occasioned by pain in the neck, that of Esau by pain in the teeth! **5—7.**] Jacob's wives and children attracting Esau's attention, are presented to him and do

near and Rachel, and they bowed themselves. 8 And he
said, What *meanest* thou by all this †host which I met? † Heb. *camp.*
And he said, *These are* to find grace in the sight of my
lord. 9 And Esau said, I have abundance, my brother;
keep that thou hast unto thyself. 10 And Jacob said, Nay,
I pray thee, if now I have found grace in thy sight, thou
wilt receive my present at my hand: for therefore I have
seen thy face, as though I had seen the face of God, and
thou wast pleased with me. 11 Take, I pray thee, my
blessing that is brought to thee; because God hath dealt
graciously with me, and because I have everything. And
he urged him, and he took *it*. 12 And he said, Let us take
our journey, and let us go, and I will go by thy side.
13 And he said unto him, My lord knoweth that the chil-
dren *are* tender, and the flocks and herds giving suck *are*
with me: and if men should overdrive them one day, all
the flock will die. 14 Let my lord, I pray thee, pass over
before his servant: and I will lead on softly, according to
the pace of the cattle that goeth before me and according
to the pace of the children, until I come unto my lord
unto Seir. 15 And Esau said, Let me now leave with thee
some of the folk that *are* with me. And he said, What need-
eth it? let me find grace in the sight of my lord. 16 ¶ So

reverence before him. The order observed here confirms the ordinary interpretation of ver. 2. **8—11.** The *present* next attracts Esau's attention. The same word (*Mahanah*) is again used as before.

9, 10.] Esau's generous answer does not satisfy Jacob, because the non-acceptance of the offered gift would leave doubtful the fact of entire reconciliation. Jacob might truly say, not in mere compliment, that the sight of Esau's face had been to him as the sight of God's face, discerning as he did in his brother's altered mind to him a sign of the divine favour. **13, 14.**] The excuse was genuine. Tender children, such as many of Jacob's were, would be injured, and flocks in milk, or with young, would die even with a day's overdriving; and therefore could not keep pace with Esau and his men. Observe Jacob addresses Esau always as "*my lord*," but Esau speaks to Jacob as "*my brother*." The one had a guilty conscience, which forbade him to touch on the brotherly relation; the other was clear in this matter.

pass over, in ver. 14, must be apparently understood as applying to Jordan. But we find Jacob next at Succoth, E. of Jordan: see below. And it does not appear why Esau should have to cross Jordan to get to Seir. The whole scene of this interview seems to need better localizing than it has yet met with. Again, it would seem from this verse as if Jacob also were directing his course toward Seir; and this is hardly met by saying, as Keil, that he probably meant to visit Esau at Seir at some subsequent time. **15.**] Esau is anxious that his brother should have an escort from among his followers. We can hardly fail to see in this reply a lingering of mistrust, if not of his brother, yet of his wild followers. The rendering is somewhat uncertain. It may be as in A. V., which, in doubt, I have retained; or it may be as Kalisch gives it: "*wherefore do I thus find* grace in the eyes of my lord?" Other renderings are given:

Esau returned that day on his way unto Seir. 17 And Jacob
journeyed to Succoth, and built him an house, and made
booths for his cattle: therefore the name of the place is
s See ch. xxviii. 21. called Succoth [Booths]. 18 ¶ And Jacob came [s] in peace
to the city of Shechem, which *is* in the land of Canaan,
when he came from Padan-aram; and pitched his tent
before the city. 19 And he bought a parcel of a field,
where he had spread his tent, at the hand of the children
t Josh. xxiv. 32. Job xlii. 11, only. of Hamor, Shechem's father, for an hundred [t] pieces of
money. 20 And he erected there an altar, and called it

the LXX. have, "*Why this? it is enough, that I have found grace in thy sight, my lord;*" the Vulgate, "*There is no need: this is all I want, to find,*" &c. On any of these the sense is the same. **17.**] **Succoth** is another of those places whose site is as yet wholly unascertained, and our view as to even its proximate situation must depend on the whole theory which we adopt as to the meeting-place of Jacob and Laban. Mr. Grove (*Biblical Dict.*) says, "From the itinerary of Jacob's return it seems that Succoth lay between Peniel, near the ford of the torrent Jabbok, and Shechem (compare Gen. xxxii. 30, and xxxiii. 18). In accordance with this is the mention of Succoth in the narrative of Gideon's pursuit of Zebah and Zalmunna (Judg. viii. 5—17). His course is eastward—the reverse of Jacob's—and he comes first to Succoth and thence to Penuel, the latter being further up the mountain than the former (ver. 8, 'he went up thence'). . . . It would appear from this passage that it lay to the East of Jordan, which is corroborated by the fact that it was allotted to the tribe of Gad (Josh. xiii. 27)." Jerome also sets it "on the other side of Jordan, in the district of Scythopolis," so that it cannot by any probability be the place generally called by this name, which is W. of Jordan and considerably N. of Jabbok (*Wady Zurka*); and known also as Scythopolis and Bethshean: nor again with *Sakut*, which Burckhardt thought he had identified as Succoth, also on the W. side of the Jordan. It would appear that Jacob lived for some time in Succoth. Knobel calls this improbable, seeing that he was returning to his father's house. But as Keil suggests, he might have gone thence and visited his father: and his great establishment could not well have found place with Isaac. Besides, it appears that Dinah was grown up when he came to Shechem, and she must have been hardly more than an infant when he left Laban. **18.**] There is considerable uncertainty about the construing of this verse. It seems very improbable that the word Salem should be a proper name, as the A. V., after the LXX. and Vulgate, has rendered it. No such place is known in the neighbourhood of Sichem (Nablus), nor mentioned elsewhere in the Bible. The meaning is far more probably "in peace," and the reference is to ch. xxviii. 21, where, in his prayer, Jacob speaks of coming again to his father's house in peace. And so it is taken by most of the Hebraists. On **Shechem,** see ch. xii. 6, 8. **19.**] This is the first possession of land, *as land*, by the Patriarchs in the country of Promise. In ch. xxxvii. 12 we find that Jacob, then dwelling at Hebron, had his flocks at Shechem. The **piece of money** here mentioned is expressed by an unusual word (reff.), *Kesitah*. Of this word two interpretations have been given. 1. *A lamb*, as A. V. in margin here, following the LXX., Vulgate, old Syriac, Samaritan Pentateuch, and the Targum of Onkelos. But Gesenius remarks that there is nothing in the etymology favouring this, and that in the patriarchal days the practice of barter had given place to that of purchasing by weighed silver: see ch. xxiii. 16; xlvii. 16. 2. The other interpretation makes the *Kesitah* a *piece of money*, or a precious metal, of some kind: of what value it is quite uncertain. This is favoured by Acts vii. 16, which must refer to this transaction. Some have supposed the medium to have been a coin impressed with the *figure of a lamb:* but there is no reason to suppose that coined money was at this time in use. The word *Kesitah* comes from a root signifying

El-elohe-Israel [God (El), the God of Israel]. XXXIV.
1 And Dinah the daughter of Leah, which she bare unto
Jacob, went out to see the daughters of the land. 2 And
Shechem the son of Hamor the Hivite, prince of the
country, saw her; and he took her, and lay with her, and
[u] ravished her. 3 And his soul clave unto Dinah the
daughter of Jacob, and he loved the damsel, and [v] spake
unto the heart of the damsel. 4 And Shechem spake unto
his father Hamor, saying, Get me this damsel to wife.
5 And Jacob heard that he had [w] defiled Dinah his daughter:
now his sons were with his cattle in the field: and Jacob
held his peace until they were come. 6 ¶ And Hamor the
father of Shechem went out unto Jacob to commune with

u Judg. xix. 24; xx. 5. 2 Sam. xiii. 22. Lam. v. 11.
v ch. l. 21. Hos. ii. 14.

w vv. 13, 27. Num. xix. 13. 2 Kings xxiii. 10. Ps. lxxix. 1. Ezek. xviii. 6, &c.; xxii. 11; xxiii. 17.

to weigh, or *balance*. **20.**] This whole transaction was an act of faith on the part of Jacob. The purchase of land, and that in the very place where God had first promised Abraham that the land should be his, shewed his conviction in the certainty of that promise as renewed to him and his seed: the erection of an altar on this his own land connected the act of purchase with the God in whose promise he trusted: and the naming of that altar bespoke special faith in the symbolic meaning of the name which God had given him, and its endurance in his posterity. In the building of an altar on that spot he had been preceded by Abraham, ch. xii. 7.

XXXIV. *Dinah's seduction by Shechem; the vengeance taken on him and his by Simeon and Levi.* **1.**] Dinah was apparently about thirteen when this happened, an age at which Oriental maidens are ripe for marriage. She, as already remarked on ch. xxxiii. 17, was but a child when Jacob left Padan-aram; but there had been a considerable time spent in Succoth. Joseph, who was not far from the same age as Dinah, was seventeen when he was sent to his brethren, ch. xxxvii. 2. There is no absolute fixity in any of these suggested dates; but neither is there any assignment of dates which would render this history improbable. The idea that Dinah must have been a mere child at this time has nothing in the narrative to support it, and the implication in ch. xxxiii. 17 is against it.

Observe, this is Jacob's first great trouble, and in it he is the victim of deceit on the part of his own sons, as he had, in his time deceived his own father. **1.**] No absolute blame is conveyed in this mention of Dinah's act, but there can be no doubt that it is mentioned here for warning, and as having led to the deplorable consequences which followed. **2.**] The proceeding was merely the carrying out of that which had been in two cases with Sarah, and in one with Rebekah, stopped before its sad issue. According to the usual practices of heathen society, it had nothing noteworthy in it. But it is already strongly condemned and thought matter of the sternest revenge in the patriarchal family. Nothing can more strikingly shew the different moral atmosphere of the two societies. For **the Hivite**, see ch. x. 17. As regards the fact, it should be remarked that no gradual temptation and seduction is described, but an act of violence, as will be seen by referring to the use of the same word in the reff. This ought to have been carefully observed in the English version, especially as the verb in vv. 5, 13, 27, is another, and really signifies to *defile*. It would therefore appear that Dinah suffered, rather than consented to, the penalty of her vain curiosity.

3.] Notwithstanding, there was true affection between the two. Shechem spoke to her heart, i. e. strove to gain her affection: see reff. **4.**] For this was the parents' matter: see ch. xxi. 21; xxiv. 1, &c.

5.] The verb used here (see above) is not the same as that in ver. 2. Its usage will be seen in reff. Jacob **held his peace**, i. e. took no step: see 2 Sam. xix. 11. It

him. 7 And the sons of Jacob came out of the field when
they heard *it*: and the men were grieved, and they were
x = Deut. xxii. 21. Judg. xix. 23. 2 Sam. xiii. 12. Hos. ii. 10. y Josh. vii. 15. Judg. xx. 6, 10.
very wroth, because he had [x] wrought folly [y] in Israel in
lying with Jacob's daughter; which thing ought not to
be done. 8 And Hamor communed with them, saying,
The soul of my son Shechem longeth for your daughter:
I pray you give her him to wife. 9 And make ye mar-
riages with us, *and* give your daughters unto us, and take
our daughters unto you. 10 And ye shall dwell with us:
z ch. xiii. 9; xx. 15.
and the land shall be [z] before you; dwell and trade ye
therein, and get you possessions therein. 11 And Shechem
said unto her father and unto her brethren, Let me find
grace in your eyes, and what ye shall say unto me I will
a Exod. xxii. 17. 1 Sam. xviii. 25, only.
give. 12 Ask me never so much [a] dowry and gift, and I
will give according as ye shall say unto me: but give me
the damsel to wife. 13 And the sons of Jacob answered She-
b = 2 Chron. xxii. 10 (Ps. cxxxvii. 5 ?).
chem and Hamor his father deceitfully, and [b] laid a plot,
because he had defiled Dinah their sister: 14 and they
said unto them, We cannot do this thing, to give our sis-
ter to one that is uncircumcised; for that *were* a reproach
unto us: 15 but in this will we consent unto you: If ye
will be as we *be*, that every male of you be circumcised;
16 then will we give our daughters unto you, and we will
take your daughters to us, and we will dwell with you,
and we will become one people. 17 But if ye will not
hearken unto us, to be circumcised; then will we take our

would appear, from Jacob's speech in ver. 30, that he was inclined to compromise the matter. 7.] The expression **wrought folly in Israel** manifestly belongs to a later time (see reff.), and betrays the hand of a subsequent editor. It may have been used by Moses, as it was by Joshua (ref.); but could hardly have been found in any document dating previously to the constitution of a community known by the name Israel. The last clause of the verse is a weighty testimony, on the part of the sacred writer, against the enormity of the crime. The words are still simpler than would appear: the notion of *ought not* is only implied in them: **which is not done**, is not the custom, is the literal rendering: see a similar construction in ch. xx. 9; xxix. 26. **8. your daughter**] Spoken to the father and the brothers, as being her natural guardians: see ver. 17. **10. the land shall be before you**] Free to your choice: see reff. 12.] The **dowry** (reff.) was the present which the bridegroom gave to the parents or relatives of the bride. The case provided for in ref. Exod. is in all features but one the same as this. The **gift** was the present to the bride. The two are distinguished in the narrative, ch. xxiv. 53. 13.] The ordinary interpretation, "*and said,*" or "*and spoke,*" is rejected by the Hebraists,—Gesenius, Knobel, Keil, all adopting the rarer sense of the Hebrew verb *davar*, found without doubt in reff. 2 Chron. and perhaps in the Psalms also. Onkelos gives "*and spoke subtilly;*" the Vulgate, "*being angry.*" 17.] On **our daughter**, see ver. 8. 19.] Shechem had no hesitation in

daughter, and we will be gone. 18 And their words
pleased Hamor, and Shechem Hamor's son. 19 And the
young man deferred not to do the thing, because he had
delight in Jacob's daughter: and he *was* more honoured
than all the house of his father. 20 ¶ And Hamor and
Shechem his son came unto the gate of their city, and
communed with the men of their city, saying, 21 These
men *are* peaceable with us; therefore let them dwell in
the land, and trade therein; for the land, behold, *it is*
large on all sides before them; let us take their daughters
to us for wives, and let us give them our daughters. 22
Only herein will the men consent unto us for to dwell
with us, to be one people, if every male among us be cir-
cumcised, as they *are* circumcised. 23 *Shall* not their cat-
tle and their substance and every beast of their's *be* our's?
only let us consent unto them, and they will dwell with
us. 24 And unto Hamor and unto Shechem his son
hearkened all that went out of the gate of his city; and
every male was circumcised, all that went out of the gate
of his city. 25 ¶ And it came to pass on the third day,
when they were sore, that two of the sons of Jacob, Simeon
and Levi, Dinah's brethren, took each man his sword,
and came upon the city boldly, and slew all the males.
26 And they slew Hamor and Shechem his son with the
[c]edge of the sword, and took Dinah out of Shechem's
house, and went out. 27 The sons of Jacob came upon

c Exod. xvii. 13. Num. xxi. 24. Deut. xiii. 15 Josh. vi. 21, &c.

complying: the words do not imply that he forthwith *did* that which was proposed, but are anticipating. The latter clause does not mean that his disposition was more honourable, but that he stood in the highest place of public honour and esteem, and his consent would therefore ensure that of all. **20.**] On **the gate of their city**, on the place of assembly and council, see ch. xxiii. 4—10. **21.**] Literally, **it is large of hands to their faces**, i. e. it is large to right and left before them. **23.**] By **cattle**, as in ch. iv. 20, is meant pasturing and grazing flocks and herds, and by **every beast** is meant beasts of burden, as camels and asses (Num. xxxii. 26). **25.**] Reuben seems to have taken no part, being, as firstborn, especially responsible to his father: see ch. xxxvii. 21, ff.; xlii. 22. Simeon and Levi were the two next of Dinah's brothers. Quotations are given from travellers in the East, illustrating the severity with which brothers avenge insult to a sister's honour. Burckhardt gives a case in which three brothers endeavoured to kill their sister's betrothed, merely on account of some innocent caress. **26.**] The expression **with the edge** (lit. the **face**, mouth) **of the sword** (reff.) denotes relentless execution. For anything that we gather from the narrative itself, Dinah was detained against her will. Nothing has been said to imply that she returned the affection of Shechem.

27.] This verse is not coupled to those which went before, and hence some have regarded vv. 27—29 as an insertion.

the slain, and spoiled the city, because they had defiled
their sister. 28 They took their sheep, and their oxen,
and their asses, and that which *was* in the city, and that
which *was* in the field, 29 and all their wealth, and all
their little ones, and their wives took they captive, and
spoiled even all that *was* in the house. 30 And Jacob
said to Simeon and Levi, Ye have troubled me to [d]make
me to stink among the inhabitants of the land, among the
Canaanites and the Perizzites: and I *being* few in number,
they shall gather themselves together against me, and slay
me; and I shall be destroyed, I and my house. 31 And
they said, Should he deal with our sister as with an har-
lot? XXXV. 1 And God said unto Jacob, Arise, go up
to Beth-el, and dwell there: and make there an altar
unto † God, that appeared unto thee when thou fleddest

d Exod. v. 21. 1 Sam. xiii. 4. 2 Sam. x. 6.

† El.

Keil objects to this that the insertor would have taken care to put in the copula also, and regards the abruptness as characteristic of the transaction, which is surely improbable. **The sons of Jacob** are apparently the *other* sons of Jacob, as the Vulgate renders. It is no objection to this that no blame is laid on them in their father's dying words in ch. xlix. Simeon and Levi were the chief perpetrators of the crime. **30.**] On the **Canaanites and Perizzites,** see ch. xii. 6; xiii. 7. **few in number** is literally **people (men) of number**, i. e. a body of persons easily counted. The fear expressed by Jacob was a very natural one, and might have come to pass, but for the reason given in ch. xxxv. 5. That this was not the only cause of Jacob's horror at the conduct of his sons is shewn by his dying speech, ch. xlix. 5, where their moral delinquency is fully asserted. **31.**] This had been done, in that she had first fallen victim to Shechem's lust, and then had been kept in his house. The exasperated brothers keep out of view altogether, like angry men, any circumstances on the other side. The whole history points to what was so often Israel's sin in after time—the double fault of mingling with the idolatrous people around them, and using immoral means to vindicate their national pre-eminence. Compare e. g. the whole of Judges iv., v.

XXXV. **1—15.** *Jacob by divine command goes to Bethel. God renews to him the promise and the change of name: and he renews the name Bethel.* It was now many years (not less than 30) since Jacob had made the vow to JEHOVAH in Bethel. This vow he had not as yet performed. And now the divine command enjoins on him immediately to do so. Kalisch thinks, and with probability, that one reason which had hitherto hindered him may have been, that whereas the performance of the vow would imply an entire devotion of him and his to JEHOVAH (see its terms, ch. xxviii. 20—22), the state of his household with regard to the retention of strange gods would by no means permit this. Certainly this view falls in well with our vv. 2—4, in which he inaugurates his journey to Bethel by clearing his household of objects of idolatrous worship. Several things in this narrative appear like repetitions of what has been related before. The re-naming of Jacob, ver. 10; the naming of Bethel, ver. 15; the setting up of a monument, ver. 14; coupled with the fact that in all this history the divine name is Elohim, whereas in all that other about Bethel (ch. xxviii. 10—22), it is JEHOVAH: these considerations make it at least probable that the sources of our narrative are not one, but several. **1.**] God (JEHOVAH) had *appeared* to him, ch. xxviii. 13. Knobel says this statement is not exact, as there was no actual appearance in ch. xxviii. But surely the words "behold Jehovah stood above it" cannot well be otherwise understood.

from the face of Esau thy brother. 2 Then Jacob said
unto his household, and to all that *were* with him, [e]Put
away the strange gods that *are* among you, and be [f]clean,
and [g]change your garments: 3 and let us arise, and go
up to Beth-el; and I will make there an altar unto God,
who answered me in the day of my distress, and was with
me in the way which I went. 4 And they gave unto
Jacob all the strange gods which *were* in their hand, and
all their [h]earrings which *were* in their ears; and Jacob hid
them under the oak which *was* by Shechem. 5 And they
journeyed: and the [i]terror of God was upon the cities
that *were* round about them, and they did not pursue after
the sons of Jacob. 6 ¶ So Jacob came to Luz, which *is*
in the land of Canaan, that *is*, Beth-el, he and all the
people that *were* with him. 7 And he built there an altar,
and called the place El-beth-el [God of Bethel]: because
there God was revealed unto him, when he fled from the
face of his brother. 8 But Deborah Rebekah's nurse died,
and she was buried beneath Beth-el under an oak: and

e Exod. xx. 3—5, 23. Ezek. xx. 7, 18; xxxvii. 23.
f Exod. xxix. 4; xl. 12. Lev. viii. 6.
g Exod. xix. 10, 14. Num. viii. 7. Zech. iii. 3—5.
h Isa. iii. 20. See Deut. xviii. 10.
i Ezek. xxvi. 17; xxxii. 23—32.

2—4.] The strange gods have been partly already accounted for by Rachel having stolen her father's Teraphim (ch. xxxi. 19, 34); and it seems probable from ch. xxxi. 53, compared with Joshua xxiv. 2, that Jacob's camp followers and servants were partly made up of idolaters. Such a mixture was prohibited among the worshippers of Jehovah (see reff.), and would defile His sanctuary (Ezek. v. 11; xxii. 3, f.; xxxvi. 18; compare 2 Kings xxi. 4). **change your garments**] See reff. The garments bore a considerable part afterwards in the provisions concerning Levitical cleanness and uncleanness: see Levit. xiii. to xv.

3.] God had answered Jacob throughout the days of his distress, and more especially in his deliverances from Laban and from Esau. **4.**] "Earrings were frequently used as amulets, believed to arrest evil, or to act as a charm; they were often covered with allegorical figures or mysterious sentences, according to the deities to which they were consecrated; they formed therefore one of the ordinary instruments of superstitious usages." Abridged from Kalisch. See also reff. **hid them**] i. e. buried them. In the repetition of this same act of purification by Joshua (Josh. xxiv. 26) mention is again made of an oak (or terebinth) at Shechem. The Hebraists tell us that we must not understand by this term any particular tree, but one tree among many. **5.**] **the terror of God**, which held back the cities from taking vengeance on Jacob's sons for the massacre at Shechem, was evidently a supernatural panic instilled by God into their minds, not the fear of God, as commonly understood. The word itself occurs only here; but its cognates are used in the same sense in reff.; and we have *the fear of Jehovah* similarly used in Exod. xxiii. 27; 2 Chron. xiv. 14. **6.**] On **Luz** and **Bethel**, see on ch. xxviii. **7.**] **was revealed** is not the same word as *appeared* in ver. 1, and should have been kept distinct in the A. V. The verb is here plural, and perhaps not without reason, as it was a vision of God accompanied by the holy angels. **8.**] The occasion of this being mentioned is not clear, nor how Deborah, who had accompanied Rebekah to Canaan, ch. xxiv. 59, came in the train of Jacob. Some have supposed that she may have been sent from his mother according to her promise, ch. xxvii. 45. May it not have well been that on Rebekah's death, which probably had happened before this, she may

the name of it was called Allon-bachuth [Oak of weeping].
9 ¶ And God appeared unto Jacob again, when he came
out of Padan-aram, and blessed him. 10 And God said
unto him, Thy name *is* Jacob: thy name shall not be
called any more Jacob, but Israel shall be thy name: and
he called his name Israel. 11 And God said unto him, I
j El Shaddai: see ch. xvii. 1. *am* j God Almighty: be fruitful and multiply; a nation
and a company of nations shall be of thee, and kings shall
come out of thy loins; 12 and the land which I gave
Abraham and Isaac, to thee I will give it, and to thy
seed after thee will I give the land. 13 And God went
up from him in the place where he talked with him. 14
And Jacob set up a pillar in the place where he talked
with him, a pillar of stone: and he poured a drink offer-
ing thereon, and he poured oil thereon. 15 And Jacob

have been transferred to the favourite son of her foster-child? She was sure to have been much about him in his infancy. We have before remarked that Jacob must be supposed to have visited Isaac at Hebron before this. It is noticeable, that the great prophetess Deborah dwelt under a palm-tree not far from this neighbourhood (Judg. iv. 5), between Bethel and Ramah. **the name of it was called,** literally [people], **called its name.** This word, *bachuth* for mourning, occurs only here, and a similar word, *bechith*, with the same meaning, only in ch. l. 4, in a portion attributed by Knobel to the same writer as this. **9—15.**] It is hardly possible to imagine this a continuous portion of the same narrative with what we have just been reading. Doubtless ingenious reasons may be discovered why it should be so accounted, but they are very far-fetched, and only credible by those who earnestly wish to believe them. The furthest that the unbiassed reader can go in their direction is to conclude that this appearance is one not related before; that it is taken from some document independent of that which contained the change of name in ch. xxxii.; and that the change, which as matter of accurate detail took place on that occasion, is here generally related. It is of course possible that this appearance may have been taken as an opportunity for solemnly ratifying the change of name then made; but if we hold this, we must be prepared for the improbability of ten years having elapsed, during which the name Israel must have been in use, between the first change and this ratification. And then there is nothing in ver. 15 to imply that this was a *renewal* of the name Bethel: the whole narrative, vv. 9—15, stands by itself and could not be taken, except for considerations foreign to itself, as other than a first account of the things narrated. This is one of the places which seem to me to stamp almost with certainty the composition of Genesis out of independent documents.

9.] The words **when he came out of Padan-aram** can hardly be fitted into the course of this chapter's history, but are a generalizing introduction to the incident about to be related. Jacob had now been ten years or more in Canaan, dwelling at Succoth, dwelling at Shechem. **10.**] On the signification of the new name, see ch. xxxii. 28. **11.**] The blessing is expressed in terms strongly reminding us of ch. xvii. 1—8, where see notes. It is a solemn renewal of the patriarchal promises to Jacob: and that in an appearance of God to him face to face, as He had appeared to Abraham: compare ch. xvii. 22. The language is singularly and studiedly correspondent. **14.**] Before (ch. xxviii. 8) he had poured oil on the pillar, now he adds a drink-offering, viz. a libation of wine.

15.] Kalisch endeavours to treat this as if it were a different place from that

called the name of the place where God spake with him,
Beth-el. 16 ¶ And they journeyed from Beth-el; and
there was [k]some distance to come to Ephrath: and Rachel [k]ch. xlviii. 7. 2 Kings v. 19
travailed, and she had hard labour. 17 And it came to
pass, when she was in hard labour, that the midwife said
unto her, Fear not; thou shalt have this son also. 18
And it came to pass, as her soul was in departing, (for
she died) that she called his name Ben-oni [Son of my
grief]: but his father called him Benjamin [Son of hap-
piness]. 19 And Rachel died, and was buried in the way
to Ephrath, which *is* Bethlehem. 20 And Jacob set a
pillar upon her grave: that *is* the pillar of Rachel's grave
unto this day. 21 ¶ And Israel journeyed, and spread his
tent beyond the tower of Edar. 22 ¶ And it came to
pass, when Israel dwelt in that land, that Reuben went
and lay with Bilhah his father's concubine: and Israel
heard *it*. Now the sons of Jacob were twelve: 23 the
sons of Leah; Reuben, Jacob's firstborn, and Simeon,
and Levi, and Judah, and Issachar, and Zebulun: 24 the
sons of Rachel; Joseph, and Benjamin: 25 and the sons

which he had named Bethel in ch. xxviii. But there is nothing to support such an idea. 16—20.] *Birth of Benjamin. Rachel's death and burial.* 16.] **some distance**, literally, **a distance of land.** There is something pathetic about the precise designation of the spot, so sad in memory to the patriarch. It would seem as if the notice had come from him before whose eyes that tract of land, with the elevated Bethlehem at the end of it, had remained unforgotten in after life: compare ch. xlviii. 7, where the expression occurs as here, and in the mouth of Jacob. The LXX. has a curious addition here: it runs, "*And Jacob left Bethel, and pitched his tent opposite the tower of Gader* (see below, ver. 21): *and it came to pass, when he drew near to Chabratha, to come to Ephratha, Rachel,*" &c. The Vulgate has also a curious rendering, "But going out thence he came in the spring time to the country which leads to Ephrata." The tomb of Rachel is one of those sites in Palestine which can hardly be questioned. The traditional spot is about half an hour north of Bethlehem. The present building is merely "an ordinary Moslem tomb of a holy person, a small square building of stone with a dome, and within it a tomb in the ordinary Mohammedan form, the whole plastered over with mortar." *Biblical Dict.* 17.] It was this very confidence, that she should have another son, that she expressed at Joseph's birth, ch. xxx. 24. On the well-known grave of Rachel, see 1 Sam. x. 2. The **unto this day** gives no certain date, but evidently belongs to a period later than Moses; to a time when the sites of the Land of Promise were known to the Jews by dwelling in it.

21, 22.] *Reuben's deed of shame.*

21.] **Migdal-eder**, or the tower of Edar (flocks), meaning probably a watchtower for the guarding of the flocks (see 2 Kings xviii. 8; 2 Chron. xxvi. 10; xxvii. 4), is said by Jerome to be 1000 paces from Bethlehem. It is mentioned only here, and is at present unknown. 22.] Jacob's sin is visited on him by degrees, stroke after stroke. The notice, **Israel heard it**, points to this, and serves, besides, to connect this account with the mention of this deed in the last speech of Jacob, ch. xlix. 4. The LXX. adds at the end of the verse, "And it ap-

of Bilhah, Rachel's handmaid; Dan, and Naphtali: 26
and the sons of Zilpah, Leah's handmaid; Gad, and
Asher: these *are* the sons of Jacob, which were born to
him in Padan-aram. 27 ¶ And Jacob came unto Isaac
his father unto Mamre, unto the city of Arbah, which *is*
Hebron, where Abraham and Isaac sojourned. 28 And
the days of Isaac were an hundred and fourscore years.
29 And Isaac gave up the ghost, and died, and was
gathered unto his people, *being* old and full of days: and
his sons Esau and Jacob buried him. XXXVI. 1 Now
these *are* the generations of Esau, who *is* Edom. 2 Esau
took his wives of the daughters of Canaan; Adah the
daughter of Elon the Hittite, and Aholibamah the daugh-
ter of Anah the daughter of Zibeon the Hivite; 3 and

peared wicked in his sight." The use of *Israel* for Jacob in this small portion is remarkable. See ch. xxxvii. 3; xlv. 28; xlvi. 30; l. 2. It is found in all these places in connexion with solemnity or pathos.

26—29.] *Jacob's return home, and Israel's death.* The notice in ver. 26 is not strictly correct, for Benjamin was born in Canaan after his return. Such a matter is of no consequence where it occurs, but should warn us not to press similar notices, the incorrectness of which is not so obvious.

27.] See ch. xiii. 18; xxiii. 2. **29.**] In ch. xlix. 31 the place of Isaac's burial is said, as might have been expected, to have been the cave of Machpelah, which Abraham purchased for a burying-place (ch. xxiii. 19, f.). The history of Isaac is brought to an end here, because the object of the sacred narrative is henceforth Jacob and his fortunes, and he is now established in his father's house at Hebron. Isaac really survived Jacob's return to Hebron 12 years. This may be seen as follows: Isaac was 60 when Jacob was born (ch. xxv. 26), consequently Jacob was 120 at his father's death. But he was 130 at his migration to Egypt (ch. xlvii. 9), which therefore was 10 years after. At that time Joseph was between 39 and 40 (compare ch. xli. 46, 47, and ch. xlv. 6). But, seeing he was 17 when he was sold into Egypt (ch. xxxvii. 2), and 23 years elapsed between that and Jacob's migration, Isaac must have survived Joseph's selling into Egypt between 12 and 13 years. Hence it also follows that Joseph was sold immediately on Jacob's coming to Hebron.

XXXVI. *Esau and the Edomites.* As in ch. xxv. the history gives the genealogies of Abraham's descendants by other wives in order to dispose of them, and to treat the line of Isaac, so here it gives the genealogies of the descendants of Esau in order to have done with them and to advance in the line of Jacob. In both cases the races enumerated are those which in subsequent times had to do with Israel.

1—8.] *Esau's wives and sons. His removal to Mount Seir, and its cause.*

1.] **Esau** was called **Edom**, as related ch. xxv. 30. The same notice is appended in vv. 8, 19, 43. **2, 3.**] There is considerable difficulty about the names of Esau's wives. Comparing this account with the previous one in ch. xxvi. 34, xxviii. 9, we find that two of the three names are entirely different. There it is said that Esau took 1. Judith, the daughter of Beeri the Hittite; 2. Bashemath, the d. of Elon the Hittite; 3. Mahalath, the d. of Ishmael, sister of Nebaioth; whereas here the d. of Elon the Hittite appears as Adah, and Ishmael's d., the sister of Nebajoth, as Bashemath. It is hardly possible, using one's common sense, not to recognize some confusion here. Both accounts have Bashemath as one of Esau's wives. According to ch. xxv. she is d. of Elon the Hittite; according to this account, she is d. of Ishmael. This is one element of confusion. One woman could not answer both these descriptions, and it is drawing a little too largely on our credulity to ask us

Bashemath Ishmael's daughter, sister of Nebajoth. 4 And
Adah bare to Esau Eliphaz; and Bashemath bare Reuel;
5 and Aholibamah bare Jeush, and Jaalam, and Korah:
these *are* the sons of Esau, which were born unto him in
the land of Canaan. 6 And Esau took his wives, and his
sons, and his daughters, and all the persons of his house,
and his cattle, and all his beasts, and all his substance,
which he had got in the land of Canaan; and went into
the country from the face of his brother Jacob. 7 For
their riches were more than that they might dwell toge-
ther; and the land wherein they were strangers could not

to accept two wives of Esau both called Bashemath. Both accounts cannot be accurate. Then the third wife, who in ch. xxv. is *Judith*, the d. of *Beeri* the *Hittite*, is here *Aholibamah*, the d. of *Anah* the d. of *Zibeon* the *Hivite*. And, as if to make confusion worse confounded, it appears from vv. 20, 25 that Aholibamah was the d. of Anah the son of Zibeon, the son of Seir the *Horite*. And even there we have some apparent confusion between two Anahs, one the son, and the other the grandson, of Seir: for although it would at first sight seem that the Anah of ver. 25 is the son of Seir, taken in his order between Zibeon and Dishon, yet from the express description of Anah in ver. 24 it would seem as if it were he that is taken up in ver. 25, which view is confirmed by Aholibamah being mentioned as his daughter, who, as we were before told, was [grand] daughter of Zibeon. Another similar element of confusion is found again in ver. 26, where Dishon, another of the sons of Seir, in his order, is again synonymous with a Dishon son of Anah in ver. 25. The various shifts resorted to by those commentators who are determined to reconcile at all hazards are more amusing than creditable, and are really not worth recounting. The only honest conclusion must be with Kalisch, "We are obliged to confess that the Hebrew text, though containing several important coincidences, evidently embodies two accounts, irreconcileably different." And even thus we shall still require the hypothesis that subsequent changes have further confused the two accounts.

The coincidences are—1. That Esau had three wives. 2. That one was a daughter of Elon the Hittite. 3. That another was a daughter of Ishmael, and sister of Nebaioth. 4. That one of the three was called Bashemath. How any one, with these data before him, can resist the inference that Genesis is compounded of various independent documents, entirely passes comprehension. Only two of the wives were daughters of Canaan, properly speaking, even as they are described *here*. As the genealogy of Aholibamah is given vv. 20, 25, *she* was also not a Canaanite, for the Horites seem to have been the aboriginal inhabitants: see ch. xiv. 6; Deut. ii. 12. But this does not apply to her description here. It is quite capricious to alter Hivite into Horite *here*, as even Knobel proposes: and for any purposes of harmonizing, useless, as will be seen from what has been said. In fact, it would, while removing the discrepancy in the Gentile descriptions of Aholibamah, introduce another into these, vv. 2, 3. **4, 5.**] *Esau's five sons.* Of these we may observe—1. That the eldest is synonymous with the friend of Job, who is called (comp. ver. 11) the Temanite: 2. That the second is synonymous with the father-in-law of Moses, Exod. ii. 18, there called "*priest of Midian*."

6—8.] The cause of Esau's removal to Mount Seir apparently operated after Jacob's full return to Hebron, and taking possession, in his father's extreme old age, of all that was Isaac's; and we have here recorded not the cause of Esau's first dwelling at Seir, but that of his final and entire removal. Jacob was the acknowledged head of the house, and the swarm cast off was that of the really elder, but now by force of circumstances become the younger brother. **cattle and beasts,** as often before, the former being the sheep and kine, the latter the

bear them because of their cattle. 8 Thus dwelt Esau in
mount Seir: Esau *is* Edom. 9 ¶ And these *are* the gener-
ations of Esau the father of the Edomites in mount Seir:
10 these *are* the names of Esau's sons; Eliphaz the son of
Adah the wife of Esau, Reuel the son of Bashemath the wife
of Esau. 11 And the sons of Eliphaz were [1]Teman, Omar,
Zepho, and Gatam, and Kenaz. 12 And Timna was con-
cubine to Eliphaz Esau's son; and she bare to Eliphaz
Amalek: these *were* the sons of Adah Esau's wife. 13
And these *are* the sons of Reuel; Nahath, and Zerah,
Shammah, and Mizzah: these were the sons of Bashemath
Esau's wife. 14 ¶ And these were the sons of Aholibamah,
the daughter of Anah the daughter of Zibeon, Esau's

1 Jer. xlix. 7, 20. Ezek. xxv. 13. Amos i. 12. Hab. iii. 3.

beasts of burden, asses and camels. **the country**] Heb. the land = went forth; hardly as Kalisch, "into *another* country."

Mount Seir is the mountain ridge extending along the east side of the valley of Arabah, from the Dead Sea to the Elanitic Gulf. The name signifies *rough*, or *rugged.* "The view from Aaron's tomb on Hor, the centre of Mount Seir, is enough to shew its appropriateness. The sharp and serrated ridges, the jagged rocks and cliffs, the straggling bushes and stunted trees, give the whole scene a sternness and ruggedness almost unparalleled." Mr. Grove, *Biblical Dict.*, whose art. see. On **Esau is Edom,** see above. **9—28.**] *Genealogy of the sons of Esau. And herein* (10—13) *the sons of Adah and Bashemath.* Observe these two of Esau's wives have their sons and their grandsons enumerated, whereas of Aholibamah (ver. 14) only the sons appear. The same distinction is observed when the dukes are enumerated below. Of these names, **Eliphaz** and **Reuel** have been observed on before. **Teman** is elsewhere in Scripture the name of an Edomitish territory (see reff.). Its inhabitants enjoyed a repute for wisdom (Jer. xlix. 7; Baruch iii. 22, 23), and from it came Eliphaz the Temanite, Job's wisest friend. Knobel makes it probable that Teman was in N.E. Idumæa. Eusebius and Jerome mention a *Thaiman*, 15 Roman miles from Petra. See on vv. 34, 42. **Omar** is recognized by Knobel in the present name of an Arab tribe, *Beni-Ammer*, in N. Edom and S. Palestine. Another Arab tribe in S. Palestine is called *Ammareh.* **Zepho**] In 1 Chron. i. 36 called *Zephi.* Knobel mentions a place *Szafieh* or *Szophia* (Safieh in Van de Velde's map), S. of the Dead Sea, where many Arab tribes fix their winter-quarters. But he does not regard the identification as certain. **Gatam**] In the LXX. *Gotham.* See ver. 16. Knobel compares *Jodham*, the name of an Arab tribe; but there is no certainty. **Kenaz** represents the Kenezites, Num. xxxii. 12; Josh. xiv. 14, of whom Caleb was one, and Othniel his brother, Josh. xv. 17; Judg. iii. 9—11. See note on ch. xv. 19. The name Kenaz was borne by a grandson of Caleb, 1 Chron. iv. 15 (but the text is doubtful). From ver. 42 Kenaz was also a town. **12.**] **Timna,** again, is a place, ver. 40. It is a question much debated, whether the Amalek mentioned here is or is not the ancestor of the well-known people of that name. The mention of the Amalekites in ch. xiv. 7 (see there), coupled with the Amorites, certainly seems to imply that that people were existing at that early period. If so, then this Amalek must be, as Knobel and others suppose, distinct from that other, and probably that of a mere portion of the great Amalekite people. The same seems a lawful inference from xxiv. 20: see there.

13.] *The second division of the Edomites.* None of the names in this verse are traceable among the Arab tribes. The old geographers mention a tribe *Sameni*, who may be connected with Shammah, but nothing is known of their habitat. **14.**] *The third division.* Its two former

wife: and she bare to Esau Jeush, and Jaalam, and
Korah. 15 ¶ These *were* [m]sheiks of the sons of Esau: m Zech. ix. 7; xii. 5, 6. See also Jer. xiii. 21. Prov. xvi. 28.
the sons of Eliphaz the firstborn *son* of Esau; sheik
Teman, sheik Omar, sheik Zepho, sheik Kenaz, 16 sheik
Korah, sheik Gatam, *and* sheik Amalek: these *are* the
sheiks *that came* of Eliphaz in the land of Edom; these
were the sons of Adah. 17 ¶ And these *are* the sons of
Reuel Esau's son; sheik Nahath, sheik Zerah, sheik
Shammah, sheik Mizzah: there *are* the sheiks *that came*
of Reuel in the land of Edom; these *are* the sons of Ba-
shemath Esau's wife. 18 ¶ And these *are* the sons of
Aholibamah Esau's wife; sheik Jeush, sheik Jaalam,
sheik Korah: these *were* the sheiks *that came* of Aholi-
bamah the daughter of Anah, Esau's wife. 19 These *are*
the sons of Esau, who *is* Edom, and these *are* their sheiks.
20 ¶ [n]These *are* the sons of Seir the Horite, who [o]inhabited n 1 Chron. i. 38—42.
the land; Lotan, and Shobal, and Zibeon, and Anah, 21 o See Exod. xxiii. 31. Num. xxxii. 17. Judg. i. 33.
and Dishon, and Ezer, and Dishan: these *are* the sheiks
of the Horites, the children of Seir in the land of Edom.
22 And the children of Lotan were Hori and Hemam; and
Lotan's sister *was* Timna. 23 And the children of Shobal
were these; Alvan, and Manahath, and Ebal, Shepho, and

names are untraceable; the latter, **Korah**, is found in the Wady *Kurahy* (*Kurazeh* in Van de Velde's map), S.E. of the Dead Sea.

15—19.] *The sheikhs, or leaders of the Edomite tribes.* Knobel maintains that the word *Aluph*, here used of all these, is not an individual, the chief of the tribe, but the tribe or *gens* itself. But he is opposed by the general consent of commentators: see reff. In the following list the name Korah occurs among the sons of Eliphaz, where it is not found in the previous enumeration,—and again among those of Aholibamah. This is probably owing to some mistake. The Samaritan text omits the name among the sons of Eliphaz, but it is not to be trusted in this list, as it evidently *corrects*, e. g. it has in ver. 2 Mahalath for Bashemath, to accord with ch. xxviii. 9. **20—30.**] *The genealogy of the Horites, the inhabitants of the land*, i. e. before the Edomites came in (Deut. ii. 12, 22). This genealogy must be inserted on account of their subsequent connexion with the Edomites, as it is not the habit of Genesis to give pedigrees of mere heathen races, unconnected with the main stream of the sacred history. The **Horites** signify properly dwellers in caves, from the Hebrew *Hor*, a cave. The land of Edom is full of "holes in the rocks." See Job xxx. 6. To this day the picture of wretchedness given in that passage is realized among the lower tribes of the land of Edom. Seven divisions of the Horites are mentioned, and are deduced from **Seir** as their ancestor.

22.] The name **Lotan**, Knobel recognizes in a wild and inhospitable tribe, the Lyathineh, in the neighbourhood of Petra. **Hori** again reminds us of the troglodyte habits of the race: see above. **Hemam** is recognized in a town mentioned by geographers ancient and modern as S. of Petra on Mount Sherah. On **Timnah**, see above, ver. 12. **23.**] **Shobal** is the name used by the chroniclers of the Crusades for the part of Arabia S. of Kerek, i. e. for Edom; but they refer this name to Ishbak, ch. xxv. 2. See also Judith iii. 1 in the Vulgate. **Alvan**

M

Onam. 24 And these *are* the children of Zibeon; both
Ajah, and Anah: this *was that* Anah that found the warm
springs in the wilderness, as he fed the asses of Zibeon his
father. 25 And the children of Anah *were* these; Dishon,
and Aholibamah the daughter of Anah. 26 And these
are the children of Dishon; Hemdan, and Eshban, and
Ithran, and Cheran. 27 The children of Ezer *are* these;
Bilhan, and Zaavan, and Akan. 28 The children of
Dishan *are* these; Uz, and Aran. 29 These *are* the sheiks
that came of the Horites; sheik Lotan, sheik Shobal, sheik
Zibeon, sheik Anah, 30 sheik Dishon, sheik Ezer, sheik
Dishan: these *are* the sheiks *that came* of Hori, accord-
p 1 Chron. i. 43—50. ing to their sheiks in the land of Seir. 31 ¶ p And
these *are* the kings that reigned in the land of Edom,

is supposed to be reproduced in the *Alawin*, a tribe of evil repute N. of Akaba. **Manahath**] Ptolemy mentions a place westward of Petra called *Monuchiatis*, which possibly is connected with this name. **Shepho** is perhaps connected with Mount *Shafeh*, N. of Akaba. **Ebal** and **Onam** are untraceable. **24.**] **Zibeon** is wholly unknown. **Ajah** is traced in the *Haiwat*, a tribe of evil repute N. of the Elanitic Gulf. On **Anah** being the son of Zibeon, see on ver. 1. The translation *mules* in the A. V. (*giants* in the Samaritan Pentateuch and in Onkelos) seems to be abandoned, and **warm springs** supposed to be the right one. These might be the warm springs in the *Wady el Asal*, S. of the Dead Sea, or perhaps those yet hotter springs in the *Wady Hamad*. **25.**] There is some confusion in this list, as before noticed on ver. 1. This Anah is evidently the son, not the grandson, of Seir, as the pedigree is not pursued beyond the second generation from Seir. **children** is literally **sons**, a term elsewhere used as the technical one in genealogies even where only one son is mentioned, e. g. ch. xlvi. 23; Num. xxvi. 8; 1 Chron. i. 41 (where Dishon only is mentioned); ii. 8. **26.**] The name **Hemdan** is traced in a portion of the tribe Omran, called *Humady*, E. and S.E. of Akaba, and also N. of Petra, and further N. still, in the land of Moab. **Eshban** is traced in another portion of the same tribe called *Usbany*. Ithran and Cheran are unknown; as also are **27.**] **Ezer**, and **Zaavan**; **Bilhan** is very uncertain; but **Akan** is found in a tribe on the Elanitic Gulf, named by the old geographers Acheni, and a place Achana, mentioned in Eusebius, where David is supposed to have built ships. **28.**] **Uz** is in all probability connected with the country of Job,—see Mr. Bevan's art. in *Biblical Dict.*, and note on Job i. 1. Pliny mentions a tribe named *Areni* in East Idumæa. But some suppose that *Aram* should rather be read, and that we have here a record of a mingled tribe of Edomites and Aramæans. Knobel supposes **Dishon** and **Dishan** mere forms of the simpler *Dish*, which word is found in the Arab race Deish, mentioned by geographers as dwelling near the Dedanites. **29, 30.**] This list of sheikhs of the Horites is coincident with that of the sons of Seir. **31—39.**] *List of Edomite kings*. The perplexing portion of ver. 31 is the addition of the words which close it. It is hardly possible in any spirit of fairness to regard them as other than a token of at least the clause itself being written after the kingdom in Israel had been established. Those interpreters who are determined to make all things square have managed to wrest them into a prophetic declaration, dependent on the promise to the Patriarchs that kings should descend from them (ch. xvii. 6; xxxv. 11): others have connected them with the provisions of Moses concerning the kingdom, Deut. xvii. 14—20. Of course we do not deny that either of these explanations is possible. The question for us is not that, but whether any such explanation is natural, or would have been thought

before there reigned any king over the children of
Israel. 32 And Bela the son of Beor reigned in Edom:
and the name of his city *was* Dinhabah. 33 And Bela
died, and Jobab the son of Zerah of [q]Bozrah reigned in q Isa. xxxiv. 6;
his stead. 34 And Jobab died, and Husham of the land of lxiii. 1. Jer. xlix. 13, 22.
Temani reigned in his stead. 35 And Husham died, and Amos i. 12.
Hadad the son of Bedad, who smote Midian in the field
of Moab, reigned in his stead: and the name of his city
was Avith. 36 And Hadad died, and Samlah of Masrekah
reigned in his stead. 37 And Samlah died, and Saul of
Rehoboth *by* the river reigned in his stead. 38 And Saul
died, and Baal-hanan the son of Achbor reigned in his
stead. 39 And Baal-hanan the son of Achbor died, and
Hadad reigned in his stead: and the name of his city *was*
Pau; and his wife's name *was* Mehetabel, the daughter of
Matred, the daughter of Mezahab. 40 And these *are* the
names of the sheiks *that came* of Esau, according to their
families, after their places, by their names; sheik Timnah,

of, unless for a preconceived purpose. There is to our mind far less violence done to our faith by supposing this clause, or even the whole list of Idumæan kings, to be a later insertion, than by such (as it seems to me) forcing of the plain sense of words. None of these kings of Edom are known. In the triumphant song of Moses and the children of Israel, Exod. xv. 15, mention is made of the *sheiks* of Edom; but in Num. xx. 14, ff., we find Moses asking permission of the *king* of Edom to pass through his land. So that it is perhaps not to be assumed that the rule of sheiks in Edom was superseded by that of kings. **32.**] It is curious to find so near a sound to Balaam son of Beor in the **Bela son of Beor** of this verse. The Jewish expositors remark on the similarity. **Dinhabah** is not known. **33.**] **Bozrah** is known to us as an Edomite city from reff. The name survives in the village *Busaireh*, midway between Petra and the Dead Sea. **34.**] On **Temani**, see ver. 11. **35.**] This defeat of Midian is otherwise quite unknown to us. **36.**] The name **Masrekah** signifies *place of grapes*, and hence Knobel has thought that it may be pointed out by large ruins between Petra and Schobek, described by Burckhardt, where a tribe dwells largely cultivating grapes, exporting raisins in abundance to Gaza, and selling them to the Syrian pilgrims. **37.**] **Rehoboth** is a very common name. It has been by some supposed to be on the Euphrates (see Mr. Grove, *Biblical Dict.*), but it is difficult to see how that can be. Eusebius and Jerome speak of a place Robotha in Edom in their time: and the word *nahar*, here rendered **river**, is used of small brooks as well as of great rivers. **39.**] From the circumstance of this **Hadar** (called in 1 Chron. i. 50 Hadad, apparently in error) not being said to have died, and from the particular enumeration of the names of his wife and her father and grandfather, it has been not without probability supposed that this king of Edom was reigning at the time of the writer: and if so, this may have been the king of whom Moses requested safe passage as related in Num. xx. 14, ff. In 1 Chron. i. 51 the historian has inserted the supplementary notice, "Hadad died also."

40—43.] *The sheikhs of Edom, and their chief towns.* There were 13 tribes (vv. 11—14), and only 11 towns are named. Therefore some tribes had no town, being, it may be supposed, nomads. On **Timnah**, see ver. 12. Most of these places are unknown. **Aholibamah** means *dwelling on high*, and is probably to be sought on the

sheik Alvah, sheik Jetheth, 41 sheik Aholibamah, sheik
Elah, sheik Pinon, 42 sheik Kenaz, sheik Teman, sheik
Mibzar, 43 sheik Magdiel, sheik Iram: these *be* the sheiks
of Edom, according to their habitations in the land of
their possession: this *is* Esau the father of the Edomites.
XXXVII. 1 And Jacob dwelt in the land wherein his
r ch. ii. 4; v. 1; vi. 9; x. 1; xi. 10, 27; xxv. 12, 19; xxxvi. 1, 9. father was a stranger, in the land of Canaan. 2 r These
are the generations of Jacob. Joseph, *being* seventeen
years old, was feeding the flock with his brethren; and
he was a lad with the sons of Bilhah, and with the sons
of Zilpah, his father's wives: and Joseph brought unto his
father their evil report. 3 Now Israel loved Joseph more
than all his children, because he *was* the son of his old age:
and he made him a coat of *many* colours. 4 And when his
brethren saw that their father loved him more than all his

highest part of Mount Seir. **Elah**, otherwise *Elath*, says Knobel, now *Ailah* on the Red Sea. **Pinon** appears to be the same as *Punon*, a place of encampment of the Israelites, where Moses lifted up the brazen serpent (compare Num. xxi. 9 with xxxiii. 42). There were there brass (copper) mines, to which afterwards many Christian confessors were condemned. It is described in the patristic writings as between Petra and Zoar. On **Kenaz** and **Teman**, see ver. 11. Knobel thinks that **Mibzar** represents Petra. The meaning of the word is a fortress, and Petra (rock) was so called from its extraordinary strength: see Jer. xlix. 16, 17; Obad. 3; also Ps. cviii. 10 (lx. 9); 2 Kings xiv. 7, and note. Eusebius and Jerome mention a large village *Mabsara* in Gabalene which belonged to Petra. **Magdiel** signifies the praise of God, and Knobel thinks it may have been the site of a temple. **Iram** is unknown. The LXX. here and in 1 Chron. have for this name *Zaphoin*.

XXXVII.—L. *The history of Jacob.* All that is now left is to pursue the fortunes of Jacob. And the whole story of Joseph is for this purpose most important. It is the introduction to the migration of Jacob and his family into Egypt, on which depended the subsequent history of the chosen people.

1.] The copula is by the Vulgate rendered "But." and doubtless there is a slightly adversative force intended. The Edomites, inhabitants of Mount Seir, have been before us. Esau had quitted the land of promise, and branched off from the line of the Covenant blessing; but Jacob remained there. **in the land wherein his father was a stranger,** thus recalling the oft-repeated promise of God, **in the land of Canaan**, thus specified by name. Here then we have the posture of the heir of the promises—dwelling in Canaan, and waiting on Providence to unfold his future course.

2.] Now the writer passes with this formal title (see above on reff.) to the history of Jacob for the rest of the sacred book. Jacob's previous acts and annals belong to the history of Isaac. Literally, **was feeding** (tending) **with his brothers among the sheep.** In the next clause it is expressed that he served under his brothers, Bilhah's and Zilpah's sons. It was their place to instruct him in the work of a shepherd. The word for **evil report** is derived from a root signifying to *creep*, or *approach insidiously*. No slur is intended on the character of Joseph, with which, as Kalisch well remarks, depravity and meanness were totally at variance.

3.] Joseph was born when his father was 90. See note, ch. xxxv. 29. On the use of the name Israel in passages of pathos, see above, on ch. xxxv. 22. The expression here rendered **a coat of many colours**, and literally **a tunic of parts**, occurs again, 2 Sam. xiii. 18, of the

brethren, they hated him, and could not speak peaceably
unto him. 5 ¶ And Joseph dreamed a dream, and he told
it his brethren: and they hated him yet the more. 6 And
he said unto them, Hear, I pray you, this dream which I
have dreamed: 7 for, behold, we *were* binding sheaves in
the field, and, lo, my sheaf arose, and also stood upright;
and, behold, your sheaves stood round about, and made
obeisance to my sheaf. 8 And his brethren said to him,
Shalt thou indeed reign over us? or shalt thou indeed
have dominion over us? And they hated him yet the
more for his dreams, and for his words. 9 ¶ And he
dreamed yet another dream, and told it his brethren,
and said, Behold, I have dreamed a dream more; and,
behold, the sun and the moon and the [s] eleven stars made
obeisance to me. 10 And he told *it* to his father, and to
his brethren: and his father rebuked him, and said unto
him, What *is* this dream that thou hast dreamed? Shall
I and thy mother and thy brethren indeed come to bow
down ourselves to thee to the earth? 11 And his brethren
envied him; but his father observed the saying. 12
¶ And his brethren went to feed their father's flock in
Shechem. 13 And Israel said unto Joseph, Do not thy

s See 2 Kings xxiii. 5. Job xxxviii. 32.

garment worn by king's daughters. Another interpretation of ver. 3 is that whereas the ordinary garment for youth in the East is simply a body coat without sleeves reaching to the knees, this was with sleeves and reaching to the feet. So Josephus here.

5—11.] His brethren's hatred is increased, and his father's rebuke incurred, by his two ambitious dreams. **8.**] **his dreams**—the fact of his having thus dreamt: **his words**—the fact of his having told them. Or does this last mean, his continued evil report of them to their father? **9, f.**] First he tells the second dream to his brethren with whom he was, and then to his father and his assembled (or, the rest of his) brethren at home. This second dream related not only, as the first, to his brethren, but to his father and mother also. **10.**] In Jacob's rebuke, the words "I and thy mother" have been regarded as an inconsistency, considering that Rachel had been some time dead. Some of those who repudiate this have drawn from them an inference that Jacob looked for a resurrection. But both are wrong. The inconsistency vanishes when we come to reflect that it was as much in Joseph's dream, and Jacob merely recites it in interpreting it: and as to the other view, surely it was not in the other world that the dream was to find its fulfilment. It *never was* fulfilled: for Leah, who only could have been regarded as standing in Rachel's place to Joseph, died before the migration into Egypt: compare ch. xlvi. 8, ff., with xlix. 31. Knobel connects the 11 stars, Joseph himself being the twelfth, with the fact that the signs of the Zodiac were not unknown to the Israelites (reff.). The word for **observed** in the LXX. is very nearly that used by St. Luke when he relates that "His mother kept all these things," ch. ii. 19. **12—24.**] *His brethren plot his death. Reuben dissuades it.*

12.] In ch. xxxiii. 19 we hear of Jacob's buying a field in Shechem. It would seem that he had there a station for his flocks.

13.] It would appear that Joseph had

brethren feed the flock in Shechem? come, and I will
send thee unto them. And he said to him, Here *am I.*
14 And he said to him, Go, I pray thee, see whether it be
well with thy brethren, and well with the flocks; and
bring me word again. So he sent him out of the vale of
Hebron, and he came to Shechem. 15 And a certain man
found him, and, behold, *he was* wandering in the field:
and the man asked him, saying, What seekest thou? 16
And he said, I seek my brethren: tell me, I pray thee,
where they feed *their flocks.* 17 And the man said, They
are departed hence; for I heard them say, Let us go to
Dothan. And Joseph went after his brethren, and found
them in Dothan. 18 And when they saw him afar off,
even before he came near unto them, they conspired
against him to slay him. 19 And they said one to another,
Behold, this lord of dreams cometh. 20 Come now there-
fore, and let us slay him, and cast him into some pit, and
we will say, Some evil beast hath devoured him: and we
shall see what will become of his dreams. 21 And Reuben
t ver. 22. heard *it*, and he [t]delivered him out of their hands; and
said, Let us not kill him. 22 And Reuben said unto them,

left his brethren and was living at home (see ver. 4); but his father wishes him again to consort with them. There is besides some trace of anxiety in Jacob's mind for fear his sons may have been involved in some evil matter. **14.**] The sending of a lad of seventeen, and one so beloved, all the way from Hebron to Shechem, is a noticeable feature in the narrative. He appears, from ver. 15, to have gone alone. **17.**] **Dothan** is only mentioned in 2 Kings vi. 13—19, as the scene of the miracle of Elisha's servant's eyes being opened to see the heavenly hosts which guarded his master. It is apparently mentioned in the Book of Judith, iv. 6; vii. 3; viii. 3, as Dothaim. It seems from Judith iii. 9, where however the words in the original "near Dotæa," are printed in our English Bibles, without a shadow of authority, "*near unto Judæa*" (!) to be on the S. side of the plain of Jezreel, between Scythopolis and Geba. According to Eusebius and Jerome it lay 12 Roman miles N. of Samaria. And just in that place travellers have found a mound still called "Tell Dothan," with a ruined aqueduct and other remains of antiquity at its base. See Van de Velde's Memoir to accompany the map of Palestine, p. 308. Dr. Thomson (*Land and Book*, p. 466) says, "The neighbourhood affords the very best pasturage: and at the base of the mound is a fountain where the brethren of Joseph may have watered their flocks." **18**, f.] The Christian reader can hardly fail to be reminded of the language of our Lord's parable, Matt. xxii. 38, nor to apply the parallel.

19.] The expression, **lord of dreamers,** is used in bitter scorn. **20.**] The name Dothaim, of which Dothan is, says Kalisch, a contracted form, signifies double cistern. "I am not aware," says Dr. Thomson, "that there still exist old cisterns about Dothaim, but there are very few ancient sites where they are not to be found." "The traditional 'pit,' at the N. extremity of the Sea of Gennesareth, is much too far Northward." Kalisch. **21.**] We have seen on ch. xxxiv. 25 that Reuben, as the firstborn, had a peculiar responsibility. **22. lay no**

Shed no blood, *but* cast him into this pit that *is* in the
wilderness, and [u]lay no hand upon him; that he might [u] ch. xxii. 12. Exod. xxiv.
deliver him out of their hands, to bring him back to his 11. Deut. xiii. 9 (Acts xii. 1).
father again. 23 ¶ And it came to pass, when Joseph was
come unto his brethren, that they stript Joseph of his
coat, the coat of *many* colours that *was* on him; 24 and
they took him, and cast him into a pit: and the pit *was*
empty, *there was* no water in it. 25 And they sat down to
eat bread: and they lifted up their eyes and looked, and,
behold, a company of Ishmaelites came from Gilead with
their camels bearing tragacanth and [v]balm and [w]ladanum, [v] Jer. viii. 22; xlvi. 11; li. 8.
going to carry *it* down to Egypt. 26 And Judah said unto [w] ch. xliii. 11, only.
his brethren, What profit *is it* if we slay our brother, and
conceal his blood? 27 Come, and let us sell him to the
Ishmaelites, and let not our hand be upon him; for he *is*
our brother *and* our flesh. And his brethren were con-
tent. 28 Then there passed by Midianites merchantmen;
and they drew and lifted up Joseph out of the pit, and

hand upon him] i. e. put him not to death: see reff. It is a strange feature in the moral constitution of the brethren that they could be persuaded to satisfy their revenge and imagine that their guilt was less, by letting Joseph perish in the pit, rather than shed his blood. On this use of cisterns, see Jer. xxxviii. 6; Lam. iii. 53. **23.**] See on ver. 3. According to Eastern habits, it would be his only garment. He entered Egypt naked, as was the custom with slaves and captives, Isa. xx. 4, in strange contrast to his subsequent array of pomp, ch. xli. 42.

25.] The highway from Gilead to Egypt still passes by the Tell Dothaim, to Ramleh, Gaza, and Egypt. The first mentioned of these articles of commerce is pronounced to be the gum of the *Astragalus tragacantha*, a thorny shrub found throughout the East, figured in Tristram's *Nat. Hist. of Bible*, p. 394; the second, *balm*, is elsewhere connected with Gilead (reff.): it was a very precious gum obtained from the balsam tree, almost peculiar to Palestine. See Mr. Drake's art. in the *Biblical Dict.* and Tristram's *Nat. Hist. of the Bible*, p. 337, where the plant is figured. The third item, erroneously rendered in the A. V. (here and in ref.) *myrrh*, is the **ladanum**, or gum of the *cistus creticus*, said to have been originally combed from the beards of goats which browse upon the plant, but now beaten from the shrub by a kind of whip, from which it is afterwards scraped. See *Biblical Dict.* and Tristram, p. 458, where the plant is figured. **26.**] Judah's speech shews that during the meal, and in Reuben's absence, the purpose had been altered, and the first plan of slaying Joseph again adopted. On this view, which is Knobel's, **conceal his blood** means, escape detection for his murder. Kalisch takes another view, and thinks that during the meal their conscience troubled them, and Judah only gave expression to their thoughts that "blood concealed" was blood still; meaning by blood concealed, his obscure death in the pit.

28.] The notice contained in the first clause seems to belong to a different account from that which we have been as yet reading. The idea maintained by some commentators (even Keil here) that the same persons in the course of the same sentence could be Ishmaelites and Midianites, will hardly be entertained except by those who are determined to carry through a thing at all hazards. In ch. xxxix 1 it is the Ishmaelites who sold Joseph into Egypt; in ch. xl. 15 he describes himself as "stolen out of the land of the Hebrews." All such variations are not

x ch. xx. 16; xxxiii. 19; xlv. 22. Judg. ix. 4, xvi. 5. 2 Kings v. 5, al.

sold Joseph to the Ishmaelites for [x] twenty *pieces* of silver:
and they brought Joseph into Egypt. 29 ¶ And Reuben
returned unto the pit; and, behold, Joseph *was* not in the
pit; and he rent his clothes. 30 And he returned unto
his brethren, and said, The child *is* not; and I, whither
shall I go? 31 And they took Joseph's coat, and killed a
kid of the goats, and dipped the coat in the blood; 32 and
they sent the coat of *many* colours, and they brought *it* to
their father; and said, This have we found: know now
whether it *be* thy son's coat or no. 33 And he knew it,
and said, *It is* my son's coat; an evil beast hath devoured
him; Joseph is without doubt rent in pieces. 34 And
Jacob rent his clothes, and put sackcloth upon his loins,
and mourned for his son many days. 35 And all his sons
and all his daughters rose up to comfort him; but he re-
fused to be comforted; and he said, For I will go down
into the [y] grave unto my son mourning. Thus his father
wept for him. 36 And the Midianites sold him into Egypt
unto Potiphar, an officer of Pharaoh's, chief of the guard.
XXXVIII. 1 And it came to pass at that time, that Judah

y Num. xvi. 30. Deut. xxxii. 22. Job xi. 8; xiv. 3. Prov. xxx. 16. Isa. v. 14. Hab. ii. 5.

to be overridden, but to gather instruction from. It is clear that there is nothing in them which invalidates the consistency of the narrative, or they would not have been allowed to remain together in the text.

twenty pieces] Or shekels: the original has no word; see reff. **29, 30.**] Reuben comes again to the cistern, in pursuance of his plan of ver. 22, but finds not Joseph. **whither shall I go?**] i. e. what will become of me? **35.**] This announcement is startling after the deed which they have done. But there is no limit to human hypocrisy. **the grave** is *Sheol*, the place of departed spirits. The A. V. sometimes renders it by *hell*, sometimes by *the pit*. **36.**] The word here is *Medanim*, whereas in ver. 28 it was *Midianim:* and from ch. xxv. 2, Medan and Midian were two different descendants of Abraham.

Potiphar is the abbreviated form of *Potipherah:* see ch. xli. 50. The LXX. express both by *Petiphres*. The word rendered officer is literally eunuch; but this name appears to have been given to others among royal officers than those to whom it properly belonged. In ch. xl. 2 the same term is applied to the butler and baker. Potiphar was captain or chief of the executioners, for so the expression literally means. He appears, from ch. xxxix. 20, to have have had the charge of the royal prison.

XXXVIII. *The history of Judah and his daughter-in-law Tamar*. The object of this parenthetical chapter seems to be to shew how near the offspring of Jacob were to falling into the habits and loathsome sins of the Canaanitish peoples; and to pave the way for the history of their removal into the land of Egypt, which took place by means of Joseph's being sold and carried thither. At the same time it defines and accounts for the two main branches in the kingly line of Judah.

1.] Judah seems to have intended to break away from the house of his father, but by the hint given in ver. 26 to have been shocked by the enormity of the sins in which he thus became involved, and to have returned again. The *time* is marked, by the fact that Judah was still with his brethren at the sale of Joseph into Egypt, as being after that incident. He *went down*, because Hebron, where Jacob dwelt, is in

went down from his brethren, and turned in to a certain
Adullamite, whose name *was* Hirah. 2 And Judah saw
there a daughter of a certain Canaanite, whose name *was*
Shuah; and he took her, and went in unto her. 3 And
she conceived, and bare a son; and he called his name Er.
4 And she conceived again, and bare a son; and she called
his name Onan. 5 And she yet again conceived, and bare
a son; and called his name Shelah: and he was at Chezib,
when she bare him. 6 And Judah took a wife for Er his
firstborn, whose name *was* Tamar. 7 And Er, Judah's
firstborn, was wicked in the sight of the LORD; and
the LORD slew him. 8 And Judah said unto Onan, Go
in unto thy brother's wife, and marry her, and raise up
seed to thy brother. 9 And Onan knew that the seed
should not be his; and it came to pass, when he went in
unto his brother's wife, that he spilled *it* on the ground,
lest that he should give seed to his brother. 10 And the
thing which he did displeased the LORD: wherefore he
slew him also. 11 Then said Judah to Tamar his daughter
in law, Remain a widow at thy father's house, till Shelah
my son be grown: for he said, Lest peradventure he die

the mountain country of Judah (Josh. xv. 54), and **Adullam** (see Josh. xv. 35) in the plain (or valley, ib. 33). This place (Josh. xii. 15) was the seat of a Canaanitish king: it was in its neighbourhood that David sheltered in a cave from the pursuit of Saul (1 Sam. xxii. 1, 2); it was from hence that the three mighty men broke through the host of the Philistines and fetched David the water from the well at Bethlehem (2 Sam. xxiii. 13, ff.). Rehoboam built one of his forts there (2 Chron. xi. 7), which was afterwards celebrated (Micah i. 15). After the captivity it was still an inhabited town (Neh. xi. 30), and is mentioned later still in 2 Macc. xii. 38. The site has never been satisfactorily identified. Van de Velde believes it to be Deir Duppân, about two hours N. of Beit Jiboin (Eleutheropolis). The neighbourhood consists of limestone hills, pierced with many caves. **2.**] Notice that **Shuah** is the name, not of Judah's wife, but of her father: see ver. 12. **5.**] **Chezib** is not mentioned elsewhere, but is probably identical with *Achzib* (Josh. xv. 44; Micah i. 14), and *Chozeba* (1 Chron. iv. 22), in the low country of Judah. In the place in 1 Chron. the men of Chozeba are numbered among the *sons of Shelah*. They had, in the taking possession of the land of promise, gravitated to the birthplace of their ancestor, and its neighbourhood. In connexion with this circumstance the mention of that birthplace here is remarkable. **6.**] The name **Tamar** in Hebrew signifies a palm-tree, but this is no token that she was of Semitic blood. The names of Melchizedek and Abimelech are parallel cases. **7.**] There is no detailed explanation of the reason of the death of Er, but it would seem by what follows, ver. 10, to have been something connected with the peculiar sins which brought destruction on the Canaanitish races. **8.**] On the law and practice of *leviratic* marriage (so called from the Latin levir, a brother-in-law) see note on Deut. xxv. 5, ff. and Matt. xxiii. ff.

11.] From Levit. xxii. 13 we learn that it was usual for a widow without children to return to her father's house. Judah had no intention to give Tamar to Shelah, although he professed it. He had the fear with which the story of Tobit has familiar-

also, as his brethren *did*. And Tamar went and dwelt in
her father's house. 12 ¶ And in process of time the
daughter of Shuah, Judah's wife, died; and Judah was
comforted, and went up unto his sheepshearers to Timnath,
he and his friend Hirah the Adullamite. 13 And it was
told Tamar, saying, Behold thy father in law goeth up to
Timnath to shear his sheep. 14 And she put her widow's
garments off from her, and covered her with a vail, and
wrapped herself, and sat in the gate of Enaim, which *is*
by the way to Timnath; for she saw that Shelah was
grown, and she was not given unto him to wife. 15 When
Judah saw her, he thought her *to be* an harlot; because
she had covered her face. 16 And he turned unto her by
the way, and said, Go to, I pray thee, let me come in unto
thee; (for he knew not that she *was* his daughter in law.)
And she said, What wilt thou give me, that thou mayest
come in unto me? 17 And he said, I will send *thee* a kid
from the flock. And she said, Wilt thou give *me* a pledge,
till thou send *it?* 18 And he said, What pledge shall I
give thee? And she said, Thy signet, and thy string,
and thy staff that *is* in thine hand. And he gave them
her, and came in unto her, and she conceived by him. 19
And she arose, and went away, and laid by her vail from
her, and put on the garments of her widowhood. 20 And

ized us, that she was a fatal wife, bringing death on her successive husbands. **12.**] The situation of Timnah, or Timnatha (for Timnath appears to be an error) is uncertain. It seems to have been Judah's station for his flocks, and to have been above where he was before. It is perhaps the Timnah in Josh. xv. 57, a town in the mountain country of Judah. See Mr. Grove's article in the *Biblical Dict.* It must be distinguished from a frontier town of Dan and Judah between Bethshemesh and Ekron, in the plain, Josh. xv. 10; xix. 43 (in the latter place called Timnathah). On sheep-shearing feasts, see 1 Sam. xxv. 4; 2 Sam. xiii. 23. **14.**] See Judith x. 3. The covering herself with a veil was to prevent her recognition by Judah: but the act seems also to have some reference to the character she was assuming: see Job xxiv. 15. The subsequent expression, **wrapped** or covered **herself**, perhaps indicated some act subsequent to the mere veiling herself—possibly the wrapping some large mantle over her. There is some doubt about the place where she sat by the way. I have given it as the LXX. and the Samaritan, and Kalisch, Knobel, and Keil. Others think it is the passage by two fountains. If we take the proper name, Enaim may perhaps be the same as Enam, in the low country of Judah, Josh. xv. 34. **17.**] The present of a kid is found in Judg. xv. 1 as sent from Samson to his wife. **18.**] She chooses those things that might best identify Judah. The signet was worn inside the garments, suspended round the neck with a silk string (Cant. viii. 6; Jer. xxii. 24; Hag. ii. 23). Both these she asks for, and for the staff in his hand. Herodotus tells us that every Babylonian carried a staff, adorned with a carving of some flower, or fruit, or animal.

Judah sent the kid by the hand of his friend the Adullamite, to receive *his* pledge from the woman's hand: but he found her not. 21 Then he asked the men of that place, saying, Where *is* the harlot, at Enaim by the way side? And they said, There was no harlot in this *place*. 22 And he returned to Judah, and said, I cannot find her; and also the men of the place said, *that* there was no harlot in this *place*. 23 And Judah said, Let her take *it* to her, lest we be shamed: behold, I sent this kid, and thou hast not found her. 24 ¶ And it came to pass about three months after, that it was told Judah, saying, Tamar thy daughter in law hath played the harlot; and also, behold, she *is* with child by whoredom. And Judah said, Bring her forth, and let her be burnt. 25 When she *was* brought forth, she sent to her father in law, saying, By the man, whose these *are*, *am* I with child: and she said, Discern, I pray thee, whose *are* these, the signet, and string, and staff. 26 And Judah acknowledged *them*, and said, She hath been more righteous than I; because that I gave her not to Shelah my son. And he knew her again no more. 27 ¶ And it came to pass in the time of her travail, that, behold, twins *were* in her womb. 28 And it came to pass, when she travailed, that *the one* put out *his* hand: and the midwife took and bound upon his hand a scarlet thread, saying, This came out first. 29 And it came to pass, as he drew back his hand, that, behold, his brother came out: and she said, How hast thou broken forth? *this* breach *be* upon thee: therefore his name was called Pharez [Breach]. 30 And afterward came out his brother,

21.] The name by which Hirah calls her is literally a holy woman. In the horrid religious rites of the goddess Ashtoreth the priestesses or female devotees were harlots, who sat and solicited the passers-by: see Jer. iii. 2; Ezek. xvi. 25; Baruch vi. 43.

23.] The meaning is, then, since we cannot find her, let her keep the pledge, notwithstanding its superior value, lest we incur shame on account of the business.

24.] The punishment of burning for unchastity was afterwards by the law reserved for the daughters of priests: see Levit. xxi. 9. And Knobel thinks that this sentence was pronounced upon Tamar as being now by marriage one of the holy race. Had she merely been punished as the betrothed of Selah, she would have been stoned: see Levit. xx. 10; Deut. xxii. 23, ff.; Ezek. xvi. 40; John viii. 5.

26.] Judah recognizes in this the retribution for his own injustice to Tamar, and an apology for her crime. But inasmuch as Hebrew customs afterwards sanctioned by the law (Levit. xviii. 15; xx. 12) condemned such an act as incest, he repeated it not.

29.] Most commentators regard the saying of the midwife as allusive to the division of the kingdom, by which a breach

that had the scarlet thread upon his hand: and his name
was called Zarah [Sunrise]. XXXIX. 1 And Joseph was
brought down to Egypt; and Potiphar, an officer of
Pharaoh, captain of the guard, an Egyptian, bought him
of the hands of the Ishmaelites, which had brought him
down thither. 2 And JEHOVAH was with Joseph, and he
was a prosperous man; and he was in the house of his
master the Egyptian. 3 And his master saw that JEHOVAH
was with him, and that JEHOVAH made all that he did to
prosper in his hand. 4 And Joseph found grace in his
sight, and he served him: and he made him overseer over
his house, and all *that* he had he put into his hand. 5
And it came to pass from the time *that* he had made him
overseer in his house, and over all that he had, that JE-
HOVAH blessed the Egyptian's house for Joseph's sake;
and the blessing of JEHOVAH was upon all that he had in
the house, and in the field. 6 And he left all that he had
in Joseph's hand; and with him he knew not ought, save
the bread which he did eat. 7 ¶ And Joseph was *a* goodly
person, and well favoured. And it came to pass after

was made in the sovereignty of the house of David, which came of the line of Pharez.

The chronology of this chapter and of the events which depend on it is not easy. Jacob was at least 88 at the time of Judah's birth, seing he was 78 at the time of his flight to Haran, and served 7 years before he married Leah, and this was his fourth son by her (see ch. xxix. 31—35), some time having elapsed before she bore him any children (ib. 20, 25, 31). And he was 130 at the time of his migration to Egypt (ch. xlvii. 9). So that we have barely 42 years' interval. But in that time Judah has grown up sons, has grandsons by their widows, one of whom has two sons, Hezron and Hamul, who went down into Egypt with Jacob and his family (ch. xlvi. 12). All this may have been, but requires the utmost limits of possibility in each case, for 3 × 14 = 42,—and Shelah, the *youngest* of the three sons, was grown up before Judah's intercourse with Tamar.

XXXIX. *Joseph in Potiphar's house and in prison.* The question as to the probable date of Joseph's arrival in Egypt is too difficult and complicated for treatment in these notes. It will be found discussed at length in Mr. Stuart Poole's article in the *Biblical Dictionary*. On the whole, it seems probable that the date was about 1900 B. C., under the dynasty of shepherd kings, who ruled mainly in Lower Egypt. On Potiphar and his office, see notes, ch. xxxvii. 36.

2—5.] Notice the introduction of the sacred name JEHOVAH for the first time into Joseph's history. He seems to have held the same place in his master's house which Eliezer held in Abraham's (ch. xv. 2; xxiv. 2).

6.] The words are literally, **knew not any thing with him,** i. e. says Knobel, in company, in partnership, with Joseph: the association with one so careful and faithful enabled him to do without personal knowledge of his affairs. But this committal of his affairs to Joseph did not extend to anything concerning his food, for that would have been an abomination: see on ch. xliii. 32. So also Keil. The concluding words of this verse introduce what follows.

7.] We are told by both ancient and modern writers that female chastity ever has been at a low ebb in Egypt. In the case of one particular mentioned in the note on ch.

these things, that his master's wife cast her eyes upon
Joseph; and she said, Lie with me. [8] But he refused,
and said unto his master's wife, Behold, my master wot-
teth not what *is* with me in the house, and he hath com-
mitted all that he hath to my hand; [9] *there is* none
greater in this house than I; neither hath he kept back
any thing from me but thee, because thou *art* his wife:
how then can I do this great wickedness, and sin against
God? [10] And it came to pass, as she spake to Joseph
day by day, that he hearkened not unto her, to lie by
her, *or* to be with her. [11] And it came to pass on a certain
day, that he went into the house to do his business; and
there was none of the men of the house there within. [12]
And she caught him by his garment, saying, Lie with
me: and he left his garment in her hand, and fled, and
got him out. [13] And it came to pass, when she saw that
he had left his garment in her hand, and was fled forth,
[14] that she called unto the men of her house, and spake
unto them, saying, See, he hath brought in an Hebrew
unto us to mock us; he came in unto me to lie with me,
and I cried with a loud voice: [15] and it came to pass,
when he heard that I lifted up my voice and cried, that
he left his garment with me, and fled, and got him out.
[16] And she laid up his garment by her, until his lord
came home. [17] And she spake unto him according to
these words, saying, The Hebrew servant, which thou
hast brought unto us, came in unto me to mock me: [18]
and it came to pass, as I lifted up my voice and cried,
that he left his garment with me, and fled out. [19] And
it came to pass, when his master heard the words of his
wife, which she spake unto him, saying, After this manner
did thy servant to me; that his wrath was kindled. [20]
And Joseph's master took him, and put him into the

xxxvii. 36, being accurate, some explanation may be suggested of the incident here.

9.] The God-fearing character of Joseph is nobly brought out by his plain and decisive reply. Compare ch. xlii. 18.

14.] From ch. xliii. 32 we learn that the Hebrews were an abomination to the Egyptians, so that the name she uses was calculated to enlist the servants on her side.

20.] It has been suggested that Potiphar could not have altogether believed the report of his wife, seeing that such a crime on the part of a slave would certainly have met with a much severer punishment. Potiphar was able to do what he did, being by his office supreme over the prison and its inmates. From ch. xl. 3 we learn further that the prison was in Potiphar's house, and

prison, a place where the king's prisoners *were* bound:
and he was there in the prison. 21 ¶ But JEHOVAH was
with Joseph, and shewed him mercy, and gave him favour
in the sight of the keeper of the prison. 22 And the
keeper of the prison committed to Joseph's hand all the
prisoners that *were* in the prison; and whatsoever they
did there, he was the doer *of it.* 23 The keeper of the
prison looked not to any thing *that was* under his hand;
because JEHOVAH was with him, and *that* which he did,
JEHOVAH made *it* to prosper. XL. 1 And it came to pass
after these things, *that* the butler of the king of Egypt
and *his* baker had offended their lord the king of Egypt.
2 And Pharaoh was wroth against two *of* his officers,
against the chief of the butlers, and against the chief of
the bakers. 3 And he put them in ward in the house of
the captain of the guard, into the prison, the place where
Joseph *was* bound. 4 And the captain of the guard
charged Joseph with them, and he served them: and they
continued a season in ward. 5 ¶ And they dreamed a
dream both of them, each man his dream in one night,
each man according to the interpretation of his dream,
the butler and the baker of the king of Egypt, which
were bound in the prison. 6 And Joseph came in unto
them in the morning and looked upon them, and, behold,
they *were* distressed. 7 And he asked Pharaoh's officers
that *were* with him in the ward of his lord's house, saying,
Wherefore are your faces sad to day? 8 And they said

under his own superintendence. The two accounts are not, as Knobel suggests, discrepant, but in perfect accord. The **keeper of the prison**, in our vv. 21—23, is obviously an inferior officer, who was charged with the actual discipline of the prison: and the commission, given to Joseph in ch. xl. 4, by Potiphar, is quite what might be expected on the report of the keeper, joined to his own high value for his former steward.

XL. *Joseph interprets the dream of the chief butler and the chief baker.* The two officers (or eunuchs) here mentioned were of high standing, and Potiphar (for *he* was chief of the guard or of the executioners) put them under the charge of Joseph, who also waited on them. The commentators have in this place disquisitions on the use of wine in Egypt, which is thought to present some difficulty. There is of course none about the interpretation of the office — "one who makes to drink," or the cupbearer,—since it is fully defined by the dream. But it is said by Herodotus and Plutarch, that the culture of the vine, and wine altogether, were unknown to the Egyptians. But this has been abundantly disproved by representations of the vine and the winepress on the monuments of the earliest dynasties; and Herodotus in other portions of his history implies that both were well known. See also Num. xx. 5; Ps. lxxviii. 47; cv. 33. **5.**] Each man according to the interpretation seems to mean, each man a diverse dream, as also the

unto him, We have dreamed a dream, and *there is* no in-
terpreter of it. And Joseph said unto them, Do not
interpretations belong to God? tell me *them*, I pray you.
9 And the chief butler told his dream to Joseph, and said
to him, In my dream, behold, a vine *was* before me; 10 and
in the vine *were* three branches: and it *was* as though it
budded, *and* its blossoms shot forth; and the clusters
thereof brought forth ripe grapes: 11 and Pharaoh's cup
was in my hand: and I took the grapes, and pressed them
into Pharaoh's cup, and I gave the cup into Pharaoh's
hand. 12 And Joseph said unto him, This *is* the interpret-
ation of it: The three branches *are* three days: 13 yet
within three days shall Pharaoh [z]lift up thine head, and z 2 Kings xxv. 17.
restore thee unto thy place: and thou shalt deliver
Pharaoh's cup into his hand, after the former manner
when thou wast his butler. 14 But think on me when it
shall be well with thee, and shew kindness, I pray thee,
unto me, and make mention of me unto Pharaoh, and
bring me out of this house: 15 for indeed I was stolen
away out of the land of the Hebrews: and here also have
I done nothing that they should put me into the dungeon.
16 When the chief baker saw that the interpretation was
good, he said unto Joseph, I also *was* in my dream, and,
behold, *I had* three baskets of white *bread* on my head: 17
and in the uppermost basket *there was* of all manner of
food for Pharaoh, the work of the baker; and the birds
did eat them out of the basket upon my head. 18 And
Joseph answered and said, This *is* the interpretation

interpretations were diverse. **8.**] Observe again Joseph's reference to God. **11.**] Some (e. g. Rosenmuller) have thought that this has reference to the fact asserted by Herodotus (see above), and that the process described does not imply the use of fermented wine. But this can hardly be, as we have representations of drunken persons on the ancient Egyptian monuments: and the reason for the form of action must be obscure. Possibly it may have been merely a symbolism belonging to the dream: the juice squeezed into the cup signifying the wine which ultimately should result from such squeezing. Compare Zech. iv. 12, where the pouring of oil (in the vision) from the olive branches into the lamps is exactly parallel. **14, f.**] We may observe at once Joseph's faith, and his charity. He has hope in the future notwithstanding all adverse appearances; and, in pleading his own innocence, he says not an angry word against any who had mistreated him. **15.**] He mentions the fact of his abduction from his father's house by the simple name of stealing or abducting him, shewing the caution of one who would not involve his brethren in disgrace before a stranger: and he names the land of Canaan, the land of the Hebrews, to identify himself with that race, rather than with the Canaanites. **19.**] The explanation seems to be

thereof: The three baskets *are* three days: [19] Yet within
three days shall Pharaoh lift up thy head from off thee,
and shall hang thee on a tree; and the birds shall eat thy
flesh from off thee. [20] ¶ And it came to pass the third
day, *which was* Pharaoh's birthday, that he made a feast
unto all his servants: and he lifted up the head of the
chief butler and of the chief baker among his servants.
[21] And he restored the chief butler unto his butlership
again; and he gave the cup into Pharaoh's hand: [22] but
he hanged the chief baker: as Joseph had interpreted to
them. [23] Yet did not the chief butler remember Joseph,
but forgat him. XLI. [1] And it came to pass at the end
of two full years, that Pharaoh dreamed: and, behold, he
stood by the river. [2] And, behold, there came up out of
the river seven well favoured kine and fatfleshed; and
a Job viii. 11, only they fed in the [a] sedge. [3] And, behold, seven other kine
came up after them out of the river, ill favoured and lean-
fleshed; and stood by the *other* kine upon the brink of the
river. [4] And the ill favoured and leanfleshed kine did eat
up the seven well favoured and fat kine. So Pharaoh
awoke. [5] And he slept and dreamed the second time:
and, behold, seven ears of corn came up upon one stalk,

that the chief baker was to beheaded, and his body hung up in disgrace: see Deut. xxi. 22, 23; Josh. x. 26; 2 Sam. iv. 12.

XLI.] *Pharaoh's dreams, and Joseph's interpretation of them.* **1.**] **the river** (stream), where the scene is in Egypt, or *the river of Egypt* (ch. xv. 18; see note there), are the usual appellations of the Nile in the O. T. But the word for these two is not the same: the former (*ha-yeor*), **the stream**, is used here and in Exodus, whereas in the other expression it is *Nahar Mizraim*, the former being the ordinary word for "river." The word here used is said to be derived from an Egyptian root signifying a dyke or channel, and never is applied as a proper name to other than the Nile, except in Dan. xii. 5, ff., where it means the Tigris. **2.**] The word for **sedge**, or **reed-grass**, is *achoo*, also an Egyptian word. It is remarkable that the LXX., making their version in Alexandria, preserve this word as it is; "they fed in the *achi:*" and so the Coptic translator, also an Egyptian, both shewing that the word as written was well understood by them. In ref. the LXX. render the word by *butomus* (rush). Jerome explains it to mean, "all the green plants that grow in the marsh." In Isa. xix. 7, where there is no such word in the Hebrew, the LXX. have, "the green *achi* all round the river." **3, 4.**] The second dream exactly corresponds. On the symbolism of both it may be remarked, that the Nile is the *condition* of fertility in Egypt, and that the *bull* (Osiris) was the symbol of the Nile. The *cow*, on the other hand, in the hieroglyphical paintings, represents the earth, agriculture, and food. And Isis,—to whom the cow was especially sacred, and who is represented horned, and also under the form of a cow,—is the goddess of the all-nourishing earth, or of the land fructified by the Nile. On the further signification, see note, ver. 26. **5–8.**] The second dream interprets itself. The seven ears on one stalk is supposed to point to the *triticum compositum*, or Egyptian wheat, of which this is a

rank and good. 6 And, behold, seven thin ears and
blasted with the east wind sprung up after them. 7 And
the seven thin ears devoured the seven rank and full ears.
And Pharaoh awoke, and, behold, *it was* a dream. 8 And
it came to pass in the morning that his spirit was troubled;
and he sent and called for all the [b] magicians of Egypt,
and all the wise men thereof: and Pharaoh told them his
dream; but *there was* none that could interpret them unto
Pharaoh. 9 ¶ Then spake the chief butler unto Pharaoh,
saying, I do remember my faults this day: 10 Pharaoh
was wroth with his servants, and put me in ward in the
captain of the guard's house, *both* me and the chief baker:
11 and we dreamed a dream in one night, I and he; we
dreamed each man according to the interpretation of his
dream. 12 And *there was* there with us a young man, an
Hebrew, servant to the captain of the guard; and we told
him, and he interpreted to us our dreams; to each man
according to his dream he did interpret. 13 And it came
to pass, as he interpreted to us, so it was; me he restored
unto mine office, and him he hanged. 14 ¶ Then Pharaoh
sent and called Joseph, and they brought him hastily out
of the dungeon: and he shaved *himself*, and changed his
raiment, and came in unto Pharaoh. 15 And Pharaoh
said unto Joseph, I have dreamed a dream, and *there is*
none that can interpret it: and I have heard say of thee,
that thou canst understand a dream to interpret it. 16 And

b ver. 24. Exod. vii. 11, 22; viii. 3, 14; xv. 9, 11. Dan. i. 20; ii. 2, 10, 27; iv. 7, 9; v. 11, only.

peculiarity. "The East wind, blowing from the sandy steppes and deserts in the vicinity of the Red Sea, and from the Arabic peninsula, often withers the vegetation of Lower Egypt, and completely destroys the labour and the hopes of the husbandman." Kalisch. The word rendered **magicians** comes from a root signifying to *cut in*, or *engrave*, or *scratch* (other conjectural derivations may be seen in Kalisch's note). These persons were those elsewhere called the *Hiero-grammateis*, those whose duty it was to inscribe the hieroglyphical inscriptions. Jannes and Jambres are cited by Eusebius as the chiefs of the Hierogrammateis. The word occurs only (see reff.) in this Egyptian portion of the Pentateuch and in the Book of Daniel, which imitates the diction of the earlier Scriptures. **9.**] By his **sins**, the chief butler means partly his offence against his king, partly his forgetfulness of his benefactor. **11.**] See on ch. xl. 5.

14.] The fact of Joseph having shaved himself is in striking accord with the Egyptian custom, which was to let the beard and hair grow in mourning only—otherwise most scrupulously shaving: whereas the Hebrews cultivated the hair and beard and shaved in token of mourning (see 2 Sam. x. 4, 5; Isa. xv. 2; Jer. xvi. 6; xli. 5; Amos viii. 10). He changed his raiment, from the ordinary habit of the prison to that of ordinary life or even of festal rejoicing. The fact of his having it in his power to do so shews that he was not treated as ordinary prisoners are: see ch. xxxix. 22, 23. **16.**] **It is not in me,** literally, *not unto me*, i. e. without me. Notice again, as characteristic of

Joseph answered Pharaoh, saying, *It is* not in me: God
shall give Pharaoh an answer of peace. 17 And Pharaoh
said unto Joseph, In my dream, behold, I stood upon the
bank of the river: 18 and, behold, there came up out of
the river seven kine, fatfleshed and well favoured; and
they fed in the sedge: 19 and, behold, seven other kine
came up after them, poor and very ill favoured and lean-
fleshed, such as I never saw in all the land of Egypt for bad-
ness: 20 and the lean and the ill favoured kine did eat up
the first seven fat kine: 21 and when they had eaten them
up, it could not be known that they had eaten them; but
they *were* still ill favoured, as at the beginning. So I
awoke. 22 And I saw in my dream, and, behold, seven
ears came up in one stalk, full and good: 23 and, behold,
c here only. seven ears, [c] withered, thin, *and* blasted with the east
wind, sprung up after them: 24 and the thin ears devoured
the seven good ears: and I told *this* unto the magicians;
but *there was* none that could declare *it* to me. 25 ¶ And
Joseph said unto Pharaoh, The dream of Pharaoh *is* one:
God hath shewed Pharaoh what he *is* about to do. 26 The
seven good kine *are* seven years; and the seven good ears
are seven years: the dream *is* one. 27 And the seven thin
and ill favoured kine that came up after them *are* seven
years; and the seven empty ears blasted with the east
wind shall be seven years of famine. 28 This *is* the thing
which I have spoken unto Pharaoh: What God *is* about
to do he sheweth unto Pharaoh. 29 Behold, there come
seven years of great plenty throughout all the land of
Egypt: 30 and there shall arise after them seven years of
famine; and all the plenty shall be forgotten in the land
of Egypt; and the famine shall consume the land; 31 and
the plenty shall not be known in the land by reason of
that famine following; for it *shall be* very grievous. 32 And

Joseph, the immediate reference to God. What follows is literally, "**God will answer the peace of Pharaoh,**" a pregnant construction, meaning, "God will give the answer, and that answer such an one as shall be for the welfare of Pharaoh." **17—24.**] ***Pharaoh tells his dream,*** but not in the very words of the previous narrative, adding some particulars, e. g. the end of ver. 19 and 21. The first epithet of the thin ears in ver. 22 is added, and is a word occurring here only in this sense. It seems to signify *dry* or *hard*, but it is said to be uncertain. Gesenius owns to having no clue to its interpretation. The LXX. and the Vulgate omit all rendering of it. **25—36.**] *Joseph's interpretation of the dream, and advice thereupon.* **32.**] See

for that the dream was doubled unto Pharaoh twice; *it is*
because the thing *is* established by God, and God will
shortly bring it to pass. 33 Now therefore let Pharaoh
look out a man discreet and wise, and set him over the
land of Egypt. 34 Let Pharaoh do *this*, and let him ap-
point officers over the land, and take up the fifth part of
the land of Egypt in the seven plenteous years. 35 And
let them gather all the food of those good years that come,
and lay up corn [d]under the hand of Pharaoh, and let d 2 Kings xiii. 5. Isa. iii. 6.
them keep food in the cities. 36 And that food shall be
for store to the land against the seven years of famine,
which shall be in the land of Egypt; that the land be not
cast off through the famine. 37 ¶ And the thing was good
in the eyes of Pharaoh, and in the eyes of all his servants.
38 And Pharaoh said unto his servants, Can we find *such
a one* as this *is*, a man in whom the Spirit of God *is?*
39 And Pharaoh said unto Joseph, Forasmuch as God hath
shewed thee all this, *there is* none so discreet and wise as
thou *art:* 40 thou shalt be over my house, and according
unto thy word shall all my people be ruled: only in the
throne will I be greater than thou. 41 And Pharaoh said
unto Joseph, See I have set thee over all the land of
Egypt. 42 And Pharaoh took off his ring from his hand,
and put it upon Joseph's hand, and arrayed him in vest-
ures of fine linen, and put a gold chain about his neck;

1 Kings xi. 9; Job xxxiii. 14; Ps. lxii. 11.

33, f.] Joseph gives this advice, as emboldened by the position which his interpretation of Pharaoh's dream had given him. But it is done in all simplicity, with that openness which characterized Joseph: compare his bearing to his temptress, ch. xxxix. 9; to the chief baker, ch. xl. 18. **34. take up the fifth part**] i. e. lay on a tax of a fifth of the produce. **35. under the hand**] i.e. subject to the control: see reff.

37—42.] *The exaltation of Joseph.* Pharaoh and his court are at once struck with the appositeness of the interpretation, and unhesitatingly adopt it as the true one. The Spirit of God was shewn to be in him, both by the interpretation, and by the wisdom of words with which he had followed it up. **40.**] There is some difficulty in the phrase rendered, **according to thy word shall my people be ruled.** Some of the Hebraists (e. g. Gesenius, Knobel) render it, "*on thy mouth shall my people kiss,*" and interpret it of the kiss of homage. But most of the others believe the meaning to be as in the text, objecting that the kiss of homage was reserved for princes. **57.**] The signet-ring (the Hebrew word for which is derived from a root signifying to dip, because the ring is dipped in the sealing matter to make the impression) has always conveyed the power of the wearer, and the royal signet carried with it the authority of the ring: see Esther iii. 10; viii. 2. On the vestures of fine linen we may remark that the priesthood, the foremost caste of Egypt, wore only linen and cotton garments, and no woollen. The golden chain is found adorning the neck of persons of distinction in the Egyptian wall-paintings. **43.**] i. e. his

43 and he made him to ride in the second chariot which he
† Literally, before his face, Abrech. had; and they cried † before him, Bow the knee: and he
made him *ruler* over all the land of Egypt. 44 And
Pharaoh said unto Joseph, I *am* Pharaoh, and without
thee shall no man lift up his hand or foot in all the land
of Egypt. 45 And Pharaoh called Joseph's name Zaphnath-paaneah [Saviour of the world, *or* Revealer of secrets];
and he gave him to wife Asenath the daughter of Poti-
e ver. 50. ch. xlvi. 20, only. pherah priest of [e]On. And Joseph went out over *all* the
land of Egypt. 46 ¶ And Joseph *was* thirty years old
when he stood before Pharaoh king of Egypt. And
Joseph went out from the presence of Pharaoh, and went
throughout all the land of Egypt. 47 And in the seven
plenteous years the earth brought forth by handfuls.
48 And he gathered up all the food of the seven years,
which were in the land of Egypt, and laid up the food in
the cities: the food of the field, which *was* round about
every city, laid he up in the same. 49 And Joseph
gathered corn as the sand of the sea, very much, until he
left numbering; for *it was* without number. 50 And unto
Joseph were born two sons before the years of famine
came, which Asenath the daughter of Poti-pherah priest
of On bare unto him. 51 And Joseph called the name of

chariot was the next to the royal state chariot in splendour. The word *Abrech*, rendered "*Bow the knee*," is of entirely obscure origin. It is not known whether it is Hebrew or Egyptian. The marginal rendering in the A.V., "tender father," is allowed to be a mistake. On the whole the rendering of the A. V. is that most approved, though by no means certain. I have therefore placed the literal rendering in the margin. **44.**] **I am Pharaoh,** i. e. king, which the name implies; I have power to decree this. **45.**] The name given to Joseph has been variously understood. Jerome interpreted it in the Vulgate *Salvator Mundi* (Saviour of the world); and the LXX. write it *Psonthomphanech*, which may perhaps be made in Coptic to mean this. It has been also rendered "*the revealer of mysteries*," so Onkelos, and the old Syriac. Kalisch prefers the former. It has been before remarked on ch. xxxvii. ult., that **Poti-pherah** is the same name as Potiphar. The signification is, *one who belongs to Râ*, or *the sun*. The priestly caste was the royal caste also. The kings chosen out of the military caste were adopted into the priestly caste, and taught the mysteries known to it alone. That this was the case with Joseph is evident from ch. xliv. 5. **On** was the popular name of Beth-shemesh or Heliopolis, these names meaning *the house or city of the Sun*. The Egyptian sacred name was Ha-Râ, with the same signification. Cyril of Alexandria, living in Egypt, says *On* signifies the sun also. It was on the E. side of the Pelusian branch of the Nile, just below the point of the Delta, and about 20 miles N.E. of Memphis. For all particulars about it, see Mr. Stuart Poole's art. in the *Biblical Dict.* **46.**] Respecting the chronology of Joseph's life, see above on ch. xxxv. 29. **49.**] The astonishing fertility of the Egyptian corn has been shewn by the results of sowing grains found in ancient tombs and mummy-cases. **51.**] Connected with the naming

the firstborn Manasseh [Making to forget]: For God,
said he, hath made me forget all my toil, and all my
father's house. 52 And the name of the second called he
Ephraim [Double fruitfulness]: For God hath caused me
to be fruitful in the land of my affliction. 53 ¶ And the
seven years of plenteousness, that was in the land of
Egypt, were ended. 54 And the seven years of dearth be-
gan to come, according as Joseph had said: and the dearth
was in all lands; but in all the land of Egypt there was
bread. 55 And when all the land of Egypt was famished,
the people cried to Pharaoh for bread: and Pharaoh said
unto all the Egyptians, Go unto Joseph; what he saith
to you, do. 56 And the famine was over all the face of
the earth: and Joseph opened all the storehouses, and
sold unto the Egyptians; and the famine waxed sore in
the land of Egypt. 57 And all countries came into Egypt
to Joseph for to buy, because that the famine was sore in
all lands. XLII. 1 Now when Jacob saw that there was
corn in Egypt, Jacob said unto his sons, Why do ye look
one upon another? 2 And he said, Behold, I have heard
that there is corn in Egypt: get you down thither, and
buy for us from thence; that we may live, and not die.
3 ¶ And Joseph's ten brethren went down to buy corn in
Egypt. 4 But Benjamin, Joseph's brother, Jacob sent
not with his brethren; for he said, Lest peradventure
mischief befall him. 5 And the sons of Israel came to
buy *corn* among those that came: for the famine was in

of Joseph's first son is the question first raised in the fifth century by Theodoret, how it came to pass that in all this time during which Joseph was in highest power in Egypt, he had never communicated with his father. Surely it is no sufficient answer to this to say, with Keil, that the overwhelming sense of God's wondrous purposes for him in Egypt so occupied his mind, as to preclude the thought of such communication. The problem must be left unsolved; and is, we cannot help feeling, further complicated by the apparent prominence into which his forgetfulness of his father's house is thrust by the naming of this his first-born son. That he retained affectionate remembrance of his father's house is not, as some apologists say, shewn by the expression **the land of my affliction** below. It was this, in virtue of his slavery and imprisonment, not of his exile from home. His subsequent affectionate treatment of his father and his brethren only increases the difficulty of his long silence. **53—57.**] *The famine.*

56.] The storehouses are literally, ***all*** *in which* [*there was*] *in them*, viz. corn.

XLII.—XLV.] *Joseph and his brethren.*

1.] **look one upon another**, in want of counsel, and despair. **4.**] Benjamin was emphatically the son of Jacob's old age. But at this time he was a grown-up man, and at the migration into Egypt had ten sons: see ch. xlvi. 21. **5.**] **among those that came** is graphically expressed in the

f Eccl. vii. 19, viii. 8; x. 5. (Ezek. iv. 20; vii. 24.) Dan. ii. 10, 15; iv. 17, 25, 26, 32; v. 21, 29, only.

the land of Canaan. 6 And Joseph *was* the [f]governor over
the land, *and* he *it was* that sold to all the people of the
land: and Joseph's brethren came, and bowed down them-
selves before him *with* their faces to the earth. 7 And
Joseph saw his brethren, and he knew them, but made
himself strange unto them, and spake roughly unto them;
and he said unto them, Whence come ye? And they
said, From the land of Canaan to buy food. 8 And Joseph
knew his brethren, but they knew not him. 9 And Joseph
remembered the dreams which he dreamed of them, and
said unto them, Ye *are* spies; to see the nakedness of
the land ye are come. 10 And they said unto him, Nay,
my lord, but to buy food are thy servants come. 11 We
are all one man's sons; we *are* true *men*, thy servants
are no spies. 12 And he said unto them, Nay, but to
see the nakedness of the land ye are come. 13 And they
said, Thy servants *are* twelve brethren, the sons of one
man in the land of Canaan; and, behold, the [g]youngest
is this day with our father, and one [h]*is* not. 14 And
Joseph said unto them, That *is it* that I spake unto you,
saying, Ye *are* spies: 15 hereby ye shall be proved: By

g little one: see ch. ix. 24.
h ch. v. 24.

Hebrew, in the midst of those that came: the crowd approached and were scrutinized by Joseph, and in the midst of them were his brethren. 6.] The word rendered governor, *Shalit*, is, except here, said to be only found in the books contemporary with and following the captivity. *Salatis* is given by Josephus as the title of the first shepherd-king. The root is found in the title *Sultan*. Joseph's dreams (compare ver. 9) were not literally fulfilled, his father being absent; nor, as observed on ch. xxxvii. 10, could they ever be, seeing that his mother was dead. But in spirit they were. Joseph recognized his brothers, they having been already grown-up men when he was sold, and retaining now their former costume; they did not recognize him, who had grown from boyhood to manhood, and besides was in a habit and with adornment strange to their eyes, and spoke a tongue not understood by them. It might well be suspected that they were spies, especially if the time usually assumed for their visit, that of the dynasty of the shepherd-kings, be correct. For this dynasty, we are told by Manetho, was ever in fear of invasion from the then powerful Assyrians; and Josephus says that on that account they fortified the Eastern side of Egypt. Hence men arriving from Asia, and especially Jacob's sons, who from their Chaldaic origin were more like the Eastern Semitic peoples than Canaanites, might well arouse suspicion as to their being Assyrian spies. The nakedness of the land may well refer to its being easily accessible, having fewer strong places than other countries. 11.] The force of this answer lies in the improbability that one man would expose so large a number of his family to the perilous life of spies, who found no quarter when detected. **true**, literally **upright**, men, not bearing a double character.

14.] i. e. what I said is still not disproved, but awaits disproof as follows, to be gathered from your own account of yourselves.

15.] Joseph swears **by the life of Pharaoh**. See similar instances among the Hebrews themselves, 1 Sam. xvii. 55; 2 Sam. xi. 11, both, however, in addresses to the king. A

the life of Pharaoh ye shall not go forth hence, except
your youngest brother come hither. 16 Send one of you,
and let him fetch your brother, and ye shall be kept in
prison, that your words may be proved, whether *there be*
any truth in you: or else by the life of Pharaoh surely ye
are spies. 17 And he put them all together into ward
three days. 18 And Joseph said unto them the third day,
This do, and live; *for* I fear God: 19 if ye *be* true *men*,
let one of your brethren be bound in the house of your
prison: go ye, carry corn for the famine of your houses:
20 but bring your youngest brother unto me; so shall your
words be verified, and ye shall not die. And they did so.
21 ¶ And they said one to another, We *are* verily guilty
concerning our brother, in that we saw the anguish of his
soul, when he besought us, and we would not hear; there-
fore is this distress come upon us. 22 And Reuben an-
swered them, saying, Spake I not unto you, saying, Do not
sin against the child; and ye would not hear? therefore,
behold, also his blood is required. 23 And they knew not

similar form occurs in the address of Abigail to David, 1 Sam. xxv. 26, so that it was not confined to royalty. Knobel suggests that Joseph may have feared that they had treated Benjamin as they had treated himself, and took this way of easing his anxiety.

16, 17.] His first proposal is a severe one, and tended to bring them to that sense of their guilt which they afterwards expressed.

18—20.] This second proposal is more merciful. It is introduced by the assertion **I fear God**, implying that he did not wish to press matters with harsh severity against them, nor to assume their obnoxious character as proved, before they had the opportunity of answering his challenge to disprove it. This do and live, i. e. by doing this, take the only way of escape from the death which awaits you as spies. Luther well remarks, that these hard-hearted men were to be broken and rendered penitent. Their lie, "*one is not*," had shewn them to be hardened in and careless about their great sin. This moved Joseph to try their hearts more thoroughly. The trial was certainly unpleasant enough, and yet proceeded from an intention perfectly void of anger, towards them. "I," adds Luther characteristically, "should have handled them more roughly." By the words, "**and they did so**," the following narrative is anticipated, as Joseph proposed, so it took place.

21, ff.] The frame of mind which it was Joseph's object to produce was produced. To this many things must have contributed; among them, doubtless, the contrast between their treatment of their brother and that which they were now receiving. They had consigned him, innocent, to death by starvation, while they, though presumed to be guilty as spies, were to receive bread for the hunger of their households, and to have a chance of final escape. There is no need, in interpreting this verse, to suppose, as Knobel does, any discrepancy of varying accounts. The whole hangs together perfectly well. Selling a lad into slavery was surely a crime which an awakened guilty conscience might well represent to itself as equivalent to his murder.

22.] It is remarkable that this charge is laid upon them by Reuben, who at the time (ch. xxxvii. 22) was the one who counselled them to "shed no blood." The mask is dropped from his self-deceit, and he sees that that cruelty which he advised was in reality nothing short of that which they had

that Joseph understood *them*; for the interpreter was be-
tween them. [24] And he turned himself about from them,
and wept; and returned to them again, and communed
with them, and took from them Simeon, and bound him
before their eyes. [25] ¶ Then Joseph commanded to fill
their vessels with corn, and to restore every man's money
into his sack, and to give them provision for the way: and
thus did he unto them. [26] And they laded their asses
with the corn, and departed thence. [27] And as one of
them opened his sack to give his ass provender at the halt-
ing place, he espied his money; for, behold, it *was* in his
sack's mouth. [28] And he said unto his brethren, My money
is restored; and, lo, *it is* in my sack: and their heart failed
them, and they were afraid, saying one to another, What
is this *that* God hath done unto us? [29] ¶ And they came
unto Jacob their father unto the land of Canaan, and told
him all that befell unto them; saying, [30] The man, *who is*
the lord of the land, spake roughly to us, and took us for
spies of the country. [31] And we said unto him, We *are*
true *men*; we are no spies: [32] we *be* twelve brethren, sons
of our father; one *is* not, and the youngest *is* this day
with our father in the land of Canaan. [33] And the man,
the lord of the country, said unto us, Hereby shall I know

intended. But more is done by this speech of Reuben's: see on ver. 24. **23.**] Joseph had completely put on the Egyptian. According to the usual views of the time at which this happened, the kings of Egypt were of Semitic origin, but doubtless all public matters were transacted in the Egyptian language. **the interpreter**] i. e. the official court interpreter. **24.**] This first softening of Joseph's is not enough, nor does it turn him from his fixed purpose of bringing Benjamin to Egypt. He takes Simeon, the second in age, because Reuben the eldest, besides being the natural leader of them all in their journey and return, had shewn himself at Shechem, and again by his words here, the best affected towards Joseph. Whether, as Knobel conjectures, there was any special reason, besides his being second in age, which made him take Simeon, we cannot say. Certainly his subsequent characterization by his father (ch. xlix. 5) is not *against* the assumption that he might have been among the most active in the sin against Joseph. **25, ff.**] They appear to have had, besides their vessels or sacks of corn for the famine of their households, each a sack for provender for their asses by the way. It was at the mouth of this sack that Joseph had the money placed. And when they came to rest for the night (it is deceptive to think of the place as answering in any sense of the word to our *inn*) one of them opened his sack to give provender to his ass (and to those of the rest, for this is implied by ver. 35), and found the money. **28.**] **their heart failed them,** literally, **went out**: they had no courage left. They were evidently on their return to be charged with being thieves as well as spies, and they regard this as another item in God's retribution for their sin. **29, ff.**] The generally unfavourable character of their report is borne out by the discovery of their money in every sack. It now appears certain that they are to be hardly dealt with on their return.

that ye *are* true *men;* leave one of your brethren *here* with
me, and take *food for* the famine of your households, and
be gone: 34 and bring your youngest brother unto me:
then shall I know that ye *are* no spies, but *that* ye *are* true
men: so will I deliver you your brother, and ye shall
traffick in the land. 35 ¶ And it came to pass as they
emptied their sacks, that, behold, every man's bundle of
money *was* in his sack: and when *both* they and their
father saw the bundles of money, they were afraid. 36 And
Jacob their father said unto them, Me have ye bereaved
of my children: Joseph *is* not, and Simeon *is* not, and ye
will take Benjamin *away:* on me come all these things.
37 And Reuben spake unto his father, saying, Slay my
two sons, if I bring him not to thee: deliver him into my
hand, and I will bring him to thee again. 38 And he
said, My son shall not go down with you; for his brother
is dead, and he is left alone: if mischief befall him by the
way in the which ye go, then shall ye bring down my
gray hairs with sorrow to the grave. XLIII. 1 And the
famine *was* sore in the land. 2 And it came to pass, when
they had eaten up the corn which they had brought out of
Egypt, their father said unto them, Go again, buy us a
little food. 3 And Judah spake unto him, saying, The
man did solemnly protest unto us, saying, Ye shall not see
my face, except your brother *be* with you. 4 If thou wilt
send our brother with us, we will go down and buy thee
food: 5 but if thou wilt not send *him,* we will not go
down: for the man said unto us, Ye shall not see my face,

36.] Jacob's argument of complaint is, that on him all this comes: it is to them matter of negotiation, but to him of loss and sorrow, for it is *his* children who are being wasted away by it. **37, f.**] To this Reuben, the firstborn and responsible, answers that not on his father's children alone shall the stroke descend—he will venture his own as pledges for the safety of Benjamin. It must be owned to be somewhat of a strange way of ensuring the safety of a *son,* to add two grandsons to the loss if such should happen. **38.**] But the aged father will not be persuaded: his heart is wrapped up in his youngest son.

XLIII.] *Joseph's brethren visit Egypt a second time, taking with them Benjamin.*

2] Jacob seems to have forgotten the condition of their again going down to Egypt.

3—10.] Judah did not state the matter accurately, if the account in ch. xli. be exact; for Joseph, according to that account, had not enquired as he here states: it was true that circumstances had forced it out of them, but that did not amount to what he here says. But it would appear, from ch. xliv. 19, that this, and not that, was what really happened. See note there. It has been suggested that Judah intervened because Reuben had already tried his utmost in vain, and Levi, who was next eldest, was implicated in the affair about Shechem, and

except your brother *be* with you. 6 And Israel said,
Wherefore dealt ye *so* ill with me, *as* to tell the man
whether ye had yet a brother? 7 And they said, The man
asked us straitly of our state, and of our kindred, saying,
Is your father yet alive? have ye *another* brother? and
we told him according to the tenor of these words: could
we certainly know that he would say, Bring your brother
down? 8 And Judah said unto Israel his father, Send
the lad with me, and we will arise and go; that we may
live, and not die, both we, and thou, *and* also our little
ones. 9 I will be surety for him; of my hand shalt thou
require him: if I bring him not unto thee, and set him before thee, then let me bear the blame for ever: 10 for except
we had lingered, surely now we had returned this second
time. 11 And their father Israel said unto them, If *it
must be* so now, do this; take of the pride of the land in
your vessels, and carry down the man a present, a little
balm, and a little honey, spices, and myrrh, nuts, and
almonds: 12 and take other money in your hand; and the
money that was brought again in the mouth of your sacks,

therefore unacceptable to his father. **9.]** **let me bear the blame for ever** is literally, **I shall sin to thee all the days.** See the faithfulness of Judah to his undertaking, ch. xliv. 18, ff. It was this which affected Joseph so that he could no longer refrain, ch. xlv. 1. **11.]** On the use of Israel for Jacob, see above, ch. xxxv. 22. **If** *it must be*, or **If** *it is*: if that is really the state of the case. **the pride of the land** is literally, **the song of the land**, i. e. that for which the land is celebrated. See a similar expression in Jer. li. 41, where, however, the Hebrew word is not the same as here. The practice of conciliating great men by presents is still universal in the East. Compare ch. xxxii. 14, ff.; 1 Kings x. 25; Matt. ii. 11. The items of the present are—(1) balm or balsam, explained at ch. xxxvii. 25; (2) honey. This is probably not honey of bees, which was probably, as now, very plentiful in Egypt, but the thick inspissated juice or jelly of grapes, which still is manufactured in Palestine and exported from Hebron to Egypt. In Ezek. xxvii. 17 it seems to be this honey which is spoken of; (3) tragacanth, explained at ch. xxxvii. 25; (4) ladanum, ditto; (5) pistachio-nuts, the fruit of the *pistachia vera*, a tree allied to the terebinth, found in dry and rocky situations, and consequently not common in Lower Egypt. Aleppo is still famous for pistachio-nuts. "They are of the shape of the almond, but rounder and glossy, generally of a pretty red hue when fresh, and the kernel a bright green, with the flavour of the walnut." Tristram. (6) Almonds hardly need explanation. The Hebrew name signifies to hasten, the almond being the first of all trees to shew its blossoms in the spring. Hence a play on words in Jer. i. 11, 12, where see note. From the fact of almonds forming part of this present, it would seem that the tree was not common in Egypt. A paltry objection has been brought against this part of the narrative, that the sending of these articles by Jacob is incongruous, in the presence of famine in Palestine. But (1) every one of these articles may have been kept in store; and (2) none of them are of that kind which would necessarily be affected by such seasons as would cause the failure of wheat. **12.]** The meaning is not, as would appear from the A. V.,

carry *it* again in your hand; peradventure it *was* an over-
sight: 13 take also your brother, and arise, go again unto
the man: 14 and [i]God Almighty give you mercy before — i El Shaddai. See ch. xvii. 1; xxxv. 11.
the man, that he may send away with you your other
brother, and Benjamin. If I be bereaved *of my children*,
I [j]am bereaved. 15 ¶ And the men took that present, — j See 2 Kings vii. 4. Esth. iv. 16 (John xix. 22).
and they took double money in their hand, and Benjamin;
and rose up, and went down to Egypt, and stood before
Joseph. 16 And when Joseph saw Benjamin with them,
he said to him that was over his house, Bring *the* men
into the house, and slay, and make ready; for *these* men
shall dine with me at noon. 17 And the man did as
Joseph bade; and the man brought the men into Joseph's
house. 18 And the men were afraid, because they were
brought into Joseph's house; and they said, Because of
the money that was returned in our sacks at the first time
are we brought in; that he may cast himself upon us, and
fall upon us, and take us for bondmen, and our asses.
19 And they came near to him that was over Joseph's
house, and they communed with him at the door of the
house, 20 and said, [k]O sir, we came indeed down at — k ch. xliv. 18. Exod. iv 10, 13.
the first time to buy food: 21 and it came to pass, when
we came to the inn, that we opened our sacks, and, behold,
every man's money *was* in the mouth of his sack, our
money in full weight: and we have brought it again in

that they were to take *three* payments,—double money *besides* that which was in their sacks—but that they were to take money of *a second*, i. e. the same, amount. And so they describe what they had done, though not with the same Hebrew word, ver. 22. **14.**] El Shaddai, see as in marg. **mercy,** literally, **bowels**: see on ver. 30. There is a characteristic difference in the mode of mentioning the two, **your other brother, and Benjamin.** **15.**] **double money** is right here: the Hebrew words are in different order. **16.**] As before (ch. xlii. 7), it seems that all who came to buy passed before Joseph, so that he distinguished his brethren among the crowd, and Benjamin with them. The objection which has been here again found, that the higher castes of the Egyptians ate no animal food, only shews the ignorance of the objectors. We know abundantly from Herodotus and other authorities that it was only from certain animals that the royal and priestly castes abstained, and only certain among them that abstained altogether: and the eating of birds was general. **18.**] They think that they are treated in this exceptional way for the purpose of judgment upon them for their theft. **cast himself** is literally, **roll himself**: see Job xxx. 14. **20.**] **O sir** appears to be literally, **Pray, sir,**—"*we pray thee, sir,*" LXX. The same phrase is found in reff. **21.**] The divergence here from the more exact account given in ch. xlii. 27, 35 is no more than was natural under the circumstances. In relating to a stranger, especially one of whom we are in awe, we are apt to suppress details, even at the expense of some trifling inaccuracy. Truth in such cases is not the

our hand. 22 And other money have we brought down in
our hands to buy food: we cannot tell who put our money
in our sacks. 23 And he said, Peace *be* to you, fear not:
your God, and the God of your father, hath given you
treasure in your sacks: I had your money. And he
brought Simeon out unto them. 24 And the man brought
the men into Joseph's house, and gave *them* water, and
they washed their feet; and he gave their asses provender.
25 And they made ready the present against Joseph came
at noon: for they heard that they should eat bread there.
26 ¶ And when Joseph came home, they brought him the
(l ch. xxiv. 10; xxxv. 4. Num. xxii. 7.) present [l]which *was* in their hand into the house, and bowed
themselves to him to the earth. 27 And he asked them of
their welfare, and said, *Is* your father well, the old man of
whom ye spake? *Is* he yet alive? 28 And they answered,
Thy servant our father *is* in good health, he *is* yet alive.
And they bowed down their heads, and made obeisance.
29 And he lifted up his eyes, and saw his brother Ben-
jamin, his mother's son, and said, *Is* this your younger
brother, of whom ye spake unto me? And he said, God
(m 1 Kings iii. 26. Amos i. 11. Isa. xlvii. 6; ver. 14. Zech. vii. 9, al. See Phil. ii. 1; Philem. 7, 12.) be gracious unto thee, my son. 30 And Joseph made
haste; for his [m]heart yearned upon his brother: and he
sought *where* to weep; and he entered into *his* chamber,

coincidence of details, but the identity of result. **23.**] The steward is in his master's secret, and acts under confidential orders. **Peace be to you** is here not the mere formula of greeting, but a mode of reassuring: compare the same use in Judg. vi. 23. There is nothing in the steward's following words to imply that he, or any of Joseph's household, had renounced idolatry. The meaning intended to be conveyed by them to those whom they addressed was, that their family tutelar God had cared for them in this manner. *We* know, and they knew who this God was: but all we can fairly infer from the steward's words is that the frequent mention of such a family God by his master had impressed him, and suggested the words in the deception which, after all, he was playing on his hearers. Literally, **your money came to me.**
25.] Their feelings must have wonderfully altered since they were brought to the house, ver. 18. **27.**] Joseph's question is literally, **Is there peace to your father . . ?** and their answer, **There is peace to thy servant our father.** The same expression with the same meaning occurs in Joab's treacherous words to Amasa, 2 Sam. xx. 9.

29.] There is nothing in the address **my son** tending in any way to disturb the chronology of Jacob's family. Joseph's position, as well as his superior age, if, even of a few years, would justify the expression. Of course it must be confessed that there is throughout something to us in the estimate of Benjamin and the words used respecting him, inconsistent with the idea that he was at this time father of 10 sons (ch. xlvi. 21, where see notes). In ver. 8 and ch. xliv. 30—34, he is "*the lad*," "*a little child*," in ch. xliv. 20. But this is not affected by the passage now before us. **30.**] **his heart**, literally, **his belly, yearned**, literally, **waxed hot**. The expression is a

and wept there. 31 And he washed his face, and went
out, and refrained himself, and said, Set on bread. 32 And
they set on for him by himself, and for them by them-
selves, and for the Egyptians, which did eat with him, by
themselves: because the Egyptians might not eat bread
with the Hebrews; for that *is* an abomination unto the
Egyptians. 33 And they sat before him, the firstborn ac-
cording to his birthright, and the youngest according to
his youth: and the men marvelled one at another. 34 And
he took *and sent* messes unto them from before him: but
Benjamin's mess was five times so much as any of their's.
And they drank, and [n]were merry with him. XLIV.
1 And he commanded him that was over his house, saying,
Fill the men's sacks *with* food, as much as they can carry,
and put every man's money in his sack's mouth. 2 And
put my cup, the silver cup, in the sack's mouth of the
youngest, and his corn money. And he did according to
the word that Joseph had spoken. 3 As soon as the morn-
ing was light, the men were sent away, they and their
asses. 4 *And* when they were gone out of the city, *and*
not *yet* far off, Joseph said unto him that was over his
house, Up, follow after the men; and when thou dost
overtake them, say unto them, Wherefore have ye re-
warded evil for good? 5 *Is* not this *it* in which my lord

n ch. ix. 21. 1 Sam. i. 14. 2 Sam. xi. 13. Cant. v. 1. Isa. xxix. 9. Jer. xxv. 27. Hag. i. 6, al.

familiar one in the O. and N. T.: see reff. **31.**] After washing away the traces of his emotion, he orders the table to be spread. **32.**] Historians describe to us the extreme exclusiveness of the Egyptians. They kept all the castes separate at meals: Joseph himself, as chief minister of state, or perhaps as belonging by marriage to the priestly caste, eats by himself, the members of his suite and court by themselves, and the Hebrews separate again. Herodotus tells us that an Egyptian never kissed a Greek, nor would use a knife or other implement belonging to a Greek, nor would eat even lawful flesh if cut by a Greek. See on ch. xxxix. 6. **33.**] Doubtless this was done to produce in them the impression that Joseph was possessed of supernatural insight: compare ch. xliv. 5, 15. **34.**] This was the practice in the East, by way of honouring guests: see 1 Sam. ix. 23, f. It is frequently mentioned in the Homeric poems, where the largest and best pieces are reserved for eminent guests, or double portions, as at the Spartan common meals for the kings, as related by Herodotus. The number **five** seems to have been in especial regard in Egypt: see ch. xli. 34; xlv. 22; xlvii. 2, 24; Isa. xix. 18. The reason is stated to have been, that the Egyptians recognized only five planets. The older versions translate the word which we render **were merry** more coarsely—*inebriati sunt*, as the Vulgate. And there is hardly any escaping this, seeing that it is the identical word used of Noah in Gen. ix. 21 and in many other places (reff.), where it is impossible to suppose any more favourable interpretation admissible.

XLIV. *Joseph's further device to detain his brother. Judah's deprecation.* **5.**] "The ancient Egyptians, and still more the

drinketh, and whereby indeed he divineth? ye have done
evil in so doing. 6 ¶ And he overtook them, and he
spake unto them these same words. 7 And they said unto
o ch. xviii. 25; ver. 17. him, Wherefore saith my lord these words? [o]Be it far
from thy servants to do according to this saying: 8 be-
hold, the money, which we found in our sacks' mouths,
we brought again unto thee out of the land of Canaan:
how then should we steal out of thy lord's house silver or
gold? 9 With whomsoever of thy servants it be found,
both let him die, and we also will be my lord's bondmen.
10 And he said, Now also *let* it *be* according unto your
words: he with whom it is found shall be my servant;
and ye shall be blameless. 11 Then they speedily took
down every man his sack to the ground, and opened every
man his sack. 12 And he searched, *and* began at the
eldest, and ended at the youngest: and the cup was found
in Benjamin's sack. 13 Then they rent their clothes, and
laded every man his ass, and returned to the city.
14 ¶ And Judah and his brethren came to Joseph's house;
for he *was* yet there: and they fell before him on the
ground. 15 And Joseph said unto them, What deed *is*
this that ye have done? wot ye not that such a man as I
can certainly divine? 16 And Judah said, What shall we

Persians, practised a mode of divination from goblets. Small pieces of gold and silver, together with precious stones, marked with strange figures and signs, were thrown into the vessel, after which certain incantations were pronounced, and the evil demon was invoked; the latter was then supposed to give the answer, either by intelligible words, or by pointing to some of the characters on the precious stones, or in some other more mysterious manner. Sometimes the goblet was filled with pure water, upon which the sun was allowed to play, and the figures thus formed, or which a lively imagination fancied it saw, were interpreted as the desired omen: a method of taking auguries still employed in Egypt and Nubia. The goblets were usually of a spherical form; and from this reason, as well as because they were believed to teach man all natural and many supernatural things, they were called 'celestial globes.' Most celebrated was the magnificent vase of turquoise of the wise Jemsheed, the Solomon among the ancient Persian kings, the founder of Persepolis; and Alexander the Great, so eager to imitate Eastern manners, is said to have adopted the sacred goblets also." Kalisch. The LXX. render the Hebrew word *Gevia* by *Kondu*, which seems to have been the Egyptian name; the Hindoo priests still call their sacred vessels *Kundi*. The word rendered **divineth** (*nichesh*) means to hiss like a serpent (*nachash*), and hence to murmur incantations. There is no proof that Joseph himself really practised this divination: the whole intent is to inspire terror into his brethren, and impress them with his supernatural character. **12, 13.**] Now took place the true proof of them. Would they give up Benjamin, their father's darling, as they had before got rid of Joseph? or would they faithfully defend him that had been entrusted to them? In ver. 17 Joseph tests them by proposing to separate Benjamin from them. Judah answers for the rest,

say unto my lord? what shall we speak? or how shall
we clear ourselves? God †hath found out the iniquity of † HA-ELOHIM.
thy servants: behold, we *are* my lord's servants, both we,
and *he* also with whom the cup is found. 17 And he said,
Be it far from me to do so: *but* the man in whose hand
the cup is found, he shall be my servant; and as for you,
get you up in peace unto your father. 18 ¶ Then Judah
came near unto him, and said, Oh my lord, let thy serv-
ant, I pray thee, speak a word [p]in my lord's ears, and let p ch. l. 4. Sam. xviii. 23, al.
not thine anger burn against thy servant: for thou *art* even
as Pharaoh. 19 My lord asked his servants, saying, Have
ye a father, or a brother? 20 And we said unto my lord,
We have a father, an old man, and a child of his old age,
a little one; and his brother is dead, and he alone is left
of his mother, and his father loveth him. 21 And thou
saidst unto thy servants, Bring him down unto me, that
I may set mine eyes upon him. 22 And we said unto my
lord, The lad cannot leave his father: for *if* he should leave
his father, *his father* would die. 23 And thou saidst unto
thy servants, Except your youngest brother come down
with you, ye shall see my face no more. 24 And it came
to pass when we came up unto thy servant my father, we
told him the words of my lord. 25 And our father said,
Go again, *and* buy us a little food. 26 And we said, We
cannot go down: if our youngest brother be with us, then
will we go down: for we may not see the man's face, ex-
cept our youngest brother *be* with us. 27 And thy servant
my father said unto us, Ye know that my wife bare me

as having in the previous pleading with his father (xliii. 8, ff.) guaranteed the safety of Benjamin: see note there. And this is why prominence is given to him in ver. 14. The moment Benjamin was in peril Judah, as the responsible party, comes to the front. Joseph was still in his house, waiting, doubtless, the issue of the device. **18, ff.**] Kalisch justly calls this pleading speech of Judah's "one of the masterpieces of Hebrew composition." Its beauty mainly consists in the simple and pathetic statement of facts. Luther says, 'I would that I could pray so well to our Lord God, as Judah prays here to Joseph, for it is a perfect example of prayer and of the earnestness which should be in prayer." **in my lord's ears,** i. e. pressingly and intimately: see reff. **19.**] This is the same statement as we have had from the brethren to their father, ch. xliii. 7, and it hence appears that it was the exact state of the case, or Judah would not have ventured to appeal to Joseph's recollection of it. **20.**] On the words **a little one**, see note, ch. xliii. 29. **his brother is dead**] See on ch. xlii. 22. **22.**] Literally, **he will leave his father, and he will die.** **27—29.**] The sayings of Jacob on several occasions, and indeed that which he may be *supposed* to have said, are put together. **my wife**] Hardly because he counted Rachel his only true wife,

two *sons*: 28 and the one went out from me, and I said,
Surely he is torn in pieces; and I saw him not since:
29 and if ye take this also from me, and mischief befall
him, ye shall bring down my gray hairs with sorrow to
the grave. 30 Now therefore when I come to thy servant
my father, and the lad *be* not with us; seeing that his
q 1 Sam. xviii. q soul is bound up in the lad's soul; 31 it shall come to
pass, when he seeth that the lad *is* not *with us*, that he will
die: and thy servants shall bring down the gray hairs of
thy servant our father with sorrow to the grave. 32 For
thy servant became surety for the lad unto my father, say-
ing, If I bring him not unto thee, then I shall bear the
blame to my father for ever. 33 Now therefore, I pray
thee, let thy servant abide instead of the lad a bondman
to my lord; and let the lad go up with his brethren.
34 For how shall I go up to my father, and the lad *be* not
with me? lest peradventure I see the evil that shall come
on my father. XLV. 1 Then Joseph could not refrain
himself before all them that stood by him; and he cried,
Cause every man to go out from me. And there stood no
man with him, while Joseph made himself known unto
his brethren. 2 And he wept aloud: and the Egyptians
and the house of Pharaoh heard. 3 And Joseph said unto
his brethren, I *am* Joseph; doth my father yet live? And
his brethren could not answer him; for they were troubled
at his presence. 4 And Joseph said unto his brethren,
Come near to me, I pray you. And they came near.

nor would such a thought surely have been uttered by a son of Leah's. It is, however, remarkable, that in the enumeration in ch. xlvi. Rachel is emphatically called "*Jacob's wife*," which title is not given to Leah.

32.] As in ch. xliii. 9, the concluding words are literally, "*I shall have sinned to my father all the days.*"

XLV. *The recognition. Joseph sends for his father.* **1.**] The pleading of Judah has conquered, not the determination of Joseph, which had no real existence, but his power of repressing his feelings. But he will not have the Egyptians know the details of his brethren's crime and his own secret history. **2.**] Literally, **he uttered his voice in weeping.** As he did so, his own suite outside and that of Pharaoh heard him (not, heard *of* it): this conclusion of the verse is manifestly connected with the fact of his weeping *aloud*. We must therefore infer that Joseph's official residence was in, or close by, the royal palace. In ver. 16 we are told that the news of that which had happened were told in Pharaoh's house; but that was a distinct matter. **3.**] The question which their former intelligence had again and again solved is again asked by Joseph. But this is an exquisite stroke of truth. He now has entered into a different relation with them. The "old man, your father," is now become "my father." Before, it was a question of courtesy; but now, of love. **4.**] He calls them nearer, and

And he said, I *am* Joseph your brother, whom ye sold
into Egypt. 5 Now therefore be not grieved, nor angry
with yourselves, that ye sold me hither: for God did send
me before you to preserve life. 6 For these two years
hath the famine *been* in the land: and yet *there are* five
years, in the which *there shall* neither *be* ploughing nor
harvest. 7 And God sent me before you to preserve you
a [r]remnant in the earth, and to save your lives by a great [r] 2 Sam. xiv. 7. Jer. xliv. 7.
deliverance. 8 So now *it was* not you *that* sent me hither,
but God: and he hath made me a father to Pharaoh, and
lord of all his house, and a ruler throughout all the land
of Egypt. 9 Haste ye, and go up to my father, and say
unto him, Thus saith thy son Joseph, God hath made me
lord of all Egypt: come down unto me, tarry not: 10 and
thou shalt dwell in the land of Goshen, and thou shalt be
near unto me, thou, and thy children, and thy children's
children, and thy flocks, and thy herds, and all that thou
hast: 11 and there will I nourish thee; for yet *there are*
five years of famine; lest thou, and thy household, and
all that thou hast, come to poverty. 12 And, behold, your
eyes see, and the eyes of my brother Benjamin, that *it is*
my mouth that speaketh unto you. 13 And ye shall tell
my father of all my glory in Egypt, and of all that ye
have seen; and ye shall haste and bring down my father
hither. 14 And he fell upon his brother Benjamin's neck,

gives them more detailed proof, at the same time fathoming by his simple words the very depth of that guilt with which their conscience was charging them, and endeavouring to remove it. **5.**] As Luther remarks, "You sold me, but God bought me for His good purposes." **8.**] So in 1 Macc. xi. 32, King Demetrius writes to his *father* Lasthenes. 2 Chron. ii. 12; iv. 16. **10. the land of Goshen**] Otherwise called (ch. xlvii. 11) "*the land of Raamses.*" Knobel says that the Elohist alone knows it by this latter name. It was to the East of the Nile as lying nearest to the immigrants from Canaan; and neither at this time, nor in the history of the Exodus, do we hear of any crossing of the river. But it must have extended to the Nile, witness the hiding of the infant Moses, and the regrets for the fish which they used to eat in Egypt (Num. xi 5). The LXX. render the word here and in ch. xlvi. 34 by "*Gesem of Arabia:*" and we know from Herodotus and Strabo that the ancients reckoned the Eastern cities of Egypt, Heliopolis and Heroopolis, as in Arabia. So that it was to the N.E. of Egypt, where even now is the most fertile part (see ch. xlvii. 6, 11) and in the neighbourhood of the capital, where Joseph dwelt.

11.] **come to poverty** is literally, **become a possession**, i. e. be sold into slavery. This was really the case with the Egyptians themselves as the result of the famine: see ch. xlvii. 19, ff. **12.**] He challenges any possible thought that might doubt his identity, appealing to all, and to that one who knew him best. Probably, in this his speech to them, he had resumed a peculiar and familiar way of speech by which he might be infallibly known to be their brother.

and wept; and Benjamin wept upon his neck. 15 More-
over he kissed all his brethren, and wept upon them: and
after that his brethren talked with him. 16 ¶ And the
fame thereof was heard in Pharaoh's house, saying,
Joseph's brethren are come: and it pleased Pharaoh well,
and his servants. 17 And Pharaoh said unto Joseph, Say
unto thy brethren, This do ye; lade your beasts, and go,
get you unto the land of Canaan; 18 and take your father
and your households, and come unto me: and I will give
you the good of the land of Egypt, and ye shall eat the
fat of the land. 19 Now thou art commanded, this do ye;
take you carriages out of the land of Egypt for your little
ones, and for your wives, and bring your father, and come.
20 And let not your eyes spare your furniture; for the
good of all the land of Egypt *is* your's. 21 And the chil-
dren of Israel did so: and Joseph gave them carriages,
according to the [s]commandment of Pharaoh, and gave
them provision for the way. 22 To all of them he gave
each man changes of raiment; but to Benjamin he gave
three hundred *pieces* of silver, and five changes of raiment.
23 And to his father he sent after this *manner;* ten asses
laden with the good things of Egypt, and ten she asses
laden with corn and bread and meat for his father by the
way. 24 So he sent his brethren away, and they departed:
and he said unto them, See that ye fall not out by the

[s] Exod. xxxviii. 21. Job xxxix. 27. Eccl. viii. 2.

15.] Only after he had thus embraced them and wept over them, have they courage to talk with him. **16—20.**] *Pharaoh's invitation to them to come to Egypt.* The promise of **the good of the land, the fat of the land,** does not here seem to refer to their being located in Goshen, but to bountiful and rich supply of their present wants: see ver. 23, and ch. xxiv. 10. The king orders Joseph to send carriages for their transport, and we know that Egypt was from of old rich in carriages and horses: see ch. xli. 43; xlvi. 29; l. 9; Exod. xiv. 6, ff.; xv. 1, 4, 19; also 1 Kings x. 28, f.; Isa. xxxi. 1; xxxvi. 9. **20.**] Make no trouble at leaving behind your possessions in Canaan, household furniture, and the like. The word is literally **your utensils,** articles of household use. **21.**] **commandment,** literally, **mouth**: see reff. **22.**] Joseph, to confirm his friendly feeling to them, dismisses them with costly presents—giving, as before, five times as much to Benjamin as to the others, besides a rich present in silver. Garments were and are the usual present in the East: see Judges xiv. 12; 2 Kings v. 5, 22, f. **24.**] He was afraid that they might begin to discuss and allot the blame belonging to each for selling him into Egypt. This, to quarrel, or fall out, is the sense of the same Hebrew word in Prov. xxix. 9; Isa. xxviii. 21. On the other hand, Kalisch, Gesenius, and others maintain the sense "*Be not afraid;*" meaning, of any after plot of mine to terrify or bring you back as before. So the Hebrew word in Exod. xv. 14; Deut. ii. 25; 1 Sam. xiv. 15, al. But surely the former sense is the better; and Knobel brings a grammatical objection against the other. **25—28.**] *They*

way. 25 ¶ And they went up out of Egypt, and came
into the land of Canaan unto Jacob their father, 26 and
told him, saying, Joseph *is* yet alive, and he *is* governor
over all the land of Egypt. And Jacob's heart fainted,
for he believed them not. 27 And they told him all the
words of Joseph, which he had said unto them: and when
he saw the carriages which Joseph had sent to carry him,
the spirit of Jacob their father revived: 28 and Israel said,
Is is [t] enough; Joseph my son *is* yet alive: I will go and
see him before I die. XLVI. 1 And Israel took his
journey with all that he had, and came to Beer-sheba, and
offered sacrifices unto the God of his father Isaac. 2 And
God spake unto Israel in the visions of the night, and said,
Jacob, Jacob. And he said, Here *am* I. 3 And he said,
I *am* God, the God of thy father: fear not to go down
into Egypt; for I will there make of thee a great nation:
4 I will go down with thee into Egypt; and I will also
surely bring thee up *again*: and Joseph shall put his hand
upon thine eyes. 5 And Jacob rose up from Beer-sheba:
and the sons of Israel brought Jacob their father, and
their little ones, and their wives, in the carriages which
Pharaoh had sent to carry him. 6 And they took their
cattle, and their goods, which they had gotten in the land
of Canaan, and came into Egypt, Jacob, and all his seed
with him: 7 his sons, and his sons' sons with him, his
daughters, and his sons' daughters, and all his seed
brought he with him into Egypt. 8 ¶ And these *are* the
names of the children of Israel, which came into Egypt,

t Exod. ix. 28. Num. xvi. 3, 7. 2 Sam. xxiv. 16. 1 Kings xix. 4.

reach, and at length persuade, Jacob.

26.] **fainted** is perhaps literally, **remained cold.** He had had too much experience of deceit to believe easily a strange tale like this. **27.**] Warmth and life returned to his spirit. **28.**] The phrase **It is enough** renders the simple Hebrew word *rav*, i. e. **much**: see reff.

XLVI.] *Jacob's migration to Egypt.* **1—7.**] He came from Hebron: see ch. xxxvii. 14. Abraham and Isaac had called on the name of the Lord Jehovah at Beersheba: see ch. xxi. 33; xxvi. 25. It may well be that the mind of Jacob was not easy at leaving the land of promise, and he wished to perform an act of solemn adhesion to the God of his fathers in prospect of the new life that awaited him in Egypt. It is true, God had predicted this very migration in a vision to Abraham, ch. xv. 13—16, but that may not have been before Jacob's mind, couched as it was in somewhat mysterious terms. **4.**] The promise, **I will surely bring thee up again,** does not refer to the bringing up of Jacob when dead, to be buried in Canaan,—for there was in that no Divine interposition,—but to the bringing up his descendants at the Exodus, which is ever said to have been God's act, with his mighty hand and outstretched arm. **8—28.**] Catalogue of Jacob's sons, grandchildren, and great-grandchildren who went down

Jacob and his sons: Reuben, Jacob's firstborn. 9 And
the sons of Reuben; Hanoch, and Phallu, and Hezron,
and Carmi. 10 ¶ And the sons of Simeon; Jemuel, and
Jamin, and Ohad, and Jachin, and Zohar, and Shaul the
son of a Canaanitish woman. 11 ¶ And the sons of Levi;
Gershon, Kohath, and Merari. 12 ¶ And the sons of
Judah; Er, and Onan, and Shelah, and Pharez, and Zarah:
u ch. xxxviii. 7—10. but Er and Onan [u]died in the land of Canaan. And the
sons of Pharez were Hezron and Hamul. 13 ¶ And the
sons of Issachar; Tola, and Phuvah, and Job, and Shim-
ron. 14 ¶ And the sons of Zebulun; Sered, and Elon,
and Jahleel. 15 These *be* the sons of Leah, which she bare
unto Jacob in Padan-aram, with his daughter Dinah: all
the souls of his sons and his daughters *were* thirty and
three. 16 ¶ And the sons of Gad; Ziphion, and Haggi,
Shuni, and Ezbon, Eri, and Arodi, and Areli. 17 ¶ And
the sons of Asher; Jimnah, and Ishuah, and Isui, and
Beriah, and Serah their sister: and the sons of Beriah;
Heber, and Malchiel. 18 These *are* the sons of Zilpah,
whom Laban gave to Leah his daughter, and these she
bare unto Jacob, *even* sixteen souls. 19 The sons of Rachel
Jacob's wife; Joseph, and Benjamin. 20 ¶ And unto
Joseph in the land of Egypt were born Manasseh and
Ephraim, which Asenath the daughter of Poti-pherah
priest of On bare unto him. 21 ¶ And the sons of Benja-
min *were* Belah, and Becher, and Ashbel, Gera, and
Naaman, Ehi, and Rosh, Muppim, and Huppim, and Ard.
22 These *are* the sons of Rachel, which were born to Jacob:
all the souls *were* fourteen. 23 ¶ And the sons of Dan;
Hushim. 24 ¶ And the sons of Naphtali; Jahzeel, and
Guni, and Jezer, and Shillem. 25 These *are* the sons of
Bilhah, which Laban gave unto Rachel his daughter, and
she bare these unto Jacob: all the souls *were* seven. 26 All

into Egypt. The children are ranged according to their mothers, as are those of Esau in ch. xxxvi. 9, ff. **9—15.** *The six sons, and daughter of Leah.* The whole number of these, excluding Er and Onan, is 32. But seeing that they are stated to be 33 in ver. 15, and that "*Jacob and his sons*" are mentioned in ver. 8, it is plain that *he himself* is reckoned to this first lot. **16—18.**] *The two sons of Zilpah, Leah's maid, and their children, sixteen in number.* **19—22.**] *Rachel's two sons, and their children, fourteen in number.* **23—25.**] *Bilhah's two sons, and their children, seven in number.* **26, f.**] So that we have 33 + 16 + 14 + 7 = 70. But of these Jacob himself and Joseph and his two sons are not counted in ver. 26, so

the souls that came with Jacob into Egypt, which came
out of his loins, besides Jacob's sons' wives, all the souls
were threescore and six; 27 and the sons of Joseph, which
were born him in Egypt, *were* two souls: all the souls of
the house of Jacob, which came into Egypt, *were* three-
score and ten. 28 ¶ And he sent Judah before him unto
Joseph, to direct his face unto Goshen; and they came
into the land of Goshen. 29 And Joseph made ready his
chariot, and went up to meet Israel his father, to Goshen,
and [v] presented himself unto him; and he fell on his neck,
and wept on his neck a good while. 30 And Israel said
unto Joseph, Now let me die, since I have seen thy face,
because thou *art* yet alive. 31 And Joseph said unto his
brethren, and unto his father's house, I will go up, and
shew Pharaoh, and say unto him, My brethren, and my
father's house, which *were* in the land of Canaan, are come
unto me; 32 and the men *are* shepherds, for their trade
hath been to feed cattle; and they have brought their
flocks, and their herds, and all that they have. 33 And it
shall come to pass, when Pharaoh shall call you, and shall

v ch. xii. 7; xvii. 1; xviii 1; xxvi. 2, 24; xxxv. 1, 9; xlviii. 3.

that 66 are left: and, adding in these four, we have (as in ver. 27) 70. Several remarks occur to us on this catalogue. (1.) The LXX. in ver. 27 insert the following words: "*There were also sons of Manasseh, which his Syrian concubine bare unto him; Machir. And Machir begat Galaad. And the sons of Ephraim the brother of Manasseh; Sutalam and Taam: and the sons of Sutalam; Edom.*" And in ver. 27, to correspond with this addition of five persons, they make the whole number 75. This appears to have been put together by the aid of our ch. l. 23, and Num. xxvi. 29, 35. This reckoning is followed by Stephen (Acts vii. 14), who as a Hellenistic Jew naturally goes by the LXX. (2.) The list is probably neither complete nor accurate, and must be regarded rather as a formal than as an historical document. For (*a*) there were all Jacob's *daughters*, ch. xxxvii. 35, and our ver. 7, and his *sons' daughters*, ver. 7, of whom no mention is made except in the two cases of Dinah and Serah. (*b*) The whole difficulty respecting the progeny of Judah (see notes on ch. xxxviii. 29), as also that regarding Benjamin's ten sons (ver. 21), is most likely to be solved not by stretching the limits of probability so as to make all square with fact, but by regarding such catalogues as this as rather formal than historical. (3.) On the variations in names and their forms between this account and those in Num. xxvi. and in 1 Chron. 11, ff. see notes in those places. **28—34.**] *Meeting of Jacob and Joseph.* Judah appears to have been sent straight to Joseph, to obtain from him directions as to the land of Goshen, and then to have returned to his father with the directions and to have guided them into the land of Goshen. Here the LXX. have "*sent Judah before him to Joseph to meet him at Heroopolis, at the land of Ramesses;*" and in the next verse where we have, after the Hebrew, **to Goshen,** they have "*to Heroopolis.*" See above on ch. xlv. 10. **29.**] **presented himself** is literally **appeared,** a word almost reserved for divine appearances (reff.): and Knobel thinks it is used here as according with the royal pomp with which Joseph was invested.

went up is used of going to Goshen which was N. of Memphis: but again in ver. 31 **go up** is used of going from Goshen

say, What *is* your occupation? 34 that ye shall say, Thy
servants' trade hath been about cattle from our youth even
until now, both we, *and* also our fathers: that ye may
dwell in the land of Goshen; for every shepherd *is* an
abomination unto the Egyptians. XLVII. 1 Then Joseph
came and told Pharaoh, and said, My father and my
brethren, and their flocks, and their herds, and all that
they have, are come out of the land of Canaan; and, be-
hold, they *are* in the land of Goshen. 2 And from among
his brethren he took five men, and presented them unto
Pharaoh. 3 And Pharaoh said unto his brethren, What
is your occupation? and they said unto Pharaoh, Thy
servants *are* shepherds, both we, *and* also our fathers.
4 They said moreover unto Pharaoh, For to sojourn in the
land are we come; for thy servants have no pasture for
their flocks; for the famine *is* sore in the land of Canaan:
now therefore, we pray thee, let thy servants dwell in the
land of Goshen. 5 And Pharaoh spake unto Joseph, say-
ing, Thy father and thy brethren are come unto thee:
6 the land of Egypt *is* before thee; in the best of the land
make thy father and brethren to dwell; in the land of
Goshen let them dwell: and if thou knowest *any* men of
activity among them, then make them rulers over my
cattle. 7 And Joseph brought in Jacob his father, and
set him before Pharaoh: and Jacob blessed Pharaoh.

to Pharaoh, either because that was to the royal presence, or because it was up the stream of the Nile. **34.**] It might seem strange that such a direction should be given under the reign of the shepherd-kings, assuming that this was the period of Jacob's visit. But Knobel well suggests that they could not change the thoughts and customs of the Egyptians, which this describes. The offer to Jacob and his sons of the best of the land and of comparative separation from the Egyptians, would seem rather to favour the idea that the shepherd-kings were reigning.

XLVII. **1—12.**] *Joseph presents his father and five of his brethren to Pharaoh. A possession is assigned them in the land of Rameses.* **from among his brethren** is literally, **from the end of his brethren,** and some have supposed that Joseph presented only the weakest, who would not be likely to be taken as soldiers by Pharaoh. But it seems clear, from the use elsewhere, that the word must be sometimes taken as meaning **from the number of,** i.e. from among. So Gesenius and Kalisch. On the use of the number five, see above, on ch. xliii. 34. **3, f.**] They answer as Joseph had bidden them, ch. xlvi. 33. **7.**] It has been asked why the father was not introduced first. The answer, I conceive, will be found in the fact that the sons represented the occupation of the family, on which would depend the situation of their location in the land. Theirs was the business interview; his was one only of form and courtesy. The "blessing" spoken of seems to have been that which was customary at greeting (compare ch. xxvii. 23, where this blessing is distinct from the more solemn one that follows), and not any marked form of benediction such as

8 And Pharaoh said unto Jacob, How old *art* thou? 9 And
Jacob said unto Pharaoh, The days of the years of my
wanderings *are* an hundred and thirty years: few and
evil have the days of the years of my life been, and have
not attained unto the days of the years of the life of my
fathers in the days of their wanderings. 10 And Jacob
blessed Pharaoh, and went out from before Pharaoh.
11 ¶ And Joseph placed his father and his brethren, and
gave them a possession in the land of Egypt, in the best
of the land, in the land of Rameses, as Pharaoh had com-
manded. 12 And Joseph nourished his father, and his
brethren, and all his father's household, with bread, ac-
cording to *their* families. 13 ¶ And *there was* no bread in
all the earth; for the famine *was* very sore, so that the
land of Egypt and the land of Canaan fainted by reason
of the famine. 14 And Joseph gathered up all the money
that was found in the land of Egypt, and in the land of
Canaan, for the corn which they bought: and Joseph

the mystic interpreters have ascribed to Jacob in the character of heir of the promise. So also in ver. 10, at their parting. Probably it is intended that Jacob approached and left Pharaoh with some such words as "God save the king," or "O king, live for ever:" compare 2 Sam. xvi. 16; Dan. ii. 4; v. 10.

9.] Jacob's answer is characteristic. He feels that his life is drawing to an end, and compares his 130 years with the 175 of Abraham (ch. xxv. 7) and the 180 of Isaac (ch. xxxv. 28): they seem to him *few*, and when he thinks how they have been spent—all those years of exile and servitude, followed by wandering and then by cruel deceit and mourning—they seem to him evil also. And they were years of wandering, well called a *pilgrimage*, as were those of his fathers. It is well, however, to retain here the simpler term wanderings, as from this passage pilgrimage is so wedded to its figurative meaning as to have lost all allusion to the wandering from which occasion was first found for its use. **11.**] The *land* of Rameses is mentioned here only. The *city* (Rameses or Raamses) is mentioned Exod. i. 11; xii. 37; Num. xxxiii. 3, 5. On the probable situation, and other particulars connected with the name, see Mr. Stuart Poole's art. in the *Biblical Dict.* **13—26.**] *Increase of the famine; Joseph's policy, and its results.*

13.] The famine was universal, and the two countries with which the Hebrews were connected are especially mentioned as being exhausted by it. **14.**] Much questioning has arisen over the policy of Joseph as related in this passage. Kalisch spends eight pages of virtuous indignation over his cruel and treacherous behaviour, and puts the enquiry to which he offers no satisfactory answer, "Is not his person, described in so bright and almost sublime traits, at once stained by the execrable meanness of sacrificing the happiness of a nation to subservient sycophancy for a tyrannical dynasty?" But we may remark, that his animadversions all proceed on one assumption, quite unwarranted by the history, viz. that the people of Egypt were aware of, and believed, the approach of the years of famine. Doubtless the fact of Pharaoh's dreams, their interpretation and the elevation of Joseph in consequence, were matters of publicity. But what a wide interval there is between this and a personal prevision on the part of the people for the coming want, any one knows who has any experience of the popular mind. The people's own confession that Joseph had saved their lives (ver. 25) includes a confession of their own improvidence. Assum-

brought the money into Pharaoh's house. 15 And when
money failed in the land of Egypt, and in the land of
Canaan, all the Egyptians came unto Joseph, and said,
Give us bread: for why should we die in thy presence?
for the money faileth. 16 And Joseph said, Give your
cattle; and I will give you for your cattle, if money fail.
17 And they brought their cattle unto Joseph: and Joseph
gave them bread *in exchange* for horses, and for the flocks,
and for the cattle of the herds, and for the asses: and he
[w]fed them with bread for all their cattle for that year.
18 When that year was ended, they came unto him the
second year, and said unto him, We will not hide *it* from
my lord, how that our money is spent; my lord also hath
our herds of cattle; there is not ought left in the sight of
my lord, but our bodies, and our lands: 19 wherefore shall
we die before thine eyes, both we and our land? buy us
and our land for bread, and we and our land will be serv-
ants unto Pharaoh: and give *us* seed, that we may live,
and not die, that the land be not desolate. 20 And Joseph
bought all the land of Egypt for Pharaoh; for the Egypt-
ians sold every man his field, because the famine prevailed
over them: so the land became Pharaoh's. 21 And as for
the people, he removed them into *the* cities from *one* end

w Exod. xv. 13. 2 Chron. xxviii. 15; xxxii. 22. Ps. xxiii. 2; xxxi. 3. Isa. xl. 11; xlix. 10; li. 8.

ing that, we may fairly say that many data are wanting before we can pronounce on the relative change made in their state by the results of Joseph's policy. It is impossible for us to say whether the condition of nominal serfdom in which it left them, coupled as it was with the change mentioned in ver. 21, were not preferable to their former one. At all events, this ground is safe: until we know very much more of the political and economical state of the people we are by no means justified in branding with reproach, still less in supposing that the sacred writer means to brand with reproach, a character so high and generous as Joseph's is throughout described. The intention evidently is to produce on the mind of the reader an impression of a combination on the part of Joseph of wisdom and humanity, together with steadfast loyalty to his royal master. And I submit that we are in no position to find fault with that impression. **17.**] The animals of Egypt are enumerated in Exod. ix. 3, where see note. ***He* fed *them*** is literally, He **led** them: it is the same word as in ref. Exod., *Thou . . . hast* **guided** *them in thy strength*, &c. But it appears also to import *feeding* or *caring for:* possibly from the pastoral relation: as the command rendered, "*Feed my sheep*" (John xxi. 16) is literally, "*Lead, or shepherd, my sheep*." This idea is borne out by the reff. **18.**] It is literally, "**Now that our money and our herd of cattle is spent unto my lord,**" the construction being what is called a pregnant one. **19.**] **Wherefore shall we die . . . both we and our land?** is another example of the same construction. The latter clause is explained at the end of the verse, where it is said, **that the land be not desolate.** **21.**] The land having become Pharaoh's, the habitations on it were his also. And in pursuance of this right Joseph removes the people into the cities, congregating them together from their previous scattered life in the fields. This

of the borders of Egypt even to the *other* end thereof.
22 Only the land of the priests bought he not; for the
priests had a portion *assigned them* of Pharaoh, and did eat
their portion which Pharaoh gave them: wherefore they
sold not their lands. 23 Then Joseph said unto the people,
Behold, I have bought you this day and your land for
Pharaoh: lo, *here is* seed for you, and ye shall sow the
land. 24 And it shall come to pass in the increase, that
ye shall give the fifth *part* unto Pharaoh, and four parts
shall be your own, for seed of the field, and for your food,
and for them of your households, and for food for your
little ones. 25 And they said, Thou hast saved our lives:
let us find grace in the sight of my lord, and we will be
Pharaoh's servants. 26 And Joseph made it a law over
the land of Egypt unto this day, *that* Pharaoh should have
the fifth *part;* except the land of the priests only, *which*

had the obvious advantage of locating them close to the corn-magazines, besides other collateral political advantages. The Samaritan Pentateuch and the LXX. have followed another reading of this verse, which makes the sense to be, "*he enslaved them to him* (Pharaoh) *as bondmen.*" And this reading is preferred by Knobel. But Keil (p. 277, note) has shewn that it is very improbable. **22.**] **portion** has been understood in two ways: (1) which is Kalisch's interpretation, that they had a definite portion of *land* constitutionally allotted them, which they could not alienate. But surely this does not agree with the text which speaks of their *eating* the portion given them by Pharaoh (an expression no way explained by Kalisch's admission that it applied only to their time of actual service as priests). And besides, how would a fixed freehold of land have helped them in time of famine? (2) which is surely right, the priests had daily rations from the king, so that, although their lands were rendered useless by the famine, they had no reason to sell them. Traces of this practice are found in Herodotus' account of Egypt (ii. 37), and in Diodorus Siculus (i. 73, 75). The former says of the Egyptian priests, "and they enjoy no few advantages. For they do not consume nor expend any of their private resources, but have sacred provisions of corn food baked for them, and an ample allowance for each of flesh of geese and of beeves day by day.'

24.] The royalty here proposed for the occupiers of the land to pay does not, says Knobel, appear exorbitant. The tenth of the produce of the soil, and also of the flocks, seems to have been a common royal tribute: see 1 Sam. viii. 15, 17, and note, Levit. xxvii. 30. The kings of Syria received from the conquered Jews (1 Macc. x. 30) a third of the seed (i. e. cereal crops), and half the fruit of the trees. The Messenians had to pay half the produce of the land to the Spartans (Pausanias): and still heavier proportions are stated to be paid by modern tributaries, e.g. in Ispahan the occupiers of royal lands, who have seed also furnished them, have to pay back three-fourths of the produce.

25.] We have before cited this as a testimony that, however we may fail entirely to see through it, Joseph's policy was at least regarded by the subjects of it as popular.

26.] Knobel remarks, that this account is confirmed by history. Diodorus Siculus relates that the only possessors of land in Egypt were the king, the priestly and the warrior-caste: from these the occupiers rented the land. Herodotus also (ii. 168) names the warrior-caste as land-owners, while here we have named as such only the king and the priests. But this may be explained. In another place (ii. 141) Herodotus relates that Sethos (contemporary with Sennacherib and Isaiah) took away from the

became not Pharaoh's. 27 ¶ And Israel dwelt in the land
of Egypt, in the country of Goshen; and they had posses-
sions therein, and grew, and multiplied exceedingly.
28 And Jacob lived in the land of Egypt seventeen years:
so the whole age of Jacob was an hundred forty and seven
years. 29 And the time drew nigh that Israel must die:
and he called his son Joseph, and said unto him, If now
I have found grace in thy sight, put, I pray thee, thy
hand under my thigh, and deal kindly and truly with me;
bury me not, I pray thee, in Egypt: 30 but I will lie with
my fathers, and thou shalt carry me out of Egypt, and
bury me in their burying-place. And he said, I will do
as thou hast said. 31 And he said, Swear unto me. And
he sware unto him. And Israel bowed himself upon
the bed's head. XLVIII. 1 And it came to pass
after these things, that *one* told Joseph, Behold, thy
father *is* sick: and he took with him his two sons, Ma-

warrior-caste the portions of land which previous kings had given them. Evidently then the warriors obtained their grants of land from some king subsequent to the time of Joseph. **27—31.**] *Israel multiplies. Jacob has an interview with Joseph in prospect of his death.* **27.**] Is evidently anticipatory, corresponding with Exod. i. 7.

29, f.] This sending for Joseph in anticipation of death is entirely distinct from that in ch. xlviii., where we read of the actual approach of death in Jacob's last sickness. On the form of oath here prescribed, see ch xxiv. 2, note. The promise is exacted here in general terms, which Jacob again exacts of all his sons, ch. xlix. 29, ff., in detail. The performance of it by them is related ch. l. 4—13. The concluding words of this chapter have been the subject of a curious, and in the estimation of sober men, a childish mistake. Their literal rendering is as in A. V. And similarly the Vulgate, —*Israel adored God, turning to the head of the bed.* But the LXX. here, as also the ancient Syriac and Latin versions, have, "*and Israel worshipped upon the top of his staff.*" The writer of the Epistle to the Hebrews (xi. 21), following as usual the LXX., thus quotes the verse: and the Vulgate *there* has strangely and erroneously rendered, "*and adored the top of his staff.*" It would hardly be credited were it not the disgraceful fact, that this is the chief authority cited by the Romish Church for the adoration of images! The whole ambiguity has arisen from the Hebrew word, *mth*, signifying, with one set of vowel points, a bed (*mittah*), and with another, a staff (*matteh*). But the LXX. themselves have translated the same word *bed* two verses further on, ch. xlviii. 2. See the whole discussed in my note on the passage in Hebrews. Kalisch thinks that the words have no reference to any act of worship, but merely mean that Jacob, having sat up (see ch. xlviii. 21) to speak to Joseph and to exact and receive his oath, lay down again. Knobel, with more likelihood (compare esp. Heb. xi. 21), thinks that it was an act of reverence in thankfulness to God for the fulfilment of his last wish. See a similar act of David's, 1 Kings i. 47.

XLVIII. *Jacob's last sickness. His adoption and blessing of Joseph's two sons.*

1.] **one told Joseph**—the verb is indefinite; merely, it was told to Joseph. So also in ver. 2. Joseph is supposed by Kalisch to have taken with him his sons, as apprehensive that they, being half-Egyptian, might miss their part in the family inheritance. But it seems more probable that the design of Jacob, expressed in ver. 5, was previously known to him. The sons were

nasseh and Ephraim. 2 And *one* told Jacob, and said,
Behold, thy son Joseph cometh unto thee: and Israel
strengthened himself, and sat upon the bed. 3 And
Jacob said unto Joseph, †God Almighty appeared unto † El Shaddai.
me at Luz in the land of Canaan, and blessed me, 4 and
said unto me, Behold, I will make thee fruitful, and
multiply thee, and I will make of thee a multitude of
people; and will give this land to thy seed after thee *for*
an everlasting possession. 5 ¶ And now thy two sons,
which were born unto thee in the land of Egypt before I
came unto thee into Egypt, *are* mine; Ephraim and Ma-
nasseh shall be mine, as Reuben and Simeon. 6 And thy
issue, which thou begettest after them, shall be thine, *and*
shall be called after the name of their brethren in their
inheritance. 7 And as for me, when I came from Padan,
Rachel died by me in the land of Canaan in the way, when
yet *there was* but a little way to come unto Ephrath: and
I buried her there in the way of Ephrath; the same *is*
Beth-lehem. 8 And Israel beheld Joseph's sons, and said,
Who *are* these? 9 And Joseph said unto his father, They
are my sons, whom God hath given me in this *place*. And
he said, Bring them, I pray thee, unto me, and I will bless
them. 10 Now the eyes of Israel were dim for age, *so that*
he could not see. And he brought them near unto him;

about 22 years old: see ch. xli. 50.

2. strengthened himself] i.e. exerted himself, used all his strength, to receive his son.

3.] On El Shaddai, see ch. xvii. 1; and on the incident referred to, ch. xxviii. 13, 19.

5.] Joseph himself had been adopted among, and was reckoned to, the Egyptians (see ch. xli. 45), but his place among Jacob's sons, so far from remaining empty, shall be doubly filled—by his two sons, who shall rank with their uncles, and be as truly progenitors of tribes as the two elder of those, Reuben and Simeon. In point of numbers in the second year after the Exodus, these two together exceeded all their uncles except Judah (Num. i. 33, 35. Kalisch has fallen into the mistake of numbering the warriors of Judah 47,000 instead of 74,000): and at another time, "after the plague," they exceeded all, Judah included.

6.] But any future sons of Joseph were not to be Jacob's, i. e. not named as his sons, but to rank under the heads of Ephraimites and Manassites, and thus to be Joseph's only. We do not read of any more such sons: if there were such, they and their progeny were simply merged among the Ephraimites and Manassites (Num. xxvi. 28—37; 1 Chron. vii. 14—29; Josh. xvi., xvii.) See a long account of the fortunes of the two tribes of Ephraim and Manasseh in Kalisch on this place.

7.] The mention of Rachel, Jacob's beloved wife, comes in opportunely, seeing that by the last-mentioned arrangement her memory had been in some measure compensated for the fewness of her children. See ch. xxxv. 16, and note on the peculiar local designation of the spot of the sad event. Some interpret **by me** to mean *at my side*: but Kalisch denies this, and explains it as merely meaning that she was taken from him.

8.] Jacob knew Joseph's sons perfectly, but did not discern them owing to his imperfection of sight. And probably

and he kissed them, and embraced them. 11 And Israel
said unto Joseph, I had not thought to see thy face: and,
lo, God hath shewed me also thy seed. 12 And Joseph
brought them out from between his knees, and he bowed
himself with his face to the earth. 13 And Joseph took
them both, Ephraim in his right hand toward Israel's left
hand, and Manasseh in his left hand toward Israel's right
hand, and brought *them* near unto him. 14 And Israel
stretched out his right hand, and laid *it* upon Ephraim's
head, who *was* the younger, and his left hand upon Ma-
nasseh's head, guiding his hands wittingly; for Manasseh
was the firstborn. 15 ¶ And he blessed Joseph, and said,
The God, before whom my fathers Abraham and Isaac did
x ch. xvii. 1. y Ps. xxiii. 1; xxviii. 9. [x]walk, the God which [y]fed me all my life long unto this
day, 16 the Angel which redeemed me from all evil, bless
the lads; and let my name be named on them, and the
name of my fathers Abraham and Isaac; and let them
grow into a multitude in the midst of the earth. 17 And
when Joseph saw that his father laid his right hand upon
the head of Ephraim, it displeased him: and he held up

since he last saw them they had grown from boyhood to maturity. **12.**] The young men had been standing at Jacob's knees as he sat upon the couch and embraced them. It is surely mere perversity, when Knobel says that the Elohist, as shewn by ver. 8, thinks of them as little children. In all probability they had been kneeling before Jacob, and did so again when they were brought up to be blessed. **14.**] The act of laying on of hands, here for the first time mentioned, is found in Num. xxvii. 18—23; Deut. xxxiv. 9; Matt. xix. 13; Acts vi. 6; viii. 17, &c., as accompanying benediction or investiture with office, and has been retained throughout the Christian Church in both these senses. The words rendered **guiding his hands wittingly** may also mean **crossing his hands**: but the leading Hebraists prefer the other rendering.

15.] **Joseph**, i.e. Ephraim and Manasseh, his representatives. We have the same form of comprehension of the two in the dying blessing of Jacob, ch. xlix. 22; of Moses, Deut. xxxiii. 13, ff. **16.**] The Angel cannot be a created Angel, but as in reff. the Angel of God's presence: the Messenger who spake with Divine authority and as Himself Divine. We must not be hasty to see, with the more fanciful of the orthodox commentators, an indication of the doctrine of the Blessed Trinity in this threefold appellation of God. For there is in reality and in honest truth no such hidden meaning in the words. Our imaginative friends lay a stress on the verb bless, being not in the plural but in the singular. But how should it be in the plural, seeing that each designation belongs to one and the same God? Surely the God, before whom Abraham and Isaac walked, the God who fed Jacob, the God who manifested Himself to him in delivering him from evil, is one and the same. Much mischief is done unwittingly to the truth of Christianity by obtruding on all occasions these remote and fanciful allusions, and it will be a happy time for Scriptural exegesis when it shall everywhere keep back and pass them by. There are abundance of direct and undeniable foreshadowings of Christian doctrine without entering on doubtful ground.

my name] Israel: and let them be counted Abraham's seed and Isaac's. There is special reference to the blessing of the Divine

his father's hand, to remove it from Ephraim's head unto
Manasseh's head. 18 And Joseph said unto his father,
Not so, my father: for this *is* the firstborn; put thy right
hand upon his head. 19 And his father refused, and said,
I know *it*, my son, I know *it*: he also shall become a
people, and he also shall be great: but truly his younger
brother shall be greater than he, and his seed shall become
a multitude of nations. 20 And he blessed them that day,
saying, In thee shall Israel bless, saying, God make thee
as Ephraim and as Manasseh: and he set Ephraim before
Manasseh. 21 And Israel said unto Joseph, Behold, I die:
but God shall be with you, and bring you again unto the
land of your fathers. 22 Moreover I have given to thee
one portion above thy brethren, which I took out of the
hand of the Amorite with my sword and with my bow.
XLIX. 1 And Jacob called unto his sons, and said,

promise on the seed of Abraham and (ch. xxi. 12) of Isaac. **19.**] **I know** *it*, i.e. am aware of the relative ages of the youths. The prophecy began to be fulfilled even in the time of Moses, for in Num. i. 33, 35, in the second year after the Exodus, Ephraim numbered 8300 more than Manasseh. But in Num. xxvi. 34, 37, "after the plague," we have the ratio more than reversed, for whereas Manasseh has 52,700, Ephraim has but 32,500, and is indeed, with the exception of Simeon, the smallest of the tribes. But, later, Ephraim assumed the chief place among all the northern tribes, and the name became identical with that of Israel itself. The commencement of this rise was probably under Joshua, himself an Ephraimite. The various steps of its rise and progress are admirably given in Mr. Grove's article "Ephraim" in the *Biblical Dict.* It would exceed my limits even to summarize them. **20.**] On **In thee shall Israel bless,** see the discussion of Knobel's view of ch. xii. 3. The difference of this meaning and that is well expressed by Kalisch,—"The tribe of Joseph was only regarded as an *example* of prosperity for the rest of the Hebrews, whereas the Israelites were viewed as the *cause* of blessing for all the other nations." **21, f.**] Connected with Jacob's prophecy of the return of his race to Canaan, is his apportionment, corresponding to the division of the tribe of Joseph, of two lots of the land of promise to him. The designation of the land as taken out of the hand of the Amorite (an apparently general name for the dwellers on the mountains: see on ch. xiv. 7) by Jacob's sword and bow is spoken in the anticipatory spirit of a prophet, assuming as done that which his descendants should do. See the expression repeated, in form of expression almost verbatim, Josh. xxiv. 12.

XLIX. **1—32.**] *Jacob's dying prophecy.* Respecting the authenticity and prophetic significance of this portion, we may remark, that there seems to be nothing which tends to throw the slightest doubt on either, except the *a priori* assumption of the rationlists, that prophecy is impossible. No charge is brought against its style or diction as inconsistent with the rest of the sacred book which relates to this period; no betrayal is found of adaptation to after circumstances by minute accuracies of prophetic detail: the whole is vague and mysterious, rather foreshadowing dimly, than describing recognizably what afterwards happened to the tribes. On the whole, we may safely say that, granting any one of the circumstances which invest Jacob with a sacred character, or any one of the incidents which connect him with a Divine calling and covenant, then the fact of his delivering such a discourse as this, reaching into the future of his sons, carries no difficulty with it and need provoke no in-

Gather yourselves together, that I may tell you
That which shall befall you [z]in the latter days.
2 Gather yourselves together, and hear, ye sons of Jacob;
And hearken unto Israel your father.
3 ¶ Reuben, thou *art* my firstborn,
My might, and the [a]beginning of my strength,
The excellency of dignity, and the excellency of power:
4 Boiling over like water, thou shalt not excel;

z Num. xxiv. 14. Deut. iv. 30; xxxi. 29. Isa. ii. 2. Jer. xxiii. 20; xxx. 24; xlviii. 47; xlix. 39. Ezek. xxxviii. 16. Dan. x. 14. Hos. iii. 5. Mic. iv. 1.

a Deut. xxi. 17. Ps. lxxviii. 51; cv. 36.

credulous question. To those who hold no such peculiar character to have belonged to the patriarch, not this discourse only, but the whole history, must be divested of foundation in fact. And it is really curious to study the rationalist commentaries here. All sorts of periods are assigned to the poem: that of Moses, that of Joshua, that of Saul, that of David, that of Solomon, that of the divided kingdom: further they cannot carry it, as the Samaritan Pentateuch would refute the hypothesis. In each of these periods ingenious writers have found especial fitness in the words, till the brain reels with the confusion worse confounded. All this gives way to simplicity and verisimilitude, if we will but give the old story credence and believe that the dying man of God spoke these words as here given to us. Difficulties enough there are in them; but those very difficulties are its best apology. Were we reading a post-event prophecy, we should be pretty sure not to meet with them.

1.] This is apparently consecutive on what was last related. **in the latter days,** literally, **in the sequel of the days** (see reff.), found nearly exclusively in prophetic passages, and especially in Messianic prophecies. Perhaps we ought not to define the reference of the time more closely than by regarding it as pointing to *aftertimes* generally.

3, 4.] Reuben, the firstborn, appears in many points not to have been by any means the worst of the brethren. He took no part in the deed of violence and treachery against the Shechemites (ch. xxxiv.); he dissuaded his brethren from the murder of Joseph, and wished to restore him to his father (ch. xxxvii. 22, 29; see also xlii. 22); he offered to become surety for the safety of Benjamin (ch. xlii. 37). But the dark spot of his life, and one which abode upon the mind of his father,—so that he disregarded his offered suretyship for Benjamin,—was his foul sin with Bilhah his father's concubine (ch. xxxv. 22). First, Jacob gives him, more by way of contrast than of praise, his rightful description of pre-eminence and dignity as firstborn. We have already seen, on more than one occasion, the value in which the birthright was held, and the kind of pre-eminence which it gave. Jacob himself had purchased it of Esau (ch. xxv. 31): the firstborn had the social pre-eminence (ch. xliii. 33), claimed a right to admonish the rest (xlii. 22), took on him special responsibility (xxxvii. 21; xlii. 37). In Isaac's blessing of Jacob (xxxvii. 29) lordship over his brethren is conveyed to him; and in Deut. xxi. 17 the right of the firstborn is described as consisting in a double portion of the inheritance. The word rendered **strength** also signifies *grief*, and is so given by the Vulgate. But it would seem as if the two verses, 3 and 4, were intended to be in contrast, and so this meaning would be alien from the former of them. There are some wonderful renderings of the latter portion of the verse, e. g. that of the LXX., "hard to be borne, hard in thy self-will;" that of the Samaritan, "*excelling in pride and excelling in imprudence;*" that of Onkelos, if it can be called a translation at all, "*Thou shouldest have received three portions,—birthright, priesthood, and kingdom.*" The Vulgate has, "*first in gifts, greater in command.*"

4.] But this pre-eminence Reuben has by his licentiousness forfeited. The metaphor is from the bubbling over of water in boiling; it is a form of the same word which is rendered *lightness* in Jer. xxiii. 32, and *light* (both with reference to the character of false prophets) in Zeph. iii. 4. It is here a substantive with an abstract meaning: "*ebullition,*" as Kalisch has it.

thou shalt not excel] i. e. shalt not hold thy place of dignity as firstborn. The transition to the third person at the end of the verse is also found in vv. 9, 26. It seems here to take place in a kind of horror, and

Because thou wentest up to thy father's bed;
Then defiledst thou *it*: he went up to my couch.
5 ¶ Simeon and Levi *are* brethren;
Weapons of cruelty *are* their swords.
6 My soul, come not thou into their secret:
My [b]glory, be not thou united with their assembly:
For in their anger they slew men,

b Ps. vii. 6; xvi. 9; xxx. 12; lvii. 8.

to be addressed as it were to the other sons.

5—7.] *Simeon and Levi.* We know nothing of the two "brethren" except the deed of treachery and cruelty here dwelt upon, and the fact, unaccounted for in the history, that Joseph chose Simeon to remain bound as an hostage in Egypt. In the expression, **are brethren**, more is meant than the mere fact of birth: they were also joined in a brotherhood of dishonour and cruelty. The renderings of the latter part of the verse are very various. That of the A. V. seems to have hardly any authority. The LXX. has (and so nearly the Samaritan), "they accomplished the iniquity of their purpose;" the Vulgate, "warring vessels of iniquity;" the Syriac, "vessels of madness by their nature;" the Targum of Onkelos, "being men of courage, they did a brave deed in the land of their pilgrimage." This may serve to shew how great is the difficulty of deciding. The rendering in the text is that of the great majority of Hebraists. A summary of the others may be seen in Kalisch, p. 744.

6.] **my glory** is used, as in reff., for the centre and treasure of my personal being. Similarly we have used "mine only one," Ps. xxii. 21; xxxv. 17. The last words of the verse appear without doubt to require the rendering in the text. The verb may import "overthrew, digged down," but the substantive cannot, except by an alteration in the vowel pointing of the present Hebrew text. On the concluding words of the verse we may remark, that they furnish no mean argument for the genuineness of the prophecy, seeing that they contain no allusion to the subsequent exaltation of the tribe of Levi to the exclusive honour of the priesthood and service of the tabernacle. It is a remark of Bp. Wordsworth's, that it is "very honourable to Moses, the great Hebrew leader and lawgiver, who was himself of the tribe of Levi, that he has recorded these words of reproof and censure from the lips of Jacob." But surely it is descending to a lower view of Genesis than the Bishop usually takes, to see in it only a reflection of the personal character of Moses. Perhaps it is hardly possible to trace the fulfilment of these words in the subsequent fortune of the tribes. It is true that Simeon at the second numbering by Moses (Num. xxvi. 14) had sunk to the lowest population of all the tribes, and that it is altogether passed over in the blessing of Moses in Deut. xxxiii.; and it is even nearer to the purpose that in the allotting of the land, Simeon had no proper division of its own, but only certain cities within the lot of Judah (Josh. xix. 1—9). On the other hand in 1 Chron. iv. 24—43, commonly cited to bear out this view, it is given as a reason for the emigration of the Simeonites, their great increase and prosperity, the opposite being predicated of one family only, that of Mishma, ver. 27. Whatever countenance however the view might be supposed to find as regards Simeon, is entirely absent when we come to the case of Levi. The sentence pronounced here on the brethren is one of punishment for treachery and cruelty. To find in the scattering of the Levites through all Israel in the most honourable of all positions, that of ministers of God, a fulfilment of such a sentence, is surely mere trifling: compare Num. iii. 12, 45; viii. 5 to end; Deut. xxxiii. 10. To say again that the curse here pronounced was afterwards turned to blessing, is only an evasion; for if so, how can it be said in any sense to have been fulfilled? Had the tribes spoken of been Dan, the idolater, and Benjamin, the object of his brethren's vengeance, something might have been said for the fulfilment in their subsequent fortunes. As it is, we must regard the words as referring to their being deposed from their right of primogeniture, and giving place to the younger Judah. They were united as brothers in their powerful deed of treachery and blood; but such union should not prevail: it should be divided and scattered, and they too, like Reu-

[c] Neh. ix. 24, 37. Dan. xi. 3, 16.

And in their [c]selfwill they hamstrung oxen.
7 Cursed *be* their anger, for *it is* fierce;
And their wrath, for it is cruel:
I will divide them in Jacob,
And scatter them in Israel.
8 ¶ Judah, thou art he whom thy brethren shall praise:
Thy hand *shall be* on the neck of thine enemies;
Thy father's children shall bow down before thee.
9 Judah *is* a lion's whelp:
From the prey, my son, thou art gone up:
He stooped down, he couched as a lion,
And as an old lion; who shall rouse him up?
10 The [d]sceptre shall not depart from Judah,

[d] =Num. xxiv. 17. Ps. xlv. 6. Isa. xiv. 5. Ezek. xix. 11, 14. Amos i. 5. Zech. x. 11.

ben, should enjoy no leadership over the family. **8—12.**] *Judah.* The first clause of ver. 8 contains an allusion to the name Judah, which (ch. xxix. 35) signified *praise.* Already in his lifetime, Judah was distinguished among the brethren. It was he who prevented the intended murder of Joseph (xxxvii. 26), who guaranteed the safety of Benjamin (xliii. 8), and made a noble pleading in order to fulfil it (xliv. 14, ff.), and who was sent before to Joseph as the herald of Jacob's arrival. And correspondent to this pre-eminence were the fortunes of the tribe of Judah. It was the most populous at both the numberings (Num. i. 27; xxvi. 22); it had the precedence in the marches through the wilderness (Num. x. 14); to it belonged Bezaleel, the architect of the tabernacle (Exod. xxxi. 2; xxxviii. 22), and Caleb, one of the only two of those alive at the Exodus who were allowed to enter the land of promise (Num. xiii. 6, 30; xiv. 6, 30), and who received the patriarchal city of Hebron as his portion. Judah, in the division, got the whole of S. Canaan. To follow the fortunes of this distinguished tribe afterwards would be superfluous. All may be included in "*our Lord sprang out of Juda,*" (Heb. vii. 14). The literal rendering is **Judah, thou, thy brethren shall praise thee**: we have similar constructions in ch. xvii. 4; xxiv. 27.

The idea of the lion is already before the speaker, and as the paw of the lion seizes the neck of the prey, so he represents Judah as having his **hand on the neck of his enemies.** In the concluding clause the period of Judah's sovereignty under David and Solomon is prophesied. In ch. xxvii. 29, in the similar promise made to Jacob, the bowing down is predicated of his *mother's* sons. This expression would not, if used here, include all the tribes, which it is evidently intended to do. It was now well known, by experience in the case of Joseph, what these words imported. **9.**] Judah, the kingly tribe, is likened to the lion, the king of beasts, who has taken his prey in the plain and is returning to his mountain habitation (Cant. iv. 8), a description eminently fitting Judah, whose lot was in the hills, and their forays in the level country of the Philistines (Judg. i. 18, f.; 2 Sam. v. 17—21). In Deut. xxxiii. 20 Gad, in v. 22 Dan, and in Num. xxiii. 24; xxiv. 9, the whole of Israel, is likened to a lion. It is from this prophecy that the remarkable title of *the Lion of the tribe of Judah* is given to Christ, Rev. v. 5. **10.**] This verse is distinctly a prophecy of government in the line of Judah, and of its continuance up to a certain point. What that point is depends on the meaning of the difficult and unexampled word Shiloh. The common understanding of that word is that it designates Christ, and that the prophecy found its fulfilment in the extinction of the Idumæan kingdom of Herod soon after the birth of our Lord. Historically, this view is entirely untenable. For the kingdom in the line of Judah came entirely and irrecoverably to an end nearly 600 years before that date. For 50 years Judæa was subject to the Chaldæans; then for 200 years a province of Persia; then for 163 years under the suc-

Nor a lawgiver from between his feet,
Until Shiloh come;
And unto him *shall be* the obedience of nations.

cessors of Alexander. When the Jews regained their independence they were ruled by the Maccabees, who were of the tribe of Levi, not of Judah; 63 years before Christ Palestine was conquered by Pompey and became subject to Rome. And Herod, who was probably not a Jew at all, was merely a tributary of Rome. If there be any meaning in words, the sceptre had departed from Judah many hundred years before the birth of Christ. It is very well for the maintainers of this theory to say that "the determination of this question is of minor importance;" in real fact it is of primary and essential importance: and the very commentator from whom the above words are quoted, rejects other interpretations as "receiving no confirmation from history," whereas of the common one he refuses to let history be the criterion. Nor again will any fiction, such as that the lineage of Christ traced by St. Matthew through Abraham and David is a *royal* lineage, or that the words of the angel to the Virgin Mary, "the Lord God shall give to him the throne of his father David," imply that David's kingdom had never ceased, serve to defend the commonly received interpretation as to the continuance of royal power in and its departure from the tribe of Judah. Whether the word may designate Christ, is quite independent of this forcing of the course of history. The words of the prophecy do not necessarily imply *any departure* of that which is meant by the sceptre, or ruler's staff, from Judah. They are quite consistent with this remaining in Judah until and including the event mentioned. If they import only the preeminence enjoyed by Judah in possessing the royal city of David and being the first tribe and that which gave name to the chosen people, this indeed, unlike the actual kingdom, though for a time suspended, was restored, and never ceased until Christ came and lifted the tribe to yet more glorious eminence. But let us now consider the words themselves. The term for sceptre means a rod, or sprout; it is the ordinary term for *tribe* (ver. 16, e. g.), the tribes being regarded as sprouts from the main stem. It is also used for the rod of correction (2 Sam. vii. 14; Job ix. 34; Ps. lxxxix. 32; Prov. x. 13, al fr.), and finally for the rod of government, a sceptre: see reff. And there can be no doubt that such is the meaning here. The word rendered *lawgiver* in the A.V. seems rather to signify again a sceptre, or staff or rod of office, which in figures of kings, e. g. those at Persepolis, rests on their body and is held between their feet. Others, taking the meaning *lawgiver*, regard the words **between his feet** as applying to progeniture, as in Deut. xxviii. 57, "the young one that cometh *from between her feet;*" and so the LXX. and Vulgate render, "*out of his thighs:*" and Onkelos, "*from his children's children.*" See 2 Kings xviii. 27; Isa. vii. 20; Ezek. xvi. 28. A similar way of speaking is found in Jer. xxx. 21. We now come to consider the word SHILOH, in which lies the kernel of the whole difficulty. First, there is a variation among the Hebrew MSS. as to the form of the word itself, tending to cast some doubt upon its meaning. Of the principal versions, the LXX. renders, "*until the things reserved for him shall come;*" the Vulgate, "*until he shall come, who is to be sent;*" the old Syriac, "*until he comes whose it is.*" The Samaritan has, "*until the peaceful one come;*" the Targum of Onkelos, "*until the Messiah come, whose is the kingdom.*" The rendering now preferred by many learned Hebraists would take Shiloh as the well-known city of that name, being the abode of the tabernacle and place of assembly of Israel. This view is taken by Bleek, Hitzig, Ewald, and Kalisch. But this interpretation, 1. In no way fulfils the historical conditions. Judah's *royal* leadership did not commence at all before the assembling of Israel at Shiloh: and in whatever sense the sceptre, &c., be understood, Judah's glories were more after than before that event. And 2. The mention of a local name of so little import at the time would be very unnatural. The only other instance in this prophecy is that of Zidon, ver. 13, a place well known from the most ancient times, ch. x. 19. Our choice seems to lie, in the uncertainty about the genuine Hebrew word itself, between the two allusions—(1) to *peace*, or *the peaceful one*, (2) to

11 Binding his foal unto the vine,
And his ass's colt unto the choice vine;
He washed his garments in wine,
And his clothes in the blood of grapes:
12 His eyes being dark with wine,
And his teeth white with milk.
13 ¶ Zebulun dwelleth at the shore of the sea;

sending. If the former be adopted, then the primary reference may be to Solomon, with the great Messianic reference behind. And there seems to be some support for this in the words of David, 1 Chron. xxviii. 3, ff. There he recounts to the princes of Israel how God would not suffer him, a man of blood, to build *His* temple; then he proceeds, "Howbeit Jehovah the God of Israel chose me before all the house of my father to be king over Israel for ever; for He hath chosen Judah to be the ruler: and of the house of Judah, the house of my father: and among the sons of my father He liked me, to make me king over Israel; and of all my sons (for Jehovah hath given me many sons) he hath chosen Solomon my son to sit upon the throne of the kingdom of Jehovah over Israel." Now Solomon signifies *peaceable*, and this very reason is alleged in 1 Chron. xxii. 9 why he was chosen to build God's temple. He was a "man of rest" (ib.). So that this exposition, especially when joined with what follows (see below), has much to recommend it, in the midst of the uncertainty. If we take the second view proposed, and consider the mysterious word to be connected with *sending*, we have in favour of this the somewhat obscure allusion in the saying of Moses, Exod. iv. 13, where he says, "Send, O Lord, by the hand which thou wilt send" (the verb being there used from which, among others, this word may be derived), or the hardly less obscure allusion in John ix. 7, where it is said that Siloam "is by interpretation, *Sent*." In this case the word will apply to the Messiah alone. The subject will be found well discussed in Mr. Twisleton's art. in the *Biblical Dict.* "Shiloh" (who takes the *local* view), and in Bp. Wordsworth's Commentary in this place, and most fully of all by Keil, in his Commentary.

In the midst of all the uncertainty we have this hardly deniable meaning, that the leadership, the royal pre-eminence, of Judah, should wax onward till the Prince of Peace, or till He who was *to be sent*, should come: then attaining its climax in the *obedience of the nations* to Him whose name is, for whatever reason, SHILOH. This last rendering is preferred by the Hebraists to that in the A. V. **11, 12.**] These words refer to the fertility and abundance of Judah's lot in the land of promise. "The vine will be so abundant that the people will tie to it their animals, as if it were a common tree; the wine will be valued no higher than the water in which garments are washed." Kalisch. Compare the saying about Solomon 1 Kings x. 27; also Job xxix. 6; Judg. iii. 18; Amos ix. 13. The ass, besides being the ordinary beast of burden, is the symbol of peace: see Zech. ix. 9. The territory of Judah produced the best wine in Canaan: see what is related of the neighbourhood of Hebron, Num. xiii. 23; of Engedi, Cant. i. 14; compare also 2 Chron. xxvi. 10; and had also abundant pastures, 1 Sam. xxv. 2; Amos i. 1; 2 Chron. xxvi. 10. **13.**] *Zebulun*, the sixth son of Leah (ch. xxx. 20), is placed before his elder brother Issachar (ib. 18) for no reason that we can assign. His name signifies *dwelling*, and hence perhaps the form of the prophecy, though the same verb from which Zebulun is derived is not used here. Zebulun occupied parts in the N. E. of Palestine, between Asher and Naphtali to the N. and Issachar to the S. (Josh. xix. 10—16, 27, 34), extending in the E. to the Sea of Tiberias (Matt. iv. 13), and in the W. to Mount Carmel and the Mediterranean (Josh. xix. 11),—to the borders of Phœnicia (Zidon). But this is doubted by both Keil and Knobel, who say that so much is not found in the division related by Joshua, only in Josephus, who says that Zebulun dwelt about Carmel and the sea and reached to Ptolemais (Acre). Still if this were so at any time, the prophecy had its

Even at the shore of ships;
And his side is next unto Zidon.
14 ¶ Issachar *is* a strong ass
Couching down between two burdens:
15 And he saw rest that *it was* good,
And the land that *it was* pleasant;
And bowed his shoulder to bear,
And became a servant unto tribute.
16 ¶ Dan shall judge his people,
As one of the tribes of Israel.
17 Let Dan be a serpent by the way,
An adder in the path,

fulfilment. At all events it is hereby saved from the imputation of being a description after the event, of Joshua's or David's time. We hear nothing of Zebulun in the patriarchal history. On the subsequent fortunes of the tribe, compare Num. i. 30; xxvi. 27; Judg. i. 30; iv. 6, 10; v. 14, 18; vi. 35; xii. 11, 12; and Mr. Grove's article in the *Biblical Dict.* **14, 15.**] *Issachar*, the fifth son of Jacob by Leah (ch. xxx. 17), was also of no note among the brethren. But the tribe became famous by taking part in the war of Deborah and Barak against Jabin, Judg. v. 15. Their portion was in the midst of the land, and contained the fertile and beautiful plains of Jezreel, Esdraelon, and Megiddo. There seems no historic trace of the tribe having become (as Kalisch asserts) averse from war and fulfilling the character here predicted. We find them in 1 Chron. vii. 1—5 described as valiant men of might; again we have them taking a lead in the measures by which David was established as king in Hebron, and described as "men that had understanding of the times, to know what Israel ought to do." One of the judges, Tola (Judg. x. 1). was of this tribe, and two of the kings of Israel, Baasha and Elah his son (1 Kings xv. 27—xvi. 10).

16—18.] *Dan.* The sons of Leah are now exhausted, and those of Bilhah and Zilpah are taken. Of these, Dan is the eldest (ch. xxx. 6). The prophecy, as in the case of Zebulun, plays on the name, which (see as above, ch. xxx. 6) means, "*judge.*" In order to understand it, we must briefly recall the history of the tribe. In the division of the land, Dan's portion is that lying W. of Benjamin and Ephraim, and N. of the Philistines (Josh. xix. 46—48), extending to the sea (Josh. xix. 46; Judg. v. 17), and touching Judah on the S. E. It was the smallest of all the portions, and because it was too little, the Danites conquered Leshem (Laish), far north at the foot of Lebanon, and called it Dan (Josh. xix. 47; Judg. xviii. 1, ff.). That portion was still further circumscribed by the Amorites, who forced the Danites from their fertile plains into the mountain (Judg. i. 34). So the tribe fell away, and became divided, the northern portion into idolatry (Judg. xviii. 14—31), while the southern portion, partly perhaps owing to mixed marriages with the Canaanites, partly from its own insignificance, dwindled away, became in fact absorbed into Judah (even in Joshua's time various Danite cities are also reckoned to Judah, comp. Jer. xix. 41, with xv. 33, and with 2 Chron. xi. 10). Once indeed in the history Dan comes to the front in the person of its great hero Samson (Judg. xiii.—xvi.); but in later times it altogether drops out. There is no genealogy of Dan in 1 Chron. ii.—xii., and no mention of the tribe in the sealing of the 144,000 in Rev. vii. We may observe that the tribe furnished one of the two artificers of the tabernacle, Aholiab (Exod. xxxi. 6), and also Hiram or Huram, the artificer of Solomon's temple (2 Chron. ii. 14; in 1 Kings vii. 14 he is said to have been of Naphtali). With regard to the prophecy, the sense of ver. 16 seems to be, in reference to Samson, that Dan, though not one of the leading tribes, should yet take his part in the government of Israel. In ver. 17 we have perhaps an allusion to the surprise and conquest of Laish, or perhaps again a

That biteth the horse heels,
So that his rider falleth backward.
18 I have waited for thy salvation, O LORD.
19 ¶ Gad, a troop shall press him:
But he shall press upon the heel.
20 From Asher is fatness, his bread:
And he shall yield royal dainties.
21 ¶ Naphtali *is* a hind let loose:
He giveth goodly words.

further description of the heroic course of Samson. The **adder** is "the *cerastes hasselquistii* of naturalists, the well-known horned snake, a small serpent of a sandy colour with pale brown or sometimes blackish irregular spots, rarely exceeding a foot or 18 in. in length, and well known in the sandy deserts of Abyssinia, Egypt, the Sahara, and Arabia Petræa." Tristram. Its habit, Dr. T. goes on to state, is to coil itself, usually in the camel's footmark, in the sand, and thence suddenly to dart out on any passing animal. Horses are in the greatest terror when one is seen ahead. **18.**] Some commentators refer these words to the prophecy, and believe them to answer to the prayer of Samson, Judg. xvi. 28. Others regard the words as an exclamation of the dying patriarch, longing for his dissolution. The objection, that such an ejaculation would hardly have found a place in a prophecy like this, is weighty: but it does not reach to denying that the words may be an ejaculation, in prospect of the wars and struggles of Israel, and spoken in Israel's name. And so the principal commentators take them: e. g. Kalisch, Delitzsch, Keil, Knobel. A reference beyond this, to the great final Messianic salvation for Israel, has been generally acknowledged by all who recognize the higher significance of O. T. history. Even in the later Targums (as cited by Keil) the Messianic sense is fully acknowledged. Some of the Fathers saw in ver. 17 a prophecy of Antichrist, who was to spring out of Dan, as our Lord out of Judah. **19.**] *Gad* was the eldest son of Zilpah, Leah's maid (ch. xxx. 10, 11). On his name, see text and note there. The rendering, "*a troop cometh*" there, seems to have been introduced owing to the drift of the prophecy here. The portion of Gad was about the centre of the country E. of Jordan, embracing, with Reuben, half Gilead (Deut. iii. 12), half the land of the Amorites (Josh. xiii. 25). The tribe came to distinction in the person of Jephthah (Judg. xi., xii.). The character of the tribe was fierce and warlike: compare the blessing of Moses, Deut. xxxiii. 20, and the description of the Gadites who joined David in the wilderness, 1 Chron. xii. 8: see also the remarkable narrative, 1 Chron. v. 18—22. And this is well described by the restless and predatory habits indicated in the prophecy. **20.**] *Asher* was the second son of Zilpah, ch. xxx. 13. His portion was from Carmel to the Phœnician frontier (Josh. xvii. 10, 11; xix. 24–31; Judg. i. 31, 32). In the latter of these places we learn that Asher was unable to drive out the Canaanites, but dwelt among them. Their teritory was eminently fertile; and in the blessing of Moses, Asher is described as "dipping his foot in oil" (Deut. xxxiii. 24, where see further notices). The meaning seems to be, the food or bread which comes of Asher is fat. There is perhaps a play on the name Asher (blessed). By the latter clause of the verse seem to be foretold the rich exports which this territory should send to its neighbours: see Ezek. xxvii. 17; Acts xii. 20. The tribe seems to have loved ease, and kept away from the wars of Israel (Judg. v. 17, 18); it never furnished any judge or hero to Israel; it is omitted in the list of rulers (1 Chron. xxvii. 16—22) in David's time. **21.**] *Naphtali* was the second son of Bilhah (ch. xxx. 8). The territory of the tribe was bounded on the W. by Asher, S. by Zebulun, E. by Manasseh, and N. by the valley which separates the two ranges of the Lebanon: see further on Deut. xxxiii 23. The great glory of the tribe was the victory under Deborah and

22 ¶ Joseph *is* a fruitful bough,
A fruitful bough by a well;
The branches run over the wall:
23 They harassed him, and shot at him,
And hated him, *even* the masters of arrows.
24 But his bow abode in strength,
And the [e]arms of his hands were made strong
From the hands of the Mighty *One* of Jacob,
From whence, the [f]Shepherd, the [g]stone of Israel:
25 From the God of thy father, he shall help thee;
And the †Almighty, he shall bless thee
With blessings of heaven from above,
Blessings of the deep that lieth under,
Blessings of the breasts, and of the womb:
26 The blessings of thy father have prevailed above the blessings of the eternal mountains,

e = Job xxii. 8. Ps. lxxvii. 15.

f ch. xlviii. 15. Ps. lxxx. 1.
g Deut. xxxii. 4. Isa. xvii. 10; xxx. 29.

† SHADDAI.

Barak (Judg. iv., v.), the latter of whom was sprung from it. And to this the words of the prophecy are generally referred. But considerable doubt rests on their meaning. The LXX., followed by Ewald, render, *Naphtali is a stately tree* (*terebinth*, Ew.), *having beautiful branches* (*he hath a goodly crest*, Ew.). The old Syriac gives it, *Naphtali is a swift messenger*. But the A. V. is preferred by most of the Hebraists, varying however between **let loose** and **graceful** or **tall.** Knobel renders the adjective, *hunted, pursued.* The simile is supposed to denote swiftness, and perhaps to have connexion with the name of Naphtali's hero, Barak, which signifies *lightning*. The second part of the verse is generally taken as referring to the triumphal song of Deborah and Barak, Judg. v. It is impossible to mention these interpretations, without feeling on what wholly uncertain ground we are treading throughout our comments on this chapter.

22—26.] *Joseph*, here treated as one, not divided into the two tribes Ephraim and Manasseh. This is to be accounted for by remembering that this is properly the blessing of the twelve *sons of Jacob*, and not, although this is in some sense predicated of them in ver. 28, the twelve tribes of Israel. The first point adduced is Joseph's fruitfulness: see before on ch. xlviii. 16—19. The literal rendering of ver. 22 is, "**Son of a fruit-tree is Joseph, son of a fruit-tree over a well: daughters ascend over a wall.**" But it is said to be a Hebrew usage to employ the word *sons*, and *daughters*, for the branches and twigs of a tree. It does not, however, appear that the same word (*ben*) as here is elsewhere found in this sense, but other like words are, e. g. *suckling* (masc.) in Job xiv. 7; Isa. liii. 2,—and fem. in Ezek. xvii. 22; Ps. lxxx. 11. This interpretation is the general one, though we must confess that it has not the slightest possible support in anything but consent of interpreters. The other interpretations have found no favour, and are not worth recounting. **23.**] It is no small argument against the common interpretation of ver. 22, that the figure which it introduces is entirely dropped in this verse. These words are supposed to point at the constant wars of the Ephraimites with the neighbouring Ituræans, Hagarenes, &c.: see also Josh. xvii. 16—18. **24**] **the arms** here are not weapons, but limbs. The word is used here as in reff. to signify *strength.* **25.**] The portions of Ephraim and Manasseh were among the choicest of all the land of promise, Deut. xxxiii. 13. The blessings of the breast and the womb are probably to be understood generally, of fertility and fecundity, of course including the increase of herds and flocks, and the provision of milk, in the land one of whose praises it was, that it *flowed with milk.*

26.] This verse has been very vari-

The delight of the everlasting hills:
They shall be on the head of Joseph,
And on the crown of the head of him that was separate from his brethren.
27 ¶ Benjamin shall ravin *as* a wolf:
h Ps. lv. 17; xcii. 2. Eccl. xi. 6. [h]In the morning he shall devour the prey,
[h]And at night he shall divide the spoil.
28 ¶ All these *are* the twelve tribes of Israel: and this *is*
it that their father spake unto them, and blessed them;
every one according to his blessing he blessed them. 29
And he charged them, and said unto them, I am to be
i ver. 17; ch. xxv. 8; xxxv. 29. Num. xx. 26. Deut. xxxii. 50. [i]gathered unto my people: bury me with my fathers in
the cave that *is* in the field of Ephron the Hittite, 30 in
the cave that *is* in the field of Machpelah, which *is* before
Mamre, in the land of Canaan, which Abraham bought

ously understood. According to the rendering of the A. V., the meaning is, in reference to Joseph's future distinction among the tribes, that Jacob's blessing of him has had more effect than the blessing of Jacob's ancestors on *him*, even to the bound of the height of the mountains above the earth. The rendering in the text is that given by the LXX., following the reading of the Samaritan Pentateuch, and approved by Gesenius, Kalisch, and Knobel, and is defended by Hab. iii. 6, where nearly the same Hebrew expression is used as here, and by the parallel passage in the blessing of Moses, Deut. xxxiii. 15. The latter part of the verse is repeated in the blessing of Moses, Deut. xxxiii. 16. The Hebrew of the last clause of the verse contains three words only, as does the last clause but one, which is in parallelism with it, and is literally, **and-to-the-crown-of-the-head-of-the-Nazarite** (separated, or consecrated one) **of-his-brethren**: and similarly the Vulgate renders these last words. The meaning is, of him that is, by distinction and superiority of blessing, separated, distinguished among his brethren. Kalisch would render it crowned, which the word will also bear, and would refer it to the kingdom of Ephraim.

28.] *Benjamin*, the youngest, has ascribed to him the character of a warrior eager for spoil. And this was borne out in the history of the tribe. Although one of the smallest in Israel, it maintained its warlike repute through even desperate fortunes. It took part in the great victory over Sisera (Judg. v. 14), and afterwards maintained a war against all Israel on account of the outrage at Gibeah (Judg. xx.). Of this tribe sprung the judge Ehud (Judg. iii. 15); and it bore the sceptre in the person of the first king of Israel, Saul. The warlike character of the Benjaminites appears in other places in the history: compare 2 Sam. ii. 15 (Judg. xx. 15, 16); 1 Chron. viii. 40; xii. 2; 2 Chron. xiv. 8; xvii. 17. **in the morning . . . and at night**] i. e. at all times: see reff.

28.] The tribes are *twelve*, according to the actual number of the *sons* of Jacob who were gathered together to receive his dying blessing; not thirteen, as they were in matter of fact when Genesis was written. Jacob is said to have *blessed* them all, notwithstanding that some of the prophecies respecting them (e. g. Reuben, Simeon, Levi, and in some measure Issachar) are unfavourable. The term is used therefore only in a looser meaning; and it is qualified by the last clause of the verse, implying that the blessing was modified according to the circumstances of each. **29—33.**] *Last charge, and death, of Jacob.* On **gathered unto my people**, see note, ch. xxv. 8. The promise had been before exacted from Joseph, ch. xlvii. 29—31. And indeed he alone had the power to carry it out. But it is here repeated in presence of them all, and not without a reference to the harmonious co-

with the field, of Ephron the Hittite for a possession of a
buryingplace, 31 (there they buried Abraham and Sarah
his wife; there they buried Isaac and Rebekah his wife;
and there I buried Leah.) 32 A purchase of the field and
of the cave that *is* therein from the children of Heth. 33
And when Jacob had made an end of commanding his
sons, he gathered up his feet into the bed, and [j] yielded up j ch. vi. 17; vii. 21; xxv. 8; xxxv. 29, al.
the ghost, and was gathered unto his people. L. 1 And
Joseph fell upon his father's face, and wept upon him, and
kissed him. 2 And Joseph commanded his servants the
physicians to embalm his father: and the physicians em-
balmed Israel. 3 And forty days were fulfilled for him;
for so are fulfilled the days of those which are embalmed:
and the Egyptians mourned for him threescore and ten
days. 4 And when the days of his mourning were past,
Joseph spake unto the house of Pharaoh, saying, If now I
have found grace in your eyes, speak, I pray you, in the ears

operation of all the sons in the burial: see ch. l. 15, ff. There is no ground for seeing any inconsistency in the two accounts (Knobel). On all particulars respecting the burial-place, see ch. xxiii., and notes.

31.] The burial of Sarah is related ch. xxiii. 19; that of Abraham, xxv. 9; that of Isaac, xxxv. 29. That of Rebekah, and that of Leah, are here first mentioned. Such simple particulars belong to a narrative which sprung not out of careful subsequent arrangement, but out of the fragmentary notices of real life. **32.**] Ver. 31 is parenthetical, and ver. 32 resumes. **33.**] Jacob had made an effort, and sat upon the bed to receive Joseph; and apparently had so remained during the blessing of his sons. In this attitude his feet were probably out of bed, over the side of the couch. He now gathered them into the bed, and lay down.

On **yielded up the ghost**, see reff. and note on ch. xxv. 8.

L. **1—13.**] *Jacob's burial.* **2.**] In Egypt, which was renowned as the home and centre of medical science, there were physicians for every portion of the body, and thus many would naturally be attached to the suite of Joseph. Herodotus tells us that the embalmers were a separate class of men. This may have become the case by the time that historian wrote (Cent. V. before Christ), or the embalmers may have been under the orders of the physicians. The body of Jacob was embalmed perhaps as a matter of course, seeing he was connected with one high in office, perhaps as being about to be transported to Canaan. **3.**] The historians, Herodotus and Diodorus Siculus, give 70 days as the time occupied by the process of embalming. But their description, as remarked above, applies to times long subsequent to these; and, besides, not only in many particulars are they not in accord with each other, but the existing evidence of mummies does not bear out their accounts. A very full resumé of the subject will be found in Kalisch, pp. 768—775. The Israelites mourned for Aaron (Num. xx. 29) thirty days only,—and the same for Moses (Deut. xxxiv. 8): see also Deut. xxi. 13. But Jacob was mourned for as a king, who was honoured in Egypt by 72 days' mourning. **4, 5.**] It is naturally questioned, why Joseph should speak to the court, and not to Pharaoh himself. Various answers have been given: some supposing that Joseph's office had ceased with the years of famine; others, that another Pharaoh had succeeded during the 28 years since Joseph was appointed. But the more probable and generally accepted answer is that Joseph was in a state of mourning, dur-

of Pharaoh, saying, [5] My father made me swear, saying,
Lo, I die: in my grave which I have digged for me in the
land of Canaan, there shalt thou bury me. Now therefore
let me go up, I pray thee, and bury my father, and I will
come again. [6] And Pharaoh said, Go up, and bury thy
father, according as he made thee swear. [7] ¶ And Joseph
went up to bury his father: and with him went up all
the servants of Pharaoh, the elders of his house, and all
the elders of the land of Egypt, [8] and all the house of
Joseph, and his brethren, and his father's house: only
their little ones, and their flocks, and their herds, they
left in the land of Goshen. [9] And there went up with him
both chariots and horsemen: and the company was very
great. [10] And they came to the threshing-floor of Atad,
which *is* beyond Jordan, and there they mourned with a
great and very sore lamentation: and he made a mourn-
ing for his father seven days. [11] And when the inhabit-
ants of the land, the Canaanites, saw the mourning in the

ing which it was the custom to neglect the personal appearance, and that thus he could not well appear before Pharaoh. Be this as it may, it is no small mark of truthfulness in a narrative when such enquiries have to be made as to matters beneath the surface.

digged] Seeing that this was not literally the case, Knobel supposes the Hebrew word ought to be otherwise read, and to signify *bought*. But surely there is no need for this. In a second-hand report of a transaction, what is more usual than the use of a common term of this kind, even though the actual fact may not be described by it? The very word is used of King Asa's sepulchre, "*which he had digged for himself*," in 2 Chron. xvi. 14; but no one supposes that he really had done this. **6—9.**] *The journey.* We may observe that in this portion, as in ch. xlvii. 29 ff., *Joseph* is the one responsible person and actor, whereas in vv. 12, 13 "*his sons*" are the agents. This is traced (?) to the separate narratives of the Jehovist and Elohist, vv. 12, 13 being regarded as consecutive on ch. xlix., and *this* portion of the narrative as following on ch. xlviii. end. **10, 11.**] The halt and the special mourning appear to have taken place as here described, and then the family alone to have gone on to Hebron. There have been grave doubts about the situation of the halting-place and the direction of the journey. One or two things may be laid down. (1) There is no accounting for the circuitous character of such a journey, ignorant as we are of the circumstances of the times with regard to obstruction by war or hostile tribes; (2) **beyond Jordan** cannot surely be interpreted as written from the position of Moses on the E. of Jordan, but must bear its accustomed meaning, i. e. E. of the Jordan. We are wholly ignorant of the site of the "floor of Atad." Jerome places it at Beth-hoglah, between Jericho and the river, i. e. to the W. of Jordan; but his writing at Bethlehem, still calls it "*beyond* Jordan." He derives the name Beth-hoglah, *place of encircling*, from the dancing round, after the manner of mourners. Two points have been cited as evidence on the respective sides: (*a*) the fact that after this mourning, Jacob was carried *into the land of Canaan*, implying that it was *outside* Canaan; (*b*) that the inhabitants of the land, the Canaanites, saw the mourning, and therefore it must have been *in* Canaan. On the former point, perhaps much stress must not be laid: see above. On the latter we may say, that though on the E. of the Jordan, the place may have been visible from the other side.

floor of Atad, they said, This *is* a grievous mourning to
the Egyptians: wherefore the name of it was called Abel-
mizraim, which *is* beyond Jordan. 12 And his sons did
unto him according as he commanded them: 13 for his sons
carried him into the land of Canaan, and buried him in
the cave of the field of Machpelah, which Abraham bought
with the field for a possession of a burying-place of Ephron
the Hittite, before Mamre. 14 ¶ And Joseph returned
into Egypt, he, and his brethren, and all that went up with
him to bury his father, after he had buried his father. 15
¶ And when Joseph's brethren saw that their father was
dead, they said, Joseph will peradventure hate us, and will
certainly requite us all the evil which we did unto him.
16 And they sent a messenger unto Joseph, saying, Thy
father did command before he died, saying, 17 So shall ye
say unto Joseph, Forgive, I pray thee now, the trespass
of thy brethren, and their sin; for they did unto thee evil:
and now, we pray thee, forgive the trespass of the servants
of the God of thy father. And Joseph wept when they
spake unto him. 18 And his brethren also went and fell
down before his face; and they said, Behold, we *be* thy
servants. 19 And Joseph said unto them, Fear not: for
am I in the place of God? 20 but as for you, ye thought
evil against me; *but* God meant it unto good, to bring to
pass, as *it is* this day, to save much people alive. 21 Now

On the whole, this must remain a point uncleared. The name, **the floor of Atad,** may be from the name of its possessor (2 Sam. xxiv. 16; 1 Chron. xiii. 9), or from the fact of the buck-thorn (in Hebrew *Atad*) growing about the spot. The threshing-floor was a circular space, cleared and smoothed for the purpose. **Abel-mizraim,** as at present pointed in our Hebrew text, signifies not the *mourning*, but the *meadow*, of the Egyptians. But the vowel points are traditional only, and date from no earlier than the 6th century after Christ. **12, 13.**] See above. **15—21.**] *Joseph's brethren fear his anger after their father's death. He reassures them.* **15.**] The literal rendering is, *If* (as we say, *suppose*) Joseph should hate us and, &c., the sentence breaking off unfinished, and requiring a filling up, "*that would be our ruin,*" or the like. We have a similar construction in Ps. xxvii. 13. **16.**] **they sent,** from Goshen to Memphis. It has been suggested that probably Benjamin was the messenger. There is no reason for charging the brethren with inventing this command of their father. **18.**] They were encouraged by the report of the messenger, and themselves came to Memphis to Joseph. **19—21.**] Joseph cannot regard himself as in God's place, to see through the motives and deserts of men. God had had mysterious and beneficent designs which were accomplished even by the carrying out of their evil thoughts against himself: and with God it was for him to leave it. Knobel remarks on ver. 21 that it assumes the famine to be still going on; but surely this need not be so taken. His **nourishing** of them need not mean more than taking protective care of them. And

therefore fear ye not: I will nourish you, and your little
ones. And he comforted them, and spake kindly unto
them. 22 ¶ And Joseph dwelt in Egypt, he, and his
father's house: and Joseph lived an hundred and ten
years. 23 And Joseph saw Ephraim's children of the third
generation: the children also of Machir the son of Ma-
nasseh were born upon Joseph's knees. 24 And Joseph
said unto his brethren, I die: and God will surely visit
you, and bring you out of this land unto the land which
he sware to Abraham, to Isaac, and to Jacob. 25 And
Joseph took an oath of the children of Israel, saying, God
will surely visit you, and ye shall carry up my bones from
hence. 26 So Joseph died, *being* an hundred and ten years
old: and they embalmed him, and he was put in a coffin
in Egypt.

as it is this day refers to the abiding result of his care during the famine, as you see by the present state of Egypt.

22—26.] *Death of Joseph.* **23.**] He saw Ephraim's **sons of the third,** i. e. either, sons *belonging to,* or sons *of,* the third generation. If the former, then his (Joseph's) great,—if the latter, his great-great—grandchildren. Ephraim is put first, as having been preferred to Manasseh in the blessing, ch. xlviii. 8, ff. **were born,** i. e. placed when new-born, for his recognition and blessing. See ch. xxx. 3. **24.**] Joseph, in faith (Heb. xi. 22) in the promises of God (ch. xlvi. 4), prophesies the Exodus, and commands the removal of his own body accordingly. So strong is his faith in the event, that he does not command them to carry him immediately to Canaan. Or perhaps he knows that after his death there would be no one with sufficient authority to carry out such a command.

The mummy of Joseph was put, as was the duty of the embalmers, in a chest of wood, such as may be seen in our museums to this day. And when the children of Israel went up from Egypt they carried it with them, Exod. xii. 19.

THE SECOND BOOK OF MOSES,

CALLED

EXODUS.

I. 1 And these *are* the names of the children of Israel,
which came into Egypt; every man and his household
came with Jacob. 2 Reuben, Simeon, Levi, and Judah,
3 Issachar, Zebulun, and Benjamin, 4 Dan, and Naphtali,
Gad, and Asher. 5 And all the souls that came out of the
loins of Jacob were seventy souls: and Joseph was in
Egypt *already*. 6 And Joseph died, and all his brethren,

Title.] In the Hebrew this book is known as *Shemoth* (the names), or *We-eleh Shemoth* (and these are the names), from the opening words. In the LXX. and the Vulgate the title is the *Exodus*, or *going out*, from the main historical subject of the book, or rather of its former portion, ch. i. to xv. 21.

I. *The increase of Israel, and their oppression in Egypt.* In order to the setting forth of the former of these, the book begins (1—7) by a statement of the names and number of the children of Israel who went down into Egypt. **And**] By the connecting particle the unity of this second book with the first is declared. The words **with Jacob** may be connected with the former part of the verse, as in all the ancient versions, which came into Egypt with Jacob; or with the latter, as in the A. V., which follows the punctuation of the present Hebrew text. Kalisch maintains the former arrangement, considering that the other impairs the simplicity of the sense. The last words are literally, **man and his house came.** **2**, f.] The arrangement of the sons is, as in Gen. xxxv. 23—26, according to their mothers, only Joseph is here omitted, for the reason given in ver. 5.

5.] The number of seventy is made out thus: the sons' wives not being counted, we have (1) 11 sons: (2) as in Gen. xlvi. 8, ff., 4 sons of Reuben, 6 of Simeon, 3 of Levi, 3 and 2 grandsons of Judah, 4 of Issachar, 3 of Zebulun, Dinah, 7 sons of Gad, 4 and 1 daughter of Asher, and 2 grandsons, 10 sons of Benjamin, 1 of Dan, 4 of Naphtali, = 66 in all: to whom must be added Joseph and his 2 sons, excepted from the immigrants but having come out of the loins of Jacob: and—for there can hardly be a doubt of this—Jacob himself, not fulfilling the latter condition, but included amongst the immigrants.

The "for" of the A. V. tends to mislead: the original has "and," meaning that Joseph (and his household, as by ver. 1) being in Egypt already, must be added to the others. **6.**] The death of Joseph has been before related in Gen. l. 26. It is however recapitulated here as formally introducing the close of the former period of Israel's Egyptian life. Knobel regards this as the relation of the event by the Elohist, the Jehovist having inserted the former mention.

7.] In this statement we have almost reproduced the terms of the blessing pro-

and all that generation. 7 And the children of Israel were
fruitful, and increased abundantly, and multiplied, and
waxed exceeding mighty; and the land was filled with
them. 8 ¶ Now there arose up a [a]new king over Egypt,
which knew not Joseph. 9 And he said unto his people,
Behold, the people of the children of Israel *are* more and
mightier than we : 10 come on, let us deal wisely with them;
lest they multiply, and it come to pass, that, when there fall-
eth out any war, they join also unto our enemies, and fight
against us, and get them up out of the land. 11 Therefore
they did set over them taskmasters to afflict them with their
burdens. And they built for Pharaoh [b]store-cities, Pithom

a = Deut. xxxii. 17. Judg. v. 8. Eccl. i. 9. Isa. xlii. 9. Ezek. xi. 19, &c.

b 1 Kings ix. 19. 2 Chron. viii. 4, 6; xvi. 4; xvii. 12; xxxii. 28.

nounced upon Noah, Gen. viii. 17; ix. 7. The words, **and the land was filled with them,** cannot be understood of the land of Goshen alone, which was (Gen. xlvii. 27; ch. ix. 26, al.) the especial habitation of Israel, but must mean the whole land of Egypt, as is also implied in ch. v. 12, and by the statement in ch. iii. 22, that the Israelites were interspersed among the Egyptians. **8—14.**] *The oppression of Israel by the Egyptians.* The **new king** who arose appears not to have been merely *another* king, in ordinary succession, but a king of a new dynasty, foreign to the traditions and maxims of his predecessors. The Hebrew word here used for new occurs in reff. in the same distinctive sense. Josephus gives this fact thus: "the kingdom having passed into another dynasty." This might well be, as dynasties of different origin and character rapidly succeeded one another in the early history of Egypt. There is a remarkable expression in Isa. lii. 4, which would seem to indicate that this oppressor of Israel was of Assyrian extraction; and the same appears to be implied in Isa. x. 24, 26. The question, under what historically-known kings of Egypt the oppression, and the Exodus, respectively took place (for it is hardly likely that they were under the same) is one of great difficulty and uncertainty, and any discussion of it would far pass the limits of a note. The reader is referred to Mr. Stuart Poole's article in the *Biblical Dict.*, where he will find a short discussion of the matter. **9.**] It seems somewhat strange that the Israelites were more in number than the native subjects of this king. Hence we may infer either that the language is that of exaggeration to stir up alarm in the people, or that this king reigned over only a portion of Egypt, and feared the hostility of the other portion. "Till the times of Sesostris," says Kalisch, "Egypt was not united under one mighty ruler, but it consisted of almost as many states as it comprised cities, or at least districts, without connexion or unity. Although Thebes maintained during a long epoch a predominant influence, it had constantly to resist the dangerous and powerful rivalry of Memphis, which became later the chief residence of the Egyptian kings, and to repel the hostilities of many other colonies, which, mostly founded and governed by priests, had sufficient resources to maintain their autonomy." **10.**] See on last verse. From the concluding words, **and get them up out of the land,** it appears that the Israelites are already dealt with as a subject people important to be retained in the country. This is the spirit which pervades the dealings of the subsequent Pharaoh of the Exodus, and which is openly shewn in ch. xiv. 5. **11.**] The object was to crush down their spirits and to check their multiplying. Aristotle mentions this as a means whereby tyrants keep down their people, and cites the Egyptian pyramids as examples. The cities which the Israelites were compelled to build were **store-cities,** not, as the A. V. seems to imply, for the laying up of treasure, but for the storing of the fruits of the earth: see reff. **Pithom**] All that is with any definiteness known about this city is that the name may safely

and Raamses. 12 But the more they afflicted them, the more
they multiplied and grew. And they were c distressed be-
cause of the children of Israel. 13 And the Egyptians made
the children of Israel to serve with rigour: 14 and they
made their lives bitter with hard bondage, in morter, and
in brick, and in all manner of service in the field, *and* with
all their service, wherein they made them serve with
rigour. 15 ¶ And the king of Egypt spake to the Hebrew
midwives, of which the name of the one *was* Shiphrah, and

c Gen. xxvii. 46. Lev. xx. 23. Num. xxi. 5; xxii. 3. 1 Kings xi. 25. Prov. iii. 11. Isa. vii. 6, 16.

be assumed identical with *Patumus* of Herodotus. The name is compounded of Pa, the same prefix as occurs in Bu-bastis (Pi-beseth or Pa-bast) and Bu-siris, signifying *abode*, and Tum or Atum, a name of the sun: and we have *Thoum* as the name of a city near to, or in, the district of Heliopolis.

Raamses] There seems no doubt that this and the **Rameses** of ch. xii. 37 (see note there, and also on Gen. xlvii. 11) represent the same place, and that a town in the land of Goshen, on its western side. The *name* is that of several Egyptian kings, but seems to afford no clue as to the date of the Exodus. It is remarkable that the LXX. give this sentence thus, *and they built strong cities for Pharaoh, both Peitho, and Ramesses, and On, which is Heliopolis.* Mr. Stuart Poole, whose articles on both names are well worth consulting, sums up, "As we find Thoum and Patumus and Rameses in or near to the land of Goshen, there can be no reasonable doubt that we have here a correspondence to Pithom and Raamses, and the probable connexion of both with Heliopolis confirms the conclusion. It is remarkable that the Coptic version of Gen. xlvi. 28 mentions Pithon for, or instead of, the *Heroöpolis* of the LXX. (see there)." Josephus interprets Raamses to *be* Heliopolis, which is hardly likely, as this latter is called On in the sacred text, and as the LXX., writing in Egypt, distinguish the two.

12.] Their policy not succeeding, the Egyptians conceived a loathing and disgust for the children of Israel, so the Hebraists understand the word rendered *were grieved* by the A. V. And this sense is amply borne out by the reff. But the same word is used of the feeling of Moab because of the children of Israel in Num. xxii. 3, and that certainly was not abhorrence so much as distress and alarm.

13, 14.] There seems to be an advance in the narrative of the hardships inflicted on the Israelites. The "burdens" in ver. 11 were public works: these verses indicate that they were generally made private slaves. When this also failed to stop their increase, the unnatural measure of vv. 15, ff. was adopted. The illustration of these former details is found in the subsequent history, see ch. v.: and that of **all service in the field** refers probably to the hard labour of watering the ground: see Deut. xi. 10. Josephus, Ant. ii. 9, gives as examples of their works, the digging of canals to the Nile, and making dams,—the building of the pyramids, and of walls round the cities.

and **with**] This last clause depends, like the rest of the verse, on **they made their lives bitter**, above. "Rossellini gives a highly interesting drawing, copied from the walls of a tomb near Thebes and generally believed to represent the oppressed Israelites making bricks under the Egyptian taskmasters." Kalisch. The drawing is from the tomb of Rekshara, an officer of the court of Thothmes III. about 1444 B.C. It is given in the *Biblical Dict.* under Brick, vol. i. p. 229.

15—22.] *The king commands the slaughter of the male infants. The midwives disobey.* It has been much debated whether these midwives were Hebrews or Egyptians. Josephus supposes the latter; and several modern interpreters adopt his view, mainly influenced by the improbability of Pharaoh having given orders to Hebrew women. But surely the improbability is far greater that the Hebrew women should have allowed themselves to have been delivered by Egyptians; and the whole narrative, names included (see, however, below), presupposes that these women were servants of the true God. If we adopt the other view, we must render, instead of **the Hebrew midwives**, "*the midwives of the Hebrew women*," or,

the name of the other Puah: 16 and he said, When ye do
the office of a midwife to the Hebrew women, and see the
d Jer. xviii. 3. Prov. xxv. 11. [d]birth; if it *be* a son, then ye shall kill him: but if it *be* a
daughter, then she shall live. 17 But the midwives feared
† HA-ELOHIM: see note. †God, and did not as the king of Egypt commanded them,
and saved the men children alive. 18 And the king of
Egypt called for the midwives, and said unto them, Why
have ye done this thing, and have saved the men children
alive? 19 And the midwives said unto Pharaoh, Because
the Hebrew women *are* not as the Egyptian women; for
they *are* lively, and are delivered ere the midwife come in

as Kalisch, '*the women, who served as midwives to the Hebrews.*' But this, though apparently allowable, seems clumsy and unnecessary. Two only are mentioned, probably as being chief of their trade: so we have the chief butler and chief baker, Gen. xl. 1. **Shiphrah**, in Hebrew, *brightness*, or *beauty*. But Mr. Stuart Poole (*Biblical Dict.*) suggests that the name has also an Egyptian sound, *Phra* being *the sun:* in which case, however, the Hebrew spelling would slightly differ from that now found. **Puah**, in Arabic, *shining*. No Egyptian meaning has been given for this name. The following expression has been much controverted. The word literally signifies *two stones*, but is applied in ref. Jer. to the wheels of a potter, which, though of wood, are similar to the two mill-stones in form and motion. The similitude of creation, or birth, to the making of a potter's vessel is often found in Scripture: e. g. Job x. 9; xxxiii. 6; Isa. xxix. 16; xlv. 9; lxiv. 8; Jer. xviii. 6. Hence it has been inferred by some Hebraists that the word here signifies the place of birth, the mouth of the womb, whence the babe issues, as the vessel from the wheels of the potter. Thus recently Knobel and Keil. The two other principal interpretations are—1. That the word signifies the stools on which the women sat or knelt to be delivered, but it is objected that there is no evidence of any such having been used. 2. That it is the stone vessel,—called the stones, or being double, itself and cover, —in which the infants were washed:—but it is justly objected that both the sex would have been previously ascertained, and the best opportunity for the cruel deed passed by, before the child was brought to be washed. These considerations induce me to decide for the meaning first given, and I have expressed it by a paraphrase. **17.**] The midwives feared the true God. This could be hardly said of Egyptians, whose religion was a compound of the grossest superstitions. We must remember, however, that Joseph used the very same expression, Gen. xlii. 18, when speaking in the character of an Egyptian. **18, f.**] In judging of such a portion of the narrative, we must remember, not our own maxims of Christian morality, but the practice of the ancient books which we are reading, which is not to drive every word to the judgment-seat of a stern ethical discrimination, but to treat human actions with more allowance than is permitted to our clearer moral light. Bearing this in mind will save us from the shuffling and presuming casuistry which even Keil quotes from Augustine: "God rewarded the midwives not because they lied, but because they shewed mercy to the people of God: consequently it was not their deceit but their humanity which was rewarded;—benignity of mind, not iniquity of lying (benignitas *mentis* non iniquitas *mentientis*): and for that good, God forgave this evil." It is the bounden duty of an expositor to protest against such morality which, if applied to our own acts, would sanction any kind of deviation from truth. Some well-meaning persons have suggested that there was truth after all in the midwives' excuse, or (so Prof. Murphy) that "the mothers, hearing the order of Pharaoh, did not admit the midwife." But ver. 17 cuts away the ground from all such feeble special-pleading.
For the words **they are lively**, the Vulgate has, "*they themselves know how to deliver*

unto them. 20 Therefore God dealt well with the mid-
wives: and the people multiplied, and waxed very mighty.
21 And it came to pass, because the midwives feared God,
that he made them houses. 22 And Pharaoh charged all
his people, saying, Every son that is born ye shall cast
into the river, and every daughter ye shall save alive.
II. 1 And there went a man of the house of Levi, and
took *to wife* a daughter of Levi. 2 And the woman con-
ceived, and bare a son: and she saw him that he *was a*
goodly *child:* and she hid him three months. 3 And

themselves;" but it would appear that this interpretation originates in a mistake. Pharaoh appears to have believed the midwives, or their punishment must have followed. **21. he made them houses**] i. e. apparently blessed them with families, which in Israel was looked upon as a great blessing: see Gen. xxiv. 60; xxx. 11, 13, and as the reward of piety, Deut. vii. 14; Ps. cxxvii. 3; cxxviii. 3. **22.**] It is naturally understood, that this command applied only to the Hebrews' children. But the rabbinical traditions report that *all* male children, Egyptian as well as Hebrew, were to be thrown into the Nile, inasmuch as it had been predicted that a deliverer of Israel would arise, and it was not known whether he were to be an Egyptian or a Hebrew.

The command in our text may not have been followed out, any more than the previous one to the midwives, or it may have been only in force for a time, or it may have been but partial in its operation on Israel, who mostly dwelt in a part of Egypt far off from the Nile. This Pharaoh is (see ch. ii. 23) distinct from the Pharaoh of the Exodus, more than eighty years after. By his time Israel had multiplied even more still, and had become a powerful nation.

II. **1—10**.] *The birth and bringing up of Moses.* A more particular account of the parents of Moses is given in ch. vi. 16—20. We there learn that the man's name was Amram, and that he was son of Kohath, and grandson of Levi. The expression here used, **a daughter of Levi**, as appears from that place, is not a general but a strict description; for Amram "took him Jochebed his father's sister to wife." **2.**] Moses was not the first offspring of the marriage: Aaron and Miriam were both older; indeed, as we see here, the latter was a grown girl before Moses' birth. Knobel has hence supposed, believing the words here, by the analogy of Hos. i. 3; Gen. xxxviii. 2, f.; iv. 1, 17, to imply that the child was the firstborn of the marriage, that Aaron and Miriam were by a former wife. This view he considers to be favoured by the circumstance that Aaron and Miriam combined against Moses (Num. xii. 1), and that Miriam is described as Aaron's sister (ch. xv. 20). This hypothesis, as he himself confesses, is refuted by Num. xxvi. 59, where it is distinctly stated that Jochebed was the mother of the three; but he supposes a discrepancy between the two places. This surely is a creation of difficulties where none really exist. **2.**] Aaron had apparently been born before the cruel order for destruction of the male children. This hiding of the babe is well described by Prof. Murphy to have taken place from maternal affection, the beauty of the child, and hope in God combined. In Heb. xi. 23, the act is said to have been a fruit of faith. Trust in God was at the foundation of her deed. In the Hebrew, **goodly** is simply *tov*, **good**, the term used in Gen. i. throughout, and in ver. 31, to designate God's works as they came from His hands. This may have some connexion with Stephen's remarkable addition in Acts vii. 20, where he says that Moses was "*beautiful to* (or *in the sight of*) *God.*" Josephus relates that God appeared in a dream to Amram before the birth, and revealed to him the future greatness of the child. Thus the beautiful simplicity of the story is lost. **3.**] There may have been faith even in the form of the cradle chosen. The word *tevah*, used here for the **ark** in which the mother laid her babe, is

when she could not longer hide him, she took for him an
ark of [e] bulrushes, and daubed it with [f] slime and with [g] pitch,
and put the child therein; and she laid *it* in the flags by
the river's brink. 4 And his sister stood afar off, to wit
what would be done to him. 5 ¶ And the daughter of
Pharaoh came down to bathe at the river; and her maidens
walked along by the river's side; and when she saw the
ark among the flags, she sent her maid, and she fetched
it. 6 And when she had opened *it*, she saw the child:
and, behold, a boy weeping. And she had compassion on
him, and said, This is one of the Hebrews' children.
7 Then said his sister to Pharaoh's daughter, Shall I go
and call to thee a nurse of the Hebrew women, that she
may nurse the child for thee? 8 And Pharaoh's daughter
said to her, Go. And the maid went and called the child's

e Job viii. 11. Isa. xviii. 2; xxxv. 7, only.
f Gen. xi. 3; xiv. 10, only.
g Isa. xxxiv. 9, only.

only found besides in the narrative of the deluge. As Noah made an ark for the safety of his house, so she for that of her darling babe. The **bulrushes** are doubtless the papyrus, the triangular lofty reed which formerly grew in abundance on the marshy banks of the Nile, and was used by the Egyptians for weaving baskets, mats, sandals, and for the manufacture of *paper*, so called from the circumstance. She smears the cradle inside with bitumen (literally, she asphalted it with asphalt), to bind it together and make it soft to the infant's tender skin, and outside with pitch, to render it waterproof. **she laid it in the flags,** i. e. the tall flowering rushes (*alga nilotica*) by the brink, to prevent it from being carried away by the stream; Josephus, however, inconsistently with the sacred story, describes it as floating down when seen by the princess.

4, ff.] It can hardly have been accident that she laid the child, and set Miriam to watch, just at the place where the princess came to bathe. We can hardly suppose that the spot was not one commonly frequented for that purpose. Josephus reports the name of the princess to have been *Thermuthis;* and Kalisch quotes from Cahen (*Précis du système hiéroglyphique*) that a name *Tomrots* has been deciphered on an Egyptian monument. But Eusebius (after Artapanus) gives her name as *Merrhis;* Syncellus as *Pharia;* the Arabic traditions as *Asiat.* The seclusion in which women were kept generally in the East did not prevail in ancient Egypt. Wilkinson gives (iii. 389) a bath scene of an Egyptian lady with four maids attending her. The Egyptians ascribed sacred virtue to the Nile water; and there may have been some religious purpose in this bathing. If so, the time, as well as the place, may have been matter of special design on the part of the mother, for such ceremony was usual, especially at the time of the Nile's rising. It is observable that Josephus evades the apparent difficulty of the king's daughter thus publicly bathing by making her merely come down to walk by the river. **6.**] In the Hebrew words rendered by the A. V. "*the babe wept,*" there is no definite article. Some supposed that she knew it to be a Hebrew child by the fact of its circumcision. But this practice was common to the Egyptians also. More probably it was by inference from its exposure in the river. **7.**] Miriam acts on the spur of the princess's compassion, assuming what was in her mind regarding the child. No Egyptian woman would be likely to undertake the duty of nursing a Hebrew child: compare Gen. xliii. 32. Josephus makes it refuse the milk of the Egyptian nurses; again, inconsistently with the sacred text, according to which all this happened then and there, on the spot. **8.] the maid** is in Hebrew a word implying a grown girl. Aaron (ch. vii. 7) was but three years older than Moses, so that Miriam must

mother. 9 And Pharaoh's daughter said unto her, Take
this child away, and nurse it for me, and I will give *thee*
thy wages. And the woman took the child, and nursed it.
10 And the child grew, and she brought him unto Pharaoh's
daughter, and he became her son. And she called his name
Moses: and she said, Because I drew him out of the water.
11 ¶ And it came to pass in those days, when Moses was
h = Gen. xxi. 20.
[h] grown, that he went out unto his brethren, and looked on
their burdens: and he spied an Egyptian smiting an Hebrew,

have been by much the oldest of the three: see on ch. xiv. 20. The fact of the princess disobeying her father's command in adopting the babe, so far from being a difficulty, as some have made it, is the very impress of truth itself. If there is a thing too strong for man's laws, it is woman's heart. Witness Antigone burying her brother. **9.**] It must be understood that from this time the mother became in some sense the recognized servant of the princess, for otherwise how would she enjoy more safety with her babe than before? Hostile enquiry would be disarmed by proof that she was bringing up the child for Pharaoh's daughter. So that the proceeding could not have been altogether secret, and must have been sheltered under the power enjoyed by royalty.

10.] When her duty as nurse was over, she brings her boy to the princess, who formally adopts him. From what has been above advanced, there is no reason to assume that any secrecy was observed. In Acts vii. 22 and Philo's Life of Moses we learn that he was brought up in all the wisdom of the Egyptians. Kalisch and others have made a great point of proving that the Mosaic law was independent of this training of Moses. But surely this is a matter of very trivial importance. It is no more strange that the wisdom of Egypt should have been incorporated into the Law, than that the philosophy of Egypt should have furnished the vocabulary for expressing the doctrines of the Gospel. The name by which Pharaoh's daughter called the child has been variously interpreted. Josephus, taking the Greek form of the name, *Moüses*, says (Ant. ii. 9. 6) that the Egyptians call water *Mo*, and *uses* those who are rescued from it. But elsewhere (against Apion, i. 31) he says that *Moü* is water in Egyptian; and so Philo and others. But the interpretation given in the text here is a Hebrew, not an Egyptian, one; and the name is referred, for the sake of the Jewish readers, to the Hebrew verb *Mashah*, *drew*. See more respecting the name in Kalisch, and in Dean Stanley's art. in the *Biblical Dict.*

11—20.] *Flight of Moses to Midian.*

11.] **in those days**, i. e. in the same period of Egyptian oppression which included the birth of Moses. The expression sometimes has a very wide extent: compare Judg. xix. 1. The LXX. render, "*in those many days.*" The traditional length of the period of Moses's becoming grown (Heb. *great*, see ref.) was *forty years:* compare Acts vii. 23. The many strange accounts given of him during this period are summarized by Dean Stanley, as above. The account in Heb. xi. 24—26 simply and in the letter characterizes his act and motive when he fled, not during this time. But the attachment to his own people and to their God must have accompanied him throughout and have matured his final resolve. Even so we may infer had his patriotism been growing and coming to a head, before the incident here related could have taken place. As Stephen shews (Acts vii. 25), he must have in his mind matured his view of himself as the future deliverer and judge of Israel, before he undertook thus first to deliver and then to judge between his brethren. Faith was throughout his guiding principle, dependence on his divine mission, and on God, who called him to it.

Observe the stress laid in this verse on the word **his brethren.** It was this feeling which was uppermost in his mind, the tie which bound him to Israel, and his mission of deliverance. **12.**] Surely the commentators, ancient and modern, might have

one of his brethren. 12 And he looked this way and that
way, and when he saw that *there was* no man, he slew the
Egyptian, and hid him in the sand. 13 And when he went
out the second day, behold, two men of the Hebrews strove
i ch. xxiii. 1. Deut. xxv. 1. together: and he said to [i]him that did the wrong, Where-
fore smitest thou thy fellow? 14 and he said, Who made
j 1 Sam. xx. 4. 1 Kings v. 5. thee a prince and a judge over us? [j]intendest thou to
kill me, as thou killedst the Egyptain? And Moses feared,
and said, Surely this thing is known. 15 Now when
Pharaoh heard this thing, he sought to slay Moses. But
Moses fled from the face of Pharaoh, and dwelt in the land
of Midian: and he sat down by a well. 16 Now the priest

spared themselves the task of apologizing for this act of Moses. Augustine this time speaks the language of common sense, when he says, comparing this act with that of Peter in the garden, "Each of them, not by blameable cruelty, but by excess of brave spirit, passed the ordinary rule of justice: each through hatred of another's wickedness, the one through love of his brother, the other of his Lord, carnal in both cases, yet love, committed a sin." Yet how much better and more dignified is the account given by Stephen—"he thought they would have understood how that God by his hand was giving deliverance to them." Moses **hid him in the sand,** which shews that the place was on the border of the desert, "the sand of the desert then, as now, running close up to the cultivated tract." Stanley.

13, f.] The same consciousness of his mission influences him in his dealing with his brethren. But they did not recognize it. The fact that it was his rejection by his brethren which drove him out, not the anger of the Egyptians in the first place, is the point of Stephen's argument in adducing his example. **him that did the wrong**] literally, the wicked person—so in reff.

14. intendest] Heb. sayest—so in reff.

15.] The king is named by his title: it is not said whether it was the same under whom Moses was born. On the (in my estimation) insoluble difficulty occasioned by the expression in Heb. xi. 27, "By faith he forsook Egypt, not fearing the anger of the king," see note there. It is very difficult to say what **land of Midian** is meant. For the Midianites with whom we have been hitherto acquainted in the sacred story dwelt east of Palestine, and traded with their caravans through Palestine to Egypt: compare Gen. xxv. 1—4; xxxvii. 28, 36. And we afterwards learn of them that they, with the Amalekites and children of the East, ravaged the land of Israel, Judg. vi. 3: we have them in alliance with the Moabites, Num. xxii. 4, 7; xxv. 1, 6, 17, 18, where Moses, then on the plains of Moab, is commanded to smite them: see also Num. xxxi. 1, Josh. xiii. 21, and Gen. xxxvi. 25. If therefore this Midian be a portion of the better known land bearing that name, we must seek it on the *East* of the Red Sea and of the Sinaitic peninsula. And this is confirmed by the fact that Hobab, Moses' brother-in-law, expressed his wish to leave the camp and regain his own home, at the point where Israel was leaving Sinai and marching N. Eastwards to Edom; also that when Moses is leaving Midian on his return to Egypt, he passes Sinai and there meets Aaron coming to meet him from Egypt, ch. iv. 27. Sinai was distinct from Midian, as ch. xviii. 27 and the already cited Num. x. 30 prove. Knobel goes into the matter at some length, and adduces interesting evidence from the ancient geographers, Ptolemy and others, to shew that these Midianites were the Marani or Mariani, on the southern point of the Sinaitic peninsula. The word **dwelt** is manifestly an anticipation, and the subsequent narrative relates not to an incident happening some time during his sojourn, but to his first arrival in the neighbourhood. **the well,** not *a* well: the chief spring, the "well of Midian." **16.**] The priest of Midian appears to have held much the same position as Melchisedek at Salem

of Midian had seven daughters: and they came and drew
water, and filled the troughs to water their father's flock.
17 And the shepherds came and drove them away: but
Moses stood up and helped them, and watered their flock.
18 And when they came to Reuel their father, he said,
How *is it that* ye are come so soon to day? 19 and they
said, An Egyptian delivered us out of the hand of the
shepherds, and also drew *water* enough for us, and watered
the flock. 20 And he said unto his daughters, And where
is he? why *is* it *that* ye have left the man? call him,
that he may eat bread. 21 And Moses was content to dwell
with the man: and he gave Moses Zipporah his daughter.
22 And she bare *him* a son, and he called his name Ger-
shom [Exile]: for he said, I have been a stranger in a
strange land. 23 ¶ And it came to pass in process of time,
that the king of Egypt died: and the children of Israel

(Gen. xiv. 18). Whether he was the civil head of the tribe does not appear. The Scripture, Josephus, and Philo designate him only as their *priest:* later legends call him their chief or sheikh. He was a worshipper of the true (Semitic) God, as his name Reu-el testifies. After the words, **seven daughters**, the LXX. add "*keeping the flocks of their father Jothor.*" This plainly was so, and the young maidens in the district are even now thus employed, as modern travellers testify. **17.**] These **shepherds** were slaves, watching the flocks. We here see the same love and carrying out of justice which seem to have distinguished the character of Moses, and broke out before when he slew the Egyptian, ver. 11.

18.] The priest of Midian is here called **Reuel** or **Raguel**, but elsewhere (ch. iii. 1; iv. 18; xviii. 1, &c) **Jethro**. Some have supposed that Reuel was Jethro's father; but there seems no need for this. The LXX. in this very passage (see above) use both names for the same person. And Knobel has pointed out that **Reuel** or Raguel (see Gen. xxxvi. 4; 1 Chron. ix. 8; Tobit vi. 10) may well have been the personal name, Jether or **Jethro** that of office, signifying as it does *pre-eminence.* **19.**] They took Moses for an Egyptian from his dress, or his speech, or perhaps from his report of himself. **20.**] Characteristic of Eastern hospitality. The benefactor ought to have been invited in to partake of the family meal: on the expression compare Gen. xxxi. 54. **21**, f.] An agreement was made, i. e. that Moses should remain, probably serving Jethro, as Jacob did Laban. And the social result was the same: he married Jethro's daughter. Knobel supposes she is intended by the Cushite (Ethiopian) woman in Num. xii. 1. See there. **22.**] Notwithstanding his apparent settlement in the family of Jethro, Moses regards his sojourn as a state of banishment, for he names his firstborn **Exile.** He sighs after his own people and God's covenant. We learn from ch. iv. 24 ff. more of the cause of this—that Zipporah his wife had no sympathy with him in this matter. See, on the naming of his other son, ch. xviii. 4. These names form a link which keeps the life of Moses continuous through the long break of forty years. **23—25.**] These verses are in fact the introduction to the great change related in the following chapter. **in process of time** is literally, **in these many days**, viz. from the birth of Moses to that of his son in Midian. Whether this king were the same as the one mentioned in ch. i. 8 f. is uncertain. Probably he was the Pharaoh from whom Moses fled. This new king was the Pharaoh of the Exodus. On his accession the children of Israel had reason to hope for a change in their oppressed condition, in which hope,

sighed by reason of the bondage, and they cried, and their
cry came up unto God by reason of the bondage. 24 And
God heard their groaning, and God remembered his
covenant with Abraham, with Isaac, and with Jacob. 25
And God looked upon the children of Israel, and God
[k]had respect unto *them*. III. 1 Now Moses kept the flock
of Jethro his father in law, the priest of Midian: and he
led the flock to the [l]back of the desert, and came to the
[m]mountain of God, *even* to Horeb. 2 And an angel of JEHOVAH appeared unto him in a flame of fire out of the

k **knew**, Gen. xxxix. 6. Job xxxiv. 4. Ps. cxliv. 3.
l Josh. viii. 2. Judg. xviii. 12.
m ch. iv. 27; xviii. 5; xxiv. 13. 1 Kings xix. 8. See Num. x. 33.

however, they were bitterly disappointed. They renewed their earnest prayers for deliverance, and God heard them. Compare Deut. xxvi. 7. The last words are literally, **and God knew**, no pronoun *them* being expressed: the verb is used in a similar sense in ref.

III., IV. *The call of Moses; his return into Egypt.* 1.] It is characteristic of the Sinaitic peninsula, that only the **flock** of Jethro is named here and in ch. ii. 16, and no herds; there being no fodder for larger cattle, only sheep and goats, asses and camels, and no kine, are kept in Sinai. On the name Jethro, see on ch. ii. 18. Jethro's home was divided from Horeb by desert. And Moses crossed to the back part (as spoken of from Jethro's home) of this desert, and came to Horeb. This would be intelligible if Jethro dwelt near the present Ras Mohammed, at the S. apex of the peninsula. The neighbourhood of Mount Sinai was fertile and abounding with springs (see Stanley, *Sinai and Palestine*, p. 18), and is even now the resort of the Bedouin tribes during the summer heats. Josephus describes it as "admirable for pasture, abounding in excellent grass." Ant. ii. 12, 1. Stephen, in Acts vii. 30, describes this as happening "*in the desert of Mount Sinai.*" The relation of the names Horeb and Sinai has not been exactly defined. Dean Stanley's account is—"1. In Exodus, Leviticus, and Numbers *Sinai* is always and exclusively used for the scene of the giving of the Law, *Horeb* being only used twice—for the scene of the burning bush and of the striking of the rock, Exod. iii. 1; xvii. 6, are doubtful; Exod. xxxiii. 6 is ambiguous. 2. In Deuteronomy *Horeb* is substituted for *Sinai*, the former being always used, the latter never, for the Mountain of the Law. 3. In the Psalms the two are used indifferently for the Mountain of the Law. 4. In 1 Kings xix. 8 it is impossible to determine to what part, if to any special part, *Horeb* is applied." *Sinai and Palestine*, p. 29. The words **of God** are omitted by the LXX. This designation is found in reff., and doubtless arose from the great theocratic significance of the mountain in after times. Knobel regards the use of the phrase as a mark of the later narrator, to whom he refers this portion of the history. But at the same time he acknowledges, judging from vv. 5, 18, that Horeb was before this a holy place of pilgrimage to the ancient Arabs. 2.] **an angel of Jehovah** is very shortly shewn to be God Himself. We have before had examples of this, and shall have again: see Gen. xvi. 7, 13; xxi. 17, 18; xxii. 11, 12; xxxi. 11, 13; xlviii. 15, 16; ch. xiii. 31, compared with xiv. 19; xxiii. 20—23; Judg. vi. 11—16; xiii. 20—23; Hosea xii. 4, 5. Knobel remarks upon this, that though in most cases, and especially in the later O. T. books, the angel appears as separate from God and a being of a different kind, in these places of the pre-captivity books he seems to be one with God Himself, the Hebrew word for angel being in its original meaning, *work* or *service*, and then a *delegate* or *messenger*. **the bush** appears to be used much as it is now with regard to the wild parts, e. g. of Australia; the coppice, or thorn-thicket. The name of the bush, *Seneh*, which probably has given its appellation to Sinai itself, is that of the wild thorny acacia (*Mimosa nilotica*) which everywhere abounds still in the peninsula. The fire is the symbol of the Divine presence: see ch.

midst of the bush : and he looked, and, behold, the bush
[n]**burned with fire, and the bush *was* not [o]consumed. 3**
And Moses said, I will now [p]turn aside, and see this
great sight, why the bush is not burnt. 4 And when
JEHOVAH saw that he turned aside to see, God called
unto him out of the midst of the bush, and said, Moses,
Moses. And he said, Here *am* I. 5 And he said, Draw
not nigh hither: [q]put off thy shoes from off thy feet,
for the place whereon thou standest *is* holy ground. 6
And he said, I *am* the God of thy [r]father, the God of
Abraham, the God of Isaac, and the God of Jacob. And
Moses hid his face ; for he was afraid to look upon God.
7 ¶ And JEHOVAH said, Seeing I have seen the affliction
of my people which *are* in Egypt, and have heard their
cry by reason of their taskmasters ; for I know their sor-
rows ; 8 and I am come down to deliver them out of the
hand of the Egyptians, and to bring them up out of that
land unto a good land and a large, unto a [s]land flowing
with milk and honey ; unto the place of the Canaan-

n Deut. iv. 11 ; v. 23.
o lit. *eaten* ; so Num. xxi. 28 ; xxvi. 10. Job xv. 34, &c.
p Judg. xiv. 8. Ruth iv. 1.
q Josh. v. 15.
r = ch. xv. 2 ; xviii. 4. See 2 Kings xx. 5. 2 Chron. xxi. 12.
s ver. 17 ; ch. xiii. 5 ; xxxiii. 3. Lev. xx. 24. Num. xiii. 27 ; xiv. 8 ; xvi. 14. Deut. vi. 3 ; xi. 9 ; xxvi. 9, 15 ; xxvii. 3 ; xxxi. 20. Josh. v. 6. Jer. xi. 5 ; xxxii. 22. Ezek. xx. 6, 15.

xix. 18 ; xxiv. 17 ; 1 Kings xix. 12 ; Ezek. i. 27, 28 ; viii. 2 (Heb. x. 27 ; xii. 29, &c.). See also Gen. xv. 17 ; Isa. iv. 5 ; also ch. xiii. 21, where Jehovah went before Israel in a pillar of fire. In the case before us the fire was not a burning, only a shining, flame ; the thorn-bush was seen among and through it, but was not consumed by it. The symbolizing interpreters have seen in the fiery thorn-bush an emblem of Israel in the furnace of Egypt, but not consumed, Ps. cxviii. 18. But this seems a confusion of figure. Far better, if we must pursue into symbolism, take the direct significance—Israel the lowly thorn-bush—the fire, the Divine presence, sparing to consume. Kalisch reminds us that the Scottish Church has chosen for its emblem the burning bush, with the motto "nec tamen consumebatur" (and yet it was not consumed). **3.**] The vision was seen beside the way or mountain path which Moses was taking. He had to **turn aside** (reff.) to approach the bush. **4.**] The practice of removing the sandals on entering sacred places, and even houses on visits of courtesy, has ever been, and still is, general in the East (see Knobel and Keil here). The same command, in almost the same words, is given to Joshua in ref. The place was **holy ground**, on account of its vicinity to the Divine presence. **6.**] The words **thy father**, as in reff., are to be taken collectively, as representing the whole of the patriarchs with whom God's covenant was made. It will be remembered that our Lord adduces this self-designation of God against the Sadducees, as proving that the fathers were still living unto God. It may serve as a caution against the driving everything into theological symbolism, to state that some ancient and some modern commentators see the doctrine of the Blessed Trinity in the "threefold" mention of God in this verse. But, first, the mention is *fourfold ;* and, secondly, such an allusion, if consistently carried out, would lead to an inference respecting the three patriarchs distinctively, as preposterous as it is unwarranted.

Moses **hid his face**, as did Elijah on the same spot (1 Kings xix. 13), and as do even the seraphim ministering round the throne (Isa. vi. 2). Compare also Deut. xviii. 16, and Acts xxii. 11. **7—10.**] **I am come down**—anthropologically said, as in Gen. xi. 5. This is the first designation of the land of Canaan in these terms of high laudation, which are hereinafter frequently repeated : see reff. Knobel states that the expression

ites, and the Hittites, and the Amorites, and the Periz-
zites, and the Hivites, and the Jebusites. 9 And now,
behold, the [t] cry of the children of Israel is [t] come unto
me: and I have also seen the oppression wherewith the
Egyptians oppress them. 10 Come now therefore, and I
will send thee unto Pharaoh, that thou mayest bring
forth my people the children of Israel out of Egypt. 11
¶ And Moses said unto God, Who *am* I, that I should
go unto Pharaoh, and that I should bring forth the
children of Israel out of Egypt? 12 And he said, Cer-
tainly I will be with thee; and this *shall be* a token
unto thee, that I have sent thee: When thou hast
brought forth the people out of Egypt, ye shall serve God
upon this mountain. 13 And Moses said unto God, Be-
hold, *when* I come unto the children of Israel, and shall
say unto them, The God of your fathers hath sent me unto
you; and they shall say to me, What *is* his name? what
shall I say unto them? 14 And God said unto Moses, I
AM THAT I AM: and he said, Thus shalt thou say unto
the children of Israel, I AM hath sent me unto you. 15
And God said moreover unto Moses, Thus shalt thou say

t Gen. iv. 10; xviii. 13; xix. 13.

never occurs in the original document, but only in the supplemental narrations. The expression is proverbial rather than literal. The chief glory of Palestine consisted in corn, oil, and wine, which can only be proverbially included in the words. By **honey** some understand the sweet juice of the grape, as in Gen. xliii. 11, where see note. But if the words are proverbial, it may not be necessary so strictly to define them. The six nations at that time inhabiting Canaan are specified: see Gen. x. 15; xv. 20, and notes. **9.**] **the cry . . . . is come**: see reff. **11, 12.**] Moses, who once claimed to be a ruler and deliverer, has, remarks Keil, learnt humility in the school of Midian, and mistrusts himself for so great a mission. Rather, it is the Divine presence which has taught him to "abhor" himself, Job xlii. 5, 6. The same self-depreciation as a messenger to Pharaoh is found again ch. vi. 12. **12.**] The pledge was redeemed by the long sojourn of Israel at the base of Sinai, the establishing of God's covenant with them there, and the setting up there of the tabernacle of God's presence. To believe in the pledge required faith, as well as to obey the command; but in our weakness we are more apt to gird ourselves to great and indefinite duties, when they are bound on to definite and concrete facts: and He who gave this token, knew what was in man. **13, f.**] The Egyptians had various gods, and Israel, long used to their practices, would be sure to enquire after the name of the **God of their fathers** whose messenger Moses was: how was HE to be named to them? **14.**] God, in this holy reply, asserts and explains the sacred name Jehovah, by which He was not now first known: compare Gen. xv. 7, and note on ch. vi. 3. That name is explained to have its root in the eternal self-existence of God. God is that which He is; He is the eternal self-existent one. And this simplicity of His self-existence is to be the main point of His designation to Israel: say to them, I AM (EHYEH) hath sent me. And **15.**] This root of the Divine name is to be further specified in the name itself, JEHOVAH. The very form of the command may serve to shew that this sacred name was no new one. "JEHOVAH **the God of your**

unto the children of Israel, Jehovah, the God of your
fathers, the God of Abraham, the God of Isaac, and the
God of Jacob, hath sent me unto you: this *is* my name for
ever, and this *is* my memorial unto all generations. 16 Go,
and gather the elders of Israel together, and say unto them,
Jehovah, the God of your fathers, the God of Abraham,
of Isaac, and of Jacob, appeared unto me, saying, I have
surely regarded you, and that which is done to you in
Egypt: 17 and I have said, I will bring you up out of the
affliction of Egypt unto the land of the Canaanites, and
the Hittites, and the Amorites, and the Perizzites, and the
Hivites, and the Jebusites, unto a land flowing with milk
and honey. 18 And they shall hearken to thy voice: and
thou shalt come, thou and the elders of Israel, unto the king
of Egypt, and ye shall say unto him, Jehovah the God of
the Hebrews hath [u] met with us: and now let us go, we

[u] ch. iv. 24; v. 3. Num. xxiii. 3, 4, 16

fathers" was, of necessity, an appeal to previous, though perhaps too much forgotten, knowledge of Him who was thus announced to them. No strange new name would have recalled to them the God of their fathers. By the closing words of the verse, this name is to be the enduring appellation of God to the Jewish people. It is well known that the Jews do not, and have not for ages, pronounced this name, and that the very vowels with which it is to be enunciated are matter of dispute, having been lost and replaced by others from the word Adonai, Lord, which they use instead of this name. Our English version, by following that example, has occasioned much confusion and loss of force in passages like the present, where it is of importance.

Observe, that this saying of God to Moses stamps for all ages the Unity and Personality of God as the centre of belief respecting Him. It is beside the scope of this commentary to enter into speculations respecting the name itself. They will be found in abundance in Knobel's commentary, and a full summary in Mr. Wright's article in the *Biblical Dict.* **16.**] The elders appear to have been the heads (or *sheikhs*) of the houses in the tribes. We meet with them in ch. iv. 29; xii. 21; xix. 7, and in all these places as the representatives of the whole people. They accompany Moses, or Moses and Aaron, on weighty occasions, as in ver. 18 here, ch. xvii. 5, 6; xviii. 12; xxiv. 1, 9. Their existence and office seems to infer an organization in Israel, which must have arisen in Egypt before the days of their oppression began. **18.**] In the subsequent history it does not appear that the elders of Israel ever accompanied Moses and Aaron into Pharaoh's presence.

hath met with us] i. e. specially appeared to us, and given us intimation of that which follows. There certainly is a difficulty about the terms of this message to Pharaoh, hardly to be got over, as some commentators, e. g. Keil, Kalisch, Wordsworth, &c., attempt to do. Their explanation is, that God, foreseeing the hard-heartedness of Pharaoh, instructs them to approach him first, not with a demand of dismission from his land, which he would be sure to refuse, but with the more moderate one of a three days' journey to sacrifice: and that when this had been proffered, conceded, and then the permission retracted, God instructed Moses and Aaron to make the fuller demand of entire dismission (ch. vi. 10). Unfortunately, the facts do not bear out this. Long after ch. vi. 10, the three days' journey was still demanded; and when Pharaoh conceded (ch. x. 8—11) all that that request really included, but not all that the ulterior design required, the concession was rejected. The whole proceeding surely must tend to confirm in the ingenuous

beseech thee, three days' journey into the wilderness, that
we may sacrifice to Jehovah our God. 19 ¶ And I am sure
that the king of Egypt will not let you go, no, not by a
mighty hand. 20 And I will stretch out my hand, and
smite Egypt with all my wonders which I will do in the
midst thereof: and after that he will let you go. 21 And
I will give this people favour in the sight of the Egyptians:
and it shall come to pass, that, when ye go, ye shall not
go empty: 22 but every woman shall [v] ask of her neigh-
bour, and of her that sojourneth in her house, jewels of
silver, and jewels of gold, and raiment: and ye shall put

[v] *ask*, Josh. xix. 50. Judg. v. 25; viii. 26. 1 Sam. i. 17, 20; xii. 13, and very frequently. *borrow*, Exod. xxii. 14. 2 Kings iv. 3; vi. 5.

mind the impression that was before made by the history of the midwives, that we are not here in the region of what is now recognized and upheld as the morality of Christians. Those who are determined to evade this conclusion in the reading of the O. T. are compelled to have recourse to those shifts and evasions of special pleading which more than anything serve the cause of unbelief. The futility of the account attempted here is manifest; for if "God knew that Pharaoh would not grant to the Israelites even that just and moderate request, and that by refusing this, his pride and obstinacy would become so manifest to all, that everybody must acknowledge the judgments and punishments inflicted upon Pharaoh as just and fully merited" (Kalisch), it might in a moment be replied on Pharaoh's behalf, that he was not deceived by the milder request, but refused it in his wisdom, seeing behind it the design of final departure. In this way do such interpretations undo their own work.

19.] It might be added to the foregoing observations, that in the Divine words themselves no such issue as the failure or success of the mere scheme of a three days' journey to sacrifice is thought of: the "letting them go" is throughout used of their final dismissal and of nothing else. The simple account to be given by the honest Scripture student, however it may offend our more elevated and enlightened views of morality, is this, that God has in view, and speaks of to Moses, the ultimate and entire deliverance of Israel from Egypt; that He was pleased to sanction, and even to order, Moses to obtain this deliverance under the pretext of a three days' journey to sacrifice. Further we need not search. This was God's will then: we know His will now. If Scripture itself asserts the imperfection of the former dispensation, why should we be restlessly anxious evermore to disprove that imperfection? Knobel regards the idea of the three days' journey as peculiar to the later narrator, and maintains that the original history knew only of the demand of entire dismission as in ch. vi. 10. The last words of the verse are variously rendered. Knobel, with the LXX., Vulgate, Luther, de Wette, and others, give them "*unless by a mighty hand*," i. e. without the influence of God's mighty judgments; but Kalisch and other Hebraists maintain that the Hebrew word introducing the clause cannot mean "*unless*," but must be rendered, as in A. V., **no, not**, or **not even**. In support of this latter it may be remembered that, even after all the plagues, Pharaoh retracted his permission when he saw that the Israelites were gone.

21, 22.] Here again our commentators are much exercised to justify the morality of the Divine announcement. Surely they might have spared themselves the trouble. The **borrowing** and **lending** took place not in a strict and proper sense; but the oppressed people spoiled their oppressors by means of the anxiety of the latter to get rid of them under the pressure of dire calamity. And this is shewn by the fact that the verb rendered in the A. V. "*borrow*" has not necessarily this meaning. It simply means **ask, demand**, and is so rendered in more than a hundred places where it occurs (see reff.), and only in very few can the signification of borrowing or lending be held, and even then the general meaning of *ask*, including the particular case of borrowing, will suffice. It was a borrowing with-

them upon your sons, and upon your daughters; and ye
shall spoil the Egyptians. IV. 1 And Moses answered
and said, But, behold, they will not believe me, nor hearken
unto my voice: for they will say, JEHOVAH hath not ap-
peared unto thee. 2 And JEHOVAH said unto him, What
is that in thine hand? And he said, A [w] rod. 3 And he said,
Cast it on the ground. And he cast it on the ground, and
it became a serpent; and Moses fled from before it. 4 And
JEHOVAH said unto Moses, Put forth thine hand, and take
it by the tail. And he put forth his hand, and caught it,
and it became a rod in his hand: 5 that they may believe
that JEHOVAH, the God of their fathers, the God of Abra-
ham, the God of Isaac, and the God of Jacob, hath ap-
peared unto thee. 6 ¶ And JEHOVAH said furthermore unto
him, Put now thine hand into thy bosom. And he put his
hand into his bosom: and when he took it out, behold, his
hand *was* leprous as [x] snow. 7 And he said, Put thine

w Exod. &c., freq. 1 Sam. xiv. 27, 43. Ps. cx. 2. Isa. xxviii. 27. Micah vi. 9, al.

x Num. xii. 10. 2 Kings v. 27.

out intent to return, and a lending without hope of receiving again. When Knobel, on the other side, tries to shew that the borrowing was for the pretended sacrifice, that the people might offer in festal raiment, we reply that at the last dire catastrophe there is no question of the pretended sacrifice. Pharaoh, when he comes to himself again after the terror, has no idea that Israel is encamped three days off in the wilderness and will again return; but at once says, ch. xiv. 5, "*Why have we done this, that we have let Israel go from serving us?*" On **ye shall put them upon your sons, and upon your daughters,** Knobel remarks, that the children of both sexes of the Fellahs in Egypt to this day go naked, and the same probably was the case with the Hebrews as a servile race. The spoiling of Egypt was but the right of Israel, who had been so long spoiled of just wages by servile oppression.

IV. **1—9.**] *The distrust of Moses, and God's reassurance of him by two miraculous signs, and promise of a third.* The distrustful assertion of Moses was in fact a questioning of the very words of God (ch. iii. 18), "*they shall hearken to thy voice.*" But God condescended to his infirmity and reassured him. When his distrust reaches its height at ver. 10, he earns a sharp rebuke and a peremptory command. The distrust in this case was prompted by the fact of Israel's degraded and apparently God-forsaken state, and the withdrawal of Divine appearances since the patriarchal days.

2.] The **rod** of Moses was perhaps his shepherd's staff. The word, in its signification of *branch*, is that commonly used to designate the *tribes* of Israel. It is not the word used for the shepherd's *rod* or *staff* in Ps. xxiii. 4. **3, 4.**] There was doubtless symbol here. The rod was emblematic of Moses' power of ruling or guiding. This power becomes to him a danger, as he apprehended a danger which he was even now fleeing from; but when grasped, it becomes a rod in his hand,—leads him on to new degrees of leadership and power. Such might be the effect of the miracle on the mind of Moses himself; on the people it would at once produce the belief required.

5.] The form of the verse, in the second person, shews that it continues the words of the Lord from the last command, after a pause for the effect of Moses' obedience to that command. This sign was exhibited not only to the Israelites (ver. 30), but also to Pharaoh, ch. vii. 10, ff. **6, 7.**] *The second sign;* leading him to see that God, who could delegate to him the power of producing and healing the deadly disease

hand into thy bosom again. And he put his hand into his
bosom again; and plucked it out of his bosom, and, be-
hold, it was turned again as his *other* flesh. 8 And it shall
come to pass, if they will not believe thee, neither hearken
y See Ps. xix. 2. Job xii. 7. to the y voice of the first sign, that they will believe the
y voice of the latter sign. 9 And it shall come to pass, if
they will not believe also these two signs, neither hearken
unto thy voice, that thou shalt take of the water of the
river, and pour *it* upon the dry *land:* and the water which
thou takest out of the river shall become blood upon the
dry *land.* 10 ¶ And Moses said unto JEHOVAH, I beseech
thee, O my Lord, I *am* not a man of words, neither here-
tofore, nor since thou hast spoken unto thy servant, for I
am slow of mouth, and slow of tongue. 11 And JEHOVAH
said unto him, Who hath made man's mouth? or who
maketh the dumb, or deaf, or the seeing, or the blind?
have not I JEHOVAH? 12 Now therefore go, and I will be
with thy mouth, and teach thee what thou shalt say. 13
And he said, O my Lord, send, I pray thee, by the hand

of leprosy, was fully able to empower him for the work which He required. Keil, guided by the words of Moses, Num. xi. 11, 12, understands the symbolism to refer to Israel, first in its degraded state, then in its state of liberation by Moses. Bp. Wordsworth unites both views. The white leprosy (reff.) was that form with which the Hebrews were best acquainted and the most difficult of cure. See art. "Leper" in *Biblical Dict.* **8, 9.**] *The third sign*, kept in reserve in case of the failure of the two others to convince the people. If Moses was endowed with the power to turn the Egyptians' boast, the salutary and life-giving water of the Nile, into blood, it was a pledge that his delegated power should prevail over all the power of Egypt. See this sign expanded into a general plague, ch. vii. 10, ff. **the voice of the first . . . of the latter sign,** i. e. the testimony, or intent, of the signs. **10—17.**] Moses' distrust is not yet overcome. His personal gifts are not in his estimation equal to the mission with which he is entrusted. And especially in the matter of speech. The word rendered *O* in A. V. is said to be a contracted form of **I pray thee,** or **I beseech thee**; and its meaning to be equivalent to "May it please thee,"—a form of deprecation of displeasure, which Moses anticipated. **heretofore** is literally **yesterday or the day before.** The slow of mouth and slow of tongue seems to point to some natural defect in speech. Neither by nature was Moses an apt speaker, nor had this infirmity been removed since God had begun to speak to him. The difficulty of expression under which he physically laboured continued even in making these replies to the Divine vision. Only thus it seems to me can we understand his words; a mere incapacity for eloquence would not thus be spoken of, as unaffected by the short time which had elapsed during his conference with God. **11, 12.**] By this rebuke, accompanied with a promise of Divine help, every reasonable ground of Moses' backwardness was taken away. And now he is driven to the real reason of it—his want of will to undertake the Divine mission.

13.] The request is equivalent to praying God to send by some other than himself. Some have seen a mystic prophetic sense in the words, and held them to mean that God should send Him whom He was about some day to send, viz. the Messiah, to work this deliverance. **14.**] God's anger is kindled by the backwardness of

of him whom thou wilt send. 14 And the anger of JEHOVAH
was kindled against Moses, and he said, Do I not know
Aaron the Levite thy brother, that he can speak well?
And also, behold, he cometh forth to meet thee: and when
he seeth thee, he will be glad in his heart. 15 And thou shalt
speak unto him, and put the words in his mouth: and I
will be with thy mouth, and with his mouth, and will teach
you what ye shall do. 16 And he shall be thy spokesman
unto the people: and he shall be, *even* he shall be to thee
instead of a mouth, and thou shalt be to him instead of
God. 17 And thou shalt take this rod in thine hand,
wherewith thou shalt do the signs. 18 ¶ And Moses went
and returned to Jethro his father in law, and said unto
him, Let me go, I pray thee, and return unto my brethren
which *are* in Egypt, and see whether they be yet alive.
And Jethro said to Moses, Go in peace. 19 And JE-
HOVAH said unto Moses in Midian, Go, return into Egypt:
for all the men are dead which sought thy life. 20 And
Moses took his wife and his sons, and made them to ride
upon [z] the ass, and he returned to the land of Egypt: and

z So Josh. xv. 18. 1 Sam. xxv. 20. 2 Sam. xvii. 23; xix. 27. 1 Kings xiii. 13.

Moses to undertake the mission. It is difficult to say why Aaron should be designated **the Levite**, seeing that Moses was a Levite also, and that the official meaning of a Levite was not yet assigned, and, had it been, would not have furnished the reason of which we are in search. Kalisch seems to come nearest to giving it—that the expression is perhaps used as more special and extended designation of Aaron, as in the case of "thy son, thy only one whom thou lovest, Isaac." But this hardly seems enough. **16.**] On this is grounded the close relation between Moses and Aaron, which we find subsisting throughout.

17, ff.] It were useless to deny with some of the commentators, that there are in this narrative abundant traces of different sources of the history, and various fragmentary notices. The mention of the rod comes in somewhat strangely here after all that has been implied concerning it in vv. 1—9, which would make his taking it with him a matter of course. The notice in ver. 18 continues the history which has extended from ver. 1; but again the notice in ver. 19 seems to betoken the commencement of a new and distinct account of Moses parting from Midian. After the distinct command given to him in ver. 12, it is strange to find the idea of returning into Egypt announced de novo, and a totally different reason assigned for the return. It is plainly futile to say with Keil, that when Moses had obtained Jethro's consent to his journey, God further stimulates him to it, by assurance that all danger in Egypt was over. Any ingenuous child may see that such is not the spirit of the narrative. **20.**] The two boys, Gershom (ch. ii. 22) and Eliezer (ch. xviii. 4), were therefore of tender age, and the marriage of Moses must have taken place far on in the forty years of his stay in Midian. This again is an inference we should hardly have drawn from ch. ii. 21, 22. We have but one son spoken of there, and again but one son in ver. 25. Knobel suspects that not *banaiv*, his *sons*, but *beno*, his *son*, ought to be read. But it is much more probable that the fragmentary character of the history has occasioned the variations. **the ass**, because it is assumed that such a beast of burden belonged to the household; so in reff. **the rod of God**]

Moses took the rod of God in his hand. [21] And JEHOVAH
said unto Moses, When thou goest to return into Egypt,
see that thou do all those wonders before Pharaoh, which
I have put in thine hand: but I will harden his heart, that
he shall not let the people go. [22] And thou shalt say unto
Pharaoh, Thus saith JEHOVAH, Israel *is* my son, *even* my
firstborn: [23] and I say unto thee, Let my son go, that he
may serve me: and if thou refuse to let him go, behold,
I will slay thy son, *even* thy firstborn. [24] ¶ And it came
a Gen. xlii. 27. to pass by the way in the [a] halting place, that JEHOVAH

The rod of vv. 1—5, afterwards so famous. Knobel points out that this rod is evermore in the Jehovistic portions of the narrative in the hand of Moses, and that he works his wonders with it—the smiting of the Nile (ch. vii. 15, 17), the hail (ch. ix. 23), the locusts (ch. x. 13), the passage of the Red See (ch. xiv. 16), the water from the rock (ch. xvii. 5; Num. xx. 8, ff.), the fight with the Amalekites (ch. xvii. 9); whereas in the Elohistic portions it is ever found in *Aaron's* hand, and he is the wonder-worker, stretching it out at Moses' command: e. g. at the turning into a serpent (ch. vii. 9, f.), the waters into blood (ch. vii. 19, f.), the plague of frogs (ch. viii. 5), the flies (ch. viii. 12, f.). But Knobel himself seems to furnish the key to the difference when he further suggests that this shepherd's staff of Moses (ver. 2) hardly seems to be the same with the rod of Aaron, which is paralleled with the rods of the Egyptian magicians, ch. vii. 12. If the two rods were different, the whole is consistent. The prevalence of the rod in ancient literature, as designating prophets and holy men, is remarkable. Chryses the priest in Homer, and Tiresias the prophet, Circe the enchantress, and Hermes the divine messenger, and Cassandra the prophetess in Æschylus, bear the staff as their ensign of office: and the Roman augurs were known by their *lituus*, or bent staff, which they carried, and used in taking their auguries. **21.**] literally, **see all the wonders that I have put in thy hand, and thou shalt do them before Pharaoh,** &c. This is the first mention of doing the wonders before Pharaoh—hitherto it had been before *the people*. Reference is made to God's wonders which He would do in the midst of Egypt, ch. iii. 20. On the **hardening of Pharaoh's heart** much discussion has been spent in vain. When it is all done, we are no nearer to a solution of the Divine sovereignty and human freewill than we were before. Each is true, the one from the idea of God, the other from the idea of man; and further than that we shall never attain. Bp. Wordsworth has a statistical table by which he shews that it is said six times that the Lord hardened Pharaoh's heart, but it is first said seven times that Pharaoh hardened his own heart: "Pharaoh's will was therefore free." And this is a fair sample of the sort of argument used on the matter. **22, 23.**] The first nine plagues wrought by the intervention of Moses should but harden Pharaoh's heart; therefore God Himself would intervene with a greater than these. The tenth plague was announced by Moses (ch. xi. 4, f.), but wrought by God Himself (xii. 29). The similitude of Israel to God's *son* is frequent: compare Hos. xi. 1; Isa. xlv. 11; lxiii. 8. He is also God's beloved, or firstborn, Jer. xxxi. 9; Ps. lxxxix. 27; Mal. i. 6; ii. 10. See also Deut. xiv. 1, 2; xxxii. 18; and ch. xix. 5. **that they may serve me**] See ch. iii. 18, and note.

24—26.] This surprising occurrence must be accounted for by remembering that Moses was an Israelite, bound to God by the covenant of circumcision, and that he was bringing his family to Egypt uncircumcised, having apparently conceded this point to the national habits of his wife. God had attached to the neglect of circumcision the penalty of death (Gen. xvii. 14). *How* God met with him we are left to surmise: possibly in a dangerous stroke of illness or sudden incapacity, as would appear from his inability to circumcise his own child. This

[b] met him, and sought to kill him. 25 Then Zipporah took [b] ch. iii. 18, reff.
a sharp [c] stone, and cut off the foreskin of her son, and [c] Isa. v. 28. Ezek. iii. 9. See Josh. v. 2.
cast *it* at his feet, and said, Surely a bloody husband *art*
thou to me. 26 So he let him go: then she said, A bloody
husband *thou art*, because of the circumcision. 27 ¶ And
JEHOVAH said to Aaron, Go into the wilderness to meet
Moses. And he went, and met him in the mount of God,
and [d] kissed him. 28 And Moses told Aaron all the words [d] Gen. xxxiii. 4. 2 Sam. xix. 39; xx. 9. ch. xviii. 7.
of JEHOVAH who had sent him, and all the signs which
he had commanded him. 29 ¶ And Moses and Aaron
went and gathered together all the elders of the children
of Israel: 30 and Aaron spake all the words which JE-
HOVAH had spoken unto Moses, and did the signs in the
sight of the people. 31 And the people believed: and
when they heard that JEHOVAH had visited the children of
Israel, and that he had looked upon their affliction, then

took place not in the *inn*, for there were not and are not in the East any buildings corresponding to our inns (see on ref.), but at the resting-place for the night. The **sharp stone** was a knife of flint, such as were used before metals were common, and as are found even now in great numbers near the haunts of ancient peoples. It is said to have been retained as the instrument of circumcision, on account of the fancied injury done by metal to the wound. See Josh. v. 2. The Egyptians, Herodotus tells us (ii. 86), used flint knives to open the bodies for embalming. And Pliny (H. N. xxxv. 12) says the priests of Cybele used similar instruments for castration: so Catullus also in his Atys. "Even now," says Kalisch, "those Jewish male children who die before the eighth day from their birth are circumcised with stone knives." It is difficult to say what exactly was done by Zipporah; at *whose* feet she cast the foreskin of her son (on the *singular*, see above on ver. 20, that it was Eliezer, and he a new-born babe, there is not a particle of ground to infer); or to whom she addressed the words. Kalisch supposes that she put the prepuce at the boy's own feet (it is literally, **made [it] to touch his feet**), and addressed the words to *him*, seeing that a newly circumcised child was called "a bridegroom of the covenant." But this seems unlikely. Zipporah would hardly be aware of this Jewish name, if it then existed; and even if she were, the child could in no sense be said to be a bridegroom *to her*. It is much more probable that it was at the feet of Moses, and that the words were addressed to *him*. In ver. 26 we have the real order of the incidents: the performance of the rite was followed by the deliverance of Moses from the peril, whatever it was: and when that was accomplished, *then* she called him a bridegroom of blood, in reference to his life having been bought, and himself as it were re-married to her, at the price of the child's blood. It is probable that Zipporah and her sons were sent back from this spot, for we find in ch. xviii. 2 f. that they had been during the Exodus in Midian.

27, f.] God had already given Aaron the command to go and meet his brother, where he spoke with Moses in Midian, and announced his coming to meet him. Moses returns by Mount Horeb; probably that was the accustomed way, in which he would be likely to meet Aaron. The brothers salute one another after the Eastern manner: see reff.

29—31.] The two brothers at once proceed to perform the Divine command, Aaron acting as the spokesman (ver. 16), and recounting God's dealings with Moses. We may notice that Aaron also did the signs, not Moses: see above on ver. 20. As God had announced (iii. 18), the people believed, viz. that God had sent Moses and Aaron for

they bowed their heads and worshipped. V. 1 And after-
ward Moses and Aaron came, and said to Pharaoh, Thus
saith JEHOVAH, the God of Israel, Let my people go, that
they may hold a feast unto me in the wilderness. 2 And
Pharaoh said, Who *is* JEHOVAH, that I should obey his
voice to let Israel go? I know not JEHOVAH, neither will
I let Israel go. 3 And they said, The God of the Hebrews
hath [e] met with us: let us go, we pray thee, three days'
journey into the desert, and sacrifice unto JEHOVAH our
God; lest he fall upon us with pestilence, or with the
sword. 4 And the king of Egypt said unto them, Where-
fore do ye, Moses and Aaron, disturb the people from their
works? get you unto your burdens. 5 And Pharaoh said,
Behold, the people of the land now *are* many, and ye make
them rest from their burdens. 6 And Pharaoh commanded
the same day the [f] taskmasters of the people, and their
[g] officers, saying, 7 Ye shall no more give the people

e ch. iii. 18, reff.

f Job iii. 18. Isa. iii. 12; lx. 17. Zech. x. 4.

g Num. xi. 16. Deut. i. 15; xvi. 18. Josh. viii. 33; xxiv. 1, 4. 2 Chron. xxvi. 11, al.

their deliverance. That this their faith did not always hold out is no objection to the entireness of their first belief. Compare ch. vi. 9. It must be remembered that this was the first excitement of the Divine messages: suffering and time blunted their ardour afterwards.

V. 11—19.] *Moses and Aaron report God's command to Pharaoh. The oppression of Israel increased thereby.* At this first application there is no mention of signs and wonders: it is merely a report of the command of Jehovah. This name is unknown to Pharaoh,—a sufficient proof, as Kalisch remarks, that it was not Egyptian in its origin; a proof also that Israel's worship hitherto had not been that of Jehovah by name, otherwise the appellation would not have been unknown to the king. And this shews that this sacred name was, not now first made known, but brought into formal and special use as that of Israel's God, in compliance with the Divine command of ch. iii. 15. It was a solemn revival of the confession of the God of their fathers: see ch. iv. 31; also note, chap. vi. 3, and Lev. xvii. 7. **3.**] The demand is again repeated, in the form of a request, and grounded on the now better explained fact, that their national God—possibly the term Hebrews extended more widely in Pharaoh's mind, and was one of more majesty than the now degraded name of Israel—had met with (reff.) them,—i. e. given them a command: and a fear is expressed which Moses' own experience (ch. iv. 24) warranted, lest the neglect of the Divine command might be visited with deadly judgments. **4, 5.**] But Pharaoh views the whole as an attempt to make Israel idle, and, inasmuch as they are now numerous, to render them dangerous to his government, ch. i. 10, 11. In consequence, Pharaoh proceeds to make the labour of the people yet more sore and oppressive. **6.**] **taskmasters**, literally **drivers**, the very word used in modern slave-countries: see reff. The **officers** were apparently Israelites, subordinated to the taskmasters, and accountable to them for the performance of the daily tale of work. "Even now the Arabic Fellahs, whose position is very analogous to that of the Israelites described in our text, are treated by the Turks in the same manner. Arabic overseers have to give an account of the labours of their countrymen to the Turkish taskmasters, who often chastise them mercilessly for the real or imputed offences of the Arabic workmen." Kalisch, citing modern travellers. On the use of the title (*Shoterim*), see reff. **7.**] Sun-hardened bricks, made of clay mixed with chopped straw, form the ordinary material of the ancient Egyptian buildings. It seems to be quite a mistake to regard, as

[h] straw to make brick, as heretofore: let them go and
gather straw for themselves. 8 And the tale of the bricks,
which they did make heretofore, ye shall lay upon them;
ye shall not diminish *ought* thereof: for they *be* idle;
therefore they cry, saying, Let us go *and* sacrifice to our
God. 9 Let there more work be laid upon the men, so
that they may be occupied therein, and may not regard
vain words. 10 ¶ And the taskmasters of the people went
out, and their officers, and they spake to the people, say-
ing, Thus saith Pharaoh, I will not give you straw. 11 Go
ye, get you straw where ye can find it: yet not ought of
your work shall be diminished. 12 So the people were
scattered abroad throughout all the land of Egypt to
gather [i] stubble instead of straw. 13 And the taskmasters
[j] were urgent, saying, Fulfil your works, the task of the
day on its day, as when there was straw. 14 And the
officers of the children of Israel, which Pharaoh's task-
masters had set over them, were beaten, *and* demanded,
Wherefore have ye not fulfilled your task in making brick
both yesterday and to day, as heretofore? 15 ¶ Then the
officers of the children of Israel came and cried unto Pha-
raoh, saying, Wherefore dealest thou thus with thy serv-

h Gen. xxiv. 25. Judg. xix. 19, al.

i ch. xv. 7. Isa. v. 24; xlvii. 14. Joel ii. 5. Nah. i. 10. Obad. 18.
j Josh. x. 15; xvii. 15. Prov. xix. 2.

Luther has done in his version, the straw (properly, chopped or comminuted straw, and so in reff.) as used for burning the bricks. Our rendering, **straw to make brick**, which is that of the LXX. and Vulgate, gives the right view. Brick-kilns were not unknown in Egypt, compare Jer. xliii. 9; but the other method of making brick was the prevalent one. See *Biblical Dict.* i. p. 229, where is an engraving of captives making bricks at Thebes. Some of the sun-baked bricks are without straw; but this was not to be the case here: the labour of the people was to be increased by their having to seek straw for themselves.

12.] The people had, besides their brick-making, to collect stubble which might serve as chopped straw. It was usual, as shewn in almost all the reff., to *burn* the stubble when thoroughly dry, which thus served as manure for the succeeding crop. The gathering of stubble by the children of Israel must therefore have taken place after harvest, and before the wheat was sown which was still in the ground at ch. ix. 32, where see note on the various times of the plagues. **13, 14.**] The Egyptian 'drivers' were severe (literally, **strait**, or **tight**: see on Josh. xvii. 15) on the Hebrew officers, and would not hear even of any distribution of the tasks over more time to allow of the gathered stubble being brought in: they required **the task of the day on its day.** Such is the literal rendering, and it gives more vividness to the description. "It will be known to our readers, that even at present the rule of the stick is generally prevalent in many parts of the East. Neither rank, learning, nor old age can protect against the ruthless tyranny of the stick." Kalisch.

15—19.] "The kings of Egypt probably held on certain days a sort of open court or divan, as usual in Oriental monarchies, when every subject was allowed to appear to seek justice or to claim redress." Kalisch. **and they say to us, Make brick,** is literally, **"and bricks, saying to us, make."**

ants? 16 There is no straw given unto thy servants, and
they say to us, Make brick: and, behold, thy servants *are*
† Heb. *sin*. beaten, and thy people † are blamed. 17 But he said, Ye
are idle, *ye are* idle: therefore ye say, Let us go *and* do
sacrifice to JEHOVAH. 18 Go therefore now, *and* work; for
there shall no straw be given you, yet shall ye deliver the
tale of bricks. 19 And the officers of the children of Israel
did see *that* they *were* in evil *case*, after it was said, Ye shall
not minish *ought* from your bricks of your daily task. 20
¶ And they met Moses and Aaron, who stood in their way,
as they came forth from Pharaoh: 21 and they said unto
them, JEHOVAH look upon you, and judge; because ye
have made our savour to be abhorred in the eyes of Pharaoh, and in the eyes of his servants, to put a sword in
their hand to slay us. 22 And Moses returned unto JE-
HOVAH, and said, Lord, wherefore hast thou *so* evil en-

The meaning of the concluding words of the verse has been much controverted. The A. V., which makes them mean merely "*thy servants* (*we*) *are beaten for a fault which is not ours, but that of thine own people*," seems to stand almost alone. The two lines of interpretation may be described as being, 1. That which applies **thy people** to the *Egyptians*; **and thy people sins**. This, which is the rendering of the Targum of Onkelos, and many others, including of the moderns Keil and Kalisch, is a more serious form of that adopted by the A. V. It is not merely "we are punished for the fault of thy people;" but, "thy people incurs guilt, commits sin, by this proceeding." But, 2. The view which takes thy people as meaning the *Israelites* is much better supported, and it would appear more correct. The LXX. have, "*thou wilt therefore do injustice to thy people*;" and so the Vulgate, "*injustice is done against thy people*;" and the Samaritan Pentateuch, "*thou doest injury to thy people*;" but in the *Version*, "*the fault is with thee*." The old Syriac has "*thou sinnest against thy people*." Of modern Hebraists, Knobel is strong for the reference of **thy people** to *Israel*. His note is, "literally, **and thy people sins**, i. e. Israel, which is yet thy people, is involved in sin and reckoned guilty (Gen. xliii. 9), are treated as offenders and not as a people belonging to thee, the king." It seems certainly in favour of this, that there is not in the original any such contrast as the "*but*" expresses, nor any such emphasis as is given by "*thine own*." It is simply, "**and thy people sins**." It is also in favour of it that the distinction between thy servants, the officers, who were beaten, and thy people, the Israelites, who were blamed, is a very natural one: and the saying, in the mouth of persons petitioning for mercy, much more natural than one which would imply flying in the face of the king, by whose order the straw had been withheld. I have therefore adopted the second view. **20—23.**] The fears of Moses begin to be realized: Israel shrinks back at the first appearance of discouragement, and Moses and Aaron are stigmatized as the cause. **20.**] Literally, **who stood for the meeting of them**, to hear from them what had been their success with the king. On the figure **our savour**, &c., see Gen. xxxiv. 30. By the last words is meant that their inopportune interference had furnished to Pharaoh a definite handle, as it were a weapon presented to him, wherewith to crush Israel. **22, 23.**] Thereupon Moses **returned to Jehovah**, i. e. sought Him with his old feeling of backwardness; returned to his work of deprecating the mission on which God had sent him. What had happened was not provided for in God's previous announcements to him, and was too much for his present faith. The re-

treated this people? why *is* it *that* thou hast sent me? 23
For since I came to Pharaoh to speak in thy name, he
hath done evil to this people; neither hast thou delivered
thy people at all. VI. 1 Then JEHOVAH said unto Moses,
Now shalt thou see what I will do to Pharaoh: for with a
strong hand shall he let them go, and with a strong hand
shall he drive them out of his land. 2 And God spake
unto Moses, and said unto him, I *am* JEHOVAH: 3 and I
appeared unto Abraham, unto Isaac, and unto Jacob, by

fusal of Pharaoh, and his coercion by signs and wonders, this was before him, but not the increase of the oppression at the very first endeavour.

VI. **1—8.**] *God replies to Moses.* **1.**] All this shall turn out, not to the greater affliction of Israel, but to the ultimate discomfiture of Pharaoh, and the high-handed deliverance of Israel. Compare ch. xii. 31—39. **2,** ff.] *God renews His commission and His self-revelation to Moses.* The occasion of this solemn inauguration of the mission of Moses and Aaron is taken to insert the genealogical notice of the heads of the houses of the tribes until Levi, from whom the descent of Moses and Aaron is given. The whole of this portion is remarkably illustrative of the fragmentary and compound character of this part of the history. This is still further shewn by what follows with regard to the Divine name. **2, 3.**] These verses have been the *crux* of interpreters. It may be well to put the reader in possession of the two principal views respecting them. Knobel, who adheres rigidly to the Elohistic and Jehovistic division of the narrative, writes as follows: The writer assumes three degrees of revelation and knowledge of God, confining himself naturally to Israel, and the line from Adam leading up from Israel to Adam. The first is the time before Abraham. To the patriarchs of this period God was only the Godhead generally: at that time He revealed Himself not to human knowledge with more distinctness than generally as the Godhead; men knew Him only as a higher Divine Being above themselves, without having any more accurate idea of Him. For this period the writer uses only the most general designation of God in the O. T., the name ELOHIM, *Godhead*, but never represents God as introducing Himself to men until the declaration "I am Elohim," and grounding any revelation on that appellation. The second step is the period from Abraham to Moses. To the patriarchs of this time God came nearer: He *appeared* to them, which He had not done before; He designated Himself to them as EL SHADDAI, the *Powerful*, the *Almighty*: they had not only a general idea of the Godhead, but knew God more definitely as the Mighty and Powerful One, compared with whom the Godheads imagined by others had no power. For this period the writer keeps in his narrative the designation ELOHIM: the name EL SHADDAI is found only in the mouth of God (Gen. xvii. 1; xxxv. 11; Exod. vi. 3) or in those of the patriarchs (Gen. xxviii. 3; xlviii. 3), who however also use ELOHIM (Gen. xxviii. 4; xxxix. 9; xl. 8; xli. 16, 25, 28, 32). Parallel with this are the Edomite speakers in the Book of Job, who belong to the pre-Mosaic period, and who use only the Divine names ELOAH, EL, and SHADDAI. The third step is the time after Moses. It was he who first learned, by Divine revelation, that God, who was known by the patriarchs before Abraham as the Godhead generally, and by the patriarchs since Abraham as the eminently mighty, was the only, or the alone true, God. To him God named Himself as JEHOVAH, *the Being*, the One only truly existent God, besides whom there is, there veritably exists, no other God (see on ch. iii. 14). Henceforth the writer uses for the most part this name of God. In his narrative, the advance of worship paid to God corresponds to the advance of knowledge of God. Before Abraham, it was only walking with God (Gen. v. 22, 24; vi. 9); after Abraham, circumcision and drink offering (Gen. xvii. 10, ff.; xxxv. 14); after Moses, sanctuary, priesthood, offering, festal times, formal purity, and generally, a detailed cultus. "It is," adds Knobel,

the name of [k]God Almighty, but by my name JEHOVAH
was I not known to them. 4 And I have also established
my [l]covenant with them, to give them the land of Canaan,
the land of their sojournings, wherein they sojourned. 5
And I have also heard the groaning of the children of
Israel, whom the Egyptians keep in bondage; and I have
remembered my covenant. 6 Wherefore say unto the
children of Israel, I *am* JEHOVAH, and I will bring you
out from under the burdens of the Egyptians, and I will
rid you out of their bondage, and I will redeem you with a
[m]stretched out arm, and with great judgments: 7 and I
will take you to me for a people, and I will be to you a
God: and ye shall know that I *am* JEHOVAH your God,
which bringeth you out from under the burdens of the
Egyptians. 8 And I will bring you in unto the land, con-

k EL SHADDAI. Gen. xvii. 1; xxviii. 3; xxxv. 11; xliii. 14; xlviii. 3; xlix. 25. Num. xxiv. 4, 16. Ruth i. 20, 21. Ps. lxviii. 14; xci. 1. Isa. xiii. 6. Ezek. i. 24; x. 5. Joel i. 15. Job, passim.

l Gen. xvii. 7, 8; xxvi. 3; xxxv. 12.

m Deut. iv. 34; v. 15; vii. 19, &c. 1 Kings viii. 42. 2 Kings xvii. 36. Ps. cxxxvi. 12. Jer. xxvii. 5, al.

"labour in vain to reduce into harmony with the clear and definite view of the Elohist, the Jehovistic narrations of the knowledge and worship of God in the pre-Mosaic period." Opposed to this view is that of those who maintain that the name JEHOVAH had been long in use, both in the period before Abraham and in that between Abraham and Moses, but that its full significance as *the* appellation of Israel's covenant-God was now first brought out. It is but fair to say here that Knobel's theory, as he states it above, can only be carried out by a considerable amount of arbitrary tampering with the Hebrew text, and that appearances, to the fair and unprejudiced reader, are certainly in favour of the other. The pre-Abrahamic patriarchs, the post-Abrahamic, knew the sacred name JEHOVAH as *an* appellation of God, but not as *the* appellation by which He chose to reveal Himself. Very much of Knobel's note is true: there were undoubtedly these steps in the revelation of the Godhead, to be followed by other and clearer revelations, as the Sun of Righteousness approached the eastern horizon; but as with those latter, so with these former, that which was one day to be clearly revealed was not totally unknown up to that day, but was known only in an imperfect and shadowy manner. This name JEHOVAH, little used, fallen perhaps into disuse (ch. iv. 31) in Israel, was from this time brought out in all its divine meaning, and made to be the One and ordinary name of the God of Israel. EL SHADDAI, see above in the extract from Knobel, is God the mighty, or, as otherwise explained, a reduplication of the idea of might, from *ool*, to be strong, and *Shadad*, to exert power; it is found only in the places mentioned in reff. with the exception of the whole of Job, where it is the usual appellation of God, occurring no less than 31 times. In Genesis (probably always, see on Gen. xlix. 25) and here only (besides Ezek. x. 25) is the EL expressed: elsewhere the name is simply SHADDAI. The appearance of God to *Isaac* by this name is not recorded in the history, but Isaac uses the name in blessing Jacob, Gen. xxviii. 3. **4.**] The covenant was established separately with each one of the three patriarchs: see reff. **5.**] God *remembered* His covenant, for it was made not only with the patriarchs themselves, but with their seed after them for ever. See especially Gen. xvii. 7, 19. **6.**] The promise of deliverance is here made more in detail, and the manner of it specified. This is the first occurrence of the expression **a stretched-out arm**, afterwards so frequent (reff.). **7.**] This is a renewal of the promise to Abraham and his seed after him, in Gen. xvii. 7. It was formally fulfilled in the declaration prescribed to Moses at Sinai, ch. xix. 5. **8.**] The continual repetition of the covenant promise in connexion with the name JEHOVAH marks forcibly the inauguration of that sacred name as the future appellation of the God of Israel.

cerning the which I did swear to give it to Abraham, to
Isaac, and to Jacob; and I will give it you for an herit-
age: I *am* JEHOVAH. 9 ¶ And Moses spake so unto the
children of Israel: but they hearkened not unto Moses for
[n] depression of spirit, and for cruel bondage. 10 And JE- n Num. xxi. 4. Job xxi. 4.
HOVAH spake unto Moses, saying, 11 Go in, speak unto
Pharaoh king of Egypt, that he let the children of Israel
go out of his land. 12 And Moses spake before JEHOVAH,
saying, Behold, the children of Israel have not hearkened
unto me; how then shall Pharaoh hear me, who *am* of
uncircumcised lips? 13 And JEHOVAH spake unto Moses
and unto Aaron, and gave them a charge unto the children
of Israel, and unto Pharaoh king of Egypt, to bring the
children of Israel out of the land of Egypt. 14 ¶ These
be the heads of their fathers' houses: The sons of Reuben

I did swear] Literally, lift up mine hand: see Gen. xiv. 22, reff. This oath is recorded in Gen. xxii. 16, ff.; see xxvi. 3.

9.] The words of the A. V. "*anguish of spirit*," if taken in the primitive meaning of anguish, from angustiæ, narrowness, exactly express the meaning of the original. But now *anguish* has lost this reference to *narrowness*, and simply implies *exceeding distress*. It is better therefore to take some expression which may more nearly represent the original. Kalisch has "*shortness of breath*," which is too material and has even a touch of absurdity. The best word which occurs is **depression**, implying some weight depressing.

11.] We have in this message again no trace of the three days' journey to sacrifice: it is a simple command to set the children of Israel free. So also in ch. vii. 2; xi. 10, being, as Knobel maintains, the uniform testimony of the original Elohistic narrative.

12.] Here again appears the characteristic backwardness of Moses. He replies **before Jehovah**, lit. **in the face of Jehovah**, shewing that a Divine appearance is recorded: so also in ver. 30. The expression **uncircumcised lips** is found only here and in the repetition, ver. 30. It must of course be taken figuratively, and according to the analogy of an *uncircumcised ear* (Jer. vi. 10), i. e. an ear not that cannot hear, but that will not hearken (ib. v. 21; Isa. vi. 10); an *uncircumcised heart* (Lev. xxvi. 41; Deut. x. 16; Jer. iv. 4; ix. 26), i. e. a heart slow to feel and to obey. The **uncircumcised lips** will thus mean lips, not, as some have thought, physically long and protruding, but slow to speak, and inapt, as in ch. iv. 10, 11. This natural infirmity of Moses again recurs as an excuse why he should not report God's command to Pharaoh.

13.] This verse again gives a general statement of the Divine command to Moses and Aaron, and apparently in connexion with vv. 26, 27; this introducing, and those closing, the genealogical table which leads to the identification of this Moses and Aaron. It seems far better thus to account for this verse than, as Knobel, to take it as a reply to Moses' question in ver. 12, by the association of Aaron with him.

14—27.] The genealogy of Moses and Aaron, following upon the solemn mention of the eminent brothers. It comes in contextually and appropriately, and those who have treated it as a fragment which has found its way into the text have certainly made a mistake. The genealogy mainly concerns Aaron, as the elder brother, and the progenitor of the Jewish priesthood.

14.] **the heads of their fathers' houses** are the chiefs of the families, e. g. the *sons* of Reuben, &c., enumerated below. The genealogical table begins with the families of the first-born son of Israel, then proceeds with those of the second, thus coming regularly to Levi the third, in the line of descent from whom are Aaron and

the firstborn of Israel; Hanoch, and Pallu, Hezron, and
Carmi: these *be* the families of Reuben. 15 And the sons
of Simeon; Jemuel, and Jamin, and Ohad, and Jachin, and
Zohar, and Shaul the son of a Canaanitish woman: these
are the families of Simeon. 16 ¶ And these *are* the names of
o Gen. x. 32; xxv. 13. the sons of Levi °according to their generations; Gershon,
and Kohath, and Merari: and the years of the life of Levi
were an hundred thirty and seven years. 17 ¶ The sons of
Gershon; Libni, and Shimi, according to their families.
18 And the sons of Kohath; Amram, and Izhar, and Hebron,
and Uzziel: and the years of the life of Kohath *were* an
hundred thirty and three years. 19 And the sons of
Merari; Mahali and Mushi: these *are* the families of Levi
according to their generations. 20 And Amram took him
Jochebed his father's sister to wife; and she bare him
Aaron and Moses: and the years of the life of Amram
were an hundred and thirty and seven years. 21 ¶ And
the sons of Izhar; Korah, and Nepheg, and Zithri. 22
And the sons of Uzziel; Mishael, and Elzaphan, and
Zithri. 23 And Aaron took him Elisheba, daughter of
Amminadab, sister of Naashon, to wife; and she bare him

Moses, for the sake of whom the table is inserted. **14—16.**] The sons of Reuben and of Simeon and of Levi are the same, and under the same names, as in Gen. xlvi. 9, 10, which see. Compare also Num. xxvi. 5; 1 Chron. v. 3; iv. 24; vi. 1, 16. After their enumeration the years of Levi's life are stated, besides the additional particular that the sons of Levi are to be given **according to their generations** or begettings (reff.). **17,** ff.] It is to be observed that no account is given in this genealogy at what age the sons in each case were begotten, and in consequence it is impossible by its means to arrive at any definite chronological conclusion as to the final result. I have dealt with the matter as far as the length of the sojourn of Israel in Egypt is concerned in the note on ch. xii. 40. These grandsons of Levi appear again Num. iii. 18—20. See also Num. xxvi. 57, ff. **20.**] Also definitely stated in Num. xxvi. 59. This kind of marriage was afterwards forbidden by the law: see Levit. xviii. 12. The LXX., Vulgate, and old Syriac in consequence make Jochebed to be Amram's cousin, "*the daughter of his father's brother,*" LXX. After the words **Aaron and Moses,** the LXX. and Samaritan Pentateuch add, "*and Miriam their sister,*" probably from Num. xxvi. 59. **21.**] Compare Num. xvi. 1; 1 Chron. vi. 37, 38. **22.**] Lev. x. 4; Num. iii. 20. No family of the third son, Hebron, is named here: but in Num. iii. 27; xxvi. 58, we read of "*the family of the Hebronites.*" See also 1 Chron. xxvi. 23, 30, 31, in which two last verses some names are mentioned. See more particulars concerning them in 1 Chron. xv. 9; xxiii. 19; xxiv. 23; xxvi. 31. **23.**] See Ruth iv. 19, 20; Matt. i. 4. **Naashon** was (Num. i. 7) prince of Judah during the journey through the wilderness. Thus Aaron, the third from Levi by the father's side, and the second by the mother's, wedded Elisheba, the fifth in descent from Judah. Such inequalities, startling at first sight, are not uncommon even now in families, and were doubtless of much more frequent occurrence at the period of this history. On **Nadab** and **Abihu,** see ch. xxiv. 1, 9; xxviii. 1; Lev.

Nadab, and Abihu, Eleazar, and Ithamar. 24 And the
sons of Korah; Assir, and Elkanah, and Abiasaph: these
are the families of the Korhites. 25 And Eleazar Aaron's
son took him *one* of the daughters of Putiel to wife; and
she bare him Phinehas: these *are* the heads of the fathers
of the Levites according to their families. 26 These *are*
that Aaron and Moses, to whom JEHOVAH said, Bring out
the children of Israel from the land of Egypt [p] according to their armies. 27 These *are* they which spake to Pharaoh king of Egypt, to bring out the children of Israel
from Egypt: these *are* that Moses and Aaron. 28 ¶ And
it came to pass on the day *when* JEHOVAH spake unto
Moses in the land of Egypt, 29 that the Lord spake unto
Moses, saying, I *am* JEHOVAH: speak thou unto Pharaoh
king of Egypt all that I say unto thee. 30 And Moses
said before JEHOVAH, Behold, I *am* of uncircumcised lips,
and how shall Pharaoh hearken unto me? VII. 1 And
JEHOVAH said unto Moses, See, I have made thee a god to

p ch. xii. 51. Num. i. 3, 52; ii. 3, 9, ff.; x. 14, 18, 22; xxxiii. 1. See ch. vii. 4; xii. 17, 41.

x. 1; Num. iii. 2—4; xxvi. 60, f.; on **Eleazar**, Num. iii. 32; xix. 3. He succeeded his father in the office of high priest, Num. xx. 26, 28, al.; was the colleague of Joshua in distributing Israel's inheritance in the land of promise, Josh. xiv. 1; xix. 51; xxi. 1; and survived Joshua, Josh. xxiv. 33.

Ithamar held office with his brethren as priest, ch. xxviii., was appointed to preside over the Levites in the work of the tabernacle, ch. xxxviii. 21; Num. iv. 28, 33, but is not elsewhere mentioned in the Pentateuch, but see 1 Chron. xxiv. 4—6. Eli the high priest was of the house of Ithamar (see on 1 Chron. xxiv. 2), and the high priesthood remained in this line till Solomon (1 Kings ii. 26, 27) thrust out Abiathar, and substituted Zadok of Eleazar's line. **24.**] On Korah and his sons, see Num. xxvi. 10, 11, from which it appears that, notwithstanding what is stated in Num. xvi. 32, 33, "*the children of Korah died not.*" **25.**] Nothing is known of **Putiel.** In the more modern Jewish traditions he is identified with Jethro the Midianite (!) see *Biblical Dict.*

Phinehas is frequently mentioned in the sacred history: see Num. xxv. 6, ff.; xxxi. 6; Josh. xxii. 13. He was high priest at the time of the outrage at Gibeah and the war against Benjamin, Judg. xx. 27, 28. There is a slight intimation in this verse of the age of the narrative. It was written after the birth of Phinehas, but probably before that of any more descendants of the direct priestly line.

26, 27.] The genealogy having now adduced all requisite particulars respecting the descent and families of Aaron and Moses, the history formally identifies them as the same Aaron and Moses who were commissioned to deliver Israel, and who spoke to Pharaoh in course of that their mission. Aaron stands first in the mention immediately following the genealogy. He was the elder, and the genealogy had mainly concerned him. But Moses stands first at end of ver. 27 when the history is about to be resumed, as officially by his mission the chief. On the expression, used of Israel, **according to their armies,** see reff. It is attributed by Knobel to the Elohist alone. **28—30.**] A taking up again and recapitulation of vv. 2, 11, 12.

VII. **1—7.**] *General declaration by God of His commission to Moses and Aaron, and summary of the history which is to follow.*

1.] God replies to the distrustful question of Moses by declaring the exact parts of himself and Aaron in that which He would do with them. The two brothers (see also ch. iv. 16) are to stand, as regards Pha-

Pharaoh: and Aaron thy brother shall be thy prophet.
2 Thou shalt speak all that I command thee: and Aaron
thy brother shall speak unto Pharaoh, that he send the
children of Israel out of his land. 3 And I will harden
Pharaoh's heart, and multiply my signs and my wonders
in the land of Egypt. 4 But Pharaoh shall not hearken
unto you, that I may lay my hand upon Egypt, and bring
q ch. vi. 26; xii. 41, 51. Num. i. 3; ii. 32. forth [q]mine armies, my people the children of Israel, out
of the land of Egypt by great judgments. 5 And the
Egyptians shall know that I *am* JEHOVAH, when I stretch
forth mine hand upon Egypt, and bring out the children
of Israel from among them. 6 And Moses and Aaron did
as JEHOVAH commanded them, so did they. 7 And Moses
was fourscore years old, and Aaron fourscore and three

raoh, in the relation in which God Himself and a prophet inspired by Him stand to His people. The one is to be the inspirer and commander of the other. And precisely so we find it in vv. 9, 19; ch. viii. 5, 16; but not beyond that. After that (e. g. in ch. viii. 20, ff.; ix. 1, ff., 10, ff., 22, ff., 29; x. 12, f., 21, f.) the wonders are done either immediately by the Divine act or through the intervention of Moses alone. **3.**] See on ch. iv. 21. **4.**] **lay my hand,** i. e. in a hostile manner, compare ch. iii. 20; ix. 3. **5.**] The Egyptians were to be convinced that Jehovah was the true God, by their own false gods falling before Him (ch. xii. 12): but this was a knowledge of discomfiture, not of conversion; Israel was by the same series of judgments to acquire the same knowledge (ch. x. 2); but this was to be a knowledge of conversion and attachment. God's sword is two-edged. **6.**] This verse contains the summary of the following history; and the next specifies the exact date in the lives of the two brothers at the time of the plagues and the Exodus.

VII. **8**—XII. **36.**] *The plagues of Egypt, and deliverance of Israel.* It would much exceed the limits of these notes to follow Knobel through his setting forth of the supposed Elohistic and Jehovistic portions of this narrative, and Keil through his refutation of the same. We may fairly say that, as usual in such cases, there has been exuberance of fancy and want of precision on the one side, Knobel having failed to make out his distinctions in several cases, both as to the historical and verbal differences between the two narrators: and on the other side the common, and to us unaccountable, timid anxiety to derive the whole narrative from one and the same pen at one and the same time. While we may not follow into all its particularities the Elohistic and Jehovistic theory, common sense and honesty cannot surely deny the coexistence in our present Exodus of various streams of narration, dropped and taken up alternately, the circumstantial assumptions of the one independent of those of the other. No discredit is thereby cast upon the entire history as we now have it, and the hypothesis of consequent incoherence in the whole can only be justified by the previous hypothesis of incapacity and want of intelligence in the ultimate author of the history. The authority and significance of the whole are much more effectually maintained by those who readily acknowledge the obvious phenomena of the compound text, than by those who in timid anxiety for the fate of a pre-conceived theory, employ page after page in fighting against them. This is strikingly shewn in the procedure of Keil, who in his zeal to shew the identity of the narrators of the various miracles, entirely sets aside the positive assertion of the sacred text in ch. ix. 22, 23 respecting the command being given to Moses, and the rod stretched forth by him,—saying that both had reference to Aaron, but that in consequence of the employment of Aaron's agency having been so many times related, it is not now specified. No such foe as the over-zealous advocate.

years old, when they spake unto Pharaoh. 8 ¶ And
JEHOVAH spake unto Moses and unto Aaron, saying, 9
When Pharaoh shall speak unto you, saying, Shew a
miracle for you: then thou shalt say unto Aaron, Take
thy rod, and cast *it* before Pharaoh, *and* it shall become a
serpent. 10 ¶ And Moses and Aaron went in unto Pha-
raoh, and they did so as JEHOVAH had commanded: and
Aaron cast down his rod before Pharaoh, and before his
servants, and it became a [r] serpent. 11 Then Pharaoh also [r] See note.
called the wise men and the sorcerers: now the magicians
of Egypt, they also did in like manner with their enchant-
ments. 12 For they cast down every man his rod, and
they became serpents: but Aaron's rod swallowed up their
rods. 13 And Pharaoh's heart was hardened, and he

8, 9.] God gives a preliminary direction as to a sign before Pharaoh, corresponding to, but on the face of the history independent of, the sign to be shewn to the people in ch. iv. 2, ff., 21. We may observe that whereas in those former places Moses was to shew the sign, now, in strict correspondence with the words of God in ver. 1, it is Aaron: and the rod, which in ch. iv. was that of Moses, is now that of Aaron, the text admitting no other interpretation. See below. **10—13.**] This direction is carried out. Here first we meet with the sorcerers of Egypt. Some of the commentators trouble themselves and their readers to prove that these were mere impostors or jugglers. But the sacred text evidently implies their genuineness as magicians, gifted with supernatural power. Nor does Scripture anywhere deny to the agents of the evil one the possession of supernatural gifts: see especially 2 Thess. ii. 9. These magicians, or Hierogrammateis, of Egypt, were of great fame. See on Gen. xli. 8; and for fuller particulars, Mr. Stuart Poole's careful and able article "Magicians" in the *Biblical Dict.* Tradition preserved the names of two of the principal of these Egyptian wise men, as *Jannes* and *Jambres*: see on 2 Tim. iii. 8. It is to be observed that the Hebrew word here used for **serpent** is not that used in ch. iv. 2, ff. (*nachash*, so Gen. iii. 1, and generally), but *tannin*, a *monster* (Gen. i. 21). See below on vv. 14—18. **12.**] The spirit of the narrative is not that the magicians' acts were imposture, and that of Moses and Aaron genuine, but that the two coincided up to a certain point, and after that the power of the magicians failed: compare ch. viii. 19. Even here the superiority of Jehovah is shewn by Aaron's rod, in its changed form as a serpent, swallowing up theirs. **14—25.**] *The plague of turning the Nile into blood.* It is hardly possible to resist the evidence of our having here two distinct forms of the narrative blended together. In the former Moses is alone. The command is given him to go and meet Pharaoh with the rod which was turned into a serpent (*nachash*, not *tannin*, as in vv. 10, 13), viz. that which he had in his hand, ch. iv. 2, ff. In the other (ver. 19) Moses is commanded to order Aaron to take his (Aaron's) rod, and stretch out his hand, &c. In the former it is the *river* which is to be smitten, in the other, all the waters in Egypt. In the former we have the object specified—the journey to serve God in the wilderness, which also appeared in the corresponding narrative, ch. iii. 18. Again, the narrative in ver. 20, with the hardly noticeable exception of the words "*Moses and Aaron*," joins naturally to vv. 14—18. The river only is mentioned, he (Moses) lifts up the rod; Pharaoh turns (from the meeting, ver. 15) to his house; the Egyptians obtain water by digging round about the river (ver. 24), which hardly agrees with ver. 19, nor could the magicians have done so with their enchantments, if all the waters in Egypt had previously become

hearkened not unto them; as JEHOVAH had said. 14 ¶ And
JEHOVAH said unto Moses, Pharaoh's heart is [s]stubborn, he
refuseth to let the people go. 15 Get thee unto Pharaoh
in the morning; lo, he goeth out unto the water; and
thou shalt stand by the river's brink against he come;
and the rod which was turned to a serpent shalt thou take
in thine hand. 16 And thou shalt say unto him, JEHOVAH
the God of the Hebrews hath sent me unto thee, saying,
Let my people go, that they may serve me in the wilder-
ness: and, behold, hitherto thou wouldest not hear. 17
Thus saith JEHOVAH, In this thou shalt know that I *am*
JEHOVAH: behold, I will smite with the rod that *is* in mine
hand upon the waters which *are* in the river, and they
shall be turned to blood. 18 And the fish that *is* in the
river shall die, and the river shall stink; and the Egypt-
ians shall [t]lothe to drink of the water of the river. 19 ¶
And JEHOVAH spake unto Moses, Say unto Aaron, Take
thy rod, and stretch out thine hand upon the waters of
Egypt, upon their streams, upon their rivers, and upon
their ponds, and upon all their pools of water, that they

s literally, *heavy*, ch. iv. 10 (twice); viii. 24; ix. 3, &c.; xvii. 12; xviii. 18. Prov. xxvii. 3, al.

t Isa. i. 14. Jer. vi. 11.

blood, as there would have been none left to operate upon. Take out ver. 19 (and the words "*and Aaron*," from ver. 20, but this is not necessary,—Moses and Aaron may well have carried out the command given to Moses alone), and all the narrative runs smoothly and continuously. But it requires a strong bias in favour of the unity of the history, to maintain that after a distinct command to Moses to go and meet Pharaoh, and a direction what to say to him, another new command to the two brothers, both covering a portion of the other, and extending beyond it, should be inserted between the utterance of and the obedience to that former order. **14.**] On the word which I have rendered **stubborn**, see reff. **15.**] Pharaoh perhaps went out each morning, or on some special day, to pay the accustomed honour to the Nile: see on ch. ii. 5. Some suppose it was to see how high the water had risen, it being in the time of the inundation; but if so, **the river's brink** would hardly be so definitely named. On the rest of the verse, see above. **16.**] See on ch. iii. 18. **18.**] The Nile abounded in all kinds of **fish**, enough not only for food in Egypt, but for considerable trade in exportation. See Num. xi. 5; Isa. xix. 8. **shall lothe** is a good paraphrase. The verb is literally shall **labour**, or **weary themselves** (reff.). The LXX. rendering, *shall not be able*, is not so good here, though it came to that: see vv. 21, 25. **19.**] On this verse as belonging to another form of the narrative, see above, and compare ver. 9, where the general command is given, of which this ordering of Aaron by Moses is an example. Knobel, in his anxiety to make the whole of this (vv. 19—25) the narrative of the Elohist, maintains that only the Nile and its derivative waters are intended in this verse. But surely, though by far the greater part of the water in Egypt is derived from this source, such an acceptation of the verse is impossible. There was both well and cistern water in Egypt. Besides the greater stores of water, even the lesser ones in vessels at home, whether stone troughs where they purified the Nile water with almond-paste, or wooden bowls for common use, should be turned into blood. To deny this, in anxiety to provide the magicians with water (ver. 22)

may become blood; and *that* there may be blood through-
out all the land of Egypt, both in *vessels of* wood, and in
vessels of stone. 20 And Moses and Aaron did so, as JE-
HOVAH commanded; and he lifted up the rod, and smote
the waters that *were* in the river, in the sight of Pharaoh,
and in the sight of his servants; and all the waters that
were in the river were turned to blood. 21 And the fish
that *was* in the river died; and the river stank, and the
Egyptians could not drink of the water of the river; and
the blood was throughout all the land of Egypt. 22 And
the magicians of Egypt did so with their enchantments:
and Pharaoh's heart was hardened, neither did he hearken
unto them; as JEHOVAH had said. 23 And Pharaoh
turned and went into his house, neither did he [u]set his [u] ch. ix. 21. 2 Sam. xiii. 20.
heart to this also. 24 And all the Egyptians digged
round about the river for water to drink; for they could
not drink of the water of the river. 25 And seven days
were fulfilled, after that JEHOVAH had smitten the river.
VIII. 1 And JEHOVAH spake unto Moses, Go unto Pha-
raoh, and say unto him, Thus saith JEHOVAH, Let my

is to deal unfairly with the text. The words "*vessels of*" are necessarily understood both times. **20.**] See above. Either (1.) The brothers carried out what God had commanded Moses alone; or (2.) The words **and Aaron** may have been the result of arranging the compound history. The latter would appear likely from what follows, for **he lifted** seems better to correspond to what went before than to ver. 19. Observe that, as in ver. 17, it is here **the waters that are in the river** which are smitten. **22.**] The magicians took water, not belonging strictly to the waters that were in the river, and by their arts turned it into blood. This again would hardly fit ver. 19. It has been suggested that they might have obtained water from the land of Goshen; but such matter is altogether outside the narrative, which says nothing here of what befell Israel. As far as it shews, they suffered as well as the Egyptians. We first read of the severance made between the two peoples in ch. viii. 22. **23.**] viz. from the interview commanded in ver. 15. On setting the heart, i. e. giving serious practical attention, see reff. **24.**] Here, again, it would seem, if all vessels and stores of water in Egypt had been filled with blood, that the resource here mentioned would have led to labour in vain; but if only the river were affected, the labour here described would have been worth their while. **25.**] This state of the river lasted a whole week. Or, perhaps, we are to connect these words with ch. viii. 1, and understand thence that seven days elapsed between the smiting of the river and the next speaking of Jehovah to Moses. That would, in fact, imply the same thing, as no remission of the plague is recorded. With the various rationalistic speculations as to a natural cause for this phenomenon, we have no concern. It is described in our narrative as supernaturally caused, by Divine command and for a special purpose. These speculations seem to have been peculiarly attractive in this instance, as even Keil indulges in them. A notice and summary refutation of them may be seen in Mr. Stuart Poole's article on the Plagues of Egypt in the *Biblical Dict.*

VIII. **1—15.**] *The second plague—of frogs.* We may observe that the same ap-

people go, that they may serve me. 2 And if thou refuse
to let *them* go, behold, I will smite all thy borders with
the [v]frogs: 3 and the river shall bring forth frogs abund-
antly, which shall go up and come into thine house, and
into thy bedchamber, and upon thy bed, and into the
house of thy servants, and upon thy people, and into thine
[w]ovens, and into thy kneading-troughs: 4 and the frogs
shall come up both on [x]thee, and upon [x]thy people, and
upon all [x]thy servants. 5 ¶ And JEHOVAH spake unto
Moses, Say unto Aaron, Stretch forth thine hand with thy
rod over the streams, over the rivers, and over the ponds,
and cause frogs to come up upon the land of Egypt. 6
And Aaron stretched out his hand over the waters of
Egypt; and the frogs came up, and covered the land of
Egypt. 7 And the magicians did so with their enchant-
ments, and brought up frogs upon the land of Egypt. 8
¶ Then Pharaoh called for Moses and Aaron, and said,
Intreat JEHOVAH, that he may take away the frogs from
me, and from my people; and I will let the people go,
that they may do sacrifice unto JEHOVAH. 9 And Moses
said unto Pharaoh, Glory over me: when shall I intreat

v here, and Ps. lxxviii. 45; cv. 30, only.

w Lev. ii. 4; vii. 9; xxvi. 26.

x vv. 9, 11, 21; ch. ix. 14; x. 6. See ver. 3.

parent intermingling of narratives occurs here as was before noticed on ch. vii. 19. First, Jehovah commands Moses to go to Pharaoh and announce the coming plague. There we have the infliction of the plague, preceded by a command to Moses to tell Aaron to stretch forth his rod, &c. **2.**] **the frogs**, viz. which always were present in myriads in Egypt, but were now to be multiplied into a plague. In the language of hieroglyphics, the figure of the frog signifies *multitude*. But this infliction is something totally distinct from the ordinary swarming of these animals in Egypt. Mr. Poole (as above) notices that this plague was peculiarly distressing to the Egyptians because the frog was among their sacred animals. Knobel adduces at considerable length the testimonies of travellers as to the swarming of frogs in Egypt. They are ordinarily kept under by the ibis and the stork. The month of their appearing is September, whereas this plague was evidently in the spring. **3, 4.**] They were to come both into all places and domestic vessels, and on the persons of all. In these kneading vessels and ovens would be prepared the king's own food, as in Gen. xl. 17. **5.**] See on ch. vii. 19. Here, as there, in the corresponding former narrative, the river only is mentioned; in the other, all the waters of Egypt. **7.**] Again we find some difficulty in imagining the course of incidents. If the general swarming of frogs had taken place and was going on, how could the magicians do the same? We are driven to suppose that the plague took place by paroxysms, day by day, or at some intervals: and that during some lull of the swarming the magicians had power to produce it. **8.**] The spirit of Pharaoh begins to be broken by the infliction. His magicians, it seems implied, could imitate but could not remove the plague. He sends for Moses and Aaron (so also ver. 25; ch. ix. 27; x. 16) to intercede with Jehovah that the plague may be removed.

9. Glory over me] The meaning of this somewhat difficult expression seems to be, that Moses recognizes in Pharaoh's request a confession of the power of Jehovah, and in order to make that power appear

for thee, and for thy servants, and for thy people, to de-
stroy the frogs from thee and thy houses, *that* they may
remain in the river only? 10 And he said, To morrow.
And he said, *Be it* according to thy word: that thou
mayest know that *there is* none like unto JEHOVAH our
God. 11 And the frogs shall depart from thee, and from
thy houses and from thy servants, and from thy people;
they shall remain in the river only. 12 And Moses and
Aaron went out from Pharaoh: and Moses cried unto
JEHOVAH because of the frogs which he had brought upon
Pharaoh. 13 And JEHOVAH did according to the word of
Moses; and the frogs died out of the houses, out of the
villages, and out of the fields. 14 And they gathered them
together upon heaps: and the land stank. 15 But when
Pharaoh saw that there was [y]respite, he hardened his y Esth. iv. 14.
heart, and hearkened not unto them; as JEHOVAH had
said. 16 ¶ And JEHOVAH said unto Moses, Say unto
Aaron, Stretch out thy rod, and smite the dust of the
land, that it may become gnats throughout all the land of
Egypt. 17 And they did so; for Aaron stretched out his
hand with his rod, and smote the dust of the earth, and

to him in its almightiness abases *himself*, as the advocate, to nothing in the presence of Pharaoh, his client—as much as to say, "Thou hast now taken the only and certain way for the removal of the plague: it is for thee to say *when*, and it shall be removed: I am only the doer of thy bidding with Him who is all powerful." The ancient versions do not give the word thus, but render it, "*Appoint a time to me.*" Modern Hebraists, however, with some slight modification of explanation, adopt the other rendering. So Knobel, Keil, Kalisch, &c. **The river** was the proper and accustomed place of the frogs. **10.**] By Pharaoh's saying To-morrow, the interview was probably at night. **12.**] **because of the frogs**, is literally, **because of the matter** (or war) **of the frogs. brought upon**] Literally, **appointed to. 13.**] In the words, **the houses, the villages, and the fields**, we have another form of expression from that in ver. 3, betokening perhaps an independent source. **14. upon heaps**] Literally, **heaps, heaps. 15. respite**] Literally, **breathing**, ref.

16—19.] *The third plague—of gnats.* Here the warning given on the two previous occasions, by sending Moses to Pharaoh, drops out, and we take up the narrative at the command to Moses to order Aaron to stretch out his rod: see on ch. vii. 19, and on ver. 5. **16.**] The fertile dark earth of the valley of the Nile was also one of the deities of Egypt; and this in its turn becomes changed into a plague to its worshippers. The word rendered *lice* by the A. V. (Kinnim) is, it seems confessed, to be interpreted **gnats** or **mosquitos.** The LXX., who are of considerable authority as writing in Egypt, render it thus, and Knobel and others give abundant extracts from travellers, and authors ancient and modern, to the same effect. **17.**] The same difficulty occurs as before, see on ver. 7, but can hardly be similarly met. The failure of the magicians in this instance is explained by Knobel to have been caused by the differing nature of the plague. The former wonders were only bringing forth, and changing into, things already existing, whereas this was a new creation. But surely there was just as

the gnats were in man, and in beast; all the dust of the
land became gnats throughout all the land of Egypt. 18
And the magicians did so with their enchantments to
bring forth gnats, but they could not: so there were gnats
upon man, and upon beast. 19 Then the magicians said
unto Pharaoh, This *is* the finger of God: and Pharaoh's
heart was hardened, and he hearkened not unto them; as
JEHOVAH had said. 20 ¶ And JEHOVAH said unto Moses,
Rise up early in the morning, and stand before Pharaoh;
lo, he cometh forth to the water; and say unto him, Thus
saith JEHOVAH, Let my people go, that they may serve
me. 21 Else, if thou wilt not let my people go, behold, I
will send the [z]swarm upon thee, and upon thy servants,
and upon thy people, and into thy houses: and the houses
of the Egyptians shall be full of the swarm, and also the
ground whereon they *are*. 22 And I will sever in that
day the land of Goshen, in which my people dwell, that
no swarm shall be there; to the end thou mayest know

z here, and Ps. lxxviii. 45; cv. 31, only. See ch. xii. 38. Neh. xiii. 3.

much a new creation in educing the swarms of frogs, or in bringing blood out of water. The reason of the failure is not given.

19.] The connexion of this verse has been somewhat obscured by our promiscuous use of the Divine names. The magicians do not acknowledge the plague as the work of Jehovah, Israel's God, but as a work of divine agency, of God in their own sense,—and not that of Moses and Aaron. What Moses and Aaron did, they could do: but this in which they had failed, was no work of men, but of God. So they disparage, instead of exalting, the agency of Moses and Aaron, and the result is that Pharaoh's heart is hardened. Compare the remarkable allusion to this answer in Isa. xix. 11, ff.

20—32.] *The fourth plague—of—?* (see below). In this case the commission of Moses to forewarn Pharaoh is related as in the two first plagues; but the subsequent account of the ordering of Aaron to perform the wonder is not given. It is in this case the act of Jehovah Himself, ver. 24. As in ch. vii. 15, Moses is to meet Pharaoh as he goes forth early to the water: see there.

21.] It is a difficult and apparently unanswerable question, of what this plague consisted. The Hebrew text has simply **swarms**, nothing being added to indicate of what the swarms were to be. Consequently very various conjectures have been made. *Flies* are perhaps the most probable, if one kind of animal only is to be understood, which from the context seems to be the case. The fly (Isa. vii. 18) was characteristic of Egypt, and is described by travellers as the greatest plague there even at this day, settling on the tender parts of the eyes and nose and irritating almost to madness both man and beast. The LXX., whose authority is great on Egyptian matters, render, "*the dog-fly*," upon which Jerome ventured an ingenious conjecture, changing one letter, that it should be, *a mixture of flies*, as A. V. in reff. Psalms. Kalisch supposed the swarm to have consisted of *beetles*, and gives travellers' descriptions of the swarms, and the destructive habits of those insects. In this uncertainty, I have thought it best to leave the literal Hebrew. The best supply perhaps would be "of insects;" but even then we should be foreclosing a matter which the text leaves open. **22.**] This is the first mention of a difference between Egypt and Israel in the matter of the plagues. There may have been before a personal and providential distinction. Now for the first time it is territorial. **22.**] Pharaoh was to be convinced, as Knobel well remarks—(1.)

that I *am* JEHOVAH in the midst of the earth. 23 And I
will put [a]redemption between my people and thy people : a Ps. cxi. 9; cxxx. 7. Isa. l. 2.
to morrow shall this sign be. 24 And JEHOVAH did so ; and
there came a grievous swarm into the house of Pharaoh, and
into his servants' houses, and into all the land of Egypt: the
land was corrupted by reason of the swarm. 25 ¶ And
Pharaoh called for Moses and for Aaron, and said, Go ye,
sacrifice to your God in the land. 26 And Moses said, It
is not meet so to do; for we shall sacrifice the abomination of the Egyptians to JEHOVAH our God: lo, shall we
sacrifice the abomination of the Egyptians before their
eyes, and will they not stone us? 27 We will go three
days' journey into the wilderness, and sacrifice to JEHOVAH
our God, as he shall command us. 28 And Pharaoh said,
I will let you go, that ye may sacrifice to JEHOVAH your
God in the wilderness; only ye shall not go very far
away: intreat for me. 29 And Moses said, Behold, I go
out from thee, and I will intreat JEHOVAH that the swarm
may depart from Pharaoh, from his servants, and from his
people, to morrow: but let not Pharaoh deal deceitfully
any more in not letting the people go to sacrifice to JEHOVAH. 30 And Moses went out from Pharaoh, and in-

That Israel's God was the inflicter of the plagues; (2.) That He had power over Egypt also; (3.) That He was everywhere the highest Power,—the only true God. **23.**] The word rendered *division* in the A. V. is acknowledged to bear no such meaning. In reff. it is redemption, and the verb from which it is derived is the ordinary word for *to redeem*. The *distinction* was in fact a redemption for Israel, only preliminary to that greater redemption at the Passover: and it might fairly be said to be placed *between them* and the Egyptians, who had it not.

24.] The swarm appears to have covered the face of the earth, and to have defiled everything. **25.**] See on ver. 8. This is a further step in the impression made on Pharaoh. He is ready to consent to the sacrifice, provided it is **in the land**, but has no idea of letting Israel go. **26.**] This objection of Moses is understood in two different ways. Some, with whom are Knobel and Kalisch, suppose it to mean that the children of Israel would have to sacrifice to Jehovah animals which it was not lawful in Egypt to kill, and to the killing of which death was attached as the penalty. The Egyptians held the cow, and in some parts the goat, sacred, and these animals could not be sacrificed as was the practice of Israel, without danger in Egypt. But others, among whom are Keil and Hengstenberg, suppose it to mean that the Israelites would not comply with the Egyptian rules about cleanness and fitness in the sacrificed animals, and so their sacrifices would be in the eyes of Egypt abominations. The former interpretation seems the more probable. **28.**] Pressed by the present plague, Pharaoh concedes the journey of three days into the wilderness. The concluding words are addressed to Moses and Aaron, and do not include the people. They are taken up again in vv. 29, 30.

29.] Moses had been once deceived (ver. 15), and therefore warns Pharaoh against repeating the treachery. Afterwards (ch. ix. 30) he becomes better accustomed to Pharaoh and his people.

treated JEHOVAH. 31 And JEHOVAH did according to the
word of Moses; and he removed the swarm from Pharaoh,
from his servants, and from his people; there remained
not one. 32 And Pharaoh hardened his heart at this time
also, neither would he let the people go. IX. 1 Then
JEHOVAH said unto Moses, Go in unto Pharaoh, and tell
him, Thus saith JEHOVAH the God of the Hebrews, Let
my people go, that they may serve me. 2 For if thou re-
fuse to let *them* go, and wilt hold them still, 3 behold, the
b Job xiii. 21; xxiii. 2. [b]hand of JEHOVAH is upon thy cattle which *is* in the field,
upon the horses, upon the asses, upon the camels, upon the
oxen, and upon the sheep: *there shall be* a very grievous
murrain. 4 And JEHOVAH shall sever between the cattle
of Israel and the cattle of Egypt: and there shall nothing
die of all *that is* the children's of Israel. 5 And JEHOVAH
appointed a set time, saying, To morrow JEHOVAH shall
do this thing in the land. 6 And JEHOVAH did that thing
on the morrow, and all the cattle of Egypt died: but of
the cattle of the children of Israel died not one. 7 And
Pharaoh sent, and, behold, there was not one of the cattle
of the Israelites dead. And the heart of Pharaoh was

IX. 1—7.] *The fifth plague — murrain* This narrative again belongs to the same class as ch. vii. 14—18; viii. 1—4, 20—24. The commission is given to Moses only: he is to go and speak to Pharaoh. In this case the narrative of the plague is confined to this narrator, and finds no place in the recital of the other. 3.] In the Hebrew, the words **a very grievous murrain** are in opposition with **the hand of Jehovah** above. The form which this adverse hand was to take was that of a heavy pestilence. Of the animals named, **horses** are uniformly associated with Egypt: see on Deut. xvii. 16, and compare Gen. xlvii. 17 and ch. xiv. 9, 23; xv. 1; **asses** as well as mules are found continually represented on the Egyptian monuments; **camels** are very seldom, if at all, thus found. See a conjecture on this in the note Gen. xii. 16. **Oxen** and **sheep** require no notice. See again Mr. Stuart Poole's interesting article on the Ten Plagues, *Biblical Dict.* 4.] See ch. viii. 22. Between this and the following verses it is to be understood that the message was delivered and had no effect on Pharaoh.

6.] The words **all the cattle of Egypt died** must not be literally understood, for in ver. 19, a portion of the same narrative as this (see on ver. 13), we find the cattle spoken of as still existing. Even the strictest of the literalists acknowledge this here, but find it convenient to ignore such acknowledgment in other places. By comparing ver. 25 with ch. x. 12 it is plain that we must take the general statements of the history with a very wide allowance. And in common fairness it must be observed, if this is undeniably the case in some cases where the history itself is its own witness, how can we justify resisting a similar wide understanding of the narrative in other cases? What right have we to deal with the word of God deceitfully, and to choose for ourselves when we shall fight for the letter, and when we shall give it up? 7.] The distinction was perhaps interpreted by Pharaoh as meaning that in this case the God of the Hebrews had prevailed; but there might be a reverse, and the Egyptian gods might hereafter get the advantage. He regards it as a mere contest of national

hardened, and he did not let the people go. 8 ¶ And
JEHOVAH said unto Moses and unto Aaron, Take to you
handfuls of [c]ashes of the [d]furnace, and let Moses sprinkle
it toward the heaven in the sight of Pharaoh. 9 And it
shall become small dust in all the land of Egypt, and
shall be a [e]boil breaking forth in [f]blisters upon man, and
upon beast, throughout all the land of Egypt. 10 And
they took [c]ashes of the furnace, and stood before Pharaoh;
and Moses sprinkled it up toward heaven; and it became
a boil breaking forth *with* blisters upon man, and upon
beast. 11 And the magicians could not [g]stand before Moses
because of the boils; for the boil was upon the magicians,
and upon all the Egyptians. 12 And JEHOVAH hardened
the heart of Pharaoh, and he hearkened not unto them;

c here only.
d Gen. xix. 28; ch. xix. 18, only.
e Levit. xiii. 18, &c. Deut. xxviii. 27, 35. 2 Kings xx. 7. Job ii. 7. Isa. xxxviii. 21, only.
f here only.
g Ps. cxlvii. 14. Prov. xxvii. 7. Dan. viii. 7.

deities. **8—12.**] *The sixth plague—boils and blisters.* This portion of the narrative, specifying the joint commission of Moses and Aaron, ranges with ch. vii. 8—13, 19—24; viii. 5—7, 16—19. Knobel thinks that in the original narrative this followed the plague of flies, viii. 16—19, and preceded the death of the first-born, ch. xii. 1, ff. In the progress of the history, we now come from the infliction of plagues on the comforts of life, and on possessions; to its incidence on the *persons* of the Egyptians. **8.**] The **furnace** appears to have been that for smelting metal (or perhaps for burning lime, in which case, as Bp. Wordsworth remarks, Egypt would be stricken through another of the sources of her pride; her pyramids and treasure cities having come out of the lime-kiln), and the ashes to have been the slack, or drossy soot, left or thrown out after use. It was to be sprinkled toward heaven, to indicate its dispersion through the air over all the land, as in ver. 22 the rod was to be stretched toward heaven, the quarter whence the hail was to come. Kalisch mentions a barbarous custom of burning human victims in certain cities of Egypt consecrated to the evil genius Typhon, and scattering their ashes in the air "in hope that with the dust the blessings of heaven would spread over the country." If this were so, it would at least give significance to the act here enjoined.
in the sight of Pharaoh implies another audience. It would appear from the other portion of the narrative that he might commonly be met going to the river in the morning (ch. vii. 15; viii. 20). **9.**] Various notices have been collected of dire eruptive diseases prevalent in Egypt; but they are no further to our present purpose than as shewing a predisposition in the climate and people to produce the miraculous effect here recorded. It will be observed that *beasts* are here mentioned, notwithstanding what is said in ver. 6: see there, and on ver. 19. **10.**] There seems to be here a transference of action from Aaron to Moses, which appears for the first time in this portion of the narrative. When the two act together, which they now do in taking the handfuls, Moses, as the more immediate representative of God, does the act of power without delegation to Aaron.
11.] The position of the magicians becomes more and more degraded. Not only are they powerless (ch. viii. 14), but they are themselves afflicted with the plague, and totally discomfited. On the form of expression, see reff. **12.**] Here for the first time we read that **Jehovah hardened the heart of Pharaoh.** Without going into the fanciful distinctions between this and the former expressions (ch. vii. 13; viii. 15, 19, 32; ver. 7), which some have discovered, we may say that it is at least implied that the very progress of the Divine judgments resulted in a corresponding insensibility to their purpose. God Himself was the agent in hardening Pharaoh's heart, inasmuch as the more he was afflicted the more he became stubborn and wilful in resistance.

as JEHOVAH had spoken unto Moses. 13 ¶ And JEHOVAH
said unto Moses, Rise up early in the morning, and stand
before Pharaoh, and say unto him, Thus saith JEHOVAH
the God of the Hebrews, Let my people go, that they
may serve me. 14 For I will at this time send all my
plagues upon thine heart, and upon thy servants, and
upon thy people; that thou mayest know that *there is*
none like me in all the earth. 15 For now I might stretch
out my hand, and smite thee and thy people with pesti-
lence; and thou shouldest be cut off from the earth. 16 But
† Heb. *made thee to stand.* in truth for this *cause* have I † spared thee, for to shew *in*
thee my power; and that my name may be declared
throughout all the earth. 17 As yet exaltest thou thyself
against my people, that thou wilt not let them go? 18
Behold, to morrow about this time I will cause it to rain
a very grievous hail, such as hath not been in Egypt since
the foundation thereof even until now. 19 Send therefore
now, *and* gather thy cattle, and all that thou hast in the
field; *for upon* every man and beast which shall be found

Observe that all ideas of a progress in the form of expression being consistently maintained, are erroneous; inasmuch as in ver. 35 we have again the former expression, simply, **the heart of Pharaoh was hardened.**

13—34.] *The seventh plague—hail.* Here again we meet with that portion of the narrative in which Moses alone receives the commission and acts upon it (see above, ch. vii. 14—18; viii. 1—4, 20—24; ix. 1—7). Here again we have no concurrence of the narratives, but all is confined to one narrator, known by Knobel, &c., as the Jehovist, or later supplementer. **13.**] In the same terms, Moses is commissioned in ch. vii. 15; viii. 20. It was the time when the king went to the river, perhaps for his devotions. **14. thine heart**] i. e. *thyself*: see Jer. iv. 18; also ib. ver. 10. On the combination here, see ch. viii. 4, reff. in the same narrative. The object of the plagues is to bring to Pharaoh and his people the knowledge of the supreme and exclusive Godhead of Jehovah. **15.**] God might have at once cut off Pharaoh and his people, but thus afflicted them short of destruction, to give an example of His power, and to declare His name upon earth. The rendering adopted for this verse is that approved by the principal Hebraists. St. Paul quotes this verse in Rom. ix. 17, with the Greek word signifying *have raised thee up*: see note there. Whichever sense we take, the meaning comes to the same. God's maintenance of Pharaoh was with a view to shew His mighty power, and to spread the knowledge of His name. Observe, that these threatening words serve for a general introduction to the three final plagues which follow. **17.**] This verse need not be interrogative: it is more naturally merely declarative: "Thou still exaltest thyself, &c. Well then, as a consequence of this," &c. But in English we express this meaning by the interrogative and the answer. **18.**] **since the foundation thereof** is expressed in ver. 24, **since it became a nation.** Thunderstorms, accompanied by hail, are not unknown in Egypt, but are of rare occurrence, and almost universally harmless. This their occasional and comparatively light character is implied by the description here. **19—21.**] See on vv. 6, 9. Observe, that there is here a command given which would put a distinction between those Egyptians who feared the threatening of Jehovah and those who set not their heart unto

in the field, and shall not be brought home, the hail shall
come down upon them, and they shall die. 20 He that
feared the word of JEHOVAH among the servants of Pha-
raoh made his servants and his cattle flee into the houses:
21 and he that [h]set not his heart unto the word of JE- h ch. vii. 23. 2 Sam. xiii. 26.
HOVAH left his servants and his cattle in the field. 22 ¶
And JEHOVAH said unto Moses, Stretch forth thine hand
toward heaven, that there may be hail in all the land of
Egypt, upon man, and upon beast, and upon every herb
of the field, throughout the land of Egypt. 23 And Moses
stretched forth his rod toward heaven: and JEHOVAH sent
[i]thunder and hail, and the fire came down upon the earth; i *voices*, see ch. xix. 16; xx. 18. Ps. xxix. 3, 9.
and JEHOVAH rained hail upon the land of Egypt. 24 So
there was hail, and fire [j]mingled with the hail, very j Ezek. i. 4.
grievous, such as there was none like it in all the land of
Egypt since it became a nation. 25 And the hail smote
throughout all the land of Egypt all that *was* in the field,
both man and beast; and the hail smote every herb of the
field, and brake every tree of the field. 26 Only in the land
of Goshen, where the children of Israel *were*, was there no
hail. 27 ¶ And Pharaoh sent, and called for Moses and
Aaron, and said unto them, I have sinned this time: JE-
HOVAH *is* righteous, and I and my people *are* the sinners.

it, i. e. regarded it not. On the expression *fearing the* word of the Lord, see Prov. xiii. 13. **22, ff.**] The morrow is come, and the threat is fulfilled. We have here, as before in ch. vii. 15, 17, the rod of Moses appointed and used as the instrument of inflicting the plague. In the other portion of the narrative it is Aaron who is to stretch forth the rod at the command of Moses: see ch. vii. (8, 9), 19; viii. 5, 16.
thunder] Literally, **voices**: see reff.
fire, i. e. lightning, **came towards, upon, the earth**. **24. fire mingled with the hail**] Some understand fire conglomerated into balls in the midst of the hail: the expression is **fire comprehending,** or **infolding itself,** as in ref. Ezek. The meaning may be lightning continuous, seeming like one mass of fire (so Knobel), or lightning flashing, infolding itself, among the hail.
25.] Here again the general language must be taken by the reader in a modified sense. For we find (ch. x. 12) that there was still left enough by the hail to make its demolition by the locusts a heavy plague. See remarks upon ver. 6. **26.**] This and the locusts are supernatural plagues, in the time of their incidence and their intensity only. Otherwise they keep the characteristics of ordinary occurrences, and amongst these is this, of partiality as to location of the thunderstorm: in Goshen there was none. **27—34.**] *The effect upon Pharaoh; the removal of the plague by intercession of Moses; Pharaoh's heart again hardened.* **27.**] Pharaoh's confession reaches further than before, even to the acknowledgment of personal guilt: Jehovah is in the right,—he and his people in the wrong. But it is only **this time**: he does not include the former times. It is a touch of nature in the narrative, that the spirit of Pharaoh is dismayed by the awful and to him unusual terrors of the thunderstorm. At such times even the bravest and hardest are frequently affrighted by an unaccount-

k Gen. xlv. 28. Num. xvi. 3. 28 Intreat JEHOVAH (for *it is* [k]enough) that there be no
more voices of God and hail; and I will let you go, and
ye shall stay no longer. 29 And Moses said unto him,
As soon as I am gone out of the city, I will spread abroad
my hands unto JEHOVAH; *and* the thunder shall cease,
neither shall there be any more hail; that thou mayest
know that the earth *is* JEHOVAH'S. 30 But as for thee and
thy servants, I know that ye will not yet fear JEHOVAH
God. 31 And the flax and the barley was smitten: for
the barley *was* in the ear, and the flax *was* bolled. 32 But
l Isa. xxviii. 25. Ezek. iv. 9, only. the wheat and the [l]spelt were not smitten: for they *were*
not grown up. 33 And Moses went out of the city from
Pharaoh, and spread abroad his hands unto JEHOVAH:
and the thunders and hail ceased, and the rain was not
poured upon the earth. 34 And when Pharaoh saw that
the rain and the hail and the thunders were ceased, he
sinned yet more, and hardened his heart, he and his serv-
ants. 35 And the heart of Pharaoh was hardened, neither
would he let the children of Israel go; as JEHOVAH had
spoken by Moses. X. 1 And JEHOVAH said unto Moses,
Go in unto Pharaoh: for I have hardened his heart, and
the heart of his servants, that I might shew these my
signs before him: 2 and that thou mayest tell in the ears

able panic. **28.**] On **it is enough**, see reff. The words **voices of God** should be preserved in the translation, as being alluded to by Moses below. **29.**] Moses was to pray when he got out of the city, perhaps to some holy place of prayer. We find him, in ch. vi. 12, ordered to go from the presence of God **in** to Pharaoh. Possibly this may have to do with the certainty of Pharaoh's knowledge that the earth is Jehovah's, that Moses could not pray in a city of the Egyptians, but in a place separate and dedicated to Jehovah. **30.**] Moses knows that notwithstanding this Pharaoh will *not* fear Jehovah Elohim, as God. He had spoken of the voices of God, it was true, but did not yet fully acknowledge Him who was God in truth. **31, 32.**] *Notice of the effects of the plague.* Barley becomes ripe in Egypt in March, and was generally cut in April. See on this as a chronological notice, on ch. xii. 1. Flax was much cultivated in Egypt; in fact, that country was the linen market of the ancient world (Kalisch). The flax was bolled or balled, had its little ball-like seed-vessels on it. The grain expressed in the A. V. by "*rie*" is agreed to be **spelt**, rye not being cultivated so far south. The Egyptians made bread of spelt.
not grown up] Literally, **were dark**, or were as yet nonapparent or but recently grown up.
33.] Recapitulates ver. 29, with the additional notice that the storm had been accompanied with pouring rain,—a marvel in Egypt. **34.**] **sinned yet more**, in allusion to his own confession, ver. 27, to which the addition of **his servants** also refers. **35.**] Knobel refers this verse, which seems to repeat the foregoing, to the other or Elohist's portion of the narrative, on account of expressions used only by him.
X. **1—20.**] *The eighth plague—the locusts.* This belongs to the same narrative as ch. ix. 13—34. **1, 2.**] We have the

of thy son, and of thy son's son, what things I have
[m]wrought in Egypt, and my signs which I have done [m] 1 Sam. vi. 6; xxxi. 4.
among them; that ye may know that I *am* JEHOVAH. Num. xxii. 29.
3 And Moses and Aaron came in unto Pharaoh, and said
unto him, Thus saith JEHOVAH God of the Hebrews, How
long wilt thou refuse to humble thyself before me? let
my people go, that they may serve me. 4 Else, if thou
refuse to let my people go, behold, to morrow will I bring
the locusts into thy border: 5 and they shall cover the
[n]face of the earth, that one cannot be able to see the earth: [n] Num. xi 7; xxii. 5, 11.
and they shall eat the residue of that which is escaped,
which remaineth unto you from the hail, and shall eat
every tree which groweth for you out of the field: 6 and
they shall fill thy houses, and the houses of all thy serv-
ants, and the houses of all the Egyptians; which neither
thy fathers, nor thy fathers' fathers have seen, since the
day that they were upon the earth unto this day. And
he turned himself, and went out from Pharaoh. 7 And
Pharaoh's servants said unto him, How long shall this [o] ch. xxiii. 33; xxxiv. 12.
man be a [o]snare unto us? let the men go, that they may Deut. vii. 16. Josh. xxiii. 13.
serve JEHOVAH their God: knowest thou not yet that Job xl. 24. Isa. viii. 14, al.

same end of God's dealings with Pharaoh specified, ch. iv. 21; vii. 5. See also, with reference to the similar effect on Pharaoh himself, ch. ix. 13—16. But we have here for the first time the far-reaching purpose announced, of the transmission by report of these Jehovah's wonderful dealings from generation to generation in Israel. As a sample of this transmission, see Ps. lxxviii. and cv. For **what things I have wrought in Egypt**, the LXX. have, "*how I have mocked the Egyptians*" (see 2nd and 3rd reff.), and the Vulgate, "*how many times I have afflicted the Egyptians.*" But the A. V. appears to be right. **3.**] Moses is commanded—Moses and Aaron obey. We may infer that the same was the case on the other occasions where it is not so specified, and thus the two narratives approximate. **that they may serve me**] viz. in the sacrifice in the wilderness: see ver. 7.

4.] On the locusts see below, note on vv. 14, 15. **5**] **the face,** literally, **the eye,** of the earth (see reff.), i. e. its appearance, its *outlook.* **6.**] **which,** i. e. **such locusts as:** see ver. 14. The A. V. has rendered the Hebrew literally, trusting to the context for a right understanding of the English sentence, in which the relative would properly apply to "*the houses.*" He, i. e. Moses, though Moses and Aaron were represented in ver. 3 as speaking jointly.

7.] Now for the first time the courtiers of Pharaoh are dismayed with the prospect of the coming ruin. It is minutely characteristic, that this happens on the threatening of the locusts: see below on vv. 14, 15.

a snare] A net or trap, to catch us for our ruin: see reff. **man** is not expressed in the Hebrew, so that the ancient versions have understood it, this matter: the LXX. render, "*How long shall this be a disgrace to us?*" and the Vulgate, "*How long shall we suffer this offence?*" But the A. V. is preferred by the Hebraists. **the men**] "They mean," says Knobel, "as is shewn by what follows, not the whole people, but the *men* only." Keil, on the other hand, says, *Ha-anoshim* means not the *men*, but the people. The courtiers wish for the dismission of the whole people, which Moses demanded; but Pharaoh, on the other hand,

Egypt is destroyed? 8 And Moses and Aaron were brought
again unto Pharaoh: and he said unto them, Go, serve
JEHOVAH your God: *but* who *are* they that shall go?
9 And Moses said, We will go with our young and with
our old, with our sons and with our daughters, with our
flocks and with our herds will we go; for we *must hold*
a feast unto JEHOVAH. 10 And he said unto them, Let
JEHOVAH be so with you, as I will let you go, and your
little ones: see, evil is in your purpose. 11 Not so: go
now ye *that are* men, and serve JEHOVAH; for that ye did
desire. And they were driven out from Pharaoh's pre-
sence. 12 ¶ And JEHOVAH said unto Moses, Stretch out
thine hand over the land of Egypt for the locusts, that
they may come up upon the land of Egypt, and eat every
herb of the land, *even* all that the hail hath left. 13 And
Moses stretched forth his rod over the land of Egypt, and
JEHOVAH brought an east wind upon the land all that
day, and all *that* night; *and* when it was morning, the
east wind brought the locusts. 14 And the locusts went

will only allow the dismission of the *men* (*Haggevarim*). And it would appear, from the absence of examples of the use of the former more general term for the male sex only, that Keil is right. **8.**] **who are they that shall go?** literally, **who and who (are) the goers?** **9.**] The law required only the presence of the males at the sacred feasts: see ch. xxiii. 17; xxxiv. 23; Deut. xvi. 16; but customarily all took part therein. Compare Deut. xvi. 11, 14; 1 Sam. i. 7; Luke ii. 41, ff. The women also took part in the religious pilgrimages of the Egyptians. **10.**] As much as to say, I only wish that the help of your God may be as likely to you as it is that I should give in to this request. **evil is in your purpose**] Literally, **is before you.** Pharaoh shews them that he suspects treacherous intent in their request. So Knobel, Keil, and Kalisch, after the LXX. and Vulgate. The other rendering, "*evil is before you*," i. e. "*you are in peril and seeking your ruin*," is that of the A. V. and various interpreters. The Targum of Onkelos unites both: "*see that the evil which you think to do stands against yourselves.*"

12—15.] *The performance of the threat.* Here again Moses is the sole agent.

locusts] It would exceed the limit of a note to cite the descriptions of travellers and residents in the East, in ancient and modern times, of the destructive ravages of these insects. One of the most terrible and graphic is that in the prophet Joel, i. 6—ii. 11. Others may be found in Mr. Houghton's art. in the *Biblical Dict.*, in Dr. Tristram's *Nat. Hist. of the Bible*, p. 306, and in Kalisch's notes here. In these, every particular of the account here is substantiated in the minutest manner. Only in the past years of 1868 and 1869 the N. of Palestine has been twice devastated by locusts in the manner here described.

12.] **all that the hail hath left:** see above on ch. ix. 6, 25. **13.**] We are told in the accounts above referred to that it is commonly the S.W. wind which brings the locusts to Egypt, from Libya. But the difference between this and an ordinary visitation was, the magnitude and universality of it (locusts commonly visiting only a circumscribed portion of land), and accordingly the east wind blows all day and all night, bringing the locusts from a more than usual distance, and in vaster quantities.

up over all the land of Egypt, and rested in all the
borders of Egypt: very grievous *were they;* before them
there were no such locusts as they, neither after them
shall be such. 15 For they covered the face of the
whole earth, so that the land was darkened; and they did
eat every herb of the land, and all the fruit of the trees
which the hail had left: and there remained not any
green thing in the trees, or in the herbs of the field,
through all the land of Egypt. 16 ¶ Then Pharaoh called
for Moses and Aaron in haste; and he said, I have sinned
against JEHOVAH your God, and against you. 17 Now
therefore forgive, I pray thee, my sin only this once, and
intreat JEHOVAH your God, that he may take away from
me this death only. 18 And he went out from Pharaoh,
and intreated JEHOVAH. 19 And JEHOVAH turned a mighty
strong wind of the sea, which took away the locusts, and
cast them into the Red sea; there remained not one locust
in all the borders of Egypt. 20 But JEHOVAH hardened
Pharaoh's heart, so that he would not let the children of

14.] On the latter part of the verse, compare Joel ii. 2. **15.**] The land was darkened, i. e. the face of the earth was covered with them: compare ver. 5. Some understand it that while flying, they obscured the light of the sun (Joel ii. 10), which is the testimony of travellers respecting their coming swarms; but on account of the immediately preceding words and of ver. 5, this does not seem so probable here.

16—20.] *The favourable but evanescent effect upon Pharaoh.* Now first Pharaoh hastens to send for Moses and Aaron; now first he becomes conscious, not only of offence generally, but of sin against Jehovah, and against Israel; but we may observe that whatever his penitent expressions may *imply*, there is this time no promise of granting the demand of Israel. The request to intercede for him is put more as a personal matter—he would bear anything but this one fatal infliction. His repentance is one of terror only. It has been superficially objected that the **wind of the sea** must have been written in Palestine, because there only can the west wind, which would take away the locusts into the Red Sea, be thus called. But to say nothing of the reply, that the Hebrew language, which grew up in the patriarchal sojourn in Palestine, would keep this term, just as an Italian in Holland would call the north wind a tramontane (Bp. Wordsworth), we must remember that it is a pure assumption that this was a *west* wind: a wind of the sea, coming from the N. W., would exactly do what is required, as the Red Sea is S. E. from Egypt. **the Red Sea**] Literally, **the Sea of Suph**, here first mentioned. There is considerable doubt to what the name *Suph* refers. It has generally been interpreted *sea-weed;* but this has been of late questioned, and Knobel, who has devoted some space to the inquiry (on ch. xiii. 18), inclines to think that the name means *reed*. He decides, however, against the idea that the sea was named merely from the fact of reeds existing on its banks, but believes, mainly on the ground of the absence of the article *ha* before *Suph*, that there must have been some town of that name, after which the Western arm was called. Knobel sees in the occurrence of some unusual terms, e. g. "*the children of Israel*" (as also in ch. ix. 35), for which this narrator usually has "*the people*," the "*darkening of the ground*," ver. 15, "*this death*," ver. 17, &c.,—the fact that "*every*

Israel go. [21] ¶ And JEHOVAH said unto Moses, Stretch
out thine hand toward heaven, that there may be darkness
over the land of Egypt, even darkness *which* may be felt.
[22] And Moses stretched forth his hand toward heaven;
and there was a thick darkness in all the land of Egypt
three days: [23] they saw not one another, neither rose any
from his place for three days: but all the children of
Israel had light in their dwellings. [24] ¶ And Pharaoh
called unto Moses, and said, Go ye, serve JEHOVAH; only
let your flocks and your herds be stayed: let your little
ones also go with you. [25] And Moses said, Thou must
give us also sacrifices and burnt offerings, that we may
sacrifice unto JEHOVAH our God. [26] Our cattle also shall
go with us; there shall not an hoof be left behind; for
thereof must we take to serve JEHOVAH our God; and we
know not with what we must serve JEHOVAH, until we
come thither. [27] ¶ But JEHOVAH hardened Pharaoh's

tree" is mentioned in ver. 5, and only "*the fruit of the trees*" in ver. 15, and that there is no mention in ver. 15 of the threatened visitation of the houses in ver. 6, that the "Jehovist" has probably taken ver. 12—20 word for word from some older source.

21—26.] *The ninth plague—darkness.* This follows without announcement or threat to Pharaoh, and without any act in his presence, differing thereby from the similarly unannounced plague of the boils in ch. ix. 8, ff., which was produced in Pharaoh's presence. This narrative also belongs to the "Jehovist" as the last. **21.**] The closing words of the verse have been interpreted in two ways—(1.) As A. V., with the LXX., Vulgate, Samaritan Pentateuch (not Version), and the majority of commentators, **and one shall feel, or handle the darkness**; it shall be so thick that it shall be like a palpable substance; (2.) With the Jerusalem Targum, Le Clerc, and others, *men shall grope in the darkness.* But the Hebraists object to this that the verb only means this in another *voice* from that used here. **22.**] **a thick darkness** is literally, **a blackness of darkness,** the doubling of the same word carrying the signification of intensity. **23.**] The natural phenomenon of which this miraculous darkness has been supposed to have been an intensification is shewn by Mr. Stuart Poole in the *Biblical Dict.* (art. "Plagues") to have had little or no correspondence with what is here described. Neither the simoom, with its sand-storms, nor the hot electrical wind called the Chamsin, produces actual darkness: the former lasts no more than a few minutes, and the latter is not thicker than a yellow fog. It is noticeable, however, that the LXX. seem to connect the plague with one of these, for they render in ver. 22 for **a thick darkness,** "*darkness and mist and tempest.*" By this distinction, now made sharper than ever, between the Egyptians and the Israelites, was clearly shewn the Divine wrath on the one, and the Divine favour on the other. **24—26.**] The immediate effect on Pharaoh. This time it is Moses alone who is sent for: see above ch. ix. 27, and x. 16. A progress is visible in the breaking down of Pharaoh's obstinacy; now he will allow all the people to go—only the flocks and herds are to be fixed, or stayed,—apparently as a pledge for their own return, for the king seems to have suspected treachery throughout. **26.**] **not an hoof,** i. e. not the most insignificant part of our flocks and herds. **27—29.**] But Pharaoh, confirmed in his suspicion and hardened in proportion to his resistance to

heart, and he would not let them go. 28 And Pharaoh
said unto him, Get thee from me, take heed to thyself,
see my face no more; for in *that* day thou seest my face
thou shalt die. 29 And Moses said, Thou hast spoken well,
I will see thy face again no more. XI. 1 And JEHOVAH
said unto Moses, Yet will I bring one plague *more* upon
Pharaoh, and upon Egypt; afterwards he will let you go
hence: when he shall let *you* go, he shall surely thrust
you out hence altogether. 2 Speak now in the ears of the
people, and let every man ask of his neighbour, and every
woman of her neighbour, jewels of silver, and jewels of
gold. 3 And JEHOVAH gave the people favour in the sight
of the Egyptians. Moreover the man Moses *was* very
great in the land of Egypt, in the sight of Pharaoh's serv-

the Divine will, withdraws his consent on this last condition being insisted on. More than this, he drives Moses from his presence, and threatens death to him if he ever enters it again. Moses accepts the condition, knowing that the last plague would work its own effect without a formal demand. On the comparison of this with ch. xi. 8, see below.

XI. **1—3.**] We have here an announcement of the tenth and final plague; directions connected with the departure of the people; and a notice of the estimation in which Moses was held in Egypt. The narrative is here curiously broken and intermingled. It seems hardly worth while, as even Knobel has done, to attempt to arrange the sections so as to fit one another. He supposes that our vv. 4—8 continue without break the narrative ch. x. 24—29, and that the words of Moses, v. 4, ff., followed during the same final interview with Pharaoh. But, considering that Pharaoh again sent for Moses and Aaron, ch. xii. 31, the continuity of the narrative is hardly preserved by this. It is better surely to take these final notices as general,—either undated, except by the context,—or as implying that in spite of the threat of Pharaoh and the declaration of Moses (x. 28, 29), other interviews did take place. The connecting notices in the text are too slender to build any consistent hypothesis upon. Of all which have been built, the most untenable is that of Bp. Wordsworth, that Moses "received a Divine message in Pharaoh's presence (a message, be it remembered, directed towards the people more than towards Pharaoh, and followed by a historical notice regarding its result), and proceeded to utter it" (which he did not, for the speech of Moses vv. 4—8 is entirely distinct from that message, and can only, with the most ingenious contrivance, be connected with the first clause of it). Equally futile is Kalisch's attempt to account for the place of the section by beginning it, "And the Lord had said. . . ." There is absolutely no difference between the original words here, and in the places referred to below.

1, 2.] This declaration and command fall, by their terms, into the period after the ninth and before the tenth plague. They are introduced by the same words as similar Divine intimations throughout the history: compare ch. iv. 21; vi. 1, 2, 10, 29; vii. 1, 14, 19; viii. 1, 5, 16, 20; ix. 1, 13, 22; x. 1, 12, 21; there is not the least intimation that they hold any other place than that which this analogy would assign them, viz. of one of the progressive revelations of God to Moses as to his course with regard to Pharaoh and the people. **2, 3.**] This had been foreshadowed by God in ch. iii. 21, 22, and we have the carrying out of it in ch. xii. 35, 36. On the substitution of **ask** for "*borrow*" of the A. V., see on ch. iii. 22. The notice of the greatness of Moses can neither be used *against* his authorship, as has been done by many, nor *for* it, as Bp. Wordsworth. The question is not, as he puts it, between what Moses himself would have written,

ants, and in the sight of the people. 4 And Moses said,
Thus saith JEHOVAH, About midnight will I go out into the
midst of Egypt: 5 and all the firstborn in the land of
Egypt shall die, from the firstborn of Pharaoh that sitteth
upon his throne, even unto the firstborn of the maidserv-
ant that *is* behind the mill; and all the firstborn of beasts.
6 And there shall be a great cry throughout all the land
of Egypt, such as there was none like it, nor shall be like
it any more. 7 But against any of the children of Israel
shall not a dog move his tongue, against man or beast:
that ye may know how that JEHOVAH doth put a differ-
ence between the Egyptians and Israel. 8 And all these
thy servants shall come down unto me, and bow down
themselves unto me, saying, Get thee out, and all the
p Deut. xi. 6; Judg. viii. 5. people that [p]follow thee: and after that I will go out.

and what "a forger" would have written. By putting the dilemma thus, the real alternative of some one other than Moses, and yet *not a forger*, is adroitly kept out of sight. **4—8.**] *Announcement by Moses of the last great plague.* We have no notice here when and to whom Moses made this. But from ver. 8 it was manifestly to Pharaoh, and in his presence. From what has been said above, we can hardly suppose it to have been at the same interview as that which ended at ch. x. 29: see the previous note. **about midnight**] *What* midnight is not specified, nor I conceive can we go into such accurate detail with the fragmentary history as to reason with Keil upon the interposition of the ordinance of the passover, and at least 4 days: see ch. xii. 3, ff. We do not know whether this announcement may not have been made on the very evening preceding the Exodus. The notice of ch. xii. 1 is in its very terms indefinite as to time: see there. The anthropomorphical expression, **I will go out into the midst of Egypt,** is reproduced in ch. xii. 12, in the form **I will pass through the land of Egypt.** The figure is not uncommon in the O. T.

The **mill** consisted of two stones placed on the ground, the upper one turned by two women sitting face to face, both holding the handle: see Matt. xxiv. 41, the *Land and the Book*, pp. 526-7, and Mr. Wright's art. "Mills" in *Biblical Dict.* The distinctive sense of *behind* the mill has not been explained; the LXX. and the Vulgate render "*at* the mill," "*by* the mill." The **firstborn** enjoyed throughout the East great and exclusive privileges: compare the history of Esau and Jacob, and see Gen. xlix. 3, and the legal provision of Deut. xxi. 16. Compare also ch. iv. 23. **6.**] **such as,** literally, **which,** as in ch. ix. 18. **7.**] The same proverbial expression of **not a dog moving his tongue** is found Josh. x. 21; Judith xi. 19. On the difference put between the Egyptians and Israel, see ch. viii. 23; ix. 4. **8.**] This announcement was doubtless fulfilled when, ch. xii. 33, the Egyptians urged the people to depart; but from ch. xii. 31 it was Pharaoh himself who sent for Moses and Aaron, and urged them to get them forth and their people. Knobel adduces the similar instance of difference in detail between ch. iii. 18 and v. 1. **shall come down**] This phrase is used, according to Knobel, because the king's palace is conceived as standing on a greater elevation than ordinary dwellings; Kalisch, however, denies this, and refers it to the Hebrew idiom, whereby going from a higher place in dignity to a lower is thus expressed. The two come virtually to the same. **that follow thee,** literally, **are at thy feet:** see reff. The notice, that Moses **went out from Pharaoh in a great anger,** literally, **a heat of anger,** though it might be joined

And he went out from Pharaoh in a great anger.
9 And JEHOVAH said unto Moses, Pharaoh shall not
hearken unto you; that my wonders may be multi-
plied in the land of Egypt. 10 And Moses and Aaron did
all these wonders before Pharaoh: and JEHOVAH hardened
Pharaoh's heart, so that he would not let the children of
Israel go out of his land. XII. 1 And JEHOVAH spake
unto Moses and Aaron in the land of Egypt, saying, 2
This month *shall be* unto you the beginning of months: it
shall be the first month of the year to you. 3 ¶ Speak ye
unto all the congregation of Israel, saying, In the tenth
day of this month they shall take to them every man a
lamb, [q]according to the [r]house of *their* fathers, a lamb for

[q] ch. vi. 11. 2 Chron. xxv. 5; xxxv. 12.
[r] Gen. vii. 1; xxx. 30. Prov. xxxi. 15.

not unnaturally to ch. x. 29, yet does not seem the most appropriate phrase to describe the calm acceptance of Pharaoh's threat there related. The anger *may have been there* when he spoke, ch. x. 29, but it was *latent*, not in a fury, as here. **9.**] A general notice, how Jehovah revealed to Moses the fruitlessness of all his words to move the stubborn heart of Pharaoh. If it belongs specially to this particular time in the history, the multiplication of the wonders refers to the two greatest which followed, viz. the death of the firstborn, and the overthrow of Pharaoh's host in the Red Sea. But it, like the following notice, may perhaps be general, and not to be confined to this particular time. **10.**] A general notice of God's wonders done by His commissioned servants, and Pharaoh's hardness of heart, before the great concluding catastrophe, which is also introduced by the first enjoined ordinance of Israel's new life, ch. xii. 1—28. It is impossible to read the conclusion of this chapter without being reminded of the very similar ending of the chapter in St. John (xii.) which precedes the narrative of the great Passover itself: compare especially John xii. 37, "*Although he had done all these miracles before them, yet believed they not on Him*,"—in words almost the reproduction of those used here.

XII. **1—28.**] *The ordinance of the Passover.* The deliverance from Egypt was as it were the birthday of Israel as God's special people (see ch. vi. 6, 7, and compare the imagery of Hosea ii. and Ezek. xvi.). The great ordinance therefore which was to introduce and celebrate this deliverance was instituted *in Egypt itself.* Hence the mention of this in ver. 1; hence the appointed beginning of the year with the month of the Exodus. In the passage 1—28, 1—14 contains the Lord's command for the institution of the Passover; 15—20, the same for the feast of unleavened bread; 21—28, the delivery of the command respecting the passover to Israel by Moses. **1.**] This portion of the law given in Egypt is introductory to the main body, given in Sinai and in the plains of Moab. **2. This month**] viz. the month then present; in the writing ascribed by Knobel and others to the original (Elohistic) writer, always known as the *first month* (ch. xl. 2, 17; Lev. xxiii. 5; Num. ix. 1; xxviii. 16; xxxiii. 3): in the supplementary portions as the month of *Abib*, i. e. the month of ears, when the corn comes into ear (ch. xiii. 4; xxiii. 15; xxxiv. 18; Deut. xvi. 1). After the captivity it was known as Nisan (Neh. ii. 1; Esth. iii. 7). It very nearly coincides with our April. From this time the Jews appear to have had two beginnings of the year; according to the *sacred* reckoning, with the month Abib, the "*first* month;" according to the *civil* reckoning, with the month Tisri, the seventh month. See on all the minutiæ of these reckonings Mr. Stuart Poole's articles "Chronology" and "Year," in the *Biblical Dict.* **3.**] The **congregation** were to be addressed through their *elders*: see ver. 21. **every man a lamb** is afterwards explained in detail to mean one for a family or

an house: 4 and if the household be too little for the lamb,
let him and his neighbour next unto his house take *it* ac-
s ch. xvi. 16. cording to the number of the souls; every man [s]according
to his eating shall make your count for the lamb. 5 Your
lamb shall be without blemish, a male of a year old: ye
shall take *it* out from the sheep, or from the goats: 6 and
ye shall keep it up until the fourteenth day of the same
month: and the whole assembly of the congregation of

a combination of families: see below. **according to the house of their fathers**] See reff.: in the repetition of this command, ver. 21, it is, **according to your families**, lit. **generations.** The meaning is that the passover-companies were not to be promiscuously composed, but to consist each of one family, or (ver. 4) compounded of two families, or even of more, as would appear if the last clause of ver. 4 were followed out. The ordinary number fixed among the Jews was *ten*. That this number was not strictly adhered to appears from our Lord's last Passover, in which He sat down with the Twelve, Matt. xxvi. 23. At this first institution all apparently were to partake. When the laws of cleanness and uncleanness were introduced, the legally unclean were to postpone it for a month: see Num. ix. 9—11.

5. without blemish] See on 1 Pet. i. 19, and note, John i. 29. Every offering to God was to be unblemished, Lev. xxii. 19, ff. **a male**] So with all animals offered in burnt-offering, Lev. i. 3, 10.

of a year old] Literally, son of a year, which expression is always used of one who has completed the portion of time named. So Isaac is a son of eight days (Gen. xxi. 4) when circumcised (see Lev. xxi. 3); in Lev. xxvii. 5—7 the expression is five times used, and each time as signifying the completion of the five years, twenty years, &c. So in ch. xxx. 14; Num. i. 3, and elsewhere. Jonah's gourd was "*son of the night*" when it had grown the night through, Jonah iv. 10. So that "*of the first year*" (A. V.) is hardly accurate. The time is fixed as being that of perfected symmetry and full vigour.

or from the goats] This alternative does not seem to have been allowed by Jewish tradition, which permitted the lamb only to be offered. Knobel and Ewald imagine, led by Deut. xvi. 2; 2 Chron. xxx. 24; xxxv. 7, that subsequently bullocks also were offered at the passover. But in Deut. xvi. 2 "thy flock and thy herd" seems only a general formula, and in Chron. it is not implied that the bullocks were for the passover offering. **6.**] The **four days keeping up** has been by some supposed to have reference to the *four generations* (Gen. xv. 16) during which Israel had been "kept up" in Egypt preparatory to becoming God's special people. Others think that it was to allow time for Israel to think of and converse of God's mercies to them in their deliverance; but this fails to give any account of the four days. **in the evening**] See margin. The interpretations of the obscure phrase are various. I give them from Kalisch's report. (1.) The Targum of Onkelos has "*between the two suns*," which in Talmudical language is said to mean between sunset and the time when the sun's light disappears in the west, and to include about an hour and twenty minutes. So also the Karaite Jews, the Samaritans, and the Arabians. (2.) Kimchi and other Jewish interpreters explain it, between the full westering of the sun, i. e. the beginning of the lengthening of the shadows, to his disappearance. Against this Kalisch quotes (but?) Deut. xvi. 6, where it is commanded to kill the passover "*at even, at the going down of the sun*," and objects that the words here cannot apply to the *afternoon*. (3.) Still less admissible is the view that the former evening began with the *first* westering of the sun at noon. This is refuted by ch. xxix. 39, 41, where this same expression is used of the time of evening sacrifice, which cannot have been at noon. (4.) The traditionally accepted time, acted upon in the temple service, was between about 3 p. m., when the heat begins to decrease, till sunset; or, as described by Josephus (B. J. vi. 9, 3), from the ninth to the eleventh hour. And this seems the most probable,

Israel shall kill it †in the evening. 7 And they shall † Heb. *between the two evenings.*
take of the blood, and strike *it* on the two side posts and
on the upper door post of the houses, wherein they shall
eat it. 8 And they shall eat the flesh in that night,
roast with fire, and unleavened bread; *and* with t bitter t Lam. iii. 15.
herbs they shall eat it. 9 Eat not of it raw, nor sodden at
all with water, but roast *with* fire; his head with his legs,
and with the purtenance thereof. 10 And ye shall let no-
thing of it remain until the morning; and that which re-

though it may have arisen not so much out of an interpretation of the words in the text as out of a necessary extension of the time when so large a number of victims had all to be slain in the temple. Hitzig holds that the two evenings are the periods immediately preceding and following sunset, and between the two evenings, the precise moment of sunset. And certainly this derives some support from Deut. xvi. 6, though practically obedience to it would have been impossible, even at the first institution. See this further illustrated in note to Matt. xxvi. 17—19, and Rev. S. Clark's article on "Passover" in the *Biblical Dict.* **the whole assembly**] Not that it was to be killed *in assembly*, but in each house. The words set forth the generality of the obligation. Afterwards, the Levites killed it for the people, see 2 Chron. xxx. 17 (though ver. 15 leaves it undecided as to the generality of the people); xxxv. 3—11; Ezra vi. 20. **7.**] The regular practice under the law was to sprinkle the altar with the blood of the offering, Lev. i. 5; iv. 5. But in Egypt, where there was no tabernacle and no altar, each house was the place of offering, and was treated as an altar. Of houses as well as of cities, the door, or gate, was the representative part: see ch. xx. 10; Deut. v. 14; xii. 17, &c. The door consisted of lintel, posts, and threshold. Of these the two former only were to be sprinkled, as the blood on the threshold would be liable to be trodden underfoot (Keil). The sprinkling was significant of atonement and cleansing from sin, for it was to be performed (ver. 22) with hyssop, invariably used in the law when cleansing from sin was symbolized, Lev. xiv. 49, ff.; Num. xix. 18, f. **they shall take**, i. e. the father of each household where the passover was eaten. Very early this part of the duty began to fall away: we find in Deut. xvi. 5 the concentration to the place of the tabernacle, and by inference to the ministers of the tabernacle, already begun. When this was so, the sprinkling of the doors could no longer be carried out.

8, 9.] **in that night**, viz. the night between the 14th and the 15th of the month.

roast with fire] The passover lamb was to be roast with fire, apparently that the analogy between it and the burnt-offering might be as far as possible complete. In ordinary sacrifices the *part offered* to the Lord was consumed by fire; the portion of the offerers was boiled (1 Sam. ii. 13, ff.: see also ch. xxix. 31; Lev. vi. 21; viii. 31; Num. vi. 19; Ezek. xlvi. 20, 24; Zech. xiv. 21). In burnt-offerings all the flesh was burnt (Lev. i. 9); and in the passover, the entireness of the lamb was of the very essence of the ordinance, symbolizing the community of God's people in the one body: compare 1 Cor. v. 7; x. 17, and the carrying out of the same symbolism with regard to the crucified body of the Lord, the real Paschal Lamb, John xix. 33, ff. **unleavened bread** was to be eaten with it, leaven (see below) being generated of corruption, and so symbolic of decay and foulness: subsequently in the law, this prescription of unleavenedness was extended over all offerings of a cereal character: see Lev. ii. 11.

with (literally, **upon**) **bitter herbs** (literally, **bitternesses**, see ref.). These are variously interpreted as wild lettuce, endive, chicory; and it seems agreed that the bitterness as the foundation of the meal symbolized the bondage of Egypt, *upon* which supervened the Lord's deliverance, represented by the passover. **9.**] See above. **10.**] This same rule, that nothing was to be left over the day of offering, was enacted respecting the sacrifice of peace-offerings (Lev. vii. 15), and of sin-offer-

maineth of it until the morning ye shall burn with fire.
11 ¶ And thus shall ye eat it; *with* your [u]loins girded,
your [v]shoes on your feet, and your [w]staff in your hand;
and ye shall eat it in [x]haste: it *is* a passover unto JE-
HOVAH. 12 For I will pass through the land of Egypt in
that night, and will smite all the firstborn in the land of
Egypt, both man and beast; and against all the gods of
Egypt I will execute judgment: I *am* JEHOVAH. 13 And
the blood shall be to you for a token upon the houses
where ye *are*: and when I see the blood, I will pass over
you, and the plague shall not be upon you for destruction,
when I smite the land of Egypt. 14 And this day shall

u 1 Kings xviii. 46. 2 Kings iv. 29.
v Josh. ix. 5,13. Acts xii. 8.
w Gen. xxxii. 10. 2 Kings iv. 29. Mark vi. 8.
x Deut. xx. 3. 2 Kings vii. 15. Ps. xxxi. 22.

ings (ib. iv. 12, 20, 21). **11.**] It is obvious that this injunction as to the manner of eating the Passover applied only to the first time of its celebration in Egypt. The **loins** were to be girded—the long loose robes bound up round the waist; the **sandals on the feet,** as was the custom when a long or rough journey was to be undertaken; the **staff in the hand,** betokening the same purpose; and it was to be eaten **in haste,** literally, in trepidation or anxiety, see reff., as the occasion was fearful and urgent. **it is a passover unto Jehovah**] The word *pesach* here first occurring, it will be well to give an account of it. The following is mainly taken from Keil: "The word *pesach* comes from *pasach*, properly *to spring* or *to hop*, from which meaning two significations are derived—(1.) to *limp* or *be lame, halt*, 1 Kings xviii. 21; 2 Sam. iv. 4, al.; (2.) To *pass over*, mostly used figuratively in the sense of to *spare;* and so here, vv. 13, 23, 27, of the *passing* of the angel of destruction *over* the door sprinkled with blood. Hence the word *pesach* came into use,—for the *lamb* itself, the instrument whereby the passing over was insured, so vv. 21, 27; 2 Chron. xxxv. 1, 13, al.,—for the *preparation* of the lamb by Divine ordinance for the feast, or the *celebration* of the feast itself, so ver. 11 (this place); Lev. xxiii. 5; Num. ix. 6, al.; and lastly, it was transferred to the whole seven days of the feast of unleavened bread, which began with the passover meal, Deut. xvi. 1—8, and to the offerings brought during that period, Deut. xvi. 2; 2 Chron. xxxv. 1, 7." **12, 13.**] *Explanation of the name pesach or passover.* **in that night**] "*This* night" of the A. V. is not a necessary rendering, and does not agree with the facts, for the words were spoken before the tenth day of the month, and the night was that of the fourteenth. The same Hebrew words are rendered **in that night,** ver. 8. It is very doubtful what is intended by the **judgment against all the gods of Egypt.** In Num. xxxiii. 4, the words are repeated, and connected with the burying of the first-born. Hence it has been supposed that the destruction of the first-born is meant by the phrase, seeing that among them would be many animals worshipped by the Egyptians. Calvin supposes that the judgment would consist in the demonstration of the worthlessness of the help and guardianship of Egypt's gods. But it must be confessed that both these explanations fall short of any satisfactory elucidation of the words. The Pseudo-Jonathan gives a perhaps more likely interpretation, when he refers it to a destruction of the images of Egypt's gods: "*the molten images shall liquefy, those of stone shall be smitten in pieces, those of earth be broken up, those of wood shall be burnt to ashes:*" compare 1 Sam. v. 3, f. We have very similar denunciations in Isa. xix. 1; Jer. xliii. 13; xlvi. 25; Ezek. xxx. 13, in three of which places is a distinct reference to the destruction of the *images*. But if this is meant, there is of course far more beneath it: the gods of Egypt are demoniac powers, and Jehovah's discomfiture of them, beginning with the failure of the magicians, was to be consummated this final night. **13.**] On the words, **I will pass over you**, see above. **14.**] That day,—the fourteenth of Abib,—

be unto you for a memorial; and ye shall keep it a feast
to JEHOVAH throughout your generations; ye shall keep
it a feast by an ordinance for ever. 15 Seven days shall
ye eat unleavened bread; even the first day ye shall put
away leaven out of your houses: for whosoever eateth
anything leavened from the first day until the seventh
day, that soul shall be cut off from Israel. 16 And in the
first day *there shall be* an [y]holy convocation, and in the
seventh day there shall be an [y]holy convocation to you; no
manner of work shall be done in them, save *that* which
every man must eat, that only may be done of you. 17
And ye shall observe *the feast of* unleavened bread; for in
this selfsame day have I brought your armies out of the
land of Egypt: therefore shall ye observe this day in your

y Levit. xxiii. 2, 3, 4, 7, 8, 24, 27, 35, 36, 37. Num. xxviii. 18, 25, 26; xxix. 1, 7, 12.

was to Israel (see above) the birthday of new life unto JEHOVAH, therefore its celebration had for him an everlasting significance. And now that the true Israel is brought in, and the real Passover sacrificed, the significance has not ended. There is no more any sanctity of times and seasons (Col. ii. 16, 17), but the great deliverance of humanity effected in our Passover is for us also an everlasting celebration.

15—20.] *Prescriptions for the seven days' feast of unleavened bread, to follow the celebration of the passover.* There is some difficulty about the *place* of these directions. Either they were not actually given till after the Exodus, or the second clause of ver. 17 is spoken by anticipation, of God's purpose as a thing accomplished. The question must be regarded in combination with the declaration of our vv. 34, 39, which assign a pragmatic reason for Israel's bread being unleavened during the days following the passover. See also on ver. 21. This being so, it seems to me that we have no resource but to suppose that these directions (vv. 15—20) were given after the Exodus, but have been in the arrangement of the history inserted here, to relate at once the complete institution of the passover ordinance. So Kalisch and Keil. Indeed, the narrative itself leads to the same conclusion, for the general formal terms of ver. 18, **In the first month, on the fourteenth day of the month,** do not correspond with the purely occasional wording of vv. 2, 3, **this** month, the tenth day of **this** month. And the command to put away leaven out of the houses looks like a subsequent command to that in ver. 8, which would follow as matter of course on it if a synchronous part of the same command.

15.] There is some little uncertainty left here as to the precise time of the prescribed absence of the leaven from the houses. From all that has been said on the subject it would appear that the **putting away of leaven** was to take place on the fourteenth, on the evening of which day the passover was sacrificed; so that the **eating of unleavened bread,** beginning with the passover feast, would last through seven days, from the evening of the fourteenth till the evening of the twenty-first. The terms, first day and seventh day, in our verse, are obviously used of the duration of the feast. During this time there was to be no leaven "in all thy quarters in the land of promise," ch. xiii. 7

16.] **an holy convocation**, i. e. an assembly for religious worship; literally, **a convocation of holiness**: compare Num. x. 2; Ezek. xlvi. 3, 9. For the use of the word, see reff. The prescription of abstinence from work is a lighter one than that which applied to the Sabbaths. This prohibition only regarded servile work (Lev. xxiii. 7); that extended to all work whatever, even making a fire, seething and baking (ch. xvi. 23; xxxv. 3).

17.] On the chronological inference, see above, ver. 15. The reason here given is a symbolical one. The purity of the new life of Israel, begun with this day, is to be free from all the leaven of Egypt (compare Matt

generations by an ordinance for ever. 18 ¶ In the first
month, on the fourteenth day of the month at even, ye
shall eat unleavened bread, until the one and twentieth
day of the month at even. 19 Seven days shall there be
no leaven found in your houses: for whosoever eateth that
which is leavened, even that soul shall be cut off from the
z ver. 48, reff. congregation of Israel, whether he be a stranger, or [z] born
in the land. 20 Ye shall eat nothing leavened; in all your
habitations shall ye eat unleavened bread. 21 ¶ Then
Moses called for all the elders of Israel, and said unto
a Judg. iv. 6; v. 14; xx. 37. Job xxi. 33. them, [a] Go and take you a lamb according to your families,
and kill the passover. 22 And ye shall take a bunch of
hyssop, and dip *it* in the blood that *is* in the bason, and
strike the lintel and the two side posts with the blood that
is in the bason; and none of you shall go out at the door
of his house until the morning. 23 For JEHOVAH will pass
through to smite the Egyptians; and when he seeth the
blood upon the lintel, and on the two side posts, JEHOVAH
will pass over the door, and will not suffer the destroyer to

xvi. 5—12; 1 Cor. v. 8). And for this reason it was, that contempt of this command was to be visited with cutting off from Israel. But the ordinance arose out of, and was commemorative of, the haste in which Israel was thrust out of Egypt: see vv. 34, 39. **18—20.**] *More detailed directions.* On the wording, see above. The **stranger** is by some (as Keil) supposed to mean the non-Israelite and uncircumcised, who sojourns, be it temporarily or for life, among Israel; by others (as Kalisch), the so-called *proselyte of righteousness*, who was circumcised and in every respect an Israelite. Kalisch also supposes those **born in the land** not to mean the Israelites, but the descendants of proselytes. But the other view seems simpler. Kalisch's objection that the sojourners could not be cut off from the congregation of Israel because they never belonged to it, looks formidable, but is not really, as the words may be used in their widest meaning.

21—28.] *Report by Moses of the Divine command to the elders of Israel*, in which it may be observed that there is no report of the ordinance of unleavened bread, but of that of the passover only. **22.**] The rendering of the A. V., "*Draw out and take*," though defended by Kalisch, is impugned by Knobel and Keil; and the LXX. and Vulgate render as the text, taking the verb intransitively. The same word is used thus in reff. **22.**] This part of the detail of the ordinance is now introduced for the first time. About the **hyssop**, there has been much controversy as to what plant it was. It will come before us again on Lev. xiv. 4, as the ordained vehicle of purification by blood. Dr. Tristram (*Nat. Hist. of the Bible*, p. 455, ff.) believes it to be the caper plant, and shews that it fulfils all the conditions of the use of the hyssop in the Bible. Others have seen in it a species of thyme, or origanum. The Hebrew word *ezob* being simply reproduced in the Greek of the LXX. and the Latin of the Vulgate, we have no data except the uses of the plant. It is something in favour of Dr. Tristram's view, that the caper is to this day known by the Arabs as *asuf*, a name nearly akin to *ezob*. See also Mr. Wright's article in the *Biblical Dict.*, and Dean Stanley, *Sinai and Palestine*, p. 21. The injunction that none is to leave his house that night is one of security, as only where the blood was sprinkled would safety be found. **23.**] The **destroyer** seems to be the obvious and

come in unto your houses to smite *you*. 24 And ye shall
observe this word for an ordinance to thee and to thy sons
for ever. 25 And it shall come to pass, when ye be come
to the land which JEHOVAH will give you, according as he
hath promised, that ye shall keep this service. 26 And it
shall come to pass, when your children shall say unto you,
What mean ye by this service? 27 that ye shall say, It *is*
the sacrifice of a passover unto JEHOVAH, who passed over
the houses of the children of Israel in Egypt, when he
smote the Egyptians, and delivered our houses. And the
people bowed the head and worshipped. 28 And the
children of Israel went away, and did as JEHOVAH had
commanded Moses and Aaron, so did they. 29 ¶ And it
came to pass, that at midnight JEHOVAH smote all the
firstborn in the land of Egypt, from the firstborn of Pha-
raoh that sat on his throne unto the firstborn of the cap-
tive that *was* in the dungeon; and all the firstborn of

natural interpretation of the Hebrew word. So the LXX. take it, and so the writer to the Hebrews, following the LXX. But this does not pass altogether unquestioned. Knobel urges that the very same Hebrew word is used in ver. 13 in the sense of *destruction*,—that there is not in the whole history any mention of an angel employed in destroying the Egyptians, but that in vv. 12, 13, 23, 27, 29, it is Jehovah alone who goes through the land smiting the Egyptians, executing judgment on their gods, and passing over the houses of Israel. He also urges, what will be variously estimated according as the theory is or is not adopted, that the Elohist never mentions an angel in his whole work. On the same side is Kalisch. We may perhaps venture to clear the ground by observing that there is really no implication of an *angel* in the use of the personal word, but only a dark and mysterious allusion to Him who destroyed. The *angel* is imported apparently from the subsequent narrative of the plague in David's time, 2 Sam. xxiv. 15—17. It is obvious that Ps. lxxviii. 49 cannot be alleged here, being entirely vague and general, and capable of interpretation as referring to all the plagues indiscriminately. **24.**] **this word**, viz. the injunction as to the passover. **25.**] So also ch. xiii. 5. Knobel regards vv. 24—27 as an insertion of a later writer, and adduces the use of the word "*service*" in this sense as found here and in xiii. 5, but never in the Elohistic account. **27.**] The people—the elders, ver. 21, only were present,—signify, and in ver. 28 carry out their obedience to the Divine command. In the latter verse it is obvious that the words apply only to that part of the command which admitted of immediate performance, viz. vv. 21, 22.

29—36.] *The slaying of the first-born in Egypt. The deliverance of Israel.*

29. at midnight] Of what day is understood from the narrative, by comparing ver. 6 with ver. 12. It was between the fourteenth and the fifteenth of the month. It is quite in vain to attempt to base this event on the ordinary pestilences common in Egypt. It was altogether above nature, and wrought by Jehovah Himself. Even if we could find a natural basis for the other plagues, there is none for this. In the mention of every first-born dying we must not imagine that every person died of whatever age who was a first-born, but that those sons and daughters who were first born in their father's house, and as yet undivided from it, died. Compare ch. xi. 5, where "*the maidservant that is behind the mill*" answers to **our captive that was in the dungeon.**

cattle. 30 And Pharaoh rose up in the night, he, and all
his servants, and all the Egyptians; and there was a great
cry in Egypt; for *there was* not a house where *there was*
not one dead. 31 ¶ And he called for Moses and Aaron
by night, and said, Rise up, *and* get you forth from among
my people, both ye and the children of Israel; and go,
serve JEHOVAH, as ye have said. 32 Also take your flocks
and your herds, as ye have said, and be gone; and bless
me also. 33 And the Egyptians were urgent upon the
people, that they might send them out of the land in
haste; for they said, We *be* all dead *men*. 34 And the
people took their dough before it was leavened, their
kneadingtroughs being bound up in their clothes upon
their shoulders. 35 And the children of Israel did accord-
ing to the word of Moses; and they asked of the Egypt-
ians jewels of silver, and jewels of gold, and raiment: 36
and JEHOVAH gave the people favour in the sight of the

30.] This cry was prophesied, ch. xi. 6. We hear of another cry at midnight, Matt. xxv. 5. The last clause of the verse was literally true of every house that was really a house, a family complete. In all such statements the exceptions readily suggest themselves. See similar general statements to be similarly taken, Isa. lvii. 1; Jer. v. 1; Micah vii. 2. **31.**] There is no discrepancy with ch. x. 29, as the circumstances were such as might well account for the resolve being broken, even if it had not been already (ch. xi. 8); nor with ch. xi. 8, for the fact of Pharaoh's sending for Moses and Aaron does not exclude that of multitudes of afflicted Egyptians crowding to him with the request to be gone. The words of Pharaoh in his terror combine the two, the granting of the actual request of Moses, to go and serve Jehovah, with an assumption and desire of that which he had all along suspected to be the real motive of their journey,—the entire departure from Egypt. **32.**] The **flocks** and the **herds** had been the subject of dispute after the last plague, ch. x. 29. There does not appear any reason for supposing with Knobel that the king's urgency was only for a temporary absence. In ch. xiv. 5 it is not that the Egyptians had been deceived, but that they had been so soft-hearted as to let Israel go, which is expressed in their words of self-reproach. **bless me also**] These again are the words of a heart for the time thoroughly softened and broken by the loss of his first-born. When they prayed to Jehovah, it was not now to be for mere deliverance from this or that plague, but for mercy and favour in his distress. **33.**] The Egyptians were afraid, not lest this particular plague should extend further, for it had been definitely announced that it should smite the first-born only, but lest some other terrible plague should take off those who remained. **34.**] See below on ver. 39. Even without that further notice, this would shew that the command to keep the seven days' feast of unleavened bread was not yet known to them: they intended to leaven the dough, had not haste prevented them; the kneading-troughs contained the dough. The **clothes** here spoken of were the outer cloaks of a square shape, which when worn were thrown over the inner clothing, and at other times were used for wrapping and carrying various things. **35, 36.**] Here again (see previous remarks on ch. iii. 22), there is not a word in the text about borrowing or lending (see on ref. 1 Sam.). The Hebrews demanded, and the Egyptians in their panic encouraged them to demand, the articles mentioned. The

Egyptians, and they [b] encouraged them to ask. And they
[c] spoiled the Egyptians. 37 ¶ And the children of Israel
journeyed from Rameses to Succoth, about six hundred

[b] 1 Sam. i. 28.
[c] Gen. xxxi. 9, 16. 1 Sam. xxx. 22. Ps. cxix. 43.

verb is the same in both verses: **they asked**, in ver. 35,—**they made them**, i. e. encouraged them, **to ask**, in ver. 36. We may observe that the proceeding is nowhere treated as one coming into question at all as to its morality; and that speculations on this matter, such as are freely indulged in by the commentators, are at least out of place. It is remarkable how prominent a part this circumstance, the enriching of Israel at the cost of the Egyptians, has played since the first announcement of the Exodus to Abraham: compare Gen. xv. 14; ch. iii. 21, 22; xi. 2, 3, in which latter place it would almost appear that the process must have begun even before the last plague. It was regarded all the way through as a lawful booty gained from enemies, who had long oppressed and defrauded them. **37—42.**] *The Exodus from Egypt.* The whole portion from this point to ch. xiii. 22 is singularly made up of detached fragments, which it is almost impossible to assign to their various writers. Ver. 39 repeats again matter already related vv. 33, 34; ver. 51 reproduces ver. 41, the terms only being varied; vv. 43—49 repeat with additional particulars, but without any specification as to time, the ordinance already given vv. 3—10, 21—27; ver. 50 is the echo of ver. 28. Then in ch. xiii., vv. 1, 2 relate to an ordinance taken up again in 11, 12, ff., but broken in upon by another ordinance, vv. 3—10; ver. 9 is reproduced in ver. 16; the main narrative, with the Divine name Elohim and not Jehovah, is resumed, or rather taken up, from the very point of the Exodus, in vv. 17—19, and the notice of the bones of Joseph inserted; and then the resumption of the journey from Succoth, joining to our ver. 37, ff., takes place at ver. 20, ending with the notice of the pillar of cloud and fire as the token of Jehovah's presence. Without undertaking to apportion these several pieces as some have done, I submit that common fairness requires the recognition of them as independent fragments put together at some time when the writing of the whole history was undertaken; such putting together not detracting from the character of the narrative, nay, betokening reverent care on the part of the sacred writer in conserving the original accounts. To resist this evidence of various origin and compound character seems to me to be as foolish as it is unfair. It may happen at some time that we may be able by careful distinction of diction and of character to assign each portion to its separate writer. If this has not at present been satisfactorily done, it is not for orthodox commentators on that account to cast discredit on all reverent examination of the composition of the sacred text, and to maintain its absolute unity and contemporaneity in spite of plain evidence.

37.] The children of Israel set out, as here related, from Rameses (see ch. i. 11), a town on the western side of the land of Goshen. Their departure was probably towards the morning (see Num. xxxiii. 3) of the fifteenth of Abib. The result of the last plague having been definitely announced by God some days before, it is reasonable to suppose that all preparation would have been made for departure, and the route agreed on, so that there might be no delay. Very considerable uncertainty rests upon the geography of the Exodus. We do not know exactly where Rameses is to be placed, and the name Succoth (tabernacles or tents) is too vague to admit of local assignment. At the same time, there is no improbability, as has been sometimes represented, in the account of their first three days' journey. *Days'* journeys they certainly appear to have been, for when the host spent more than one day between station and station, it is specially noticed: see Num. xxxiii. 8, and x. 33; also ch. xv. 22. The three first of these embrace together a distance of about forty-five miles, giving fifteen miles a day. This might easily be accomplished by the men (and strong women) on foot, and the children and the feeble on beasts of burden. Let it be remembered—(1.) That all possible haste would be made; (2.) That in mentioning the places of bivouac, the head-quarters of the camp alone would be specified; the "mixed multitude" might be lagging behind.

The *number* here stated has appeared to some incredible. But it has been again and again shewn that for such a fertility as is pre-

thousand on foot *that were* men, beside children. 38 And a
mixed multitude went up also with them; and flocks, and
herds, *even* very much cattle. 39 And they baked un-
leavened cakes of the dough which they brought forth out
of Egypt, for it was not leavened; because they were
thrust out of Egypt, and could not tarry, neither had they
prepared for themselves any victual. 40 ¶ Now the so-
journing of the children of Israel, which they sojourned

dicated of Israel in Egypt, the reckoning is not only within bounds of probability, but actually moderate. If there were about 600,000 *men* (the exact number was 603,550, besides the Levites, who were 22,000. Compare Num. ii. 32; iii. 39), there would be about 2,400,000 in all. Now, if the time of the sojourning was (see below) 215 years = 7 generations, and 70 persons went down into Egypt, an ordinary average of children per family would produce the number, allowing for a moderate intermarrying with Egyptian wives. On the supposed difficulty of sustenance for such a multitude during the journeys in the wilderness, see note on ch. xvi. 3. **38.**] This **mixed multitude** seems to have consisted of Egyptians and other non-Israelites: see ch. ix. 20, where we read of some that feared the word of Jehovah among the Egyptians, x. 7; xi. 3. We hear of them again in Num. xi. 4; Deut. xxix. 11. **39.**] We here have the reason why they ate unleavened bread during the first days after the Exodus. On this circumstance was founded the ordinance of the feast of unleavened bread, the institution of which has been anticipated in vv. 15—20. **40.**] This chronological notice as it stands in the Hebrew text is positive and definite. Those who accept that text as the very words of Divine inspiration have no right to set it aside on account of its difficulty, as has been done, e. g. by Bishop Wordsworth, on the testimony of the Samaritan Pentateuch and the LXX. The matter stands thus: In Gen. xv. 13 Jehovah foretold to Abram that his seed was to be a stranger in a land not theirs, and should serve the people of that land and be afflicted by them, for 400 years,—the round number being there taken,—the land being, on any fair interpretation, one and the same land, and the afflicting people whom Israel were to serve, one and the same people. The attempts to evade this are beneath notice. In agreement with the prophecy, we have it here stated that the sojourning of Israel in Egypt was 430 years: and the assertion is made still more definite by the addition that on the very day which ended that period, the hosts of Jehovah left Egypt. But there is here an insuperable difficulty, patent in the text itself. For, from ch. vi. 20, Amram, father of Moses, married Jochebed, his father Kohath's sister, and daughter of Levi. Now, allowing the very utmost period of Levi's life, the length of which is stated (ch. vi. 16) at 137 years, for the birth of Jochebed (an allowance put out of the question by the tenor of the Abrahamic history);—seeing that Levi was about 45 when Jacob went into Egypt, and Moses was 80 at the Exodus, we should have 137 — 45 = 92 years after the going down to Egypt, for Jochebed's birth. We may reduce this by 40 years at least, even thus making Jochebed to be born in the 97th year of Levi's life. So that we shall have 430 — 52 — 80 = 298, for Jochebed's age when Moses was born, which of course involves an impossibility. In seeking for a solution, we may observe that the Samaritan text and the LXX. here have "*the sojourning of the children of Israel which they* (the Alexandrine MS. of the LXX. adds, *and their fathers*) *sojourned in the land of Egypt, and the land of Canaan, was four hundred and thirty years:*" and that this, although entirely discrepant from the Hebrew text, represents the same account of the matter as that adopted by St. Paul in Gal. iii. 17, where he makes the law 430 years subsequent to the promise made to Abraham. Josephus also (*Ant.* ii. 15. 2) gives the same account. And it has been very commonly adopted by Jewish and Christian writers. Probably it is the true account: but let it be observed that it simply sets aside the sacred text.

in Egypt, *was* four hundred and thirty years. 41 And it
came to pass at the end of the four hundred and thirty
years, even the selfsame day it came to pass, that all the
hosts of JEHOVAH went out from the land of Egypt. 42 It
is a night to be observed unto JEHOVAH for bringing them
out from the land of Egypt: this *is* that night of JEHOVAH
to be observed unto all the children of Israel in their
generations. 43 ¶ And JEHOVAH said unto Moses and
Aaron, This *is* the ordinance of the passover: There shall
no [d]stranger eat thereof: 44 but every man's servant that d Gen. xvii. 12, 27. Levit. xxii. 25.
is bought for money, when thou hast circumcised him,
then shall he eat thereof. 45 A [e]foreigner and an hired e Gen. xxiii. 4. Lev. xxv. 6. Ps. xxxix. 13.
servant shall not eat thereof. 46 In one house shall it be
eaten; thou shalt not carry forth ought of the flesh abroad

That text is accepted as the truth of the matter by many considerable names, e. g. in later times, Kalisch, Keil, and Knobel. **41.**] **the selfsame day** (literally, **in the body of this day**) would seem to imply that the day of Israel's departure, viz. the fifteenth day of Abib, exactly corresponded with the day of Jacob's coming into Egypt. For we surely cannot maintain with Keil that the selfsame day has no reference to the period mentioned, but only indicates the fifteenth of Abib before (ver. 12, ff.) mentioned. **42.**] There are various interpretations of this verse, containing as it does a word (*shimmurim*) used here only. The expression both times is **a night of watchings,** or **preservings.** Some Jewish interpreters understand the word the first time as applying to the watch which Jehovah kept over his people, and the second time of the watch which the Jews were to keep in commemoration of this. So also in substance Keil. To this double meaning Kalisch very naturally objects, as also to the sense of *watching* altogether, seeing that such an observance was never part of the Jewish practice on that night. He contends for the sense given by the A. V., which is also upheld by Knobel and by Gesenius, a kindred word, from the same root, being often used for the observations or celebrations of sacred rites.

43—49.] *Repeated and more detailed injunctions as to the passover.* The pertinence of this insertion here is supposed to consist in the circumstance (ver. 38) of a mixed multitude having gone up out of Egypt with Israel. But this may well be questioned, seeing that the passover was celebrated previously to the Exodus, and to the attachment of this multitude. Far more probably it belongs to the completion of all the primary prescriptions regarding the rite and its accompanying ordinances, which are here collected, before the wilderness-journey is entered upon. The substance of this portion of the Divine command is to set forth the strictly theocratic and Israelitish character of the ordinance. **no stranger,** literally, **no son of a stranger,** as being outside the people of Jehovah. **44.**] But all the families of Israel were bound to observe it, and in consequence all who by incorporation had become members of such families. This could be done by circumcision only. For **man's servant,** Kalisch prefers "*male servant.*" **45.**] **A foreigner** represents the word commonly rendered by **sojourner,** the stronger word being requisite here, to mark that he is one outside Israel, and not merely a casual Israelitish visitor. The same is understood of the hired servant—that he is hired from without, not a brother. **46.**] This further particularizes injunctions already virtually given in vv. 4, 9, 10. *Unity* was the great essential ground-feature of the symbolism. There was to be no division, either of the victim or of the partakers. All were to belong to the sacred people, and all in their social (betokening their national) completeness were to partake of one sacrifice. The Christian will not fail to perceive the

out of the house; neither shall ye break a bone thereof.
47 All the congregation of Israel shall keep it. 48 And
when a stranger shall sojourn with thee, and will keep the
passover to JEHOVAH, let all his males be circumcised, and
then let him come near and keep it; and he shall be as
one that is [f]born in the land: but no uncircumcised person
shall eat thereof. 49 One law shall be to him that is
[f]homeborn, and unto the stranger that sojourneth among
you. 50 Thus did all the children of Israel; as JEHOVAH
commanded Moses and Aaron, so did they. 51 And it
came to pass the selfsame day, *that* JEHOVAH did bring the
children of Israel out of the land of Egypt by their armies.
XIII. 1 And JEHOVAH spake unto Moses, saying, 2
Sanctify unto me all the firstborn, whatsoever openeth
the [g]womb among the children of Israel, *both* of man and
of beast: it *is* mine. 3 ¶ And Moses said unto the people,
Remember this day, in which ye came out from Egypt, out
of the [h]house of bondmen; for by strength of hand JE-

f ver. 19. Lev. xvi. 29; xxiii. 42; xxiv. 22. Ps. xxxvii. 35 (see note there).

g Num. iii. 12; xii. 12. Job x. 18. Hos. ix. 14.

h ver. 14. ch. xx. 2. Deut. v. 6; vii. 12; vii. 8; viii. 14; xiii. 5, 10. Josh. xxiv. 17.

deep significance of this, which it is not the object of this commentary to point out. The last clause of this verse is adduced by St. John (xix. 36) as having been literally fulfilled in the body of Christ, our Passover. **48.**] This further specifies circumcision as the one condition of admission to the partaking of the passover, and that not of individual only but of the whole family of him who wished to participate. In the covenant made with Abraham's seed, all *families* of the earth were to be blessed. **49.**] **One law**, viz. that of the absolute necessity of circumcision in all cases: in other words, of the absolute co-extensiveness of the rite with the theocracy. **homeborn,** see reff.: i. e. an Israelite.

50, 51.] *Closing formulæ*, found also in vv. 28, 41. It seems far more natural to take ver. 50 thus, as simply helping to close in the narrative of the Exodus itself, than with Knobel and Keil, after some of the Jewish interpreters, as anticipatory, and referring to subsequent occasions when the children of Israel had the opportunity of fulfilling these precepts, e. g. Num. ix. 4, 5, where the same general notice is appended. Ver. 51 forms the solemn close to the history of Israel in Egypt. **the selfsame day**] Again literally, in the body of the day, is repeated as a sort of refrain, hardly as applying to the day when the immediately preceding commands were given.

XIII. **1—16.**] *Ordinances belonging to the passover. The setting apart of the first-born* (1, 2); *the commemorating of the day of the Exodus* (3, 4); *the seven days' feast of unleavened bread to be observed in the land of promise* (5—10); *the setting apart of the first-born to be similarly observed* (11—16). On the separate portions, see below. **1, 2.**] These commands appear to have been given in Succoth, the first halting station of Israel. On the ground of this sanctifying, or setting apart for Jehovah of the first-born, see below, on ver. 15. Here, the command is simply given, without the reason or the details there appended. Knobel assigns this to the original Elohistic narrative, and finds this confirmed by the expressions used. **3, 4.**] Injunction to remember the day of their deliverance from Egypt, followed, vv. 6—10, by the ordinance of the seven days' feast of unleavened bread. The whole is parallel with ch. xii. 14—20, and, like that, is introduced by mention of the hallowing of the day itself of their deliverance. It is in fact the same narrative under a differing form, and with the addition of the command to make the injunction

HOVAH brought you out from this *place:* there shall no
leavened bread be eaten. 4 This day came ye out in the
month Abib. 5 ¶ And it shall be when JEHOVAH shall
bring thee into the land of the Canaanites, and the Hit-
tites, and the Amorites, and the Hivites, and the Jebusites,
which he sware unto thy fathers to give thee, a land
[i]flowing with milk and honey, that thou shalt keep this i ch. iii. 8, reff.
service in this month. 6 Seven days thou shalt eat un-
leavened bread, and in the seventh day *shall be* a feast to
JEHOVAH. 7 Unleavened bread shall be eaten seven days;
and there shall no leavened bread be seen with thee,
neither shall there be leaven seen with thee in all thy
quarters. 8 ¶ And thou shalt tell thy son in that day,
saying, *This is done* because of that *which* JEHOVAH did
unto me when I came forth out of Egypt. 9 And it shall
be for a sign unto thee upon thine hand, and for a me-
morial between thine eyes, that the law of JEHOVAH may
be in thy mouth: for with a strong hand hath JEHOVAH
brought thee out of Egypt. 10 Thou shalt therefore keep j Judg. xi. 40; xxi. 19. 1 Sam. i. 3 ii. 19.
this ordinance in his season [j]from year to year. 11 ¶ And

a sign and a memorial, and its reason. **the house of bondmen**] So literally, and so rendered by the A. V. at Deut. vii. 8, a comparison derived from the strong room or building in which slaves were kept at night, chained, and whence they were sent out to their work in the morning: see reff.

4.] The expression literally is, **This day are ye coming out.** The Exodus was then going on, not yet accomplished. **the month Abib**] This is the first time that the month is so named. See note on ch. xii. 2.

5.] Parallel with ch. xii. 28. Five principal nations of the promised land are here mentioned: see Gen. xv. 19, where ten are named, but not the Hivites; ch. iii. 8, 17, where six are named, including all these and adding the Perizzites; Deut. vii. 1, where seven are named, including all these and adding the Girgashites and Perizzites. These two last are added here by the Samaritan text and the LXX. On the various tribes named, see on Gen. x. 15—17. The enumeration of these tribes, the mention of the land flowing with milk and honey, and of the oath of Jehovah, are all stated to be characteristic of the supplemental, or Jehovist, narrator (Knobel).

6, 7.] Parallel to ch. xii. 15—20, varying in the last day only of the seven here specified as a solemn feast, whereas there both the first and last are mentioned.

8.] See ch. xii. 26, 27: that, however, is said of the ordinance of the passover.

9.] These words appear to be used both here and in ver. 16 not in a material but a figurative sense. I deal with *phylacteries* on ver. 16, where the expression is more material than here. But it is here that the lawgiver's aim is made apparent, **that the law of Jehovah may be in thy mouth,** which would be the effect not of a literal and outward, but of an inward and spiritual compliance with the precept.

10.] Literally, **from days to days,** i. e. as often as the days come round, as we say, from year to year: see reff.

11—16.] *Repetition, with additional detail, of the ordinance of setting apart the first-born.* It, like the feast of unleavened bread, is to come into force after the entry into the promised land. The further details respecting the firstlings of beasts are given in ch. xxii. 30; Num. xviii. 15—18. Those of

it shall be when JEHOVAH shall bring thee into the land
of the Canaanites, as he sware unto thee and to thy
fathers, and shall give it thee, 12 that thou shalt set apart
k ver. 2, reff. unto JEHOVAH all that openeth the [k]womb, and every
firstling that cometh of a beast which thou hast; the
males *are* JEHOVAH'S. 13 And every firstling of an ass
thou shalt redeem with a lamb; and if thou wilt not redeem
it, then thou shalt break its neck: and all the firstborn of
man among thy sons shalt thou redeem. 14 ¶ And it
l Gen. xxx. 33. shall be when thy son asketh thee [l]in time to come, say-
ing, What *is* this? that thou shalt say unto him, By
strength of hand JEHOVAH brought us out from Egypt,
from the house of bondmen: 15 and it came to pass, when
Pharaoh would hardly let us go, that JEHOVAH slew all
the firstborn in the land of Egypt, both the firstborn of
man, and the firstborn of beast: therefore I sacrifice to
JEHOVAH all that openeth the womb, being males; but all
the firstborn of my children I redeem. 16 And it shall be
m Deut. vi. 8, xi. 18, only. for a token upon thine hand, and for [m]frontlets between

clean beasts were not redeemable, but were absolutely the Lord's. **13.**] The ass is taken as the most obvious example of the unclean among beasts: the order to redeem extended to all the unclean, Num. xviii. 15. The **first-born of man** were to be redeemed at a price of five shekels each, Num. iii. 46, 47; xviii. 16. The firstling might be devoted by vow to the Lord as being His already: see Lev. xxvii. 26, f. All further details see in the places referred to.

14, 15.] The account to be given of this ordinance to future generations: viz. that when Jehovah destroyed all the first-born of man and beast in the land of Egypt, He spared for Himself all the first-born of Israel, both man and beast. We afterwards learn (Num. iii. 12, f.) that the first-born were originally destined to the special service of Jehovah, but that he afterwards took the Levites instead of them. **in time to come** is literally, **to-morrow**, so in ref.

16.] The same method is taken as in ver. 9, of impressing on the children of Israel the importance of the ordinance and the duty of observing it. On these verses, and on Deut. vi. 8; xi. 18, the Talmudists and other Jewish interpreters (e. g. even Kalisch) ground the practice of wearing tephillin or phylacteries: see Matt. xxiii. 5. These tephillin, in the form to which, through tradition, they have attained, "consist of small square leather boxes, those of the *hand* with one leather thong, which is tied round the left arm and the fingers; those of the *head* with a double thong, which hangs down at both sides of the head. The box contains, on parchment strips, the following four sections from the Pentateuch: 1. About the sanctification of the first-born, Exod. xiii. 1—10. 2. Further precepts about the same subject, vv. 11—16. 3. The observance of the law and its injunction to the rising generation, Deut. vi. 4—9. And, 4. The blessing attending the strict adherence to the Divine precepts, Deut. xi. 13—21." Kalisch. The four passages are in fact those respecting which the supposed command to bind them is given. That the whole interpretation is erroneous will be seen at once by comparing such passages as Prov. iii. 3; vi. 21; vii. 3; Cant. viii. 6; Isa. xlix. 18; Jer. xxii. 24; Hag. ii. 23. When Kalisch objects to the adducing of these passages, that they are poetical, it is simply begging the question. We main-

thine eyes: for by strength of hand Jehovah brought us
forth out of Egypt. 17 ¶ And it came to pass, when Pha-
raoh had let the people go, that God led them not *through*
the way of the land of the Philistines, although that *was*
near; for God said, Lest peradventure the people repent
when they see war, and they return to Egypt: 18 but
God made the people to turn by the way of the wilderness

tain that these are poetical likewise, and that it is impossible to dissociate the poetical element from these sayings of Moses. What, for example, is the *stretched-out arm*, the *strength of hand*, with which Jehovah brought them out of Egypt? What is such an expression as the law of the Lord being in their mouth, but poetical? What right have we to require that the one shall be interpreted literally of texts worn on the brow and hand, and to dispense with interpreting the other that texts shall be carried in the mouth? And what Kalisch urges, of commands being attached to texts in Deut. vi. 9 and xi. 20 which cannot be taken figuratively, such as "*Thou shalt write them on the door-posts of thine house and on thy gates*," and consequently themselves requiring a literal interpretation, is equally futile. If this be so, then each command stands on its own ground. Those who wish to see more particulars respecting the phylacteries will find them in Kalisch on this place, and Mr. Farrar's article "Frontlets" in *Biblical Dict.* The word here used for **frontlets** (*totaphoth*) is of uncertain derivation. The Jewish name for phylacteries, *tephillin*, is not found in Scripture, nor is there any trace of the practice of wearing them before the captivity. It has been supposed that the Jews learned it from the Babylonians, among whom Jerome tells us it was prevalent. There can be no doubt that it was a superstition of late date. It is rejected by the Karnite Jews, who maintain the figurative sense of these passages. **17—19.**] A notice, in which remarkably enough the name Elohim stands instead of Jehovah, which has been used as yet, with the exception of passages in chapters i.—iii., throughout the whole book. This seems to indicate distinctness of origin for this incorporated fragment. Even those who are fondest of finding subjective reasons for the change of the Divine names have, as far as I have seen, abstained here. Seeing that Israel was especially the people of Jehovah, and is here spoken of as under His special guidance, we might expect to find that His special name here if anywhere.

17.] Succoth, their first station, seems to have been the general rendezvous after their hasty flight, and from thence their journey proper began. From that point (somewhere on the E. of Egypt, and S. E. probably of Rameses) to Palestine, through the land of the Philistines, the usual caravan way, is but short. "From Rameses to Gaza is a straight and much frequented way of eight to ten days, either northwards, through the pass of Djebel-el-Tih, or more eastwards, through that of Djebel-el-Edshmeh; and the sons of Jacob journeyed, in not many days, from Palestine to Egypt to buy corn.' Kalisch. The Philistines were known as a warlike people, who would not have allowed Israel to enter Palestine without resistance, for which (see ch. xiv. 10, ff.) the people were not as yet prepared. **18.**] The independence of this portion of the account is also shewn by the fact that this way must have been previously determined on by Moses in consequence of what had been Divinely announced to him in ch. iii. 12. Both reasons concurred; indeed, the one here stated may have been in the Divine purpose the leading one, involving the other

the wilderness of the Red Sea] Again, and usually, **the Sea of Suph**, first mentioned in ch. x. 19, where see note. They turned southward, towards the desert lying between the cultivated land and the Western Gulf. They went up harnessed, i. e. in arms and in rank, not in a loosely arranged multitude. Such is the alleged meaning of the word, which occurs here and in reff. only. Some connect it with the numeral *five*, and explain it *five in a rank*. But the more probable connexion of the word is with *loins*, and the account of it, that it implies *with their loins girt*. The LXX. curiously render, "*The children of Israel went up in the fifth gen-*

n Josh. i. 14; iv. 12. Judg. vii. 11, only.

of the Red sea: and the children of Israel went up [n]har-
nessed out of the land of Egypt. 19 And Moses took the
bones of Joseph with him: for he had straitly sworn the
children of Israel, saying, God will surely visit you; and
ye shall carry up my bones away hence with you. 20 ¶
And they took their journey from Succoth, and encamped
in Etham, in the edge of the wilderness. 21 And JEHOVAH
went before them by day in a pillar of a cloud, to lead
them the way; and by night in a pillar of fire, to give
them light; to go by day and night: 22 he took not away
the pillar of the cloud by day, nor the pillar of fire by
night, *from* before the people. XIV. 1 And JEHOVAH
spake unto Moses, saying, 2 Speak unto the children of
Israel, that they turn and encamp before Pi-hahiroth, be-

eration, &c. **19.**] Notice respecting the bones of Joseph: see Gen. l. 24, 25. **20.**] *Second journey — Succoth to Etham.* The situation of **Etham** is placed by Mr. Stuart Poole (art. "Exodus" in *Biblical Dict.*) at the present *Seba Biar*, or seven wells, where the cultivated land ceases, about three miles from the western sides of the ancient head of the gulf. It lies at the S. of the bitter lakes through which the present Suez canal passes. The wilderness here is called in Num. xxxiii. 8, "*the wilderness of Etham*," but in our ch. xv. 22, "*the wilderness of Shur*" (see Gen. xvi. 7). **21, 22.**] *The pillar of fire and cloud.* From this point Israel left inhabited land and journeyed through the wilderness; and Jehovah Himself undertook their guidance, until they came again to a peopled land. An analogy has been found between the pillar of fire and cloud and the kindled fire which went before caravans or armies in the East. Quintus Curtius relates of Alexander, as he went through Babylonia and Susiana, that "he set a pole (*vertica*) which could be seen on every side, over the royal tent, which shewed a signal conspicuous to all, seen as a fire by night and as smoke by day." And such notices are interesting and useful, except when they are treated as accounting for and exhausting the theocratic narrative. All that we can say of them is, that Jehovah may have been pleased to base upon an existing practice His method of manifesting His guarding and leading presence to His people. We are in this narrative not in the region of the legendary and mythical, but of the supernatural and Divine. This daily and nightly presence was by means not of two pillars, but of *one*: see ch. xiv. 24; see also vv. 19, 20; xl. 38; Num. ix. 15, 16. In it was present "*the angel of God*" (ch. xiv. 19), i. e. the Divine presence personally; in it appeared "*the glory of Jehovah*," ch. xvi. 10; xl. 34; Num. xv. 1, 42. It was an elementary appearance, made use of by Him who appointed and rules the elements, to signify to His people His immediate presence and guardianship: see other notices of this continued miracle in Num. x. 34; xiv. 14; Deut. i. 33; Neh. ix. 12; Ps. cv. 39; also notes on ch. xxxiii. 9; Num. xii. 5; Deut. xxxi. 15. **22.**] **He took not away**, viz. from this time: the narrative, treating of the beginning of the journey, does not specify the end of this appearance.

XIV. *Passage of the children of Israel through the Red Sea, and destruction of Pharaoh and his hosts.* The questions of detail will be treated as they arise in the text. In the discussion of the probable locality, the reader is referred to Mr. Stuart Poole's article "Red Sea, passage of" in the *Biblical Dict.*

2.] They had hitherto, according to the view above taken, been going eastward up the valley known as the Wady-el-Tumeylât. At the end of that valley lay Etham, or Seba Biar. From that point they were to

tween °Migdol and the sea, over against Baal-zephon: be- o See Gen. xi. 4. Josh. xv.
fore it shall ye encamp by the sea. 3 And Pharaoh will 37. Judg. viii. 17. Isa.
say of the children of Israel, They *are* entangled in the v. 2, al.
land, the wilderness hath shut them in. 4 And I will
harden Pharaoh's heart, that he shall follow after them;
and I will be honoured upon Pharaoh, and upon all his host;
that the Egyptians may know that I *am* JEHOVAH. And
they did so. 5 ¶ And it was told the king of Egypt that
the people fled: and the heart of Pharaoh and of his serv-
ants was turned against the people, and they said, Why
have we done this, that we have let Israel go from serving

turn (literally, **return**, but on no hypothesis can the literal sense be pressed), and evidently *southward*, for thus only could it be said that the wilderness had shut them in; and they were to encamp by the sea, i. e. by what was then the western shore of the western gulf. **before Pi-hahiroth**] This is most probably an Egyptian word, *Pi* being the article, and Hah- or Hach-iroth the real name: the signification being "*the bed of reeds.*" There is a tract with this very name (in Arabic, *Ghuweyhet-el-boos*) about the spot even now; but in the change which has taken place in the situation of the gulf, a natural feature of this kind would be liable to shift. **Migdol** is akin to the Hebrew expression for a military watch-tower, or look-out in a vineyard (see reff.). Perhaps there may have been such a tower on one of the hills near the sea, or a place named after one. The name occurs again as a local one in Egypt, Ezek. xxix. 10; xxx. 6; Jer. xliv. 1; xlvi. 14. See Mr. Stuart Poole's art. "Migdol" in *Biblical Dict.* **over against Baal-zephon**] That much stress is not to be laid upon any distinction between the words **before** and **over against** will be seen by their being indifferently used here, in ver. 9, and in Num. xxxiii. 7, where the people are said to have encamped "*before Migdol,*" and in ver. 8 that they departed "*from before Hahiroth.*" All that can be decided is that Migdol and Baal-zephon must have been opposite to one another, and the latter behind Pi-hahiroth with reference to the Israelites. The name has by almost all commentators been connected with Typhon, "a place sacred to Typhon," an idea which Mr. Stuart Poole characterizes as a very bold conjecture, seeing that we have no ground for considering the name Typhon to be either Egyptian or Semitic. He inclines to give the word a Hebrew derivation, and suppose it to be named from a watch-tower on the frontier, like Migdol. See his art. as above.

3.] The object of this change of route is distinctly stated to have been to produce this inference in the mind of Pharaoh. This being so, it must evidently be treated as a deviation from the way for a special purpose, and cannot be involved in any considerations regarding the natural route to be taken. **And**, i. e. **and then**, the result which will follow. **4.**] This would shew itself in that hardness of heart, which seemed broken down by the last great plague, returning and inducing Pharaoh to attempt to recover his nation of slaves.

5—9.] *Pursuit by the Egyptians.*

5.] It certainly seems implied in the previous verses that the change of route there enjoined would cause Pharaoh to imagine that the people had lost themselves. This he would learn by scouts, or by the return of some of the mixed multitude, ch. xii. 38. In this portion, however, the mere flight of the people is the moving cause of Pharaoh's regret and of his pursuit. The two portions are independent, but not inconsistent. In matter of fact, the two might very naturally combine. But a natural interpretation of the narrative will require a delay of some days at Pi-hahiroth, during which Pharaoh might receive the news which should lead him to the inference in ver. 3. The regret described would naturally have place on the next day after the Exodus, after the burial of the first-born. There is perhaps a trace in the narrative of Pharaoh's having

p = Num. xxi. 23, 23. Deut. ii. 32; iii. 1.
q ch. xv. 4.

us? 6 And he made ready his chariot, and took his [p] people
with him: 7 and he took six hundred chosen chariots, and
all the chariots of Egypt, and [q] captains over every one of
them. 8 And JEHOVAH hardened the heart of Pharaoh
king of Egypt, and he pursued after the children of Israel:
and the children of Israel went out with an high hand.
9 But the Egyptians pursued after them, all the horses
and chariots of Pharaoh, and his horsemen, and his army,
and overtook them encamping by the sea, beside Pi-hahi-
roth, before Baal-zephon. 10 ¶ And when Pharaoh drew
nigh, the children of Israel lifted up their eyes, and, be-
hold, the Egyptians marched after them; and they were sore
afraid: and the children of Israel cried out unto JEHOVAH.
11 And they said unto Moses, Because *there were* no graves
in Egypt, hast thou taken us away to die in the wilder-
ness? wherefore hast thou dealt thus with us, to carry us
forth out of Egypt? 12 *Is* not this the word that we did
tell thee in Egypt, saying, Let us alone, that we may
serve the Egyptians? For *it had been* better for us to serve
the Egyptians, than that we should die in the wilderness.
13 ¶ And Moses said unto the people, Fear ye not, stand

now discovered that the pretext of a three days' journey was only to cover the design of final flight; but, as before observed (see on ch. x. 10), this seems to have been suspected by the king throughout. **6, 7.**] Pharaoh took his **people,** i. e. his army: see reff. Egypt was always celebrated for its chariots and horses: see Isa. xxxi. 1; xxxvi. 9. There is some doubt about the word the rendering of which by the A. V. *captains,* I have preserved because no other seems to have established a preference over it. It seems to import "*third men;*" Jerome explains it, officers of the second rank after the king; but some believe it to mean captain over the three who are supposed to have been the complement of the war-chariot. Again, **over every one of them** is rendered by the Vulgate, *over all his host.*

8.] The latter clause imports that Israel did not escape ignominiously, as such pursuit would naturally suggest, but went out with the high hand of Jehovah over them (Isa. xxvi. 11), publicly and triumphantly. Or the high hand may refer to their own lofty spirit and warlike attitude, as in Job xxxviii. 15. **9.**] The expression **his army** here can hardly be understood of infantry, which would be unsuitable for so rapid a pursuit. We find only chariots and cavalry mentioned in the triumphant song, ch. xv. So that the fighters from and attendants on the chariots must probably be meant. On the situation of the camp, see above. **10.**] **the Egyptians,** literally, **Egypt.** They cried to Jehovah, but not in faith; only as men in peril and distrust. **11.**] The Israelites remembered the vast necropolis attached to several of the cities in Egypt, and "looked with Egyptian horror at the prospect that their carcases should be left on the face of the wilderness." Mr. Stuart Poole.

12.] This refers perhaps to the speech of the officers to Moses and Aaron in ch. v. 21; but it doubtless had happened often during the grievous and increased oppression of the people in Egypt: compare ch. vi. 9. **13.**] The LXX. render, moved perhaps by the consideration that Israel did actually see again the Egyptians dead, "in the manner in which ye have

still, and see the salvation of JEHOVAH, which he will
shew to you to day: for the Egyptians whom ye have
seen to day, ye shall see them again no more for ever.
14 JEHOVAH shall fight for you, and ye shall [r]hold your r Gen. xxxiv. 5.
peace. 15 ¶ And JEHOVAH said unto Moses, Wherefore
criest thou unto me? speak unto the children of Israel
that they go forward: 16 but lift thou up thy rod, and
stretch out thine hand over the sea, and divide it: and
the children of Israel shall go on dry *ground* through the
midst of the sea. 17 And I, behold, I will harden the
hearts of the Egyptians, and they shall follow them: and
I will get me honour upon Pharaoh, and upon all his
host, upon his chariots, and upon his horsemen. 18 And
the Egyptians shall know that I *am* JEHOVAH, when I
have gotten me honour upon Pharaoh, upon his chariots,
and upon his horsemen. 19 ¶ And the angel of God,
which went before the camp of Israel, removed and went
behind them; and the pillar of the cloud went from be-
fore their face, and stood behind them: 20 and it came be-
tween the camp of the Egyptians and the camp of Israel;
and it was a cloud and darkness, but it gave light by
night: so that the one came not near the other all the

seen the Egyptians to-day ye shall see them no more for ever." But this is objected to by the Hebraists. **15.**] The narrative leaves it to be understood that Moses, after what he had said to the people, betook himself in prayer to God. **16.**] He is commanded to lift up his rod, to shew the direct agency of God in the matter. In vv. 24, 26, 27 we hear of Moses *stretching out his hand* over the sea, but nothing of the rod. This is in agreement with the features of the two narratives throughout: see ch. iv. 20, and note there. If the children of Israel advanced before the miracle took place, then indeed was Heb. xi. 29 signally verified, that "they passed *by faith* through the Red Sea." **19, 20.**] On the **angel of God**, see note above, ch. xiii. 21. There is a difficulty in the rendering of ver. 20. Literally, in the Hebrew, it stands thus: **and it was cloud and darkness, and illuminated the night.** The general view has been that the pillar presented darkness to the Egyptians, but light to the Israelites. Thus the Targums, and almost all the interpreters, including Kalisch, Knobel, and Keil. But surely this is not necessary, and does not correspond to the words of the text. Those words simply state again of the pillar, in its changed position, that which we had before heard of it in ch. xiii. 23, that it was (in its ordinary state by day) a pillar of cloud,—cloud and darkness,—but gave light by night. And thus the purpose of which the last clause announces the fulfilment was answered. It divided the two hosts by day with a barrier of cloud, by night with a barrier of fire. On the common acceptation, the words **by night** are altogether superfluous and out of place. The pillar could only be a cloud and darkness to the Egyptians *by day*, for by night all is darkness; whereas it could only give light to Israel *at night*, for by day all is light. So that thus there would be no simultaneous contrast. See Josh. xxiv. 7, where it is only said that Jehovah *put darkness between* Israel and the Egyptians. **21.**] On the stretching

night. [21] And Moses stretched out his hand over the sea;
s Job xii. 17,19. Ps. cxxv. 5. Ezek. xxxii. 14. and Jehovah caused the sea to [s]part by a strong east
wind all that night, and made the sea dry, and the waters
were divided. [22] And the children of Israel went into
the midst of the sea upon the dry *ground:* and the waters
were a wall unto them on their right hand, and on their
left. [23] ¶ And the Egyptians pursued, and went in after
them in the midst of the sea, *even* all Pharaoh's horses,
his chariots, and his horsemen. [24] And it came to pass,
that in the morning watch Jehovah looked unto the
t Gen. xxxii. 8, ff.; xxxiii. 8; l. 9. [t]host of the Egyptians through the pillar of fire and of the
cloud, and troubled the [t]host of the Egyptians, [25] and
took off their chariot wheels, and brought them into diffi-
culty: so that the Egyptians said, Let us flee from the
face of Israel; for Jehovah fighteth for them against the
Egyptians. [26] ¶ And Jehovah said unto Moses, Stretch

out the hand, see note above, ver. 16. The miraculous effect is thus described: God sent a strong east wind which beat upon that part of the sea where the passage was to take place, and drove back the waters each way. The phenomenon was by this carefully-stated circumstance kept totally distinct from any that could be produced by an unusually low tide, accompanied by an unusually strong wind. That such combinations do produce wonderful effects in the neighbourhood of Suez, is testified by travellers. But that circumstance only furnishes another instance of God being pleased to use the workings of nature as the basis for His miraculous manifestations. Jehovah caused the sea to **go**, i. e. to part: the word is rendered *lead away* in reff. Job, *run* in ref. Ezek., *lead forth* in ref. Ps. The *go back* of the A. V. hardly gives the right idea, but represents more the driving in one direction only. **dry** is literally, **dryness**: see Gen. viii. 13. **23.**] The pursuit of the Egyptians appears to have been almost immediate, so that only the pillar of fire and cloud separated the two hosts. Thus the Israelites would have for the most part safely reached the other side by the time the Egyptian host was all within the bed of the sea. It does not appear whether the Egyptians followed seeing the miracle and trusting to its continuance, or simply in the darkness and seeing the pillar move on. **24.**] The Hebrews divided the night into three watches: this was the third or morning watch, from about 2 A.M. to sunrise. We cannot infer, either from this verse or from Ps. lxxvii. 18 (which need not refer specially to this incident), that the troubling was by means of a storm. Nay, the narrative itself forbids such a rationalization, by simply relating the miraculous act of God in looking through the pillar of fire and cloud, and by implying that no tempestuous agency was on the sea till Moses lifted his hand again. As little can we understand this looking of Jehovah unto the host of the Egyptians to have been a breaking out of fire through the dark portion of the pillar, supposed in the ordinary interpretation to have been turned towards the Egyptians. It was some terrible revelation of His presence dismaying the pursuers at once. **the host,** literally, the **camp**: so in reff. **25.**] Even those who rationalize on ver. 24 are obliged to confess that the narrative here can express no other than direct agency. The interference would appear to be that God made their chariots to advance with difficulty in the rough bed of the sea, wheels coming off, and thus the whole pursuit became involved in trouble and delay. **26, 27.**] The immediate effect of the action enjoined appears to have been to cause the wind to cease by which the sea had been parted,

out thine hand over the sea, that the waters may come
again upon the Egyptians, upon their chariots, and upon
their horsemen. 27 And Moses stretched forth his hand
over the sea, and the sea returned to his strength when
the morning appeared; and the Egyptians fled against it;
and JEHOVAH overthrew the Egyptians in the midst of the
sea. 28 And the waters returned, and covered the chariots,
and the horsemen, *and* all the host of Pharaoh that came
into the sea after them; there remained not so much as
one of them. 29 But the children of Israel walked upon
dry *land* in the midst of the sea; and the waters *were* a
wall unto them on their right hand, and on their left. 30
Thus JEHOVAH saved Israel that day out of the hand of
the Egyptians; and Israel saw the Egyptians dead upon
the sea shore. 31 And Israel saw the great [u]work which
JEHOVAH did upon the Egyptians: and the people feared
JEHOVAH, and believed JEHOVAH, and [v]his servant Moses.
XV. 1 Then sang Moses and the children of Israel this
song unto JEHOVAH, and spake, saying,

u Job xxvii. 11. Ps. lxxviii. 42.

v Num. xii. 7, f. Deut. xxxiv. 5. Josh. i. 1. f., 7, 13, 15; viii. 31, 33, al.

or even to reverse its action in combination with the returning tide. The **Egyptians fled against it** (more properly, **to meet it**) is interpreted by Knobel that one part fled from the waves coming from the S., another from the opposite, and so each met the advancing sea. They could not flee the direct way, as it was blocked up by their own host.

29.] Is a repetition of ver. 22; not exact in its place here, seeing that before this Israel had passed over, but generally stated. **30.**] The circumstance of the bodies of the Egyptians being cast up on the eastern shore seems to favour the idea that an opposite or westerly wind was used to bring the sea again to its strength. **31.**] **work** is literally **hand**, as in reff. They entered the sea in faith, and the product of their deliverance was increase of faith. See the similar expression used on the effect of our Lord's first miracle, John ii. 11. Knobel remarks that the expression, Jehovah's servant, as applied to Moses, occurs only in the portions not due to the Elohist: see reff.

XV. **1—18.**] *Thanksgiving song of praise for Israel's deliverance.* Respecting this song of triumph opinions have no otherwise differed than according as men's estimates of the reality or otherwise of prophecy differ. Writers like Ewald and Knobel, with whom there is no such thing as an exaltation of human thought by Divine influence, regard every onward reaching reference in it as evidence that it was composed after the fact to which that reference is made. But, even taking such an opinion on its very lowest ground, is it likely that in the song of triumph of a people setting forth with a definite ultimate object, the return to the land of their fathers, no allusion would be made to their anticipations as regarded the entrance into that land? The course of patriarchal history, as I have endeavoured to shew in the notes, was sufficient to have suggested every allusion here made: see on ver. 17. But there is no need for us to confine ourselves to this lowest ground. Holding distinctly to the fact of a Divine leading and inspiration in the history of Israel, we see these popular yearnings and anticipations fixed, and lifted into prophecy by the Spirit who dwelt in Moses. For that his was the composition is clearly implied by the narrative. A remark of Herder's, quoted by Kalisch, is well worth remembering when

I will sing unto JEHOVAH, for he hath triumphed glori-
The horse and his rider hath he cast into the sea. [ously:

such criticisms as those of Knobel and Ewald are urged upon us: "If this poem contains parts which, it might seem, could not well have been sung in that period, it must be remembered that the temple, the holy places, and the land which the Israelites were destined to occupy, existed already clearly in God's and Moses's minds; and the latter prepared the people successfully for the exertions and sacrifices necessary for the realization of their hopes."

The ode may be divided into (*α*) the exordium, or refrain, responded to in ver. 21 by Miriam and the women, ver. 1 *b;* (*β*) three principal portions or strains, as arranged in the text; and an ascriptive conclusion, ver. 18. Of these strains the two former, vv. 2—5, 6—10, are retrospective, celebrating the overthrow of the Egyptians; the third, vv. 11—18, after a reminiscence of the same great act of God, becomes prospective, celebrating Jehovah's mercies which should follow after this same pattern of triumph. Within these larger divisions, the sentences are arranged, whether for responsive singing or merely in poetic structure, in parallelisms, as also given in the text.

All sorts of fanciful conjectures have been made as to the imagined *metre* in which the song was composed. They are not worth setting before the English reader. Not one of them has been substantiated even by the remotest probability, and the absurdity of them may be instanced by one specimen, that of Josephus and others describing the ode as composed in hexameter verse, a form of metre wholly alien from the Hebrew language.

This song is honoured among the Jews by being commonly call *Shirah*, the song, *par excellence.* "It is not only publicly recited in the synagogues on the seventh day of the passover, when the transit of the Israelites is believed to have taken place, but it has been embodied in the daily prayers." Kalisch.

1 *a.*] Introduction. It is time surely that we should claim to have done with such trifling as that set down here by Knobel, that it is "extremely improbable that the song should have been sung by all Israel immediately after the passage of the Red Sea." To take again the very lowest ground, the assertion of the text would be satisfied by what is related in ver. 21, that the burden, or refrain, of ver. 1 *b* was repeated in chorus by Miriam and the women. But we may well believe much more than this. Moments of exultant triumph have been known to inspire whole crowds with united sentiment and utterance; and when we add to this the suggestions of a specially present Divine Spirit, we may surely further believe that the host, or many of them, may have joined in exulting recitation of the principal parts of this glorious hymn, whether by previous dictation of Moses, such as must be prescribed in vv. 20, 21, or, which is less likely, in spontaneous outburst. **unto Jehovah**] i. e. in honour of, with reference to. In some parts the song is a direct address to Jehovah: compare vv. 6—8, 10—13, 16, 17. **1** *b.*] *The subject, or burden:* repeated in chorus by Miriam and the women, vv. 20, 21. The declarative singular number here is changed to the hortative plural in the chorus, ver. 21. This use of the first person singular in vv. 1, 2 makes perhaps the recitative by Moses alone probable. **hath triumphed gloriously**] I have left these words unchanged, consecrated as their sound is by the glorious chorus in Israel in Egypt. They not unfairly represent the Hebrew, which is literally, **in magnifying is magnified.** The words have a further reference than to the then present occasion. By this triumph Jehovah is magnified—His name lifted up among men. So the blessed Maiden's song of triumph, the *Magnificat;* so the future song of Moses and the Lamb (Rev. xv. 3) begins with the same strain of magnifying God. **thrown into the sea**] Description of the act from the result, which was as if they had been cast into the sea. Literally, the sea *came upon them.* To regard this (Knobel) as an inconsistency with the previous narrative is surely the merest trifling. As to the *depth* of the part of the sea which was dried, they only will find offence in it who reject the miracle, and to them the whole is fiction. Compare Neh. ix. 11. **2—5.**] *First strain.* It is not improbable that the responsive chorus of Miriam may have been given after the opening words of Moses, and

2 [w]JAH is my [x]strength and my song: — w See note. x Ps. viii. 3; xxix. 1; lxviii. 35; xcix. 4.
And is become my salvation:
This is my God, and I will glorify him:
My father's God, and I will exalt him.
3 JEHOVAH is a [y]man of war: — y Josh. xvii. 1. 2 Sam. xvii. 8.
JEHOVAH is his name.
4 Pharaoh's chariots and his host hath he cast into the sea:
And the [z]flower of his [a]captains are drowned in the — z Heb. *choice*. See Gen. xxiii. 6, reff.
5 The depths cover them: [Red sea. — a ch. xiv. 7.
They sank into the bottom as a [b]stone. — b Rev. xviii. 21.

6 Thy right hand, O JEHOVAH,
Is become glorious in power:
Thy right hand, O JEHOVAH,
[c]Dasheth in pieces the enemy. — c Judg. x. 8, only.
7 And in the greatness of thine excellency thou [d]over- — d Ps. xxviii. 5. 1 Chron. xx. 1.
[throwest them that [e]rise up against thee: — e ch. xxxii. 25. Deut. xxxiii. 11. Ps. xviii. 40.
Thou sendest forth thy wrath,
It consumeth them as stubble.

at the end of each portion or strain. JAH.] This name is the abbreviation of JEHOVAH. It seems to have passed from this song into the Psalms, where it is found 43 times: see especially Ps. lxviii. 4. Besides the Psalms, it is found only in ch. xvii. 16; Isa. xii. 2; xxvi. 4; xxxviii. 11, bis. It is frequently found in composition, as in *Hallelu-jah*, "*praise ye Jah.*" **my strength**] So literally. But the Hebraists contend that the word also means *praise*, and instance the reff. as examples. In all these, however, the primitive meaning *strength* will satisfy the context. The whole expression recurs, Ps. cxviii. 14; Isa. xii. 2, and kindred expressions in Ps. xviii. 2; xxviii. 7. **I will glorify Him**] The A. V., *I will prepare Him an habitation*, seems to be in error. The LXX., Vulgate, Syriac, and most interpreters have as the text. **3. a man of war**] i. e. one versed and mighty in war (Ps. xxiv. 8). The title is applied to men by way of honour in the reff. **4.**] On **captains**, see note, ch. xiv. 7; and on **Red Sea**, note, ch. x. 19. **5. cover them**] The Hebrew tense which has been in the A. V., and by the commentators, rendered sometimes by a *perfect*, sometimes by a *future*, according to the supposed requirements of the meaning, has been in our text with a view faithfully to preserve the original in its simplicity, uniformly rendered by a *present*. See for example, **dasheth**, ver. 6; **overthrowest, &c.**, ver. 7; and vv. 12, 14—16, ff. Those which we have rendered as *past* tenses are preterites in the Hebrew. **6—10.**] *Second strain.* **7.**] **the greatness of thine excellency**, literally, **the abundance of thine exaltation** or **height.** **thou overthrowest**] The word is commonly used of *pulling down* buildings, so Judg. vi. 28; 1 Kings xix. 10; Isa. xiv. 17, and frequently. In the reff. the sense is as here. The expression, *sending forth wrath* or *anger* is found in Ezek. vii. 3. The allusion is perhaps to the looking of Jehovah through the pillar of fire on the Egyptian host, ch. xiv. 24. The whole similitude is illustrated by Isa. ix. 18; x. 17; see also Isa. v. 24; Neh. i. 10. **8.**] **the breath of thy nostrils** was the strong east wind which caused the sea to recede: see Ps. xviii. 15. **piled up**] So Kalisch: the word is found only here, and signifies to be exalted or lifted up: see ch. xiv. 22. **the waves**] The contrast in the

8 And with the breath of thy nostrils the waters were
 The [f]waves stood upright as an [g]heap, [piled up,
The depths were congealed in the heart of the sea.
9 The enemy said, I will pursue, overtake, divide the spoil:
My [h]desire shall be satisfied upon them.
 I will draw my sword,
 My hand shall [i]destroy them.
10 Thou didst blow with thy breath, the sea covered them:
They sank as lead
 In the [j]lordly waters.

11 Who is like thee among the gods, O Jehovah?
 Who is like thee, glorious in holiness,
Fearful in praises,
 Doing wonders?

f Ps. lxxxviii. 16, 44. Isa. xliv. 3.
g Josh. iii. 13, 16. Ps. xxxiii. 7; lxxviii. 13.
h Heb. *soul.* See Gen. xxiii. 8. Deut. xii. 20, al. Eccl. vi. 7.
i Num. xiv. 12.
j Judg. v. 25. 1 Sam. iv. 8. 2 Chron. xxiii. 20. Neh. iii. 5. Ezek. xvii. 23. Nah. ii. 5; iii. 18.

original between *flowing* and *standing* is not suggested by the word *floods*, which is as often used in English of a standing water as of a flowing. **as heaps**] Kalisch prefers mounds, but one fails to appreciate the difference. The word used is of obscure derivation, but is found again in reff., and its meaning pretty clearly defined. **congealed**, or **coagulated**, as if by frost—suddenly arrested and made fast. **9**.] So the effect of sudden consecutive action is given in Judg. v. 27; Isa. xxvi. 5. Compare the well-known *Veni, vidi, vici.* **desire** is literally **soul**, but evidently to be understood as in reff. **desire** or **lust**, viz. of destruction and vengeance. **shall destroy them**] Of this meaning there can be little doubt, though the verb originally means to *possess* or *occupy.* The derived sense seems to be arrived at by that of *occupying the place of*, i. e. driving out or annihilating. The meaning in ref. is decisive. In Judg. i. 29, ff. the verb is repeatedly used for to occupy the place of, i. e. to *drive out*, expel, i. e. destroy: compare ib. 22—25. **10**. **They sank**] Knobel would connect the word thus rendered (*tsalal*) with one of the same sound signifying *clanging* or *jangling*, and would refer it to the hurtling or gurgling sound of sinking in the water; but other Hebraists, including Gesenius, are against him, and simply understand it of *sinking*, Gesenius objecting that there is no similarity in the sounds compared. **the lordly waters**] The adjective is thus rendered in ref. Judg. It is commonly used (see other reff.) to express magnificence or nobility.

11—18.] *Third strain.* We now, with a general ascription of praise to Jehovah (ver. 11) and a short reference to His recent mighty deeds (vv. 12, 13), pass on to the future,—the similar protection, safe guidance, and deliverance which He should furnish to His people in bringing them into the land of promise. **11**.] Bishop Wordsworth remarks, that the opening words of this verse, *Mi camocah ba-elim Jehovah*, were afterwards inscribed on the standards of the Maccabees in their wars against Antiochus, and that from the initial letters of these words their name of *Maccabees* was derived. **the gods** certainly are the idols of the heathen, classed by way of comparison with the true God, according to constant and undoubted usage of Scripture. See Ps. lxxi. 9; lxxxvi. 8; Isa. xliv. 10, 15; xlv. 20; xlvi. 6 al. fr., and compare 1 Cor. viii. 5, 6. Besides, we must not forget that what had passed had been specially announced by God as a judgment upon the gods of Egypt, ch. xii. 12. **glorious in holiness**] Here, as in Ps. lxxvii. 13 in A. V., the LXX. has rendered "*in the sanctuary.*" But there, as here, it cannot be doubted that **holiness** is the true rendering. Holiness is the exclusive attribute of Jehovah, the true God. It is, above all other attributes, His especial glory. It includes purity unspotted, justice unfailing, love unbounded.

12 Thou stretchedst out thy right hand,
    The earth swalloweth them. [deemest;
13 Thou leddest in thy mercy the people which thou re-
Thou guidest them in thy strength unto thy holy habita-
14 The people heard; they are afraid: [tion.
Sorrow took hold on
    The inhabitants of Philistia.
15 Then were amazed the sheikhs of Edom;
    The mighty ones of Moab,
    Trembling taketh hold on them:
All the inhabitants of Canaan melted away.
16 There falleth upon them fear and dread: [stone:
    By the greatness of thine arm they are still as a
Till these pass by thy people, O JEHOVAH,
    Till these pass by the people which thou purchasedst.
17 Thou bringest them in and plantest them in the moun-
        tain of thine inheritance:

See on ch. xix. 6. **Fearful in praises**] Man we may praise with enthusiasm, with generosity, with allowance: God we can only praise with *fear*. "He is terrible in His doing toward men" (Ps. lxvi. 5), so that all our celebration of His acts must be tempered with fear. We have to fear that our praise will be wanting in divine fitness, and excessive through human unfitness.

12.] Introduces, with the opening wonder of God's doing, the prophecy which is to follow, regarding, as Keil well remarks, that the singer regards all His wonders as implied and contained in that one. **13.**] On the rendering of the Hebrew tenses in this and following verses, see note, ver. 5. The **holy habitation** of God is the land of promise: see Ps. lxxviii. 54; Gen. xxviii. 16, 17; xxxi. 13; xxxv. 7. **14, 15.**] The inhabitants of Philistia who dwelt nearest to Egypt would first hear of the wonderful deliverance of Israel. It is no small confirmation of the genuineness of this sacred song and of its contemporaneity with the events among which it is placed, that these tribes are named in the order in which they would be likely to receive the news, and that the poetic description of the effects produced on them does not accurately in matter of fact correspond to the events. We do not learn that the Philistines or Edomites shewed any especial terror at the coming of Israel; indeed, Edom refused them a passage and obliged them to make a circuit round their land. The king of Moab indeed was afraid, and sent vainly for Balaam to curse them, but they were not allowed (Deut. ii. 9) to invade the territory of Moab, and Moab by no means ceased to be a most troublesome adversary to them: see Mr. Grove's exhaustive article "Moab" in the *Biblical Dict.* And so far were all the inhabitants of Canaan from melting away, that they were never nearly exterminated, and remained among the Israelites. No one, writing after the events had happened, could have thus expressed himself. Keil remarks that another evidence in the same direction is the classing the inhabitants of Canaan with Edom, Moab, and the Philistines,—importing a period when the command for the extirpation of the *Canaanites* had not as yet been given. On the chiefs or sheikhs of Edom, see Gen. xxxvi. 15. **16.**] See Isa. xxiii. 2. The **passing by** here spoken of is the passing through or by their territory, which would take place in the course of their journey to Canaan. Knobel, consistently with his view of the whole passage as written long *post eventum*, wants to refer the words to the passing over Jordan. On this view, see above. **17.**] **the mountain of** Jehovah's **inheritance** has been variously understood. Knobel thinks it means Canaan,

k 1 Kings viii. 13. Isa. iv. 5. A [k]place for thy dwelling didst thou make, O JEHOVAH:
l Ps. cvii. 36. Hab. ii. 12. A [l]sanctuary, O Lord, did thine hands establish.
18 JEHOVAH reigneth for ever and ever.

19 For the horse of Pharaoh went in with his chariots and
with his horsemen into the sea, and JEHOVAH brought
again the waters of the sea upon them; but the children
of Israel went on dry *land* in the midst of the sea. 20
¶ And Miriam the prophetess, the sister of Aaron, took a
timbrel in her hand; and all the women went out after
her with timbrels and with dances. 21 And Miriam an-
swered them, Sing ye to JEHOVAH, for he hath triumphed
gloriously; the horse and his rider hath he thrown into

referring to Lev. xxv. 23, and for the expression **mountain** as denoting the whole land, to Deut. iii. 25; Ps. lxxviii. 44. But this last place is used by Keil to shew that it is not the hill country or the land at all, but the mountain before signalized as God's dwelling-place by the sacrifice of Isaac. Keil further remarks, "That in ver. 17, at this early period, a mountain is already spoken of as Jehovah's habitation, denotes no 'prophecy after the event,' but is genuine prophecy, having however its natural foundation in this, that mountains were generally the site of divine service and sanctuaries, as we see Moses was fully aware, Gen. xxii. 2; Ex. iii. 1, 2. Compare such passages as Num. xxii. 41; xxxiii. 52; Mic. iv. 1, 2. In the fulfilment it is the Mount Zion, on which Jehovah reigns enthroned among His people." See Rev. xiv. 1, compared with Ps. xv. 1; Isa. lvii. 13. **the place** is Jerusalem; and in Jerusalem the temple, see reff., not the land of Canaan. And the **sanctuary** is not the tabernacle in the wilderness, which could not be said to be established, the word being ordinarily used of firm and stable erection: see reff.

18] This serves as a solemn conclusion to the whole song, ver. 19 being shewn by its style, which is narrative prose, not strictly to belong to it, but being probably inserted as explanatory. It would seem to come in as a natural appendage to the song, and to have formed part of the document containing it. The verse is included in the song in the Jewish scrolls of the law: but Kalisch remarks that the diction is perfectly prosaical, without rhythm or parallelism. Of course it will at once be seen, that it cannot form part of the same history, and from the same source, as ch. xiv. 28, 29,—repeating as it does by way of explanation the facts already given there in nearly the same words. But there is no inconsistency in detail with that passage, as some have supposed.

20.] Miriam was sister of Moses as well as of Aaron, but seems to be coupled with Aaron in order to leave Moses standing alone as the specially appointed of God to lead and to give laws to Israel: see on Num. xii. 1, 6—8, 10. She, as well as her brothers, had the gift of prophecy from God, which seems to have shewn itself in leading the women of Israel in sacred things. The (i. e. *her*) **timbrel**, *tôph* in the Hebrew, in other languages *tympanum*, *tambour*, *tabor*, *tambourine*, was apparently much what the last-named instrument is now, a hoop with a piece of parchment stretched over it, and armed with pieces of brass to make a jingling sound. It was played principally by women. See Judg. xi. 34; 1 Sam. xviii. 6; Ps. lxviii. 25; with the song and dance, Judith iii. 7; Jer. xxxi. 4; and in feasts, Isa. v. 12; xxiv. 8; but not exclusively by women: comp. 1 Sam. x. 5; 2 Sam. vi. 5. See also Job xxi. 12; Isa. xxx. 32. It is figured, as used by the modern Egyptian dancing-girls, in the art. "Timbrel" in the *Biblical Dict.*

21.] The chorus, as now in the "Israel in Egypt," consisted of the repetition of the leading strain, with the first person singular

the sea. 22 So Moses brought Israel from the Red sea,
and they went out into the wilderness of Shur; and they
went three days in the wilderness, and found no water.
23 ¶ And when they came to Marah, they could not drink
of the waters of Marah, for they *were* bitter: therefore the
name of it was called Marah [Bitterness]. 24 And the
people murmured against Moses, saying, What shall we
drink? 25 And he cried unto JEHOVAH; and JEHOVAH
shewed him a tree, *which* when he had cast into the waters,
the waters were made sweet: there he made for them a
[m]statute and an [m]ordinance, and there he [n]proved them,
26 and said, If thou wilt diligently hearken to the voice of
JEHOVAH thy God, and wilt do that which is right in his
sight, and wilt give ear to his commandments, and keep
all his statutes, I will put none of these diseases upon thee,
which I have brought upon the Egyptians: for I *am* JE-

m Josh. xxiv. 25.
n ch. xvi. 4. Deut. viii. 2, 16; xxviii. 8.

changed into the hortatory second plural.

22.—XVIII. **27.**] *The journey to Sinai. And herein* (22—27) *the journey from the Red Sea to Marah and Elim.* **the wilderness of Shur**] This name has before occurred in Genesis: see on ch. xvi. 7; xx. 1; xxv. 18. The wilderness includes the district lying E. of Egypt between the Mediterranean and the top of the Red Sea. It is called in Num. xxxiii. 8, "*the wilderness of Etham*," and Josephus renders it by "*the desert of Pelusium*." Mr. Holland, in his article on the recent survey of Sinai, says of the desert S. of Suez, "Some 12 or 15 miles from the coast, and parallel to it, runs Jebel er Rahab, appearing in the distance as a long flat-headed range of white cliffs, which form as it were a wall inclosing the desert on the N. Hence probably arose the name of the 'wilderness of Shur,' for the meaning of the name Shur is a wall."

23, ff.] A satisfactory site has been found for Marah. Howârah, at the head of Wady Amârah, where even now caravans halt in their journey to Sinai, possesses a spring at times so bitter that neither men nor camels can drink of it. There is no reason to suppose that the miraculous effect would be permanent, nor does the example of 2 Kings ii. 21 prove anything in this matter. It is manifestly idle to speculate about herbs which have the power to sweeten brackish water: the incident is related as special and miraculous, due to Divine intervention: and there our speculation ends. If there were such trees, then God founded, as so often, His miraculous action on something already familiar to men's minds. One feature distinguishes our narrative from anything which we have as yet read. It is the first which is distinctly pronounced to be typical, and gives rise to an ordinance and an instruction founded on the nature of the incident. The people murmured, therefore Jehovah proved them (see reff.) as follows. Against their murmurings He set obedience to Him: if they would change the one for the other, then He would remove from them, as typified in this deadly water (the Arabs to this day call the spring at Howârah "*destruction*"), all judgments and calamities of bodily disease, and be their Healer, as He had healed the bitter water. And this plain indication of a typical meaning in the miracle justifies the comment of the Christian Fathers, who, from Tertullian in the third century downwards, have seen in this healing tree a type of the Cross of Christ, which is set for the healing of men. Compare with this conditional promise (repeated in substance Deut. vii. 15) the corresponding threat on disobedience, Deut. xxviii. 27, 60. See also Ezek. xlvii. 7—9. We may observe that no trace is found of the name Marah, except in this Scripture narrative. **27.**] **Elim** (so named also Num. xxxiii. 9, as one of their

HOVAH that healeth thee. 27 ¶ And they came to Elim,
where *were* twelve wells of water, and threescore and ten
palm trees: and they encamped there by the waters.
XVI. 1 And they took their journey from Elim, and all
the congregation of the children of Israel came unto the
wilderness of Sin, which *is* between Elim and Sinai, on
the fifteenth day of the second month after their departing
out of the land of Egypt. 2 And the whole congregation
of the children of Israel murmured against Moses and
Aaron in the wilderness: 3 and the children of Israel said
unto them, Would that we had died by the hand of JEHO-

camping places) is generally acknowledged to be the present Wady Ghurundel, 2½ hours S.E. of Mara, and even now a famous watering-place of the Arabs. There is pretty good water, and in the rainy season a considerable stream, running into the Red Sea. Travellers speak also of the vegetation in this valley, especially the palms and tamarisks, and rank high grass. The name means *high* or *strong trees*. See Stanley, *Sinai and Palestine*, Appendix, No. 76. I may add that Mr. Holland, in his article, concurs in the abovementioned view, inclining however to place Elim on a raised plain above the S. bank of Wady Ghurundel.

XVI. *Quails and manna in the wilderness of Sin.* **1.**] Between the encampment at Elim, and the coming to the wilderness of Sin, there was, Num. xxxiii. 10, 11, an encampment by the Red Sea. But the present history, careful only about remarkable incidents, passes it over. On the topographical questions connected with this part of the route, see Stanley, *Sinai and Palestine*, pp. 37, ff. Knobel says, "They must have gone from Ghurundel to the upper end of the Wady Tayibeh, then have followed it westwards, and have encamped at its mouth near the present Ras Zelima, the distance being about 8 leagues." The further journey is much debated. The discussion will be found in Stanley, as above. The route for which there appears most to be said is that by Wady Mokatteb and Wady Feiran, leading up directly to the present or traditional Sinai. The whole of this district, described here as between Elim and Sinai, is probably the wilderness of Sin. The idea that the plain by the sea extending S. from Ras Zelima is meant, seems to be inconsistent with the definite local notice given in the text. The objection to the above suggested route, urged by Knobel, that these valleys abound with water and vegetation, and that they certainly would have been contested by the local tribes, is a weighty one: and the view maintained by him (and shared also by Keil) that the wilderness of Sin is the great sandy plateau Debbet er Ramleh, between the desert of Et-Tih and Sinai, is at least in harmony with the great features of the sacred narrative. This plateau begins near Elim and stretches S. Eastwards towards the range in which Sinai must be included. Knobel accounts for the détour to the encampment near the sea by the necessity of finding water, there being none of good quality between Ghurundel and the Wady Naseb in the direct line. But Mr. Holland, with much more reason, holds the Israelites to have gone down Wady Tayibeh to the sea, the inland détour having been occasioned by the bluff of the Hammam Pharaoan interrupting the coast march, and the wilderness of Sin to be the plain (El Murkah) extending from the mouth of W. Tayibeh for several miles. Thence he holds them to have gone up the Wady Feiran: see below.

1 *b*—**3.**] They had eaten the passover on the *fifteenth day of the first month*, therefore they had been a month coming to the wilderness of Sin, during which period their store of provision brought from Egypt had doubtless been exhausted. **Would that we had died**] Literally, **Who will grant us to have died . . . .**? A sudden death by the last fearful plague seemed to them preferable to this lingering death by famine. Compare Job xxi. 13. Kalisch demurs to this, and interprets dying **by the hand of**

vah in the land of Egypt, when we sat by the flesh pots, *and*
when we did eat bread to the full; for ye have brought
us forth into this wilderness, to kill this whole assembly
with hunger. 4 ¶ Then said Jehovah unto Moses, Be-
hold, I will rain [o]bread from heaven for you; and the o John vi. 31, ff.
people shall go out and gather every day sufficient for the
day, that I may [p]prove them, whether they will walk in my p ch. xv. 25, reff.
law, or no. 5 And it shall come to pass, that on the sixth
day they shall prepare *that* which they bring in; and it
shall be twice as much as they gather daily. 6 And Moses
and Aaron said unto all the children of Israel, At even,
then ye shall know that Jehovah hath brought you
forth from the land of Egypt: 7 and in the morning, then
ye shall see the glory of Jehovah; for that he hear-
eth your murmurings against Jehovah: and what *are* we,
that ye murmur against us? 8 And Moses said, *This shall
be,* when Jehovah shall give you in the evening flesh to
eat, and in the morning bread to the full; for that Jeho-
vah heareth your murmurings which ye murmur against
him: and what *are* we? your murmurings *are* not against
us, but against Jehovah. 9 ¶ And Moses spake unto

God to signify dying in old age and by a natural death. But this does not seem so probable. This was the third occasion of Israel's murmuring: see ch. xiv. 11; xv. 24. On the abundance in Egypt, see Num. xi. 5. **4, 5.**] *Promise of the manna.* Here observe, that the plainest declaration is made of the miraculous nature of this supply. Whatever natural phenomenon may have underlain the provision of manna, the supplying it from day to day, and the withholding it on the sixth day, were the special and immediate acts of Jehovah Himself. **every day sufficient for the day**] Literally, **the matter of the day in this day**: see Matt. vi. 11, 34. On the **proving** them, see on reff. **5.**] That is, on the sixth day, when they prepared, i. e. set in order, what they brought in, they should find it to be double the quantity which they had gathered on other days: see below on ver. 22, 23. The words do not imply any command to *gather* twice as much as on other days, as sometimes misunderstood, nor is any reason here assigned for the announcement: see again as below, and on the report to Moses by the elders, on ver. 22. **6.**] The **bread from heaven** of ver. 4 seems to have included both the quails and the manna, and Moses and Aaron received details respecting the supply, which the history does not relate. The people had said, "ye *have brought us forth:*" they were to be made to know that it was not Moses and Aaron, but Jehovah Himself. **8.**] As indicated by the italic, the sentence in the original does not contain the opening words; but the principal Hebraists agree that it needs some such clause to connect it with the foregoing.

9—12.] Here we have again one of those recapitulations so often occurring in the history, and apparently betokening independent origin, and a slightly differing report of the same or parallel incidents. The command here given might, but for what follows, be consecutive on ver. 8. But when Jehovah speaks to Moses out of the cloud, He commands him to say to them the very thing which he has already said, ver. 8, so that it would seem that ver. 9 is really consecutive on ver. 3, and that vv. 4, 5 represent in another form the words of Jehovah in ver.

Aaron, Say unto the whole congregation of the children
of Israel, Come near before JEHOVAH: for he hath heard
your murmurings. 10 And it came to pass, as Aaron
spake unto the whole congregation of the children of
Israel, that they looked toward the wilderness, and, be-
hold, the glory of JEHOVAH appeared in the cloud. 11
¶ And JEHOVAH spake unto Moses, saying, 12 I have heard
the murmurings of the children of Israel: speak unto
them, saying, At even ye shall eat flesh, and in the morn-
ing ye shall be filled with bread; and ye shall know that
I *am* JEHOVAH your God. 13 And it came to pass, that
at even the quails came up, and covered the camp: and
in the morning the dew lay round about the host. 14 And

12. In ver. 7 they were to see the glory of Jehovah in the morning, when they should have bread to the full: whereas in ver. 10 the glory appears, and out of it the announcement of the eating in the morning is made. With such evidence, we cannot surely in fairness reject the inference that parallel accounts have been united in the sacred narrative. It is quite vain, with Keil and others, to maintain that the appearance of the glory in ver. 10 is not that announced in ver. 7. **before Jehovah**] Spoken probably in anticipation of the appearance which immediately follows. Knobel understands the words as importing that space in front of the tent of Moses where afterwards the tabernacle was erected. But this seems doubtful; and much more probably, as Keil, they advanced towards the pillar of cloud. **10.**] **toward the wilderness** would be in the very direction in which they were, in their unbelief, reluctant to advance: not necessarily, as Knobel, towards Mount Sinai, as if Jehovah were considered permanently abiding there. God indicated, by this appearance, that He always went before His people and could supply them even when earthly means failed. **The glory of Jehovah** was manifested in a fiery appearance: see ch. iii. 2; xiii. 21; xl. 34; Lev. ix. 23, 24; Num. xiv. 10; xvi. 19, 42. **11.**] It is understood that Jehovah spake with Moses out of *the cloud of fire*. **12.**] It would here seem that this appearance took place on the morning *before* the quails came in the evening: compare what has been said above. **13.**] There seems no reason to depart from the ordinary rendering of the Hebrew word *selav* by **quail.** It is singular, and has the definite article: **the quail.** The whole description, here and in Num. xi. 31, 32, answers to the well-known habits of these birds, and the Arabic name for them even now is *Salwa.* In the spring they migrate northwards from Africa, and flying low, especially when wearied, are taken or come to ground in immense multitudes. Dr. Tristram says, "I have myself found the ground in Algeria, in the month of April, covered with quails for an extent of many acres at daybreak, where on the preceding afternoon there had not been one. They were so fatigued that they scarcely moved till almost trodden upon: and although hundreds were slaughtered, for two days they did not leave the district." The present writer has seen the S. coast of the island of Capri surrounded by a net on poles about four feet high at a short distance from the beach, set to catch the quails, and was told that enormous multitudes were on some days thus captured. Many more examples to the same effect are accumulated by Knobel. Pliny relates that they settle in such multitudes on the rigging of ships, as to overturn them. The Divine interference was shewn in bringing the quails to the precise spot of the Israelitish camp. The final clause of the verse is interpreted to mean that a dense mist settled round the camp, condensing in dew. **14.**] This having cleared off, the manna was found. **a small round thing**] The Hebrew word so rendered is found only here. It appears, after

when the dew that lay was gone up, behold, upon the face
of the wilderness *there lay* a small round thing, *as* small as
the hoar frost on the ground. 15 And when the children
of Israel saw *it*, they said one to another, It *is* [q] Man [i. e.
What?]: for they wist not what it *was*. And Moses said
unto them, This *is* the bread which JEHOVAH hath given
you to eat. 16 ¶ This *is* the thing which JEHOVAH hath
commanded, Gather of it every man [r] according to his eat-
ing, an omer for every man, *according to* the number of
your persons; take ye every man for *them* which *are* in
his tent. 17 And the children of Israel did so, and gathered,
some more, some less. 18 And they measured *it* with the
omer, he that gathered much had nothing over, and he
that gathered little had no lack; they gathered every man

q vv. 31, 33, 35. Num. xi 6, 7, 9. Deut. viii. 3, 16. Josh. v. 12 (bis). Neh. ix. 20. Ps. lxxviii. 24. John vi. 31, 49. Rev. ii. 17, only.

r ch. xii. 4.

all that has been said on it, to be rightly translated, or at least approximately well expressed. The variety of meaning next favoured by commentators is that of *coagulated*, or *run together*. 15.] The derivation of the name **manna** is very uncertain. The ordinary idea, that manna (Heb. *man*) carries a question, *What is this?* is perhaps the best supported. Knobel questions this, on the ground that *man* instead of *mah*, the ordinary Hebrew interrogative pronoun, could not have been put into the mouth of the Israelites by the sacred writer. But others answer to this, that the unusual form was probably the popular dialect. Knobel would derive the name from an Arabic root signifying a *gift* or a *grant*. But Keil objects that this root itself is not ancient, and is derived from the very word *manna* (*man*). So that perhaps we may safely abide by the old explanation. On the nature of the manna, see note, vv. 31, 35. The speech of Moses here, as well as God's words in ver. 4, entirely distinguish it from all merely natural produce. 16—21.] *Directions for the daily gathering of the manna, and their result.* On the **omer**, see note, ver. 36. 17, 18.] These verses stand literally thus: **And the sons of Israel did so, and they gathered; the increaser, and the diminisher. And they measured with the omer, and the increaser got nothing over, and the diminisher got nothing short**, &c. They have received two interpretations: the first, that of the ancient Jewish authorities, that every one, however little or however much he had gathered, when he came to measure the quantity in his tent, found as many omers as there were mouths in his family; the second, which is that of Calvin, Le Clerc, and Christian interpreters generally, that *the whole* which had been gathered was put into one heap, and when measured it was found exactly to fit the number of mouths, an omer for each, the superfluity of one man's gathering compensating the deficiency of another's. But surely this last is an explaining away of the simple assertion of our text, to say nothing of the great improbability of its hypothesis of *all* being poured into one great heap. The former interpretation must therefore be accepted. It involves this difficulty, that the idle gatherer would apparently thus have his family quota furnished him without his own labour, and if this were carried to the extreme, none need more than cover the bottom of his vessel, and the rest would be supernaturally supplied. But the answer would be that we are bound to understand the miracle as pre-supposing *bonâ fide* action in the too-little-gatherers. God defeated the greediness of the too-much-gatherers, and helped the weakness of the too-little-gatherers: but in the case of these latter, *aide-toi et Dieu t'aidera* was a necessary condition. And when St. Paul uses this verse as an illustration in 2 Cor. viii. 15, he distinctly assumes this condition, saying, "*where there is a ready mind*," literally, "*where readiness of mind is pre-existing*," a man is accepted according to that he hath, not ac-

according to his eating. 19 And Moses said, Let no man
leave of it till the morning. 20 Notwithstanding they
hearkened not unto Moses; but some of them left of it
until the morning, and it bred worms, and stank: and
Moses was wroth with them. 21 And they gathered it
every morning, every man according to his eating: and
when the sun waxed hot, it melted. 22 ¶ And it came to
pass, *that* on the sixth day they gathered twice as much
bread, two omers for one *man:* and all the rulers of the
congregation came and told Moses. 23 And he said unto them,
s Lev. x. 3. This *is that* which JEHOVAH said, [s]To morrow *is* a rest,
† Or, *rest.* an holy † sabbath unto JEHOVAH: bake what ye will bake,
and boil what ye will boil; and all that is over lay up for
you to be kept until the morning. 24 And they laid it up
till the morning, as Moses bade: and it did not stink,
neither was there any worm therein. 25 And Moses said,
Eat that to day; for to day *is* a sabbath unto JEHOVAH:
to day ye shall not find it in the field. 26 Six days ye

cording to that he hath not. **19.**] The manna was to serve for daily bread, not for a laid up and prospective store. Knobel reminds us that in the East the general practice is to eat bread of the same day, not of yesterday. **20.**] **it bred worms** is literally, **worms grew.**

22—30.] *Sequel of the announcement in* ver. *5.* In pursuance of the Divine announcement, when that which was gathered on the sixth day was set in order, "prepared," measured, it turned out to be twice as much as on other days, two omers per man. This miraculous circumstance, that God had given them "on the sixth day the bread of two days" (ver. 29), is reported by the rulers to Moses. Then, ver. 23, he explains to them that this was the meaning (see ref.) of what God had said, viz. of the announcement made to him by God, ver. 5, that the morrow was a rest, "a rest of holiness" to Jehovah, and *on that account* it was that the miracle had happened. In other words, the institution of the day of rest, which was coeval with the creation of man, was now to be practically put in force in Israel. Whatever observation of that day there may have been in patriarchal times, it is manifest that during the bondage in Egypt there can have been none, and by this circumstance it is to be revived. This is the simplest way of understanding all that passed. To suppose that ver. 5 contains a command to the people to *gather* twice as much on the sixth day, and that they did so, and that the rulers, ignorant of the command, came and told Moses, is to involve the narrative in inextricable difficulties. **a rest, an holy Sabbath**] Literally, **a** (**great**) **rest, a rest of holiness.** This is the first time that the word **Sabbath** occurs. It signifies **rest,** and may often be thus rendered: but its technical usage as applied to the seventh day begins with this its first occurrence, and must usually be maintained. **bake what ye will bake,** &c.] It is uncertain whether these words are to be taken as applying to the *whole* double allowance for the two days, or only to that for the sixth day. The latter seems most probable, for if the other were the case, the remainder which was kept over to the next day being cooked, could hardly be compared with that which was left over before, for it would naturally be less liable to incur putrefaction. Besides which, the very form of the sentence seems to favour this view: "bake and boil as much as you will, and that which is over lay up," &c., i. e. after baking and boiling what you will. On the other view, there would have

shall gather it; but on the seventh day, the sabbath, in it
there shall be none. 27 ¶ And it came to pass, *that* there
went out *some* of the people on the seventh day for to
gather, and they found none. 28 And JEHOVAH said unto
Moses, How long refuse ye to keep my commandments
and my laws? 29 See, for that JEHOVAH hath given you
the sabbath, therefore he giveth you on the sixth day the
bread of two days; abide ye every man in his place, let
no man go out of his place on the seventh day. 30 So the
people rested on the seventh day. 31 And the house of
Israel called the name thereof [t] Man: and it *was* like cori- t Ver. 15.
ander seed, white; and the taste of it *was* like wafers *made*
with honey. 32 ¶ And Moses said, This *is* the thing which
JEHOVAH commandeth, Fill an omer of it to be kept for
your generations; that they may see the bread wherewith
I have fed you in the wilderness, when I brought you forth
from the land of Egypt. 33 And Moses said unto Aaron, † Heb. *Man*, and so always.
Take a vessel, and put an omer full of † manna therein,

to be supplied after "all which is over,"—when you have eaten to-day's portion. It is true that in the subsequent injunctions concerning the Sabbath it is forbidden to kindle a fire on that day: but we do not absolutely know that the manna required cooking to make it eatable at all. It is observable that in ver. 25 Moses does not tell them to bake or boil the Sabbath portion, but merely "*Eat that to-day.*" **28.**] The question here is somewhat surprising, seeing that no commandments or laws had as yet been given, except those concerning the passover and the feast of unleavened bread. Israel had indeed often already murmured against God (see ch. xiv. 11; xv. 24; and ver. 2), and to this may be the reference. It can hardly be to the single command concerning the Sabbath: but the question may merely characterize generally their spirit of disobedience. **29. let no man go out of his place**] "Rabbinical tradition has from these words deduced the prohibition, that no Israelite shall go further than 2000 yards, i. e. 6 stadii, or 750 Roman paces (the Sabbath day's journey, Acts i. 12); for that was the distance of the holy tabernacle from the remotest part of the Hebrew camp." Kalisch.

31.] This comes in again as a part of an interrupted description, joining on most naturally to ver. 15, where their saying to one another, "It is *man*," leads on to the statement that this became its ordinary name. In these two places only have I retained the Hebrew word, **Man.** It seemed necessary here, where especial reference is made to the origin of the name: but the word has an awkward sound in English, and in the nine other places where it occurs (besides this chapter) I have kept to the common name. The LXX. and Vulgate have been inconsistent in their usage, sometimes giving it as *man*, sometimes as *manna.* The **coriander seed** is that of the *coriandrum sativum*, cultivated in England for confectionery, and wild in Egypt and Palestine. The seed is globular, grayish-coloured, and hollow, the surface marked with fine stripes. It has a pleasant spicy flavour. "We found it," says Dr. Tristram, "abundant in the valley of the Jordan." In Numbers xi. 8 it is said that the taste of the manna was as of fresh (or dainty) oil.

32—34.] It is to be laid up and kept for a memorial. What is meant by **before Jehovah** in vv. 32, 33 is explained by ver. 34, before the Testimony, or before the Law, i. e. the ark of the covenant, in which the Law was to be deposited, ch. xxv. 16, 21,

and lay it up before Jehovah, to be kept for your genera-
tions. 34 As Jehovah commanded Moses, so Aaron laid
it up before the Testimony, to be kept. 35 And the chil-
dren of Israel did eat the manna forty years, until they
came to a land inhabited; they did eat the manna, until
they came unto the borders of the land of Canaan. 36 Now

22. All this manifestly belongs to the somewhat later period, when the tabernacle was set up, and the ark of the covenant. The word rendered *pot* in the A. V. is found only here, and seems to be derived from a verb signifying *weaving* or *plaiting*. It was more probably a basket of some description: and so the Coptic version renders it. I have thought it better to preserve the general term **vessel**. **35.**] This notice is manifestly due to a period after the manna had ceased, and Israel had entered Canaan. By no possibility can that be true which some (e. g. Bp. Wordsworth) have maintained in anxiety to secure the authorship of Moses for every word of the Pentateuch, "this sentence shews that the Book of Exodus did not pass out of the hands of Moses till a little before his death:" for the manna did not cease till the day following the eating of the corn of Canaan on the morrow after the passover in Gilgal (Josh. v. 12); and the command to Joshua to pass over Jordan was prefaced by the words "Moses my servant is dead" (Josh. i. 2). This is only an example of a kind of criticism which needs to be entirely cleared away before the word of God can be fairly dealt with. Kalisch would change **a land inhabited** into "*the land which they were to inherit*," seeing that they did "pass, before their entrance into Canaan, through many inhabited countries, for instance, those of Sihon and Og." But he stands alone, and the rendering seems neither necessary nor allowable; whatever fragments, so to speak, of inhabited land they may have passed previously, it was Canaan which was especially and entirely to them the inhabited land. **the borders**] Heb. **the end,** i. e. as we should call it, meaning the same thing, *the beginning;* till they entered, that is, the land of Canaan. It is not meant that during the whole of this period they had no other sustenance: the herds which they had brought out of Egypt had not failed them at Sinai (ch. xxxiv. 3), nor even when they were about to pass through Edom (Num. xx. 19), nor even when the Reubenites and Gadites petitioned to be settled on the E. of Jordan (Num. xxxii. 1). It is plain that they had bread (Lev. viii. 2, 26, 31) and meal (Lev. ix. 4; x. 12; xxiv. 5, ff.; Num. vii. 13, &c.), and that they bought food and water from the Edomites (Deut. ii. 6). And from Josh. i. 11 we see that the staple of their victuals must have been other than manna, for there they are commanded to lay in three days' provision, and the manna would not keep from day to day. But it was granted to them during all this time to help out other provision, and probably it was the only food of those who could not afford the rarer and costlier kinds. It is only mentioned specially after this in Num. xi. 7, ff., at their first breaking up from Sinai, and in Num. xxi. 5, during the circuit of Edom, and after the death of Aaron. The mention in Josh. v. 12 has already been noticed. This miraculous supply, like many others of the Divine interference in this history, was grounded upon natural phenomena. The natural manna is still found in the peninsula of Sinai in May, June, and July, and most abundantly in the immediate neighbourhood of Sinai itself, —in the Wadys Feiran and Es Sheikh, Ghurundel and Taiyibeh. It distils in the warm nights, especially after rain, from the branches of the turfa, a kind of tamarisk. It falls in small balls on the ground beneath, is gathered before sunrise, and melts in the heat. It has the appearance of gum and the taste of honey, and when taken in some quantity acts as a mild purgative. So far there is an analogy. But the multiplication, and the continuance of the supply, and that without reference to production from trees, remove this incident from the realm of natural phenomena into that of supernatural. For further details concerning the manna, see the *Biblical Dict.* and Stanley, *Sinai and Palestine*, p. 26, note. **36.**] On the various Hebrew measures see Mr. Bevan's

an omer *is* the tenth *part* of an ephah. XVII. 1 And all
the congregation of the children of Israel journeyed from
the wilderness of Sin, after their journeys, according to
the commandment of JEHOVAH, and pitched in Rephidim:
and *there was* no water for the people to drink. 2 Where-
fore the people did chide with Moses, and said, Give us
water that we may drink. And Moses said unto them,
Why chide ye with me? wherefore do ye [u]tempt JEHOVAH? [u] Num. xiv. 22. Ps. lxxviii.
3 And the people thirsted there for water; and the people 18; xcv. 9; cvi. 14.
murmured against Moses, and said, Wherefore *is* this *that*
thou hast brought us up out of Egypt, to kill us and our
children and our cattle with thirst? 4 And Moses cried
unto JEHOVAH, saying, What shall I do unto this people?
they be almost ready to stone me. 5 And JEHOVAH said
unto Moses, Go on before the people, and take with thee
of the elders of Israel; and thy rod, wherewith thou
[v]smotest the river, take in thine hand, and go. 6 Behold, [v] ch. vii. 20.
I will stand before thee there upon the rock in Horeb;

art. "Weights and Measures" in the *Biblical Dict.* From Ezek. xlv. 11 we learn that the ephah was, in its turn, the tenth part of the homer. The *absolute* capacity of these measures is matter of considerable doubt. In the article above referred to the omer is given as estimated,—by Josephus at nearly nine-tenths of a gallon, by the Rabbinists at less than four-fifths.

XVII. 1—7.] *Lack of water in Rephidim; striking of the rock in Horeb.* **1. after their journeys**] i. e. (see ref.) with the intervention of some stages and encampments not here mentioned: viz. Dophkah and Alush, Num. xxxiii. 13, 14 (where see notes). Nothing particular having happened at either of these stages, they are left unnoticed by the history. **Rephidim**] i. e. *rests*, or *stays*. The situation may be approximately given. From ver. 6 and ch. xviii. 5 it was quite near to Horeb. From ch. xix. 2; Num. xxxiii. 15, the next day's encampment was in the wilderness of Sinai. The members of the recent survey were divided about the *exact* site of Rephidim, Mr. Holland placing it in the pass of El Matiyeh in the Wady es Sheikh, while the others placed it in Wady Feiran, a short distance below the spot where Wady Aleyat runs into it from Jebel Serbal. Mr. Holland's reasons for supporting his view may be seen in his article as above, and he has made a fair statement of the other side. Dean Stanley also, after Ritter, thinks that Rephidim must be in the Wady Feiran: see his *Sinai and Palestine*, pp. 40, 41, and Dr. Hayman's art. in the *Biblical Dict.* **2.**] The people tempted Jehovah in that they doubted His power or His will to supply them. See reff. **4, 5.**] This is the first mention of *stoning*. It was the ordinary capital punishment (see art. "Punishments" in *Biblical Dict.*), and from its nature was especially likely to have been resorted to in the dry and stony east as a tumultuary mode of putting to death. Of such character appears to have been the stoning of Stephen, Acts vii. 57, 58, where see notes. Moses was to take some of the elders as witnesses: the miracle was not to be seen by the people generally. We have the same care exhibited for the secrecy of the Divine works of wonder, in Gen. xix. 17; xxii. 5; xxxii. 29. **6.**] The miracle was to be wrought not by any power of Moses, but by the special presence of God on the spot. This makes the conduct of Moses and Aaron on the other similar occasion, Num. xx. 10, the more inexcusable, and the words of God there (ver. 11) more solemn: see note. The very name Horeb

and thou shalt smite the rock, and there shall come water
out of it, that the people may drink. And Moses did so
in the sight of the elders of Israel. 7 And he called the
name of the place [w] Massah [Temptation], and [x] Meribah
[Chiding], because of the chiding of the children of Israel,
and because they tempted JEHOVAH, saying, Is JEHOVAH
among us, or not? 8 ¶ Then came [y] Amalek, and fought
with Israel in Rephidim. 9 And Moses said unto Joshua,
Choose us out men, and go out, fight with Amalek: to
morrow I will stand on the top of the hill with the rod of
God in mine hand. 10 So Joshua did as Moses had said
to him, and fought with Amalek: and Moses, Aaron, and
Hur went up to the top of the hill. 11 And it came to

w Deut. vi. 16; ix. 22; xxxiii. 8.
x Num. xx. 13, 24; xxvii. 14. Deut. xxxii. 51.
y Num. xiv. 43, ff. 1 Sam. xiv. 48; xv. 1, ff.; xxvii. 8; xxx. 1, ff. 2 Sam. viii. 12.

signifies *dry and hard*, so that there was that in the command itself which set forth the paradox and the miracle. It is impossible to assign any satisfactory locality to this miracle. Some, among whom is Knobel, have supposed its site to have been the spot called by the Arabs Sassafeh, one of the highest summits of Horeb, whence the whole plain Er Rahah is commanded. But this seems unnecessary, and is against the whole evidence which points out Er Rahah as the site of the encampment before Sinai, which itself is now almost shewn to have been Ras-Sassâfeh; and also against the spirit of the narrative, for thus the miracle would be visible to the whole multitude. The traditions respecting the rock are given by Kalisch, and the probability of imposition being practised by the monks on the spot is discussed. **7.**] On difficulties attending the subsequent use of these names (reff.), see notes, Num. xx. 13.

8—16.] *Israel's fight with Amalek.* From Deut. xxv. 17, ff., it appears that the Amalekites, whose dwelling was near the Sinaitic peninsula, harassed the children of Israel, smiting the hindmost of them, being apparently jealous of this irruption of strangers into their fertile valleys round Sinai. On the question respecting the descent of this Amalek from Esau, see Gen. xxxvi. 2. The history of the Amalekites after this will be found in the various passages referred to in the margin. **9.**] This is the first mention of Joshua. He is called by this name also in ch. xxiv. 13; xxxii. 17; xxxiii. 11; Num. xi. 28; according to Knobel, all Jehovistic passages. The Elohistic narrative relates, Num. xiii. 8, 16, that his name was Oshea, and that Moses called him Joshua. The last name imports "Jehovah the Saviour," or "whose help is Jehovah," answering to the German "*Gotthelf.*" He already appears here as the commander of the armies of Israel. He was of the tribe of Ephraim, see Num. xiii. 8. **the hill** is variously assigned according to the foregoing interpretations. On **the rod of God,** see note, ch. iv. 20. **10.**] **Hur** is first here mentioned: he appears again in ch. xxiv. 14 in company with Moses and Aaron. He seems, from ch. xxxi. 2; xxxv. 30; xxxviii. 22, to have been of the tribe of Judah, and the grandfather of the eminent workman Bezaleel. He is not further mentioned in the Pentateuch. But in 1 Chron. ii. 19, 20, we learn that he was great-grandson of Judah, Caleb being his father by a second wife Ephrath (see ib. ver. 50, and iv. 4; and remarks on Josh. xiv. 6, where Caleb is called "*the son of Jephunneh the Kenezite*"). Hur is said by Josephus (*Ant.* iii. 2, 4) to have been the husband of Miriam. This, if true, might account for his association with Moses and Aaron; if fictitious, may have been an inference from that association. **11, 12.**] This is a passage the symbolism of which lies so much on the surface, that it is impossible, in exegesis, to pass it altogether by. It was the first and the most strongly marked conflict of Israel with the heathen world. It was to be plainly declared that Israel's help was from God: that conquest was not of their own strength,

pass, when Moses held up his hand, that Israel prevailed:
and when he let down his hand, Amalek prevailed. 12
But Moses' hands *were* heavy; and they took a stone, and
put *it* under him, and he sat thereon; and Aaron and Hur
stayed up his hands, the one on the one side, and the other
on the other side; and his hands were steady until the
going down of the sun. 13 And Joshua discomfited Ama-
lek and his people with the edge of the sword. 14 And
JEHOVAH said unto Moses, Write this *for* a memorial in
the book, and rehearse *it* in the ears of Joshua: for I will
utterly put out the remembrance of Amalek from under
heaven. 15 And Moses built an altar, and called the name

but simply of Him, and because they were His people. And accordingly Moses, representing Israel (by Divine direction, we may well assume, though so much is not declared), takes the rod of God, that instrument through which His power had before been exercised, and holds it up to heaven, the hand or hands being in the universally recognized position of prayer, or, if this seem importing too much into the explanation, symbolizing plainly connexion between himself and God. As long as this is maintained, Israel prevails; when it is intermitted, Israel fails. The bearing of the symbolism on Messianic typology and on the religious life of men and communities of men, is obvious, but it is not within the province of this commentary to dwell on it. The process of the action seems to have been this. Moses at first held up his right hand with the rod: when that was wearied, his left: when both were wearied singly, the two together: when this failed Aaron and Hur held up the two, both holding the rod together. Knobel remarks that **the hand** only is mentioned in other places in this book where the hand with the rod is necessarily understood: see ch. viii. 5 compared with 6; ix. 22, 23; x. 12, 13. **13.] Amalek and his people** is perhaps only a mode of indicating the Amalekites,—perhaps means the Amalekites and others who accompanied them as followers or allies. **14.**] The first mention of perpetuating the memory of an incident in a book. The expression **the book,** which is the literal rendering, seems to imply that there was a known and recognized book in which the incidents of Israel's history were entered. And this seems to receive support from other passages: see ch. xxiv. 4, 7, where we read of "*the book of the covenant.*" In xxxiv. 27 Moses is commanded to write these words, as if a recognized book, in which to write, were already in existence; in Num. xxxiii. 1, 2 we are told that Moses wrote all the journeys of the Israelites by command of the Lord; in Deut. xxviii. 61 "*the book of this law*" is spoken of: see also Num. v. 23; 1 Sam. x. 25. We may conclude that this incident was directed to be recorded in the book of the journeyings which Moses kept.

The memorandum was to be, besides being committed to writing, **enjoined in the ears of Joshua**, seeing that he would have in charge the settling of Israel in the Land of Promise, and after that settling the rooting out of Amalek was to take place: see Deut. xxv. 19. The idea of Keil, that it was merely to strengthen Joshua's trust in God, is beneath the requirement of the context. A prophecy of the result of this injunction is found in the mouth of Balaam, Num. xxiv. 20. The injunction came practically into remembrance in the days of Saul, 1 Sam. xv., but was not entirely fulfilled: see 1 Sam. xxx. 1—20; 2 Sam. viii. 11, 12: even down to Hezekiah's time; see 1 Chron. iv. 42. **15, 16.**] This altar seems not to have been erected for sacrifice, but as a memorial, as in Gen. xxxiii. 20; see this purpose fully set forth and vindicated in the case of the Reubenites, Gadites, and Manassites, Josh. xxii. 15—34. Ver. 16 is very difficult. It would really appear as if the present Hebrew text could hardly be correct.

of it Jehovah-nissi [Jehovah my banner]: 16 for he said,
† or, perhaps, banner. that a hand is on the † throne of Jah, war to Jehovah
with Amalek from generation to generation. XVIII. 1
When Jethro, the priest of Midian, Moses' father in law,
heard of all that God had done for Moses, and for Israel
his people, *and* that Jehovah had brought Israel out of
Egypt; 2 then Jethro, Moses' father in law, took Zipporah,
Moses' wife, after he had sent her back, 3 and her two
sons; of which the name of the one *was* Gershom [Exile];
for he said, I have been an alien in a strange land: 4 and
the name of the other *was* Eliezer [My God *is* help]; for
the God of my father, *said he*, *was* mine help, and delivered
me from the sword of Pharaoh: 5 and Jethro, Moses'
father in law, came with his sons and his wife unto Moses

The altar is called Jehovah-nissi, and for this naming a reason is to be rendered. As the text now stands, the reason is, **that a hand (is) on the** ***Kehs*** **of Jah, war is to Jehovah against Amalek from generation to generation.** Now this word *Kehs* is found only here, and can only be interpreted by an hypothesis of some kind. The majority of translators and commentators have supposed it to be an abbreviated form of *Kisseh, a throne*. But how should the name Jehovah-*nissi* be accounted for by the word *Kisseh*, even supposing that to be meant? The Hebrew word *nehs*, differing from *Kehs* only as the letter נ, noon, differs from כ, caph, means *standard* or *banner*, and is the very word used in the foregoing appellation, *Jehovah-nissi*. We can hardly help believing that *nehs* and not *Kehs* must be the original text. This is the view taken by Le Clerc, Michaelis, Gesenius, De Wette, Knobel, and others. In this case the meaning would be, **the hand is on the banner of Jah**, i. e. the Lord has ever His banner in His hand, is ever waging war, which would be a natural expression, especially after the long-sustained attitude of Moses, for the perpetuity of war on the part of Jehovah against Amalek. Still, we must deal with the text as we have it, in the absence of any existing various readings, however improbable its forms may appear. And it must be owned, that as it now stands the text does not seem to convey any definite meaning. The *hand on the throne* is said variously to imply an oath, and to be God's hand on His throne, or to import Moses's hand which was lifted up to God's throne in prayer, or to be Amalek's hand lifted against God's throne, i. e. His people Israel, or to be the interceding and ruling hand of Christ on God's throne. I fairly own that one of these seems to me as irrelevant as the other, and not one of them to have the remotest reference to the endurance of God's war with Amalek. I have therefore left the text in its obscurity, inserting in the margin the alternative, and as it seems to me the far more probable rendering.

XVIII. *Visit of Jethro to Moses.* On **Jethro**, see ch. ii. 18; iii. 1, ff, and notes. The interchange of the Divine names in this narrative is to be observed, but hardly can be always rendered account of. In this first verse, e. g., there seems no reason why a difference should be made, or why the reverse order should not have been adopted.

2.] There has been no previous mention of this sending back of Zipporah. It probably took place after the incident related, ch. iii. 24, 26: see note there.

3, 4.] The birth and naming of Gershom has been related, nearly in the same words, in ch. ii. 22. Nothing has hitherto been said of Eliezer, but "*his sons*" are spoken of in ch. iv. 30, see note there. The name Eliezer is in signification nearly allied to Joshua, "God" standing instead of "Jehovah." The German Gotthelf would express both.

5.] Jethro appears to have visited

into the wilderness, where he encamped at the mount of
God: 6 and he said unto Moses, I thy father in law Jethro
am come unto thee, and thy wife, and her two sons with
her. 7 ¶ And Moses went out to meet his father in law,
and did obeisance, and kissed him; and they asked each
other of *their* welfare; and they came into the tent. 8
And Moses told his father in law all that JEHOVAH had
done unto Pharaoh and to the Egyptians for Israel's sake,
and all the travail that had come upon them by the way,
and *how* JEHOVAH delivered them. 9 And Jethro rejoiced
for all the goodness which JEHOVAH had done to Israel,
whom he had delivered out of the hand of the Egyptians.
10 And Jethro said, Blessed *be* JEHOVAH, who hath de-
livered you out of the hand of the Egyptians, and out of
the hand of Pharaoh, who hath delivered the people from
under the hand of the Egyptians. 11 Now I know that
JEHOVAH *is* greater than all the gods: for in the thing
wherein they dealt proudly *he was* above them. 12 And
Jethro, Moses' father in law, took a burnt offering and

Moses at Rephidim. We already know that that encampment was close to Horeb, and here we have Moses "*encamped at the mount of God.*" The visit seems to have been after the battle with Amalek: hardly, as Kurtz supposes, in consequence of Israel's victory, or that would have been mentioned in ver. 1. Jethro came in consequence of hearing of the wonders in Egypt and of the Exodus; possibly owing to previous agreement with Moses, who was divinely informed that his march would lead him to Horeb (ch. iii. 12). **6.**] **he said**, i. e. by messengers: the meeting follows. **7, ff.**] Moses does all eastern honour to the eminence of Jethro: brings him into his tent, and informs him of the details of the deliverances of which he had generally heard, and of the passage of the Red Sea, and the victory over Amalek. Here all is to the praise of JEHOVAH, the God of Israel, whom thereby Jethro recognizes as greater than all the gods. Some understand the latter clause of ver. 11 as meaning that Jehovah had requited upon the Egyptians, by destroying them in the water, that which they had devised against the Hebrews, by casting their children into the waters. But Neh. ix. 10, where these words are plainly referred to, shew that such reference of them is too narrow, and that they apply to the whole dealings of God in requital of Egypt's pride against Israel. **12.**] It would seem as if there were some general mode of offering common to Israel, and to those who, though outside the covenant of Jehovah, yet recognized the true God. It is not said that Jethro offered to Jehovah, though he recognized His supereminent greatness: he knew Him not as *Jehovah*, not being within His covenant. This is a notable instance of intercommunion under even that dispensation which most jealously and exclusively fenced about the unity of faith and worship. The *place* was most probably that previously indicated, ch. xvi. 9, as "*before* JEHOVAH," or it might have been that the sacrifices were offered on the altar of ch. xvii. 15. But see note there. The offerings were of two kinds: the burnt offering, that which was lifted up on the altar and entirely consumed, and the thank offerings, those parts of the slain victim which were not consumed but simply offered, and then partaken of by the offerers. The various sacrifices will be explained in the places where they are enjoined. Moses is not mentioned among those that came, because he was the host, the entertainment

thank offerings for God: and Aaron came, and all the
elders of Israel, to eat bread with Moses' father in law
before God. [13] ¶ And it came to pass on the morrow, that
Moses sat to judge the people: and the people stood by
Moses from the morning unto the evening. [14] And when
Moses' father in law saw all that he did to the people, he
said, What *is* this thing that thou doest to the people?
why sittest thou thyself alone, and all the people stand by
thee from morning unto even? [15] And Moses said unto
his father in law, Because the people come unto me to en-
quire of God: [16] when they have a matter, they come
unto me; and I judge between one and another, and I do
make *them* know the statutes of God, and his laws. [17] And
Moses' father in law said unto him, The thing that thou
doest *is* not good. [18] Thou wilt surely wear away, both
thou, and this people that *is* with thee: for this thing *is*
too heavy for thee; thou art not able to perform it thy-
self alone. [19] Hearken now unto my voice, I will give
thee counsel, and God shall be with thee: Be thou for the
people to God-ward, that thou mayest bring the causes
unto God: [20] and thou shalt teach them ordinances and
laws, and shalt shew them the way wherein they must
walk, and the work that they must do. [21] Moreover thou
z See Gen. xxii. 8. Isa. xxviii. 15. shalt [z] provide out of all the people able men, such as fear
God, men of truth, hating covetousness; and place *such*

taking place in his tent. The **eating bread,** as in ref., is not to be confined to the literal sense of the words: it was the partaking of the flesh of the victim offered. It took place **before God,** i. e. in the spot where God had been worshipped by the sacrifice.

13—26.] Moses was the depository of the oracles of God for Israel, and reported to them His (then unwritten) statutes and laws. This he had hitherto done entirely in his own person. Such labour was too hard for him, and the waiting whole days during the necessary delays of decision was too hard for the people. There is nothing, as Keil supposes, improbable in Knobel's view, that the cases which arose formed the ground on which statutes and laws were based; indeed, ver. 20 seems to require such an understanding. **18.**] The literal words are, **Fading thou wilt fade.** **19.**] The meaning seems to be well expressed in the A.V., and can hardly be, as Kalisch and Keil make it, that Moses was to be to the people *instead* of God, *in the place of* God. He was to be **for them in the presence of God,** i. e. as their representative, to bring their difficulties and questions to God for decision, and on those causes, thus brought, were to be grounded (ver. 20) precedents which might rule future action. **21. provide**] Literally, **look**: see reff. There is an apparent difficulty as to the numbers of these rulers or judges: if all here mentioned were appointed for 600,000 men, their numbers would be, for the tens, 60,000; for the fifties, 12,000; for the hundreds, 6000; for the thousands, 600; in all, 78,600 rulers or judges. (The argument against this calculation in Keil is ingenious, but would go entirely to explain away the assertions of the text. His

over them, *to be* rulers of thousands, *and* rulers of hundreds,
rulers of fifties, and rulers of tens: 22 and let them judge
the people at all seasons: and it shall be, *that* every great
matter they shall bring unto thee, but every small matter
they shall judge: so make it easy for thyself, and they
shall bear *it* with thee. 23 If thou shalt do this thing, God
shall strengthen thee, and thou shalt be able to endure,
and all this people shall also go to their place in peace.
24 So Moses hearkened to the voice of his father in law,
and did all that he had said. 25 And Moses chose able
men out of all Israel, and made them heads over the
people, rulers of thousands, rulers of hundreds, rulers of
fifties, and rulers of tens. 26 And they judged the people
at all seasons: the hard causes they brought unto Moses,
but every small matter they judged themselves. 27 ¶ And
Moses let his father in law depart; and he went his way
into his own land. XIX. 1 In the third month of the
going forth of the children of Israel out of the land of
Egypt, the same day came they *into* the wilderness of Sinai.

view is that the thousands, hundreds, fifties, and tens import only greater and smaller families, and are no numerical guides at all. On his support of this view from Deut. i. 15, see there.) Either the words of vv. 24, 25 must not be taken literally, and must mean only that the principle was generally followed, or the subsequent arrangement mentioned in Num. xi. 16, ff., as prescribed by God Himself, may have been a remedy proposed for the inconveniences of this present system. See notes there. It is also somewhat surprising that in a congregation, which so frequently and largely manifested a rebellious and murmuring spirit, so large a number should have been found possessing the high qualifications here specified. Yet it would appear from the subsequent narrative that the number of those thus appointed must have been very considerable, for in Num. xxv. 5 we find Moses commanding "*all the judges of Israel*" to slay those who were joined to Baal-peor. **23.**] The rendering given of this verse is that of the LXX., approved by Gesenius and others, and seems best to suit the context. If we follow that of the A.V. the meaning will be, "*If thou do this, and it meet with the Divine approval,*" &c. **to their place**] i. e. to Canaan, the spot for which they are bound. On vv. 24, 25, see above. **27.**] Midian was no part of the Sinaitic district, but a land by itself. See on ch. ii. 15, and Num. x. 30.

XIX. *Arrival at Sinai, and preparation for the covenant.* Vv. 1, 2 contain, as is found so often in this book, two concurrent accounts of the same matter. The former part of ver. 2 connects with ch. xvii. 1, and is repeated in the enumeration in Num. xxxiii. 15, but is a chronological notice, of the same character as those in ch. xii. 41, 51; xvi. 1. In the specification, **in the third month, ... the same day,** it is uncertain what day of the month is meant. Knobel and Keil maintain that **the same day** means only *at that time*, in that month, and that no nearer date is here given, citing for this the specifications of time in Num. ix. 1; xx. 1, where however no mention of *day* is made. Kalisch renders, *in the third new moon*, but Hengstenberg and Keil have shewn that the Hebrew word is nowhere in the Pentateuch used in this sense, nor indeed necessarily anywhere else. But it must be acknowledged that, irrespectively of any

2 And they departed from Rephidim, and came *to* the
wilderness of Sinai, and encamped in the wilderness; and

question about the import of the *word*, the general inference would seem to be that **the same day** would imply the very day that it began to be the third month, i. e. the first day of the month. **2.**] This verse raises the whole question of the locality of Sinai and the place of the encampment.* In discussing this, we may perhaps be permitted to set aside at once, as not fulfilling the Egyptian conditions of the problem, the hypothesis which would place Mount Sinai much further east in Arabia, and would make the eastern arm, the present Gulf of Akaba, the Red Sea of the Israelites' passage. The spot of that passage was only three days' journey removed from their starting-point in Egypt, a description which cannot possibly answer to any point of the Gulf of Akaba. Assuming then that the present Gulf of Suez is the "Red Sea" with which we have to deal, we have to seek for Mount Sinai in the triangular piece of land which divides the two gulfs. Now there are certain conditions which any assigned mountain must fulfil. (1.) It must be easy of approach, and have before it a space large enough for the children of Israel to assemble. (2.) It must be a prominent mountain rising abruptly, or nearly so, from the underlying plain. We read of the people *standing at the nether part of the mount* (ch. xix. 7). It must also have been accessible from that plain, since *bounds were set about it* (ib. 23). (3.) There must have been plentiful supply of water and pasturage close by.

Now of the mountains within the piece of land, there are but two which in any way come up to these conditions, Jebel Serbal and Jebel Mûsa. The former of these is the most imposing feature in the peninsula, and of itself would be chosen as the likeliest spot. But (1.) It is not visible from any point of the valleys which surround its base. (2.) The two valleys (see the map), Wadys Aleyat and Ajelah, which run from its base to Wady Feiran, are filled with boulders and torrent beds, and most unsuitable for a large encampment. And there is not, as once supposed, any plain between them; on the contrary, the intervening space is a chaos of rugged mountains intersected by deep ravines. The members of the late Survey Expedition were unanimous against Jebel Serbal as having any claims to be the Sinai of the Law.

In examining Jebel Mûsa, they found as follows. The Ras Sufsâfeh, forming not a distinct mountain, but the N. portion of Jebel Mûsa, rises up precipitously from the bottom of the plain of Er Râheh to a height of about 2000 feet, and "stands out in lovely grandeur against the sky like a huge altar" (Stanley). It is bounded by Wady el Deir, "the Valley of the Convent," on the E.; Wady Shuraich, a steep and rocky valley, on the W. This last is separated by a narrow ridge (Jebel Fara) from Wady Leja, lying still further W. On the S. two smaller valleys run into Wady Sebaiyeh and separate it from the neighbouring mountains. So far, the conditions seem to be fulfilled. Some have advocated the southern and highest peak of Jebel Mûsa as being Sinai, and have placed the encampment in Wady Sebaiyeh. But that valley could hardly have been the spot. It does not lie immediately below the mountain, and there is nowhere extent enough for the camp. On the contrary, the plain of Er Râheh is the most suitable spot imaginable for the assembling of many thousands of people. It is upwards of two miles long and half a mile broad. It slopes (contrary to the statement hitherto made) towards the foot of the mountain, at about 300 yards from which there runs across the plain a low semicircular mound forming a kind of natural theatre, while further distant on either side of the plain the slopes of the enclosing mountains would afford seats to an almost unlimited number of spectators. "The members of our expedition," says Mr. Holland, "were as unanimous in their conviction that the Law was given from Ras Sufsâfeh to the Israelites assembled in the plain of Es Râheh, as they had been unanimous in rejecting Serbal as the mount of giving the Law." Particulars are afterwards adduced respecting the possible enlargement of the encampment into a neighbouring val-

* In the whole of the following note I have been helped by Mr. Holland's article on the recent "Explorations in the peninsula of Sinai."

there Israel encamped before the mount. 3 And Moses
went up unto † God, and JEHOVAH called unto him out of
the mountain, saying, Thus shalt thou say to the house of
Jacob, and tell the children of Israel; 4 Ye have seen what
I did unto the Egyptians, and *how* I bare you on [a]eagles'
wings, and brought you unto myself. 5 Now therefore, if
ye will obey my voice indeed, and keep my covenant, then
ye shall be a [b]peculiar treasure unto me above all people:
for all the earth *is* mine: 6 and ye shall be unto me a
kingdom of priests, and an holy nation. These *are* the
words which thou shalt speak unto the children of Israel.
7 ¶ And Moses came and called for the elders of the

† HA-ELOHIM.

a Deut. xxviii. 49; xxxii. 11, 12. 2 Sam. i. 23. Job ix. 26. Ps. ciii. 5. Isa. xl. 31, al.

b Deut. vii. 6; xiv. 2; xxvi. 18. 1 Chron. xxix. 3. See Eccl. ii. 8. Also Lev. xx. 26. Ps. cxxxv. 4.

ley at the mouth of Wady Leiffa, and shewing that there is no spot in the peninsula so well supplied with water as the neighbourhood of Jebel Mûsa. This point being considered as fixed, the whole route has to be arranged accordingly, and this has been done approximately by the recent survey, in a manner which I have in the main followed through the preceding chapters.

3.] Moses knew before the Exodus that the people would worship God upon this mountain (ch. iii. 12). Hither then he had led them, and on his arrival had gone up to the Divine Presence. Keil suggests that the cloudy pillar may have withdrawn itself to the mountain. However this may have been, doubtless Moses had received an intimation in obedience to which he went up. He does not appear at first to have approached the summit, nor as yet had God descended on Mount Sinai. The Divine Presence was withdrawn into the fastnesses of the mountain, and from thence Jehovah called to him. **the house of Jacob]** This is the only place in the Pentateuch where Israel is so called. This first utterance of Jehovah from Sinai opens by reminding Israel of His deliverance, and promising them special adoption as His people, on condition of obedience. **on eagles' wings]** The eagle is swift and vigorous of flight, and more than other birds careful for the flying and the safety of its young: see reff. The bird is, strictly speaking, not the eagle, but the griffon (*gryps fulvus*), the great vulture: see Dr. Tristram's account, *Nat. Hist. of Bible*, p. 172, ff. The most interesting of the reff. is that in Deut. xxxii. 11, 12, where the pertinency of this comparison is shewn by Moses, in an enlarged treatment of the similitude. **unto myself,** i. e. to Mount Sinai, where was God's earthly dwelling-place. In Rev. xii. 4 this similitude is referred to, where were given to the woman *the two wings of the great eagle, that she might fly into the wilderness.* It has been remarked that the similitude is of interest as mentioned by Moses, seeing that in Egypt the griffon vulture was sacred to the goddess of maternity. **5.]** This verse is much alluded to in the N. T., and the expressions used in it of Israel applied to the Christian Church. See Acts xx. 28; 1 Cor. vi. 20; vii. 23; Eph. i. 14; Titus ii. 14; 1 Pet. ii. 9. The expression here, a peculiar treasure, is literally a hoard or treasure specially set aside. See the same form of expression in reff., where equivalent descriptions are given of Israel. This Israel was to be, not because Jehovah was their national God and not the God of other nations also; but inasmuch as all the earth is His, He chooses out of all the nations Israel to be in an especial manner His. And this is further expanded in ver. 11, by saying that they should be to God **a kingdom of priests,** i. e. a realm the denizens of which, compared to the rest of mankind, were to be as the priests compared to the rest of a nation; in other words, **an holy nation.** See again St. Peter's use of these words 1 Pet. ii. 5, where he follows up the figure of priesthood. The expression is found in the O. T. only here. On the *holiness* of the nation and those in it, see ch. xxii. 31; Deut. xiv. 21; Isa. lxii. 12. We may observe that these words contain the

people, and laid before them all these words which JEHO-
VAH commanded him. 8 And all the people answered to-
gether, and said, All that JEHOVAH hath spoken we will
c Gen. xxxvii. 14. Deut. i. 32, 35. Josh. xxii. 32. do. And Moses [c]brought again the words of the people
unto JEHOVAH. 9 And JEHOVAH said unto Moses, Lo, I
d Ps. xviii. 11, ff.; civ. 3. Isa. xix. 1; xxix. 6. come unto thee in a [d]thick cloud, that the people may hear
when I speak with thee, and believe thee for ever. And
Moses told the words of the people unto JEHOVAH. 10
¶ And JEHOVAH said unto Moses, Go unto the people, and
sanctify them to day and to morrow, and let them wash
their clothes, 11 and be ready against the third day: for
the third day JEHOVAH will come down in the sight of all
the people upon mount Sinai. 12 And thou shalt set bounds
unto the people round about, saying, Beware to yourselves,
of going up into the mount, or touching the border of it:
whosoever toucheth the mount shall be surely put to death:
e 1 Sam. xx. 36, 37. Ps. xi. 2. 2 Kings xiii. 7, al. 13 there shall not an hand touch him, but he shall be
stoned with stones, or [e]shot with a dart; whether beast

whole substance of God's spiritual covenant with Israel, and are among the most important in the whole history. 7.] **before them**, literally, as A. V., **before their faces**, but there is no need here rather than elsewhere to express this common idiom.

8.] This was the acceptance of the covenant by the people, Moses acting strictly as mediator or go-between in the transaction. And this his mediatorship was to be substantiated (ver. 9) by the speaking of Jehovah, present in the darkness of a cloud, with Moses, and the people hearing. Then they would believe for ever in the Divine mission and authority of Moses. This substantiation of the mission of Moses was to extend to the people's hearing not of the whole law, but only of the ten commandments, for these only Jehovah spake, and added no more, Deut. v. 22; see also ch. xx. 18, 20. The darkness of clouds is the accustomed investiture of the Divine presence, see reff. The repetition of the notice that Moses told the people's words to Jehovah would almost look as if a mention of Moses having conveyed God's last announcement to them and their answer had dropped out.

10—13.] *Formal precautions to be taken in preparation for the manifestation of God.* The people were to be **sanctified**, as was the household of Jacob, Gen. xxxv. 2. Minute regulations for lustral washings are given in Levit. xv. 5, &c. They were very much used in Egypt, and were doubtless generally known in their ceremonial use in Israel. 12.] By what follows in ver. 23 it appears that this command of setting bounds was meant of placing a material fence around the bottom of the actual rise of Sinai, so that the people *could not* break through.

13.] None were to share his crime by approaching to touch him, but he was to be put to death from a distance, either by stoning or by a cast of a javelin or arrow. The literal words are, **by stoning he shall be stoned, or by shooting shall be shot**. The last clause is not without difficulty. The LXX. has an extraordinary translation: "when the voices and the trumpets and the cloud have departed from the mountain," they shall go up upon the mountain. And similarly the Targum of Onkelos, but without the additions: and the old Syriac, "when the trumpet shall be silent." This shews that the difficulty was felt, and a various reading devised to meet it. For according to the narrative, ver. 16, the trumpet sounded and the people came out and stood on the nether part of the mount, before God spoke in their hearing with Moses. The

or man, it shall not live: when the trumpet soundeth long,
they shall come up into the mount. 14 ¶ And Moses went
down from the mount unto the people, and sanctified the
people; and they washed their clothes. 15 And he said
unto the people, Be ready against the third day: come
not near a woman. 16 ¶ And it came to pass on the third
day in the morning, that there were thunders and light-
nings, and a thick cloud upon the mount, and the voice
of the trumpet exceeding loud; so that all the people that
was in the camp trembled. 17 And Moses brought forth
the people out of the camp to meet with God; and they
stood at the nether part of the mount. 18 And mount
Sinai was altogether on a smoke, because JEHOVAH de-
scended upon it in fire: and the [f]smoke thereof ascended [f] Gen. xix. 28.
as the smoke of a furnace, and the whole mount quaked
greatly. 19 And when the voice of the trumpet sounded

difficulty consists in the same term being used in the command at the end of the verse as had been used in the prohibition in ver. 12. These two actions are the same, that of going up into the mount. They were not to do it under pain of death, but when the trumpet sounded long, they were to do it. It would be an injunction of no import to order them to come up, as Knobel agrees with the LXX., &c., in supposing, *after the Divine manifestations were over.* These lasted many weeks, and these words manifestly relate to something to be done by the people during this present day's events. I cannot solve the difficulty. Keil supposes that when the trumpet gave the signal, Moses brought the people out of their boundary and up the lower hills. This agrees well with a *primâ facie* view of the narrative of vv. 16, 17, but does not satisfy the identity of the terms noticed above, nor indeed ver. 23.

trumpet] "*Yobel*, a joyful sound, *jubilum:* thence the sound of the trumpet, which was used to announce the *jubilee;* perhaps connected with the same root as *Jubal*, Gen. iv. 21. The word here used is different from that in ver. 16, 19." Bp. Wordsworth.

14, 15.] On the conclusion of ver. 15, see Levit. xv. 16—18. **16.**] **thunders**, literally **voices**: see ch. ix. 23, ff. It is added, Deut. iv. 11, that "*the mountain burned with fire unto the heart of heaven.*" This was the descent of God, announced ver. 9. Knobel remarks, "As God enters Jerusalem in the ark with shouts and blowing of trumpets (2 Sam. vi. 15; Ps. xlvii. 6; lxviii. 18, f.), so He appears on Sinai, accompanied by angels (see the LXX. Deut. xxxiii. 2 ['and the angels with Him']). Similar is the announcement of the Messiah at His coming being accompanied by angels, and one of them blowing the trumpet (Matt. xvi. 27; xxv. 31; 1 Thess. iii. 13; iv. 16)." **17.**] It would appear as if the people had been hitherto restrained within their camp, and now were brought (not all of them, but naturally a chosen portion only) out of the camp to the bounds which had been set around the mount, ver 23. These bounds were on the lower portion of the mount itself, so that the people could stand outside them and yet be **at the nether part of the mount.** But this explanation does not remove the difficulty above stated, on ver. 13. **18.**] See Ps. xviii. 7—13; Heb. xii. 18—20. **19.**] Moses enquired the Divine pleasure, and God **answered him by a voice**, i. e. spoke His commands plainly in the hearing of the people: those being the ten commandments, which follow, ch. xx. 1. That these are intended, and not a separate and preliminary voice, the whole context, and the parallel account in Deut. v., prove. But between ver. 19 and the consecutive words in ch. xx. 1 comes in another, and subsidiary

long, and waxed louder and louder, Moses spake, and God
answered him by a voice. 20 And JEHOVAH came down
upon mount Sinai, on the top of the mount: and JEHOVAH
called Moses *up* to the top of the mount; and Moses went
up. 21 And JEHOVAH said unto Moses, Go down, charge
the people, lest they break through unto JEHOVAH to gaze,
and many of them perish. 22 And let the priests also,
which come near to JEHOVAH, sanctify themselves, lest
JEHOVAH break forth upon them. 23 And Moses said
unto JEHOVAH, The people cannot come up to mount
Sinai: for thou chargedst us, saying, Set bounds about the
mount, and sanctify it. 24 And JEHOVAH said unto him,
Away, get thee down, and thou shalt come up, thou, and
Aaron with thee: but let not the priests and the people
break through to come up unto JEHOVAH, lest he break
forth upon them. 25 So Moses went down unto the people,
and said it unto them. XX. 1 And God spake all these

account of the descent of God on Sinai, and of the limitation of the people, and of the command to Moses to come up with Aaron, ending with the notice that Moses went down to the people, and spoke to them: after which the spoken commands of God in ch. xx. come in abruptly and inconsecutively. This seems the only way of understanding the insertion of vv. 20—25.

20.] This coming down of God has (see above) been already related, vv. 16, ff. The going up of Moses to the top of the mount does not seem in the order of things to have taken place till later, see ch. xx. 21. And the warning of ver. 21, ff., is in a measure correspondent to that of vv. 12, 13. Ver. 23 comes in rather curiously, and would almost seem to refer to some command not hitherto related, for we have had no order from God to set bounds *about the mount*, or to sanctify *it*. The verse is a reminiscence of ver. 12, and represents the same facts, but is otherwise expressed, and as the same narrator could hardly have given it.

21.] For it is death to man to behold God: see Gen. xvi. 13; ch. xxxiii. 20.

22.] Who are these **priests?** We have in the narrative no mention of a priesthood before ch. xxviii. 1, ff., where Aaron and his sons are specially devoted to the priestly office. The persons here mentioned must have been those, whoever they were, that exercised the office before that appointment was made. Priests of some sort there must have been (see ch. xxiv. 5), or no sacrifice could ever have been offered. Possibly they were the first-born, as the Jewish interpreters think; possibly the princes of the people, as others, and as seems perhaps implied in ver. 24, "*the priests and the people*," but we cannot speak with certainty. Whoever they were, they were to **sanctify** (specially purify) themselves, lest Jehovah, being wroth with them, visit them with vengeance. Knobel directs attention, as he has done often before, to the characteristic anthropomorphism of this parenthetic narrative. **23.**] See remarks on ver. 13, which certainly to our present understanding seems, unless violence be done in the rendering (as in A. V.), to be hardly in agreement with this. **24.**] The Divine response takes no note of the reply of Moses in ver. 23, but reiterates the command to charge the priests and the people not to break through. **25.**] After this, Knobel supposes the giving of the Decalogue followed in this narrative also. Moses went down to the people and abode with them while God spake the ten commandments. He is with the people at the end of them, ch. xx. 19, ff.

words, saying, 2 I *am* Jehovah thy God, which have

XX. 1—17.] *The ten commandments.* It would much exceed the limits of a general commentary to enter upon the various questions respecting the Decalogue. We may briefly state—1. Respecting the two reports of it contained in the Pentateuch, viz. here and Deut. v. 6—18: that this one is beyond all question the older and the more exact, as will be shewn in the notes on Deuteronomy. 2. Respecting the division into commandments: that while it is evident these were ten in number, "*the ten words,*" ch. xxxiv. 28 (see also Deut. iv. 13; x. 4), no division into these ten is suggested anywhere in the sacred text. Consequently, various divisions have been current. The oldest testimony is found in Philo, who wrote about the time of our Lord, and thus divides: (1) Strange gods, (2) Images, (3) The name of God, (4) The Sabbath, (5) Parents, (6) Adultery, (7) Murder, (8) Theft, (9) False witness, (10) Covetousness. With this Josephus agrees, except that instead of following the LXX. in the order of (6) and (7), he keeps to the Hebrew text, which is the order in the A. V. This division was followed by Calvin, and is that adopted in the Reformed Churches and by the modern Greek Catechism.

The next important division is that which unites into one commandment vv. 3—6, and divides ver. 17 into two. This has no primitive support in *both* its features, although some of the earliest Fathers seem to have made vv. 3—6 one commandment. It is first found in its completeness in Augustine, who counts ver. 17 as two, but transposes the order of the opening clauses to that found in Deut. v. 21, placing the neighbour's *wife* before his *house*: the only arrangement, be it noted, which can even seem to justify such a division of the verse. The Latin Fathers and teachers who followed adopt this division, and it is that of the Roman Catholics and of the Lutheran Church.

A third division is that which regards ver. 2 as the first commandment, vv. 3—6 as the second, and ver. 17 as the tenth. This is found mentioned as early as Cyril of Alexandria (Cent. V.), and it is stated as possible by Jerome. It is also left as possible in the uncertain earlier arrangements of Clement of Alexandria (Cent. III.) and others. It has had considerable support among the Talmudical writers and the mediæval Rabbis.

The disputes about the divisions which follow from the various punctuation of our present Hebrew text do not admit of notice in this commentary. The division which most commends itself to us is the first mentioned, provided that ver. 2, the statement of the fact that Jehovah is the God of Israel, and of His great deed of deliverance of Israel, be included in the first commandment. The division of ver. 17 into two commandments we regard as altogether illogical, the sin forbidden being one and the same, towards whatever possession of our neighbour's the desire may be. On the other hand, the sin forbidden in ver. 3 is not identical with that forbidden in vv. 4, 5, seeing that a man might have other gods than Jehovah without worshipping images.

Another question occurs, as to the division of the ten commandments between the two tables on which they were written (ch. xxiv. 12; xxxi. 18; xxxii. 15, 19; xxxiv. 1, 2, 28; Deut. iv. 13; v. 22; ix. 10, 11). And here again the more ancient evidence is also the more trustworthy, that five commandments were written on each table, for the form and distribution of the Decalogue itself support such a division. The five former commandments prescribe duties towards God and parents, the giver of all life and the earthly propagators of it; towards those set over men and higher than them. The five latter regard conduct towards equals and fellow-men. The former enjoin *piety*, the latter *probity*. To this are added the considerations—(*a*) That to each of the former five a *motive* is attached: to none, however, of the latter; (*b*) That in each of the five former the words Jehovah thy God occur, and in none of the five latter. The logical connexion of the commandments will be found under each below. It is only left to remark that it is not without reason that the Decalogue holds its supereminent and exclusive place at the head of the whole law. Its simple but comprehensive ordinances are the foundation of all that follows; and hardly anything can be found in the subsequent expansion of the Law in detail which is not grounded upon or derived from the Decalogue itself. **2, 3.**] *The first*

brought thee out of the land of Egypt, out of the house of
bondmen. 3 Thou shalt have no other gods [g]beside me.
4 Thou shalt not make unto thee any [h]graven image, or
any form that *is* in heaven above, or that *is* in the earth
beneath, or that *is* in the water under the earth: 5 thou
shalt not bow down thyself to them, nor [i]serve them: for
I JEHOVAH thy God *am* a jealous God, visiting the iniquity
of the fathers upon the children unto the third and fourth
generation of them that hate me; 6 and shewing mercy
unto the thousandth *generation* of them that love me, and

g Gen. xxxi. 50. Deut. xix. 9.

h Judg. xvii. 3, &c. 2 Kings xxi. 7. Ps. xcvii. 7. Isa. xl. 19, al.

i ch. iii. 12. 2 Kings x. 18. Isa. xix. 21. Jer. xliv. 3.

commandment. Jehovah the God of Israel to be held the only God. Knobel, from whom much that has preceded is derived, makes ver. 2 alone the first commandment. The objection to this is, that it contains no command, except by implication. It is better to regard the exclusive holding of Jehovah as God as the first commandment. Again, to regard (as Keil and others) ver. 2 as a mere introduction, and ver. 3 as the first commandment, is objectionable, as it leaves the first without a *motive*, and thus incommensurate with the others of the first table. The *motive* of this first commandment is the deliverance of Israel from Egypt. And undoubtedly this same motive is to be supplied from this first in the four remaining commandments of this table, where "*Jehovah thy God*" occurs. **no other gods**] As, e. g., the host of heaven (Deut. iv. 19): the gods of the heathen nations (ch. xxiii. 24), whose very names were not to be mentioned (ch. xxiii. 13). **beside me**] Such is the generally received interpretation, and not as A. V.; "*before me*," i.e. "*in my presence*," is possible, but does not seem so well to suit ver. 23. In our Liturgical Decalogue we have **but me**, which expresses the right meaning. The commandment, as also all those which are expressed negatively in form of prohibition, implies the opposite corresponding duty, in this case that detailed in Deut. vi. 4, 5.

4—6.] *The second commandment. Prohibition of image worship.* The *motive* of this commandment is the jealousy of God, not allowing the outward payment of worship due to Him to be given to another than Himself. Knobel's objection that unless we unite ver. 3 to this commandment, the motive, which really belongs to ver. 3 as much as to ver. 4, will be detached from that verse, will prove too much, for that motive belongs just as much to ver. 2, the exclusiveness of God's right to Israel's worship being implicitly asserted there also. And it must also be remembered that by this commandment, not so much the having other gods is forbidden as the worship of Jehovah Himself by means of images. That this is so is evident from Deut. iv. 15, where the ground of this prohibition is stated as being that they saw no form when Jehovah spoke to them. The various kinds of forms are also in that passage explained. Those **in heaven above** are (the stars and host of heaven, and) birds; those **in the earth beneath** men and beasts and land reptiles; those **in the water under the earth** fishes and water reptiles. **5.**] The **bowing down** is in prayer; the **serving**, in sacrifice, see reff. Keil remarks well, that the latter part of ver. 5 and ver. 6 apply to the first and second commandments alike (see argument against Knobel above). Jehovah is jealous (Deut. vi. 15) as Israel's only God, and will not suffer the transfer of His honour to another: see ch. xxxiv. 14; He is jealous as a spirit, invisible by man, and will not suffer that His invisible glory to be transferred to material figures: see Rom. i. 23; Isa. xlii. 8; xlviii. 11. The third generation is taken by some as the grandchildren, by others as the great grandchildren. The latter seems most probable, see ch. xxxiv. 7.

6.] Not "*unto thousands*," as the A. V., but as in the text, as is evident from Deut. vii. 9. In Hebrew, the same word serves as the cardinal and ordinal number in the case of *a thousand*. The extension of God's mercy vastly exceeds that of his wrath. It is hardly worth mentioning, as

keep my commandments. 7 Thou shalt not [j]take the name
of JEHOVAH thy God [k]in vain; for JEHOVAH will not
[l]hold him guiltless that taketh his name in vain. 8 [m]Re-
member the sabbath day, to keep it holy. 9 Six days shalt
thou labour, and do all thy work: 10 but the seventh day
shall be rest unto JEHOVAH thy God: thou shalt not do

j ch. xxiii. 1. Num. xxiii. 7. Job xxvii. 1. Ps. lxxxi. 3; cxxxix. 20.
k Ps. xii. 2; xli. 6; cxxxix. 20. Isa. lix. 4.
l ch. xxxiv. 7. 1 Kings ii. 9. Job ix. 28; x. 14. Ps. xix. 13. Jer. xxx. 11
m=ch. xiii. 3.

plain to all, that the art of sculpture is not forbidden by this commandment, nor indeed the practice of sculpture for religious uses of decoration, &c., seeing it was prescribed to Moses (ch. xxv. 18; xxvi. 31; Num. xxi. 9), and practised by Solomon with the Divine approval (1 Kings vii. 25, ff.; compare viii. 16). What is forbidden is the use of any such images as assistants to or vehicles of worship. The ordinary practice of the Romish Church is in direct violation of this commandment, and they accordingly omit it from their Decalogue in their authorized catechism, being afraid to teach it to their people.

7.] *The third commandment. Prohibition of profane use of the name of God.* Some, among whom is Kalisch, regard this commandment as directed only against *perjury:* but it manifestly is of far wider extent. The verb rendered **take** means to **take up** or **lift up**; it is applied in reff. to *raising* or uttering a false rumour, to *taking up* a parable, to *blowing up* a trumpet, to *lifting up* a prayer. Hence we may deduce, that it is here equivalent to *uttering*, raising up out of silence into speech. Some have supposed the words rendered **in vain** to mean *for a lie*, so as to sanction or bear witness to a falsehood. Doubtless this would be one, and a very marked, way of breaking the commandment; but the signification of the words is far wider, being, **into emptiness or waste**: see reff., in all of which it is rendered *vanity*. The meaning of the prohibition is as commonly understood, that the name of Jehovah is not to be invoked, used, uttered to no purpose, unadvisedly, lightly, or wantonly, much less to sanction untruth. By the last clause of the verse a connexion is established with the last commandment, where there is mention of the visiting of guilt. The word used is a remarkable one, the root signifying purification by sacrifice: Jehovah will not purify, absolve, reckon as innocent: see reff., where the Hebrew word occurs in the same sense.

8—11.] *The fourth commandment. Observance of the Sabbath day.* The first word of this commandment, **remember**, has been imagined to presuppose a foreknowledge of the ordinance here formally enjoined. But the expression, especially as qualified by the following, **to keep it holy,** hardly carries so much as this. The day was to be remembered for the sake of being kept holy, i. e. was to be thought of and observed on its weekly recurrence, not neglected and forgotten. In other words, *memory* enjoined is not so much *of the past*, as *in the future:* forget not to keep holy the sabbath day: see reff. In Deut. v. 12 the equivalent word to this Remember has no trace of memory of the past, but imports exactly as we have here interpreted, "*observe*," "*keep*." The fact, that the special honour of the seventh day dated from the Creation, remains: but it can hardly be alluded to in these words as they now stand. The *institution* of the Sabbath had been first formally brought before Israel by the doubling of the manna on the sixth day, see on ch. xvi. 22, ff.; and with this view Deut. v. 15 also agrees, where the Exodus is expressly assigned as the reason of the injunction to keep the Sabbath. In Deut. v. 12, 16, the words, "*as Jehovah thy God commanded thee*," are added to this and to the first clause of the next commandment: see there. The **keeping it holy** is afterwards explained. **9.**] This verse is not an absolute command, as some have treated it, to devote every day but the Sabbath to work, for thus it would have been contradicted by the Law itself, which prescribed days of rest which were not Sabbaths. But it is a command for the sake of the exception which is to follow; in the secondary and background of the commandment, not in its front and main regard.

10.] The seventh day, on the contrary, **shall be rest unto Jehovah**, see ch. xvi. 23. It is far better here to keep the *meaning* of the Hebrew **Sabbath**, rather than

any work, thou and thy son and thy daughter, thy man-
servant and thy maidservant and thy beast, and thy
stranger that *is* within thy gates: 11 for *in* six days JEHO-
VAH made heaven and earth, the sea, and all that in them
is, and rested the seventh day: wherefore JEHOVAH blessed
the sabbath day, and hallowed it. 12 ¶ Honour thy father
and thy mother: that thy days may be long upon the
land which JEHOVAH thy God giveth thee. 13 Thou shalt
not kill. 14 Thou shalt not commit adultery. 15 Thou

the technical term *Sabbath*, for thus we have the exception set both in contrast to the *work* which has preceded, and in connexion with Jehovah's *rest*, which follows. The persons included in the prohibition are divided by the absence of the copulative before **thy manservant**, into two classes: (1.) The family of the house, (2.) All belonging to it. The gates within which the stranger is are those of the city or village, see Deut. xiv. 21, not the doors of the private house. The general character of this prohibition is illustrated in detail in many subsequent places, as e. g. with reference to field-work, ch. xxxiv. 21; to wine-pressing and merchandise-making, Neh. xiii. 15; to bearing burdens, Jer. xvii. 21; to buying and selling generally, Amos viii. 5; to gathering wood, Num. xv. 32, ff.; to lighting fires in private houses, ch. xxxv. 3. On the addition in Deut. (v. 14), see there, and on ch. xxiii. 12. The motive of *rest* is not adduced here: see below.

11.] Here follows the *motive* for the command: the fact that God after the six days of creation rested on the seventh day, and on that account that day was a holy one. Therefore Israel, whose it was (Deut. viii. 6; x. 12; xi. 22; xxvi. 17) to walk in the ways of Jehovah their God, were to do as He did, and rest on that day. This likeness to God must not be left out of sight, as Keil maintains, seeing that it was a prominent point ever kept in Israel's view: see Lev. xi. 44; xix. 2; xx. 26. For this another motive is substituted in Deut. v. 15, see there. On the great fact referred to, see notes, Gen. ii. 2, and compare ch. xxxi. 17.

12.] *The fifth commandment. Command of honour to parents*, the *motive* being the prospect of long life in the land of promise. Observe, we are still on the ground of "duty to God," and have not yet entered on "duty to man's neighbour." This commandment, in its mention of **Jehovah thy God**, in its appending a motive to the command, in its prescribing reverence to those above a man, who stand to him in the place of God, belongs to the first, not to the second, table. The wider application of this command to all who stand in any degree in the place of parents, whether in domestic or in civil life, needs no explanation here. See the references made to this commandment in Matt. xv. 4; Eph. vi. 2. In the former of these our Lord asserts its Divine authority; in the latter, St. Paul refers to it as *the first commandment with promise:* see note there. Long life was ever esteemed under the old dispensation as happiness, and as the reward of piety. See Deut. iv. 40; v. 33; vi. 2; xi. 9; xxii. 7; 1 Kings iii. 14; on the other hand, see Prov. xx. 20; xxx. 17. In the parallel, Deut. v. 16 (cited by St. Paul as above), the words "*and that it may go well with thee*" are added. As Knobel well remarks, they may be regarded as included here also, by the mention of the happy land of promise.

13.] *The sixth commandment. Prohibition of murder.* Here (see above) begins the second table, containing those commandments which concern duties towards fellow-men. Of these the first concerns *life*, man's greatest treasure (Job ii. 4), called his *one thing* or *only one* in Ps. xxii. 24; xxxv. 17; see also our Lord's saying, Matt. xvi. 26. On the extent of this prohibition, see Matt. v. 21, 22; and in the Law itself, ch. xxi. 12, 14, 18; Lev. xix. 14; Deut. xxii. 8.

14.] *The seventh commandment. Prohibition of adultery.* Next to a man's life comes she whom he loves as one with himself: holding a place next to his own person, and far before all his goods. See Gen. ii. 24; Prov. xii. 4; xix. 14; xxxi. 10, f. See the Divine

shalt not steal. 16 Thou shalt not be a false [n]witness
against thy neighbour. 17 Thou shalt not covet thy neigh-
bour's house, thou shalt not covet thy neighbour's wife,
nor his manservant, nor his maidservant, nor his ox, nor
his ass, nor any thing that *is* thy neighbour's. 18 ¶ And
all the people [o]saw the thunderings, and the lightnings,
and the noise of the trumpet, and the mountain smoking:
and when the people saw *it*, they [p]were moved, and stood

n ch. xxiii. 1. Deut. xvii. 6; xix. 15. Ruth iv. 9—11. Isa. viii. 2, al.

o = Gen. xlii. 1. Isa. xliv. 16. Jer. xxxiii. 24.

p = Isa. vii. 2; xix. 1.

comment on this command, Matt. v. 28; and the legal extensions of it in ch. xxi. 19; Levit. xviii.; xix. 19, f., 29; xx. 10, ff., &c. The LXX. (perhaps by mere mistake, as they follow the common order in Deut. v.) put this commandment and the eighth before the sixth.

15.] *The eighth commandment. Prohibition of theft.* Next in value follow the neighbour's goods, which, like his person and his dearest possession of all, must be inviolable by us. See extensions of this literal command in ch. xxi. 33; xxii. 13, 25, ff.; Levit. xix. 13.

16.] *The ninth commandment. Prohibition of false witness against another.* It is possible to injure a neighbour without laying hands on his person, his wife, or his goods, —by that which shall put all these in peril, viz. undermining his character by false testimony against him. This, then, is also provided against. The A. V., familiar as its sound is to us, is hardly near enough to the original, which is literally, **Thou shalt not answer against thy neighbour as a witness of falsehood**: the word **witness** being not neuter, of the *thing testified*, but masculine, of *him that testifies:* see reff. On the slightly varying sentence in Deut. v. 20, see there. This command is further extended in other places, see ch. xxiii. 1 (Num. xxxv. 30; Deut. xvii. 6; xix. 15, 16, ff.); xxii. 13, ff.

17.] *The tenth commandment. Prohibition of greedy desire.* Of all the acts forbidden in this second table selfish desire is the root. Therefore it, as well as they, is forbidden. First, the **house** is not to be desired, i. e. the household (Gen. xv. 2; Job viii. 15), including all the particulars which follow,—wife, servants, cattle, goods. Thus the whole holds together as one commandment. In Deut. v. 21 the wife is put first, probably to keep the order of the seventh and eighth commandments. The same order is adopted here by the LXX., who also insert from Deut., "*nor his field,*" as does also the Samaritan text. This order is necessary for those who wish to split this tenth into two commandments. See above on ver. 1. There is no mention here of *his horse*, seeing that horses were almost practically unknown, and indeed almost forbidden to the Israelites (Deut. xvii. 16; Hos. i. 7; xiv. 3). But the LXX. version, which was made in Egypt, where horses abounded, has inserted after **his ox nor his ass,** "*nor any beast of his.*" Here the Samaritan Pentateuch has this curious and characteristic addition: "*When Jehovah thy God shall have brought thee into the land of the Canaanites, whither thou goest to possess it, thou shalt set up for thee two great stones, and thou shalt plaster them with lime, and thou shalt write upon those stones all the words of this law. And when thou shalt have passed over Jordan, thou shalt set up those stones which I command thee this day, in the Mount Gerizim, and thou shalt build there an altar to Jehovah thy God, an altar of stones: thou shalt not lift up iron upon them. Thou shalt build that altar to Jehovah thy God of unhewn stones, and thou shalt offer upon it whole burnt-offerings to Jehovah thy God, and shalt sacrifice peace-offerings, and shalt eat there, and shalt rejoice before Jehovah thy God in that mountain, beyond Jordan, behind the way of the sunsetting, in the land of the Canaanite who inhabiteth the plain opposite Gilgal, near the oak of Moreh, towards Sichem*" (see Deut. xi. 29, 30).

18—21.] Compare Deut. v. 29—33, where a fuller account is given of this same incident. The verb **saw** is used of all the objects which follow, as in reff., meaning *perceived.* **thunderings**] lit., **voices,** they **were moved,** viz. with fear, see reff.

19.] **they said unto Moses,** viz. the

afar off. 19 And they said unto Moses, Speak thou with
us, and we will hear: but let not God speak with us, lest
we die. 20 And Moses said unto the people, Fear not: for
God is come to prove you, and that his fear may be before
your faces, that ye sin not. 21 And the people stood afar
off, and Moses drew near unto the thick darkness where
God *was*. 22 ¶ And JEHOVAH said unto Moses, Thus thou
shalt say unto the children of Israel, Ye have seen that I
have talked with you from heaven. 23 Ye shall not make
with me gods of silver, neither shall ye make unto you
gods of gold. 24 ¶ An altar of earth thou shalt make unto
me, and shalt sacrifice thereon thy burnt offerings, and
thy peace offerings, thy sheep, and thine oxen: in all
places where I cause my name to be remembered I will

heads of the tribes, and the elders, as explained Deut. v. 23. All this is given there much more fully. **20.**] This coming to **prove** them has before been asserted, ch. xv. 25; xvi. 4. The awful appearance of Jehovah was to impress them with fear. In Deut. the order is given that they are to get them back into their tents again.

21.] It appears from the narrative in ch. xix. 24 that Aaron also went up into the mountain: see ch. xxiv. 1, 2. It is there stated that Moses went to the *top*: here, that he drew near to the cloud which covered the Divine presence.

22—XXII. **33.**] *The first injunctions of the Law*, divided into three heads: 1. (xx. 22—26) The prescribed form of worship; 2. Laws for Israel, (*a*) in their civil relations to one another (xxi. 1—xxiii. 13); (*b*) in their theocratic relation to Jehovah (xxiii. 14—19); 3. The place towards Israel which Jehovah would hold (xxiii. 20—33).

22—26.] The injunctions regarding worship open with recalling the positive proof just furnished to Israel, of the being and presence of Jehovah. **from heaven**, because he had **come down** on Sinai, and because Sinai itself was uplifted high in the material sky. **23.**] God is a spirit, and must be worshipped in spirit. Any material representation will not set forth Jehovah, but will be with Him, i. e. something besides Him. Those who think they worship Him through an image do not in fact worship Him alone, but *Him and the image*. **24.**] An **altar** is needed, to symbolize the lifting up of the offering presented to Jehovah in heaven. But the Divine Spirit is not to be honoured in the prime act of worship, by a wrought altar of man's device. Man's work would but unconsecrate it: it is to consist of simple earth, or if, for more endurance, stone be used, it must be unwrought. **25.**] **tool** is, literally, sword, any cutting instrument; in this case, of course, adapted for stone. These general directions, fitted for various places where God would have His name honoured by remembrance, do not come into collision with those afterwards given (ch. xxvii. 1, ff.) for the special altar to be erected in the tabernacle. These rules were to apply to such cases as Josh. viii. 30, at Ebal, where these rules are recited and recorded to have been observed: as Judg. vi. 25, at Ophrah; as Judg. xxi. 4, and 1 Sam. vii. 17, at Mizpeh; as on Mount Carmel, 1 Kings xviii. 31, f.: and we may add, as at Gilgal, where the twelve stones taken out of Jordan, "pitched" for a memorial by Joshua, were evidently an altar: compare Josh. ix. 6, 27; 1 Sam. x. 8; xi. 14, 15; xiii. 7, 9, &c. The **places where** Jehovah **caused his name to be remembered** were such as the above-mentioned, and others, where God had specially manifested Himself. We have an interesting example in Judg. xiii. 19, where God had caused His name to be remembered by the appearance of His angel, and Manoah offered sacrifice to Him on a rock, which is thence called "*the altar*," ver. 20.

come unto thee, and I will bless thee. 25 And if thou wilt
make me an altar of stone, thou shalt not build it of hewn
stone: for if thou lift up thy tool upon it, thou hast pol-
luted it. 26 Neither shalt thou go up by steps unto mine
altar, that thy nakedness be not discovered thereon.
XXI. 1 Now these *are* the judgments which thou shalt set
before them. 2 If thou buy an Hebrew servant, six years
he shall serve: and in the seventh he shall go out free for
nothing. 3 If he came in by himself, he shall go out by
himself: if he were married, then his wife shall go out
with him. 4 If his master have given him a wife, and she
have born him sons or daughters; the wife and her chil-
dren shall be her master's, and he shall go out by himself.
5 And if the servant shall plainly say, I love my master,
my wife, and my children; I will not go out free: 6 then

26.] Man approaches the altar of God as a sinner, to offer sacrifice in expiation for sin. The fruit of sin is shame, and shame after sin was (Gen. iii. 7) first connected with that portion of the body of which the manifestation is here forbidden in approaching God. This order does not seem to have been observed with regard to the altar prescribed for the tabernacle, ch. xxvii. 1, ff., which seems to have had steps (Lev. ix. 22), and on that account to have necessitated the order in ch. xxviii. 42, f.

XXI. **1—XXIII. 13.**] *Laws applying to civil relations in Israel.* And first come laws as to *personal rights* (vv. 2—11): and of those, **2—6.**] those regarding *slaves.* See Deut. xv. 12—18, where the rules are given more in detail, and are accompanied with *motives.* **2.**] An Hebrew might have sold himself into slavery from poverty (Lev. xxv. 39), or might be sold in default of restitution for theft (ch. xxii. 3). The rules here given for the Hebrew male servant hold also for the female, see Deut. xv. 12. This law about **six years'** service was modified by the institution of the year of jubilee: see Lev. xxv. 40, where it is ordained that the Hebrew slave was to be set free on the year of jubilee, come when it might. But remarkably enough, when in Zedekiah's days Jeremiah was commissioned to enforce the law, it is not the subsequent rule, of the year of jubilee, but this, of the serving six years and going free on the seventh, which is appealed to: see Jer. xxxiv. 13, 14. It hardly needs pointing out that the whole regulation rests on sabbatical grounds. The six days' work earns the seventh day's rest, and so the six years' work rest on the seventh. **3.**] **by himself,** is, literally, **with his body,** with nothing but his person, see Gen. xlvii. 18; Neh. ix. 37. **4.**] This, though in strict accordance with the law of property, was a hard rule, and in consequence is modified and softened by what follows. We shall continually find examples of this in the Mosaic law: see Lev. xxv. 39, 43, 53, al. The only wife who could be given the Hebrew bondman must have been previously a bondwoman of his master's, and as such would probably (not certainly) be a heathen. If she were a Hebrew her retention by the master would only last till the seventh year of her servitude. But it is importing too much into this simple ordinance to regard it, as some have done, as intended to discourage Hebrews from marrying heathen wives. Such a side-intention would agree but ill with the full and merciful recognition of the marriage in the next verse. **5, 6.**] Provision for the slave to retain his place if he be minded. In the parallel, Deut. xv. 16, 17, no mention is made of the motive of love for wife or children, but only of loving "*thee and thine house:*" and the ordinance is extended to bondwomen likewise. **6.**] The words **unto God** have been almost

his master shall bring him unto God: and shall bring him
to the door, or unto the door post; and his master shall
bore his ear through with an aul; and he shall serve him
q =1 Sam. i. 22. Compare then vv. 11, 28. [q]for ever. 7 ¶ And if a man sell his daughter to be a
r Gen. xx. 17; xxi. 10. Judg. ix. 18. [r]maidservant, she shall not go out as the menservants do.
8 If she please not her master, who hath betrothed her to
himself, then shall he let her be redeemed: to sell her unto
a strange nation he shall have no power, seeing he hath
s Jer. iii. 20. Mal. ii. 14. [s]dealt deceitfully with her. 9 And if he have betrothed
her unto his son, he shall deal with her after the manner
of daughters. 10 If he take unto him another woman; her

universally rendered "*before the judges.*" This would naturally be so in fact; but surely there is no need to turn translation into interpretation. Unto God will mean the same as the frequent expression "*before Jehovah*," viz. to some place of God's especial presence; and such, in the case in hand, would be a place of judgment, where the genuineness of the case might be competently judged of. In ver. 22, where *the judges* are mentioned, the word is not as here, *Elohim*, but *phelilim*. The ceremony of boring his ear against the door-post seems to have imported merely the attachment, or nailing, of him to the house. The Talmudists suppose the door-posts to have been chosen as having been sprinkled with the paschal blood, and therefore witnessing the Divine redemption and sovereignty; and the ears, as having heard God's commandments. This fancy surely would be refuted by the **door** being here first, and in Deut. exclusively, mentioned. The *door* received no paschal blood. See more in Kalisch. On the supposed reference to this in Ps. xl. 6, see notes there, and on Heb. x. 5. **for ever** has generally been understood *for life*, as in ref. But some of the Jewish interpreters understood it *till the year of jubilee*, influenced by the idea that then all property returned to its original condition: see Lev. xxv. 41. The reply, that the jubilee ordinance modified these rules made before it, will hardly hold, seeing that the same expression, for ever, is used in Deut. xv. 17.

7–11.] *The case of a Hebrew girl sold by her father.* A complication is here introduced by the nature of the case. A girl thus sold, in the then relations of society, almost naturally became the secondary wife, or concubine, of her master: see reff., where the word "*maidservant*" implies this relation. And this secondary wife possessed certain connubial rights, on which legislation was founded. She became a part of her master's family, therein differing from a male slave, and therefore was not to go out as he did. **8.**] There is a difficulty here, arising from an apparent error in the spelling of a Hebrew word. *Lo*, written as here with an *aleph*, means *not*: written with a *vau*, it means *to him*. The latter meaning would certainly seem to be here required. And the Masorites, who edited the present Hebrew text, have noted 14 other places (among them Lev. xi. 21; xxv. 30) where the same clerical error seems to have been made. We retain therefore the text of the A. V. rather than "*who hath not betrothed* (or *espoused*) *her*." In the case contemplated he is to let the father buy her back again, or to sell her to a brother Hebrew. And this because he has dealt deceitfully, or treacherously, by her, broken his covenant of marriage with her: see reff., where the same expression is used. The same rule is said (see Knobel) to be observed among the modern Arabs.

9.] This case was and is common in the East. The father buys a concubine for his son, to keep him from looser living. In such a case she is to be treated, not as a slave, but as a daughter. **10.**] There is some doubt whether the **him** apply to the father himself or to the son. In either case the rule as regards the Hebrew girl remains the same. She was not to be worse treated on account of her being associated with another who by the nature of the case

[t]flesh-meat, her raiment, and her marriage rights, shall he
not diminish. 11 And if he do not these three unto her,
then shall she go out free without money. 12 ¶ He that
smiteth a man, so that he die, shall be surely put to death.
13 And if a man lie not in wait, but God deliver *him* into
his hand; then I will appoint thee a place whither he
shall flee. 14 But if a man come [u]presumptuously upon
his neighbour, to slay him with guile; thou shalt take him
from mine altar, that he may die. 15 ¶ And he that
smiteth his father, or his mother, shall be surely put to
death. 16 ¶ And he that stealeth a man, and selleth him,
or if he be found in his hand, he shall surely be put to
death. 17 ¶ And he that curseth his father, or his mother,
shall surely be put to death. 18 ¶ And if men strive
together, and one smite another with a stone, or with *his*
fist, and he die not, but keepeth *his* bed: 19 if he rise
again, and walk abroad upon his staff, then shall he that
smote *him* be quit: only he shall pay *for* the loss of his
time, and shall cause *him* to be thoroughly healed. 20

t See Job xxxi. 31.

u ch. xviii. 11. Deut. i. 43; xvii. 13; xviii. 20.

was preferred to her. **her flesh-meat** is mentioned, being the superior kind of food, and this ordinance having in view persons who were well off and could afford a household thus described. **her marriage rights**] The word occurs only here, and is thus explained by the chief authorities. The A. V. "*duty of marriage*" means the same thing: see 1 Cor. vii. 3. **11.**] **these three**, viz. the giving her in full her meat, her raiment, and her marriage rights: not, as some, the three obligations arising out of the three cases supposed, which would rather require *one of these three.*

12—21.] *Laws relating to the taking of life.*

12.] Deliberate murder is to be punished with death, see Gen. ix. 6; Lev. xxiv. 17, and that without regard to the time when death may follow the blow. **13.**] But accidental homicide will be hereafter specially provided for: see Num. xxxv. 9, ff. By God here is to be understood God directly, without the intervention of human intent.

14.] **presumptuously**, i. e. uplifting himself to the unwarranted design of taking life: see reff. The altar seems, as with most ancient nations, to have been the place of sanctuary: see 1 Kings i. 50; ii. 28. More particulars are given respecting cases of premeditated murder in Lev. xxxv. 16, ff.; Deut. xix. 11. **15.**] Parents are next to, and in place of, God, and therefore the lifting up a hand or even the tongue (ver. 17) against them, is punishable with the heaviest of penalties. **16.**] This is limited by Deut. xxiv. 7 to the case where the stolen person was one of his brethren the children of Israel. But not the least sanction can thence be derived for modern kidnapping into slavery: for all men are now brethren. **in his hand**] i. e. that of the stealer. On ver. 17, see above, and compare Matt. xv. 4 with Mark vii. 10, and both with our ver. 1. **18, f.**] The case of heavy personal injury not resulting in death. Two things result by implication from this law:—1. That if death take place before the injured person gets about, ver. 12 comes into force. 2. That if it result after that, the striker is blameless. **the loss of his time** is literally **his rest, his sabbath**: and the last clause is, **in healing shall heal him**, i. e. shall pay his doctor's bill. The case here contemplates restoration *in soundness*. Where this was not so, the *lex talionis* prevailed: see Lev. xxiv. 19, 20.

¶ And if a man smite his servant, or his maid, with a rod,
and he die under his hand; it shall be surely avenged.
21 Notwithstanding, if he continue a day or two, it shall
not be avenged: for he *is* his money. 22 ¶ If men strive,
and hurt a woman with child, so that her fruit depart *from*
her, and yet no mischief follow: he shall be surely punished,
according as the woman's husband will lay upon him;
and he shall pay as the judges *determine*. 23 And if *any*
mischief follow, then thou shalt give life for life, 24 eye for
eye, tooth for tooth, hand for hand, foot for foot, 25 burn-
ing for burning, wound for wound, stripe for stripe. 26
¶ And if a man smite the eye of his servant, or the eye of
his maid, that it perish; he shall let him go free for his
eye's sake. 27 And if he smite out his manservant's tooth,
or his maidservant's tooth; he shall let him go free for his

20, 21.] If a slave be struck, the case is different. This applies not only to non-Hebrews. It is true (see Lev. xxv. 44, ff.) that out of these the ordinary ranks of slaves were to be supplied: but, as in ver. 2, there were certain circumstances under which Hebrews became slaves, and they then came under such rules as this. See Keil here against Knobel and others. The rod was the common instrument of punishment: see Prov. x. 13; xiii. 24; xxiii. 13; Isa. ix. 4. The method and amount of this avenging are not prescribed. The Talmudical expositors say, by death with the sword; but this obviously cannot be, or the words would have been corresponding: probably it was by a fine in proportion to the nature of the case. If the slave's life were not taken on the spot, but he lingered, no vengeance was to be taken, seeing that the slave himself was a valuable possession, and the loss of him to his master was mulct enough. It is very difficult to see the distinction between the two cases: why the avenging should apply to the former if not to the latter, and should not apply to the latter, if to the former. The reason assigned by Bp. Wordsworth, that his survival proved the injury to be "not wilful, but accidental," will hardly convince many. Keil's view that such survival would shew that the master did not intend to kill the slave on the spot is hardly better, for the supposition in ver. 20 of itself assumes this. Perhaps we do not thoroughly understand the rule.

22—27.] *Examples of personal injury and their treatment.* **22, f.**] The case supposed is that of two men fighting, and the wife of one of them interfering to part them: see Deut. xxv. 11. **her fruit depart**] Literally, **children come forth**, the plural expressing the vagueness of the supposition. It is clear that the case supposes premature birth or miscarriage, and not, as Keil imagines, the birth of a living child. Kalisch renders the last words, "*he shall bring it before the judges*:" they seem literally to be **he shall give** (pay) **by** (the intervention of) **judges**, or **arbitrators**. The fine would be for the danger occasioned to the life of the woman, and the loss to the husband by the death of the child. The LXX. have a curious rendering here: "*and her child depart from her, if it be not fully formed, he shall pay a fine according as the woman's husband shall appoint, and he shall fine it with valuation: but if it be fully formed, he shall give life for life*," &c. **23**] Mischief — to whom? Keil interprets it, to mother or child. But (see above) by hypothesis the latter perishes. It is therefore the mother that is here thought of: and the prescription is a particular case of the *lex talionis*, more generally enforced Lev. xxiv. 19, ff., where see note. **26, f.**] In the case of slaves there shall be no *lex talionis*: the punishment of the cruel master shall be the loss of his property; the recompense to the injured slave the recovery of his liberty.

28—32.] *Law in case of injury to the*

tooth's sake. 28 ¶ If an ox gore a man or a woman, that
they die: then the ox shall be surely stoned, and his flesh
shall not be eaten; but the owner of the ox *shall be* quit.
29 But if the ox were wont to push with his horn in time
past, and it hath been testified to his owner, and he hath
not kept him in, but that he hath killed a man or a woman;
the ox shall be stoned, and his owner also shall be put to
death. 30 If there be laid on him a sum of money, then
he shall give for the ransom of his life whatsoever is laid
upon him. 31 Whether he have gored a son, or have gored
a daughter, according to this judgment shall it be done
unto him. 32 If the ox shall push a manservant or a maid-
servant; he shall give unto their master thirty shekels of
silver, and the ox shall be stoned. 33 ¶ And if a man shall
open a pit, or if a man shall dig a pit, and not cover it, and
an ox or an ass fall therein; 34 the owner of the pit shall
make *it* good, *and* give money unto the owner of them;
and the dead *beast* shall be his. 35 ¶ And if one man's ox
hurt another's, that he die; then they shall sell the live
ox, and divide the money of it; and the dead *ox* also they
shall divide. 36 Or if it be known that the ox hath used
to push in time past, and his owner hath not kept him in;

person by an animal. See Gen. ix. 5. In ch. xx. 10 we see that the domestic animals are regarded as part of a man's household, and as such they come under a mode of human responsibility: see also Lev. xx. 15. The flesh was not to be eaten as being unclean, through the shedding of innocent blood, Num. xxxv. 33. The master is punished by the loss of his beast. **29.**] In the case here supposed, the master is, by his carelessness, an accomplice, as it were, in the guilt, and deserves the same punishment. But inasmuch as carelessness is not malice prepense, option is given him to commute his punishment for a fine, laid on him, as we naturally supply from ver. 22, by the slain person's relatives, and approved by the judges. **31.**] And the same law holds good in case a child of either sex under age be the victim. All the children of Israel, young and old, were holy. **32.**] If a slave or bondmaid, the penalty of blood was to be exacted from the animal, but that of carelessness was not to exceed 30 silver shekels, perhaps the ordinary price of a slave, as 50 was the price of an Israelite's freedom, Lev. xxvii. 3. See Matt. xxvii. 15; Zech. xi. 12, f. Keil remarks that other ancient nations had laws for the punishment of beasts that killed or wounded a man, but none had one for making the owner responsible, because none knew of human life in its character as the image of God.

33—36.] *Rules for cases of hurt, where not men but other animals are victims.* **33, f.**] *Case of accident by carelessness.* The causer of the death of another man's ox or ass (the two most valuable animals among the Hebrews) was to give money (naturally, the price of the living animal), and to possess the carcase.

35, f.] In the case of accidental slaughter of one man's ox by another's the live and dead animals were to be shared,—the live by sale, the dead by division. But in the case answering to that in ver. 29 the live ox is to be paid in exchange for the dead one.

he shall surely pay ox for ox; and the dead shall be his
own. XXII. 1 If a man shall steal an ox, or a sheep, and
kill it, or sell it; he shall restore five oxen for an ox, and
four sheep for a sheep. 2 ¶ If a thief be found breaking
up, and be smitten that he die, *there shall be* no *avenging*
of blood for him. 3 If the sun be risen upon him, *there*
shall be avenging of blood for him; *for* he should make full
restitution; if he have nothing, then he shall be sold for
his theft. 4 If the theft be openly found in his hand alive,
whether it be ox, or ass, or sheep; he shall restore double.
5 ¶ If a man shall cause a field or vineyard to be eaten,
and shall allow his beast to stray, and shall feed in another
man's field; of the best of his own field, and of the best
of his own vineyard, shall he make restitution. 6 ¶ If fire
break out, and catch in thorns, so that the stacks of corn,
or the standing corn, or the field, be consumed *therewith;*
he that kindled the fire shall surely make restitution. 7

XXII. **1—14.**] *Laws respecting theft, borrowing, and damage.* The different proportions in which reparation is to be made for an ox or a sheep (or goat, the Hebrew word being one for smaller cattle generally; see A. V., Isa. xliii. 23; Ezek. xxxiv. 17, 20) are due apparently to the fact that the ox, as the companion of man's labour at the plough, has a value in the eyes of its master far exceeding that of a sheep, and the loss of one might stop his tillage altogether. The law of fourfold restoration for a sheep is cited by David in reply to Nathan's famous parable, 2 Sam. xii. 6, and alluded to as a general rule by Zacchæus, Luke xix. 8. The *restoring sevenfold* of Prov. vi. 31 is perhaps only a general expression. With this verse is intimately connected ver. 4, and the difference between the two enactments is probably to be found in this, that the thief who has sold or slain the stolen animal has advanced further in crime, and has also made actual restitution of the thing stolen more difficult, and consequently the injury a deeper one. **2, 3.**] *The law in case of homicide for housebreaking.* The two second members of the sentences are literally, **no blood for him** and **blood for him**: i. e. *he shall not*, and *he shall, be the subject of avenging of blood.* The difference being, that by breaking house or fold under cover of night, he renders himself justly liable to the worst suspicion that can arise, and must suffer the consequences: if by day, there is light to discern him and his object, and he must not be blindly dealt with. As in xxi. 20, *how* his slayer is to be punished is left to the judges to determine. **4.**] On the rationale, see above on ver. 1. The literal words are, **If the theft in finding be found**, i. e. if there be no doubt about the finding. The "*certainly*" of the A. V. hardly suggests this. Again, it is literally, **from an ox even to an ass, even to small cattle.** **5.**] It is plain by the meaning of the Hebrew verb "allow to stray," and mere fact of simple restitution being ordered, that injury to a neighbour's field by accidental straying, and not by intentional encroachment, is intended. The A. V. rather favours the latter idea. The Samaritan Pentateuch and the LXX. have, "*he shall make restitution out of his own field according to its fruit. But if he eat down all the field, he shall make restitution out of the best,*" &c. **6.**] This might well be from the universal practice of burning the weeds and roots when the ground has been cleansed after the harvest. See Isa. v. 24; xlvii. 14.

7—15.] *Laws regarding things deposited or borrowed.* **7.**] **stuff**, i. e. any kind

¶ If a man shall deliver unto his neighbour money or stuff
to keep, and it be stolen out of the man's house; if the
thief be found, let him pay double. [8] If the thief be not
found, then the master of the house shall be brought unto
God, *to see* whether he have put his hand unto his neigh-
bour's goods. [9] For every matter of trespass, for ox, for
ass, for sheep, for raiment, *or* for any lost thing, which a
man declareth to be so, the cause of both parties shall come
before God; *and* whom God shall condemn, he shall pay
double unto his neighbour. [10] If a man deliver unto his
neighbour an ass, or an ox, or a sheep, or any beast, to
keep; and it die, or be hurt, or driven away, no man see-
ing *it:* [11] *then* shall an oath of JEHOVAH be between them
both, that he hath not put his hand unto his neighbour's
goods; and the owner of it shall accept *thereof,* and he
shall not make *it* good. [12] And if it be stolen from his
charge, he shall make restitution unto the owner thereof.
[13] If it be torn in pieces, *then* let him bring it *for* witness,
and he shall not make good that which was torn. [14]
¶ And if a man borrow an animal of his neighbour, and it
be hurt, or die, the owner thereof *being* not with it, he
shall surely make *it* good. [15] *But* if the owner thereof *be*

of goods whatever. In Deut. xxii. 5; Isa. lxi. 10, the word is used of garments: let him pay double, as in ver. 4. **8.**] Here again we have the expression **unto God** (*Ha-Elohim*): and I have rendered it, as in ch. xxi. 6, simply, leaving the inference to be drawn that it must be to judges sitting with theocratic power. See note there. The LXX. and Vulgate render, "*and he shall swear that he hath not,*" &c.: and this is defended by Knobel and Kalisch. But Keil impugns it, and apparently with reason. **9.**] **to be so,** viz. to be matter of trespass. On the **coming before God,** and **God condemning,** see above.

10—13.] *Of animals given in charge to another.* These rules have a reference back to the last, and would tend to define in some uncertain cases the action of the judges in ver. 9. The case here supposed would arise when a flock or herd was entrusted to a shepherd or neatherd. Cattle would often be **driven away** by the predatory expeditions of enemies; compare 1 Chron. v. 21; 2 Chron. xiv. 15; Job i. 15, 17; and a figurative use of the fact in Jer. xiii. 17. **11.**] **he,** i. e. the person to whom the trust was committed. **12.**] The A. V. "from him" does not express the original, which is *de chez lui,* from his premises, or from his custody. And herein lies the difference from the case in ver. 10. He ought to keep a guard over his own premises or charge, which would not be expected of him in the other case. See Gen. xxxi. 39. **restitution,** apparently single, or perhaps according to that prescribed in case of simple theft, viz. double. **13.**] The carcase, or part of it, would in some cases be a testimony that the depositary had exerted himself to defend the deposit (see 1 Sam. xvii. 34, f.; Amos iii. 12): or at least would substantiate the fact of the violent death. If no such evidence were forthcoming, the case would go by default against the depositary.

14, 15.] *Injury to borrowed and hired animals.* The difference made by the owner's presence would be, that he would have seen

with it, he shall not make *it* good: if it *be* an hired *thing*,
it came for its hire. 16 ¶ And if a man entice a maid that
is not betrothed, and lie with her, he shall surely endow
her to be his wife. 17 If her father utterly refuse to give
v Gen. xxxiv 12. 1 Sam. xviii. 25. her unto him, he shall pay money according to the [v] dowry
of virgins. 18 ¶ Thou shalt not suffer a witch to live. 19
¶ Whosoever lieth with a beast shall surely be put to
death. 20 ¶ He that sacrificeth unto gods, save unto JE-
w Levit. xxvii. 28, 29. 1 Sam. xv. 3. HOVAH only, he shall be [w] devoted. 21 ¶ Thou shalt
x ch. xii. 40. neither vex a [x] stranger, nor oppress him: for ye were
strangers in the land of Egypt. 22 ¶ Ye shall not afflict
any widow, or fatherless child. 23 If thou afflict them in
any wise, and they cry at all unto me, I will surely hear
their cry; 24 and my wrath shall wax hot, and I will kill
you with the sword; and your wives shall be widows, and

that the calamity was unavoidable, or if avoidable, he did not prevent it: whereas in case of his absence no evidence as to this point would exist, and in default of it judgment must go against the borrower. If it were hired, then the contract of hiring included the possibility of accident, and that was enough. But of course this implies that the injury was bonâ fide an accident, and not owing to malice, fraud, or negligence. **16, 17.**] A girl belongs to her father as long as she is unbetrothed (ch. xxi. 7), and her case is treated accordingly in connexion with the rights of property. A seducer is bound, if the father consents, to marry her whom he has seduced. (It would be well if this were also the law among ourselves: see a note of Bp. Wordsworth here.) In this case he had to pay the accustomed dowry (see on Gen. xxxiv. 12; and the somewhat different enactment in Deut. xxii. 29, where the amount is fixed at fifty pieces of silver). If the father refused his consent, the seducer was to pay a fine equal to the usual dowry of a virgin: see above. On the seduction of a betrothed virgin see Deut. xxii. 23.

18—30.] *Various enactments.* It is not easy to discover any connexion with what has preceded: and in the original the context is broken off by the dropping of the **If** which has hitherto strung together the enactments. The use of the somewhat unusual **not suffer to live** instead of "*put to death*" has been variously accounted for, but is deprived of weight by the usual expression being found in the repeated enactment, Lev. xx. 27. There too we find the masculine gender used, whereas here the feminine seems to imply the fact that such persons were most frequently of that sex.

19.] See Lev. xviii. 23; xx. 15.

20.] **shall be devoted**, *i.e.* to Jehovah, in which case death was imperative: see ref. Lev. In rendering the expression we ought not to explain it, but to keep to the expression of the original. **21—27.**] *Laws against oppression:* first of the stranger, Canaanitish and remaining among them (ref.), or not Canaanitish,—answering to their own position in Egypt: not the proselyte, as some interpreters, which would make void the *motive* assigned. The LXX. clearly, in using the word "*proselytos*," had no such meaning as that which proselyte now bears, for it adds, *ye were* "proselytoi" *in the land of Egypt.* On the sense see the fuller ch. xxiii. 9; also Lev. xix. 34; Deut. x. 19; xxiv. 18, 22. Then if not a stranger, much less the destitute and poor of your own people: the widow and fatherless. See different instances of their oppression in Isa. i. 23; Jer. v. 28; Deut. xxiv. 17; xxvii. 19; Job xxiv. 3; Isa. x. 2; Micah ii. 9; 2 Kings iv. 1; Job xxiv. 9. On the other hand, special kindnesses were to be shewn to such persons: compare Deut. xxiv. 19—21, 29; xvi. 11, 14; xxvi. 12, 13. **24.**]

your children fatherless. 25 ¶ If thou lend money to *any*
of my people *that is* poor by thee, thou shalt not be to him
as an [y]exactor, neither shalt thou lay upon him usury. 26 [y] 2 Kings iv. 1. Ps. cix. 11. Isa. l. 1.
If thou at all take thy neighbour's raiment to pledge, thou
shalt deliver it unto him by that the sun goeth down: 27
for that *is* his covering, it only *is* his raiment for his skin:
wherein shall he sleep? and it shall come to pass, when
he crieth unto me, that I will hear; for I *am* gracious.
28 ¶ Thou shalt not revile God, nor curse the ruler of thy
people. 29 ¶ Thou shalt not delay *to offer* thy [z]fulness and [z] Num. xviii. 29. Deut. xxii. 9.
thine outflowing: the firstborn of thy sons shalt thou give
unto me. 30 Likewise shalt thou do with thine oxen, *and*
with thy sheep: seven days it shall be with his dam; on
the eighth day thou shalt give it me. 31 ¶ And ye shall
be holy men unto me: neither shall ye eat *any* flesh *that is*
torn of beasts in the field; ye shall cast it to the dogs.
XXIII. 1 Thou shalt not raise a false report: put not thine

We have a similar threat in Isa. ix. 17.

25—27.] Nor may the poor and needy be oppressed in lending or in withholding the pledge. On the not taking usury see on the general command, Lev. xxii. 35, ff.: and on the restoring the garment, the more detailed injunctions, Deut. xxiv. 10, ff. **I am gracious**, i. e. merciful, taking compassion on him. The word is rendered "*gracious*" always in the A. V., seeing that of the twelve times of its occurrence it is five times coupled with "*merciful.*" **28.**] Blasphemy of God and rebellious contempt of rulers come under the same category of crime: *fear thou Jehovah and the king*, Prov. xxiv. 21; see also 1 Pet. ii. 17. Some have supposed that judges or magistrates are meant by Elohim here, and so A. V.; but, as before, it seems best to keep the name to its sacred and simple meaning where possible, and so the modern Hebraists, Gesenius, Knobel, Keil, Kalisch. Still less can the view of Josephus and some Jewish expositors be taken, that by this verse they were forbidden to speak evil of the gods of the nations. Such an idea was foreign to the Law, in which all those gods are but vanity: see ch. xxiii. 13. The punishment for blasphemy was death, Lev. xxiv. 11, ff. The reader will remember St. Paul's citation of the second of these prohibitions in Acts xxiii. 5. The word rendered **ruler** is commonly used in the law of the *chiefs of the tribes*, see Num. vii. 10, and throughout: sometimes of those of the *divisions* of the tribes, Num. iii. 24, ff.; but also of *kings*, 1 Kings xi. 34; Ezek. xii. 10, al. **29, 30.**] *Of the offering of first-fruits to God.* The literal words are, **Thou shalt not retard thy fulness and thy tear.** This term **fulness** is used only in reff., and there in the same ambiguous sense as here. Although therefore it probably means first-fruits here, it is best not to render it by an explanation, but to be faithful. By **thy tear** is meant the first and choicest of the flowing of thine oil and wine. See on the matter, ch. xxiii. 19; Deut. xxvi. 2—4. On the last clause see ch. xiii. 2, 12, and more detail on Num. iii. 12.

30.] See on Lev. xxii. 27. **31.**] The dedication of the first-born was but symbolic of the whole people being God's: see ch. iv. 22. On the injunction of the latter part of the verse see Lev. xvii. 15, where its ground, as preventing the incurring of uncleanness, is further stated. The Israelites were to be especially clean, as being God's peculiar people.

XXIII. **1—9.**] *Rules for social duties.*

1.] The two clauses are closely connected: the first leads on to the second. A false report is literally **a report of nothing-**

hand with the wicked to be a witness for violence. 2
¶ Thou shalt not follow a multitude to *do* evil; neither shalt
thou answer in a cause to decline after many to wrest
judgment: 3 ¶ Neither shalt thou give advantage to a poor
man in his cause. 4 ¶ If thou meet thine enemy's ox or
his ass going astray, thou shalt surely bring it back to him
again. 5 If thou see the ass of him that hateth thee lying
under his burden, and wouldest forbear to loose it for him,
thou shalt surely loose it with him. 6 Thou shalt not wrest
the judgment of thy poor in his cause. 7 Keep thee far
from a false matter; and the innocent and righteous slay
thou not: for I will not justify the wicked. 8 ¶ And thou
shalt take no gift: for the gift blindeth them that see, and
perverteth the matters of the righteous. 9 ¶ Also thou
shalt not oppress a stranger: for ye know the heart of a
stranger, seeing ye were strangers in the land of Egypt.

ness: as we say of a false rumour, "*there is nothing in it.*" **a witness for violence,** i. e. to bring about an oppressive act.

2.] It is disputed whether these verses are addressed to magistrates or to ordinary men. The latter seems the most probable, as there is no indication of a special reference. If so, the law will mean that none are to allow themselves, in giving testimony, to be inclined to the popular side in neglect of truth and justice. The word *judgment* is not in the original, the verb being used absolutely, but is rightly supplied: see ver. 6, where it is expressed. **3.**] Literally, **adorn a poor man,** i. e. give him additional favour on account of his being poor. The A. V. "*countenance*" may express too much,—as if it meant that a poor man was to be deterred from seeking justice. See the same enjoined Lev. xix. 15. **4, 5.**] And not only such injustice, but lack of kindly service owing to aversion to a person is forbidden. The same is re-enacted more at large in Deut. xxii. 1—4. As Bp. Wordsworth observes, this precept is preparatory to the evangelical command, "Love your enemies," Matt. v. 43—45; Rom. xii. 19—21. There is some difficulty in ver. 5. The verb rendered "*help*" in the A. V. primarily signifies to **loose** (from bands or chains), and hence, and most commonly, to **leave.** Gesenius and some others (Keil, e. g.) believe that the verb is used here first in its ordinary, and secondly in its primary, meaning: *thou shalt forbear to leave it to him* (i. e. thou shalt not leave the animal to him, to manage as he may), *thou shalt surely loose it* (the ass) *with him* (i. e. help thine enemy to free the animal from its burden). But why should not the verb be used both times in its primary sense? Why should we not render, "and wouldest forbear to loose it for him, thou shalt surely loose it with him?" Thus we need not have recourse to two senses, and all seems easy, and in accordance with the parallel, Deut. xxii. 4. The other renderings may be seen discussed in Kalisch, pp. 445-7. **6.**] Seems best to cohere with ver. 3, and vv. 4, 5 to be an insertion interrupting the context. The command is the converse of that in ver. 3,—the poor is not to be *dis*advantaged any more than advantaged on account of his poverty. **7.**] States the general principle of uprightness and equity, on the motive of the unerring judgment of the righteous God. **8.**] The custom of the East (and not of the East only) is to approach witnesses and judges with presents to win their favour. It is literally, **blindeth the open** (eyes), **perverteth the matters** (the cause) **of the righteous,** i. e. turns aside the cause of the righteous from its proper issue. See 1 Sam. viii. 3.

9.] This is not a simple repetition of ch. xxii. 21. It is placed here in reference to

10 And six years thou shalt sow thy land, and shalt gather
in the fruits thereof: 11 but the seventh *year* thou shalt
let it rest and lie still; that the poor of thy people may
eat: and what they leave the beasts of the field shall eat.
In like manner thou shalt deal with thy vineyard, *and*
with thy oliveyard. 12 Six days thou shalt do thy work,
and on the seventh day thou shalt rest: that thine ox and
thine ass may rest, and the son of thy handmaid, and the
stranger, may be [a]refreshed. 13 And in all *things* that I [a] ch. xxxi. 17. 2 Sam. xvi. 14.
have said unto you be circumspect: and make no mention
of the name of other gods, neither let it be heard out of
thy mouth. 14 ¶ Three times thou shalt keep a feast unto
me in the year. 15 Thou shalt keep the feast of unleavened
bread: (thou shalt eat unleavened bread seven days, as I
commanded thee, in the time appointed of the month Abib;
for in it thou camest out from Egypt: and none shall ap-
pear before me empty:) 16 and the feast of harvest, the
firstfruits of thy labours, which thou hast sown in the field:

doing justice, as in Deut. xxiv. 17; xxvii. 19. And we have the former motive pressed home by the reminding them that they knew the feelings of a stranger. He feels himself, as Knobel observes, enough already oppressed by his situation as such.

10—19.] *Laws about sacred times*, of which the sabbatical year is the first mentioned. The former verses of the passage, 10—12, serve as a transition from what has gone before to what follows, resting the ordinance on the interests of the poor. Then with ver. 13 the context passes to a positive ordinance. On vv. 10, 11, see Lev. xxv. 2—7, where the same commands are given more in detail. **12.**] The ground of the sabbatical year, the day of rest itself, is again enjoined, but now in strict reference to the context, not as a solemn ordinance to Jehovah, but with the motive of rest and refreshment (literally, **breathing**) to a man's cattle and dependents. **13.**] The former clause serves as a solemn conclusion and caution regarding the rules which have preceded; the latter leads on to what follows, by enforcing loyalty to Jehovah alone and repudiation of all other gods. See on the form of this command, Psal. xvi. 4; Hosea ii. 17; Zech. xiii. 2.

14—17.] *Three yearly feasts ordained.* These ordinances are repeated, and several singular features in the present context recur in ch. xxxiv. 18—26. See also Num. xxviii. 18—31; Deut. xvi. 16, 17; and 2 Chron. viii. 13. **15.**] To the recitation of what was commanded in ch. xii. 19, f. and ch. xiii. 6, f., is added the injunction, not to appear before God empty, i. e. to bring gifts according to God's bounty to each, Deut. xvi. 17. These gifts would be partly the passover lambs, of which a share was the Lord's (ver. 18), partly the thank-offerings at the passover of which we read 2 Chron. xxx. 22. This order, not to appear before God empty, which is here attached to one feast only, belongs to all three in Deut. xvi. 16, 17. **16.**] The second feast, called here **the feast of harvest,** is otherwise *the feast of weeks* (ch. xxxiv. 22; Deut. xvi. 16). It was to be kept fifty days after the waving of the sheaf of the first-fruits, Lev. xxiii. 15, f., and was hence called *Pentecost, the fiftieth.* The Jewish writer Philo calls it *the feast of first-fruits.*

The third feast is that of **ingathering,** the time of which, depending on the occurrence of harvest, is not here specified. But in Lev. xxiii. 34; Num. xxix. 12, it is fixed to the fifteenth day of the seventh month. Keil directs attention to the fact,

and the feast of ingathering, in the end of the year, when
thou gatherest in thy labours out of the field. 17 Three
times in the year all thy males shall appear before the
Lord JEHOVAH. 18 Thou shalt not offer the blood of my
sacrifice with leavened bread; neither shall the fat of my
feast remain until the morning. 19 The first of the first-
fruits of thy land thou shalt bring into the house of JEHO-
VAH thy God. Thou shalt not seethe a kid in its mother's
milk. 20 ¶ Behold, I send an Angel before thee, to keep

that it is not said "*when thou hast gathered*" (A. V.), but **when thou gatherest**: the feast was during, not at the end of, harvest. He also insists on it, that the end of the year, here spoken of, is not a formal, but only an economical description of the time, at the end of the agricultural year as measured by the works of the field. This third feast is called *the feast of tabernacles* in Lev. xxiii. 34; Deut. xvi. 16: see there.

17.] Of this nothing is said in the ordinance of these feasts, Lev. xxiii. 4, ff., but it appears in Deut. xvi. 16, with the specification of "*in the place which he shall choose.*" By the mention of males, women were not excluded: see 1 Sam i. 3, ff.; nor children, see Luke ii. 41, ff.

18, 19.] *Various ordinances relating to the manner of offering to God at these times.* **18.**] In the parallel ch. xxxiv. 25, for **offer** we have *slay*. **with** is literally **over**, not meaning local superimposition, but superaddition, i. e. while leavened bread is in thine house. As the offerer's portion, so God's (see Lev. iii. 16, and compare Lev. vii. 23—25), was to be consumed then and there. The commands here given are restricted to the three feasts: but it would appear from Lev. ii. 11; vii. 15; xxii. 30, that the same applied to all sacrifices. Keil understands *the fat of my feast* (as he would render) to refer to that of the passover only, *the* feast *par excellence*, as specified in ch. xxxiv. 25. He says the command would have been unnecessary in the case of ordinary sacrifices, as the fat was always burnt at the time of offering. **19.**] This rule refers to the second of the three feasts, and enjoins the offering in God's house of the very earliest of the fruits: see Lev. xxiii. 17 for more particulars. Perhaps also the waving of the first sheaf, Lev. xxiii. 10, is intended. The second rule (which is repeated in the same connexion in ch. xxxiv. 26, and in another in Deut. xiv. 21) is understood generally by the Jewish commentators to forbid altogether the cooking of flesh in milk: so Onkelos, "*ye shall not eat flesh with milk.*" According to this idea, **its mother's milk** is a general expression, without reference to any particular she goat. But this seems doing violence to the text: and the general view to be preferable, which regards the command to be one prohibiting an act which turns the merciful provision of the Creator for sustenance into an accomplice, as it were, in the destruction of life. The command is a precious one, as shewing the Divine care even for those natural feelings which we are apt to set down as sentimental, and to hold too much in contempt. Some suppose that the command has a reference to some pagan superstitious practice. **20—33.**] *Promises of Jehovah's presence and help by means of an angel, and directions how to reverence and obey him; also promises that Israel shall prevail over the nations of Canaan, and orders respecting their treatment of those nations.* **20.**] It is beside the purpose of this commentary to enter into a theological discussion whether or not this angel were personally identical with our blessed Lord. We know that He is the manifestation to us of the Father: but we also know that there is every difference between the way in which God spoke to the fathers by angels and messengers, and that in which He now speaks to us by His Son. On such ground we do not venture to tread, nor to affirm that because Malachi calls Christ *the Angel of the Covenant*, therefore every angel manifesting the Divine Presence and clothed with the Divine attributes must necessarily be our Lord Himself. Such speculations seem to us to lead to no result,

thee in the way, and to bring thee into the place which I
have prepared. 21 Beware of him, and obey his voice,
provoke him not; for he will not pardon your transgres-
sions: for my name *is* in him. 22 For if thou shalt indeed
obey his voice, and do all that I speak; then I will be an
enemy unto thine enemies, and an adversary unto thine
adversaries. 23 For mine Angel shall go before thee, and
bring thee in unto the Amorites, and the Hittites, and the
Perizzites, and the Canaanites, the Hivites, and the Jebus-
ites: and I will cut them off. 24 Thou shalt not bow
down to their gods, nor serve them, nor do after their
works: but thou shalt utterly overthrow them, and quite
break down their †images. 25 And ye shall serve JEHO- † or, *pillars*.
VAH your God, and he shall bless thy [b]bread, and thy [b] Isa. iii. 1; xxx. 20; xxxiii. 16.
[b]water; and I will take sickness away from the midst of
thee. 26 ¶ There shall nothing cast their young, nor be
barren, in thy land: the number of thy days I will fulfil.
27 I will send my fear before thee, and will [c]trouble all the [c] ch. xiv. 24.
people to whom thou shalt come, and I will make all thine
enemies turn their backs unto thee. 28 And I will send

and to be altogether beyond our powers. See notes on ch. iii. 2, and on the places there referred to; and, besides, ch. xxxii. 34; xxxiii. 2. In xxxiii. 14, 15 the expression is varied for "*the Face of God*" going with them. The visible method of the leading of this angel was by the pillar of fire and cloud: see ch. xiv. 19. **21.**] He is no created angel, but a form of the Divine Presence, bearing the name of Jehovah, as in ch. xiii. 21, and clothed with His attributes, and indeed identified in action (ver. 22) with Him: for it is not said, "*he* will be an enemy," &c., but "*I* will be," as equivalent: and (23) the way in which this will be shewn is by *his* going before thee, and *his* cutting off the nations. And (24, ff.) this obedience to him will be shewn by utter separation from those nations and their idolatry. Keil observes that these **images** were, strictly speaking, memorial **pillars** or engraved upright stones dedicated to their gods: and refers to 1 Kings xiv. 23, which see. On the breaking down commanded, see ch. xxxiv. 13; Num. xxxiii. 52; Deut. vii. 5, 25; xii. 2. **25,** ff.] *The temporal blessings which should follow serving Jehovah their God.* **bread and water,** as in reff., for the chief nourishments of life. On the promise of immunity from sickness, see ch. xv. 26; and the opposite set forth, Lev. xxvi. 16; Deut. xxviii. 21, ff. **26.**] See Lev. xxvi. 9; Deut. xxviii. 11; xxx. 9. The latter clause implies that thy days shall not be cut short by accident or failure of strength, but shall fill up the allotted life of man. See a similar promise with regard to the days of the Messiah, Isa. lxv. 20. **27.**] Literally, **will give thine enemies' necks toward thee**: see Psal. xviii. 40; xxi. 12; and compare Josh. vii. 8, 12. **28.**] "The hornet," says Dr. Tristram, "is abundant in the Holy Land; the species are larger than ours: instances are on record in profane history, where hornets have multiplied to such a degree as to become a pest to the inhabitants. But it is probable here—considering that nothing is related of any such material allies of Israel, and that in reff. Josh., where the hornet is stated **to have** been sent, and to have driven out Sihon and Og, we know that they were otherwise overcome—that the word is metaphorically used of a panic, and means, as Augustine inter-

d Deut. vii. 20. Josh. xxiv. 12. [d]hornets before thee, which shall drive out the Hivite, the
Canaanite, and the Hittite, from before thee. 29 I will not
drive them out from before thee in one year; lest the land
become desolate, and the beast of the field multiply against
thee. 30 By little and little I will drive them out from
before thee, until thou be increased, and inherit the land.
31 And I will set thy bounds from the Red sea even unto
the sea of the Philistines, and from the desert unto the
river: for I will deliver the inhabitants of the land into
your hand; and thou shalt drive them out before thee.
e Josh. ix. 6. 1 Sam. xi. 1. 32 Thou shalt [e]make no covenant with them, nor with their
gods. 33 They shall not dwell in thy land, lest they make
thee sin against me: for if thou serve their gods, it will
surely be a snare unto thee. XXIV. 1 And unto Moses
he said, Come up unto Jehovah, thou, and Aaron, Nadab,
and Abihu, and seventy of the elders of Israel; and wor-
ship ye afar off. 2 And Moses alone shall come near Je-

prets it, "sharp stings of fear, by which flying rumours stung them so that they fled." See Wisd. xii. 8. On ver. 29, see the fuller Deut. vii. 22. **31.**] See the boundaries given in the promise to Abraham, Gen. xv. 18. Then it was from the river of Egypt (see note there) to the Euphrates. Here, from the Red Sea to the Mediterranean, and from the desert, i. e. the Arabian desert, to the Euphrates. See also Deut. xi. 24; Josh. i. 3. These limits were approached in Solomon's time, but never seem to have been reached. The promise, be it noticed, was conditional on Israel's perfect loyalty and obedience, and the condition was never fulfilled. **32.**] Ref. Josh. was an exceptional case.

XXIV.] The narratives in this chapter are remarkably intertwined. That of vv. 1, 2, 9—11, 16, 17, proceeds continuously, and the same is the case with that of vv. 3—8, 12—15, and 18. **1.**] It is not clear on what portion of the preceding history this immediately follows. The last notice of Moses was in ch. xx. 21, where he "*drew near to the thick darkness where God was*," and received from God the "*judgments*" which have since been detailed. On this seem continuously to follow our vv. 3—8. Knobel thinks that our vv. 1, 2 follow on ch. xix. 25, where Moses had been down to speak to the people after the Divine prohibition of their ascending into the mount. And Keil's objection to this, that the words **And unto Moses he said** imply that God had been hitherto speaking to others and not to Moses (whereas on Knobel's view what had been previously spoken was the Decalogue which was addressed to the people and Moses), is not valid, for two reasons: 1. That **unto Moses he said** might very well be the transition from the general address (to Moses and the people) to the particular address to Moses himself: and, 2. That these introductory words might well be due to the arranger of the compound narrative, in order to set this notice in its present place. Knobel's view is made very probable by the same matter, of the people not going up, being here dwelt on, as there, in ch. xix. 25. See notes there. Nadab and Abihu were Aaron's two eldest sons, see ch. xxviii. 1. The idea of Bp. Wordsworth, that "their presence was required at this time because the precepts now to be delivered concerned the tabernacle and priesthood to which Aaron and his sons were to be consecrated," does not agree with the fact that *Moses alone* received all those precepts while he was forty days up in the mount, and Aaron was with the people below: compare vv. 14, 18 with

HOVAH: but they shall not come nigh; neither shall the
people go up with him. 3 ¶ And Moses came and told
the people all the words of JEHOVAH, and all the judg-
ments: and all the people answered with one voice, and
said, All the words which JEHOVAH hath said will we do.
4 And Moses wrote all the words of JEHOVAH, and rose up
early in the morning, and builded an altar under the hill,
and twelve pillars, according to the twelve tribes of Israel.
5 And he sent [f]young men of the children of Israel, which
offered burnt offerings, and sacrificed peace offerings of
oxen unto JEHOVAH. 6 And Moses took half of the blood,
and put *it* in basons; and half of the blood he sprinkled on
the altar. 7 And he took the book of the covenant, and
read in the audience of the people: and they said, All that
JEHOVAH hath said will we do, and be obedient. 8 And
Moses took the blood, and sprinkled *it* on the people, and
said, Behold the blood of the covenant, which JEHOVAH

f ch. xxxiii. 11. 2 Sam. xviii. 15. 1 Kings xx. 14. See Acts v. 6, 10.

ch. xxxii. 1. This going up was merely for the purpose of worship, i. e. of a solemn approach to God and entering into His presence: see vv. 9—11, which in the narrative follow immediately on ver. 2.

3—8. Follows upon ch. xxiii. 33, in obedience to God's command, ch. xx. 22; xxii. 1. The words of Jehovah and the judgments which Moses told the people were ch. xx. 22; xxiii. 33: not the decalogue, which the people themselves had heard. The answer of the people in ver. 3 is the same as it had been in ch. xix. 8, when, so to speak, the preliminaries of the covenant were propounded to them. **4.**] Moses now commits to writing the commands which he had received—exclusive again of the decalogue, which was engraved on tables of stone by God himself. A book has been already mentioned ch. xvii. 14, but this one would naturally be a separate one. That was of the wars of the Lord; this of the covenant, ver. 7. The altar was for the coming ceremony; the 12 stone pillars (probably in a circle round the altar) not only symbolized the 12 tribes, but possibly also indicated their places, or those of their representatives, at the ratifying of the covenant. On these 12 stones, see Josh. iv. 8, 20; 1 Kings xviii. 31, 32. **5.**] These young men are called in the Targum of Onkelos "*the first-born of the sons of Israel;*" and ch. xxii. 29 seems to favour this. The Levites were afterwards taken by God in lieu of the first-born (Num. iii. 12, 41, 45), who before that seem to have ministered in holy things. Or they may have been servants of Moses, as Joshua was: see ch. xxxiii. 11, where he is called "Moses's servant, *a young man.*" Keil prefers this view, inasmuch as not the whole people but only the 70 had part in this sacrifice. But this reasoning rests on a view of the narrative which in our opinion is quite untenable. In the present section we have nothing to do with the 70: it is the whole people who are concerned (vv. 7, 8). On **burnt-offerings**, see Lev. i.; on **peace-offerings**, Lev. iii. **6—8.**] The blood of expiation is offered to God, and sprinkled upon man, but not efficacious unless its work of cleansing as well as of clearing from guilt be performed. Therefore Moses sprinkles **half the blood on the altar**, then binds the people to the holy covenant, then sprinkles the other **half** on **the people.** The writer of the Epistle to the Hebrews includes the book of the covenant also among the things sprinkled: see notes on Heb. ix. 19. It is called **the blood of the covenant,** as that by which the covenant was ratified and became efficacious. The Christian mean-

hath made with you concerning all these words. 9 ¶ Then
went up Moses, and Aaron, Nadab, and Abihu, and seventy
of the elders of Israel: 10 and they saw the God of Israel:
and *there was* under his feet as it were a paved work of a
sapphire stone, and as it were the body of heaven in *his*
clearness. 11 And upon the nobles of the children of Israel
he laid not his hand: also they saw God, and did eat and
drink. 12 ¶ And JEHOVAH said unto Moses, Come up to
me into the mount, and be there: and I will give thee
tables of stone, with the law, and commandments which I
have written; to teach them. 13 And Moses rose up, and
his minister Joshua: and Moses went up into the mount
of God. 14 And he said unto the elders, Tarry ye here for
us, until we come again unto you: and, behold, Aaron and
Hur *are* with you: if any man have any matters to do, let
him come unto them. 15 And Moses went up into the
mount, and a cloud covered the mount. 16 And the glory
of JEHOVAH abode upon mount Sinai, and the cloud

ing of this will be seen in the Epistle to the Hebrews. It is not the place to insist on it here.

9—11.] *Continuation of* vv. 1, 2. Jehovah's command to Moses there is carried out. **10.**] They saw a form in which God was pleased to appear to them—the glorious appearance of the God of Israel. "They saw," says Knobel, "the form of God clothed in glory and splendour (see ch. xvi. 10): and accordingly the writer uses (ver. 11) not *Jehovah*, but *Elohim*." God Himself, as He is, none can see, and live, see ch. xxxiii. 20. *What* they saw we know not: clearly not so much as Moses was allowed to see, "*the form of Jehovah*," Num. xii. 8; see also ver. 1. Deut. iv. 12, 15, which by a careless observance might be supposed inconsistent with this, do not relate to the same occasion, but to that in ch. xix. 16, ff., when the decalogue was given. Compare the progression in definiteness in Isa. vi. 1, where no form of God is described; Ezek. i. 26, where HE is described as in a human form; and Dan. vii. 9, 13; and the notes on those places. The pavement of sapphire (sky blue) betokened that His footstool was heaven: and the same is indicated by the celestial clearness described. The very same particulars are found in the vision of Ezekiel, i. 26. **11.**] **The nobles** (literally, the separated, i. e. selected), apparently the same as the 70,—for none others were present,—were allowed without inquiry to see the Divine vision. God **did not lay His hand**, i. e. did not break forth (ch. xix. 22) upon them. And they partook of the sacrifice *there before God*.

12—15.] *Continuation of* vv. 3—8. After the covenant had been ratified, God called Moses up into the mount to receive the two tables. He is to **be there**, i. e. to tarry a considerable time. The principal purpose is to receive the tables (see ch. xxxi. 18), but also to receive the ordinances respecting the tabernacle, which follow. He takes Joshua with him, commending the elders, and by implication the people, to Aaron and Hur (see ch. xvii. 10) for government and guidance. In saying **here** he did not mean the very spot on the mount where he left them, but below, in contrast to himself and Joshua who were going up (see ch. xxxii. 1, ff.). Joshua went up with him, though it is not here specified: see ch. xxxii. 17.

16, 17.] *Connects with* vv. 9—11. This abiding of the glory six days on the mount does not seem to form any part of the history which we have just left, inasmuch as we are repeatedly told that Moses was in the mount

covered it six days: and the seventh day he called unto
Moses out of the midst of the cloud. 17 And the sight of
the glory of JEHOVAH *was* like devouring fire on the top of
the mount in the eyes of the children of Israel. 18 And
Moses went into the midst of the cloud, and gat him up
into the mount: and Moses was in the mount forty days
and forty nights. XXV. 1 And JEHOVAH spake unto
Moses, saying, 2 Speak unto the children of Israel, that
they bring me an offering: of every man that giveth it
[g]willingly with his heart ye shall take my offering. 3
And this *is* the offering which ye shall take of them; gold,
and silver, and [h]brass, 4 and blue, and purple, and scarlet,

g ch. xxxv. 5, 22.

h Deut. viii. 9. Job xxviii. 2.

forty days and forty nights, but not more. But it may without forcing be interwoven into the progress of that other narrative. After Moses and Joshua left the elders and went up into the mount, the glory was visible to the people below six days, and in the seventh there was a special call to Moses (heard perhaps by the people) to approach nearer to God. This would be the time of his separation from Joshua, who did not (ver. 1) come near to Jehovah. On ver. 17, see ch. xix. 18. **18.**] *Connects either with* ver. 15, *or with the preceding:* see above. On its contents, see ch. xxxiv. 28.

XXV. **1**—XXXI. 17.] *Ordinances of the Tabernacle and the Priesthood.* The whole of this portion belongs in the main to the earlier or Elohistic narrator, as also does the almost exact repetition of it all in chapters xxxv.—xl. His favourite words and expressions occur throughout them both, as will be seen by the notes. **1—9.**] The order for an offering for the sanctuary of Jehovah.

2.] The word rendered an **offering**, and constantly used in Scripture for this meaning, is derived from a root signifying *to lift,* or *make high,* such offerings being lifted up from earth and lower uses to God in heaven: see further in notes on Lev. ii. 9; vii. 32. See the result of this command, ch. xxxv. 20—29; xxxvi. 5—7. It has been well remarked by Knobel, that in the earliest or Elohistic narrative (see above) the *favourable* disposition of Israel to God and His covenant are dwelt upon; while the later narrative notes more their shortcomings and rebellions. **that giveth willingly with his heart** is literally, **whom his heart shall make willing:** see ref. **3.**] First, *metals.* The various apportionments of these in the tabernacle and its vessels will be seen as we proceed. They were used in order of value, the most precious for those things which in the symbolism were nearest to God: and the further from Him, the less costly. *Iron* is not mentioned. **brass** is not the mixture of copper and zinc now so called, which was not known to the Hebrews, but probably copper only: see reff., which have been chosen to illustrate this point. See also note on Gen. iv. 22. **4.**] Secondly, *colours.* These are *violet-purple,* then *red-purple,* then *scarlet,* or *crimson.* The first of these colours was extracted from the shell-fish called *murex,* respecting which there is considerable uncertainty. It was the precious colour worn by kings and princes, and known to us as "the purple." The second was also extracted from a shell-fish, called *purpura.* The third is expressed in the Hebrew by the words **worm of the red.** The worm is the *coccus ilicis* of Linnæus, found on the *ilex aquifolia.* Kalisch suggests that the word *vermilion* may best express the colour, having itself a worm (*vermes*) in its composition. Thirdly, *stuffs and other materials.* (*a*) **linen.** The word for this is said to be Egyptian. In Ezek. xxvii. the prophet calls fine linen by this name when speaking of Egypt (ver. 7), and by another (ver. 16) when speaking of Syria. It would seem that both cotton and linen fabrics are included in the word, but that linen alone is to be understood by it when speaking of the tabernacle and sacred uses: see notes on ch.

and [i]fine linen, and [j]goats' *hair*, 5 and [k]rams' skins dyed
red, and [l]seals' skins, and acacia wood, 6 oil for the light,
spices for anointing oil, and for sweet incense, 7 onyx
stones, and stones to be set in the ephod, and in the breast-
plate. 8 And let them make me a sanctuary; that I may
[m]dwell among them. 9 According to all that I have
shewed thee, *after* the [n]pattern of the tabernacle, and the
pattern of all the instruments thereof, even so shall ye
make *it*. 10 And they shall make an ark *of* acacia wood:
two cubits and a half *shall be* the length thereof, and a

i Gen. xli. 42. Prov. xxxi. 22, al fr.
j So Num. xxxi. 20. 1 Sam. xix. 13, 16.
k ch. xxvi. 14; xxxix. 34.
l ch. xxvi. 14; xxxix. 34. Ezek. xvi. 10.
m ch. xxix. 45; Num. v. 3; xvi. 9.
n Deut. iv. 17. 2 Kings xvi. 10. Ps. cxliv. 12.

xxviii. 42; Ezek. xliv. 17, 18. (*b*) **goats' hair**, in the Hebrew, simply **goats**, but the meaning is undoubted: compare reff.

5.] (*c*) *Leather*. On the **rams' skins dyed red**, see reff. On the other animal, which the A. V. renders *badger*, there is considerable doubt. The badger is found in *Palestine*, but can hardly have been sufficiently common in the wilderness of Sinai to have provided, as it did (ch. xxvi. 14), an outer covering for the tabernacle. The Hebrew word used (*tachash*) is easily identified, says Dr. Tristram, by the present Arabic *tuchash*, which is a general name for the various species of seals, dugongs, and dolphins, found in the Red Sea. The *dugong*, of which several species are taken in the eastern seas, is a curious marine animal of considerable size, the skin of which might well answer for the purpose of an outer covering to the tabernacle. But as the skin of the dugong is coarse and thick, and the name also includes the seal, and, as in ref. Ezek., the shoes of the Jewish ladies are said to be made of these same skins, I have thought seal-skins the more probable, or, at all events, the more intelligible English rendering. (*d*) **wood**. The *shittim* (kept in its Hebrew form by the A. V.) is the *acacia seyal*, the only timber tree of any size in the Arabian desert. Dr. Tristram describes it as a gnarled and thorny tree, somewhat like a solitary hawthorn in its habit, but much larger. The timber is very hard and close-grained, with a darker heart, and admirably adapted for fine cabinet work. It is now important in commerce as yielding the *gum Arabic*. The reader should be reminded that the acacia has no connexion with the species commonly known by that name in England, which is a papilionaceous tree, and properly called *robinia*. The real acacia is a *mimosa*, with yellow ball-like flowers. The acacias in the Sinaitic peninsula have of late been destroyed by the Arabs to make charcoal. See Stanley, p. 25. (*e*) *Oil and spices*. On the former kind, see ch. xxvii. 20, 21; Lev. xxiv. 1—4: and on the latter, ch. xxx. 23, ff. On the incense, ch. xxx. 34, ff. **7.**] (*f*) *Precious stones*. On the **onyx**, see note, Gen. ii. 12, and for the use of the precious stones (Heb. stones of fulness, a similar usage occurs ch. xxviii. 16, 17, 20; xxxi. 5, and in other places), ch. xxviii. 17, ff.; xxxix. 10, ff. The precious stones were offered by the rulers: see ch. xxxv. 27. For the ephod and the breastplate, see ch. xxviii. 4—35.

8.] The object of these offerings was to make a dwelling-place for God: see ver. 22, and the reff. **9.**] The past, **I have shewed thee**, need not, as Knobel endeavours to do, in order to establish a discrepancy between the narratives, be interpreted to mean that God had already shewn Moses the pattern spoken of, but that when the offerings should be made and the tabernacle built, then He *would have* shewn them these things. This use of the past tense is familiar to all. This pattern (see reff.) was (ver. 40) shewn to Moses *in the mount*. He there saw, not the heavenly worship itself, nor anything belonging to it, but a pattern, or representation, of the tabernacle which he was to make, which pattern, as well as the tabernacle constructed after it, was but a type of heavenly things. The mount was not heaven, only an earthly similitude of heaven. See Heb. viii. 5; ix. 23; and Acts vii. 44.

10—22.] *The ark of the testimony*. See

cubit and a half the breadth thereof, and a cubit and a half
the height thereof. 11 And thou shalt overlay it with pure
gold, within and without shalt thou overlay it, and shalt
make upon it a [o]band of gold round about. 12 And thou
shalt cast four rings of gold for it, and put *them* in the
four feet thereof; two rings in the one side of it, and two
rings in the other side of it. 13 And thou shalt make
staves *of* acacia wood, and overlay them with gold. 14 And
thou shalt put the staves into the rings by the sides of the
ark, that the ark may be borne by them. 15 The staves
shall remain in the rings of the ark: they shall not be
taken from it. 16 And thou shalt put into the ark the
testimony which I shall give thee. 17 And thou shalt make
a mercy seat *of* pure gold: two cubits and a half *shall be*
the length thereof, and a cubit and a half the breadth

o ch. xxx. 3, f.; xxxviii. 2, 11, 26; ver. 24, only.

also ch. xxxvii. 1—9. **10.**] On **shittim** or **acacia** wood, see note ver. 5. The length of the cubit (see note on Gen. vi. 15) being assumed at 21 inches, the size of the ark would be 4 ft. 4½ in. long, by 2 ft. 7½ in. broad and high, i. e. about the size of a seaman's large chest. **11. within and without.** See note on ref. Gen. This **overlaying** seems almost beyond doubt to have been *gilding*, which we know, from numerous remains, was well known and practised in Egypt. The round staves (ver. 13) and the carved flower-work in Solomon's temple (1 Kings vi. 28, 35) could hardly be overlaid with gold in any other manner. The word rendered *crown* in A. V. is derived from a verb signifying to enclose or include, and is more probably a **band.** It occurs only in reference to the ark, the table of shewbread, and the altar of incense. See reff. **12.**] The rings were to be attached not to the four *corners* (as A. V.), but to the four **feet,** so that when borne the ark might be clear and high above the shoulders of the priests. This, from its comparatively small size, might well be, the rings being not pendulous, but fixed. We see from ch. xxxii. 4 that the casting of metals was known and practised by the Israelites. **13, 14.**] On the **overlaying** see above, ver. 11. **15.**] See note on Num. iv. 6. **16.**] The **testimony which I shall give thee** is understood by Knobel to refer to the law yet to be given, as the original (Elohistic) narrative, as he apportions it, has not as yet contained anything corresponding to the decalogue. But in order to this he is obliged to regard ch. xl. 20 as an anticipatory notice, which is, to say the least, forced and unnatural. It is far more reasonable to understand the future tense as applying to the law in its completed form, when that should be. The word rendered testimony might be also translated revelation or manifestation. It occurs frequently in Exodus, Leviticus, and Numbers, but never in Deuteronomy. See ch. xvi. 34, and note.

17—22.] Directions respecting the **mercy-seat**. This, which was to be put **above upon the ark,** was the most important and significant portion of the whole of the symbolic furniture of the tabernacle. That it was a mere *cover* of the ark is (1) contrary to the meaning of the root, which is maintained by Keil never to have had the mere signification of to cover in the material sense, but always to have implied covering in a figurative sense, as of sins, and (2) also against probability, as the ark itself being all of wood, had doubtless its own covering of acacia wood, whereas this is to be made of pure gold. The LXX., seeing this, have rendered the word a cover of expiation, and the Vulgate, *expiatorium*. Our word **mercy-seat** expresses the meaning very well, as it was there that the blood of expiation was to be sprinkled, and there that Jehovah would

thereof. 18 And thou shalt make two cherubim, gold;
beaten work shalt thou make them, in the two ends of the
mercy seat. 19 And make one cherub on the one end, and
the other cherub on the other end: of the mercy seat shall
ye make the cherubim on the two ends thereof. 20 And
the cherubim shall stretch forth wings on high, covering
the mercy seat with their wings, and their faces *shall look*
one to another; toward the mercy seat shall the faces of
the cherubim be. 21 And thou shalt put the mercy seat
above upon the ark; and in the ark thou shalt put the
testimony that I shall give thee. 22 And there I will meet
with thee, and I will commune with thee from above the
mercy seat, from between the two cherubim which *are*
upon the ark of the testimony, of all *things* which I will
give thee in commandment unto the children of Israel. 23
¶ Thou shalt also make a table *of* acacia wood: two cubits
shall be the length thereof, and a cubit the breadth there-
of, and a cubit and a half the height thereof. 24 And
thou shalt overlay it with pure gold, and make thereto a
band of gold round about. 25 And thou shalt make unto
it a border of an hand breadth round about, and thou shalt
make a golden band to the border thereof round about.
26 And thou shalt make for it four rings of gold, and put
the rings in the four corners that *are* on the four feet there-
of. 27 Over against the border shall the rings be for places
of the staves to bear the table. 28 And thou shalt make

appear and manifest Himself (ver. 22). The above defended view is corroborated by the circumstance that in 1 Chron. xxviii. 11 the holy of holies is called the house of the mercy-seat. Were this a mere cover of the ark, such a name could never have been used. The mercy-seat was, as having to be laid on the ark, to be of exactly the same dimensions: see ver. 10. **18.**] *The cherubim.* On these see note, Gen. iii. 24, and the art. "Cherub" in *Smith's Biblical Dict.* All we can deduce for certain respecting them from this passage is that they had outstretched wings, and faces of some kind. They were to be beaten work, i. e. not cast, solid, but hammered out of plates; and probably, by what follows (ver. 19), out of the same plate of gold as the mercy-seat itself. In Solomon's temple the cherubs were of olive wood, gilt: see 1 Kings vi. 23—28. **20.**] **one to another**, literally, **man to his brother.** **21.**] The injunction to put into the ark the testimony is repeated apparently to remind Moses that this was to be done before the mercy-seat was superimposed. **22.**] See ch. xxx. 6, 36; Num. vii. 89. **23—30.**] *The table of shewbread.* Such tables for offerings were common to many forms of heathen temple-worship: but the ordinance of shewbread was peculiar to the worship of Jehovah. For particulars respecting the situation of this table, and the ordinance of the shewbread, see ver. 35; Lev. xxiv. 5, ff. Apparently, from vv. 24, 25, the table itself was to have a band of gold, and also the border, or wooden casing round the edge, was to have another such band. It

the staves *of* acacia wood, and overlay them with gold, that
the table may be borne with them. 29 And thou shalt
make the dishes thereof, and spoons thereof, and [p]cans
thereof, and [q]cups thereof, to pour out withal: pure gold
shalt thou make them. 30 And thou shalt set upon the
table showbread before me alway. 31 ¶ And thou shalt
make a candlestick, pure gold: beaten work shall the
candlestick be made: its [r]base and [s]shaft, its [t]cups, its
[u]knobs, and its flowers, shall be of it. 32 And six branches
shall come out of the sides of it; three branches of the
candlestick out of the one side, and three branches of the
candlestick out of the other side: 33 three cups made like
unto almonds, a knob and a flower in one branch; and
three cups made like almonds in the other branch, a knob
and a flower: so in the six branches that come out of the
candlestick. 34 And in the candlestick *shall be* four bowls
made like unto almonds, *with* their knobs and their flowers.
35 And *there shall be* a knob under two branches of the

p ch. xxxvii. 16. Num. iv. 7. 1 Chron. xxviii. 17, only.
q ch. xxxvii. 16. Num. iv. 7. Jer. lii. 19.
r Gen. xxiv. 2. Num. v. 27. al. fr.
s Gen. xli. 5. 1 Kings xiv. 15. Isa. vi. 20, al.
t Gen. xliv. 2. Jer. xxxv. 5.
u Here and ch. xxxviii., passim. Besides, Amos ix. 1. Zeph. ii. 14, only.

was (vv. 26, 27) to have rings beneath the border at the four corners where were the feet, and staves to carry it, as had the ark, and the staves were to be similar (ver. 28). In both cases the feet are named, though no direction has been given respecting them, being taken as matter of course.

29.] **the dishes** (their name implying *depth*) were apparently 130 shekels' weight each (Num. vii. 13, &c.), and were large deep vessels, probably for putting on the showbread; the **spoons** (the name meaning *a hollow hand*) were apparently 10 shekels in weight (Num. vii. 14, &c.), and were for the incense which was (Lev. xxiv. 7) to be offered with the showbread; the **cans** are in A. V. *covers;* but apparently in error: these two last-mentioned vessels belong to the drink-offerings, and these cans were apparently shallow vessels to pour the wine, while the **cups** (or jugs) were to bring the wine in. See reff., in the last of which the A. V. renders the word *cups:* as also in the last reff. for the latter word.

30.] See Lev. xxiv. 4, ff. I have altered the spelling of *shew*bread to **showbread,** as many English readers, not being aware of the import of the first syllable, pronounce it "*shoe*-bread." The Hebrew name signifies **bread of faces,** or bread of (the) face: the word for *face* existing only in the plural, we cannot determine the number in English. It seems agreed, however, that the word is to be taken as applying to God, before whom the bread was laid up: and this seems to be proved by 1 Sam. xxi. 6, where the showbread is said to have been "*taken from before the Face of Jehovah.*" The name has been very variously rendered: by the LXX. as "*loaves of presence;*" by the Vulgate as "*bread of setting forth.*" So also in the N. T., Matt. xii. 4; but in Heb. ix. 2 "*the setting forth of the loaves, which is called holy.*"

31—40.] *The golden candlestick.* This candlestick, from being of pure gold, is called in ch. xxxi. 8; xxxix. 37; Lev. xxiv. 4, "*the pure candlestick.*" All was to be pure:—the **base,** literally the thigh, or seat (reff.); the **shaft,** or main stem,—the word being *kaneh,* reed, or *cane;* the **cups,** or calyxes; the **knobs,** little balls or apples; the **flowers** (see description below). **of it,** as in ver. 19, of one piece with and forming a whole with it.

32, 33.] These branches again are shafts, canes, or stems, but subsidiary, each carrying a calyx with knob and flower **like those of an almond.** This last rendering has been doubted by Knobel and others, but apparently without reason.

34, 35.] On the *main stem,* called here **the candlestick,** are to be four such calyxes with balls and

same, and a knob under two branches of the same, and a
knob under two branches of the same, according to the six
branches that proceed out of the candlestick. 36 Their
knobs and their branches shall be of it: all of it *shall be*
one beaten work *of* pure gold. 37 And thou shalt make the
seven lamps thereof: and they shall put on the lamps
thereof, and they shall give light over against it. 38 And
the [v] tongs thereof, and the [w] snuffdishes thereof, *shall be*
pure gold. 39 *Of* a talent of pure gold shall he make it,
with all these vessels. 40 And look that thou make *them*
after their pattern, which was shewed thee in the mount.

v ch. xxxvii. 23. Num. iv. 3 1 Kings vii. 49. 2 Chron. iv. 21. Isa. vi. 6.
w ch xxvii. 3. Le . xvi. 12. Num. xvi. 37, ff. 1 Kings vii. 50. Jer. lii. 19.

ows s: i. e. each pair of branches, being three, is to spring out of such a flower-cup, and the termination of the main shaft is to be, like the rest, one such. **36.**] **of it** again, i. e. as above (vv. 19, 31), of one piece, forming one whole. **37.**] The seven lamps were to be made, and then put on the finials of the seven stems. The A. V. has taken the verb, which literally means **to cause to ascend**, as meaning *to light;* whereas it rather imports *to put up* upon the stems. This is shewn by these lamps being called *the lamps of setting up*, ch. xxxix. 37. The probable interpretation of the latter part of the verse is to be found in the circumstance that the candlestick, in the arrangement of the tabernacle (ch. xxvi. 35), was to stand toward the south, i. e. against the southern side of the holy place, and to cast its light toward the north, the side **over against it.** This it might do, either simply from its position, or by having, as Knobel supposes, small snouts or vents, out of which the wicks came, and the vents turned toward the north.

38.] The **tongs,** for pulling up and cleansing the wick, answering to snuffers for candles. The snuff-dishes, receptacles for the refuse snuff. In the reff. the same word is used for coal-vessels, or shovels, to receive coals, and is rendered *fire-pans, censers,* or *ash-pans.* **39.**] The whole mass of pure gold, out of which. beaten out and hollow, the candlestick and its fittings were to be made, was **a talent** in weight. The mass and present value of a talent of gold are matters of considerable doubt, the latter being set down variously at from £4000 to £6000 (see the elaborate but somewhat confusing art. on Weights and Measures in the *Biblical Dict.*). It is to be observed that no dimensions are prescribed for the candlestick. The Rabbis report that it was about five feet high. The interesting figure of the seven-branched candlestick, now sculptured inside the arch of Titus at Rome as carried in triumph, cannot be above 3 ft. 6 in. high, judging by the size of the men who bear it. But it (see it given in art. "Candlestick" in *Biblical Dict.*) was not apparently even the genuine successor of the original, and is adorned with fabulous Pagan griffins, which cast much doubt on its having any trustworthy resemblance even to the candlestick of the Herodian temple. **he,** i. e. whoever is entrusted with the workmanship.

all these vessels is defined in ch. xxxvii. 24 to mean merely the appurtenances of the candlestick, not any previously prescribed. Into the symbolism of the golden or pure candlestick it is not the province of this commentary to enter. In its main features it will be obvious to the reader, and it may be found elucidated by Keil and Bp. Wordsworth, the former taking the Jewish, the latter exclusively the Christian, significance. The places of Scripture which bear on the subject, and under which it will be so far found in each case treated, are Zech. iv.; Rev. i. 20; John viii. 12.

40.] See on ver. 9.

* * * * * * * *

THE END.